Microsoft®

Windows Vista

Complete Concepts and Techniques

Gary B. Shelly

Thomas J. Cashman

Steven M. Freund

Raymond E. Enger

COURSE TECHNOLOGY
CENGAGE Learning™

SHELLY
CASHMAN
SERIES®

Australia • Brazil • Japan • Korea • Mexico • Singapore • Spain • United Kingdom • United States

COURSE TECHNOLOGY
CENGAGE Learning™

Microsoft Windows Vista
Complete Concepts and Techniques
Gary B. Shelly, Thomas J. Cashman, Steven M. Freund,
Raymond E. Enger

Executive Editor: Alexandra Arnold

Senior Product Manager: Mali Jones

Associate Product Manager: Klenda Martinez

Editorial Assistant: Jon Farnham

Print Buyer: Julio Esperas

Content Project Manager: Matthew Hutchinson

Developmental Editor: Karen Stevens

Executive Director of Marketing: Cheryl Costantini

Marketing Manager: Tristen Kendall

Marketing Coordinator: Julie Schuster

QA Manuscript Reviewers: John Freitas, Serge
    Palladino, Susan Whalen

Art Director: Bruce Bond

Cover Design: Joel Sadagursky

Cover Photo: Jon Chomitz

Compositor: Gex Publishing Services

Printer: RRD Menasha

For product information and technology assistance, contact us at
Cengage Learning Academic Resource Center, 1-800-423-0563

For permission to use material from this text or product, submit all
requests online at **cengage.com/permissions**
Further permissions questions can be emailed to
permissionrequest@cengage.com

ISBN-13: 978-1-4188-5981-7

ISBN-10: 1-4188-5981-8

Course Technology
25 Thomson Place
Boston, Massachusetts 02210
USA

Cengage Learning is a leading provider of customized learning solutions with office
locations around the globe, including Singapore, the United Kingdom, Australia, Mexico,
Brazil and Japan. Locate your local office at:

international.cengage.com/region

Cengage Learning products are represented in Canada by Nelson Education, Ltd.

For your lifelong learning solutions, visit **course.cengage.com**

Printed in the United States of America
1 2 3 4 5 6 7 8 9 10 BM 09 08

Microsoft® Windows Vista
Complete Concepts and Techniques

Contents

CHAPTER FOUR

Personal Information Management and Communication

CHAPTER FIVE

Personalize Your Work Environment

CHAPTER SIX
Customizing Your Computer Using the Control Panel

Appendices

Preface

The Shelly Cashman Series® offers the finest textbooks in computer education. We are proud of the fact that our Microsoft Windows 3.1, Microsoft Windows 95, Microsoft Windows 98, Microsoft Windows 2000, and Microsoft Windows XP books have been so well received by students and instructors. With each new edition of our Windows books, we have made significant improvements based on the software and comments made by instructors and students.

Microsoft Windows contains many changes in the user interface and feature set. Recognizing that the new features and functionality of Microsoft Windows Vista would impact the way that students are taught skills, the Shelly Cashman Series development team carefully reviewed our pedagogy and analyzed its effectiveness in teaching today's student. An extensive customer survey produced results confirming what the series is best known for: its step-by-step, screen-by-screen instructions, its project-oriented approach, and the quality of its content.

We learned, though, that students entering computer courses today are different than students taking these classes just a few years ago. Students today read less, but need to retain more. They need not only to be able to perform skills, but to retain those skills and know how to apply them to different settings. Today's students need to be continually engaged and challenged to retain what they're learning.

As a result, we've renewed our commitment to focusing on the user and how they learn best. This commitment is reflected in every change we've made to our Windows Vista books.

Objectives of This Textbook

Microsoft Windows Vista: Complete Concepts and Techniques is intended for a six- to nine-week period in a course that teaches Microsoft Windows Vista in conjunction with another application or computer concepts. No experience with a computer is assumed, and no mathematics beyond the high school freshman level is required. The objectives of this book are:

- To offer an in-depth presentation of Microsoft Windows Vista
- To expose students to practical examples of the computer as a useful tool
- To acquaint students with the proper procedures to manage and organize document storage options for coursework, professional purposes, and personal use
- To help students discover the underlying functionality of Windows Vista so they can become more productive
- To develop an exercise-oriented approach that allows learning by doing

The Shelly Cashman Approach

Features of the Shelly Cashman Series Microsoft Windows Vista books include:

- **Step-by-Step, Screen-by-Screen Instructions** Each of the tasks required to complete an activity is clearly identified throughout the chapter. Now, the step-by-step instructions provide a context beyond point-and-click. Each step explains why students are performing a task, or the result of performing a certain action. Found on the screens accompanying each step, call-outs give students the information they need to know when they need to know it. Now, we've used color to distinguish the content in the call-outs. The Explanatory call-outs (in black) summarize what is happening on the screen and the Navigational call-outs (in red) show students where to click.

- **Q&A** Found within many of the step-by-step sequences, Q&As raise the kinds of questions students may ask when working through a step sequence and provide answers about what they are doing, why they are doing it, and how that task might be approached differently.

- **Experimental Steps** These new steps, within our step-by-step instructions, encourage students to explore, experiment, and take advantage of the features of Windows Vista. These steps are not necessary to complete the activities but are designed to increase the confidence with the software and build problem-solving skills.

- **Thoroughly Tested Instruction** Unparalleled quality is ensured because every screen in the book is produced by the author only after performing a step, and then each set of steps must pass Course Technology's Quality Assurance program.

- **Other Ways Boxes** The Other Ways boxes displayed at the end of most of the step-by-step sequences specify the other ways to do the task completed in the steps. Thus, the steps and the Other Ways box make a comprehensive reference unit.

- **BTW** These marginal annotations provide background information, tips, and answers to common questions that complement the topics covered, adding depth and perspective to the learning process.

- **Integration of the World Wide Web** The World Wide Web is integrated into the Windows Vista learning experience by (1) BTW annotations that send students to Web sites for up-to-date information and alternative approaches to tasks; (2) the Learn It Online section at the end of each chapter, which has chapter reinforcement exercises, learning games, and other types of student activities.

- **End-of-Chapter Student Activities** Extensive student activities at the end of each chapter provide the student with plenty of opportunities to reinforce the materials learned in the chapter through hands-on assignments. Several new types of activities have been added that challenge the student in new ways to expand their knowledge, and to apply their new skills to a project with personal relevance.

Q&A

Why does my desktop look different from the one in Figure 1–5?

The Windows Vista desktop is customizable and your work or school may have modified the desktop to meet their needs.

Other Ways

1. Right-click icon, click Open, click Empty Recycle Bin, click the Close button, click the Yes button

2. Double-click the Recycle bin icon, click Empty Recycle Bin, click the Close button, click the Yes button

BTW

Vista Capable and Premium Ready

When buying a computer, you may run across ones that are labeled Vista Capable and Vista Premium Ready. A Vista Capable computer can run the Vista Basic experience, but may need to be upgraded to support the Aero experience. Vista Premium Ready means that the computer can run Aero, but some features still may require additional hardware.

Organization of This Textbook

Microsoft Windows Vista: Complete Concepts and Techniques consists of six chapters on Microsoft Windows Vista, and four appendices.

End-of-Chapter Student Activities

A notable strength of the Shelly Cashman Series Microsoft Windows Vista books is the extensive student activities at the end of each chapter. Well-structured student activities can make the difference between students merely participating in a class and students retaining the information they learn. The activities in the Shelly Cashman Series Windows books include the following.

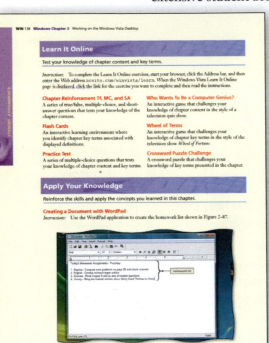

CHAPTER SUMMARY A concluding paragraph, followed by a listing of the tasks completed within a chapter together with the pages on which the step-by-step, screen-by-screen explanations appear.

LEARN IT ONLINE Every chapter features a Learn It Online section that is comprised of six exercises. These exercises include True/False, Multiple Choice, Short Answer, Flash Cards, Practice Test, and Learning Games.

APPLY YOUR KNOWLEDGE This exercise usually requires students to open and manipulate a file from the Data Files that parallels the activities learned in the chapter. To obtain a copy of the Data Files for Students, follow the instructions on the inside back cover of this text.

EXTEND YOUR KNOWLEDGE This exercise allows students to extend and expand on the skills learned within the chapter.

IN THE LAB Three all new in-depth assignments per chapter require students to utilize the chapter concepts and techniques to solve problems on a computer.

CASES AND PLACES Five unique real-world case-study situations, including Make It Personal, an open-ended project that relates to student's personal lives, and one small-group activity.

Instructor Resources CD-ROM

The Shelly Cashman Series is dedicated to providing you with all of the tools you need to make your class a success. Information about all supplementary materials is available through your Course Technology representative or by calling one of the following telephone numbers: Colleges, Universities, Continuing Education Departments, Post-Secondary Vocational Schools, and Career Colleges, Business, Industry, Government, Trade, Retailer, Wholesaler, Library and Resellers, 1-800-648-7450; K-12 Schools, Secondary Vocational Schools, Adult Education, and School Districts, 1-800-824-5179; Canada, 1-800-268-2222.

The Instructor Resources CD-ROM for this textbook include both teaching and testing aids. The contents of each item on the Instructor Resources CD-ROM (ISBN 1-4239-1179-2) are described in the following text.

INSTRUCTOR'S MANUAL The Instructor's Manual consists of Microsoft Word files, which include chapter objectives, lecture notes, teaching tips, classroom activities, lab activities, quick quizzes, figures and boxed elements summarized in the chapters, and a glossary page. The new format of the Instructor's Manual will allow you to map through every chapter easily.

SYLLABUS Sample syllabi, which can be customized easily to a course, are included. The syllabi cover policies, class and lab assignments and exams, and procedural information.

FIGURE FILES Illustrations for every figure in the textbook are available in electronic form, both with and without callouts. Use this ancillary to present a slide show in lecture or to print transparencies for use in lecture with an overhead projector. If you have a personal computer and LCD device, this ancillary can be an effective tool for presenting lectures.

POWERPOINT PRESENTATIONS PowerPoint Presentations is a multimedia lecture presentation system that provides slides for each chapter. Presentations are based on chapter objectives. Use this presentation system to present well-organized lectures that are both interesting and knowledge based. PowerPoint Presentations provides consistent coverage at schools that use multiple lecturers.

SOLUTIONS TO EXERCISES Solutions are included for the Chapter Reinforcement exercises.

TEST BANK & TEST ENGINE In the ExamView test bank, you will find our standard question types (40 multiple-choice, 25 true/false, 20 completion) and new objective-based question types (5 modified multiple-choice, 5 modified true/false and 10 matching). Critical Thinking questions are also included (3 essays and 2 Cases with 2 case-based questions each) totaling the test bank to 112 questions for every chapter with page number references, and when appropriate, figure references. A version of the test bank you can print also is included. The test bank comes with a copy of the test engine, ExamView, the ultimate tool for your objective-based testing needs. ExamView is a state-of-the-art test builder that is easy to use. ExamView enables you to create paper-, LAN-, or Web-based tests from test banks designed specifically for your Course Technology textbook. Utilize the ultra-efficient QuickTest Wizard to create tests in less than five minutes by taking advantage of Course Technology's question banks, or customize your own exams from scratch.

ADDITIONAL ACTIVITIES FOR STUDENTS These additional activities consist of Chapter Reinforcement Exercises, which are true/false, multiple-choice, and short answer questions that help students gain confidence in the material learned.

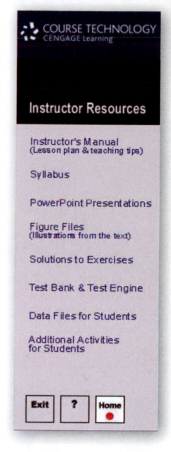

COURSE TECHNOLOGY
CENGAGE Learning

Instructor Resources

Instructor's Manual
(Lesson plan & teaching tips)

Syllabus

PowerPoint Presentations

Figure Files
(Illustrations from the text)

Solutions to Exercises

Test Bank & Test Engine

Data Files for Students

Additional Activities
for Students

| Exit | ? | Home |

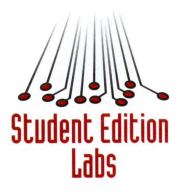

Assessment & Training Solutions

SAM 2007

SAM 2007 helps bridge the gap between the classroom and the real world by allowing students to train and test on important computer skills in an active, hands-on environment.

SAM 2007's easy-to-use system includes powerful interactive exams, training or projects on critical applications such as Word, Excel, Access, PowerPoint, Outlook, Windows, the Internet, and much more. SAM simulates the application environment, allowing students to demonstrate their knowledge and think through the skills by performing real-world tasks.

Designed to be used with the Shelly Cashman series, SAM 2007 includes built-in page references so students can print helpful study guides that match the Shelly Cashman series textbooks used in class. Powerful administrative options allow instructors to schedule exams and assignments, secure tests, and run reports with almost limitless flexibility.

Student Edition Labs

Our Web-based interactive labs help students master hundreds of computer concepts, including input and output devices, file management and desktop applications, computer ethics, virus protection, and much more. Featuring up-to-the-minute content, eye-popping graphics, and rich animation, the highly interactive Student Edition Labs offer students an alternative way to learn through dynamic observation, step-by-step practice, and challenging review questions.

Online Content

Blackboard is the leading distance learning solution provider and class-management platform today. Course Technology has partnered with Blackboard to bring you premium online content. Instructors: Content for use with *Microsoft Windows Vista: Complete Concepts and Techniques* is available in a Blackboard Course Cartridge and may include topic reviews, case projects, review questions, test banks, practice tests, custom syllabi, and more.

Course Technology also has solutions for several other learning management systems. Please visit http://www.course.com today to see what's available for this title.

CourseCasts Learning on the Go. Always Available...Always Relevant.

Want to keep up with the latest technology trends relevant to you? Visit our site to find a library of podcasts, CourseCasts, featuring a "CourseCast of the Week," and download them to your portable media player at http://coursecasts.course.com.

Our fast-paced world is driven by technology. You know because you are an active participant — always on the go, always keeping up with technological trends, and always learning new ways to embrace technology to power your life.

Ken Baldauf, a faculty member of the Florida State University (FSU) Computer Science Department, is responsible for teaching technology classes to thousands of FSU students each year. He knows what you know; he knows what you want to learn. He is also an expert in the latest technology and will sort through and aggregate the most pertinent news and information so you can spend your time enjoying technology, rather than trying to figure it out.

Visit us at http://coursecasts.course.com to learn on the go!

CourseNotes

Course Technology's CourseNotes are six-panel quick reference cards that reinforce the most important and widely used features of a software application in a visual and user-friendly format. CourseNotes will serve as a great reference tool during and after the student completes the course. CourseNotes for Microsoft Office 2007, Word 2007, Excel 2007, Access 2007, PowerPoint 2007, Windows Vista, and more are available now!

To the Student . . .   Getting the Most Out of Your Book

Welcome to *Microsoft Windows Vista: Complete Concepts and Techniques*. You can save yourself a lot of time and gain a better understanding of Microsoft Windows Vista if you spend a few minutes reviewing the figures and callouts in this section.

1 CONSISTENT STEP-BY-STEP, SCREEN-BY-SCREEN PRESENTATION

Chapter solutions are built using a step-by-step, screen-by-screen approach. This pedagogy allows you to build the solution on a computer as you read through the chapter. Generally, each step includes an explanation that indicates the result of the step.

2 MORE THAN JUST STEP-BY-STEP

BTW annotations in the margins of the book, Q&As in the steps, and substantive text in the paragraphs provide background information, tips, and answers to common questions that complement the topics covered, adding depth and perspective. When you finish with this book, you will be ready to use the Office programs to solve problems on your own. Experimental steps provide you with opportunities to step out on your own to try features of the programs, and pick up right where you left off in the chapter.

3 OTHER WAYS BOXES

Other Ways boxes that follow many of the step sequences explain the other ways to complete the task presented, such as using the mouse, Ribbon, shortcut menu, and keyboard.

4 EMPHASIS ON GETTING HELP WHEN YOU NEED IT
Chapter 1 shows you how to use all the elements of Windows Vista Help. Being able to answer your own questions will increase your productivity and reduce your frustrations by minimizing the time it takes to learn how to complete a task.

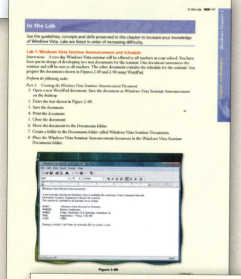

5 REVIEW, REINFORCEMENT, AND EXTENSION
After you successfully step through a project in a chapter, a section titled Chapter Summary identifies the tasks with which you should be familiar. Terms you should know for test purposes are bold in the text. The SAM Training feature provides the opportunity for addional reinforcement on important skills covered in each chapter. The Learn It Online section at the end of each chapter offers reinforcement in the form of review questions, learning games, and practice tests. Also included are exercises that require you to extend your learning beyond the book.

6 LABORATORY EXERCISES
If you really want to learn how to use the programs, then you must design and implement solutions to problems on your own. Every chapter concludes with several carefully developed laboratory assignments that increase in complexity.

About Our New Cover Look

Learning styles of students have changed, but the Shelly Cashman Series' dedication to their success has remained steadfast for over 30 years. We are committed to continually updating our approach and content to reflect the way today's students learn and experience new technology.

This focus on the user is reflected in our bold new cover design, which features photographs of real students using the Shelly Cashman Series in their courses. Each book features a different user, reflecting the many ages, experiences, and backgrounds of all of the students learning with our books. When you use the Shelly Cashman Series, you can be assured that you are learning computer skills using the most effective courseware available.

1 Fundamentals of Using Microsoft Windows Vista

Objectives

You will have mastered the material in this chapter when you can:

- Describe Microsoft Windows Vista

- Explain operating system, server, workstation, and user interface

- Log on to the computer

- Identify the objects on the Microsoft Windows Vista desktop

- Display the Start menu

- Add gadgets to Windows Sidebar

- Identify the Computer and Documents windows

- Add and remove a desktop icon

- Open, minimize, maximize, restore, and close a Windows Vista window

- Move and size a window on the Windows Vista desktop

- Scroll in a window

- Launch an application program

- Switch between running application programs

- Use Windows Vista Help and Support

- Log off from the computer and turn off the computer

1 | Fundamentals of Using Microsoft Windows Vista

What is Microsoft Windows Vista?

An **operating system** is the set of computer instructions, called a computer program, that controls the allocation of computer hardware such as memory, disk devices, printers, and CD and DVD drives, and provides the capability for you to communicate with the computer. The most popular and widely used operating system is **Microsoft Windows**. **Microsoft Windows Vista**, the newest version of Microsoft Windows, allows you to easily communicate with and control your computer.

Windows Vista is commonly used on stand-alone computers, computer workstations, and portable computers. A **workstation** is a computer connected to a server. A **server** is a computer that controls access to the hardware and software on a network and provides a centralized storage area for programs, data, and information. Figure 1–1 illustrates a simple computer network consisting of a server, three workstations, and a laser printer connected to the server.

Windows Vista is easy to use and can be customized to fit individual needs. The operating system simplifies working with documents and applications, transferring data between documents, interacting with the different components of the computer, and using the computer to access information on the Internet or an intranet. The **Internet** is a worldwide group of connected computer networks that allows public access to information on thousands of subjects and gives users the ability to use this information, send messages, and obtain products and services.

This book demonstrates how to use Microsoft Windows Vista to control the computer and communicate with other computers both on a network and over the Internet. In Chapter 1, you will learn about Windows Vista and how to use the Windows Vista user interface.

Overview

As you read this chapter, you will learn how to use the Microsoft Windows Vista graphical user interface by performing these general tasks:

- Start Windows Vista and log on
- Open the Start menu, expand and close a menu
- Work with Windows Sidebar
- Launch an application
- Switch between applications
- Add and delete icons on the desktop
- Open, minimize, restore, move, size, scroll, and close a window
- Display folder contents
- Use the Help system to answer questions
- Log off and turn off the computer

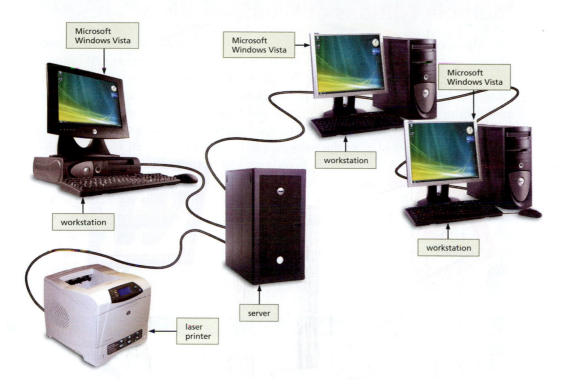

Figure 1–1

Working with Microsoft Windows Vista

Working with an operating system requires a basic knowledge of how to start the operating system, log on and off the computer, and identify the objects on the Windows Vista desktop.

1. **Determine how you will be logging on to the computer.** Depending on the setup of the computer you are using, you may need an account and password. If it is a work or educational computer, you may be assigned an account.

2. **Establish which edition of Windows Vista is installed.** Since there are different editions of Windows Vista with different features, you should know which edition is installed on the computer you will be using.

3. **Determine the permissions you have on the computer you will be using.** Each user account can have different rights and permissions. Depending on which rights and per-missions have been set for your account, you may or may not be able to perform certain operations.

4. **Determine if you have Internet access.** For some features of Windows Vista, such as help and support, there is a lot of material online that you may find useful. You will want to know if your computer has Internet access and if anything is required of you to use it.

**Plan
Ahead**

Multiple Editions of Windows Vista

The Microsoft Windows Vista operating system is available in a variety of editions. The editions that you will most likely encounter are Windows Vista Starter, Windows Vista Home Basic, Windows Vista Home Premium, Windows Vista Business, Windows Vista Ultimate, and Windows Vista Enterprise. Because not all computers are the same or even used for the same functions, Microsoft provides these various editions so that each user can have the edition that best meets their needs. **Microsoft Windows Vista Ultimate Edition** is the most complete of all of the editions and has all of the power, security, mobility, and entertainment features. **Microsoft Windows Vista Home Premium Edition** contains many of the features of Microsoft Windows Vista Ultimate Edition, but is designed for entertainment and home use. The Home Premium Edition allows you to establish a network of computers in the home that share a single Internet connection, share a device such as a printer or a scanner, share files and folders, and play multi-computer games. The network can be created using Ethernet cable or telephone wire or can be wireless. These six editions are briefly described in Table 1–1. For more information about the new features of Windows Vista and the differences between the editions, see Appendix A.

Table 1–1 Windows Vista Editions	
Edition	**Description**
Windows Vista Starter Edition	This edition is made for countries that do not have developed technology markets. It only comes with the most basic features designed for beginning computer users. It is not available in the United States, the European Union, Australia, and Japan.
Windows Vista Home Basic Edition	This edition is easy to set up and maintain, provides security and parental controls, allows access to e-mail, simplifies searching for pictures and music, and allows the creation of simple documents. It is designed for individuals who have a home desktop or mobile PC.
Windows Vista Home Premium Edition	This edition is designed for individuals who have a home desktop or mobile PC that has the additional multimedia hardware necessary for the advanced Windows media software. It includes all of the features of the Home Basic Edition plus home networking capabilities and Windows Media Center. With Windows Media Center, the computer can be used to watch and record television, play video games, listen to music, and play and burn CDs and DVDs.
Windows Vista Business Edition	This edition is the first operating system designed specifically to meet the needs of small and mid-sized businesses. This edition includes features that make it easy to keep PCs up-to-date and running smoothly, as well as powerful ways to find, organize, and share information on the road or at the office. It is designed for the work or educational environment where there is a greater need for networking, and does not contain games or the Windows Media Center.
Windows Vista Ultimate Edition	This edition is the most complete edition of Windows Vista. It includes all of the features of the other editions plus advanced power, security, mobility and entertainment capabilities and features. For example, it includes support for Windows Tablet and Touch Technology, Windows SideShow, Windows Mobility Center, Windows DreamScene, and Windows BitLocker Drive Encryption (see Appendix A, for a full description of these features).
Windows Vista Enterprise Edition	This edition was designed to help global organizations and enterprises with complex IT infrastructures to lower IT costs, reduce risk, and stay connected. This edition only is available to volume license customers who have PCs covered by Microsoft Software Assurance. This edition is most similar to the Business edition but includes more sophisticated features such as Windows BitLocker Drive Encryption (see Appendix A, for a full description of this feature).

Microsoft Windows Vista

Microsoft Windows Vista (called **Windows Vista** for the rest of the book) is an operating system that performs the functions necessary for you to communicate with and use the computer. Windows Vista is available in 32-bit and 64-bit versions for all editions except Windows Vista Starter Edition.

Windows Vista is used to run **application programs**, which are programs that perform an application-related function such as word processing. Windows Vista includes several application programs, including Windows Internet Explorer, Windows Media Player, Windows Movie Maker, and Windows Mail. **Windows Internet Explorer**, or **Internet Explorer**, integrates the Windows Vista desktop and the Internet. Internet Explorer allows you to work with programs and files in a similar fashion, regardless of whether they are located on the computer, a local network, or the Internet. **Windows Media Player** lets you create and play CDs, watch DVDs, listen to radio stations all over the world, and search for and organize digital media files. **Windows Movie Maker** can transfer recorded audio and video from analog camcorders or digital video cameras to the computer, import existing audio and video files to use in the movies you make, and send finished movies by e-mail or post them on the World Wide Web. **Windows Mail** is an e-mail program that lets you exchange e-mail with friends and colleagues, trade ideas and information in a newsgroup, manage multiple mail and news accounts, and add stationery or a personal signature to messages; it also has junk e-mail filtering and protection against fraudulent messages. Windows Vista includes other applications, depending upon the edition you are using.

Windows Vista has a number of customizations that you can perform. Depending upon how you desire to use your computer, you can change the appearance of the desktop, Sidebar, Start menu, and more. As you proceed through this book, you will learn many ways to customize your experience. To use the application programs that can be run under Windows Vista, you need to understand the Windows Vista user interface.

User Interfaces

A **user interface** is the combination of hardware and software that you use to communicate with and control the computer. Through the user interface, you are able to make selections on the computer, request information from the computer, and respond to messages displayed by the computer. Thus, a user interface provides the means for dialogue between you and the computer.

The computer software determines the messages you receive, how you should respond, and the actions that occur based on your responses. The goal of an effective user interface is to be **user-friendly**, which means that the software is easy to use by people with limited training. Research studies have indicated that the use of graphics plays an important role in helping users to interact effectively with a computer.

A **graphical user interface**, or **GUI** (pronounced gooey), is a user interface that displays graphics in addition to text when it communicates with the user. Windows Vista has two variations of GUIs: Windows Vista Basic experience and Windows Vista Aero experience. The Aero experience is not available in the Starter and Home Basic Editions.

BTW

Determining Edition Support

Before you upgrade an existing Windows system to Vista, you can determine which edition of Vista your computer will support by installing and running the Windows Vista Upgrade Advisor. To access the Windows Vista Upgrade Advisor, visit http://www.microsoft.com/windows, and then click, "Are you ready for Windows Vista?".

BTW

Vista Capable and Premium Ready

When buying a computer, you may run across ones that are labeled Vista Capable and Vista Premium Ready. A Vista Capable computer can run the Vista Basic experience, but may need to be upgraded to support the Aero experience. Vista Premium Ready means that the computer can run Aero, but some features still may require additional hardware.

Aero Experience

Aero is a three-dimensional graphical user interface. To use Aero, your computer needs to have a compatible graphics adapter and an edition of Vista installed that supports Aero. The first thing you will notice about Aero is **Aero Glass,** which is a flashy translucent glass effect around the borders of the windows that allows you to partially see the items behind the windows. **Windows Flip** and **Windows Flip 3D**, another part of the Aero experience, make switching between your applications as visual and tactile as flipping through papers on your desk.

Aero provides a simple and entertaining interface for dealing with Windows Vista. Figure 1–2 shows examples of the Basic experience and the Aero experience. The figures in this book were created in the Aero experience.

(a) Basic experience

(b) Aero experience

Figure 1–2

The Windows Vista graphical user interface was carefully designed to be easier to set up, simpler to learn, faster and more powerful, and better integrated with the Internet than previous versions of Microsoft Windows.

Launching Microsoft Windows Vista

When you turn on the computer, an introductory screen consisting of a progress bar and copyright messages (© Microsoft Corporation) is displayed. The progress bar animates continuously as the Windows Vista operating system loads. After a brief time, the Windows Vista logo appears. After the Vista logo appears, if your computer is set to start with **automatic logon**, you will be taken directly to your desktop without being asked to type a user name or password; otherwise, the Welcome screen displays (Figure 1–3).

The **Welcome screen** shows the user icons and names of every user on the computer. On the bottom left side of the Welcome screen, the **Ease of Access button** appears, which allows you to change accessibility options as long as you have permission to change them. On the bottom right side of the Welcome screen is the **Shut Down button**. Clicking the Shut Down button shuts down Windows Vista and the computer. To the right of the Shut Down button is the **Shut Down options arrow**, which provides access to a menu containing three commands, Restart, Sleep, and Shut Down. The **Restart command** closes open programs, shuts down Windows Vista, and then restarts the computer and Windows Vista. The **Sleep command** waits for Windows Vista to save your work and then turns off the fans and hard disk. To wake the computer from the Sleep state, press the Power button or lift the laptop cover, and then log on to the computer. The **Shut Down command** shuts down Windows Vista and turns off the computer.

BTW

User Icons
When a user account is created, an icon (picture) can be selected to identify the user. This user icon can be changed by using the Control Panel if you have the permission to change it. A school or work account may not allow you to change your user icon.

BTW

User Names and Passwords
A unique user name identifies each user. In the past, users often entered a variation of their name as their user name. For example, Nicki Kennedy might have chosen nickikennedy or nkennedy. Today, most Windows Vista users use their first and last name as the user name. A password is a combination of characters that allows you to access your account on the computer or your account on a network. Passwords should be kept confidential. For security purposes, schools and businesses may require you to change your password on a regular basis.

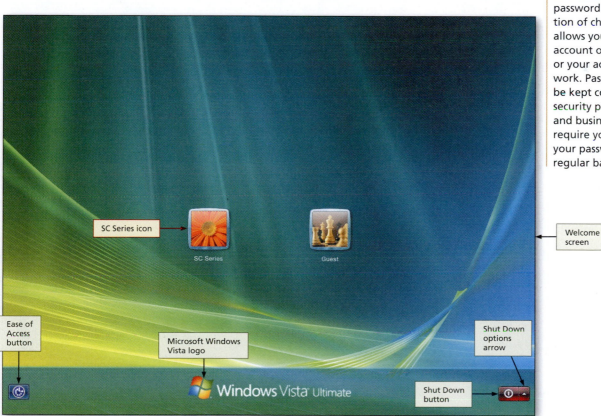

Figure 1–3

BTW

Buttons

Buttons are an integral part of Windows Vista. When you point to them, their function displays in a ToolTip. When you click them, they appear to recess on the screen to mimic what would happen if you pushed an actual button. All buttons in Windows Vista operate in the same manner.

In the middle bottom of the Welcome screen there is the Windows Vista logo and the name of your Vista edition, for example, Windows Vista Ultimate. In the middle of the Welcome screen is a list of the **user icons** and **user names** for all authorized computer users. The list of user icons and names on the Welcome screen on your computer may be different. Clicking the user icon or user name begins the process of logging on to the computer. If the user account you clicked does not require a password, then you will be taken to your desktop; otherwise, you will be prompted to enter your password to log on.

If, after logging on to the computer, you leave the computer unattended for fifteen minutes, the computer will go to sleep automatically. In **Sleep mode**, your work is saved and the computer is placed in power saving mode. When you start using your computer again, the Welcome screen will display and you will have to log on to the computer again to gain access to your account.

Logging On to the Computer

After launching Windows Vista but before working with Windows Vista, you must log on to the computer. For this section, it is assumed that automatic logon is turned off and that you have to type in a password. Logging on to the computer opens your user account and makes the computer available for use. In the following steps, the SC Series icon and the Next button are used to log on to the computer and enter a password. When you perform these steps, you will want to log on to the computer by clicking *your user icon* on the Welcome screen and typing *your password* in the text box instead of the password shown in the steps.

To Log On to the Computer

The following steps log on to the computer.

1

- Click the SC Series icon (or your icon) on the Welcome screen to display the password text box.

- Type your password in the password text box (Figure 1–4).

Q&A Why do I not see an SC Series icon?

The SC Series icon is not present as the SC Series account is not a user account on your computer.

Q&A Where is my password text box?

You will not see a password text box if your account does not require a password. You only have to select your user icon to log on.

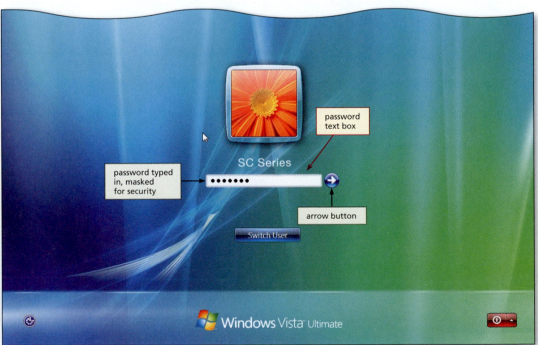

Figure 1–4

2
• Click the arrow button to log on to the computer to display the Welcome Center window and Windows Sidebar on the Windows Vista desktop (Figure 1–5).

Q&A

Why does my desktop look different from the one in Figure 1–5?

The Windows Vista desktop is customizable and your work or school may have modified the desktop to meet their needs.

Figure 1–5

Although the Windows Vista desktop can easily be tailored to your needs, it does contain some standard elements. The items on the desktop in Figure 1–5 include the Recycle Bin icon and its name in the top-left corner of the desktop, the Welcome Center window in the center of the desktop, and the taskbar at the bottom of the desktop. The **Recycle Bin** allows you to discard unneeded objects. Your computer's desktop may contain more, fewer, or different icons, depending on how the desktop was modified.

The **taskbar** shown at the bottom of the screen in Figure 1–5 contains the Start button, Quick Launch toolbar, taskbar button area, and notification area. The **Start button** allows you to launch a program quickly, find or open a document, change the computer's settings, obtain Help, shut down the computer, and perform many more tasks. The **Quick Launch toolbar** contains icons for those applications you want to be able to access quickly. The **taskbar button area** contains buttons to indicate which windows are open on the desktop. The Welcome Center button is displayed in the taskbar button area.

The **notification area** contains the Show hidden icons button, notification icons, and the current time. The **Show hidden icons button** indicates that one or more inactive icon is hidden from view in the notification area. The **notification icons** provide quick access to utility programs that are currently running in the background on your computer. A program running in the background does not show up on the taskbar, but is still working. Icons may display temporarily in the notification area when providing status updates. For example, the printer icon is displayed when a document is sent to the printer and is removed when printing is complete. The notification area on your desktop may contain more, fewer, or different icons as the contents of the notification area can change.

BTW

The Notification Area
The Show hidden icons button displays on the left edge of the notification area if one or more inactive icon is hidden from view in the notification area. Clicking the Show hidden icons button displays the hidden icons in the notification area and replaces the Show hidden icons button with the Hide button. Moving the mouse pointer off the notification area removes, or hides, the inactive icons in the notification area and redisplays the Show hidden icons button.

Also on the Windows Vista desktop is the Windows Sidebar. The **Windows Sidebar** is a long, vertical strip on the right edge of the desktop that holds mini-programs called gadgets (Figure 1–5 on the previous page). A **gadget** is a mini-program that provides continuously updated information, such as current weather information, news updates, traffic information, and Internet radio streams. You can customize your Sidebar to hold the gadgets you choose.

The Welcome Center

The **Welcome Center** is displayed when the computer is used for the first time and allows you to complete a set of tasks to optimize the computer. The tasks may include adding user accounts, transferring files and settings from another computer, and connecting to the Internet. The Welcome Center can be turned off; therefore, you may not see it on your screen. It does not have to be displayed because you do not need to use it every time you want to complete a task in Windows Vista.

To Close the Welcome Center

The following step closes the Welcome Center window. If the Welcome Center window is not visible on your screen, you do not have to perform this step.

- Click the Close button on the Welcome Center window to close the Welcome Center (Figure 1–6).

Start button

Figure 1–6

The Windows Vista Desktop

The Windows Vista desktop and the objects on the desktop emulate a work area in an office. You may think of the Windows desktop as an electronic version of the top of your desk. You can place objects on the desktop, move the objects around on the desktop, look at them and then put them aside, and so on.

Opening the Start Menu

The **Start menu** allows you to easily access the most useful items on the computer. A **menu** is a list of related commands and the **commands** on a menu perform a specific action, such as searching for files or obtaining help. The Start menu contains commands that allow you to connect to and browse the Internet, launch an e-mail program, launch application programs, store and search for documents, folders, and programs, customize the computer, obtain help, and log off and turn off the computer.

To Display the Start Menu

The following steps display the Start menu.

1

• Click the Start button on the Windows Vista taskbar to display the Start menu (Figure 1–7).

Q&A Why does my Start menu look different?

Depending upon your computer's configuration, the Start menu can look different. In a work or school environment, it may be customized for any number of reasons such as usage requirements or security issues.

Figure 1–7

2

• Click the All Programs command on the Start menu to display the All Programs list (Figure 1–8).

Q&A

Why does my All Programs list look different?

The applications installed on your computer may differ. Your All Programs list will show the applications that are installed on your computer.

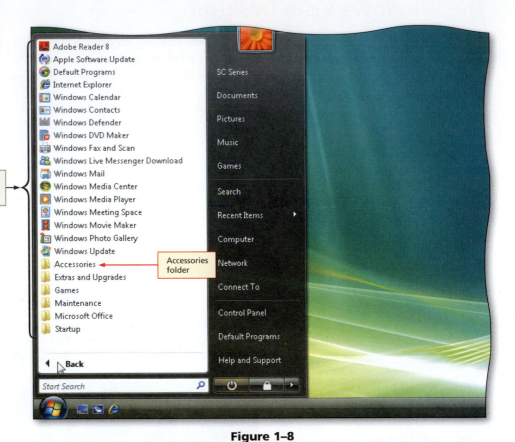

Figure 1–8

3

• Click the Accessories folder to display the Accessories list (Figure 1–9).

Q&A

What are accessories?

Accessories are application programs that accomplish a variety of tasks commonly required on a computer. Most accessories are installed with the Vista operating system, including Calculator, Snipping Tool, Windows Mobility Center (if you have a portable computer), WordPad, etc. Your Accessories list may contain additional or fewer programs.

Figure 1–9

To Scroll Using Scroll Arrows, the Scroll Bar, and the Scroll Box

A **scroll bar** is a bar that is displayed when the contents of an area are not completely visible. A vertical scroll bar contains an **up scroll arrow**, a **down scroll arrow**, and a **scroll box** that enables you to view areas that currently are not visible. In Figure 1–9, a vertical scroll bar displays along the right side of the All Programs list. Scrolling can be accomplished in three ways: (1) click the scroll arrows; (2) click the scroll bar; and (3) drag the scroll box. You **drag** an object by pointing to an item, holding down the left mouse button, and moving the object to the desired location, and then release, or **drop**, the object by releasing the left mouse button. The following steps scroll the items in the All Programs list.

1

- Click the down scroll arrow on the vertical scroll bar to display additional folders at the bottom of the All Programs list (Figure 1–10). You may need to click more than once to get to the bottom of the All Programs list.

Figure 1–10

2

- Click the scroll bar above the scroll box to move the scroll box to the top of the All Programs list (Figure 1–11). You may need to click more than once to get to the top of the All Programs list.

Q&A

Why does it take more than one click to move the scroll box to the top of the scroll bar?

There may be more applications installed on your computer than on the one in the figure; in that case, you may have to click two or more times to move the scroll box to the top.

Figure 1–11

3

- Click the scroll box and drag down to the bottom of the scroll bar and display the bottom of the All Programs list (Figure 1–12).

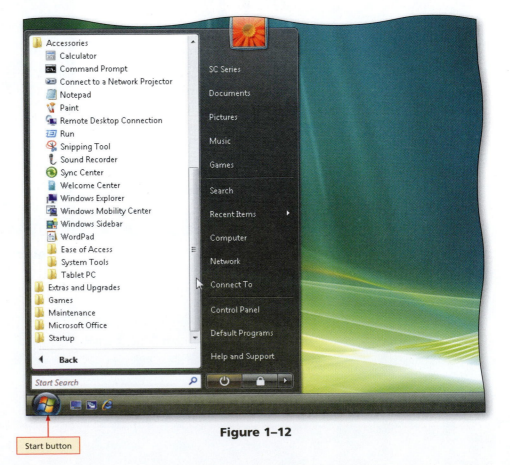

Figure 1–12

4
- Click the Start button to close the Start menu (Figure 1–13).

Start menu closed

Figure 1–13

The Computer Folder

The **Computer folder** is accessible via the Start menu. When opened, the Computer folder opens in a **folder window**. The Computer folder is the place you can go to access hard disk drives, CD or DVD drives, removable media, and network locations that are connected to your computer. You also can access other devices such as external hard disks or digital cameras that you have connected to your system.

To Open the Computer Folder Window

The following steps open the Computer folder window.

1
- Click the Start button on the Windows Vista taskbar to open the Start menu (Figure 1–14).

Computer command

Figure 1–14

2
- Click the Computer command on the right pane to open the Computer folder window (Figure 1–15).

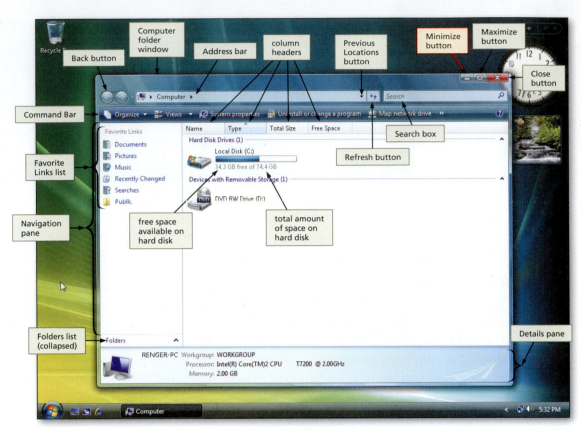

Figure 1–15

Other Ways

1. Click the Start button, right-click Computer, click Open
2. Press WINDOWS+E

Folder windows are the key tools for finding, viewing, and managing information on the computer. Folder windows have common design elements, as shown in Figure 1–15. The three buttons to the left of the **Address bar** allow you to navigate the contents of the right pane and view recent pages. On the right of the title bar are the Minimize button, the Maximize button, and the Close button, which can be used to reduce the window to the taskbar, increase the window to the full screen, or close the window.

The two right arrows in the Address bar allow you to revisit locations on the computer that you have visited using the Address bar. The **Previous Locations button** saves the locations you have visited and displays the locations using computer path names.

The **Refresh button** at the end of the Address bar refreshes the contents of the right pane of the Computer window. The **Search box** to the right of the Address bar contains the dimmed word, Search. You can type a term into the Search box for a list of files, folders, shortcuts, and programs containing that term within the location you are searching.

The **Command Bar** contains context-specific buttons used to accomplish various tasks on the computer related to organizing and managing the contents of the open window. Depending upon the selections you make in the Computer folder window, the Command Bar buttons will change to reflect the selections. For example, if you were to navigate to a DVD burner drive, the Command Bar would show the appropriate buttons for a DVD burner. The area below the Command Bar is separated into two panes; the left contains the Navigation pane and the right provides additional details organized into four columns. The **Navigation pane** on the left contains the Favorite Links section and the Folders list (shown as collapsed in Figure 1–15). The **Favorite Links list** contains your documents, pictures, music files, and more.

The four **column headers**, Name, Type, Total Size, and Free Space, that appear in the right pane allow you to sort and group the entries by each header category.

To Minimize and Redisplay a Window

Two buttons on the title bar of a window, the Minimize button and the Maximize button, allow you to control the way a window displays or does not display on the desktop. The following steps minimize and restore the Computer folder window.

- Click the Minimize button on the title bar of the Computer folder window to minimize the Computer folder window (Figure 1–16).

Q&A What happens to the Computer folder window when I click the Minimize button?

The Computer folder window remains available, but is no longer an active window. It collapses down to a non-recessed, light gray button on the taskbar.

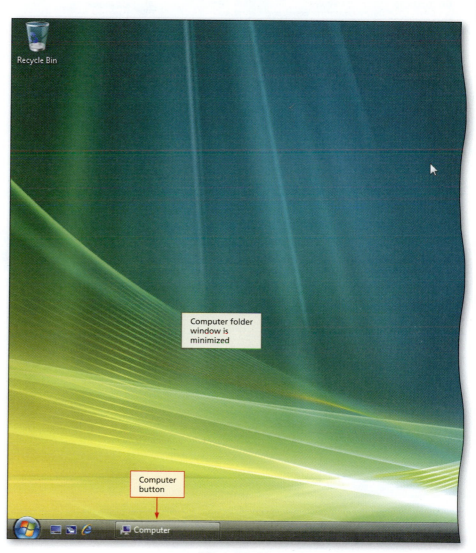

Figure 1–16

2

● Click the Computer button on the taskbar to display the Computer folder window (Figure 1–17).

Q&A

Why does the Computer button on the taskbar change?

The button changes to reflect the status of the Computer folder window. A black recessed button indicates that the Computer folder window is active on the screen. A light gray non-recessed button indicates that the Computer folder window is open but not active.

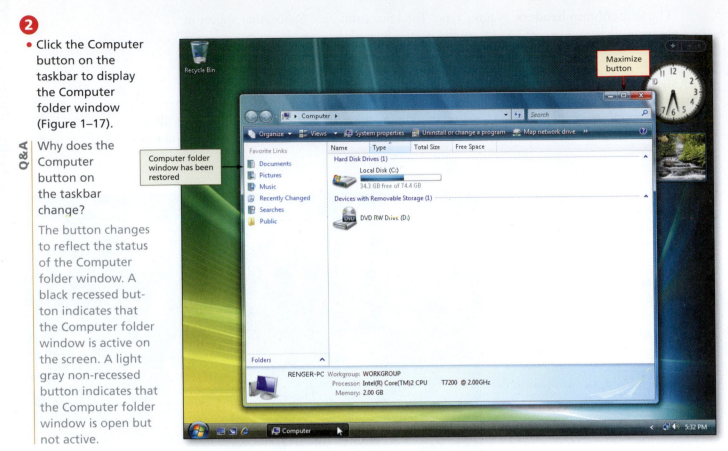

Figure 1–17

Q&A

Why do I see a picture when I click the Computer button?

Whenever you move your mouse over a button or click a button on the taskbar, a preview of the window will be displayed as part of the Aero experience.

Other Ways

1. Right-click title bar, click Minimize, in taskbar button area click taskbar button

2. Press WINDOWS+M, press WINDOWS+SHIFT+M

To Maximize and Restore a Window

Sometimes information is not completely visible in a window. One method of displaying the entire contents of a window is to enlarge the window using the **Maximize button**. The Maximize button increases the size of a window so it fills the entire screen, making it easier to see the contents of the window. When a window is maximized, the **Restore Down button** replaces the Maximize button on the title bar. Clicking the Restore Down button will return the window to the size it was before it was maximized. The following steps maximize and restore the Computer folder window.

1

• Click the Maximize button on the Computer folder window to maximize the Computer folder window (Figure 1–18).

Q&A
When a window is maximized, can you also minimize it?

Yes. Click the Minimize button to minimize the window. Clicking the button on the taskbar will return the window to its maximized size.

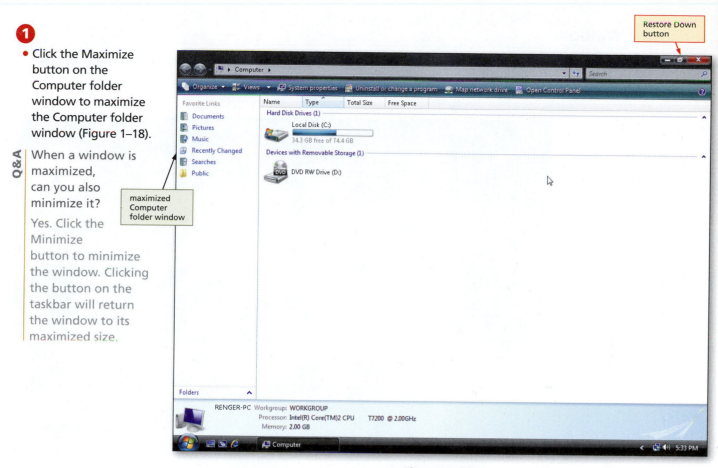

Figure 1–18

2

• Click the Restore Down button on the Computer folder window to return the Computer folder window to its previous size (Figure 1–19).

Q&A
What happens to the Restore Down button after I click it?

The Maximize button replaces the Restore Down button on the title bar.

Other Ways

1. Right-click title bar, click Maximize, right-click title bar, click Restore

2. Double-click title bar, double-click title bar

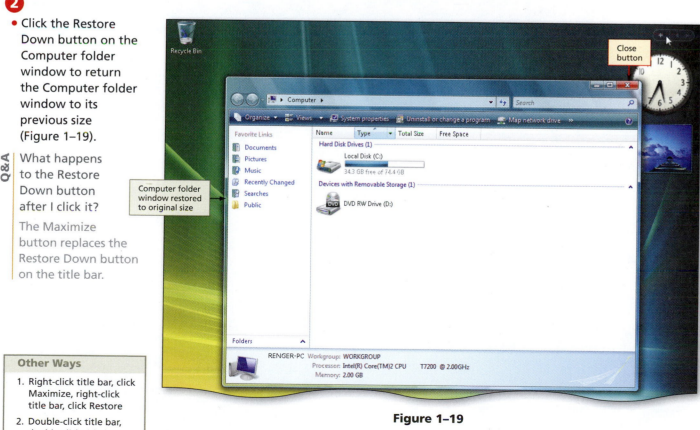

Figure 1–19

To Close a Window

The **Close button** on the title bar of a window closes the window and removes the taskbar button from the taskbar. To close the Computer folder window, complete the following step.

- Click the Close button on the title bar of the Computer folder window to close the Computer folder window (Figure 1–20).

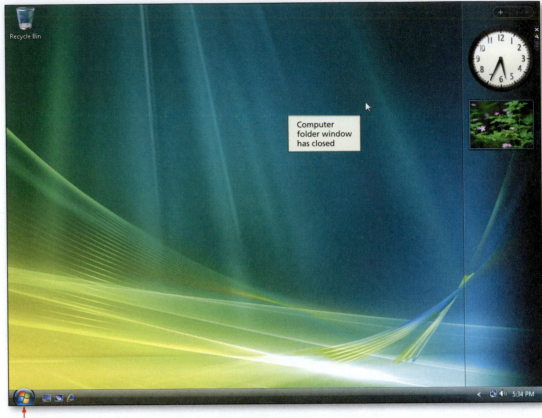

Computer folder window has closed

Start button

Figure 1–20

Other Ways

1. Right-click title bar, click Close
2. Press ALT+F4

To Add an Icon to the Desktop

Once you start doing a lot of work on your computer, you may want to add additional icons to the desktop. For example, you may want to add the Documents folder icon to the desktop for faster access. The **Documents folder window** is a central location for the storage and management of documents that Windows Vista has optimized for faster searching and organizing. The following steps add a shortcut to the Documents folder window to your desktop.

1

- Click the Start button to open the Start menu.

- Point to the Documents command on the right pane and then click the right mouse button (right-click).

- Point to the Send To command on the Documents shortcut menu to display the Send To submenu (Figure 1–21).

Q&A

What is a shortcut menu?

A shortcut menu appears when you right-click an object and contains commands specifically for use with that object.

Figure 1–21

2

- Click the Desktop (create shortcut) command on the Send To sub-menu to place a shortcut to the Documents folder on the desktop (Figure 1–22).

Q&A   Why would I want to use a shortcut menu?

Using shortcut menus can speed up your work and add flexibility to your interaction with the computer by making often used items available in multiple locations.

Q&A   Why am I unable to add an item to my desktop?

Sometimes at work or in school labs users are not allowed to customize their desktop.

Q&A   How many icons should I have on my desktop?

Icons can be added to your desktop by applications or by users; however, it is considered a best practice to keep your desktop as clutter free as possible. If you are not using an icon on the desktop, consider removing it from the desktop.

3

- Click the Start button to close the Start menu.

Figure 1–22

Other Ways

1. Right-click desktop, point to New, click Shortcut which opens the Create Shortcut Wizard, click Browse, click your user name, click Documents, Click OK button, click Next button, type shortcut name (or leave alone), click Finish

To Open a Window Using a Desktop Icon

The following step opens the Documents window using the shortcut you have just created on the desktop.

1

- Click the mouse button twice, in quick succession (double-click) on the Documents icon on the desktop to open the Documents folder window (Figure 1–23).

Q&A | What does the Documents folder window allow me to do?

The Documents folder window is designed to provide a location for you to store your commonly used files. Many programs use this location by default when opening and closing files.

Q&A | Why are the contents of my Documents folder different?

Because you have different documents and folders created on your computer, the contents of your Documents folder will be different than the one in Figure 1–23.

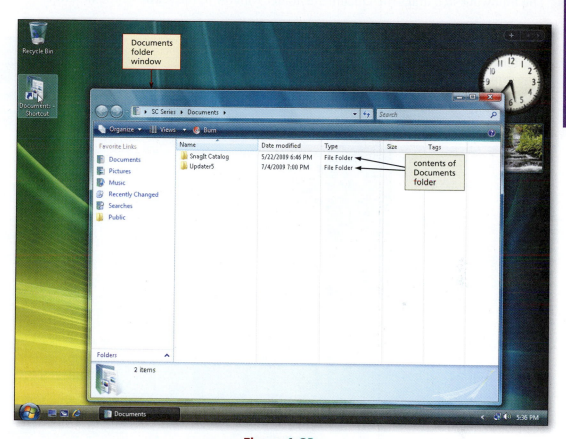

Figure 1–23

Other Ways

1. Right-click desktop icon, click Open on the shortcut menu

Double-Clicking Errors   While double-clicking an object, it is easy to click once instead of twice. When you click an object such as the Documents icon once, the icon becomes active and dimmed. To open the Documents folder window after clicking the Documents icon once, double-click the Documents icon as if you had not clicked the icon at all.

Another possible error occurs when the mouse moves after you click the first time and before you click the second time. In most cases when this occurs, the icon will appear dimmed as if you had clicked it just one time.

A third possible error is moving the mouse while you are pressing the mouse button. In this case, the icon might have moved on the screen because you inadvertently dragged it. To open the Documents folder window after dragging it accidentally, double-click the icon as if you had not clicked it at all.

To Move a Window by Dragging

You can move any open window to another location on the desktop by dragging the title bar of the window. The following step drags the Documents folder window to the center of the desktop.

1

• Drag the Documents folder window to the center of the screen, as shown in Figure 1–24.

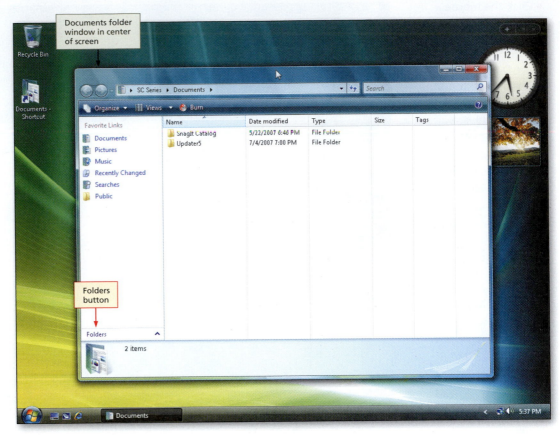

Figure 1–24

Other Ways
1. Right-click title bar, click Move, drag window

To Expand the Folders List

In Figure 1–24, the Folders list in the Documents folder window is collapsed and an up arrow appears to the right of the Folders name. Clicking the up arrow or the Folders button expands the Folders list and reveals the contents of the Folders list. The following step expands the Folders list.

1

• Click the Folders button to expand the Folders list in the Navigation pane of the Documents folder window (Figure 1–25).

Q&A

What is shown in the Folders list?

The Folders list displays a hierarchical structure of files, folders, and drives on the computer.

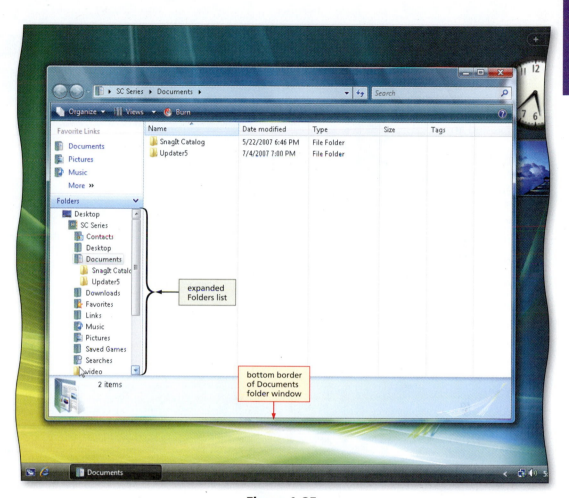

Figure 1–25

To Size a Window by Dragging

Sometimes information is not completely visible in a window. You learned how to use the Maximize button to increase the size of a window. Another method to change the size of the window is to drag the window borders. The following step changes the size of the Documents folder window.

1

- Point to the bottom border of the Documents folder window until the mouse pointer changes to a two-headed arrow.

- Drag the bottom border downward to display more of the Folders list (Figure 1–26).

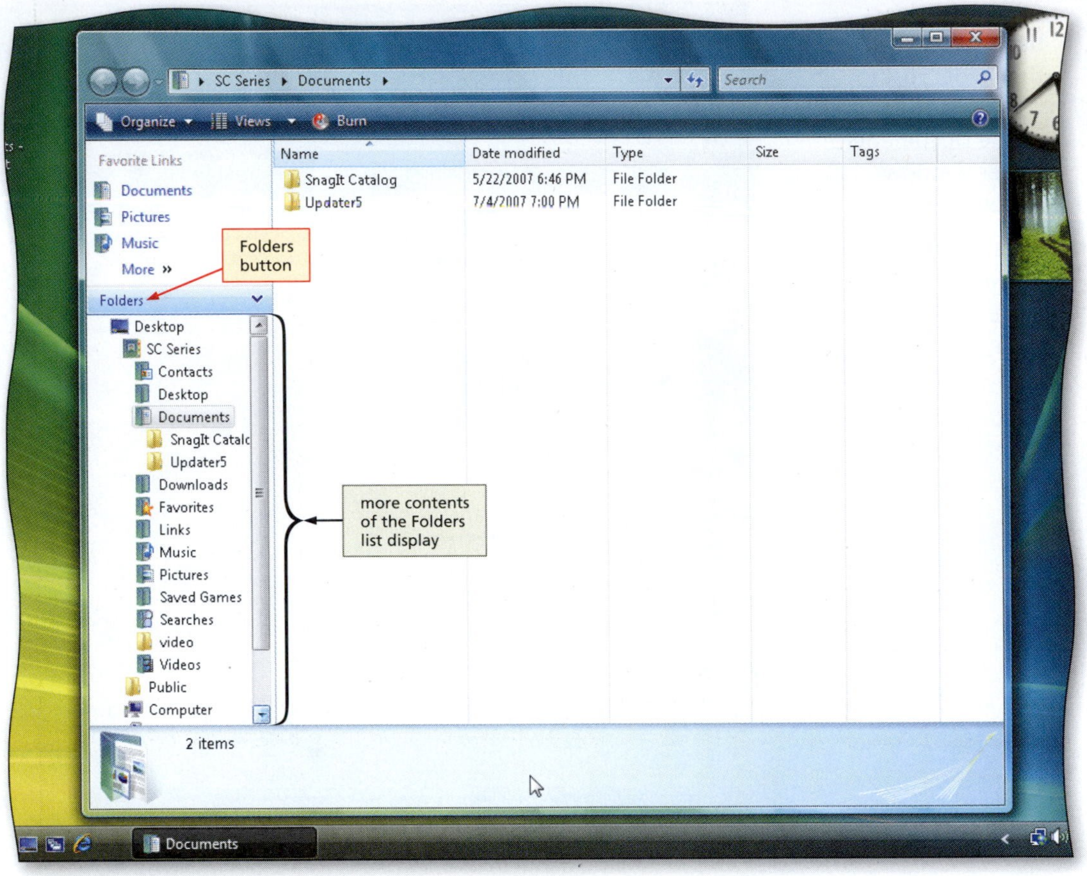

Q&A Can I drag other sides besides the bottom border to enlarge or shrink the window?

Yes, you can drag the left, right, and top borders and any window corner to resize the window.

Q&A Will Windows Vista remember the new size of the window after I close it?

Yes. Windows Vista remembers the size of the window when you close the window. When you reopen the window, it will display with the same size as when you closed it.

Figure 1–26

To Collapse the Folders List

The following step collapses the Folders list.

1

- Click the Folders button to collapse the Folders list (Figure 1–27).

Q&A

Should I keep the Folders list expanded or collapsed?

If you need to use the contents with the Folders list, it is handy to keep the list expanded. You can collapse the Folders list when the information is not needed.

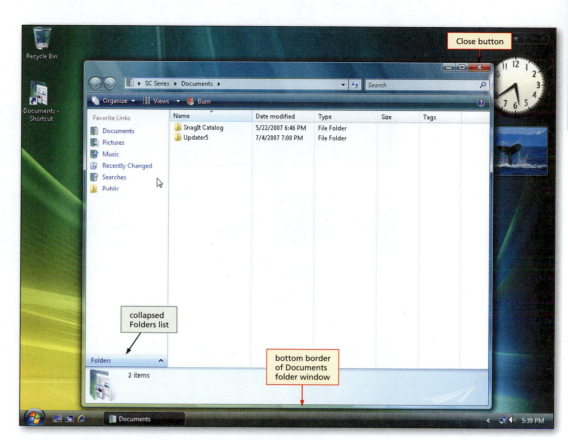

Figure 1–27

To Resize a Window

After moving and resizing a window, you may wish to return the window to its original size. To return the Documents folder window to approximately its original size, complete the following step.

1 Drag the bottom border of the Documents folder window up until the window is returned to approximately its original size.

To Close a Window

After you have completed work in a window, normally you would close it. To close the Documents folder window, complete the following step.

1 Click the Close button on the title bar of the Documents folder window to close the Documents folder window (Figure 1–28).

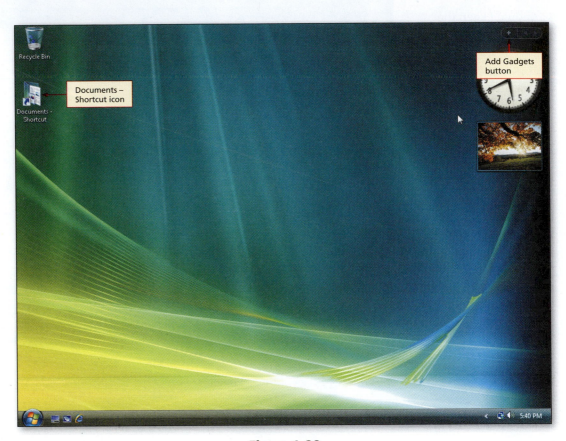

Figure 1–28

To Delete a Desktop Icon by Dragging

Although Windows Vista has many ways to delete desktop icons, one method of removing an icon from the desktop is to drag it to the Recycle Bin. The following steps delete the Documents icon by dragging the icon to the Recycle Bin.

1

• Point to the Documents - Shortcut icon on the desktop and press the left mouse button to select the icon (Figure 1–29). Do not release the left mouse button.

Figure 1–29

- Drag the Documents icon over the Recycle Bin icon on the desktop, and then release the left mouse button to place the shortcut in the Recycle Bin (Figure 1–30).

Experiment

- Double-click the Recycle Bin icon on the desktop to open a window containing the contents of the Recycle Bin. The Documents shortcut you have just deleted will display in this window. Close the Recycle Bin window.

Figure 1–30

Q&A Why did my icon disappear?

Releasing the left mouse button moved the icon from the desktop to the Recycle Bin.

> **Other Ways**
> 1. Right-click icon, click Delete, click Yes button
> 2. Right-click icon and hold, drag to Recycle Bin, release right mouse button, click Move Here

To Empty the Recycle Bin

The Recycle Bin prevents you from deleting files you actually might need. Up until the time you empty the Recycle Bin, you can recover deleted items from the Recycle Bin. The following steps empty the Recycle Bin. If you are not sure that you want to delete the files permanently in the Recycle Bin, read these steps without performing them.

- Right-click the Recycle Bin to show the shortcut menu (Figure 1–31).

- Click the Empty Recycle Bin command to permanently delete the contents of the Recycle Bin.

- Click the Yes button to confirm the operation.

> **Other Ways**
> 1. Right-click icon, click Open, click Empty Recycle Bin, click the Close button, click the Yes button
> 2. Double-click the Recycle bin icon, click Empty Recycle Bin, click the Close button, click the Yes button

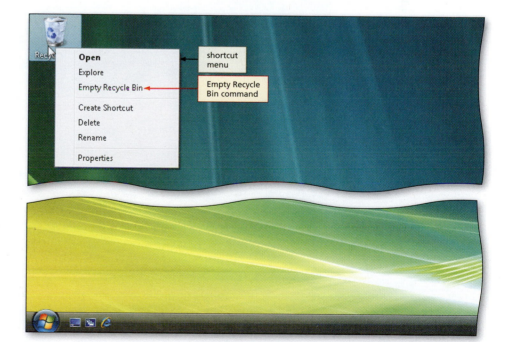

Figure 1–31

To Add a Gadget to the Windows Sidebar

The Windows Sidebar displays on the right side of the desktop and contains gadgets. Gadgets are mini-programs that display information and provide access to various useful tools. In Figure 1–13 on page WIN 15, the Windows Sidebar displays the clock and picture gadgets. The Windows Sidebar can be modified according to personal preference by adding or removing gadgets. Additional gadgets can be found in the **Gadget Gallery** or you can download gadgets from the Internet. Gadgets can include mini games, RSS feeds, and even online auction updates. In order to use gadgets, they first must be added to the Windows Sidebar. One method to add a gadget to the Windows Sidebar is to double-click the gadget in the Gadget Gallery. The following steps open the Gadget Gallery and add a gadget to the Windows Sidebar.

1

- Click the Add Gadgets button (see Figure 1-28 on page WIN 28) to open the Gadget Gallery on the desktop (Figure 1–32).

Q&A

Where can I find more gadgets?

You can download additional gadgets from http:// vista.gallery. microsoft.com, or search online to locate other gadget collections.

Figure 1–32

2

- Double-click the CPU Meter gadget in the Gadget Gallery to add the gadget to the top of the Windows Sidebar and display the performance measurements for your CPU (Figure 1–33).

3

- Click the Close button to close the Gadget Gallery.

Can I customize the Windows Sidebar?

Yes. You can select which gadgets you want to add or remove, add multiple instances of a particular gadget, and detach one or more gadgets from the Sidebar and place them on the desktop.

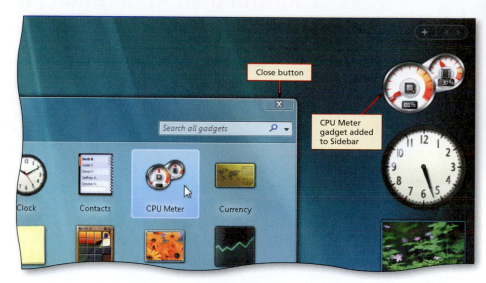

Figure 1–33

To Remove a Gadget from the Windows Sidebar

In addition to adding gadgets to the Windows Sidebar to customize your desktop, you might want to remove one or more gadgets from the Sidebar. The following steps remove a gadget from the Windows Sidebar.

1

- Point to the CPU Meter gadget to make the Close button visible (Figure 1–34).

2

- Click the Close button to remove the CPU Meter gadget from the Windows Sidebar.

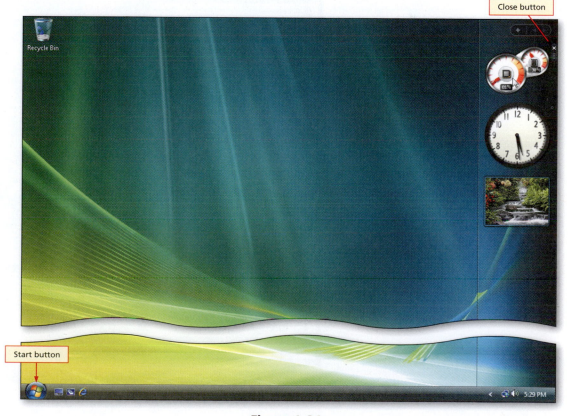

Figure 1–34

BTW

Application Programs
There are many application programs (Internet Explorer, Movie Maker, Media Player, and Windows Mail) that are installed as part of Windows Vista. Most application programs, however, such as Microsoft Office or Adobe® Photoshop®, must be purchased separately. Other application programs, like Mozilla Firefox or OpenOffice, are available for free.

Launching an Application Program

One of the basic tasks you can perform using Windows Vista is to launch an application program. A **program** is a set of computer instructions that carries out a task on the computer. An application program is a program designed to perform a specific user-oriented task. For example, a **word processing program** is an application program that allows you to create written documents; a **presentation graphics program** is an application program that allows you to create graphical presentations for display on a computer; and a **Web browser program** is an application program that allows you to explore the Internet and display Web pages.

The **default Web browser program** (Internet Explorer) appears in the pinned items list on the Start menu shown in Figure 1–7 on page WIN 11. Because the default **Web browser** is selected during the installation of the Windows Vista operating system, the default Web browser in the pinned items list on your computer may be different. In addition, you can easily select another Web browser as the default Web browser. Another frequently used Web browser is **Mozilla Firefox**.

To Start an Application Using the Start Menu

The most common activity performed on a computer is running an application program to accomplish tasks. You can start an application program by using the Start menu. The following steps open the Welcome Center using the Start menu.

- To display the Start menu, click the Start button.

- Display the Accessories list (Figure 1–35).

Figure 1–35

2

- Click the Welcome Center command to start the Welcome Center (Figure 1–36).

Figure 1–36

To Start an Application Using the Search Box

If you are unsure of where to find the application you wish to open in the Start menu, you can use the Start Search box to search for the application. **WordPad** is a popular application program available with Windows Vista that allows you to create, save, and print simple text documents. The steps on the following page search for the WordPad application using the Start Search box.

1

- Display the Start menu.

- Type wordpad in the Start Search box to have Windows Vista look for WordPad (Figure 1–37).

Q&A Why did different items display as I typed in the Start Search box?

As you type in the Start Search box, Windows Vista automatically tries to find items matching the text you enter.

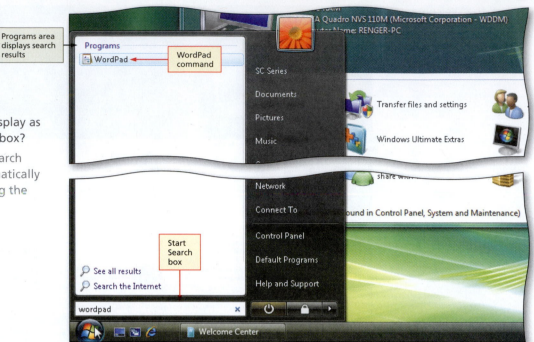

Figure 1–37

2

- Click the WordPad command in the Programs area to start WordPad (Figure 1–38).

Q&A Do I have to type the entire word before clicking the result?

No. As soon as you see the result you are looking for in the Programs area above the Start Search box, you can click it.

Other Ways

1. Open Start menu, type wordpad in the Start Search box, press ENTER

2. Open Start menu, click All Programs, open Accessories list, click WordPad

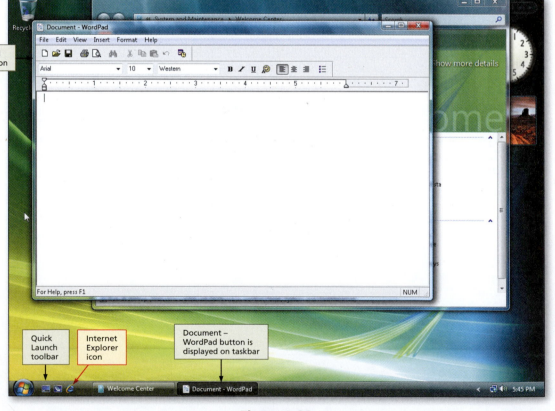

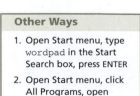

Figure 1–38

To Start an Application Using the Quick Launch Toolbar

Windows Vista allows users to access selected applications with one click of the mouse button via the Quick Launch toolbar. The following steps start the Internet Explorer application using the icon on the Quick Launch toolbar.

1

- Click the Internet Explorer icon on the Quick Launch toolbar to start Internet Explorer (Figure 1–39).

Q&A What if the Internet Explorer icon does not appear on my Quick Launch toolbar?

The Quick Launch toolbar is customizable, and yours may differ. Use one of the previous methods to open Internet Explorer instead.

Q&A Why does my Internet Explorer window look different?

Depending on your computer's setup, Internet Explorer may display a Web page other than the MSN.com Web page. For example, many school computer labs display their school's Web site when Internet Explorer first starts.

Figure 1–39

Other Ways

1. Open Start menu, click Internet Explorer
2. Press CTRL+ESC, press DOWN ARROW, press ENTER

To Switch Applications Using Windows Flip 3D

When you have multiple applications open simultaneously, invariably you will need to switch between them. Windows Flip 3D provides an easy and visual way to switch between the open applications on your computer. The steps on the following page switch from Internet Explorer to the WordPad application using Windows Flip 3D.

• Click the Switch
  Between Windows
  button on the Quick
  Launch toolbar
  to start Windows
  Flip 3D (Figure 1–40).

Q&A

Why does my
Windows Flip
not appear
three-dimensional?

Your computer is set
up to use the Basic
experience, so you
are seeing the basic
Windows Flip
which is not three-
dimensional.
Windows Flip 3D
is part of the Aero
experience.

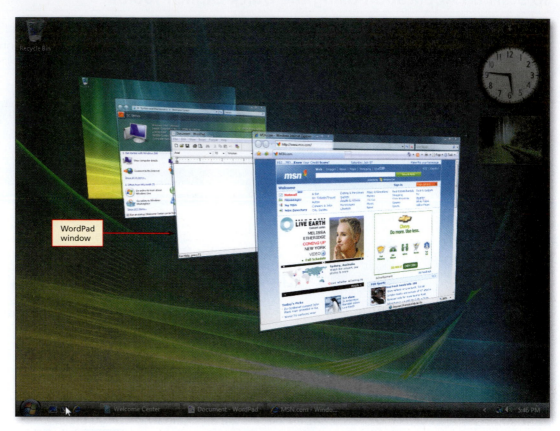

WordPad
window

Figure 1–40

• Press the TAB key
  repeatedly until the
  WordPad window
  appears at the front
  of the applica-
  tions displayed in
  Windows Flip 3D
  (Figure 1–41).

Q&A

Do I have to use the
TAB key?

You can also scroll the
mouse wheel, if your
mouse has one, until
WordPad window is
at the front.

WordPad
window

Figure 1–41

3
• Click the WordPad
window to exit
Windows Flip 3D
and make WordPad
the active applica-
tion (Figure 1–42).

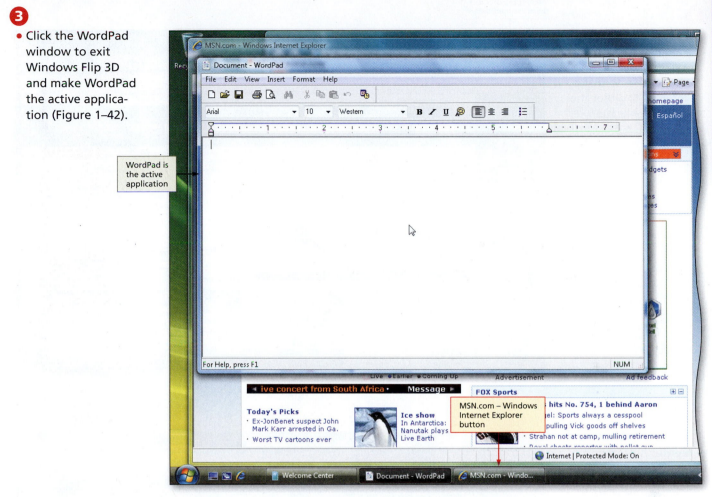

Figure 1–42

To Switch Applications Using the Taskbar

You also can switch applications using the taskbar. By clicking the button for the application, you make it
the active application and bring the window to the front. The steps on the following page switch applications using
the taskbar.

1

• Click the MSN.com - Windows Internet Explorer button on the taskbar to make Internet Explorer the active application (Figure 1–43).

Figure 1–43

2

• Click the Welcome Center button on the taskbar to make the Welcome Center the active window (Figure 1–44).

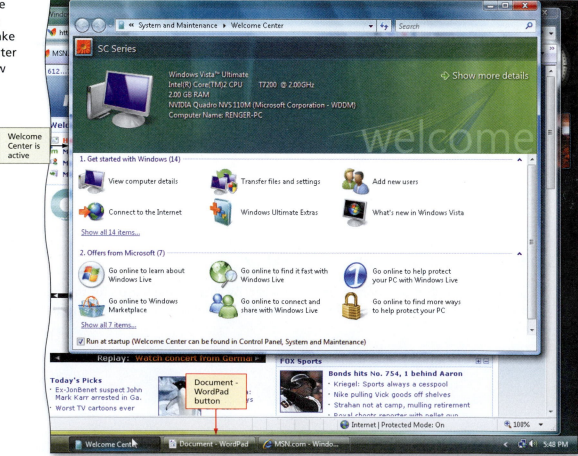

Figure 1–44

3

- Click the Document - WordPad button on the taskbar to make WordPad the active application (Figure 1–45).

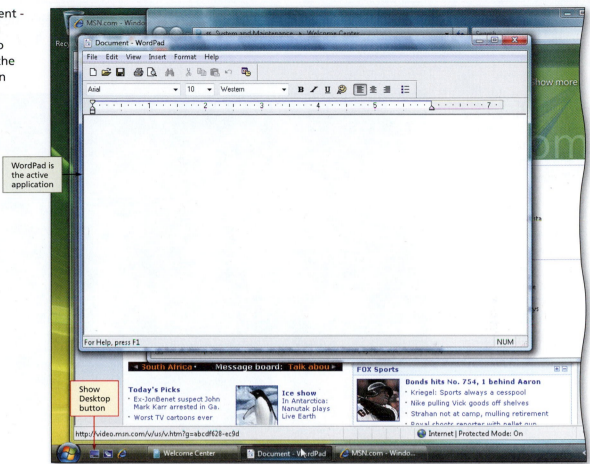

WordPad is the active application

Show Desktop button

Figure 1–45

To Show the Desktop Using the Show Desktop Button

When you have several windows open at the same time and need to reveal the desktop without closing all of the open windows, you can use the Show Desktop button on the Quick Launch toolbar to show the desktop quickly. The following step shows the desktop.

- Click the Show desktop button on the Quick Launch toolbar to show the Desktop (Figure 1–46).

Q&A

Where did the Windows Sidebar go?

When you click the Show Desktop button, it shows the desktop without the Sidebar.

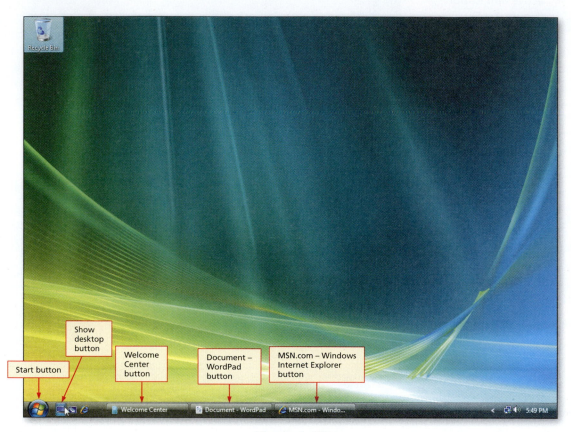

Figure 1–46

To Close Open Windows

After you are done viewing windows or using applications in Windows Vista, you should close them. The following steps close the open applications.

1 Click the Document - WordPad button on the taskbar to display the WordPad window. Click the Close button on the title bar of the WordPad window to close the WordPad window.

2 Click the MSN.com - Windows Internet Explorer button on the taskbar to display the Internet Explorer application. Click the Close button on the title bar of the Internet Explorer window to close the Internet Explorer window.

3 Display the Welcome Center and click the Close button on the title bar of the Welcome Center window to close the Welcome Center window.

Using Windows Help and Support

One of the more powerful Windows Vista features is Windows Help and Support. **Windows Help and Support** is available when using Windows Vista or when using any Microsoft application running under Windows Vista. This feature is designed to assist you in using Windows Vista or the various application programs. Table 1–2 on the next page describes what can be found in the Help and Support Center.

To Start Windows Help and Support

Before you can access the Windows Help and Support services, you must start Windows Help and Support. One method of starting Windows Help and Support uses the Start menu. The following steps start Windows Help and Support.

- Display the Start Menu (Figure 1–47).

Figure 1–47

2

- Click the Help and Support command to display the Windows Help and Support window (Figure 1–48).

- If necessary, click the Maximize button on the Windows Help and Support title bar to maximize the Windows Help and Support window.

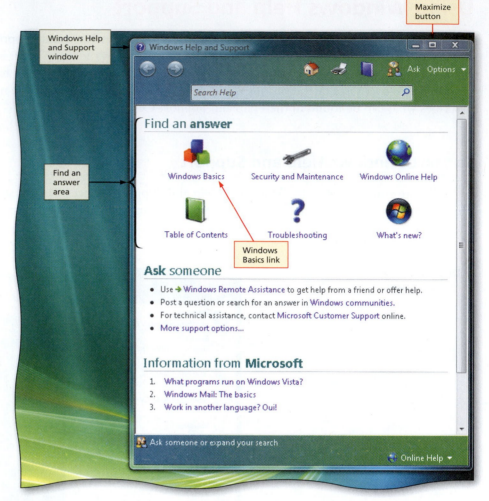

Figure 1–48

Other Ways

1. Press CTRL+ESC, press RIGHT ARROW, press UP ARROW, press ENTER
2. Press WINDOWS+F1

Table 1–2 Windows Help and Support Center Content Areas	
Area	**Function**
Find an answer	This area contains six Help topics: Windows Basics, Table of Contents, Security and Maintenance, Troubleshooting, Windows Online Help, and What's new?. Clicking a category displays a list of related subcategories and Help topics.
Ask someone	This area allows you to get help from a friend or offer help to others by using Windows Remote Assistance, post a question or search for an answer in Windows communities, and get technical assistance from Microsoft Customer Support online. Clicking the More support options link allows you to search the Knowledge Base, get in-depth technical information from Microsoft Website for IT professionals, and Windows Online Help and Support.
Information from Microsoft	This area contains links provided by Microsoft. These links are regularly updated if you are connected to the Internet.

To Browse for Help Topics in Windows Basics

After starting Windows Help and Support, your next step is to find Help topics that relate to your questions. Windows Help and Support organizes Help topics by headings and subheadings, as illustrated in Figure 1-49. The following steps use the 'Find an answer' area in the Windows Help and Support to locate a Help topic that describes how to use the Windows Help and Support.

• Click the Windows
Basics link in the
Find an answer
area to display the
Windows Basics: all
topics page
(Figure 1–49).

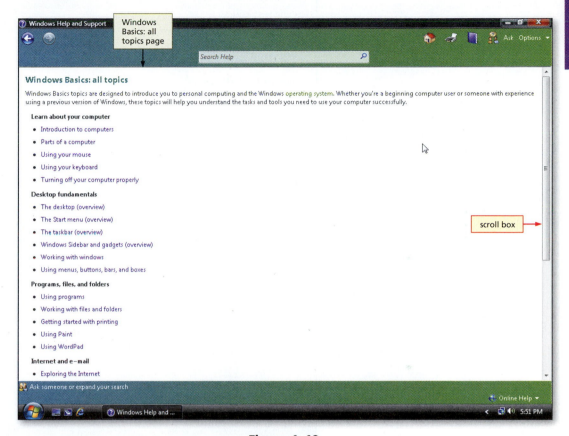

Figure 1–49

2

- Scroll down to view the Getting help link under the Help and support heading (Figure 1–50).

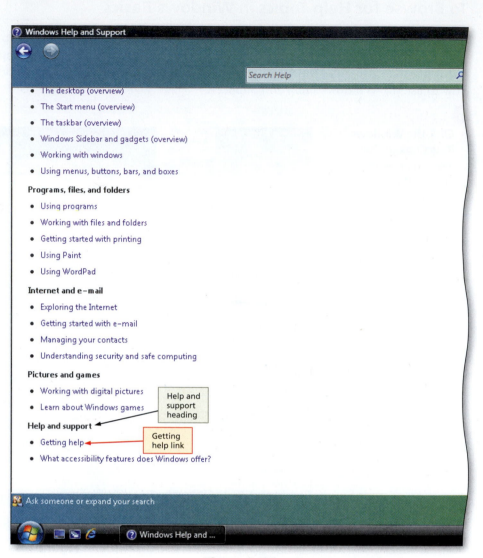

Figure 1–50

- Click the Getting help link to display the Getting help page (Figure 1–51).

- Read the information on the Getting help page.

Figure 1–51

- Click the Back button on the Navigation toolbar two times to return to the page containing the Find an answer area (Figure 1–52).

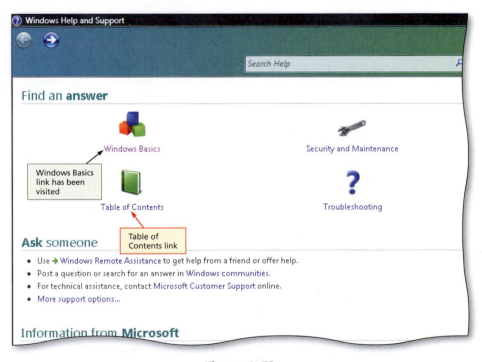

Figure 1–52

To Search for Help Topics Using the Table of Contents

A second method for finding answers to your questions about Windows Vista is to use the Table of Contents. The Table of Contents contains a list of entries, each of which references one or more Help topics. The following steps locate help and information on what you need to set up a home network.

- Click the Table of Contents link in the Find an answer area to display the Contents page (Figure 1–53).

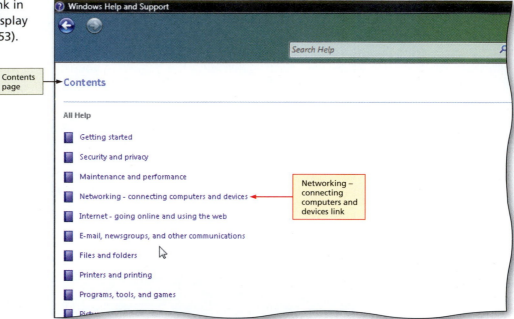

Figure 1–53

2
- Click the Networking - connecting computers and devices link on the Contents page to display the links in the Networking - connecting computers and devices topic (Figure 1–54).

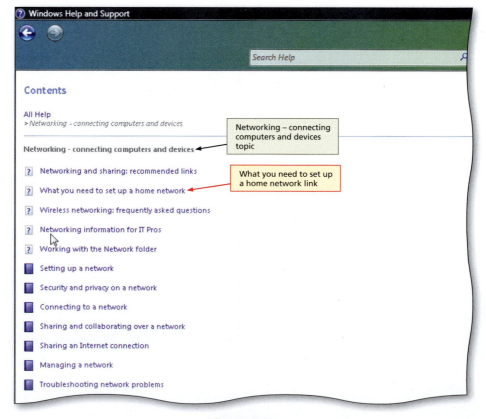

Figure 1–54

3

- Click the What you need to set up a home network link to show the What you need to set up a home network help page (Figure 1–55).

What you need to set up a home network help page

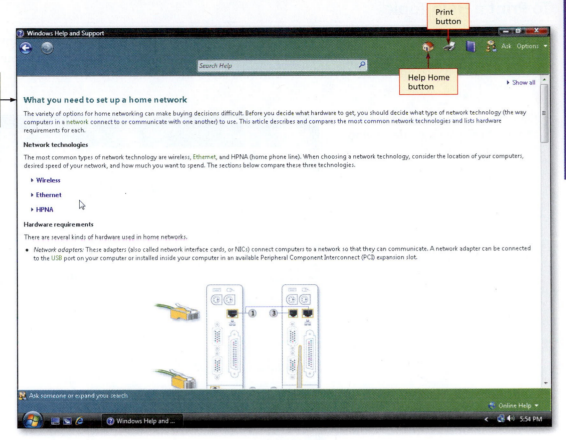

Print button

Help Home button

Figure 1–55

Other Ways

1. Press TAB until category or topic is highlighted, press ENTER, repeat for each category or topic

To Print a Help Topic

There are times when you might want to print a help topic so that you can have a printout for reference. The following steps show you how to print a Help topic. If you are unable to print from your computer (for example, you are in a school lab with no printer), read the following steps without actually performing them.

1

- Click the Print button on the Help toolbar to display the Print dialog box (Figure 1–56).

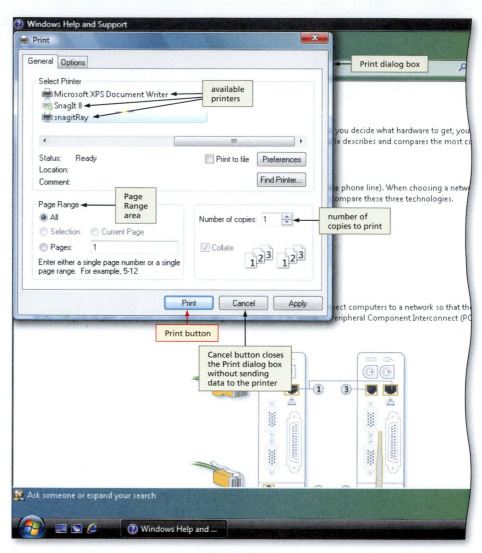

Figure 1–56

2

- Click the Print button in the Print dialog box to print the Help topic (Figure 1–57).

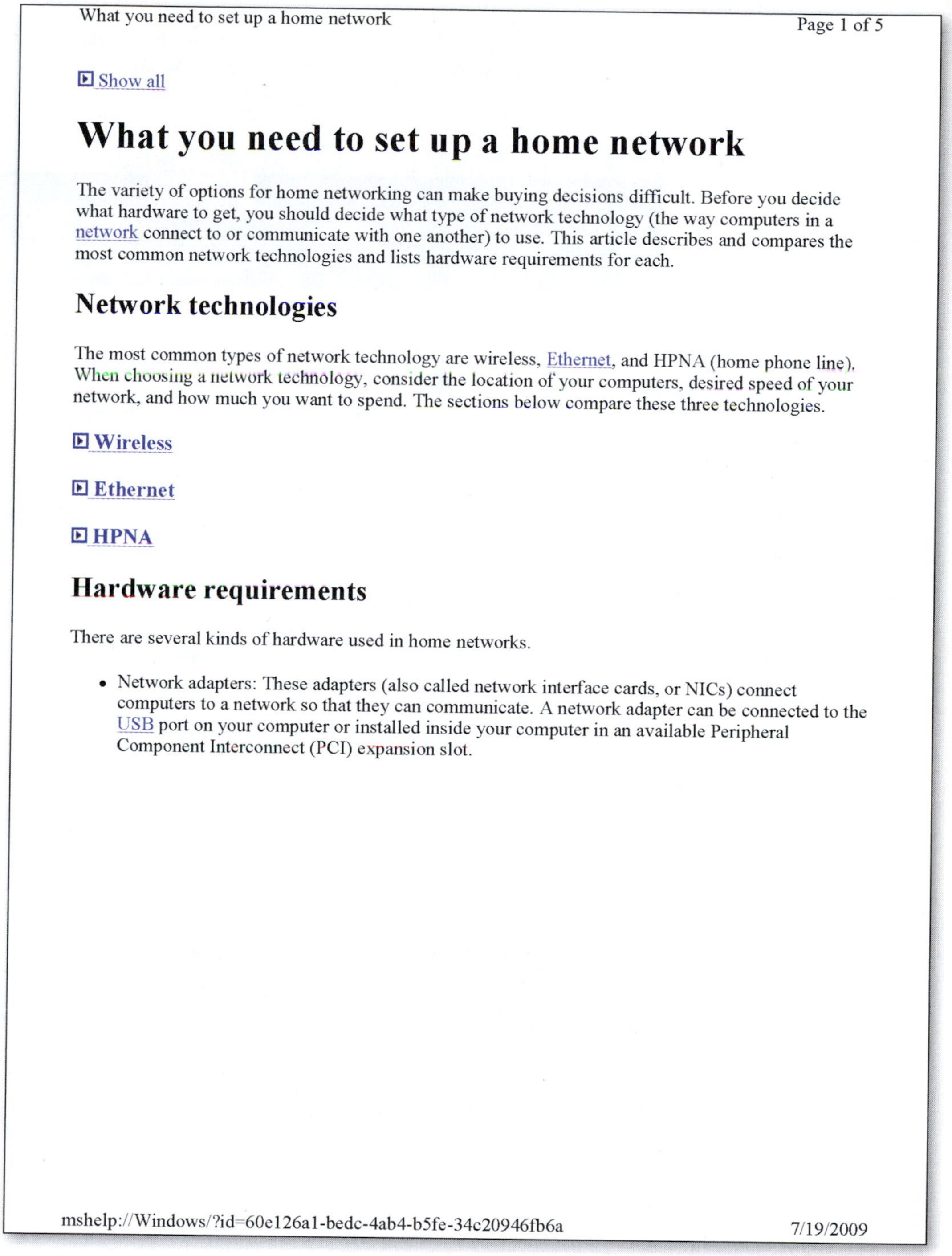

What you need to set up a home network | Page 1 of 5

▶ Show all

What you need to set up a home network

The variety of options for home networking can make buying decisions difficult. Before you decide what hardware to get, you should decide what type of network technology (the way computers in a network connect to or communicate with one another) to use. This article describes and compares the most common network technologies and lists hardware requirements for each.

Network technologies

The most common types of network technology are wireless, Ethernet, and HPNA (home phone line). When choosing a network technology, consider the location of your computers, desired speed of your network, and how much you want to spend. The sections below compare these three technologies.

▶ Wireless

▶ Ethernet

▶ HPNA

Hardware requirements

There are several kinds of hardware used in home networks.

- Network adapters: These adapters (also called network interface cards, or NICs) connect computers to a network so that they can communicate. A network adapter can be connected to the USB port on your computer or installed inside your computer in an available Peripheral Component Interconnect (PCI) expansion slot.

mshelp://Windows/?id=60e126a1-bedc-4ab4-b5fe-34c20946fb6a | 7/19/2009

Figure 1–57

To Return to the Help Home Page

1 Click the Help and Support Home button on the Navigation toolbar to return to the page containing the Find an answer area (Figure 1–58).

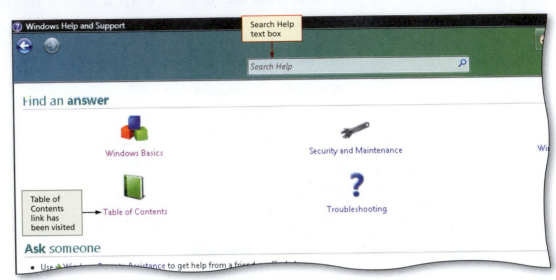

Figure 1–58

To Search Windows Help and Support

A third method for obtaining Help about Windows Vista is to use the Search Help text box in the Windows Help and Support window. The Search Help text box allows you to enter a keyword to display all Help topics containing the keyword. The following steps use the Search Help text box to locate information about computer viruses.

- Click the Search Help text box and type `virus` in the Search Help text box to provide a keyword for searching (Figure 1–59).

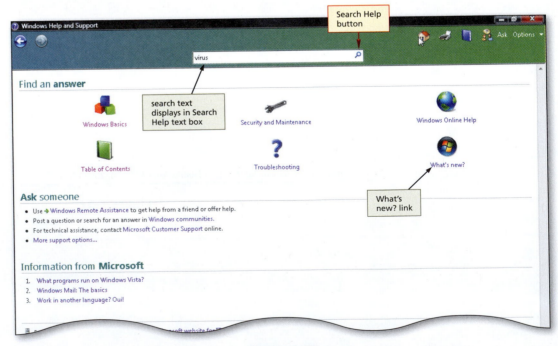

Figure 1–59

- Click the Search Help button to search for items matching virus (Figure 1–60).

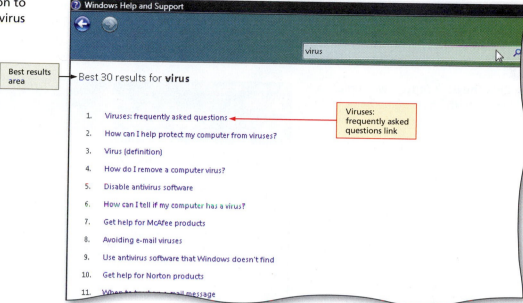

Figure 1–60

3

- Click Viruses: frequently asked questions in the Best 30 results for viruses area to display the Viruses: frequently asked questions help page (Figure 1–61).

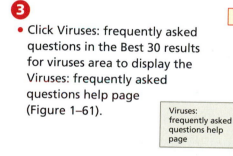

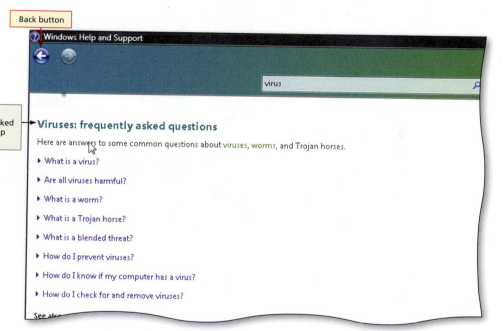

Figure 1–61

Other Ways
1. Press ALT+S, type keyword, press ENTER

When you search Help, the results of the search are sorted to produce the best matches for your keyword. When the computer is connected to the Internet, Windows Help and Support also searches the Microsoft Knowledge Base Web site for topics or articles that are relevant to the keyword you enter. The Best results area shows 30 results at a time. If there are more than 30 results for your keyword, a link will appear at the end of the Best 30 results list that lets you see more results. The total number of results will depend upon the search keywords.

To View a Windows Help and Support Demo

A fourth method for obtaining Help about Windows Vista is to view Windows Help and Support demos. The following steps, which display a demo about security, assume that you have Windows Media Player configured on your computer. If you have not yet configured Windows Media Player, please see your instructor.

• Click the Back button two times to return to the help home page containing the Find an answer area.

• Click the What's new link in the Find an answer area to display the What's new in Windows Vista Ultimate page (Figure 1–62).

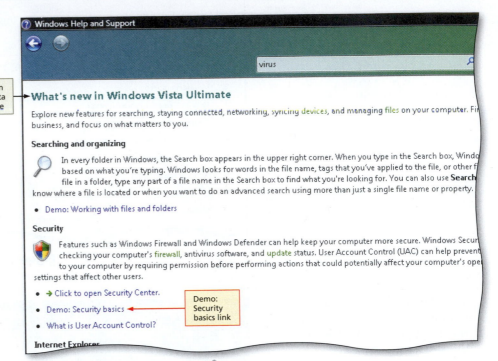

Figure 1–62

• Click the Demo: Security basics link to display the Demo: Security basics demo Help page (Figure 1–63).

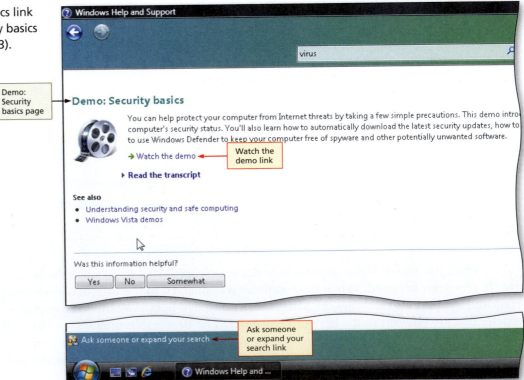

Figure 1–63

3
- Click the Watch the demo link to open the demo in Windows Media Player (Figure 1–64).

4
- Click the Close button on the title bar on the Windows Media Player window.

Figure 1–64

To Get More Help

If you do not find the results you are seeking, you can use Windows Help and Support to ask someone or find ways to expand your search. The following step opens the Ask someone or expand your search area.

1
- Click the Ask someone or expand your search link at the bottom of the Windows Help and Support window to open the Get customer support or other types of help page (Figure 1–65).

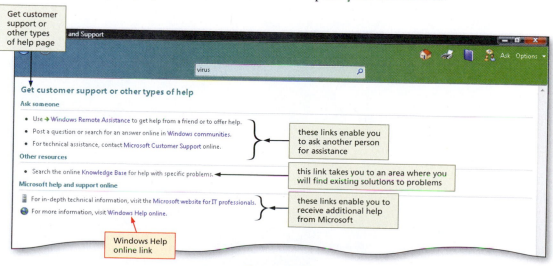

Figure 1–65

To Search Windows Help Online

Using Windows Help online allows you to search a broader range of content, get help from others, share a Help topic, or save a link to a Help topic for future reference by adding it to your favorites in Internet Explorer. The following steps open Internet Explorer to access Windows Help online.

1

- Click the Windows Help online link to open Internet Explorer and display the Windows Vista: Help and How-to Web page (Figure 1–66).

Q&A

Why am I unable to access Windows Help online?

You must have an active Internet connection to use Windows Help online.

Figure 1–66

2

• Click the Security link on the Windows Help and How-to Web page to display the Windows Vista Help: Security Web page (Figure 1–67).

Figure 1–67

To Add a Page to Favorites

When you know you will want to return to a Windows Help page in the future, you can add it to your Favorites list in Internet Explorer. The following steps add the Windows Vista Help: Security page to your Favorites.

1

• Click the Add to Favorites button to display the Add to Favorites menu, and point to the Add to Favorites command (Figure 1-68).

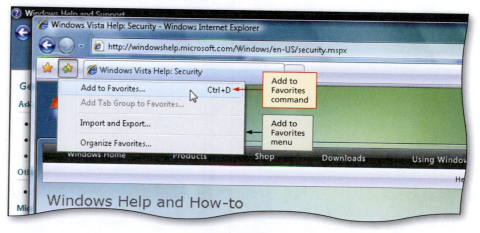

Figure 1–68

- Click the Add to Favorites command to display the Add a Favorite dialog box (Figure 1–69).

Figure 1–69

❸

- Click the Add button to add the Windows Vista Help: Security page to your Favorites list (Figure 1–70).

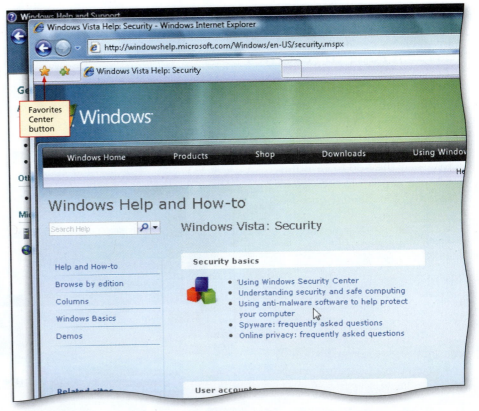

Figure 1–70

4

- Click the Favorites Center button on the Internet Explorer toolbar to display the Explorer Bar.

- If necessary, click the Favorites button on the Explorer Bar to display the Favorites list (Figure 1–71).

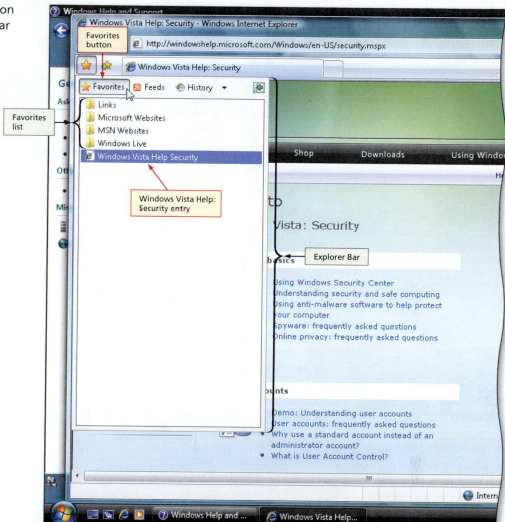

Figure 1–71

To Delete a Link from Favorites

When you are through referring to a Help topic stored in your Favorites, you may want to delete the link. The steps on the following page delete the security help page from your Favorites list.

1

• Right-click the Windows Vista Help: Security entry to display a shortcut menu (Figure 1–72).

Figure 1–72

2

• Click the Delete command to close the shortcut menu and display the Delete File dialog box (Figure 1–73).

• Click the Yes button to delete the Windows Vista Help: Security Favorite from the Favorites list.

Q&A

Why does the dialog box ask me if I want to delete a file?

Internet Explorer and Windows Vista store your favorites as small text files in a special folder on your computer. When you add a favorite, you are creating a file. When you delete a favorite, you are deleting a file.

Figure 1–73

To Close Windows Internet Explorer and Windows Help and Support

1 Click the Close button on the title bar of the Windows Internet Explorer window.

2 Click the Close button on the title bar of the Windows Help and Support Center window.

Logging Off and Turning Off the Computer

After completing your work with Windows Vista, you should close your user account by logging off from the computer. In addition to logging off, there are several options available for ending your Windows Vista session. Table 1–3 describes the various options for ending your Windows Vista session.

Table 1–3 Options and Methods for Ending a Windows Vista Session	
Area	**Function**
Switch User	Click the Start button, point to the arrow next to the Lock button, and then click the Switch User command to keep your programs running in the background (but inaccessible until you log on again), and allow another user to log on.
Log Off	Click the Start button, point to the arrow next to the Lock button, and then click the Log Off command to close all your programs and close your user account. This method leaves the computer running so that another user can log on.
Lock	Click the Start button, and then click the Lock button to deny anyone except those who have authorized access to log on to the computer.
Restart	Click the Start button, point to the arrow next to the Lock button, and then click the Restart command to shut down and then restart the computer.
Sleep	Click the Start button, point to the arrow next to the Lock button, click the Sleep command, wait for Windows to save your work to memory and then power down your computer to a low-power state. This is useful if you are expecting to return to your computer in a short amount of time.
Hibernate	Click the Start button, point to the arrow next to the Lock button, click the Hibernate command, and then wait for Windows to save your work to the hard disk and power down your computer. This is useful if you are expecting to not use your computer for a few days.
Shut Down	Click the Start button, point to the arrow next to the Lock button, and then click the Shut Down command to close all your programs and turn off the computer.

To Log Off from the Computer

Logging off from the computer closes any open applications, gives you the opportunity to save any unsaved documents, ends the Windows Vista session, and makes the computer available for other users. A logging off message will display briefly as Windows Vista logs you off. When the process is finished, the Welcome screen will appear again. At this point, another user can log on to the computer. The steps on the following page log off from the computer. If you do not want to end your session on the computer, read the following steps but do not perform them.

1

● Display the Start menu (Figure 1–74).

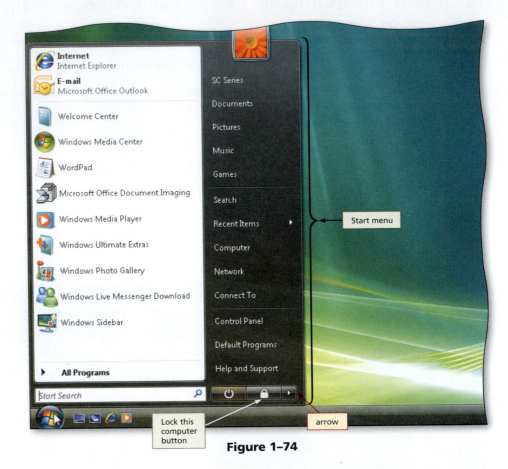

Figure 1–74

2

● Point to the arrow to the right of the Lock button to display the Shut Down options menu (Figure 1–75).

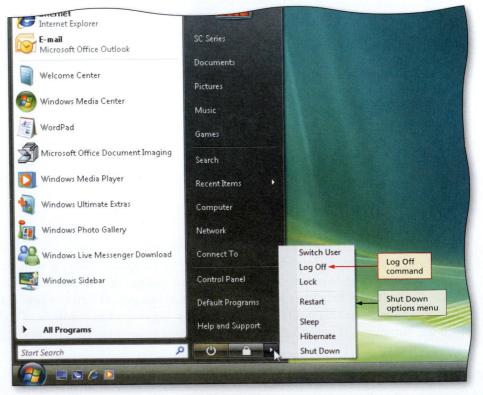

Figure 1–75

3
- Click the Log Off command, and then wait for Windows Vista to prompt you to save any unsaved data, if any, and log off (Figure 1–76).

Q&A Why should I log off the computer?

Some Windows Vista users have turned off their computers without following the log off procedure only to find data they thought they had stored on disk was lost. Because of the way Windows Vista writes data on the hard disk, it is important you log off the computer so you do not lose your work. Logging off a computer is also a common security practice, preventing unauthorized users from tampering with the computer or your user account.

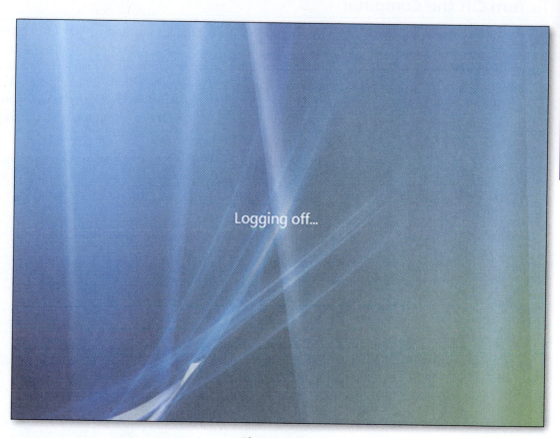

Logging off...

Figure 1–76

<table>
<tr><td colspan="2">Other Ways</td></tr>
<tr><td>1.</td><td>Press CTRL+ESC, press RIGHT ARROW, press RIGHT ARROW, press RIGHT ARROW, press L</td></tr>
</table>

To Turn Off the Computer

After logging off, you also may want to turn off the computer. Using the Shut down button on the Welcome screen to turn off the computer shuts down Windows Vista so that you can turn off the power to the computer. Many computers turn the power off automatically as part of shutting down. While Windows Vista is shutting down, a message shows stating 'Shutting down' along with an animated progress circle. When Windows Vista is done, the computer will shut off. You should not turn off your computer during this process, as you could lose data. The following step turns off the computer. However, if you do not want to turn off the computer, read the step without performing it.

• Click the Shut down button to turn off the computer (Figure 1–77).

Figure 1–77

Other Ways

1. Press ALT+F4, press DOWN ARROW, press OK

Chapter Summary

In this chapter you have learned how to work with the Microsoft Windows Vista graphical user interface. You launched Windows Vista, logged on to the computer, learned about the parts of the desktop, and added and removed a gadget from the Windows Sidebar. You opened, minimized, maximized, restored, and closed Windows Vista windows. You launched applications and used Windows Flip 3D to switch between them. Using Windows Help and Support, you located Help topics to learn more about Microsoft Windows Vista. You printed a Help topic, viewed a Help demo, and learned how to find Help topics online. You logged off from the computer using the Log Off command on the Start menu and then shut down Windows Vista using the Shut down button on the Welcome screen.

The following list includes all the new Windows Vista skills you have learned in this chapter.

1. Log On to the Computer (WIN 8)
2. Close the Welcome Center (WIN 10)
3. Display the Start Menu (WIN 11)
4. Scroll Using Scroll Arrows, the Scroll Bar, and the Scroll Box (WIN 13)
5. Open the Computer Folder Window (WIN 15)
6. Minimize and Redisplay a Window (WIN 17)
7. Maximize and Restore a Window (WIN 18)
8. Close a Window (WIN 20)
9. Add an Icon to the Desktop (WIN 21)
10. Open a Window Using a Desktop Icon (WIN 23)
11. Move a Window by Dragging (WIN 24)
12. Expand the Folders List (WIN 25)
13. Size a Window by Dragging (WIN 26)
14. Collapse the Folders List (WIN 27)
15. Delete a Desktop Icon by Dragging (WIN 28)
16. Empty the Recycle Bin (WIN 29)
17. Add a Gadget to the Windows Sidebar (WIN 30)
18. Remove a Gadget from the Windows Sidebar (WIN 31)
19. Start an Application Using the Start Menu (WIN 32)
20. Start an Application Using the Search Box (WIN 33)
21. Start an Application Using the Quick Launch Toolbar (WIN 35)
22. Switch Applications Using Windows Flip 3D (WIN 35)
23. Switch Applications Using the Taskbar (WIN 37)
24. Show the Desktop Using the Show Desktop Button (WIN 40)
25. Start Windows Help and Support (WIN 41)
26. Browse for Help Topics in Windows Basics (WIN 43)
27. Search for Help Topics Using the Table of Contents (WIN 46)
28. Print a Help Topic (WIN 48)
29. Search Windows Help and Support (WIN 50)
30. View a Windows Help and Support Demo (WIN 52)
31. Get More Help (WIN 53)
32. Search Windows Help Online (WIN 54)
33. Add a Page to Favorites (WIN 55)
34. Delete a Link from Favorites (WIN 57)
35. Log Off from the Computer (WIN 59)
36. Turn Off the Computer (WIN 62)

Learn It Online

Test your knowledge of chapter content and key terms.

Instructions: To complete the Learn It Online exercises, start your browser, click the Address bar, and then enter the Web address scsite.com/winvista/learn. When the Windows Vista Learn It Online page is displayed, click the link for the exercise you want to complete and then read the instructions.

Chapter Reinforcement TF, MC, and SA
A series of true/false, multiple-choice, and short answer questions that test your knowledge of the chapter content.

Flash Cards
An interactive learning environment where you identify chapter key terms associated with displayed definitions.

Practice Test
A series of multiple-choice questions that test your knowledge of chapter content and key terms.

Who Wants To Be a Computer Genius?
An interactive game that challenges your knowledge of chapter content in the style of television quiz show.

Wheel of Terms
An interactive game that challenges your knowledge of chapter key terms in the style of the television show *Wheel of Fortune*.

Crossword Puzzle Challenge
A crossword puzzle that challenges your knowledge of key terms presented in the chapter.

Apply Your Knowledge

Reinforce the skills and apply the concepts you learned in this chapter.

What's New in Windows Vista?
Instructions: Use Windows Help and Support to perform the following tasks.

Part 1: Launching Windows Help and Support
1. Click the Start button and then click Help and Support on the Start menu. If necessary, maximize the Windows Help and Support window.
2. Click the What's new? link in the Find an answer area in the Windows Help and Support window.

Part 2: Exploring Windows Vista Demos
1. In the Searching and organizing area, click the Demo: Working with files and folders link to display the Demo: Working with files and folders Web page (Figure 1–78), and then click the Watch the demo link. As you watch the demo, answer the questions below.
   a. The Start menu provides access to several folders. What are the three folders mentioned?

   _____

   b. How do you create a new folder?

   _____

   c. If you use a folder frequently, where should you put the folder?

   _____

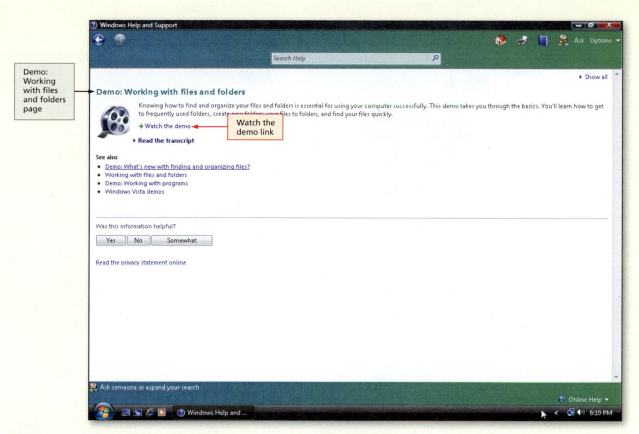

Demo:
Working
with files
and folders
page

Watch the
demo link

Figure 1–78

2. Click the Back button below the Windows Help and Support title to return to the What's new in Windows Vista Ultimate heading.

Part 3:   What's New in Security?

1. In the Security area, click the Click to open Security Center link to open the Windows Security Center (Figure 1–79 on the next page). Answer the questions below.

   a.   What are the four security essentials shown in the Windows Security Center?

   _____

   b.   Close the Windows Security Center.

   c.   In the Security area, click the Demo: Security basics link and then click the Read the transcript link.

   d.   What is the quickest way to check your computer's security status and fix security problems?

   _____

   e.   What does a firewall do?

   _____

   f.   What does it mean when all the lights in the Security Center are green?

   _____

2. Click the Back button below the Windows Help and Support title to return to the What's new in Windows Vista Ultimate page.

Continued >

Apply Your Knowledge *continued*

Figure 1–79

Part 4:   What's New in Parental Controls?

1. Scroll down to view the Parental Controls area.

   a.   In the Parental Controls area, click the What can I control with Parental Controls? link.

   b.   What can I do with Parental Controls?

   _____

   _____

   c.   After setting up Parental Controls, how can a parent keep a record of a child's computer activity?

   _____

2. Click the Back button below the Windows Help and Support title to view the topics in the Windows Help and Support window.

Part 5:   What's New in the Picture Area?

1. Scroll down the Windows Help and Support window to view the Pictures area.

   a.   In the Pictures area, click the Working with digital pictures link.

   b.   What are the two main ways to import pictures?

   _____

   _____

2. Click the Back button below the Windows Help and Support title to view the topics in the Windows Help and Support window.

Part 6: What's New in Mobile PC Features Area?

1. If necessary, scroll to view the Mobile PC features area, click the Using Windows Mobility Center link, and answer the following question.

   a. How do you open the Mobility Center?

   _____

   _____

2. Click the Close button in the Windows Help and Support window.

Extend Your Knowledge

Extend the skills you learned in this chapter and experiment with new skills. You may need to use Help to complete the assignment.

Using Windows Help and Support to Obtain Help

Instructions: Use Windows Help and Support to perform the following tasks.

1. Find Help about Windows keyboard shortcuts by typing keyboard shortcuts in the Search Help text box and then clicking the Search Help button (Figure 1–80). Click the first result listed.

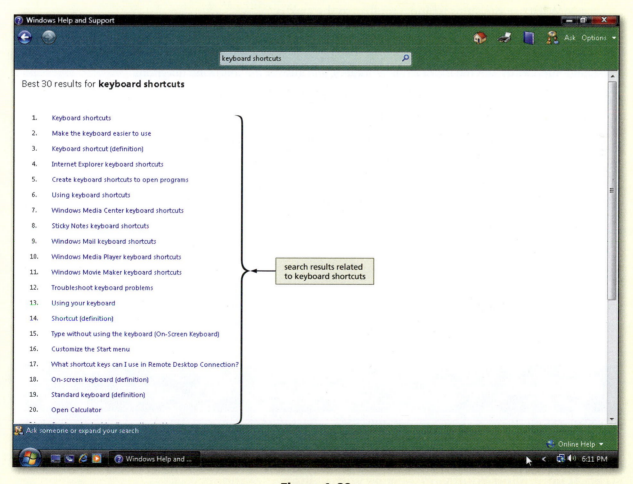

Figure 1–80

Continued >

Extend Your Knowledge *continued*

   a.   What general keyboard shortcut is used to display the Start menu?

   b.   What general keyboard shortcut is used to display the shortcut menu for an active window?

   c.   What general keyboard shortcut is used to view the properties for a selected item?

   d.   What dialog box keyboard shortcut is used to move backward through options?

   e.   What dialog box keyboard shortcut is used to display Help?

   f.   What Microsoft keyboard shortcut is used to display or hide the Start menu?

   g.   What Microsoft keyboard shortcut is used to open the Computer folder window?

2. Use the Help Table of Contents to answer the following questions.

   a.   How do you reduce computer screen flicker?

   b.   What dialog box do you use to change the appearance of the mouse pointer?

   c.   How do you minimize all windows?

   d.   What is a server?

3. Use the Search Help text box in Windows Help and Support to answer the following questions.

   a.   How can you reduce all open windows on the desktop to taskbar buttons?

   b.   How do you launch a program using the Run command?

   c.   What are the steps to add a toolbar to the taskbar?

   d.   What wizard do you use to remove unwanted desktop icons?

4. The tools to solve a problem while using Windows Vista are called **troubleshooters**. Use Windows Help and Support to find the list of troubleshooters, and answer the following questions.

   a.   What problems does the home networking troubleshooter allow you to resolve?

   b.   List five Windows Vista troubleshooters.

5. Use Windows Help and Support to obtain information about software licensing and product activation, and answer the following questions.

   a.   What is software piracy?

   b.   What are the five types of software piracy?

   c.   Why should I be concerned about software piracy?

   d.   What is a EULA (end user licensing agreement)?

   e.   Can you legally make a second copy of Windows Vista for use at home, work, or on a portable computer?

   f.   What is Windows Product Activation?

6. Close the Windows Help and Support window.

In the Lab

Use the guidelines, concepts and skills presented in this chapter to increase your knowledge of Windows Vista. Labs are listed in order of increasing difficulty.

Lab 1: Improving Your Mouse Skills with Windows Gadgets

Instructions: Perform the following steps to play a game using a gadget.

1. Click the Add Gadgets button on the Windows Sidebar. Double-click the Picture Puzzle to add it to the Sidebar. Close the Add Gadget window.

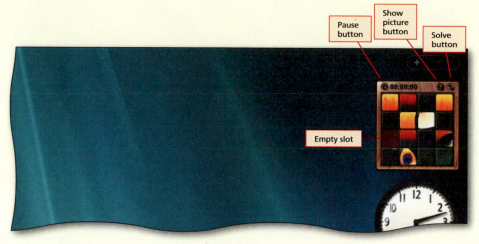

Figure 1–81

2. Click the Show picture button on the Picture Puzzle to see what the picture will look like once you solve the puzzle (Figure 1–81).

3. Play the Picture Puzzle game, by moving the puzzle tiles around by clicking on them when they are near the empty slot. Continue to rearrange the tiles until you have completed the picture (you can show the picture at any time to determine if you are close to the solution).

4. Click the Close button on the gadget to remove the gadget from the Sidebar.

In the Lab

Lab 2: Switching through Open Windows

Instructions: Perform the following steps to launch multiple programs using the Start menu and then use different methods to switch through the open windows.

Figure 1–82

Continued >

In the Lab *continued*

Part 1: Launching the Welcome Center, WordPad, and Internet Explorer
1. Click the Start button, click the All Programs command, and then click the Internet Explorer command to launch Internet Explorer.
2. Click the Start button, click the All Programs command, click the Accessories folder, and then click the Welcome Center command to display the Welcome Center.
3. Click the Start button, click the All Programs command, click the Accessories folder, and then click WordPad to launch WordPad.

Part 2: Switching through the Windows
1. Press ALT+TAB to switch to the next open window.
2. Press WINDOWS+TAB to switch to the next open window.
3. Press CTRL+ALT+TAB to view the open applications. Press TAB. Click the WordPad window to switch to WordPad.
4. Press CTRL+WINDOWS+TAB to view the open applications. Press TAB. Click the Internet Explorer window to switch to Internet Explorer.

Part 3: Report your Findings
1. What is the difference between pressing ALT+TAB and pressing WINDOWS+TAB? _____
_____

2. What is the difference between pressing ALT+TAB and CTRL+ALT+TAB? _____
_____

3. What is your favorite method of switching between windows? _____
_____

4. Besides using the keyboard shortcuts, what other ways can you switch between open windows?

Part 4: Closing the open Windows
1. Close WordPad.
2. Close Internet Explorer.
3. Close the Welcome Center.

In the Lab

Lab 3: Launching and Using Internet Explorer
Instructions: Perform the following steps to Internet Explorer to explore a selection of Web sites.

Part 1: Launching the Internet Explorer Application
1. If necessary, connect to the Internet.
2. Click the Start button and then click Internet Explorer in the pinned items list on the Start menu. Maximize the Windows Internet Explorer window.

Part 2: Exploring Microsoft's Web Site
1. Click the URL in the Address bar to highlight the URL.
2. Type www.microsoft.com in the Address bar and then press the ENTER key.

3. Answer the following questions.

    a.   What URL displays in the Address bar? _____

    _____

    b.   What window title displays on the title bar? _____

    _____

4. If necessary, scroll the Web page to view the contents of the Web page. List five links shown on this Web page. _____

5. Click any link on the Web page. What link did you click? _____
_____

6. Describe the Web page that displayed when you clicked the link? _____
_____

7. If requested by your instructor, click the Print button to print the Web page.

Part 3: Exploring Disney's Web Site
1. Click the URL in the Address bar to highlight the URL.
2. Type www.disney.com in the Address bar and then press the ENTER key.
3. What title displays on the title bar? _____
_____

4. Scroll the Web page to view the contents of the Web page. Do any graphic images display on the Web page? _____

5. Pointing to an image on a Web page and having the mouse pointer change to a hand indicates the image is a link. Does the Web page include an image that is a link? _____
_____

    If so, describe the image. _____
_____

6. Click the image to display another Web page. What window title displays on the title bar?
7. If requested by your instructor, click the Print button to print the Web page.

Part 4: Displaying Previously Displayed Web Pages
1. Click the Back button. What Web page displays? _____
2. Click the Back button twice. What Web page displays? _____
3. Click the Forward button. What Web page displays? _____

Part 5: Exploring the Shelly Cashman Series Web Site
1. Click the URL in the Address bar to highlight the URL.
2. Type www.scsite.com in the Address bar and then press the ENTER key.
3. Scroll the Web page to display the Operating Systems link, and then click the Operating Systems link.
4. Click the Microsoft Windows Vista link, and then click the title of your Windows Vista textbook.
5. Click any links that are of interest to you. Which link did you like the best? _____
_____

6. Use the Back button or Forward button to display the Web site you like the best.
7. Click the Print button to print the Web page, if requested by your instructor.
8. Click the Close button on the Internet Explorer title bar to close Internet Explorer.

Cases and Places

Apply your creative thinking and problem solving skills to design and implement a solution.

• Easier   **••** More Difficult

• 1: Researching Technical Support

Technical support is an important consideration when installing and using an operating system or an application software program. The ability to obtain a valid answer to a question at the moment you have the question can be the difference between a frustrating incident and a positive experience. Using Windows Help and Support, the Internet, or another research facility, write a brief report on the options that are available for obtaining help and technical support while using Windows Vista.

• 2: Assessing Windows Vista Compatibility

The Windows Vista operating system can be installed only on computers found in the Windows Vista hardware compatibility list. Locate three older personal computers. Look for them in your school's computer lab, at a local business, or in your house. Use Windows Help and Support and the Internet to find the Microsoft Web page that contains the Windows Vista hardware compatibility list. Check each computer against the list and write a brief report summarizing your results.

•• 3: Researching Multiple Operating Systems

Using the Internet, a library, or other research facility, write a brief report on three personal computer operating systems that are popular today. Describe the systems, pointing out their similarities and differences. Discuss the advantages and disadvantages of each. Finally, tell which operating system you would purchase and explain why.

•• 4: Importing Your Pictures

Make it Personal

Using Windows Help and Support, and the keywords, Digital Pictures, find the Working with digital pictures article. In a brief report, summarize the steps to send a photo by e-mail and process your photos on the Web. Include a description of Windows Photo Gallery.

•• 5: Researching Operating Systems in Use

Working Together

Because of the many important tasks an operating system performs, most businesses put a great deal of thought into choosing an operating system. Each team member should interview a person at a local business about the operating system he or she uses with his or her computers. Based on the interview, write a brief report on why the businesses chose that operating system, how satisfied it is with it, and under what circumstances it might consider switching to a different operating system.

2 | Working on the Windows Vista Desktop

Objectives

You will have mastered the material in this chapter when you can:

- Create and save a document in the Documents folder

- Create, name, and save a text document directly in the Documents folder

- Change the view and arrange objects in groups in the Documents folder

- Create and name a folder in the Documents folder

- Move documents into a folder

- Add and remove a shortcut on the Start menu

- Open a document using a shortcut on the Start menu

- Create a shortcut on the desktop

- Open a folder using a desktop shortcut

- Open, modify, and print multiple documents in a folder

- Store files on a USB drive

- Delete multiple files and folders

- Work with the Recycle Bin

- Work with gadgets

- Close and show the Sidebar

2 | Working on the Windows Vista Desktop

Introduction

In Chapter 2, you will be learning about the Windows Vista desktop. With thousands of hardware devices and software products available for desktop and notebook computers, users need to manage these resources quickly and easily. One of Windows Vista's impressive features is the ease with which users can create and access documents and files on the desktop. You will organize the lives of two computer users by developing and updating their daily reminder lists. You will create folders, use shortcuts, open and modify multiple documents, and work with gadgets and the Windows Sidebar.

Mastering the desktop will help you to take advantage of user interface enhancements and innovations that make computing faster, easier, and more reliable, and that offer seamless integration with the Internet. Working on the Windows Vista desktop in this chapter, you will find out for yourself how these features can save time, reduce computer clutter, and ultimately help you work more efficiently.

Overview

As you read this chapter, you will learn how to work with Windows Vista to create the documents shown in Figure 2–1 and how to use the Windows Sidebar by performing these general tasks:

- Creating and editing a WordPad document
- Moving and renaming a file
- Creating and moving a folder
- Storing and retrieving documents from a USB drive
- Deleting and restoring shortcuts, files and folders using the Recycle Bin
- Customizing and rearranging gadgets
- Hiding and showing the Sidebar

Plan Ahead

Working on the Windows Vista Desktop

Working with the Windows Vista desktop requires a basic knowledge of how to use the desktop, insert a USB drive, access the Internet, and use a printer.

1. **Determine the permissions you have on the computer you will be using.** Each user account can have different rights and permissions. Depending on which rights and permissions have been set for your account, you may or may not be able to perform certain operations.

2. **Identify how to add a USB drive to your computer.** Depending on the setup of the computer you are using, there may be several ways to add a USB drive to your computer. You should know which USB ports you can use to add a USB drive to your computer.

3. **Determine how to access the Internet.** Many gadgets can be found online, free-of-charge. You will want to know if your computer has Internet access and how to access it

4. **Ascertain how to access a printer.** In order to print, you must know which printer you can use and where it is located.

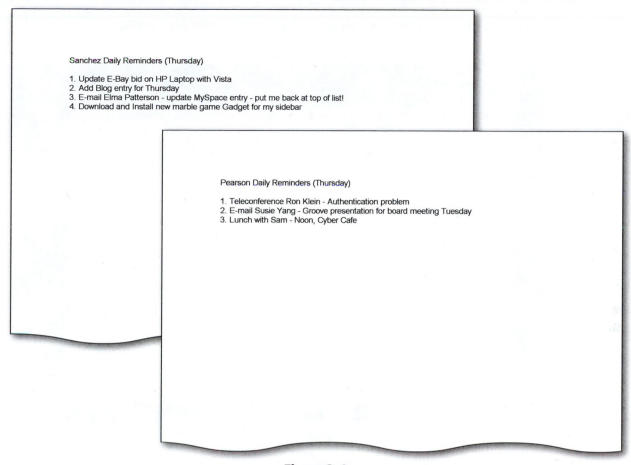

Sanchez Daily Reminders (Thursday)

1. Update E-Bay bid on HP Laptop with Vista
2. Add Blog entry for Thursday
3. E-mail Elma Patterson - update MySpace entry - put me back at top of list!
4. Download and Install new marble game Gadget for my sidebar

Pearson Daily Reminders (Thursday)

1. Teleconference Ron Klein - Authentication problem
2. E-mail Susie Yang - Groove presentation for board meeting Tuesday
3. Lunch with Sam - Noon, Cyber Cafe

Figure 2–1

Creating a Document in WordPad

As introduced in Chapter 1, a **program** is a set of computer instructions that carries out a task on the computer. An **application program** is a program that accomplishes specific tasks such as creating documents, browsing the web, or working with e-mail. For example, you create written documents with a **word processing program**, spreadsheets and charts with a **spreadsheet program**, and graphics presentations with a **presentation graphics program**. All of these applications display on your computer as you use them.

To help learn how to work with the Windows Vista desktop, you will create two daily reminders lists, one for Mr. Sanchez and one for Ms. Pearson. Because they will be reviewing their lists throughout the day, you will need to update the lists with new reminders as necessary. You decide to use **WordPad**, a popular word processing program available with Windows Vista, to create the daily reminders lists. The finished documents are shown in Figure 2–1.

You will first create the daily reminders document for Mr. Sanchez using WordPad, by launching the WordPad application program, typing the reminders, and then saving the document in the Documents folder. The **Documents folder** is created by Windows Vista as a central location for storing and managing documents and folders. In Windows terminology, this method of opening an application program and then creating a document is known as the **application-centric approach**.

To Launch a Program and Create a Document

The following steps launch WordPad and create a daily reminders document for Mr. Sanchez.

1

- Display the Start menu.

- Type wordpad in the Start Search box to prompt Windows Vista to search for the WordPad application.

- Press the ENTER key to launch the WordPad application and display the Document - WordPad window (Figure 2–2).

Q&A

Do I have to type the entire word before I press the ENTER key?

No. As soon as you see the result you are looking for at the top of the list in the Programs area above the Start Search box, you can press the ENTER key.

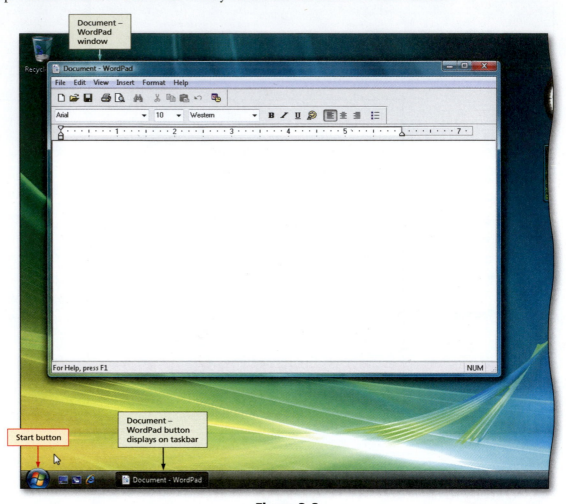

Figure 2–2

2

- **Type** Sanchez Daily Reminders (Thursday) **and then press the** ENTER **key two times.**

- **Type** 1. Update E-Bay bid on HP Laptop with Vista **and then press the** ENTER **key.**

- **Type** 2. Add Blog entry for Thursday **and then press the** ENTER **key.**

- **Type** 3. E-mail Elma Patterson - update MySpace entry - put me back at top of list! **and then press the** ENTER **key.**

- **Type** 4. Download and Install new marble game Gadget for my Sidebar **and then press the** ENTER **key (Figure 2–3).**

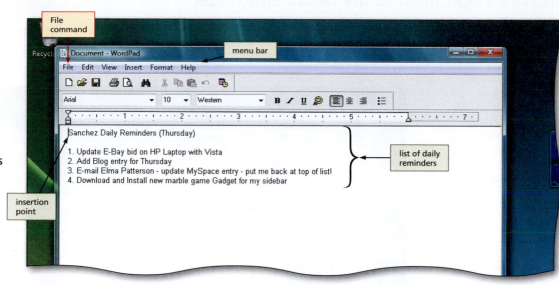

Figure 2–3

Other Ways

1. Open Start menu, type wordpad in the Start Search box, click WordPad

2. Open Start menu, click All Programs, click Accessories list, click WordPad

Saving Documents

When you create a document using a program such as WordPad, the document is stored in the main memory (RAM) of the computer. If you close the program without saving the document or if the computer accidentally loses electrical power, the document will be lost. To protect against the accidental loss of a document and to allow you to modify the document easily in the future, you should save your document. While you can save a file on the desktop, it is recommended that you save the document in a different location to keep the desktop free from clutter. For example, you can save files to the Documents folder or to a USB drive. A document saved to the Documents folder will be easier to find when searching.

When you save a document, you are creating a file. A **file** refers to a group of meaningful data that is identified by a name. For example, a WordPad document is a file; an Excel spreadsheet is a file; a picture made using Paint is a file; and a saved e-mail message is a file. When you create a file, you must assign a file name to the file. All files are identified by a **file name**. A file name should be descriptive of the saved file. Examples of file names are Sanchez Daily Reminders (Thursday), Office Supplies List, and Automobile Maintenance.

In order to associate a file with an application, Windows Vista assigns an extension to the file name of each document, which consists of a period followed by three, four, or five characters. Most documents created using the WordPad program are saved as rich text format documents with the .rtf extension, but they also can be saved as plain text with the .txt extension. A rich text format document allows for formatting of the text and insertion of graphics, which is not supported in plain text files.

Many computer users can tell at least one horror story of working on their computers for a long period of time and then losing all of their work because of a power failure or software problem. Consider this a warning: save often to protect your work.

BTW

File Names
A file name can contain up to 255 characters, including spaces. Any uppercase or lowercase character is valid when creating a file name, except a backslash (\), slash (/), colon (:), asterisk (*), question mark (?), quotation mark (''), less than symbol (<), greater than symbol (>), or vertical bar (|) as these symbols have special meaning for the operating system. Similarly, file names cannot be CON, AUX, COM1, COM2, COM3, COM4, LPT1, LPT2, LPT3, PRN, or NUL.

To Save a Document to the Documents Folder

The following steps save the document you created using WordPad to the Documents folder using the file name, Sanchez Reminders (Thursday).

1
• Click the File command on the menu bar to display the File menu (Figure 2–4).

Q&A

Why is there an ellipsis (…) following the Save As command?

The ellipsis (…) indicates that Windows Vista requires more information to carry out the command and will open a dialog box when you click the Save As command.

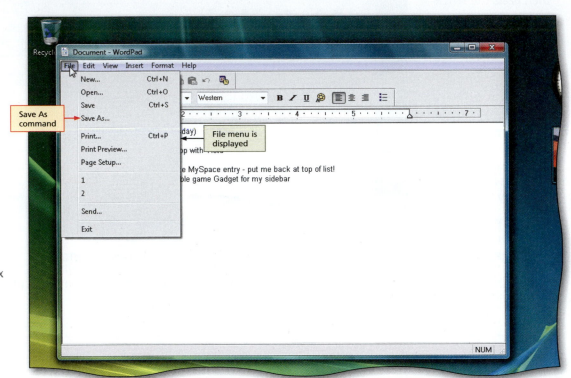

Figure 2–4

2
• Click the Save As command to display the Save As dialog box (Figure 2–5).

• Type Sanchez Daily Reminders (Thursday) in the File name text box.

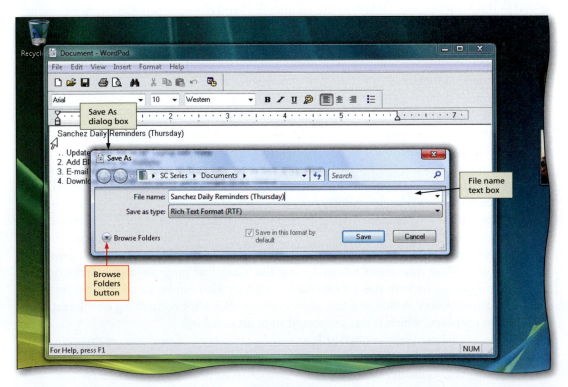

Figure 2–5

3
- Click the Browse Folders button to expand the folders list (Figure 2–6).

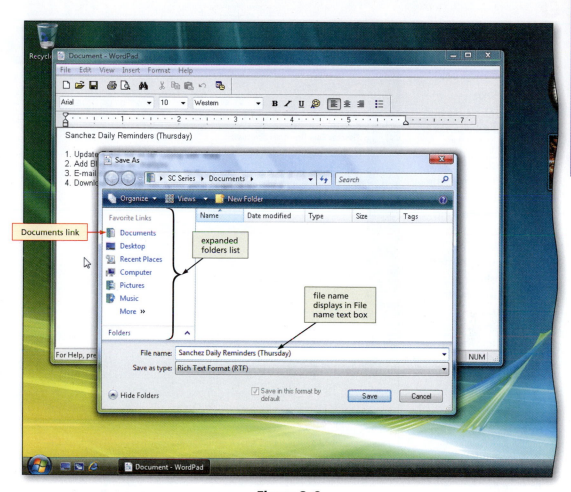

Figure 2–6

4
- Click the Documents link to select the Documents folder (Figure 2–7).

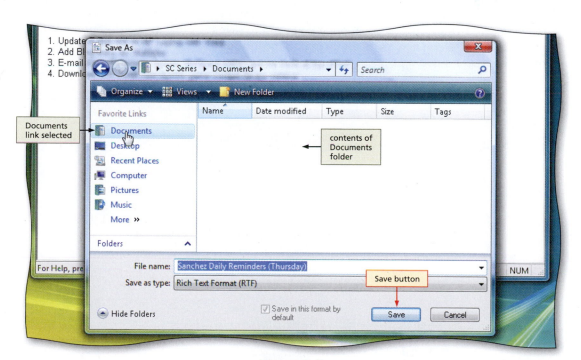

Figure 2–7

5
• Click the Save button to save the document and close the Save As dialog box (Figure 2–8).

Q&A Why did the title bar of WordPad change?

Now that you have saved the document with a file name, the file name will display on the title bar and on the button on the taskbar. The file name on the button in the taskbar button area contains an ellipsis (…) to indicate the entire file name does not fit on the button. To display the entire button name along with a live preview, point to the button.

Q&A Will I have to use Save As every time to save?

Now that you have saved the document, you can use the Save command to save changes to the document without having to type a new name or select a new storage location. If you want to save the file with a different name or to a different location, you would use the Save As command. By changing the location using the Address bar, you can save a file on the hard disk of the computer or a USB drive.

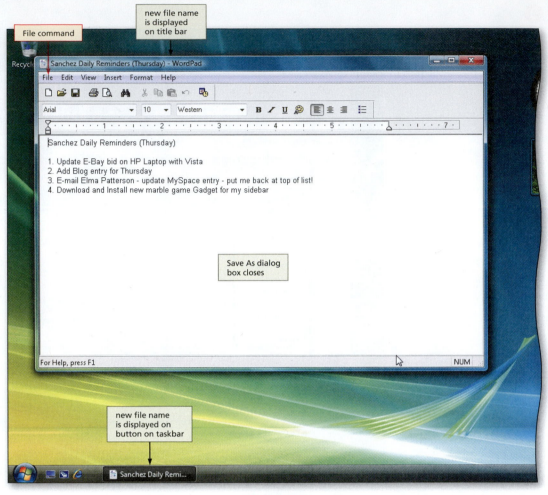

Figure 2–8

To Open the Print Dialog Box from an Application Program

Paper printouts are and will remain an important form of output for electronic documents. However, many sophisticated application programs are expanding their printing capabilities to include sending e-mail and posting documents to Web pages of the World Wide Web. One method of printing a document is to print it directly from an application program. The following steps open the Print dialog box in WordPad.

1

- Click the File command on the menu bar to display the File menu.

2

- Click the Print command to display the Print dialog box (Figure 2–9).

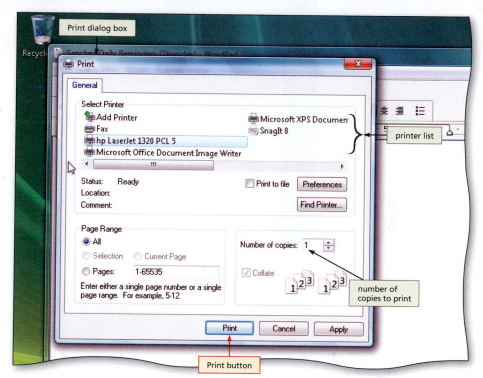

Figure 2–9

Other Ways

1. Press ALT+F, press P

The highlighted printer icon in the Select Printer area indicates that, in this case, the hp LaserJet printer is ready to print the document. Windows Vista automatically installs additional print options: an Add Printer option, a fax option, and a Microsoft XPS Document Writer option. Add Printer instructs Windows Vista to locate and identify any printers attached to the computer. Fax can be used to select a Fax device for printing or for sending a fax. The Microsoft XPS Document Writer printer allows you to create XPS documents. XPS documents look the same in print as they do on the screen and can be shared electronically with anyone who has an XPS viewer. They can be identified by the .xps extension. If you have other printers installed (such as the SnagIt 8 in Figure 2–9), you will be able to see them in the list. The highlighted printer is the selected destination for your printouts.

BTW

Printing Options
The Page Range area contains four option buttons. The option buttons give you the choice of printing all pages of a document (All), selected parts of a document (Selection), current page (Current Page), or selected pages of a document (Pages). The selected All option button indicates all pages of a document will print.

To Print a Document

The following step prints the Sanchez Daily Reminders (Thursday) document.

● Ready the printer according to the printer's instructions.

● If necessary, click the appropriate printer to select your printer.

● Click Print button to print the document (Figure 2–10).

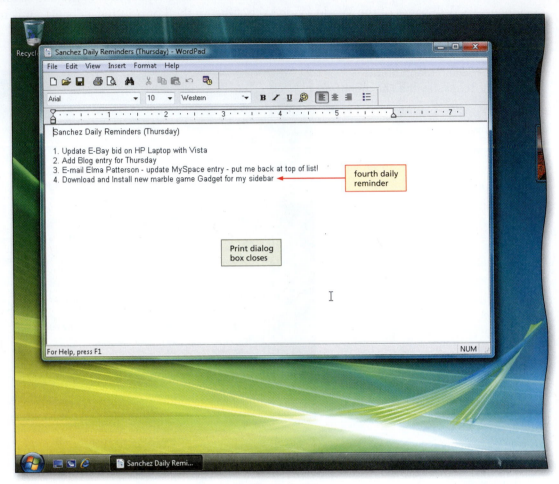

Figure 2–10

Other Ways

1. Click appropriate printer, press ENTER

To Edit a Document

Undoubtedly, you will want to make changes to a document after you have created it and saved it. For any document, your edits can be as simple as correcting a spelling mistake or as complex as rewriting the entire document. The following step edits the Sanchez Daily Reminders (Thursday) document by adding a new reminder.

1

• Click directly after the fourth daily reminder and then press the ENTER key.

• Type 5. Register for next semester's classes and then press the ENTER key (Figure 2–11).

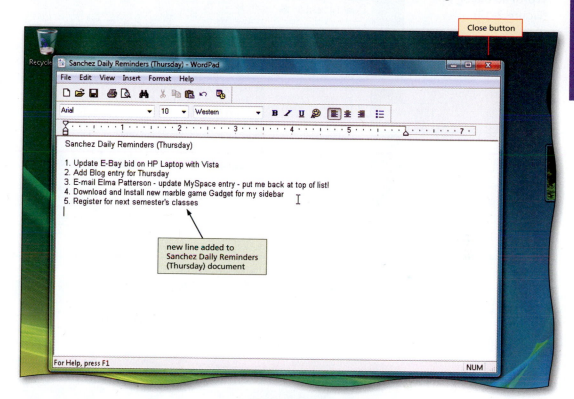

Figure 2–11

To Close and Save a Document

If you forget to save a document after you have edited it, a dialog box will display asking if you want to save your changes. This is how WordPad helps protect you from losing your work. If you choose to not save your changes, then all edits you made since the last time you saved will be lost. If you select cancel, your changes are not saved, but the document remains open and you can continue working. The following steps on the next page close and save the Sanchez Daily Reminders (Thursday) document.

1

• Click the Close
button on the
title bar to display
the WordPad
dialog box
(Figure 2–12).

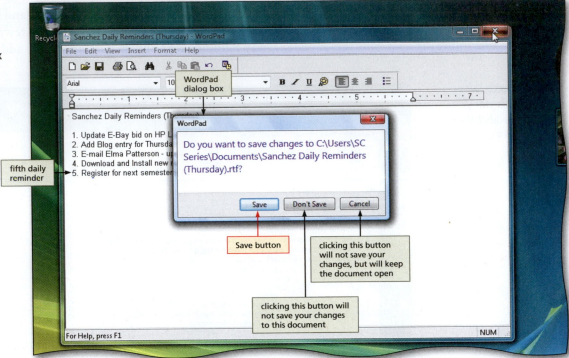

Figure 2–12

2

• Click the Save
button in the
WordPad dialog box
to save your changes
to the document
and close WordPad
(Figure 2–13).

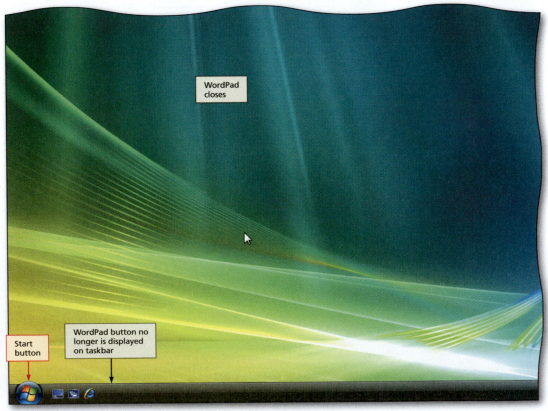

Other Ways

1. On title bar double-click
   WordPad icon, click the
   Save button

2. On title bar click
   WordPad icon, click
   Close, click the Save
   button

3. On File menu click Exit,
   click the Save button

4. Press ALT+F, press X;
   or press ALT+F4, press
   ENTER

Figure 2–13

Creating a Document in the Documents Folder

After completing the reminders list for Mr. Sanchez, the next step is to create a similar list for Ms. Pearson. Opening an application program and then creating a document (application-centric approach) was the method used to create the first document. Although the same method could be used to create the document for Ms. Pearson, another method is to create the new document in the Documents folder without first starting an application program. Instead of launching a program to create and modify a document, you first create a blank document directly in the Documents folder and then use the WordPad program to enter data into the document. This method, called the **document-centric approach**, will be used to create the document that contains the reminders for Ms. Pearson.

To Open the Documents Folder

The following step opens the Documents folder.

1

- Display the Start menu.

- Click the Documents command to display the Documents folder window (Figure 2–14).

Figure 2–14

To Create a Blank Document in the Documents Folder

The phrase, creating a document in the Documents folder, may be confusing. The document you actually create contains no data; it is blank. You can think of it as placing a blank piece of paper with a name inside the Documents folder. The document has little value until you add text or other data to it. The following steps create a blank document in the Documents folder to contain the daily reminders for Ms. Pearson.

- Right-click an open area of the Documents folder to display the shortcut menu.

- Point to the New command on the shortcut menu to display the New submenu (Figure 2–15).

Figure 2–15

2

- Click the Text Document command to display an icon for a new text document in the Documents folder window (Figure 2–16).

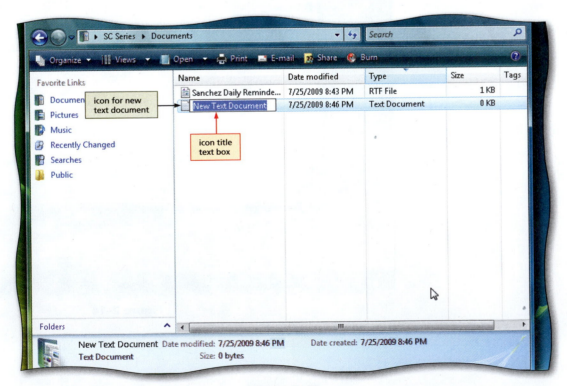

Figure 2–16

To Name a Document in the Documents Folder

After you create a blank document, you need to name the document so it is easily identifiable. In Figure 2–16, the default file name (New Text Document) is highlighted and the insertion point is blinking, indicating that you can enter a new file name. Until you name the document, the blank document will appear at the bottom of the list in the Documents folder. The following step assigns the file name, Pearson Daily Reminders (Thursday), to the blank document you just created.

1

- Type Pearson Daily Reminders (Thursday) in the icon title text box, and then press the ENTER key to assign a name to the new file and alphabetically sort the file in the Documents folder (Figure 2–17).

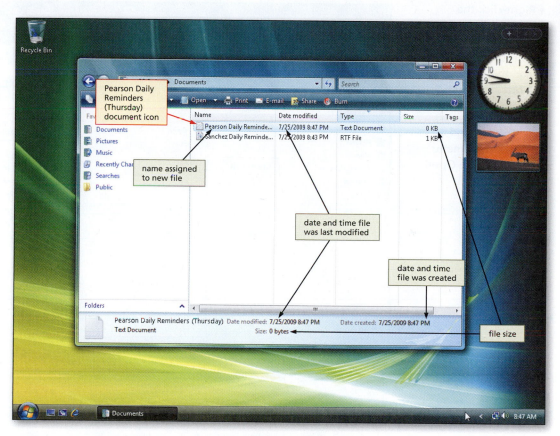

Figure 2–17

To Open a Document with WordPad

Although you have created the Pearson Daily Reminders (Thursday) document, the document contains no data. To enter data into the blank document, you must open the document. Because text files open with Notepad by default, you need to use the shortcut menu to open the file using WordPad. The following steps open a document with WordPad.

- Right-click the Pearson Daily Reminders (Thursday) document icon to display the shortcut menu.

- Point to the Open With command on the shortcut menu to display the Open With submenu (Figure 2–18).

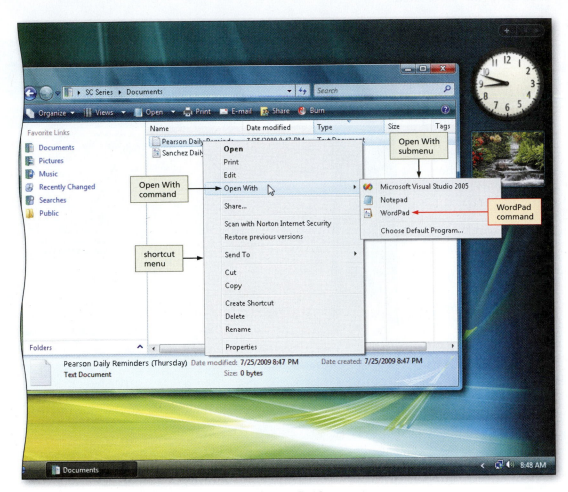

Figure 2–18

2

- Click the WordPad command on the Open With submenu to open the Pearson Daily Reminders (Thursday) document in WordPad (Figure 2–19).

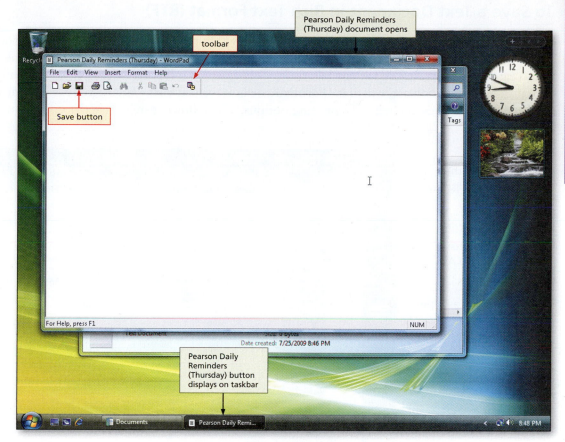

Figure 2–19

To Enter Data into a Blank Document

After the document is open, you can enter the required data by typing the text (the daily reminders) in the document. The following step enters the text in the Pearson Daily Reminders (Thursday) document.

1

- **Type** Pearson Daily Reminders (Thursday) and then press the ENTER key twice.

- **Type** 1. Teleconference Ron Klein – Authentication Problem **and then press the** ENTER **key.**

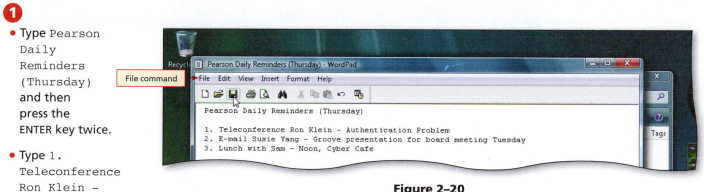

Figure 2–20

- **Type** 2. E-mail Susie Yang – Groove presentation for board meeting Tuesday **and then press the** ENTER **key.**

- **Type** 3. Lunch with Sam – Noon, Cyber Cafe **and then press the** ENTER **key (Figure 2–20).**

- Click the Save button on the toolbar to save the file.

To Save a Text Document in Rich Text Format (RTF)

Entering text into the Pearson Daily Reminders (Thursday) document modifies the document, which results in the need to save it. If you make many changes to a document, you should save the document as you work. When you created the blank text document Windows Vista assigned it the .txt extension, so you will need to use Save As to save it in Rich Text Format, which is WordPad's default format. Using the Rich Text Format will allow you to use all of WordPad's features, including formatting options. The following steps save the document in Rich Text Format.

- Click the File command on the menu bar to display the File menu.

- Click the Save As command to open the Save As dialog box.

- Click the Save as type list box arrow to display the Save as type list (Figure 2–21).

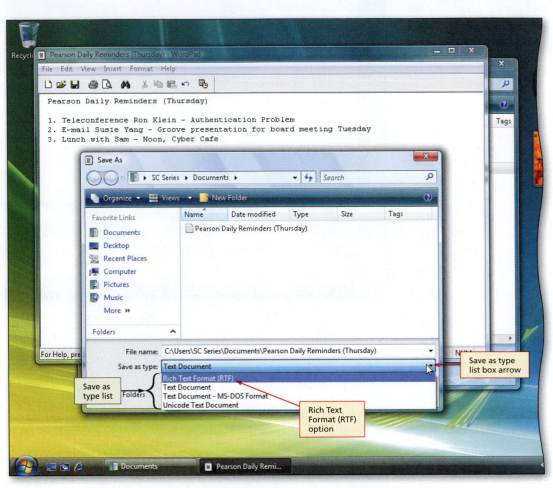

Figure 2–21

2

- Click the Rich Text Format (RTF) option to change the file type to .rtf.

- Type `Pearson Daily Reminders (Thursday).rtf` in the File name text box to change the file name (Figure 2–22).

- Click the Save button to save the document in Rich Text Format.

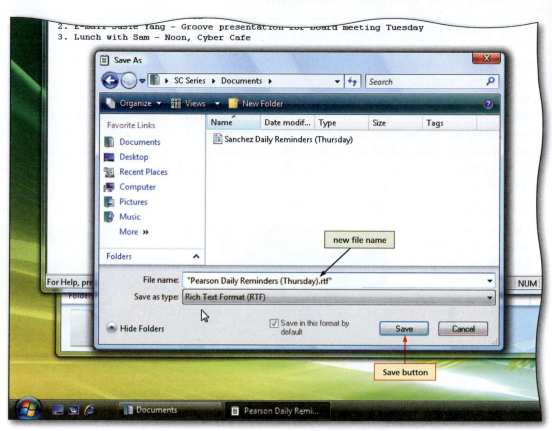

Figure 2–22

To Close the Document

You have saved your changes to Pearson Daily Reminders (Thursday), and now you can close the document.

1 Click Exit on the File menu, to close the Document and exit WordPad.

Working with the Documents Folder

Once you create documents in the Documents folder, using either the application-centric or document-centric approach, you can continue to modify and save the documents, print the documents, or create a folder to contain the documents and move the documents to the folder. Having a single storage location for documents makes it easy to create a copy of the documents so that they are not accidentally lost or damaged.

BTW

The Documents Folder
Windows Vista creates a unique Documents folder for each computer user. When you have multiple users on a single computer, having a unique central storage area for each user makes it easier to back up important files and folders.

To Change the View to Small Icons

The default view in the Documents folder (shown in Figure 2–23) is the Details view. The Details view shows a list of file folders plus common columns such as Date Modified and Type. You can use the Views button to change your view to other formats. The Small Icons, Medium Icons, Large Icons, and Extra Large Icons formats display the icons in increasingly larger sizes. When Medium, Large, or Extra Large Icon formats are selected, Windows Vista provides a Live Preview option. With Live Preview, the icons display images that more closely reflect the actual contents of the files or folders. For example, a folder icon for a folder that contains text documents would show sample pages from those documents. List view displays the files and folders as a list of names without any extra details. Tiles view displays the files and folders as tiles, which consist of an icon and icon description. With all of these views, the default arrangement for the icons is to be alphabetical by file name. The following steps change the view from the Details view to the Small Icons format.

- Click the More options arrow button next to the Views button on the toolbar of the Documents folder window to display the Views menu (Figure 2–23).

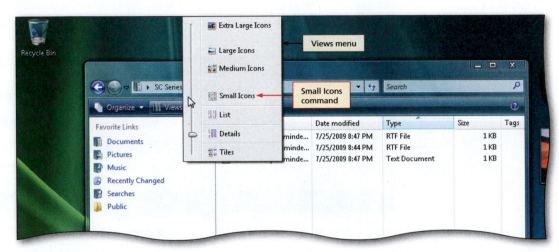

Figure 2–23

- Click the Small Icons command to display the files and folders as Small Icons (Figure 2–24).

 **Experiment**

- Select each of the options from the Views menu to see the various ways that Windows can display folder contents. After you have finished, be sure to select the Small Icons command from the Views menu.

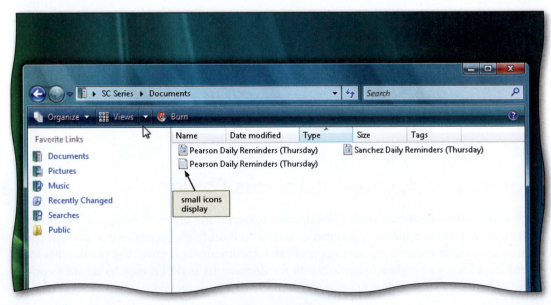

Figure 2–24

Other Ways

1. Right-click open space in the Documents folder, point to View, click Small Icons

To Arrange the Items in a Folder in Groups by Type

There are other methods of arranging the icons in the Documents folder. One practical arrangement is to display the icons in groups based upon file type. This arrangement places files of the same type (File Folder, Text Documents, Microsoft Word, Microsoft Excel, and so on) in separate groups. When a window contains many files and folders, this layout makes it faster and easier to find a particular file or folder. The following steps group the icons in the Documents folder by file type.

1

- Right-click the open space below the list of files and folders in the Documents folder to display the shortcut menu.

- Point to the Group By command to display the Group By submenu (Figure 2–25).

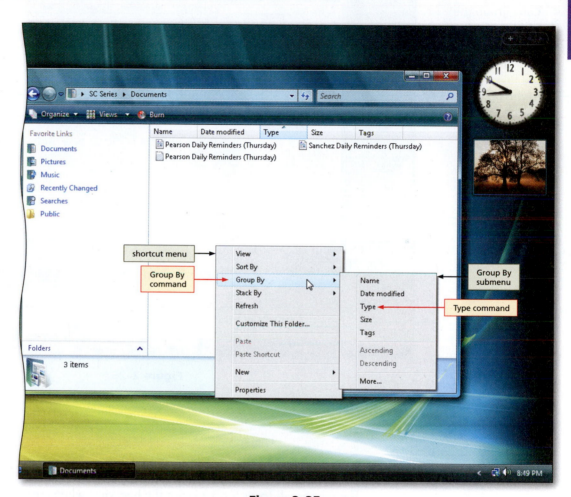

Figure 2–25

2

● Click the Type command to display the files and folders grouped by type (Figure 2–26).

Q&A

Can I group the files and folders in other ways?

You can group the files by any of the options on the Group By submenu. This includes Name, Date modified, Size, and Tags. To remove the groupings, select (None) on the Group By submenu.

Figure 2–26

Other Ways

1. Press ALT + V, press P, press T, press ENTER

To Change to Medium Icons Format

Because Small Icons format is not the best view when creating folders, you will change the view to Medium Icons.

1 Click the More options arrow button next to the Views button on the toolbar and then click the Medium Icons command to change to Medium Icons format.

To Create and Name a Folder in the Documents Folder

Windows Vista allows you to place one or more documents into a folder in much the same manner as you might take a document written on a piece of paper and place it in a file folder. You want to keep the Sanchez and Pearson documents together so you can find and reference them easily from among other text documents stored in the Documents folder. In order to keep multiple documents together in one place, you first must create a folder in which to store them. The following steps create and name a folder titled Daily Reminders in the Documents folder to store the Sanchez Daily Reminders (Thursday) and Pearson Daily Reminders (Thursday) documents.

1

• Click the Organize button on the Documents folder toolbar to display the Organize menu (Figure 2–27).

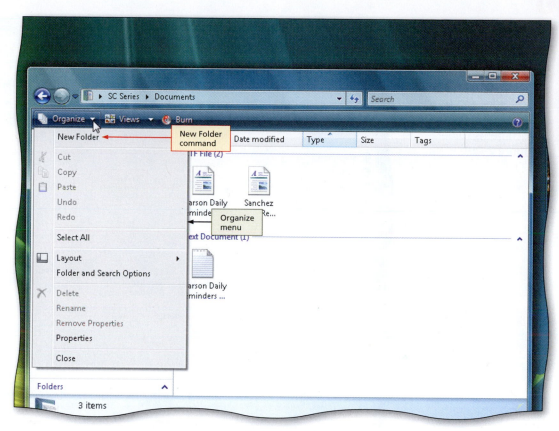

Figure 2–27

2

• Click the New Folder command on the Organize menu to create a new folder (Figure 2–28).

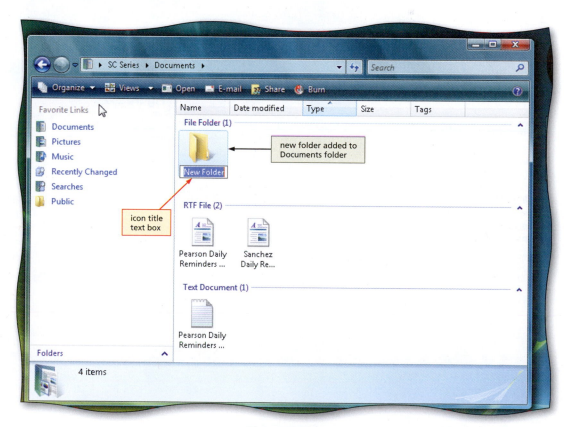

Figure 2–28

3

- Type Daily Reminders in the icon title text box and then press the ENTER key to name the folder and sort the folder in the Documents folder (Figure 2–29).

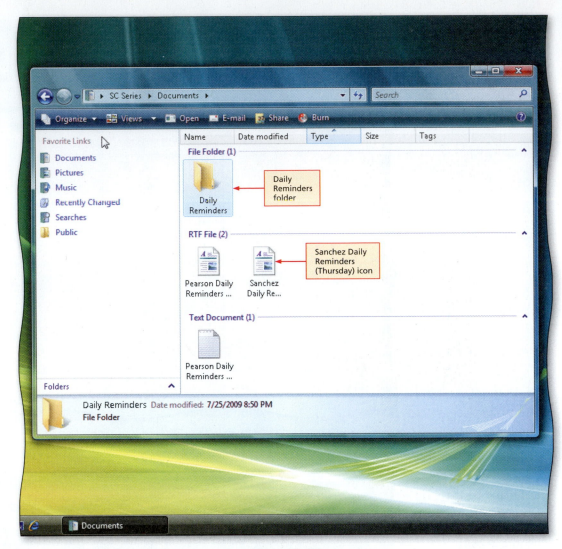

Figure 2–29

To Move a Document into a Folder

The ability to organize documents and files within folders allows you to keep the Documents folder organized when using Windows Vista. After you create a folder in the Documents folder, the next step is to move documents into the folder. The following steps move the Pearson Daily Reminders (Thursday) and the Sanchez Daily Reminders (Thursday) documents into the Daily Reminders folder.

1

• Right-click and drag (also known as right-drag) the Sanchez Daily Reminders (Thursday) icon onto the Daily Reminders folder icon to display the shortcut menu (Figure 2–30).

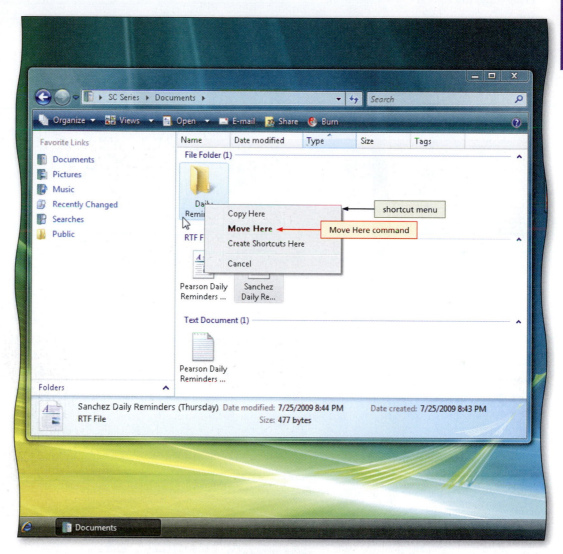

Figure 2–30

2

• Click the Move Here command on the shortcut menu to move the Sanchez Daily Reminders (Thursday) file to the Daily Reminders folder (Figure 2–31).

Q&A

What are the other options in the shortcut menu?

When you right-drag, a short-cut menu opens and lists the available options. In this case, the options are Copy Here, Move Here, Create Shortcuts Here, and Cancel. Selecting Copy Here would create a copy of the Sanchez document in the Daily Reminders Folder, Create Shortcuts here would put a link to the Sanchez document (not the file or a copy of the file) in the Daily Reminders Folder and Cancel would end the right-drag process. The options in the shortcut menu may change, depending on the type of file and where you are dragging it.

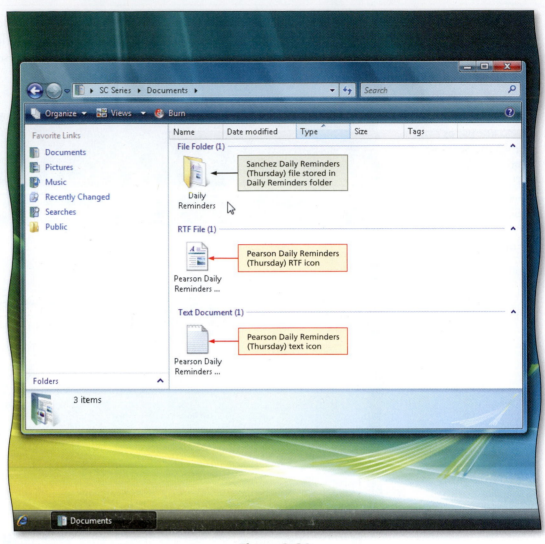

Figure 2–31

- Right-drag the Pearson Daily Reminders (Thursday) RTF icon onto the Daily Reminders icon to move it to the Daily Reminders Folder.

- Right-drag the Pearson Daily Reminders (Thursday) text icon onto the Daily Reminders icon to move it to the Daily Reminders Folder (Figure 2–32).

Q&A What happened to the Rich Text Format and Text Document groups?

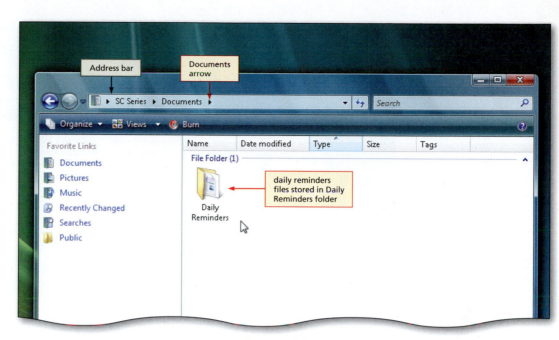

Figure 2–32

Because the documents have been moved to Daily Reminders, the groups were no longer needed. Only if there were other RTF and text documents in the Documents folder would the groupings remain.

Other Ways	
1. Drag document icon onto folder icon	2. Right-click document icon, click Cut, right-click folder icon, click Paste

To Change Location Using the Address Bar

If you would like to navigate to the folder to see if your files are there, there are several ways to do this. The easiest way in Windows Vista is to use the Address bar. The **Address bar** appears at the top of the Documents folder window and displays your current location as a series of links separated by arrows. By clicking on the arrows, you change your location. The Forward and Back buttons can be used to navigate through the locations you have visited just like the forward and back buttons in a Web browser. The following steps change your location to the Daily Reminders folder.

- Click the Documents arrow on the Address bar to display a location menu that contains a list of folders in the Documents folder (Figure 2–33).

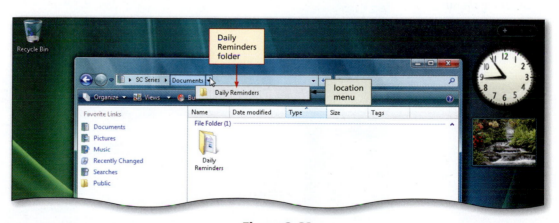

Figure 2–33

2

- Click the Daily Reminders folder on the location menu to move to the Daily Reminders folder (Figure 2–34).

Q&A

Why did the view change to Details view?

When you changed to the Medium Icons view, the change only affected the Documents folder itself, not any subfolders. Once you opened the Daily Reminders folder, the view reverted to Details view, which is the default view for folders in the Documents folder.

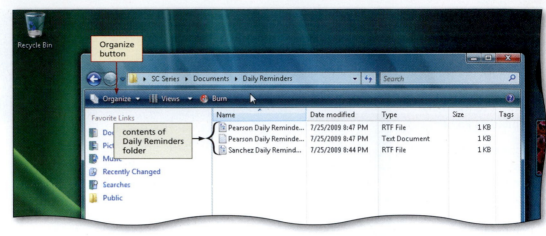

Figure 2–34

To Display and Use the Preview Pane

Now that you are in the Daily Reminders folder, you can add a Preview Pane to the layout, which will provide you with an even better Live Preview of your documents. When you select a document, the **Preview Pane** displays a live view of the document to the right of the list of files in the folder window. The following steps add the Preview Pane to the layout of the Daily Reminders folder and then show a Live Preview of the Sanchez document.

1

- Click the Organize button on the toolbar to display the Organize menu.

- Point to the Layout command on the Organize menu to display the Layout submenu (Figure 2–35).

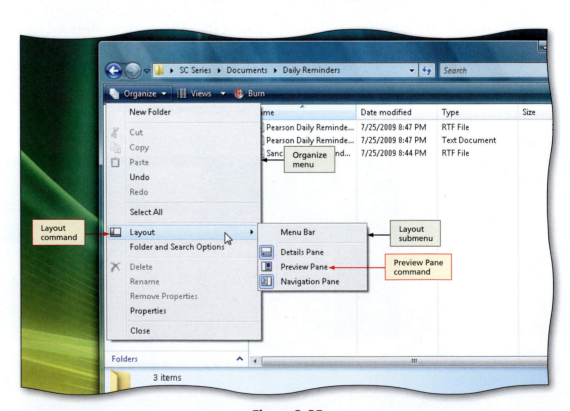

Figure 2–35

2

- Click the Preview Pane command to display the Preview Pane (Figure 2–36).

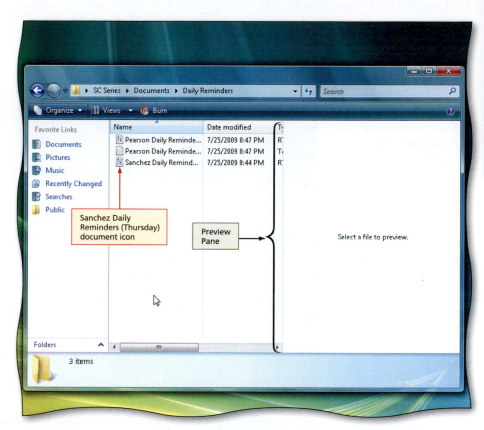

Figure 2–36

3

- Click Sanchez Daily Reminders (Thursday) document icon to display a preview of the document in the Preview Pane (Figure 2–37).

Q&A

Why did the menu bar change?

Depending upon what items are selected in the folder window, the menu bar options will change to reflect the options available to you.

Experiment

- Select different documents to see their preview in the Preview Pane.

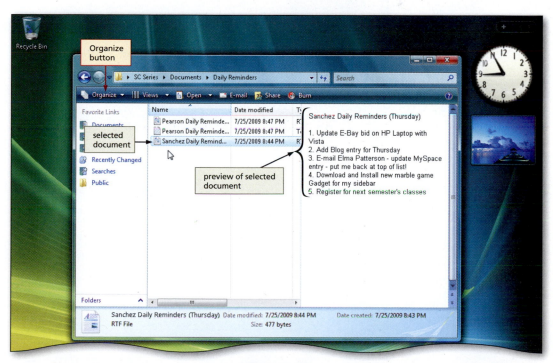

Figure 2–37

To Close the Preview Pane

After verifying that your files are in the Daily Reminders folder, you can close the Preview Pane and then use the Address bar to return to the Documents folder. The following step closes the Preview Pane.

- Click the Organize button on the toolbar to display the Organize menu.

- Point to the Layout command to display the Layout submenu.

- Click Preview Pane to close the Preview Pane (Figure 2–38).

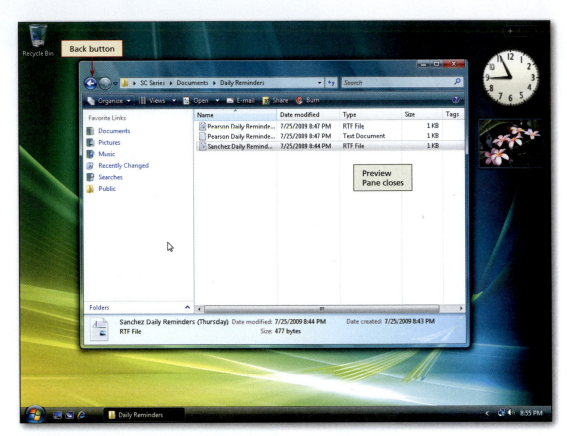

Figure 2–38

To Change Location Using the Back Button on the Address Bar

Besides clicking the arrows in the Address bar, you also can change locations by using the Back and Forward buttons. Using the Back button will allow you to return to a location that you have already visited. The following step changes your location to the Documents folder.

- Click the Back button on the Address bar to return to the Documents folder (Figure 2–39).

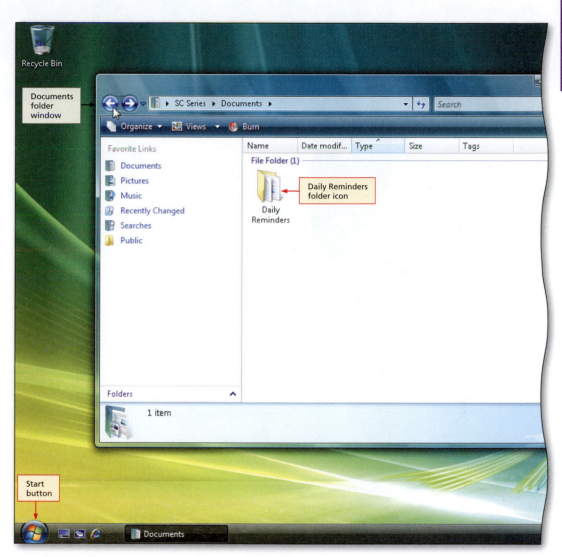

Figure 2–39

Creating Folder Shortcuts

One way to customize Windows Vista is to use shortcuts to launch application programs and open files or folders. A **shortcut** is a link to any object on the computer or on a network, such as a program, file, folder, Web page, printer, or another computer. Placing a shortcut to a folder on the Start menu or on the desktop can make it easier to locate and open the folder.

A shortcut icon is not the actual document or application. You do not actually place the folder on the menu; instead you place a shortcut icon that links to the folder on the menu. When you delete a shortcut, you delete the shortcut icon but do not delete the actual document or application. They remain on the hard disk.

To Add a Shortcut on the Start Menu

The following steps place the Daily Reminders folder shortcut on the Start menu.

1

- Drag the Daily Reminders folder icon onto the Start button to begin to add the icon to the Start menu. Do not release the left mouse button (Figure 2–40).

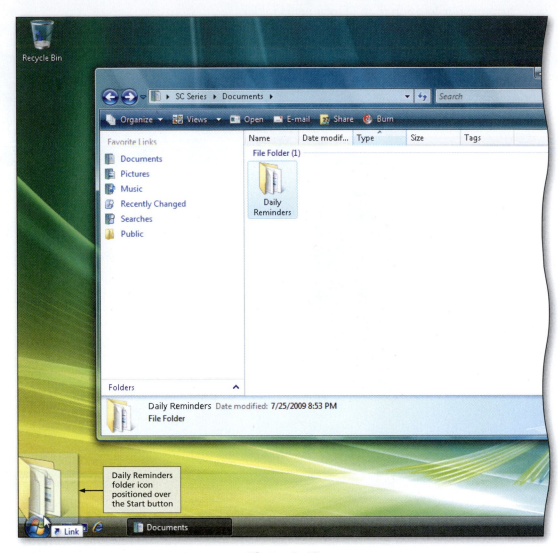

Figure 2–40

2

• Release the left mouse button to add the Daily Reminders icon to the Start menu (Figure 2–41).

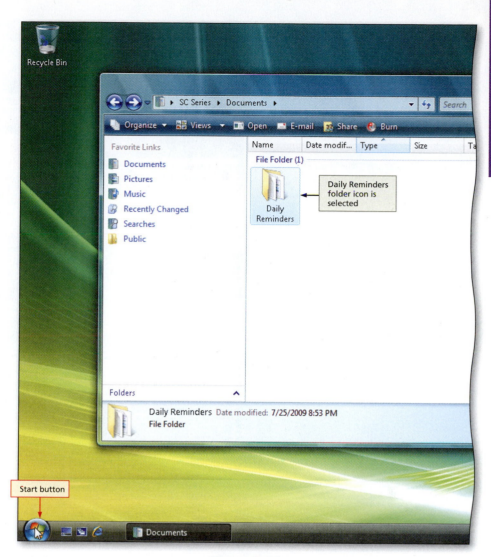

Figure 2–41

3

- Display the Start menu to see the Daily Reminders icon pinned to the Start menu (Figure 2–42).

Q&A

Can I add other shortcuts to the Start menu?

In addition to placing a folder shortcut on the Start menu, you also can place a shortcut to other objects (programs, files, USB drives, Web pages, printers, or other computers) on the Start menu in a similar manner. First display the object's icon on the desktop and then drag the icon onto the Start button.

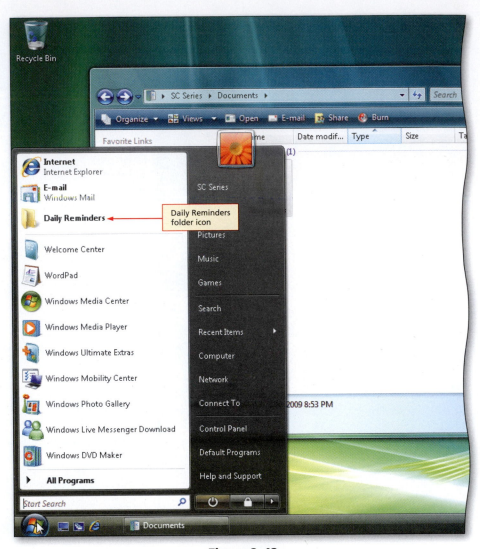

Figure 2–42

Other Ways

1. Right-drag folder icon onto Start button

To Open a Folder Using a Shortcut on the Start Menu

After placing a shortcut to the Daily Reminders folder on the Start menu, you can open the Daily Reminders folder by clicking the Start button and then clicking the Daily Reminders command. The following step opens the Daily Reminders folder from the Start menu.

1
- Display the Start Menu.

- Click Daily Reminders to open the Daily Reminders folder (Figure 2–43).

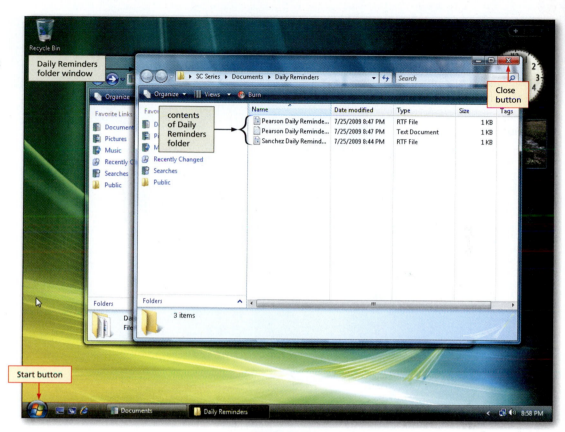

Figure 2–43

To Close the Daily Reminders Folder Window

After verifying that the folder opened correctly, you can close the window. The following step closes the Daily Reminders folder window.

1 Click the Close button on the title bar of the Daily Reminders folder window.

BTW

Deleting Shortcuts
When you delete a shortcut, you remove only the shortcut and its reference to the file or folder. The file or folder itself is stored elsewhere on the hard disk and is not removed.

To Remove a Shortcut from the Start Menu

The capability of adding shortcuts to and removing them from the Start menu provides great flexibility when customizing Windows Vista. Just as you can add shortcuts to the Start menu, you also can remove them. The following steps remove the Daily Reminders shortcut from the Start menu.

1

- Display the Start menu.

- Right-click the Daily Reminders command on the Start menu to display the shortcut menu (Figure 2–44).

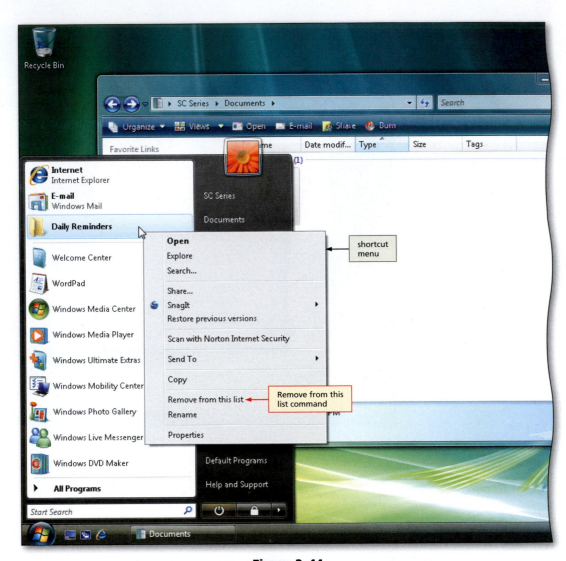

Figure 2–44

2

- Click Remove from this list command to remove the Daily Reminders shortcut from the Start menu (Figure 2–45).

- Close the Start menu.

Figure 2–45

To Create a Shortcut on the Desktop

You also can create shortcuts directly on the desktop. Windows Vista recommends that only shortcuts be placed on the desktop rather than actual folders and files. This is to maximize the efficiency of file and folder searching, which will be covered in a later chapter. The following steps create a shortcut for the Daily Reminders folder on the desktop.

1

- If necessary, click the Documents button on the taskbar to make it the active window.

- Right-click the Daily Reminders folder to display the shortcut menu.

- Point to the Send To command to display the Send To submenu (Figure 2–46).

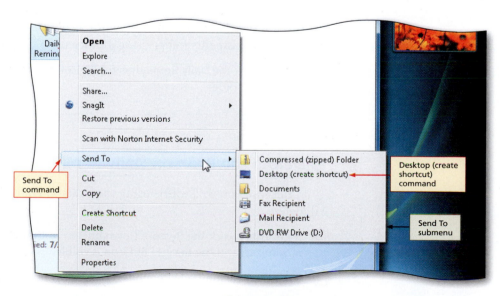

Figure 2–46

2

- Click the Desktop (create shortcut) command to create a shortcut on the desktop.

- Close the Documents folder (Figure 2–47).

Figure 2–47

Opening and Modifying Documents within a Folder

When editing a document, you can open the document directly instead of first opening the application program and then opening the document. Does this feel more natural? Research has indicated that people feel comfortable working with documents directly instead of dealing with application programs and then documents.

You have received new information to add to Mr. Sanchez's daily reminders. An Internet meeting with the sales department in the western United States has been scheduled for 3:00 p.m. and the sales department must be notified of the meeting. To add these new items to the Daily Reminders document, you first must open the Daily Reminders folder that contains the document.

To Open a Folder Using a Shortcut on the Desktop

Because you have created a shortcut on the desktop for the Daily Reminders folder, you can use the shortcut icon to open the Daily Reminders folder the same way you opened the Documents folder using a shortcut in Chapter 1.

1 Double-click the Daily Reminders folder icon on the desktop to open the Daily Reminders folder.

To Delete the Pearson Daily Reminders (Thursday) Text File

Because you will not be using the Pearson Daily Reminders (Thursday) text file, you will delete it.

1 If necessary, click the Restore Down button so that the Daily Reminders folder is not maximized and the Recycle Bin icon is visible.

2 Drag the Pearson Daily Reminders (Thursday) text icon to the Recycle Bin to delete it.

To Open and Modify a Document in a Folder

Now you need to edit the remaining documents in the Daily Reminders folder. The following steps open the Sanchez Daily Reminders (Thursday) document and add new text about the Internet meeting.

1
- Open the Sanchez Daily Reminders (Thursday) document in WordPad.

2
- Press the DOWN ARROW key seven times to move the insertion point to the end of the document.

- Type 6. Notify Sales – NetMeeting at 3:00 p.m. and then press the ENTER key to modify the Sanchez Daily Reminders (Thursday) document (Figure 2–48).

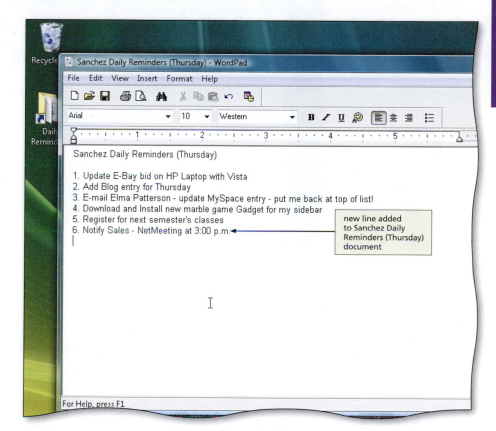

Figure 2–48

To Open and Modify Multiple Documents

Windows Vista allows you to have more than one document and application program open at the same time so you can work on multiple documents. The concept of multiple programs running at the same time is called **multitasking**. To illustrate how you can work with multiple windows open at the same time, you will now edit the Pearson Daily Reminders (Thursday) document to include a reminder to talk to Dan about Carol's birthday party. You will not have to close the Sanchez Daily Reminders (Thursday) document. The following steps open the Pearson Daily Reminders (Thursday) document and add the new reminder.

1
- Open the Pearson Daily Reminders (Thursday) document in WordPad.

Q&A

Why does the font look different in the two documents?

Since the Pearson Daily Reminders (Thursday) document was created as a text file, its font will appear different than that of the Sanchez Daily Reminders (Thursday) document. Remember, Rich Text Format documents allow for more formatting than plain text files.

2

- Press the DOWN ARROW key five times to move the insertion point to the end of the document in the WordPad window.

- Type 4. Call Dan – Birthday party for Carol and then press the ENTER key (Figure 2–49).

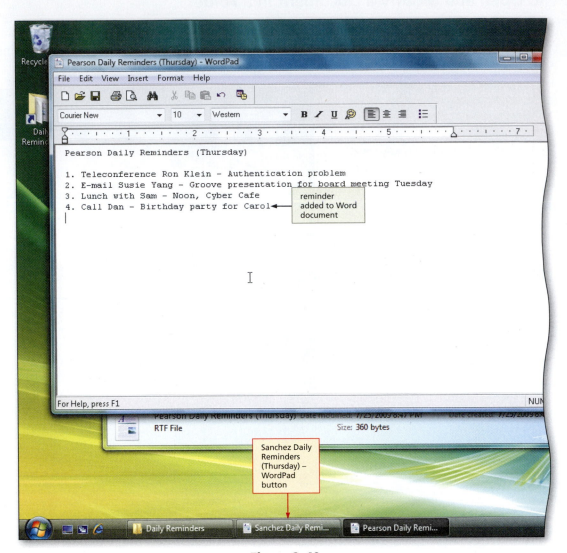

Figure 2–49

To Open an Inactive Window

After you have modified the Pearson Daily Reminders (Thursday) document, you receive information that a dinner meeting with Art Perez has been scheduled for Mr. Sanchez for 7:00 p.m. at The Crab House. You are directed to add this entry to Mr. Sanchez's reminders. To do this, you must make the Sanchez Daily Reminders (Thursday) - WordPad the active window. The following steps make the Sanchez Daily Reminders (Thursday) – WordPad window active and enter the new reminder.

1

- Click the Sanchez Daily Reminders (Thursday) - WordPad button on the taskbar to switch windows.

2

- When the window opens, type `7.`
  `Dinner with Art Perez –`
  `7:00 p.m., The Crab`
  `House` and then press the ENTER key to update the document (Figure 2–50).

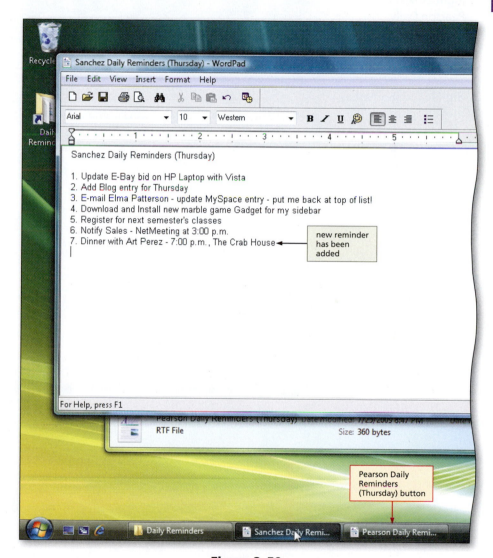

Figure 2–50

To Close Multiple Open Windows and Save Changes from the Taskbar

When you have finished working with multiple windows, close them. If the windows are open on the desktop, you can click the Close button on the title bar of each open window to close them. Regardless of whether the windows are open on the desktop or the windows are minimized using the Show the Desktop command, you also can close the windows using the buttons on the taskbar. The following steps close the Sanchez Daily Reminders (Thursday) - WordPad and Pearson Daily Reminders (Thursday) - WordPad windows from the taskbar.

- Right-click the Pearson Daily Reminders (Thursday) - WordPad button on the taskbar to display the shortcut menu (Figure 2–51).

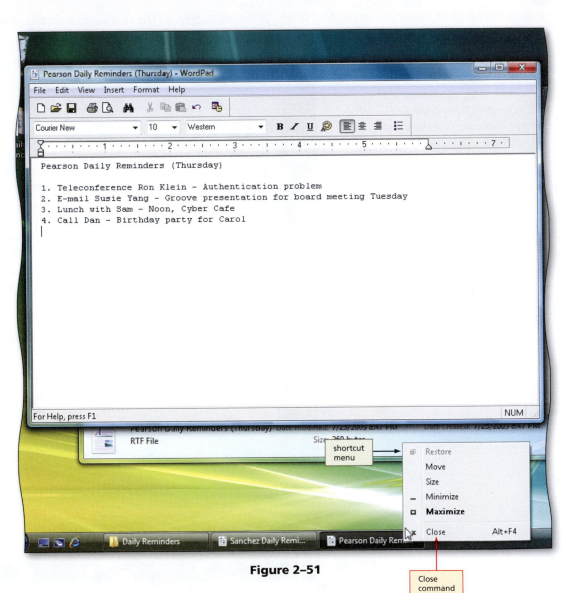

Figure 2–51

2

- Click the Close command to display the WordPad dialog box (Figure 2–52).

- Click the Save button in the WordPad dialog box to save the changes and close the document.

3

- Close and save the Sanchez Daily Reminders (Thursday) document.

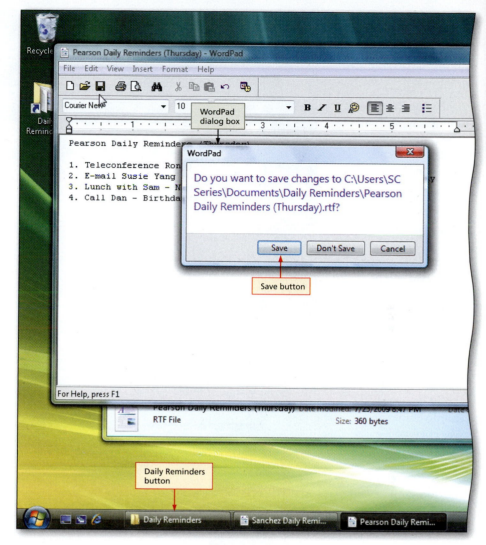

Figure 2–52

Other Ways

1. Click taskbar button, on File menu click Save, click Close button

2. Click taskbar button, on title bar click Close button, click Save button

3. Click taskbar button, on File menu click Exit, click Save button

To Print Multiple Documents from within a Folder

After you modify and save documents on the desktop, you may want to print them so you have an updated hard copy of the documents. Earlier in this chapter, you used the Print command on the File menu to print an open document. You also can print multiple documents from within a folder without actually opening the documents.

Before you can print them, you must select both of them. There are a couple of different ways to select multiple items. You can select the first item, then while holding down the CTRL key, you can select the other items, or you can select the first item, then while holding down the SHIFT key, you can select the other items. The first method works when the items you want to select are not together whereas the second method (using the SHIFT key) only works if all of the items are adjacent. The following steps on the next page print both the Sanchez Daily Reminders (Thursday) and the Pearson Daily Reminders (Thursday) documents from the Daily Reminders folder.

1
- Click the Daily Reminders button on the taskbar to make it the active window.

- Click the Pearson Daily Reminders (Thursday) icon in the Daily Reminders folder to select the icon.

- Press and hold the SHIFT key, click the Sanchez Daily Reminders (Thursday) icon, and then release the SHIFT key to select both items in the Daily Reminders folder (Figure 2–53).

2
- Click the Print button on the toolbar to print the two files.

3
- Click the Close button in the Daily Reminders window to close the Daily Reminders window.

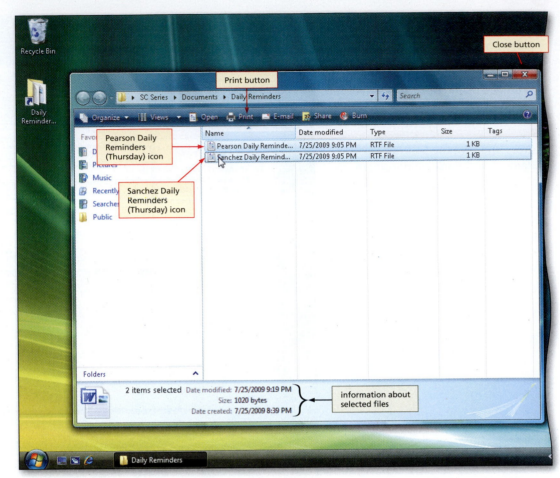

Figure 2–53

Other Ways

1. Select document icons, right-click, click Print
2. Press ALT+F, press P

BTW

Backups
Copying a file or folder to a USB drive is one way to create a backup, but often backing up files is a much more elaborate process. Most backup systems use tape or portable hard disks that contain hundreds of megabytes (millions of characters) and even gigabytes (billions of characters).

Copying a Folder onto a USB Drive

A shortcut on the desktop is useful when you frequently use one or more documents within the folder. It is a good policy to make a copy of a folder and the documents within the folder so if the folder or its contents are accidentally lost or damaged, you do not lose your work. This is referred to as making a **backup** of the files and folders. Another reason to make copies of files and folders is so that you can take the files and folders from one computer to another, for instance if you need to take a file or folder from a work computer to your home computer. A USB drive is a handy device for physically moving copies of files and folders from one computer to another.

To Copy a Folder onto a USB Drive

You want to be able to use the files you have created on another computer. To do so, you will need to copy the files to your USB drive. The following steps copy the Daily Reminders folder on to a USB drive.

1

• Insert a USB drive into an open USB port to display the AutoPlay menu (Figure 2–54).

Q&A

Why does my USB drive have a different letter?

Depending on how many devices you have connected to your computer, your USB drive might have been assigned a different letter such as F or G.

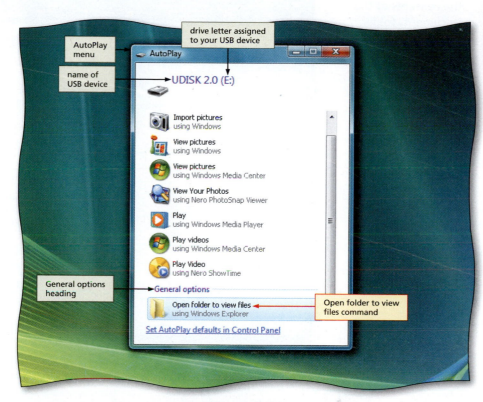

Figure 2–54

2

• Under the General options heading, click the Open folder to view files command to open a folder window (Figure 2–55).

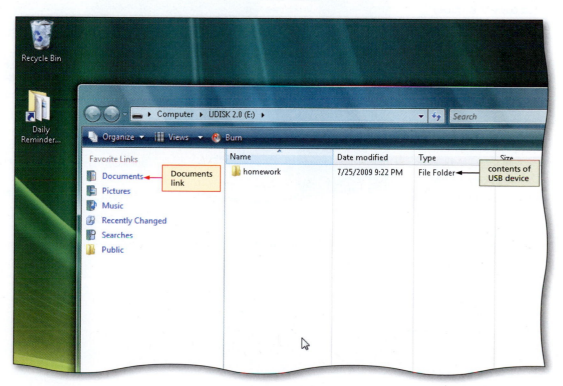

Figure 2–55

3
- Click the Documents link in the left pane to display the contents of the Documents folder.
- Right-click the Daily Reminders folder to display the shortcut menu.
- Point to the Send To command to display the Send To submenu. (Figure 2–56)

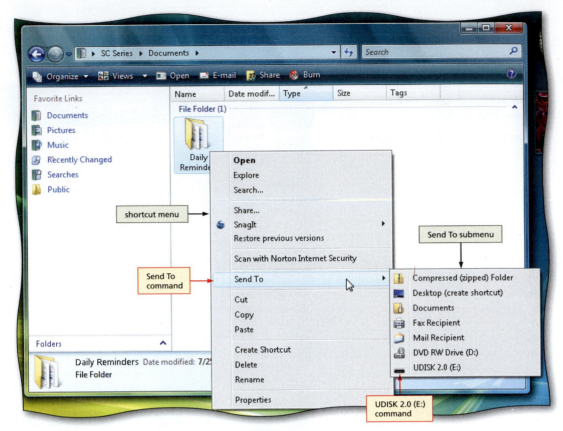

Figure 2–56

4
- Click UDISK 2.0 (E:) to copy the folder to the USB drive (Figure 2–57).

Q&A Can I back up the entire Documents folder?

Yes. It is important to regularly back up the entire contents of your Documents folder. To back up the Documents folder, display the Start menu, right-click the Documents command, click Send To on the shortcut menu, and then click the location of the backup drive.

Figure 2–57

Other Ways

1. Press ALT + F, point to Send To, click UDISK 2.0 (E:)

To Open a Folder Stored on a USB Drive

After copying a folder onto a USB drive, in order to verify that the folder has been copied properly, you can open the folder from the USB drive and view its contents. The following steps open a folder stored on a USB drive.

- Click the Back button on the Address bar of the Documents folder to return to the USB drive window (Figure 2–58).

- Double-click the Daily Reminders icon to open the folder and verify the files are in the Daily Reminders folder.

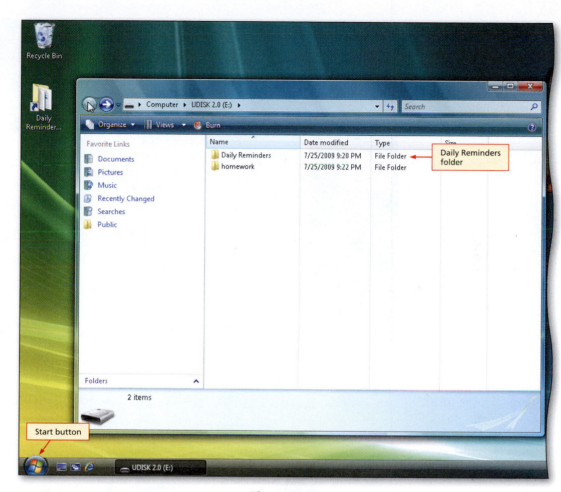

- Close the Daily Reminders folder.

- Close the USB drive window.

Figure 2–58

To Safely Remove a USB Drive

If you wish to open one of the documents in the folder stored on the USB drive you can use one of the methods covered earlier in this chapter to open and edit the file. After you are finished, you should safely remove the USB drive.

1

• Display the Start menu and then click the Computer command to open the Computer folder window (Figure 2–59).

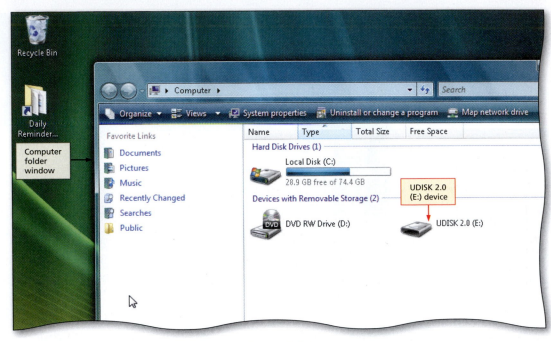

Figure 2–59

2

• Right-click the UDISK 2.0 (E:) device to display the shortcut menu (Figure 2–60).

Figure 2–60

❸

- Click the Safely Remove command on the shortcut menu to have Windows close the USB drive and display the Safe to Remove Hardware message in the Notification area (Figure 2–61).

- Remove the USB drive from the USB port.

- Close the Computer folder.

Q&A

Why do I need to safely remove the USB drive?

Even though you may not have anything open on the USB drive, Windows Vista still may be accessing it in the background. Safely removing the USB drive tells Windows Vista to stop communicating with the device. If you were to remove it while Windows Vista was still accessing it, you could lose your data stored on it.

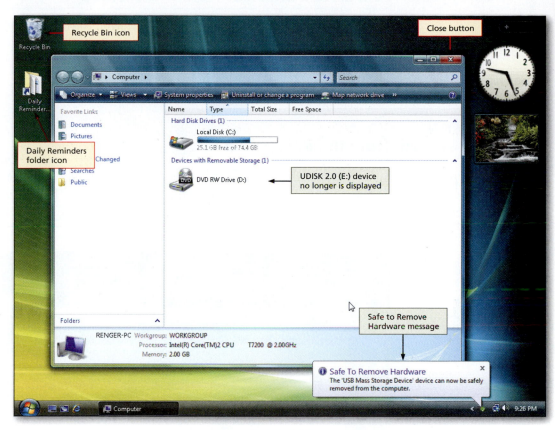

Figure 2–61

The Recycle Bin

Occasionally you will want to delete files and folders from the Documents folder. Windows Vista offers three different techniques to perform this operation: (1) drag the object to the Recycle Bin; (2) right-drag the object to the Recycle Bin; and (3) right-click the object and then click Delete on the shortcut menu.

It is important to realize what you are doing when you delete a file or folder. When you delete a shortcut from the desktop, you only delete the shortcut icon and its reference to the file or folder. The file or folder itself is stored elsewhere on the hard disk and is not deleted. When you delete the icon for a file or folder (not a shortcut), the actual file or folder is deleted. A shortcut icon includes an arrow to indicate that it is a shortcut, while a folder would not have the arrow as part of its icon.

When you delete a file or folder, Windows Vista places these items in the **Recycle Bin**, which is an area on the hard disk that contains all the items you have deleted. When the Recycle Bin becomes full, empty it. Up until the time you empty the Recycle Bin, you can recover deleted files and application programs. Even though you have this safety net, you should be careful whenever you delete anything from your computer.

To Delete a Shortcut from the Desktop

The following step removes a shortcut from the desktop.

 Drag the Daily Reminders - Shortcut icon onto the Recycle Bin icon on the desktop to move the shortcut to the Recycle Bin.

To Restore an Item from the Recycle Bin

At some point you will discover that you accidentally deleted a shortcut, file, or folder that you did not wish to delete. As long as you have not emptied the Recycle Bin, you can restore them. The following steps restore the Daily Reminders - Shortcut icon to the desktop.

- Open the Recycle Bin.

- Click the Daily Reminders - Shortcut icon to select it (Figure 2–62).

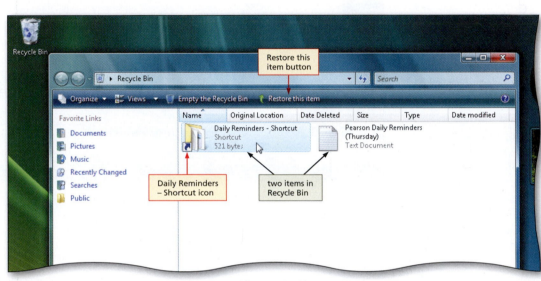

Figure 2–62

2

- Click the Restore this item button to put the Daily Reminders - Shortcut icon back on the desktop (Figure 2–63).

- Close the Recycle Bin window.

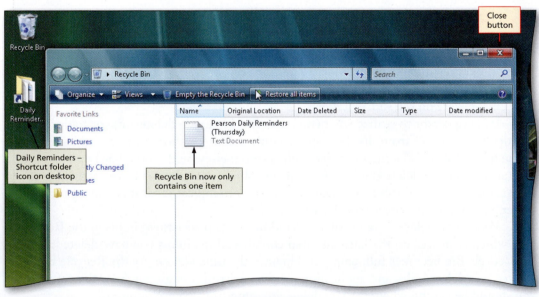

Figure 2–63

To Delete a Shortcut from the Desktop

Now you should delete the Daily Reminders shortcut icon again so that you can leave the desktop how you found it.

 Drag the Daily Reminders - Shortcut icon onto the Recycle Bin icon on the desktop.

To Delete Multiple Files from a Folder

You can delete several files at one time. The following steps delete both the Sanchez Daily Reminders (Thursday) and the Pearson Daily Reminders (Thursday) documents.

1

- Open the Documents folder.

- Open the Daily Reminders folder.

- Click the Sanchez Daily Reminders (Thursday) document to select it.

- Press and hold the CTRL key, click the Pearson Daily Reminders (Thursday) document.

- Right-click the documents to display the shortcut menu (Figure 2–64).

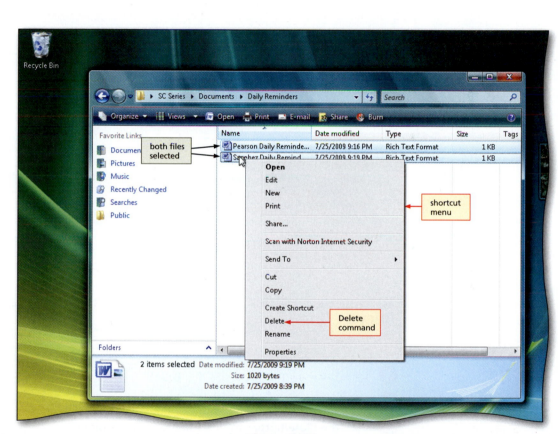

Figure 2–64

2

- Click the Delete command to display the Delete Multiple Items dialog box (Figure 2–65).

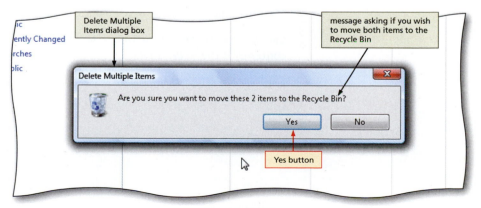

Figure 2–65

3

• Click the Yes button to move the files to the Recycle Bin (Figure 2–66).

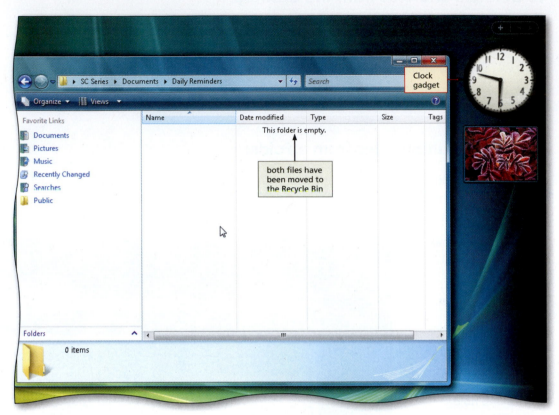

Figure 2–66

To Delete a Folder from the Documents Folder and Empty the Recycle Bin

You also can delete folders from the Documents folder using the same method.

1 Click the Documents link in the Navigation pane.

2 Delete the Daily Reminders folder.

3 Click the Close button to close the Documents folder.

4 Right-click the Recycle Bin to show the shortcut menu.

5 Click the Empty Recycle Bin command.

6 Click the Yes button in the Delete Multiple Files dialog box to permanently delete the contents of the Recycle Bin.

The Windows Sidebar

The Windows Sidebar is a vertical bar that is displayed on the side of your desktop. It is designed to contain mini-programs called gadgets. Through the use of these gadgets, the Windows Sidebar can display useful tools and information. In addition to the gadgets that come with Windows Vista, many developers are building their own gadgets. You can find new gadgets online at the Windows Vista Sidebar Web site, where they are organized into categories including games, multimedia, security, and safety, among others. Be careful if you choose to download a gadget. Not all gadgets have been created by Microsoft directly; therefore, you should verify any gadgets you download as coming from a trusted source.

To Customize the Clock Gadget

As you have learned in Chapter 1, you can add gadgets to the Windows Sidebar. You also can customize the existing gadgets. Depending on the gadget, you will have different options available to you for customizing the gadget. You decide to experiment with the Clock gadget as you would like to see a different clock design, and you would like to add your name to it. The following steps customize and personalize the Clock gadget.

1

• Right-click the Clock gadget on the Sidebar to display the shortcut menu (Figure 2–67).

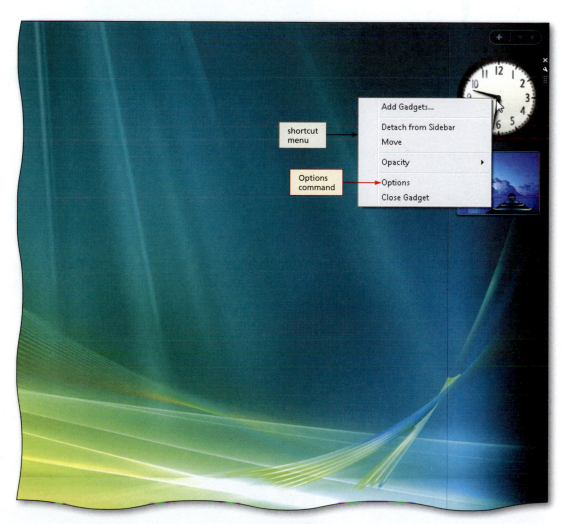

Figure 2–67

2

- Click the Options command to display the Clock dialog box (Figure 2–68).

Figure 2–68

3

- Click the Next button three times to display the neon light clock (Figure 2–69).

Figure 2–69

4

- Click the Clock name text box to select it.

- Type Steve's (or your own name) in the Clock name text box (Figure 2–70).

Figure 2–70

5

- Click the OK button to apply your changes and close the Clock dialog box (Figure 2–71).

Q&A

Do all gadgets have the same options?

Every gadget has different options. For example, the Calendar gadget can be customized to show a week or a month, not just the current day.

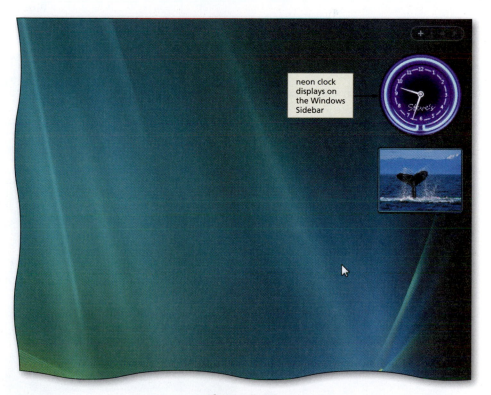

Figure 2–71

To Undo the Changes to the Clock Gadget

Although you like the new look for the Clock gadget, you decide that the original style was easier to read. You therefore want to undo the changes you have made. The following steps undo the changes to the Clock gadget.

- Right-click the Clock gadget and then click the Options command on the shortcut menu (Figure 2–72).

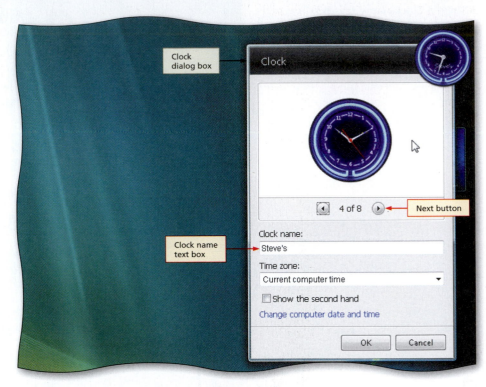

Figure 2–72

2

- Click the Next button five times to display the original clock.

- Delete the text from the Clock name text box (Figure 2–73).

- Click the OK button to apply your changes and close the Clock dialog box.

Figure 2–73

To Rearrange Gadgets on the Sidebar

Besides customizing the gadgets, you also can rearrange the gadgets on the Sidebar. Rearranging gadgets is as simple as dragging them to the location where you want. You decide to see how the gadgets would look in another arrangement. The following steps rearrange the gadgets on the Sidebar.

1

- Point to the Clock gadget to show the Move button (Figure 2–74).

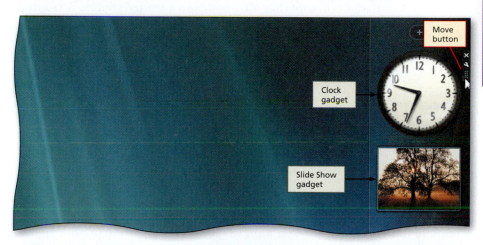

Figure 2–74

2

- Click the Move button and drag the Clock gadget below the Slide Show gadget to reposition it on the Sidebar (Figure 2–75).

Figure 2–75

3

- Point to the Slide Show gadget to show the Move button.

- Click the Move button and drag the Slide Show gadget below the Clock gadget to put the gadgets back in their original order (Figure 2–76).

Figure 2–76

Finding More Gadgets

Besides the gadgets that come pre-installed with Windows Vista, you also can find gadgets online that offer news, sports updates, entertainment, or other useful tools and information. Once you find a gadget online that you are interested in, you can download and install it on your computer. Before downloading and installing a gadget, first make sure that it comes from a trusted source. A **trusted source** is a source that has been verified to be trustworthy either by you, by a trusted friend, or by a trusted organization such as Microsoft. Trusted sources are not known to offer gadgets that contain offensive content or malicious code that could possibly damage your computer or do any other type of harm. If you download from a trusted source, you can feel secure about what you are installing on your computer. If the developer of the gadget you want to download is not a trusted source, you should not download and install the gadget.

To Search for Gadgets Online

Now you decide to go online and browse for new gadgets, although you are not going to download and install any new gadgets at this time. You just want to become familiar with what types of gadgets are available. In fact, since you have been so busy, you want to find some gadgets to provide quick relief from work, without being too distracting or time-consuming. The following steps search for gadgets online.

- Click the Add Gadgets button to display the Gadget Gallery (Figure 2–77).

Figure 2–77

2
- Click the Get more gadgets online link to open Windows Internet Explorer and display the Personalize Windows Vista Sidebar Web page (Figure 2–78).

Why do I see different gadgets on my computer?

The Windows Vista Sidebar Web site is frequently updated. Each time you search for gadgets online, different gadgets may appear.

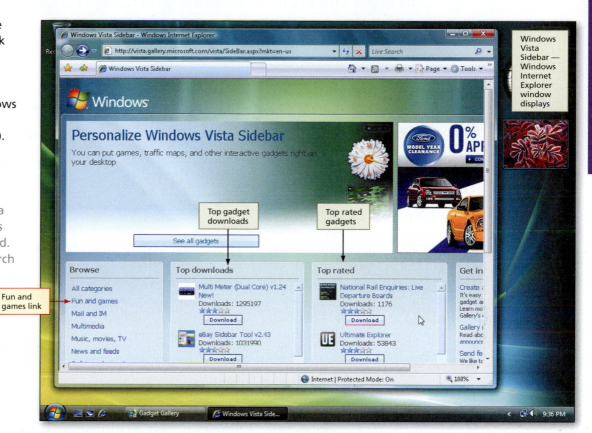

Figure 2–78

3
- Click the Fun and games link to display the gadgets in this category (Figure 2–79).

Experiment

- Try some of the other links to see what gadgets developers are creating. Take a look at the Safety and security gadgets as well as the Multimedia gadgets.

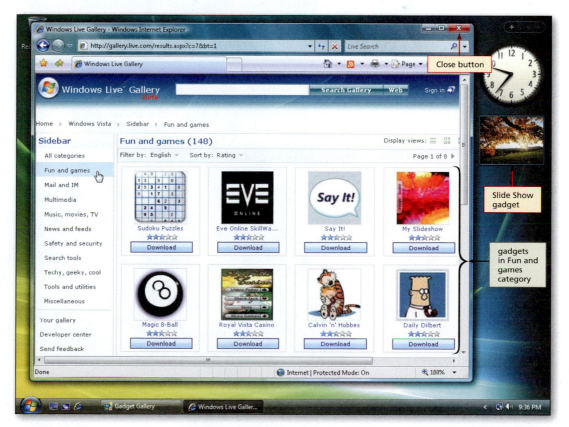

Figure 2–79

To Close the Internet Explorer and Gadget Gallery Windows

After having reviewed some of the gadgets available online, you decide to close Internet Explorer. You do not want to download gadgets yet; you want to wait until you have verified that the gadgets you want are from trusted sources. The following steps close Internet Explorer and the Gadget Gallery windows.

1 Click the Close button of the Windows Internet Explorer to close the window.

2 Click the Close button in the Gadget Gallery to close the window.

To Place a Gadget on the Desktop

Gadgets, when displayed in the Sidebar, are limited as to where they can appear. Windows Vista allows you to move a gadget from the Sidebar to other locations on the desktop. When you move a gadget off of the Sidebar, it often will change in appearance to reflect the fact that it is no longer constrained to fitting within the Sidebar. This does not mean that you can enlarge it to whatever size you want; some gadgets only expand a little when moved off of the Sidebar. You decide to see what the Slide Show gadget would look like when it is placed on the desktop, and whether you will have a better view of the pictures it displays. The following steps place the Slide Show gadget on the desktop.

- Right-click the Slide Show gadget to display the shortcut menu (Figure 2–80).

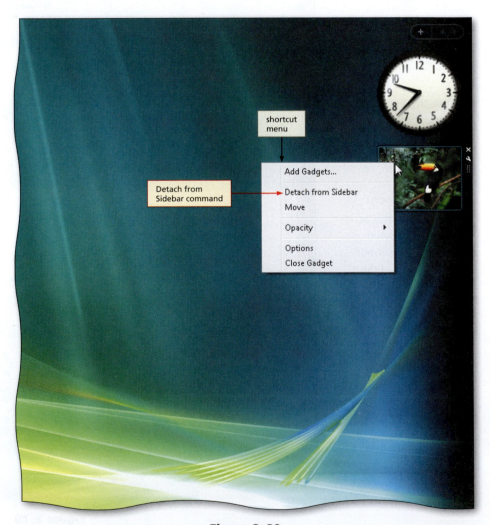

Figure 2–80

- Click Detach from Sidebar to place the Slide Show gadget on the desktop.

- Drag the Slide Show gadget to the center of the desktop (Figure 2–81).

Figure 2–81

To Remove a Gadget from the Desktop

After having placed the Slide Show gadget on the desktop, you decide to put it back on the Sidebar so that you have more of your desktop available. The following steps place the Slide Show gadget back on the Sidebar.

- Right-click the Slide Show gadget to display the shortcut menu (Figure 2–82).

Figure 2–82

2

- Click the Attach to Sidebar command to place the Slide Show gadget back on the Sidebar (Figure 2–83).

Q&A Why did the Slide Show gadget show up at the top of the Sidebar?

When you attach a gadget to the Sidebar, Windows Vista automatically places it at the top of the Sidebar.

Slide Show gadget displays on Sidebar

Figure 2–83

To Move the Slide Show Gadget

Now you move the Slide Show gadget back to its original location.

1 Click and drag the Slide Show gadget below the Clock gadget to put it back into its original position.

To Close and Show the Sidebar

You may want to hide the Sidebar to maximize and unclutter your screen while you are working with other application programs. The following steps close and then show the Sidebar.

1

● Right-click an open area of the Sidebar to display the shortcut menu (Figure 2–84).

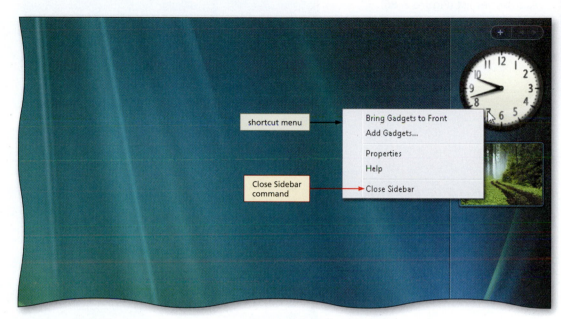

Figure 2–84

2

● Click the Close Sidebar command to close the Sidebar (Figure 2–85).

Figure 2–85

3

- Display the Start menu, click All Programs, and then click the Accessories folder to expand the Accessories list (Figure 2–86).

- Click the Windows Sidebar command to show the Sidebar.

Figure 2–86

To Log Off from the Computer

After restoring the Windows Sidebar, you decide to log off from the computer, because you are done working with it. The following steps log off your account from the computer.

1 Display the Start menu.

2 Point to the arrow to the right of the Lock this computer button to display the Shut Down options menu.

3 Click the Log Off command, and then wait for Windows Vista to prompt you to save any unsaved data, if any, and log off.

To Turn Off the Computer

The following step turns off the computer. If you are not sure whether you should turn off the computer, read the following step without actually performing it.

 Click the Shut Down button to turn off the computer.

Chapter Summary

In this chapter, you learned to create text documents using both the application-centric approach and document-centric approach. You moved these documents to the Documents folder and modified and printed them. You created a new folder in the Documents folder, placed documents in the folder, and copied the new folder onto a USB drive. You worked with multiple documents open at the same time. You placed a document shortcut on both the Start menu and on the desktop. Using various methods, you deleted shortcuts, documents, and a folder. Finally, you learned how to customize a gadget, rearrange gadgets on the Sidebar, search for new gadgets online, place a gadget on the desktop, and hide and show the Sidebar. The items listed below include all the new Windows Vista skills you have learned in this chapter.

1. Launch a Program and Create a Document (WIN 76)
2. Save a Document to the Documents Folder (WIN 78)
3. Open the Print Dialog Box from an Application Program (WIN 81)
4. Print a Document (WIN 82)
5. Edit a Document (WIN 83)
6. Close and Save a Document (WIN 83)
7. Open the Documents Folder (WIN 85)
8. Create a Blank Document in the Documents Folder (WIN 86)
9. Name a Document in the Documents Folder (WIN 87)
10. Open a Document with WordPad (WIN 88)
11. Enter Data into a Blank Document (WIN 89)
12. Save a Text Document in Rich Text Format (RTF) (WIN 90)
13. Change the View to Small Icons (WIN 92)
14. Arrange the Items in a Folder in Groups by Type (WIN 93)
15. Create and Name a Folder in the Documents Folder (WIN 94)
16. Move a Document into a Folder (WIN 97)
17. Change Location Using the Address Bar (WIN 99)
18. Display and Use the Preview Pane (WIN 100)
19. Close the Preview Pane (WIN 102)
20. Change Location Using the Back Button on the Address Bar (WIN 103)
21. Add a Shortcut on the Start Menu (WIN 104)
22. Open a Folder Using a Shortcut on the Start Menu (WIN 107)
23. Remove a Shortcut from the Start Menu (WIN 108)
24. Create a Shortcut on the Desktop (WIN 109)
25. Delete the Pearson Daily Reminders (Thursday) Text File (WIN 110)
26. Open and Modify a Document in a Folder (WIN 111)
27. Open and Modify Multiple Documents (WIN 111)
28. Open an Inactive Window (WIN 113)
29. Close Multiple Open Windows and Save Changes from the Taskbar (WIN 114)
30. Print Multiple Documents from within a Folder (WIN 115)
31. Copy a Folder onto a USB Drive (WIN 117)
32. Open a Folder Stored on a USB Drive (WIN 119)
33. Safely Remove a USB Drive (WIN 120)
34. Restore an Item from the Recycle Bin (WIN 122)
35. Delete Multiple Files from a Folder (WIN 123)
36. Customize the Clock Gadget (WIN 125)
37. Undo the Changes to the Clock Gadget (WIN 128)
38. Rearrange Gadgets on the Sidebar (WIN 129)
39. Search for Gadgets Online (WIN 130)
40. Place a Gadget on the Desktop (WIN 132)
41. Remove a Gadget from the Desktop (WIN 133)
42. Close and Show the Sidebar (WIN 135)

Learn It Online

Test your knowledge of chapter content and key terms.

Instructions: To complete the Learn It Online exercises, start your browser, click the Address bar, and then enter the Web address scsite.com/winvista/learn. When the Windows Vista Learn It Online page is displayed, click the link for the exercise you want to complete and then read the instructions.

Chapter Reinforcement TF, MC, and SA
A series of true/false, multiple-choice, and short-answer questions that tests your knowledge of the chapter content.

Flash Cards
An interactive learning environment where you identify chapter key terms associated with displayed definitions.

Practice Test
A series of multiple-choice questions that tests your knowledge of chapter content and key terms.

Who Wants To Be a Computer Genius?
An interactive game that challenges your knowledge of chapter content in the style of a television quiz show.

Wheel of Terms
An interactive game that challenges your knowledge of chapter key terms in the style of the television show *Wheel of Fortune*.

Crossword Puzzle Challenge
A crossword puzzle that challenges your knowledge of key terms presented in the chapter.

Apply Your Knowledge

Reinforce the skills and apply the concepts you learned in this chapter.

Creating a Document with WordPad
Instructions: Use the WordPad application to create the homework list shown in Figure 2–87.

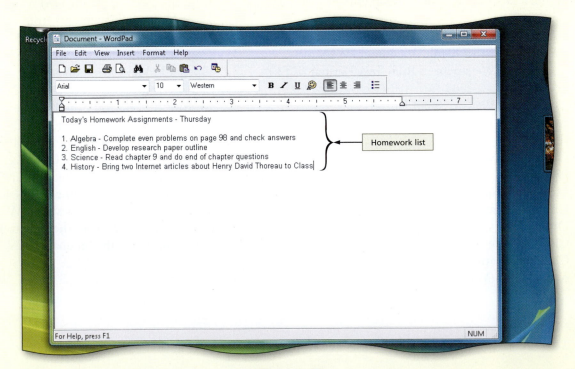

Figure 2–87

Perform the following tasks:

Part 1: Launching the WordPad Application
1. Click the Start button.
2. Launch WordPad. The Document - WordPad window displays an insertion point (flashing vertical line) in the blank area below the menu bar.

Part 2: Creating a Document Using WordPad
1. Type Today's Homework Assignments - Thursday and then press the ENTER key twice.
2. Type 1. Algebra - Complete even problems on page 98 and check answers and then press the ENTER key.
3. Type 2. English - Develop research paper outline and then press the ENTER key.
4. Type 3. Science - Read chapter 9 and do end of chapter questions and then press the ENTER key.
5. Type 4. History - Bring two Internet articles about Henry David Thoreau to Class and then press the ENTER key.

Part 3: Printing the Today's Homework Document
1. Click File on the menu bar, and then click Print to print the document.

Part 4: Save and Close the WordPad Window
1. Insert a USB drive.
2. Save your document as Homework Assignment to the USB drive.
3. Close WordPad.

Extend Your Knowledge

Extend the skills you learned in this chapter and experiment with new skills. You may need to use Help to complete the assignment.

Finding File and Folder Help

Instructions: Use Windows Help and Support to learn about files and folders.

Perform the following tasks:

Part 1: Creating a Document in the Documents Folder
1. Create a WordPad document in the Documents folder. Save the document as Working with Files and Folders.
2. Maximize the Working with Files and Folders - WordPad window.

Part 2: Launching Windows Help and Support
1. Click the Start button on the taskbar.
2. Click Help and Support on the Start menu.
3. Click Windows basics in the Find an Answer area.
4. Scroll down to Programs, files, and folders area.
5. Click Working with files and folders. The Working with files and folders page displays in the topic pane (Figure 2–88 on the next page).

Continued >

Extend Your Knowledge *continued*

Part 3: Copying a Set of Steps to the WordPad Window

1. Scroll down to the Creating and deleting files area.

2. Drag through the heading steps below the heading to highlight them.

3. Right-click the highlighted text to display a shortcut menu.

4. Click Copy on the shortcut menu.

5. Click the Working with Files and Folders button in the taskbar button area to display the Working with Files and Folders - WordPad window.

6. Right-click the text area of the WordPad window to display a shortcut menu.

7. Click Paste. The heading and steps display in the window.

8. Click File on the menu bar and then click Save to save the document.

9. Click the Windows Help and Support button in the task-bar button area to display the Windows Help and Support window.

10. Click the Back button on the navigation toolbar.

Part 4: Copying Other Headings and Steps to the WordPad Window

1. Using the procedure previously shown in Part 3, copy the following headings and steps to the WordPad window: Copying and moving files and folders, Finding your files, and Opening an existing file.

2. Click File on the menu bar and then click Save to save the document.

3. Click File on the menu bar, click Print on the File menu, and then click the Print button to print the document.

4. Close the Working with Files and Folders - WordPad window.

5. Close the Windows Help and Support window.

6. Insert a USB drive and copy the Working with Files and Folders document in the Documents folder to the USB drive.

7. Delete the Working with Files and Folders document from the Documents folder and empty the Recycle Bin.

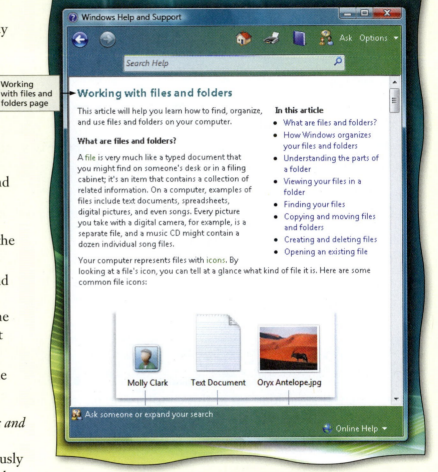

Figure 2–88

In the Lab

Use the guidelines, concepts and skills presented in this chapter to increase your knowledge of Windows Vista. Labs are listed in order of increasing difficulty.

Lab 1: Windows Vista Seminar Announcement and Schedule

Instructions: A two-day Windows Vista seminar will be offered to all teachers at your school. You have been put in charge of developing two text documents for the seminar. One document announces the seminar and will be sent to all teachers. The other document contains the schedule for the seminar. You prepare the documents shown in Figures 2-89 and 2-90 using WordPad.

Perform the following tasks:

Part 1: Creating the Windows Vista Seminar Announcement Document

1. Open a new WordPad document. Save the document as Windows Vista Seminar Announcement on the desktop.
2. Enter the text shown in Figure 2–89.
3. Save the document.
4. Print the document.
5. Close the document.
6. Move the document to the Documents folder.
7. Create a folder in the Documents folder called Windows Vista Seminar Documents.
8. Place the Windows Vista Seminar Announcement document in the Windows Vista Seminar Documents folder.

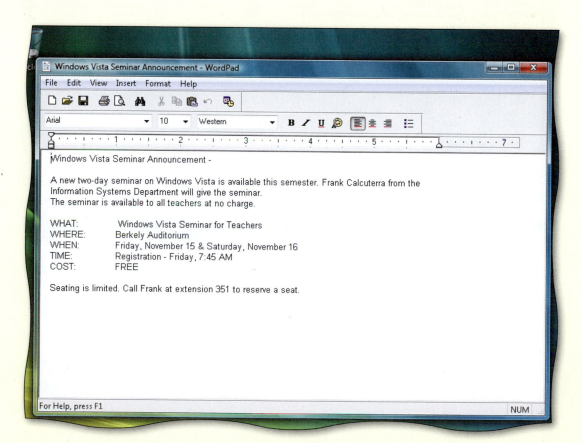

Figure 2–89

Continued >

In the Lab *continued*

Part 2: *Creating the Windows Vista Seminar Schedule Document*

1. Open a new WordPad document. Save the document as Windows Vista Seminar Schedule on the desktop.

2. Enter the text shown in Figure 2-90.

3. Save the document.

4. Print the document.

5. Close the document.

6. Move the Windows Vista Seminar Schedule document to the Documents folder.

7. Place the Windows Vista Seminar Schedule document in the Windows Vista Seminar Documents folder.

8. Move the Windows Vista Seminar Documents folder to your USB drive.

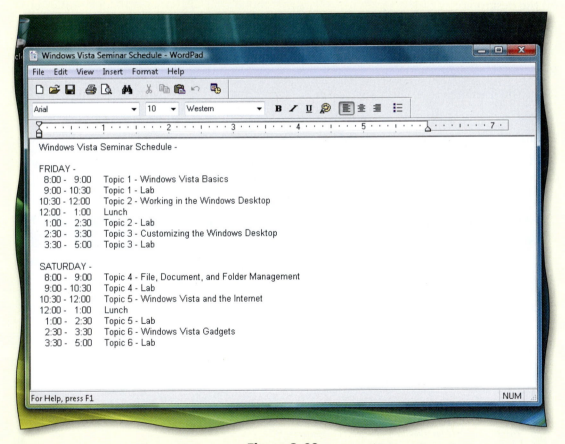

Figure 2–90

In the Lab

Lab 2: Researching Online Gadgets

Instructions: You are asked to create a list of gadgets that your company might find useful. Using the Windows Vista Sidebar Web site, you will create a gadget list that lists the gadgets and the categories in which they are located. Your boss is interested in four main categories. Create the headings shown in Figure 2–91 using the application-centric approach and WordPad. Then follow the steps to find some potentially useful gadgets online.

Perform the following tasks:

1. Start WordPad.

2. Enter the text shown in Figure 2–91.

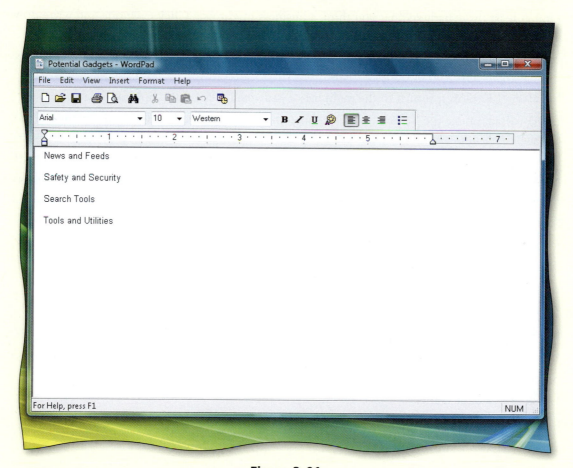

Figure 2–91

Continued >

In the Lab *continued*

3. Use Save As to save the document in the Documents folder with the file name Potential Gadgets.

4. Click the Add Gadgets button on the Windows Sidebar.

5. Click, Get more gadgets online, to open the Windows Vista Sidebar Web site.

6. Click on the link for News and feeds.

7. Find at least three gadgets that you think a business might use. Click each one and write down the name of the gadget and who developed it.

8. In WordPad, under the News and feeds heading, enter a numbered list stating the names of the three gadgets and who developed them.

9. In Internet Explorer, return to the main list of gadgets. Click on the link for Safety and security.

10. Find at least three gadgets that you think a business might use. Click each one and write down the name of the gadget, who developed it, and why it might be of use to a business.

11. In WordPad, under the Safety and Security heading, enter a numbered list stating the names of the three gadgets and who developed them.

12. In Internet Explorer, return to the main list of gadgets. Click on the link for Search tools.

13. In WordPad, under the Search Tools heading, enter a numbered list stating the names of the three gadgets and who developed them.

14. In Internet Explorer, return to the main list of gadgets. Click on the link for Tools and utilities.

15. In WordPad, under the Tools and Utilities heading, enter a numbered list stating the names of the three gadgets and who developed them.

16. Save the document.

17. Print the document from WordPad.

18. Close WordPad.

19. Insert a USB drive in an open USB port.

20. Right-click the Potential Gadgets icon in the Documents folder and then click Send To.

21. Click USB DISK.

22. Close the Documents folder.

23. Safely Remove the USB drive.

24. Close the Gadget Gallery.

25. Close Internet Explorer.

In the Lab

Lab 3: Creating, Saving, and Printing Automobile Information Documents

Instruction: For eight months, you have accumulated data about your 2006 Dodge Viper automobile. Some of the information is written on pieces of paper, while the rest is in the form of receipts. You have decided to organize this information using your computer. You create the documents shown in Figures 2-92 and 2-93 using the application-centric approach and WordPad.

Perform the following tasks:

Part 1:   Creating the Automobile Information Document

1. Create a new WordPad document. Save the document on the desktop with the file name, Automobile Information.

2. Type the text shown in Figure 2–92.

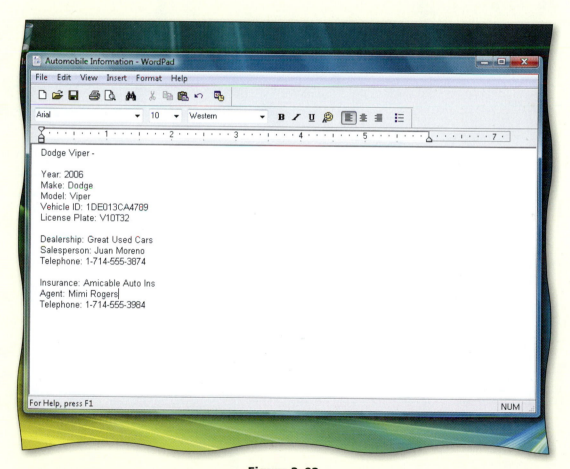

Figure 2–92

3. Save the document.

4. Print the document.

5. Create a folder in the Documents folder called Automobile Documents.

6. Place the Automobile Information document in the Automobile Documents folder.

Continued >

In the Lab *continued*

Part 2: Other Automobile Documents

1. Create the Phone Numbers document (Figure 2–93a), the Automobile Gas Mileage document (Figure 2–93b), and the Automobile Maintenance document on the desktop (Figure 2–93c).

2. Move each document into the Documents folder.

3. Print each document.

4. Place each document in the Automobile Documents folder.

5. Move the Automobile Documents folder to a USB drive.

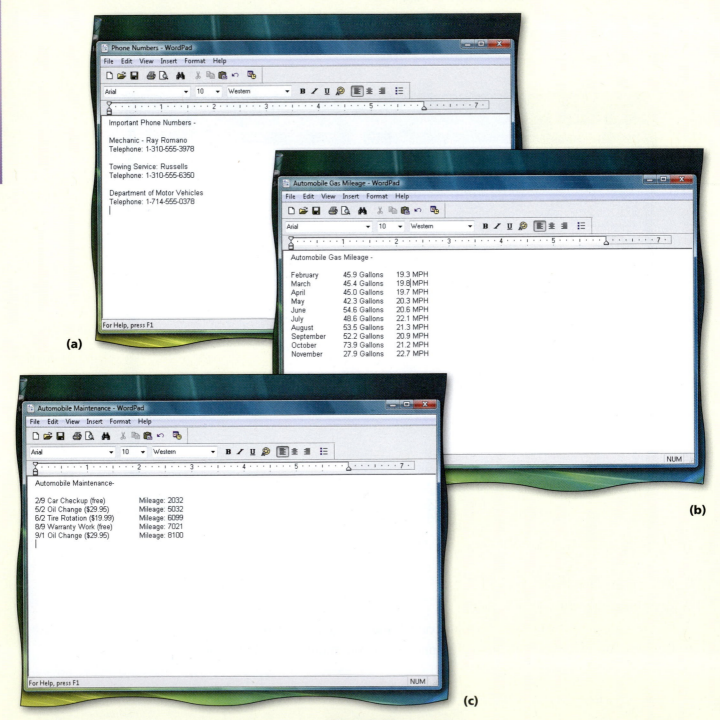

Figure 2–93

Cases and Places

Apply your creative thinking and problem solving skills to design and implement a solution.

- • Easier   •• More Difficult

• 1 Creating Employer Request List

Your employer is concerned that some people in the company are not thoroughly researching purchases of office supplies. She has prepared a list of steps she would like everyone to follow when purchasing office supplies: (1) Determine your department's need for office supplies; (2) Identify at least two Internet sites that sell the office supplies you need; and (3) Obtain prices for the office supplies from their Web sites.

Your employer wants you to use WordPad to prepare a copy of this list to post in every department. Save and print the document. After you have printed one copy of the document, try experimenting with different WordPad features to make the list more eye-catching. If you like your changes, save and print a revised copy of the document.

• 2 Locating Gadgets Online

As you have learned, the Windows Sidebar provides a place for useful gadgets. You would like to find out more about gadgets and install one for yourself. Visit the Windows Vista Sidebar Web site and find out how to get gadgets that will provide up-to-date news. Download one and try it out. Write a brief report about what you found online and what you think about news gadgets. Include the name and developer of the gadget you installed.

•• 3 Researching Retraining Costs

Retraining employees can be an expensive task for a business of any size. Many Windows Vista users believe the Windows Vista operating system is an intuitive, easy-to-learn operating system which can reduce retraining costs. Using the Internet, current computer magazines, or other resources, research this topic and write a brief report summarizing your findings. Explain those features that you think make the Windows Vista operating system an easy-to-use operating system.

•• 4 Research Gadgets for Personal Use

Make it Personal

Just like for business, there are lots of useful gadgets for you to find and use. Look online for a Multimedia gadget that will let you play a radio station or watch a TV show. Pick a few that you find interesting. Download and install them. Write a brief report comparing and contrasting them. Which one is the easiest to use? Which one is the worst? If you decide you do not like any of the ones you downloaded, try a couple of more until you find one you like. Include in your report how likely you will or will not download more gadgets to use in the future.

•• 5 Researching Course Registration Procedures

Working Together

Registering for classes can be a daunting task for incoming college freshmen. As someone who has gone through the process, prepare a guide for students who are about to register for the first time next semester. Working with classmates, research and create your guide. Your guide should be two or more documents, include a schedule of key dates and times, a description of the registration procedure, and suggestions for how students can make registration easier. Give the documents suitable names and save them in a folder in the Windows Vista Documents folder. Print each document.

3 File and Folder Management

Objectives

You will have mastered the material in this chapter when you can:

- View the contents of a drive and folder using the Computer folder window
- View the properties of files and folders
- Find files and folders from a folder window
- Find files and folders using Search
- Cascade, stack, and view windows side by side on the desktop
- View the contents of the Pictures folder window

- Open and use the Windows Photo Gallery
- View pictures as a slide show
- E-mail a picture
- View the contents of the Music folder window
- View information about an audio file
- Play an audio file using Windows Media Player
- Create a backup on a USB drive and a CD
- Restore a folder from a backup on a USB drive

3 | File and Folder Management

Introduction

In Chapter 2, you used Windows Vista to create documents on the desktop and work with documents and folders in the Documents folder. Windows Vista also allows you to examine the files and folders on the computer in a variety of other ways, enabling you to choose the easiest and most accessible manner when working with the computer. The Computer folder window and the Documents folder window provide two ways for you to work with files and folders. In addition, the Pictures folder window allows you to organize and share picture files, and the Music folder window allows you to organize and share your music files. This chapter will illustrate how to work with files in the Computer, Documents, Pictures, and Music folder windows.

Overview

As you read this chapter, you will learn how to work with the Computer, Pictures and Music folders by performing these general tasks:

- Opening and using the Computer folder window
- Searching for files and folders
- Managing open windows
- Opening and using the Pictures folder window
- Using the Windows Photo Gallery
- Opening and using the Music folder window
- Playing a music file in Windows Media Player
- Backing up and restoring a folder using a USB drive

Plan Ahead

> **Working with the Windows Vista Desktop**
> Working with the Windows Vista desktop requires a basic knowledge of how to use the Windows Vista desktop, insert a USB drive, access the Internet, and use a printer.
>
> 1. **Determine the permissions you have on the computer you will be using.** Each user account can have different rights and permissions. Depending on which rights and permissions have been set for your account, you may or may not be able to perform certain operations.
>
> 2. **Identify how to add a USB drive to your computer.** Depending upon the setup of your computer, there may be several ways to add a USB drive to your computer. You should know which USB ports you can use to add a USB drive to your computer.
>
> 3. **Determine if your computer has speakers.** Some computer labs do not provide speakers with their computers. If you are going to be using a computer in a lab, you need to know if the computer has speakers or if you will need to bring a set of headphones.
>
> 4. **Find out if you have access to the sample files installed with Windows Vista.** To complete the steps in this chapter, you will need access to the sample pictures, videos and sounds installed with Windows Vista.
>
> *(continued)*

**Plan
Ahead**

(continued)

5. **Determine if your computer has a CD or DVD burner.** Some labs do not provide CD or DVD burners. If you are going to be using a computer in a lab, you need to know if you have access to a CD or DVD burner to back up your files.

6. **Check to see if e-mail is configured.** To complete the e-mail portion of this chapter, you will need to have access to an e-mail program. You need to make sure that the e-mail program has been configured before you use it.

7. **Understand copyright issues.** When working with multimedia files, you should be aware that most pictures, movies, and music files are copyrighted. Before you use them, you should make sure that you are aware of any copyrights. Just because you can download a picture or music file from the Internet does not mean that it belongs to you.

The Computer Folder Window

As noted in previous chapters, the Start menu displays the Computer command. Selecting the **Computer command** displays a window that contains the storage devices that are installed on the computer. The Computer folder window looks very similar to the Documents folder window that you worked with in the previous chapter. This is due to Windows Vista relying on folder windows to display the contents on the computer. A **folder window** consists of an Address bar at the top, a toolbar containing variable options, a navigation pane on the left below the toolbar, a headings bar and list area on the right below the toolbar, and a Details pane at the bottom of the window. Depending upon which folder you are viewing, Computer, Documents, Pictures, etc., the folder window will display the toolbar options that are most appropriate for working with the folder contents. The toolbar of the Computer folder window shows the Organize, Views, Systems properties, Uninstall or change a program, and Map network drive buttons, but these options will change as the objects displayed change. Although the list area of the Computer window shows groupings based upon the different types of devices connected to your computer, it will display files and folders depending upon your selections.

To Open and Maximize the Computer Folder Window

The following steps open and maximize the Computer folder window so that you can view its contents.

1 Display the Start menu.

2 Click the Computer command to open the Computer folder window. If necessary, maximize the Computer folder window.

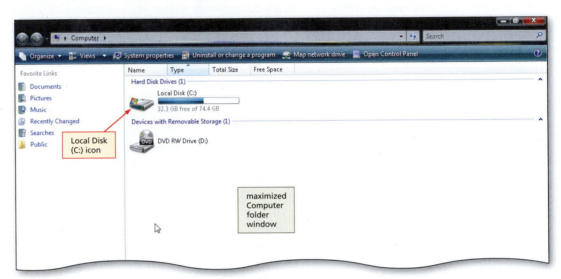

Figure 3–1

The list area of the Computer folder window is organized to group objects based upon the different types of devices connected to your computer. The Hard Disk Drives group contains the **Local Disk (C:) icon** that represents the hard disk on the computer. The **hard disk** is where you can store files, documents, and folders. Storing data on a hard disk is more convenient than storing data on a USB drive because the hard disk is faster, and generally has more storage room available. A computer always will have at least one hard disk drive, normally designated as drive C. On the computer represented by the Computer folder window in Figure 3–1, the icon consists of an image of a hard disk and a **disk label**, or title, Local Disk, and a drive letter (C:). The label is not required and may differ depending upon the name assigned to the hard disk. For example, some people label their drives based upon usage; therefore, it could be called PRIMARY (C:) where PRIMARY is the label given to the hard disk as it is the drive that houses the operating system and main programs.

The Devices with Removable Storage group contains the DVD RW Drive (D:) icon, indicating that there is a DVD burner attached to your computer. The CD RW Drive (D:) icon would indicate that your computer has a CD burner instead of a DVD burner. If your computer has a CD or DVD drive that only reads CD and DVDs, and cannot burn to the discs, you would not see the RW. **RW** is an abbreviation of rewritable, which means that the drive can write data onto read/writable CDs or DVDs. The DVD RW Drive (D:) icon represents the DVD rewritable drive attached to the computer, also known as a DVD burner. The label for the drive is DVD RW Drive, and the drive letter assigned to this drive is (D:). The icon consists of an image of a DVD disc on top of an image of a DVD drive because the drive does not currently contain a DVD. If you were to insert a CD or a DVD in the drive, such as an audio CD containing music, Windows Vista would change the icon to reflect a music CD and change the label to display the artist's name.

BTW

Icons
It is possible that some icons may display that you do not recognize. Software vendors develop hundreds of icons to represent their products. Each icon is supposed to be unique, meaningful, and eye-catching. You can purchase thousands of icons on a CD or DVD that you can use to represent documents you create.

To Display Properties for the Local Disk (C:) Drive in the Details Pane

The Details pane of a folder window displays the properties of devices, files, or folders. Every drive, folder, file, and program in Windows Vista is considered an object. Every object in Windows Vista has properties that describe the object. A **property** is a characteristic of an object such as the amount of storage space on a storage device or the number of items in a folder. The properties of each object will differ, and in some cases, you can change the properties of an object. For example, in the Local Disk (C:) properties, you would check the Space free property to determine how much space is available on the C drive. To determine the drive's capacity, you would view the Total size property. The following step displays the properties for the Local Disk (C:) in the Details pane of the Computer folder window.

1

- Click the Local Disk (C:) icon to select the drive and display the properties in the Details pane (Figure 3–2).

🔍 **Experiment**

- See what properties display for the other drives and devices shown. Click each one and note what properties display in the Details pane. Return to the Local Disk (C:) when you are done.

Q&A Why do the properties of my Local Disk differ from those in the figure?

Because the size of the drive and contents of your drive will be different than the one in the figure, the properties of the drive also will be different. Depending upon what has been installed on the drive and how it is formatted, the space used, file system, space free, and total size properties will vary.

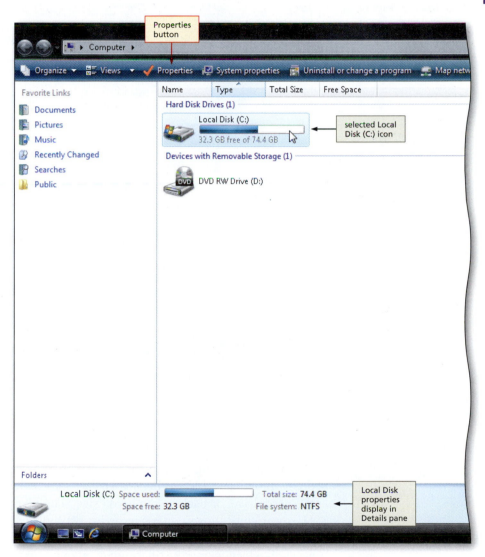

Figure 3–2

To Display the Local Disk (C:) Properties Dialog Box

The properties shown in the Details pane are just a few of the properties of the C: drive. In fact, the Details pane is used to highlight the common properties of a hard disk that most people want to know: the size of the drive, how much space is free, how much space is used, and how the drive is formatted. However, you can display much more detailed information about the hard disk. The Properties dialog box will allow you to view all of the properties of the C: drive. The following step displays the Properties dialog box for the Local Disk (C:) drive.

- Click the Properties button on the toolbar to display the Local Disk (C:) Properties dialog box (Figure 3–3).

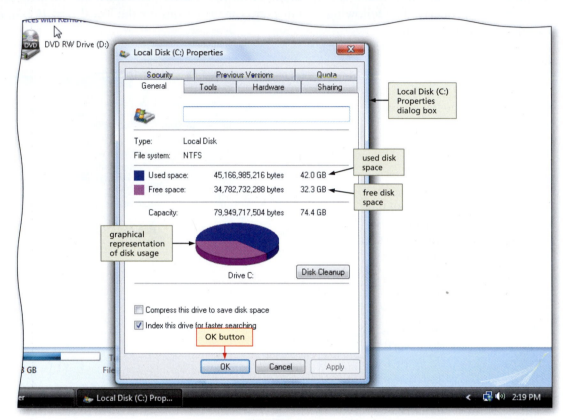

Figure 3–3

Other Ways

1. Right click the Local Disk (C:) icon, click Properties
2. Click drive icon, press ALT, on File menu click Properties
3. Select drive icon, press ALT+ENTER

The Local Disk (C:) Properties dialog box includes tabs that contain advanced features for working with the hard disk. The Tools sheet in the Local Disk (C:) Properties dialog box, accessible by clicking the Tools tab, allows you to check errors, defragment the hard drive, or back up the hard drive. The Hardware sheet, accessible by clicking the Hardware tab, allows you to view a list of all disk drives, troubleshoot disk drives that are not working properly, and display the properties for each disk drive. The Sharing sheet, accessible by clicking the Sharing tab, allows you to share the contents of a hard disk with other computer users. However, to protect a computer from unauthorized access, sharing the hard disk is not recommended. Other tabs may display in the Local Disk (C:) Properties dialog box on your computer. The Security sheet displays the security settings for the drive, such as user permissions. The Previous Versions sheet allows you to work with copies of your hard disk that are created when using backup utilities or from automatic saves. Finally, the Quota sheet can be used to see how much space is being used by various user accounts.

To Close the Local Disk (C:) Properties Dialog Box

Now that you have reviewed the Local Disk (C:) Properties dialog box, you should close it.

- Click the OK button to close the Local Disk (C:) Properties dialog box (Figure 3–4).

Figure 3–4

Other Ways

1. Click the Cancel button
2. Click the Close button
3. Press ESC

To Switch Folders Using the Address Bar

Found on all folder windows, the Address bar lets you know which folder you are viewing. A useful feature of the Address bar is its capability to allow you to switch to different folder windows by clicking on the arrow directly after the first item listed on the Address bar. Clicking the arrow displays a command menu, containing options for showing the desktop on a folder window, or switching to the Computer folder, the Recycle Bin, the Control Panel, the Public folder, your personal folder, and the Network folder. The following steps change the folder window from showing the Computer folder to showing the desktop, and then returning to the Computer folder.

- Click the arrow to the right of the computer icon on the Address bar to display a menu that contains folder switching commands (Figure 3–5).

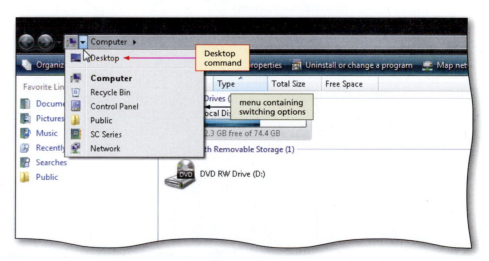

Figure 3–5

2

• Click the Desktop command to switch to viewing the contents of the desktop in a folder window (Figure 3–6).

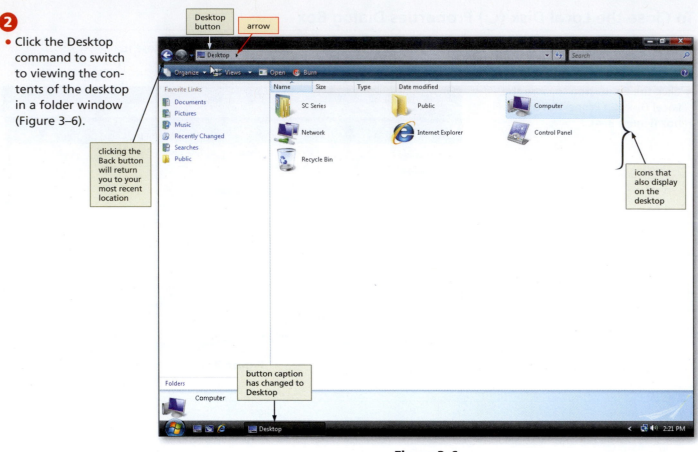

Figure 3–6

3

• Click the arrow to the right of the Desktop button on the Address bar to display a menu containing switching options (Figure 3–7).

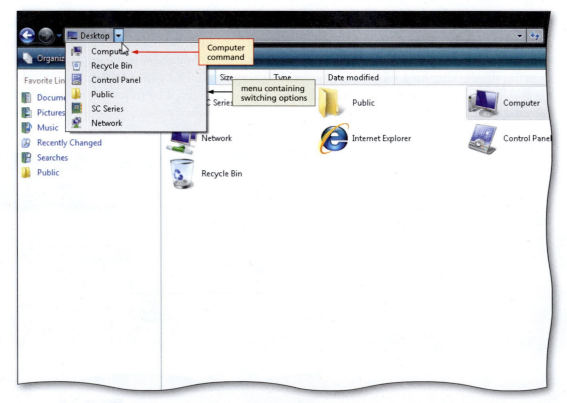

Figure 3–7

4

- Click the Computer command to switch to the Computer folder (Figure 3–8).

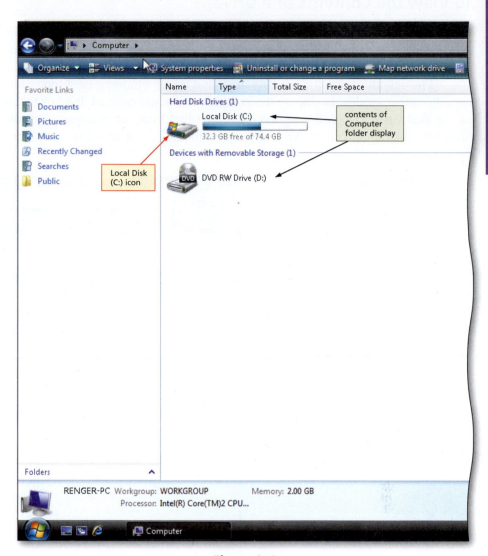

Figure 3–8

To View the Contents of a Drive

In addition to viewing the contents of the Computer folder, you can view the contents of drives and folders. In previous chapters, you have viewed windows for folders and windows for drives. In fact, the contents of any folder or drive on a computer can display in a folder window.

The default option for opening drive and folder windows, the Open each folder in the same window option, uses the active window to display the contents of a newly opened drive or folder. Because only one window displays on the desktop at a time, this option eliminates the clutter of multiple windows on the desktop. The following step illustrates the Open each folder in the same window option and displays the contents of the C: drive.

1

- Double-click the Local Disk (C:) icon in the Computer folder window to display the contents of the Local Disk (C:) drive (Figure 3–9).

Q&A

Why do I see different folders?

The contents of the Local Disk (C:) window you display on your computer can differ from the contents shown in Figure 3–9 because each computer has its own folders, application programs, and documents. The manner in which you interact with and control the programs and documents in Windows Vista is the same, regardless of the actual programs or documents.

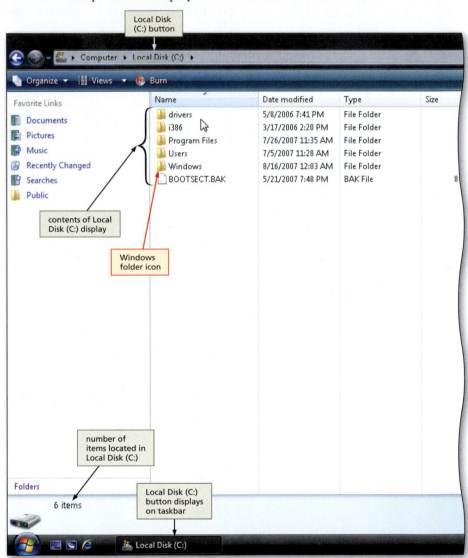

Figure 3–9

Other Ways

1. Right-click Local Disk (C:), click Open
2. Click Local Disk (C:), press ENTER

To Preview the Properties for a Folder

When you move your mouse over a folder icon, a preview of the folder properties will display in a tooltip format. A **tooltip** is a brief description that appears when you hold the mouse over an object on the screen. Not every item will cause a tooltip to display, but many times they will appear and provide useful information. The properties typically consist of the date and time created, the folder size, and the name of the folder. One folder in the Local Disk (C:) window, the **Windows folder**, contains programs and files necessary for the operation of the Windows Vista operating system. As such, you should exercise caution when working with the contents of the Windows folder because changing the contents of the folder may cause the programs to stop working correctly. The following step shows a preview of the properties for the Windows folder.

1

• Point to the Windows folder icon to display a preview of the properties for the Windows folder (Figure 3–10).

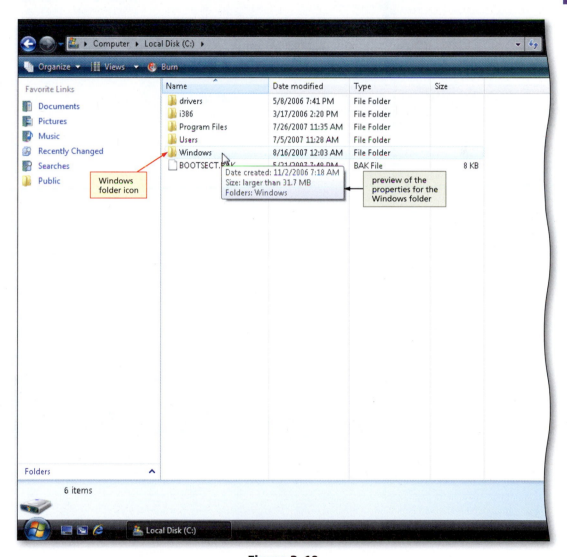

Figure 3–10

To Display Properties for the Windows Folder in the Details Pane

Just like with drives, properties of folders can be displayed in the Details pane. The following step displays the properties for the Windows folder in the Details pane of the Computer folder window.

1

• Click the Windows folder icon to display the properties in the Details pane (Figure 3–11).

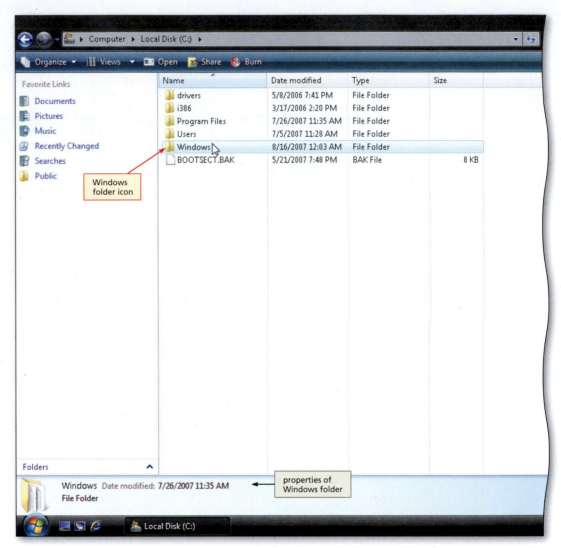

Figure 3–11

To Display All of the Properties for the Windows Folder

If you want to see all of the properties for the Windows folder, you will need to open up the Properties dialog box. The following steps display the Properties dialog box for the Windows folder.

1

- Right-click the Windows folder icon to display a shortcut menu (Figure 3–12). (The commands on your shortcut menu may differ.)

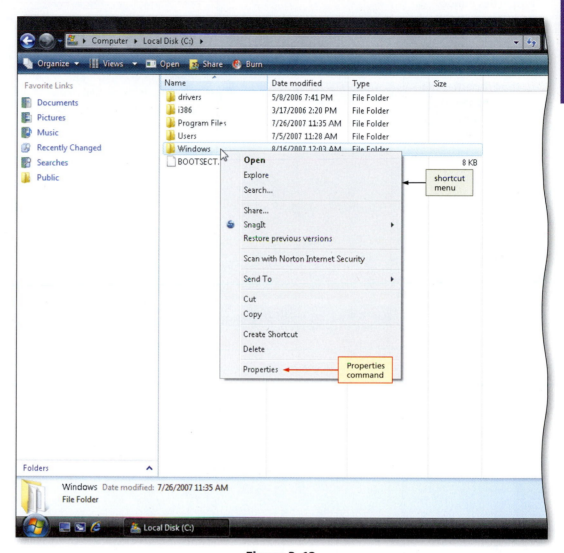

Figure 3–12

2

- Click the Properties command to display the Windows Properties dialog box (Figure 3–13).

 **Experiment**

- Click the various tabs in the Properties dialog box to see the different properties available for a folder.

Q&A Why might you want to look at the properties of a folder?

When you are working with folders, you might need to look at folders' properties in order to make changes, such as configuring a folder for sharing over a network or hiding folders from users who do not need access to them. You even can customize the appearance of a folder to be different than the default Windows folder view.

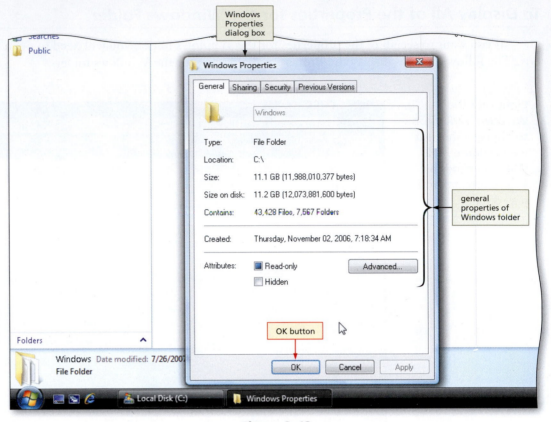

Figure 3–13

Q&A Why are the tabs of the Windows folder properties different than for the Local Disk (C:) properties?

Drives, folders and files have different properties, and therefore need different tabs. A folder's Properties dialog box typically shows the General, Sharing, Security, and Previous Versions tabs; however, depending upon your Windows Vista version and installed applications, the tabs may differ. The Properties dialog box always will have the General tab, although what it displays may differ.

To Close the Properties Dialog Box

Now that you have seen all of the properties, you should close the Properties dialog box.

1 Click the OK button to close the Windows Properties dialog box.

To View the Contents of a Folder

The following step opens the Windows folder so that you can view its contents.

1

• Double-click the Windows folder icon to display the contents of the Windows folder. If necessary, switch to Design view (Figure 3–14).

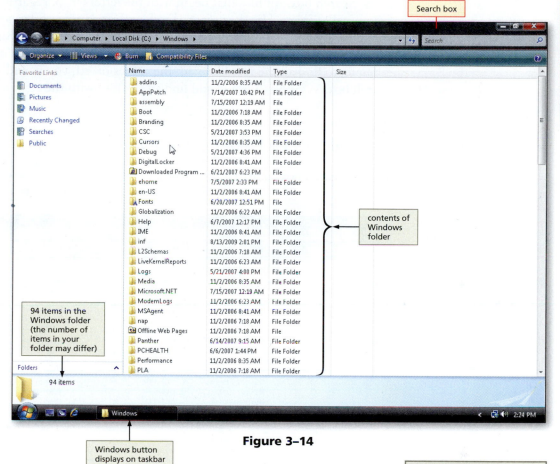

Figure 3–14

Searching for Files and Folders

The majority of objects displayed in the Windows folder, as shown in Figure 3–14, are folder icons. Folder icons always display in alphabetical order at the top of the list of objects in a folder window, before the icons for applications or files.

A folder such as the Windows folder contains many folders and files. When you want to find a particular file or folder but have no idea where it is located, you can use the Search box to find the file or folder quickly. Similar to the Search box on the Start menu, as soon as you start typing, the window will update to show search results that match what you typed. As Windows Vista is searching for files or folders that match what you entered, you will see a searching message displayed in the list area, an animated circle will attach to the pointer, and an animated progress bar will appear on the Address bar to provide live feedback as to how much of the search has been completed. When searching is complete, you will see a list of all items that matched your search criteria.

If you know only a portion of a file's name and can specify where the known portion of the name should appear, you can use an asterisk in the name to represent the unknown characters. For example, if you know a file starts with the letters MSP, you can type `msp*` in the Search box. All files that begin with the letters msp, regardless of what letters follow, will display. However, with Windows Vista's powerful search capabilities, you would get the same results if you did not include the asterisk. If you wanted all files with a particular extension, you can use the asterisk to stand in for the name of the files. For example, to find all the text files with the extension rtf, you would type `*.rtf` in the Search box. Windows Vista would find all the files with the rtf extension.

To Search for a File and Folder in a Folder Window

The following step uses the Search box to search the Windows folder for all the objects that contain 'aero'.

1

• Type `aero` in the Search box to search for all files and folders that match the search criteria (Figure 3–15).

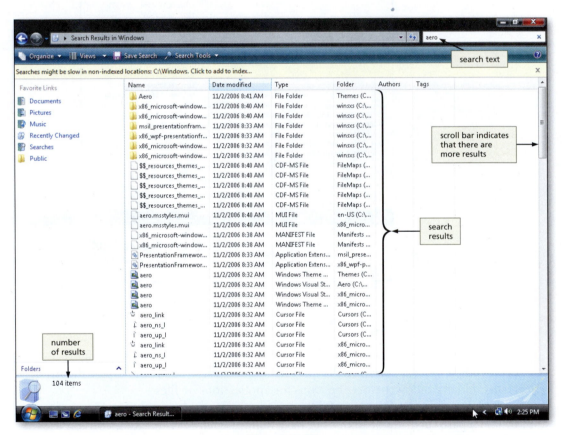

Figure 3–15

To Return to the Computer Folder Window

As you have learned, you can return to the Windows folder by clicking the Back button at the top of the folder window; however, you also can return to where you were prior to searching by clearing the Search Box. The following steps will return you to the Computer folder window.

- Double-click the search text, aero, to select it.

- Press the DELETE key to remove the search text from the Search box and redisplay all files and folders in the Windows folder (Figure 3–16).

- Click the Computer button on the Address bar to return to the Computer folder window.

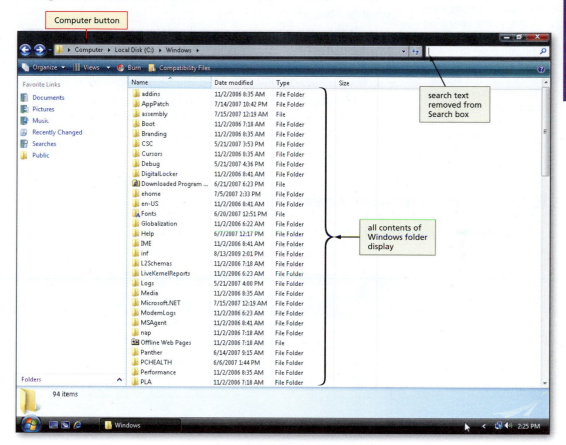

Figure 3–16

Using the Search Window to Find Files

Another way to search is to use the Search window. The Search window is accessible via the Start menu. It contains a Search box similar to the one found in the folder window, but also includes a Search toolbar. Using the Search toolbar, you can limit your search to specific types of files, including e-mail, documents, pictures, and music. The Search window also includes a link to Advanced Search options.

Using Advanced Search allows you to select a specific location to search, such as other computers on a network. Normal search only goes through the locations that have been indexed by Windows Vista. An **indexed location** is a location that has been added to the Search Index for Windows. The Search Index allows Search to find files and folders faster than without an index. Windows Vista builds this automatically as you create files and folders. Locations on Network computers are not automatically added to your computer's Search Index.

BTW

Hidden Files and Folders

Hidden files and folders usually are placed on your hard disk by software vendors such as Microsoft and often are critical to the operation of the software. Rarely will you need to designate a file as hidden. You should not delete a hidden file as doing so may interrupt how or whether an application program works. By default, hidden files and folders are not displayed in a file listing.

Advanced Search also allows you to search for files and folders by location, date, size, name, tags, and authors. You can search for a file based on when you last worked with the file, or search for files containing specific text. You also can choose to search non-indexed, hidden, and system files as well. Additionally, if you have edited the properties of a file or folder and added tags, you will then be able to find them using the Tags text box in Advanced Search.

If the search results were not satisfactory, you can refine the search by changing the file name or keywords, looking in more locations, or changing whether hidden and system files are included in the search. If no files were found in the search, a message (No items match your search) will appear in the Search Results window. In this case, you may want to double-check the information you entered or select different parameters to continue the search. For now, you will work with a basic search using the Search window, but in later chapters, you will experiment with all the features of an advanced search.

To Search for Files Using Advanced Search

The following steps search for all files with the name, forest, using Advanced Search.

1

- Display the Start menu.

- Click the Search command to display the Search Results window (Figure 3–17).

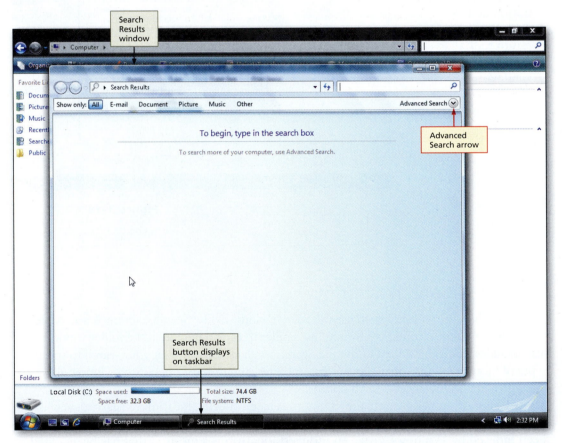

Figure 3–17

2

- Click the Advanced Search arrow to display the Advanced Search pane (Figure 3–18).

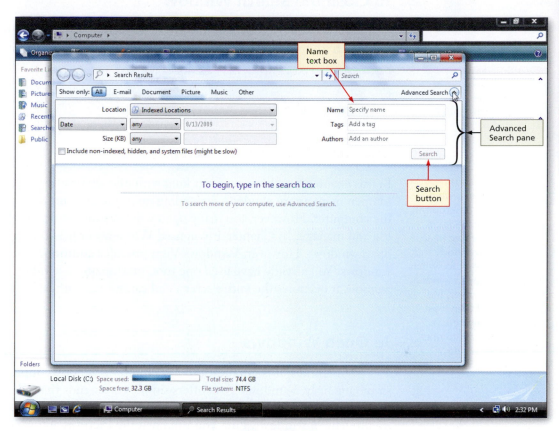

Figure 3–18

3

- Type forest in the Name text box.

- Click the Search button to search for all files and folders that match the search criteria, forest (Figure 3–19).

 Experiment

- Click the different results to view them. Consider how they match the search criteria.

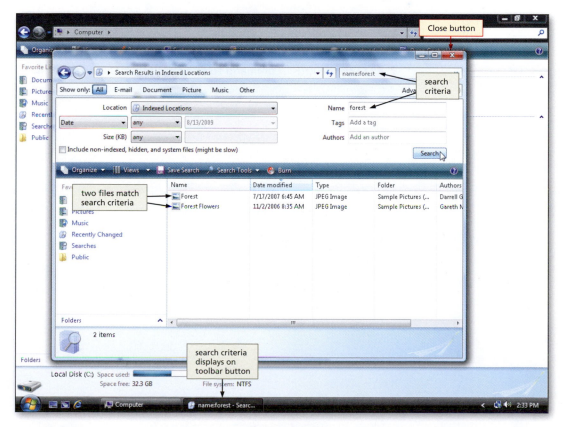

Figure 3–19

To Close the Search Window

You will be conducting more advanced searches in a later chapter; however, now that you have finished searching, you should close the Search window.

1 Click the Close button to close the Search Results window.

Managing Open Windows

In this chapter, you have been working with one window open. Windows Vista allows you to open many more windows depending upon the amount of RAM you have installed on the computer. However, too many open windows on the desktop can become difficult to use and manage. In Chapter 1, you used Windows Flip 3-D to navigate through multiple open windows. However, Windows Vista provides additional tools for managing open windows. You already have used one tool, maximizing a window. When you maximize a window, it occupies the entire screen and cannot be confused with other open windows.

To Open Windows

Sometimes, it is important to have multiple windows appear on the desktop simultaneously. Windows Vista offers simple commands that allow you to arrange multiple windows in specific ways. The following sections describe the ways that you can manage mulitple open windows. First you will open the Pictures and Music folder windows.

1 Display the Start menu.

2 Click the Pictures command to open the Pictures folder window.

3 Display the Start menu.

4 Click the Music command to open the Music folder window.

To Cascade Open Windows

One way to organize windows on the desktop is to display them in a cascade format, where they overlap one another in an organized manner. Windows Vista only cascades open windows. Windows that are minimized or closed will not be cascaded on the desktop. When you cascade open windows, the windows are resized to be the same size to produce the layered cascading effect. The following steps cascade the open windows on the desktop.

1

• Right-click an open area on the taskbar to display a shortcut menu (Figure 3–20).

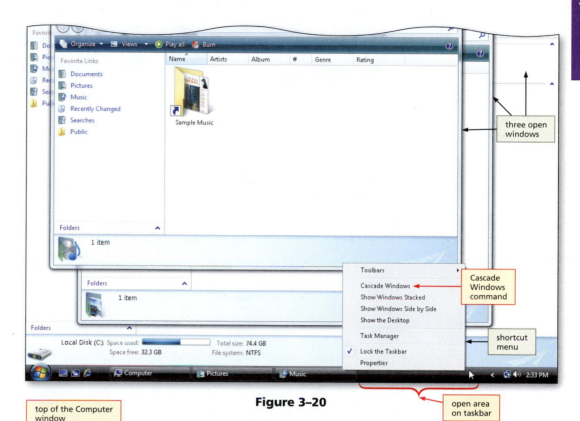

Figure 3–20

2

• Click the Cascade Windows command on the shortcut menu to cascade the open windows (Figure 3–21).

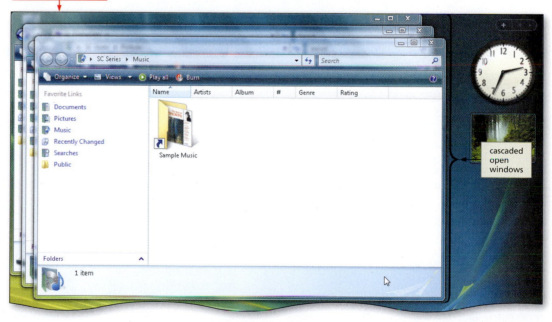

Figure 3–21

Other Ways
1. Right-click an open area on the taskbar, press D

To Make a Window the Active Window

When windows are cascaded, as shown in Figure 3–21 on the previous page, they are arranged so that you can see them easily. In order to work in one of the windows, you first must make it the active window. When you make the Computer folder window the active window, it will remain the same size and remain in the same relative position as placed by the Cascade Windows command. The following step makes the Computer folder window the active window.

1

- Click the top of the Computer folder window to make it the active window (Figure 3–22).

Q&A

What happens if I click the wrong window?

Click the remaining windows until the Computer folder window displays in the foreground.

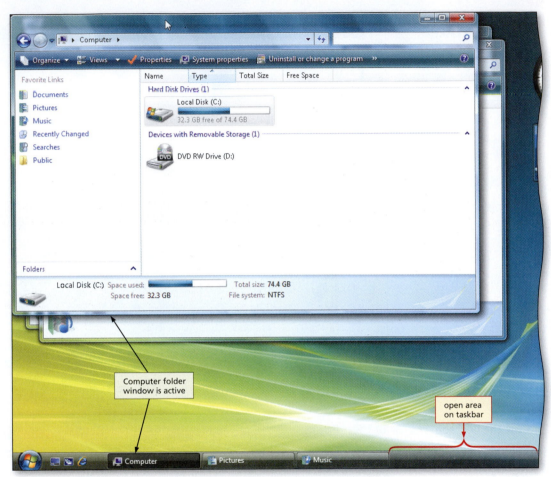

Figure 3–22

Other Ways

1. Click Computer button in taskbar button area
2. Press ALT+TAB until Computer folder window is selected, release ALT key
3. Click anywhere in window to make it active

To Undo Cascading

Now that you have seen the effect of the Cascade Windows command, you will undo the cascade operation and return the windows to the size and location they were before cascading. Depending upon the task at hand, cascading the windows may not allow you to view the contents of the windows the way you would like. The following steps undo the previous cascading of the windows.

1

• Right-click an open area on the taskbar to display the shortcut menu (Figure 3–23).

Figure 3–23

2

• Click the Undo Cascade command to return the windows to their original sizes and locations (Figure 3–24).

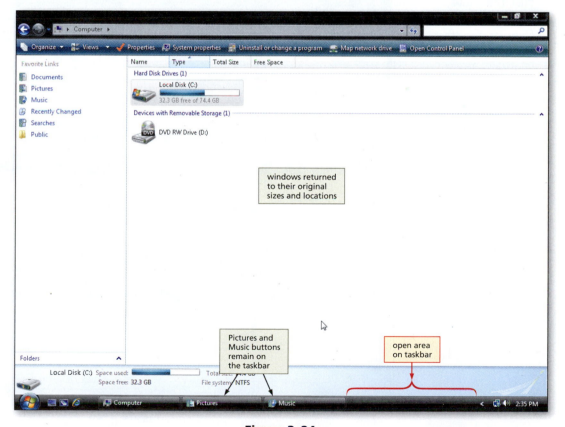

Figure 3–24

Other Ways
1. Right-click an open area on taskbar, press U
2. Press CTRL+Z

To Stack Open Windows

While cascading arranges the windows on the desktop so that each of the each of the window's title bars is visible, it is impossible to see the contents of each window. Windows Vista also can stack the open windows, which allows you to see partial contents of each window. The windows will be resized to the full width of the screen and arranged on top of each other vertically, like a stack of books. Each window will be the same size, and you will be able to see a portion of each window. The following steps stack the open windows.

- Right-click an open area on the taskbar to display the shortcut menu (Figure 3-25).

Figure 3–25

- Click the Show Windows Stacked command to stack the open windows (Figure 3–26).

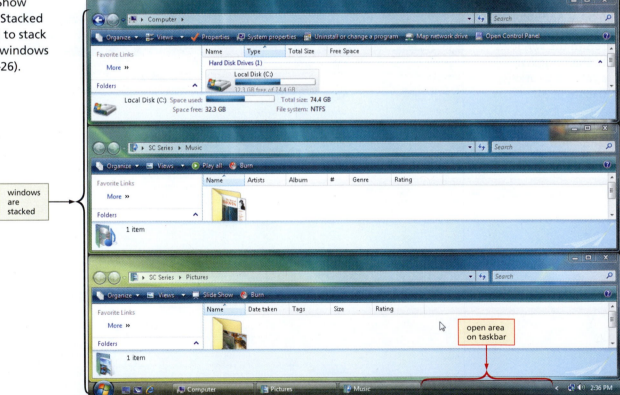

Figure 3–26

Other Ways

1. Right-click an open area on taskbar, press T until Show Windows Stacked is selected, press ENTER

To Undo Show Windows Stacked

While the stacked windows are arranged so that you can view all of them, it is likely that the reduced size of an individual window makes working in the window difficult. You will undo the stacking operation to return the windows to the size and position they occupied before stacking. If you want to work in a particular window, you should maximize the window. The following steps return the windows to their original sizes and position.

1
- Right-click an open area on the taskbar to display the shortcut menu (Figure 3–27).

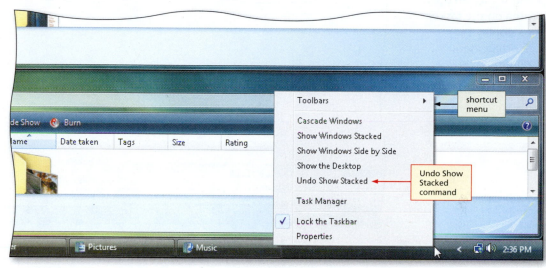

Figure 3–27

2
- Click the Undo Show Stacked command to return the windows to their original sizes and locations (Figure 3–28).

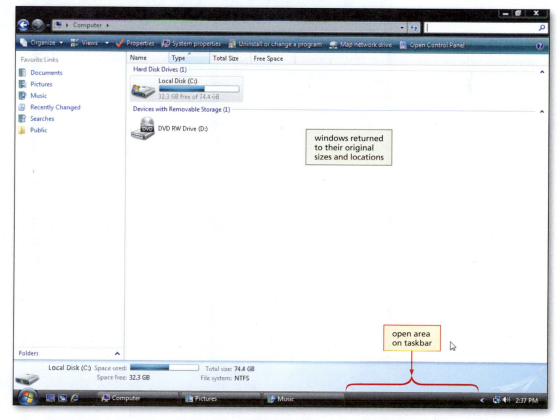

Figure 3–28

Other Ways

1. Right-click an open area on taskbar, press U
2. Press CTRL+Z

To Show Windows Side by Side

While stacking arranges the windows vertically above each other on the desktop, it also is possible to arrange them horizontally from left to right, or side by side. The Show Windows Side by Side command allows you to see partial contents of each window horizontally. The following steps show the open windows side by side.

1

• Right-click an open area on the taskbar to display the shortcut menu (Figure 3-29).

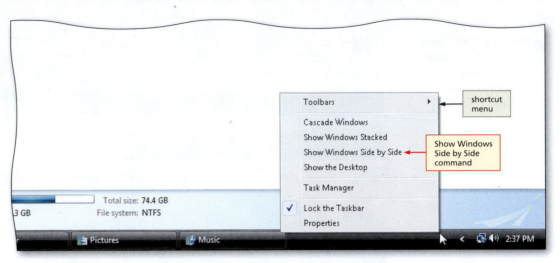

Figure 3-29

2

• Click the Show Windows Side by Side command to display the open windows side by side (Figure 3-30).

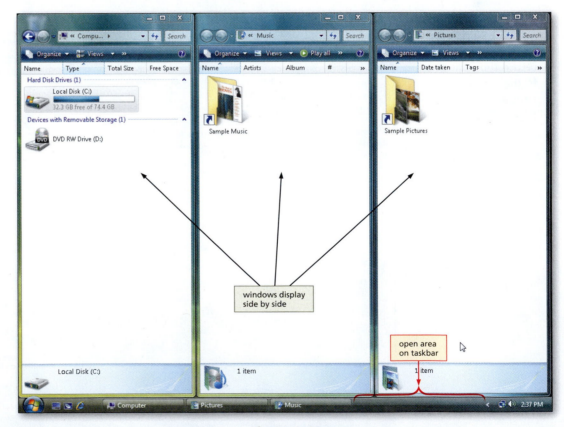

Figure 3-30

Other Ways

1. Right-click an open area on taskbar, press I

To Undo Show Windows Side by Side

The following steps undo the side by side operation and return the windows to the arrangement shown in Figure 3–28 on page WIN 173.

- Right-click an open area on the taskbar to display the shortcut menu (Figure 3–31).

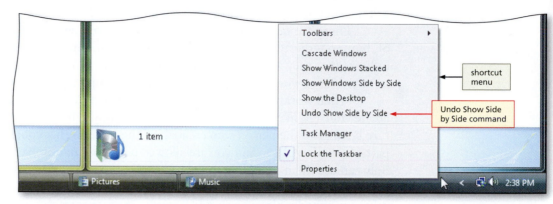

Figure 3–31

- Click the Undo Show Side by Side command to return the windows to their original sizes and locations (Figure 3–32).

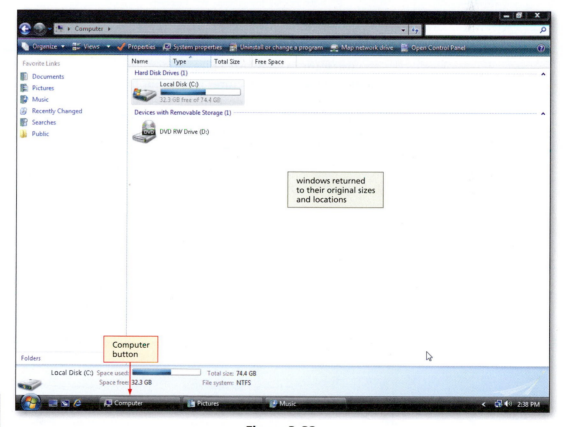

Figure 3–32

Other Ways

1. Right-click an open area on taskbar, press U
2. Press CTRL+Z

The Pictures Folder

You can organize your pictures and share them with others using the Pictures folder. The Pictures folder was created to encourage users to organize their pictures in one location. By putting all your pictures in the Pictures folder, you always know where to find your pictures. When you save pictures from a digital camera, scanner, or hard drive, by default,

Windows Vista stores the pictures in the Pictures folder. Applications that you install to work with pictures also can be saved to this folder.

Using this folder will allow you to view the pictures as a slide show, share pictures with others, e-mail pictures to friends, print pictures, publish pictures to the Internet, and order prints of a picture from the Internet. You will work with a few of the options now, and the rest will be covered in a later chapter where multimedia files will be covered in greater depth.

There are many different formats for picture files. Some pictures have an extension of .bmp to indicate a bitmap file. Other pictures might have the extension .gif extension to indicate that they are of the Graphics Interchange Format. There are too many file types to mention; however, some common ones are .bmp, .jpg, .gif, and .tif.

When working with pictures, you should be aware that most images that you did not create yourself, like other multimedia files, are copyrighted. A **copyright** means that a picture belongs to the person who created it. The pictures that come with Windows Vista are part of Windows Vista and you are allowed to use them; however, they are not yours. You only can use them according to the rights given to you by Microsoft. Pictures that you take using your digital camera are yours, because you created them. Before using pictures and other multimedia files, you should be aware of any copyrights associated with them, and you should know whether you are allowed to use them for your intended purpose.

To Search for Pictures

You want to copy three files, Monet, Psychedelic, and Pine_Lumber, from the Windows folder to the Pictures folder; but first, you have to find these files. Because the three files all have the .jpg extension, you can search for them using an asterisk (*) in place of the file name, as discussed earlier in this chapter. The following steps open the Windows folder window and display the icons for the files you wish to copy.

1 Click the Computer button on the taskbar to switch to the Computer folder window.

2 Double-click the Local Disk (C:) icon in the Computer folder window.

3 Double-click the Windows folder icon in the Local Disk (C:) window.

4 Type *.jpg in the Search box and then press the ENTER key to search for all files with a jpg file extension.

5 Scroll down the right pane of the Windows folder window until the icons for the Monet, Pine_Lumber, and Psychedelic files are visible in the right pane (Figure 3–33). If one or more of these files are not available, select any of the other picture files.

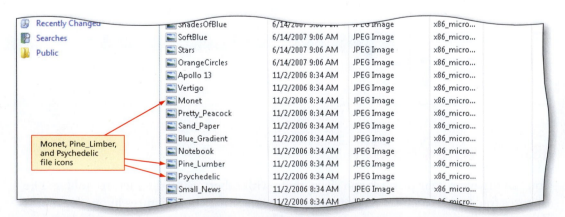

Figure 3–33

To Copy Files to the Pictures Folder

In Chapter 2, you learned how to move and copy document files on the desktop to a folder, how to copy a folder onto a USB drive, and how to delete files. Another method you can use to copy a file or folder is the **copy and paste method**. When you **copy** a file, you place a copy of the file in a temporary storage area of the computer called the **Clipboard**. When you **paste** the file, Windows Vista copies it from the Clipboard to the location you specify. You now have two copies of the same file.

Because the search results include the pictures you were looking for, you now can select the files and then copy them to the Pictures folder. Once the three files have been copied into the Pictures folder, the files will be stored in both the Pictures folder and Windows folder on drive C. Copying and moving files are common tasks when working with Windows Vista. If you want to move a file instead of copying a file, you would use the Cut command on the shortcut menu to move the file to the Clipboard, and the Paste command to copy the file from the Clipboard to the new location. When the move is complete, the files are moved into the new folder and no longer are stored in the original folder.

The following steps copy the Monet, Pine_Lumber, and Psychedelic files from the Windows folder to the Pictures folder.

1

- Hold down the CTRL key and then click the Monet, Pine_Lumber, and Psychedelic icons.

- Release the CTRL key.

- Right-click any highlighted icon to display a shortcut menu (Figure 3–34).

Q&A

Are copying and moving the same?

No! When you copy a file, it is located in both the place to which it was copied and in the place from which it was copied. When you move a file, it is located only in the location to which it was moved.

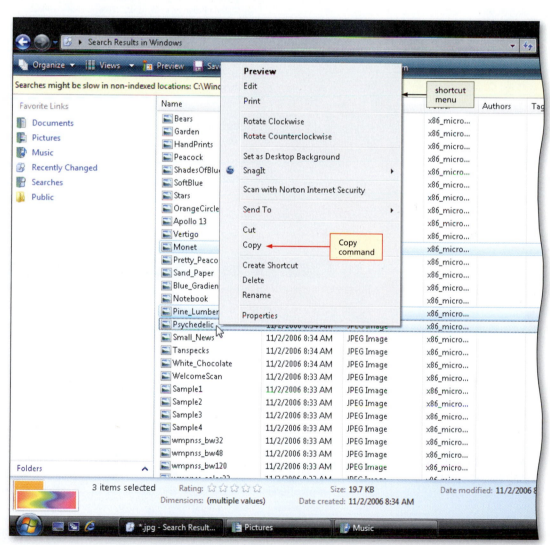

Figure 3–34

2
- Click the Copy command on the shortcut menu to copy the files to the Clipboard (Figure 3–35).

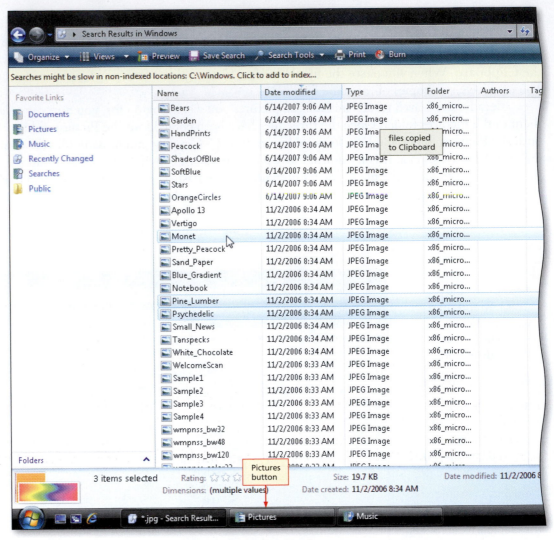

Figure 3–35

3
- Click the Pictures button on the task-bar to switch to the Pictures folder window.
- Right-click an open area of the Pictures window to display a shortcut menu (Figure 3–36).

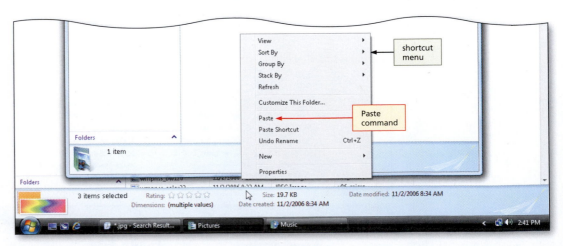

Figure 3–36

4

- Click the Paste command on the shortcut menu to paste the files in the Pictures folder (Figure 3–37).

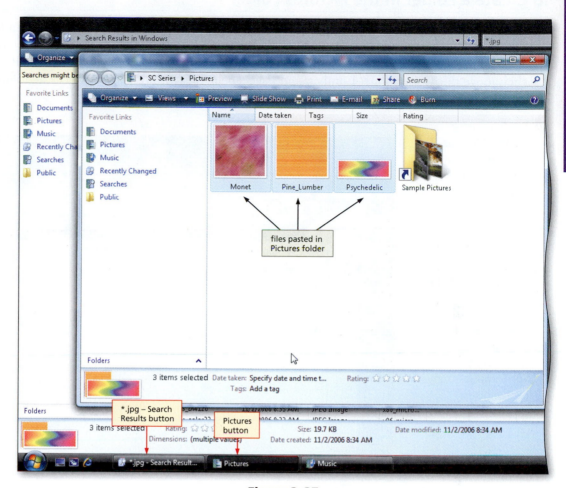

Figure 3–37

To Close the Search Results Window

You no longer need the Search Results window open, so you can close it. Whenever you are not using a window, it is a good idea to close it so as not to clutter your desktop. The following steps close the Search Results window.

1 Click the *.jpg - Search Results button on the taskbar to display the Search Results window.

2 Close the Search Results window.

Other Ways

1. Select file icons, press ALT, on Edit menu click Copy, display window where you want to store file, press ALT, on Edit menu click Paste

2. Select file icons, press ALT, on Edit menu click Copy To Folder, click arrow next to your user name, click Pictures, click Copy button

3. Select file icons, press CTRL+C, display the window where you want to store file, press CTRL+V

To Create a Folder in the Pictures Folder

When you have several related files stored in a folder with with a number of unrelated files, you may wish to create a folder to contain the related files so that you can find and reference them easily. To reduce clutter and improve the organization of files in the Pictures folder, you will create a new folder in the Pictures folder window and then move the Monet, Pine_Lumber, and Psychedelic files into the new folder. The following steps create the Backgrounds folder in the Pictures folder.

- Click the Pictures button on the task-bar to make the Pictures folder window the active window.

- Right-click any open part of the list area of the Pictures folder window to display a shortcut menu (Figure 3–38). (The commands on the shortcut menu on your computer may differ slightly.)

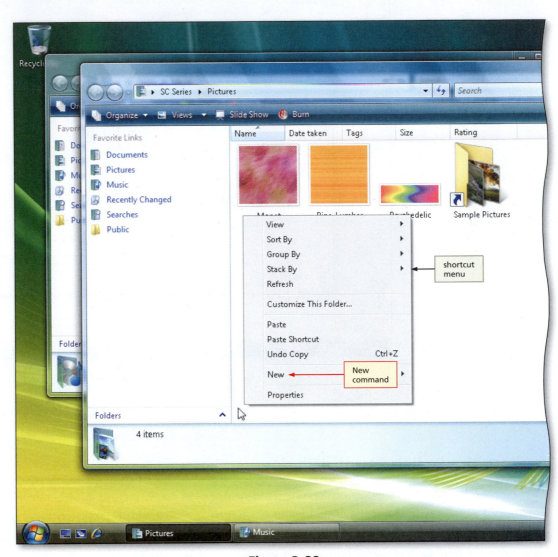

Figure 3–38

2

• Point to the New command on the shortcut menu to display the New submenu (Figure 3–39). (The commands on the New submenu on your computer may differ slightly.)

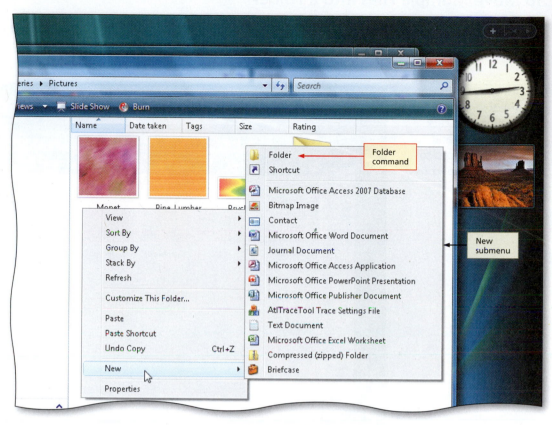

Figure 3–39

3

• Click the Folder command on the New submenu to create a new folder in the Pictures folder.

• Type Backgrounds in the icon title text box, and then press the ENTER key to assign the name to the new folder (Figure 3–40).

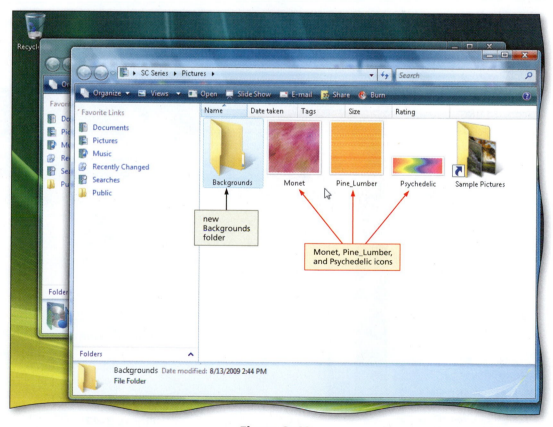

Other Ways

1. Press ALT, click File menu, point to New, click Folder, type file name, press ENTER

2. Press ALT+F, press W twice, press RIGHT ARROW, press F, type file name, press ENTER

Figure 3–40

To Move Multiple Files into a Folder

After you create the Backgrounds folder in the Pictures folder, the next step is to move the three picture files into the folder. The following steps move the Monet, Psychedelic, and Pine_Lumber files into the Backgrounds folder.

• Click the Monet icon, hold down the CTRL key, and then click Pine_Lumber and Psychedelic icons to select all three icons (Figure 3–41).

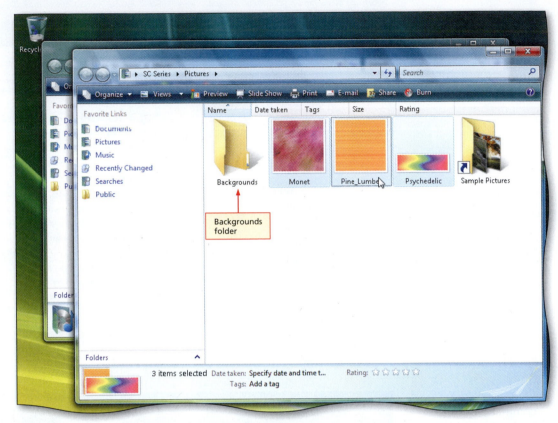

Figure 3–41

• Drag the selected icons to the Backgrounds folder, and then release the mouse button to move the files to the Backgrounds folder (Figure 3–42).

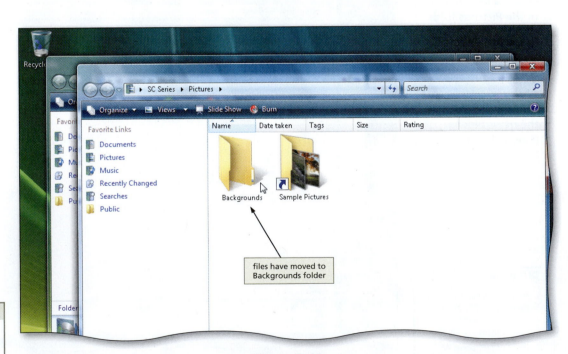

Figure 3–42

Other Ways

1. Drag icons individually to folder icon

2. Right-click icon, click Cut, right-click folder icon, click Paste

To Refresh the Image on a Folder

After moving the three files into the Backgrounds folder, it still appears as an empty open folder icon. To replace the empty folder icon with a Live Preview of the three files stored in the Backgrounds folder (Monet, Pine_ Lumber, Psychedelic), the Pictures folder window must be refreshed. The following steps refresh the Pictures folder window to display the Live Preview for the Backgrounds folder.

1

- Right-click any open part of the list area to display a shortcut menu (Figure 3–43).

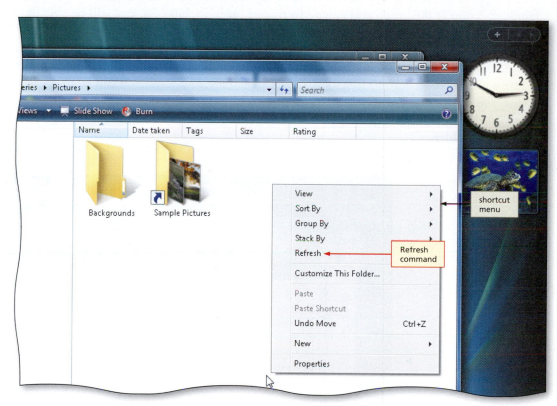

Figure 3–43

2

- Click the Refresh command to refresh the list area (Figure 3–44).

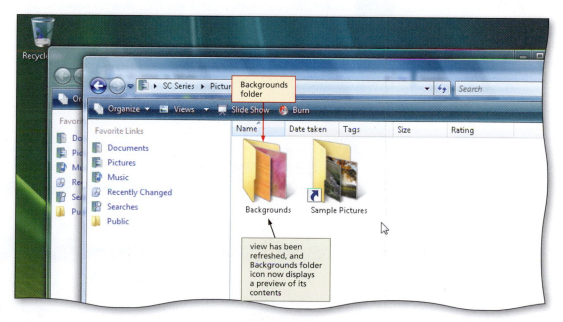

Figure 3–44

Other Ways

1. Press ALT, click View, click **Refresh**

To View and Change the Properties of a Picture

As mentioned earlier in the chapter, in Windows Vista, all objects have properties. You already have explored the properties of a drive, now you will review the properties of a picture. Picture properties include the Date taken, Tags, Rating, Dimensions, and Size. Date taken refers to the date the person created the picture. Tags are keywords you associate with a Picture file to aid in its classification. For example you could tag a family photo with the names of the people in the photo. When you create a tag, it should be meaningful. For example, if you have pictures from a family vacation at the beach and you add a title of vacation; later on, you will be able to find the file using the tag, 'vacation', in a search. Be aware that you only can search for tags that you already have created. If your family vacation photo was saved as "photo1.jpg" and tagged with the tag "vacation", you will not find it by searching for "beach" as it is not part of the name or tag. Rating refers to the ranking, in stars, that you assign to a picture. You can rate a picture from zero to five stars. Date taken, Tags, and Rating all can be changed using the Details pane. Because you do not know when the Background pictures were created, you only will change the Tags and Rating properties. The following steps display and change the Tags and Rating properties of the Monet image in the Backgrounds folder.

- Display the contents of the Backgrounds folder.

- Click the Monet icon to select it (Figure 3–45).

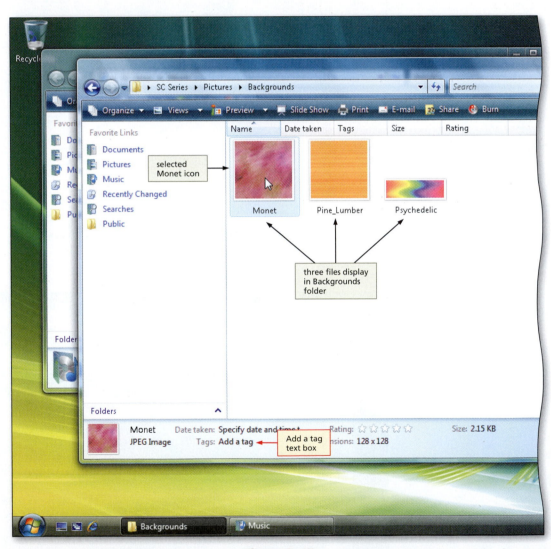

Figure 3–45

2

• Click the Add a tag text box in the Details pane to activate it (Figure 3–46).

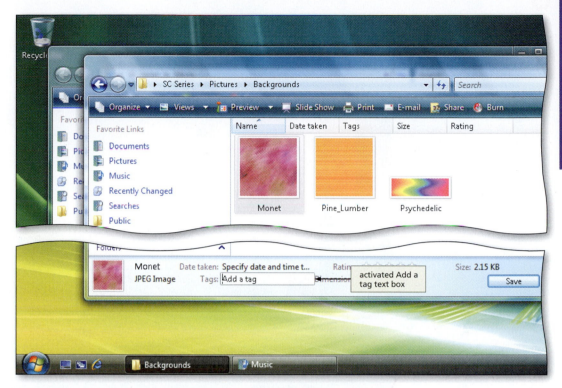

Figure 3–46

3

• Type A Work of Art in the text box to create a tag for the picture (Figure 3–47).

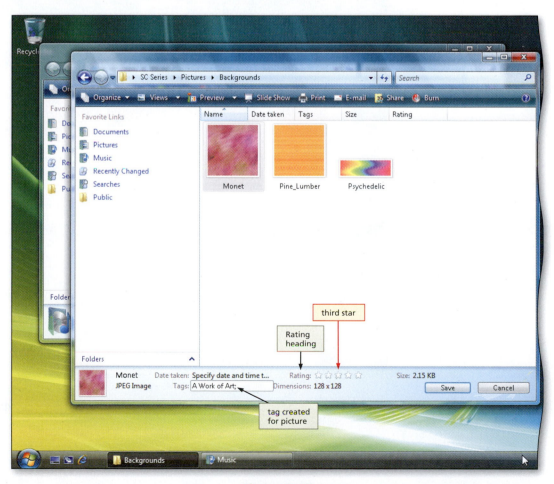

Figure 3–47

4

• Click the third star next to the Rating heading in the Details pane to assign a 3-star rating to the picture (Figure 3–48).

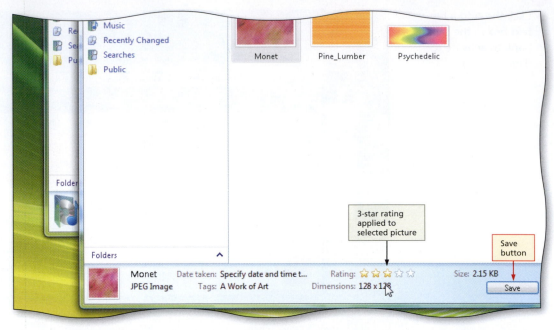

Figure 3–48

5

• Click the Save button in the Details pane to save the changes to the Tags and Rating (Figure 3–49).

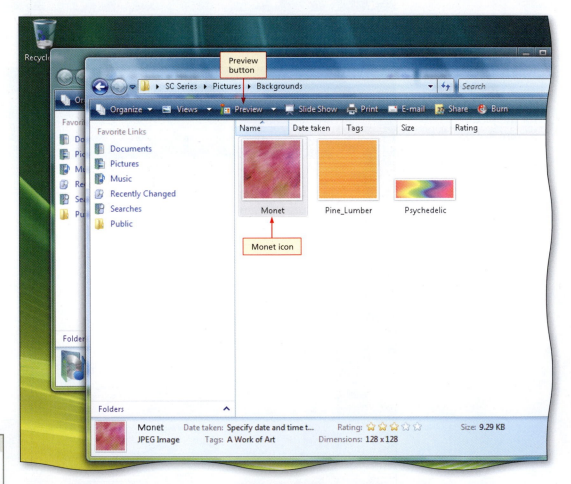

Figure 3–49

Other Ways

1. Right-click icon, click Properties, click Details tab, enter text next to Tags, click third star next to Rating, click OK

To Open a Picture in the Windows Photo Gallery

You can view the images in a folder in the Windows Photo Gallery or as a slide show. The **Windows Photo Gallery** is a program that allows you to view each image separately, and work with the pictures in your Pictures folder. It can be used to view pictures individually or as part of a slide show. A later chapter will cover the Windows Photo Gallery in more detail. For now, you will look at the basics of Windows Photo Gallery.

The buttons on the toolbar at the bottom of the Windows Photo Gallery allow you to move through the images and rotate an image clockwise or counterclockwise. The following steps display the Monet image in the Backgrounds folder in the Windows Photo Gallery.

- If necessary, select the Monet icon.

- Click the Preview button on the toolbar to open the Monet picture in the Windows Photo Gallery (Figure 3–50).

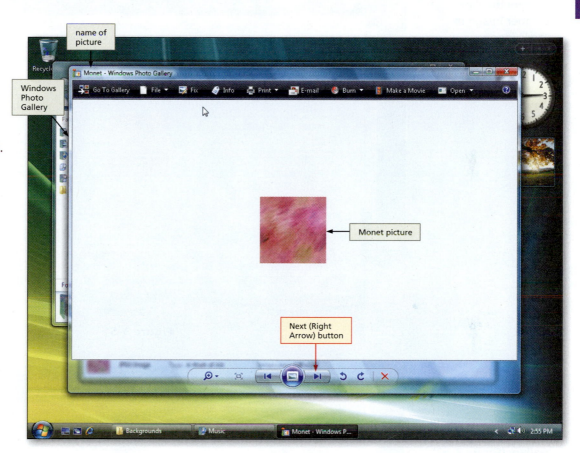

Figure 3–50

Other Ways

1. Right-click icon, click Preview

To Navigate through Your Pictures

To navigate through your pictures, you use the buttons at the bottom of the Windows Photo Gallery window. The Next (Right Arrow) button allows you to move forward to the next photo, and the Previous (Left Arrow) button allows you to move backward to the photo you already have seen. The following steps navigate through the pictures in the Backgrounds folder using the Windows Photo Gallery.

- Click the Next (Right Arrow) button to view the Pine_Lumber image in the Windows Photo Gallery (Figure 3–51).

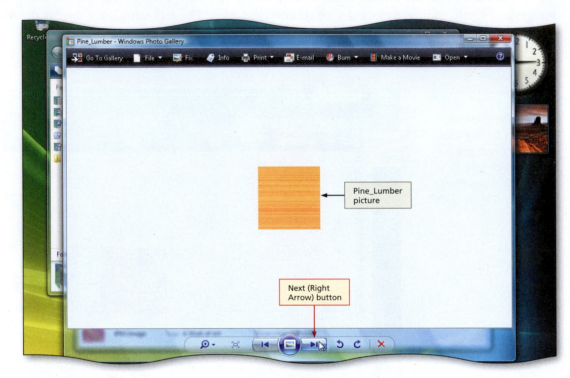

Figure 3–51

- Click the Next (Right Arrow) button to view the Psychedelic image in the Windows Photo Gallery (Figure 3–52).

Figure 3–52

To Close the Windows Photo Gallery

Now that you have seen all of the pictures, the next step is to close the Windows Photo Gallery.

1 Click the Close button to close the Windows Photo Gallery.

To View Your Pictures as a Slide Show

The **Slide Show** displays each image in the folder in a presentation format on your computer screen. Each picture will be shown one at a time while everything else on the desktop is hidden from sight. Slide Show allows you to view pictures by automatically moving through the pictures or by using the navigation buttons to view the next or previous picture. You also can rotate a picture clockwise or counterclockwise, pause the slide show, and exit the slide show. The following step opens the images in the Backgrounds folder as a slide show.

1

• Click the Slide Show button on the Pictures folder window toolbar to view the selected files as a slide show (Figure 3–53).

• Watch the show for a few seconds to see the pictures change.

Q&A Can I change the Slide Show speed?

Yes, you can use the Slide Show options button to select speeds of slow, medium and fast. The Slide Show options button is next to the Exit button.

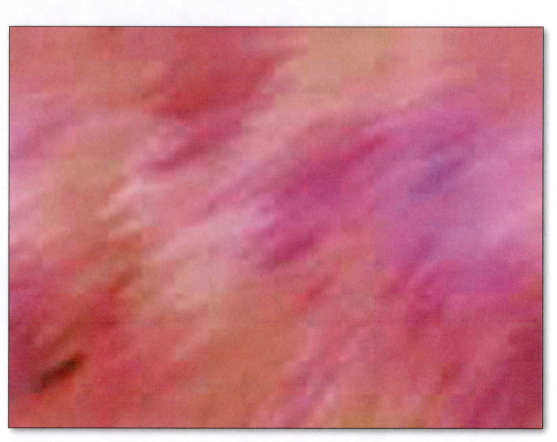

Figure 3–53

To End a Slide Show

When you are done viewing the slide show, the next step is to end it. The following steps exit the slide show.

1
- Move the mouse and then click the Exit button on the toolbar (Figure 3-54).

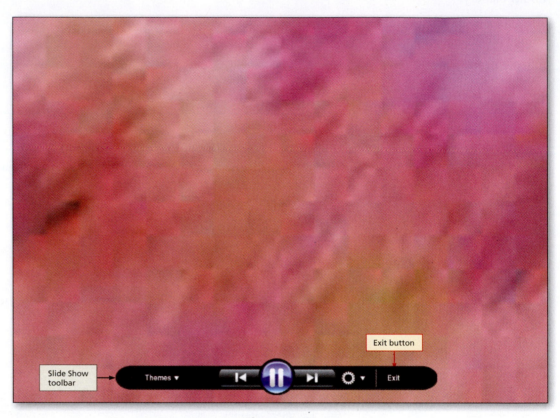

Figure 3–54

2
- Click the Exit button on the Slide Show toolbar to exit the slide show (Figure 3–55).

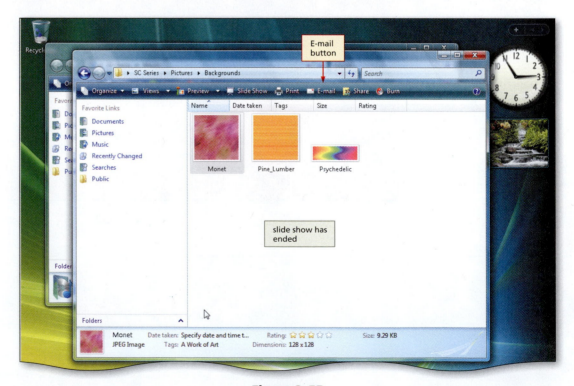

Figure 3–55

To E-Mail a Picture

Electronic mail (**e-mail**) is an important method of exchanging messages and files between business associates and friends. Windows Vista provides options to send files using the e-mail program that you have installed on your computer. Windows Vista includes the Windows Mail e-mail program, which can be configured to work with most e-mail accounts, even Web-based e-mail such as Windows Live Hotmail and Gmail.

E-mailing large images can be time-consuming and often results in the file not reaching its destination. As a result, Windows Vista makes it easy to reduce the size of an image at the time you send it. If you do not have Windows Mail configured, read but do not complete the following steps. The following steps e-mail an image to a friend.

- If necessary, click the Monet icon to select it.

- Click E-mail button on the toolbar to display the Attach Files dialog box (Figure 3–56).

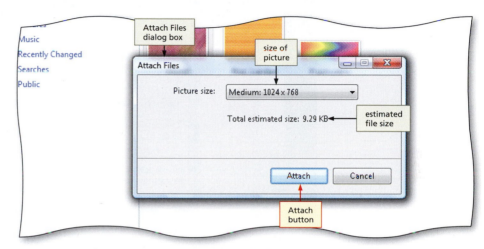

Figure 3–56

2

- Click the Attach button to compose a new e-mail message and attach the picture to the e-mail message (Figure 3–57).

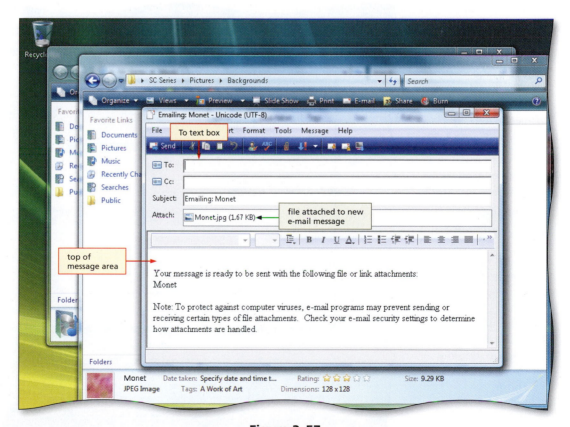

Figure 3–57

3

- Type rayenger@
  yahoo.com in the To
  text box.

- Click at the top of
  the message area.

- Type I thought
  you might like
  this picture for
  your collection.
  in the message area
  (Figure 3–58).

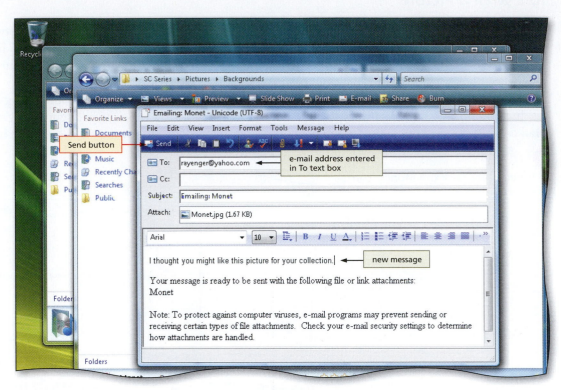

Figure 3–58

 4

- Click the Send
  button to display
  the Windows Mail
  dialog box while
  the message is send-
  ing, and to close the
  Emailing Monet -
  Unicode (UTF-8)
  window (Figure 3–59).

Q&A

Why does my
Windows Mail show
a different account?

Your computer has
been configured
to use an e-mail
account for that
machine. For exam-
ple, at home you
may set up Windows
Mail to use a Hotmail
account while at
work you would use
a company e-mail
account.

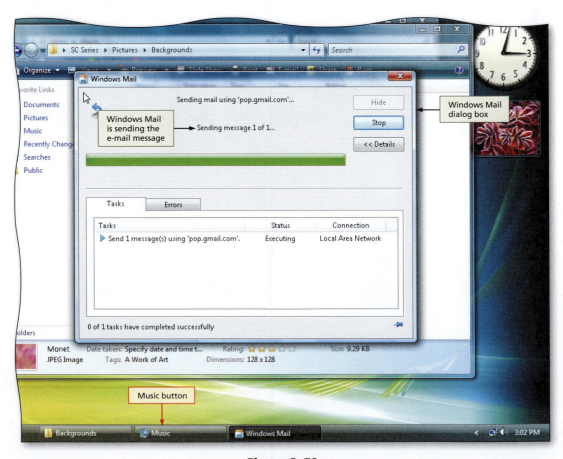

Figure 3–59

The Music Folder

The **Music** folder can be used to store your music files. If you have any digital music players installed, they will use this location by default when you download, play, rip, and burn music. When you **rip** a file, you extract the audio data from a CD and transfer it to your hard disk. After the file has been ripped, it will be in a format that is compatible with your computer as opposed to a CD player. When you **burn** music, you take files that are compatible with your computer and copy them onto a CD in the format that can be played in CD players. Some CD players can play music files in the same format as your computer; therefore, the burn process does not always result in a file format change.

You can arrange your music files into organized collections. The Sample Music folder, installed by Windows Vista, contains samples of music for you to experiment with so that you can make sure that your sound card and speakers are working properly. If you use a music program such as iTunes or Windows Media Player, you will be able to add additional music files to your collection. Music files come in a variety of formats, similar to how picture files have different formats. Common music file formats include are .wav, .wma, .mp3, .mp4, and .mid. For example, audio podcasts often are saved in the .mp3 format. You can use the Music folder window to view, organize, and play your music.

Just like other media files, you should be aware of copyrights. If you download music from the Internet, make sure that you have the right copyright to do so. It is illegal to download and share music that you do not have the rights to download and share.

To Switch to the Music Folder

You want to view the contents of the Music folder in order to understand how music is stored and arranged. To see this, you will switch to the Music window. The following step makes the Music folder the active window.

1 Click the Music button on the taskbar to display the Music folder window (Figure 3–60).

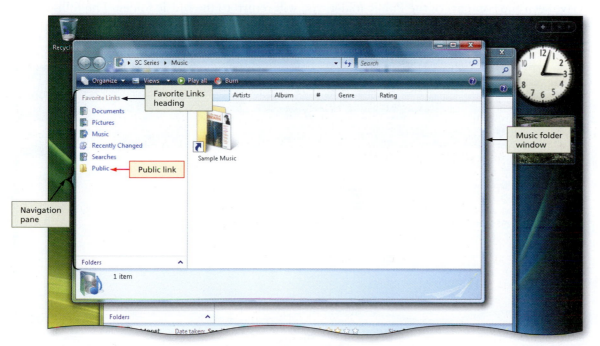

Figure 3–60

To Open the Public Folder

To see the sample music files, you will need to open the Sample Music folder. The Sample Music folder is located in the Public Music folder, although a shortcut to the Sample Music folder appears in the Music folder window. When you view the contents of the Sample Music folder, notice that the Address bar reflects the fact that you are in the Public folder. The **Public folder** contains a collection of folders that are shared amongst all of the user accounts. Anything that you want to share with other users should be placed in one of the Public folders. The following step opens the Public folder.

- Click the Public link under the Favorite Links heading of the Navigation pane to display the Public folder (Figure 3–61).

Q&A

What are Favorite Links?

The Favorite Links area contains a list of locations that you commonly use. By using Favorite Links, you quickly can go to those locations without having to search for or navigate to them. Windows Vista automatically builds this list during installation.

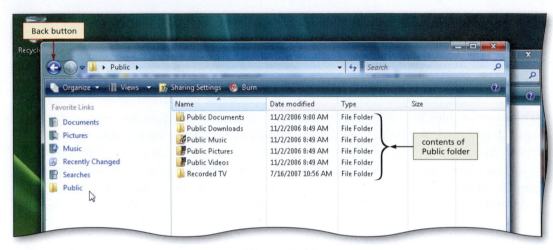

Figure 3–61

To Return to the Music Folder

Now that you have seen the contents of the Public folder, you will return to the Music folder. The following step switches back to the Music folder.

- Click the Back button on the Address bar to return to the Music folder (Figure 3–62).

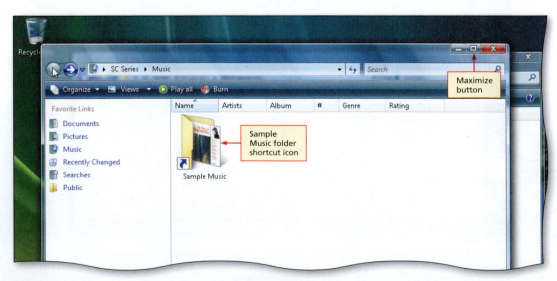

Figure 3–62

To Open the Sample Music Folder

In Figure 3–62, the Live Preview shows an album cover image. In order for an album cover to be displayed by Live Preview, your music files must include the album cover image. An album cover image usually is included when the music files are created. If you download music files, they often will have the album art included, but not every music file will have album art. You want to review the music files already installed on the computer, so you open the Sample Music folder. The following steps open the Sample Music folder.

1

• Double-click the Sample Music folder icon to open the Sample Music folder.

• If necessary, click the Maximize button to maximize the Sample Music window (Figure 3–63).

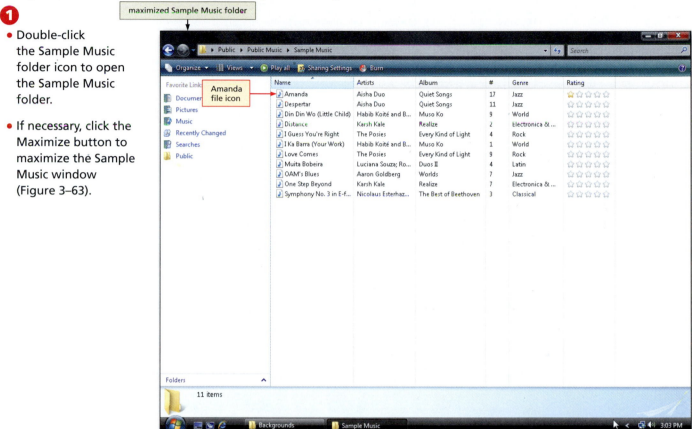

Figure 3–63

To View Information about a Music File

Similar to the Pictures folder, when you view a folder that contains music files, the folder structure and options will be specific to music files. In the Music folder, after the column titled Name, all of the remaining columns, Artists, Album, #, Genre, and Rating, are properties of the music files. The Artists column contains the name of the recording artist, while the Album column contains the name of the album that includes the song. The number symbol (**#**) indicates the track number of the song on the album, while Genre provides the classification of the music file. Finally, Rating is similar to the picture Ratings; you can rate the music files from zero to five stars.

Once you select a file, its properties display in the Details pane. As with picture files, you can use the Details pane to change the properties. The steps on the following pages display the properties of the Amanda music file in the Details pane and change the rating to four stars.

1
● Click the Amanda file icon to select the music file (Figure 3–64).

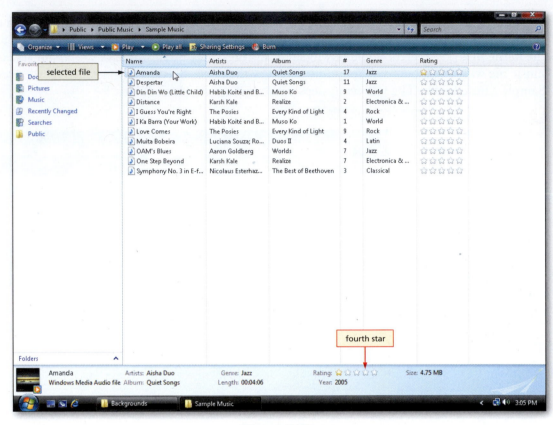

Figure 3–64

2
● Click the fourth star next to the Rating heading in the Details pane to rate the music file (Figure 3–65).

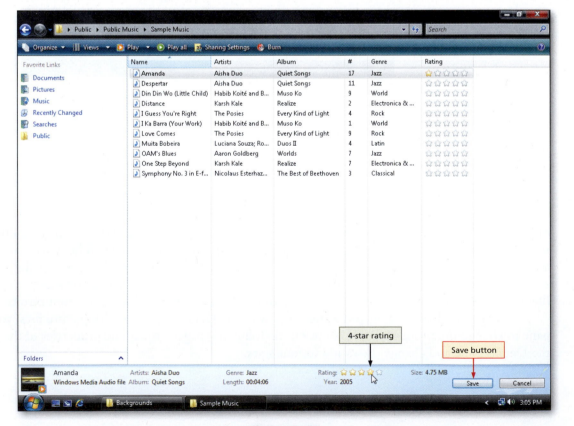

Figure 3–65

3
- Click the Save button to save the changes to the Amanda music file properties (Figure 3–66).

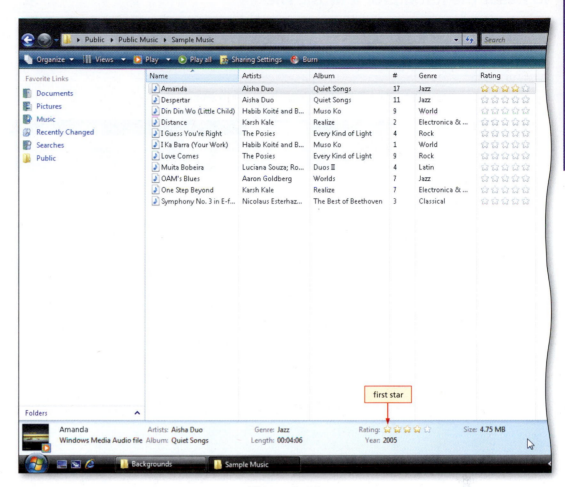

Figure 3–66

To Reset the Rating for a Music File

Because the Amanda file is in the Sample Music folder that is shared by everyone who uses this computer, you should clear your rating. However, if you are working on your own computer and you agree with the rating, you could leave the rating at four stars. The following steps will reset the rating of the Amanda file back to its original value.

• Position the mouse pointer at the left edge of the first star so that all stars appear clear, and then click the mouse.

• Click the Save button to save the changes to the Amanda music file properties (Figure 3–67).

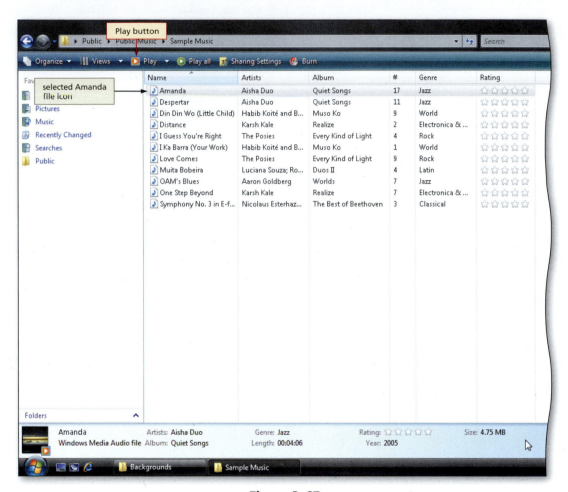

Figure 3–67

To Play a Music File in Windows Media Player

There are several ways to play a music file. The easiest way is to use the toolbar of the Music folder window. If you click the Play button, you will play the current song. Clicking the Play all button will play all of the music files in the folder. **Windows Media Player** is the default Windows Vista program for playing and working with digital media files such as music or video files.

In addition to playing music files, Windows Media Player can rip and burn music, maintain a music library, sync with portable audio players, and even download music. Windows Media Player also works with other multimedia files, including movies. The features of Windows Media Player will be discussed in a later chapter.

In Windows Media Player, there are buttons for controlling the playback of the music file. The following steps play the Amanda music file in Windows Media Player.

1

- If necessary, select the Amanda file.

- Click the Play button on the toolbar to open and play the Amanda music file in Windows Media Player (Figure 3–68).

Q&A Why am I unable to hear any music?

Check the speakers attached to your computer. Your speakers may not be turned on, or the volume may not be turned up on the speakers or computer. If you are in a lab using a computer without speakers, you will need a pair of headphones to listen to the music file.

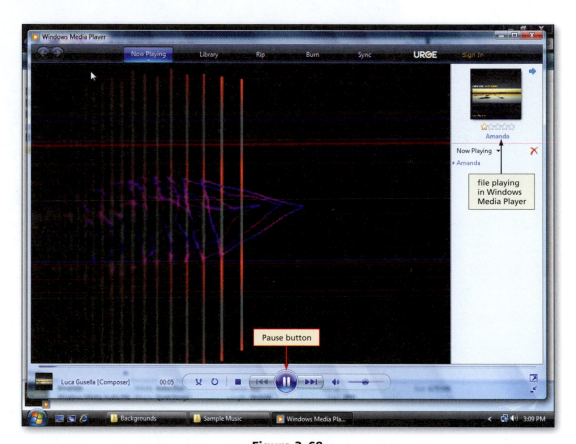

Figure 3–68

To Pause a Music File

After you have listened to the Amanda music file, you can stop playing the recording. The following step pauses the Amanda music file that is playing in Windows Media Player.

- Click the Pause button on the toolbar at the bottom of the window to pause the song in Windows Media Player (Figure 3–69).

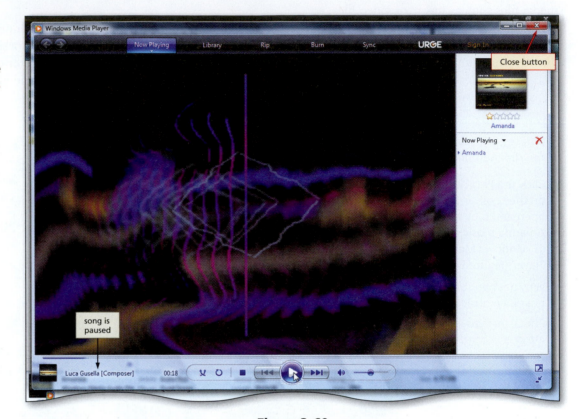

Figure 3–69

To Close Windows Media Player

Now that you are done using the Windows Media Player and the Sample Music folder window, you should close them.

1 Click the Close button on the Windows Media Player window to close the window.

2 Click the Close button on the Sample Music folder window to close the window.

Backing Up Files and Folders

It is very important that you make backups of your important files and folders. A **backup** is a copy of files and folders that are stored at a different location than the originals. While you can back up files and folders on the same drive where they were created, it is not considered as secure as backing them up to a separate drive. For example, you would not back up your C: drive files and folders on the C: drive. If something goes wrong with the C: drive, it would affect any backups stored there as well. Typically, you would store the backups on other hard drives, USB drives, CDs, DVDs, or even tape drives.

Backing up files and folders is a security aid; if something happens to your primary copy of a file or folder, you can restore it from the backup. Depending upon the size of the files and folders you are backing up, you might use a USB drive, a CD, a DVD, an external hard drive, or any other available storage device to back up your files. You might even consider creating a scheduled backup. A **scheduled backup** is a backup that is made according to dates and times that you predetermine. It always occurs on those dates and times.

After you have created a backup, you should store your backup away from the computer. Many people store their backups right by their computer, which is not a good practice, for security reasons. If a mishap occurs where the computer area is damaged, or someone steals the computer, or any other number of events occur, the backup still will be safe if it is stored in a different location. Most corporations make regular backups of their data and store the backups off site.

When you **restore** files or folders from a backup, you copy the files or folders from the backup location to the original location. If your hard disk crashes, a virus infects your computer, or an electrical surge damages your computer, you can restore the files and folders that you have stored on the backup. Before restoring files or folders, make sure that the location to where you are restoring the files is now secure. For example, before restoring files on a drive that has been infected by a virus, first make sure the virus is gone.

First, you will back up your files and folders using a USB drive. A USB drive is handy for backing up files and folders created on a computer in a classroom, computer lab, or Internet café, where you have to remove your files before you leave.

To Insert a USB Drive and Open It in a Folder Window

First you need to insert the USB drive so that you can back up your data to your USB drive. The following step inserts a USB drive and open it in a folder window.

1 Insert a USB drive into any open USB port on your computer to display the Auto Play window. Under the General Options heading, click the Open folder to view files command to open a folder window.

To Create a Backup on a USB Drive

With the USB drive connected, you are ready to make a backup. You decide to back up your Backgrounds folder. By copying this folder to the USB drive, you will be adding a measure of security to your data. The following steps copy the Backgrounds folder from the Pictures folder to the USB drive.

- Click the Backgrounds button on the task-bar to make the Backgrounds window the active window (Figure 3–70).

Figure 3–70

2
- Click the Pictures button on the Address bar to change the location to the Pictures folder (Figure 3–71).

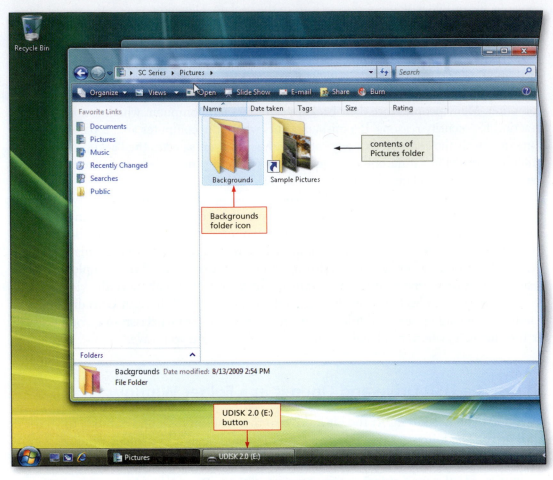

Figure 3–71

3
- If necessary, click the Backgrounds folder icon to select the Backgrounds folder.

- Right-click the Backgrounds folder to display a shortcut menu (Figure 3–72).

- Click the Copy command on the shortcut menu to copy the folder to the Clipboard.

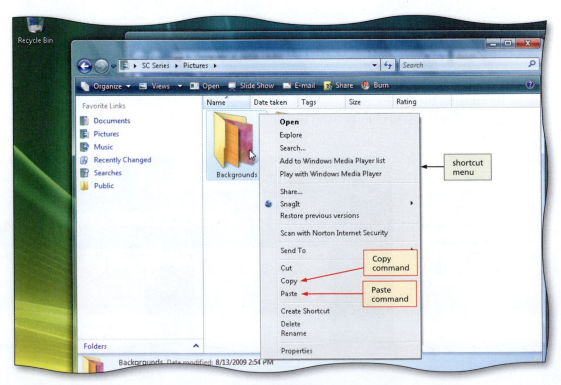

Figure 3–72

4
- Click UDISK 2.0 (E:) button on the taskbar to make the UDISK 2.0 (E:) window the active window.
- Right-click an open area in the list area to display a shortcut menu.
- Click the Paste command on the shortcut menu to paste a copy of the Backgrounds folder onto the USB drive (Figure 3–73).

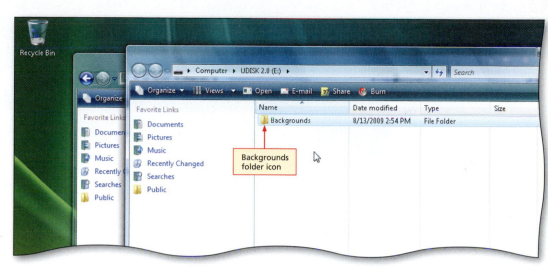

Figure 3–73

To Rename a Folder

Because the folder on the USB drive is a backup copy of the original folder, it is a good idea to change its name to reflect that it is a backup. The following steps rename the folder on the USB drive to indicate that it is a backup folder.

- If necessary, click the Backgrounds folder icon to select the Backgrounds folder.
- Right-click the Backgrounds icon to display a shortcut menu (Figure 3–74).

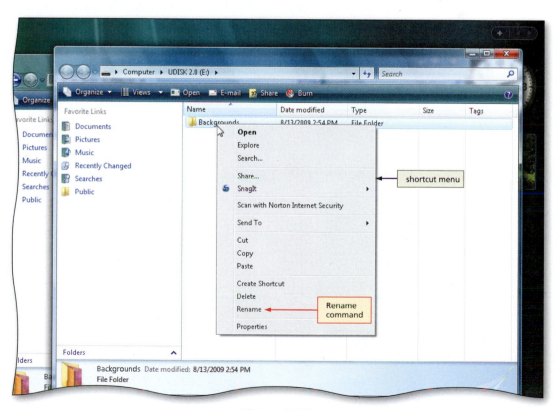

Figure 3–74

2

- Click the Rename command to open the name of the folder in a text box (Figure 3–75).

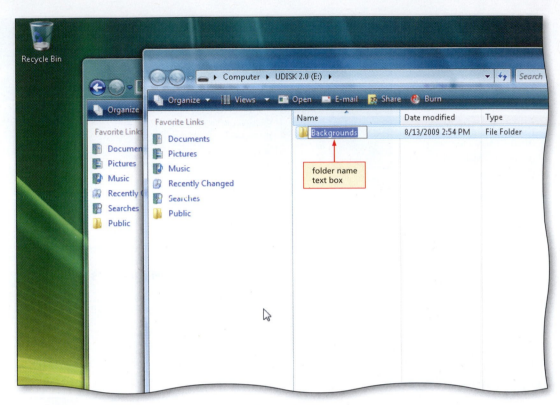

Figure 3–75

3

- Type Backgrounds – Backup as the new name for the folder (Figure 3–76).

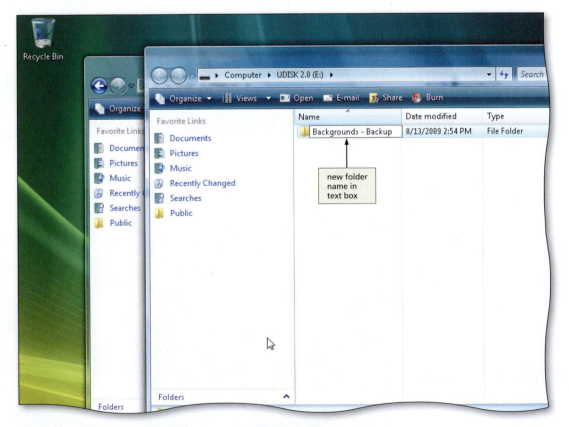

Figure 3–76

4
• Press the ENTER key to apply the new name to the folder (Figure 3–77).

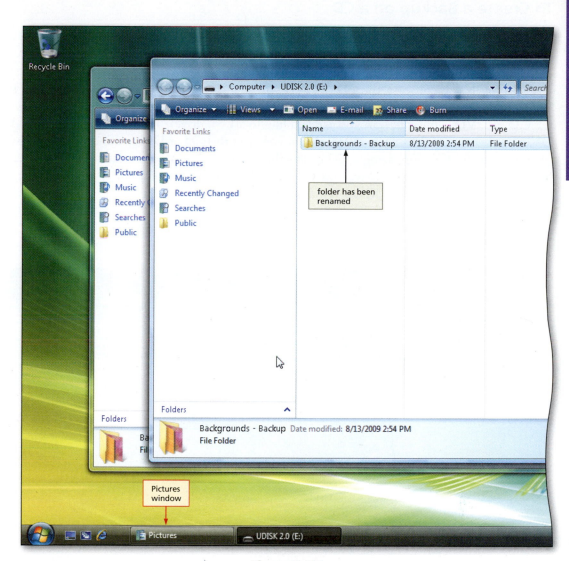

Figure 3–77

To Create a Backup on a CD

Copying a folder to a USB drive is one method of creating a backup. Another way to make a backup is to burn the files to a CD. The process of backing up files to CD requires that you have a CD or DVD drive that can write data onto CDs or DVDs. You also need a blank writable CD or DVD.

In this backup process, the CD or DVD will be formatted with the Live File System. The **Live File System** is a file storage system that allows you to add files continually to the CD or DVD until you are ready to write the data to the CD or DVD (similar to how you can add files to a USB drive). The files are not actually burned onto the CD or DVD until you eject the CD or DVD. When you eject the CD or DVD, Windows Vista finalizes the CD by burning the files onto the CD. Finalizing a CD means that the CD is prepared for later use in your computer or another computer. Because the CD is formatted with the Live File System, you only will be able to use it in computers that are formatted with the Windows XP or Windows Vista operating systems.

The following steps back up the Backgrounds folder from the Pictures folder to a blank CD. If you do not have access to a CD or DVD burner or do not have a blank CD or DVD read the following steps without performing them.

- Click the Pictures button on the taskbar to make the Pictures folder window the active window.

- If necessary, select the Backgrounds folder (Figure 3–78).

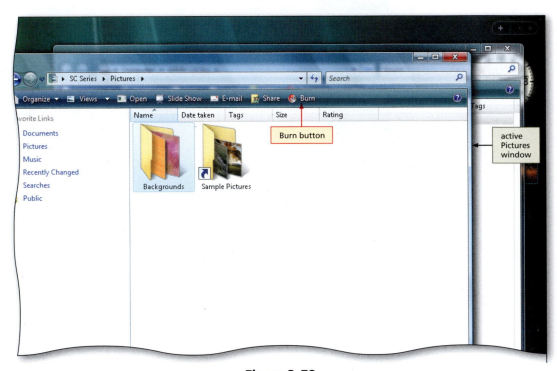

Figure 3–78

2

- Click the Burn button on the tool-bar to begin the burn process and display the Burn to Disc dialog box (Figure 3–79).

Figure 3–79

3

• Insert a blank CD into the drive to continue the burn process (Figure 3–80). If the AutoPlay dialog box displays, click the Close button to close the AutoPlay dialog box.

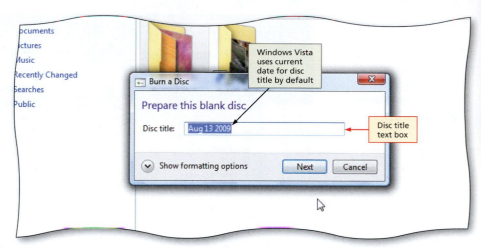

Figure 3–80

4

• Type Backup – Aug in the Disc title text box to provide a name for the disc (Figure 3–81).

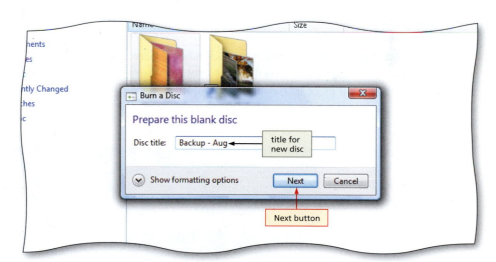

Figure 3–81

5

• Click the Next button to continue the burn process and display the Calculating time remaining dialog box that shows the progress of the burning process (Figure 3–82).

Figure 3–82

6

- Once the burning process has completed, the contents of the Backup – Aug disc appear in a new folder window (Figure 3–83).

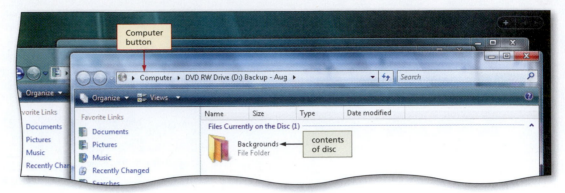

Figure 3–83

To Eject a CD

Now that the process is complete, the Backup - Aug folder is shown in a new folder window (Figure 3–83). You can continue to add files to this disc until you run out of storage space on the CD or DVD. Once you are ready to remove the disc, you eject it. Before the computer ejects the disc, the CD will be finalized. The following steps eject and finalize the CD.

1

- Click the Computer button on the Address bar to display the Computer folder window (Figure 3–84).

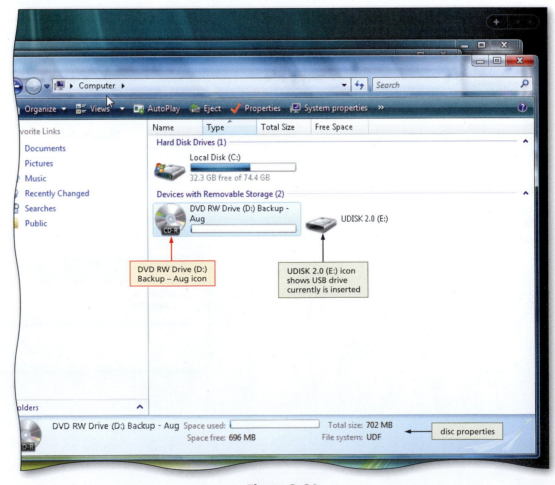

Figure 3–84

2

- Right-click the DVD RW Drive (D:) : Backup - Aug icon to display a shortcut menu (Figure 3–85). The drive name and letter may be different on your computer.

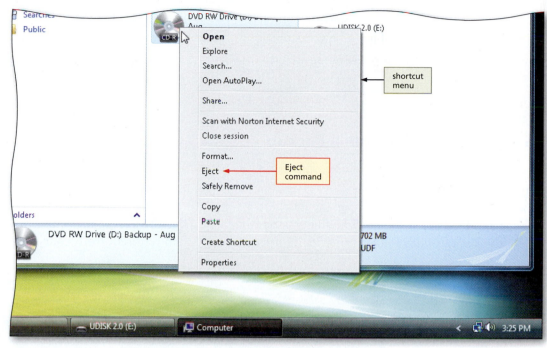

Figure 3–85

3

- Click the Eject command on the shortcut menu to have Windows Vista finalize and eject the CD (Figure 3–86).

- Remove the CD from the computer's CD drive.

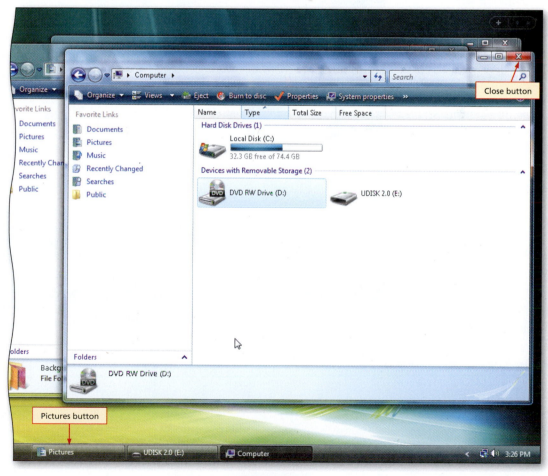

Figure 3–86

To Close the Computer Folder Window

Now that you have ejected the CD, you should close the Computer folder window. The following step closes the Computer folder window.

1 Click the Close button on the Computer folder window to close the window.

To Restore a Folder from a Backup

Whenever you need to restore a file or folder from a backup copy, you need to insert the removable media where the backup copy was stored, and then you can copy the backup to the destination drives or folders. To learn how to restore a folder from backup, you will first simulate an accidental loss of data by deleting the Background folder from the Pictures folder, and then restore the folder from the backup on your USB drive. The following steps delete the Backgrounds folder from the Pictures folder and then restore it from your backup copy.

1

- Click the Pictures button on the task-bar to make the Pictures folder window the active window (Figure 3–87).

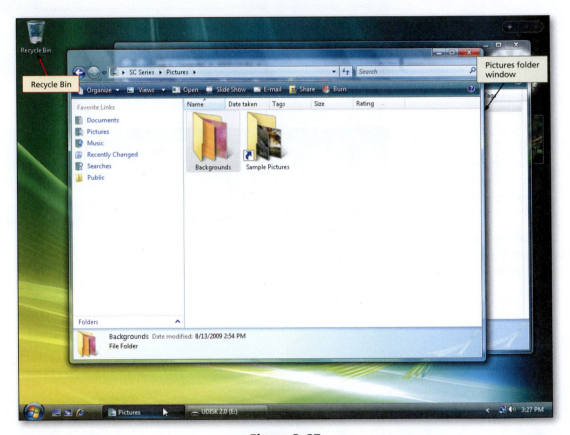

Figure 3–87

2

- Delete the Backgrounds folder to simulate an accidental loss of data.

- Empty the Recycle Bin (Figure 3–88).

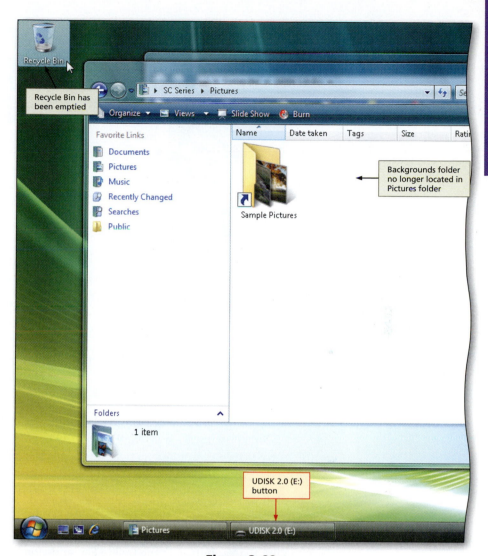

Figure 3–88

3

- Click the UDISK 2.0 (E:) button on the taskbar to make the UDISK 2.0 (E:) window the active window.

- Copy the Backgrounds - Backup folder to place a copy on the Clipboard.

- Click the Pictures button on the taskbar to make the Pictures window the active window.

- Paste the Backgrounds - Backup folder to place a copy in the Pictures folder (Figure 3–89).

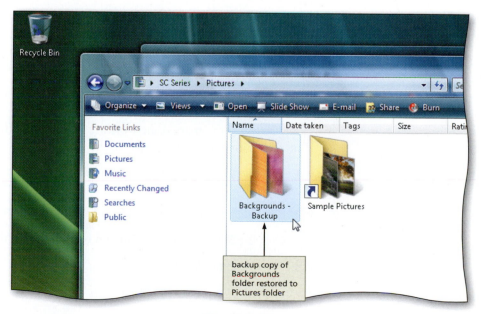

Figure 3–89

4

• Rename the folder Backgrounds to finish the restoration process (Figure 3–90).

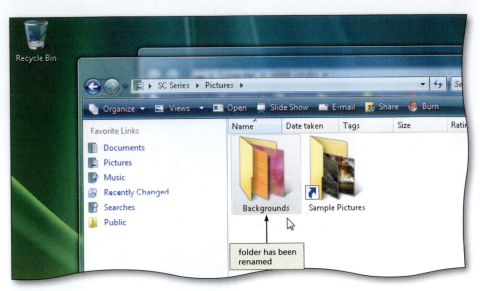

Figure 3–90

To Delete a Folder from the Pictures Folder

You now have restored the Backgrounds folder after a mishap. This process would be the same if you were working from a CD or DVD backup. To return the Pictures folder to its original state, you will delete the Backgrounds folder. The following steps delete the Backgrounds folder.

1 Right-click the Backgrounds folder to display a shortcut menu.

2 Click the Delete command on the shortcut menu.

3 Click the Yes button in the Delete Folder dialog box.

4 Close the Pictures folder.

5 Empty the Recycle Bin.

To Remove the USB Drive

Now that you are done working with the USB drive, you should safely remove it. The following steps safely remove the USB drive.

1 Click the Computer button on the Address bar of the UDISK 2.0 (E:) window to display the Computer folder window.

2 Right click the UDISK 2.0 (E:) icon to display a shortcut menu.

3 Click the Safely Remove command to prepare the drive to be removed.

4 Remove the USB drive.

5 Close the Computer folder window.

To Log Off from and Turn Off the Computer

After completing your work with Windows Vista, you should close your user account by logging off of the computer, and then turn off the computer.

1 Display the Start menu.

2 Click the Shutdown options button.

3 Click the Log Off command to Log Off of the computer.

4 Click the Shut Down button to turn off the computer.

Chapter Summary

In this chapter, you learned about the Computer folder window. You learned how to view the properties of drives and folders, as well as how to view their content. You worked with files and folders in the Pictures folder window, reviewed and changed their properties, viewed images in Windows Photo Gallery and as a slide show, and e-mailed a picture to a friend. As part of this process, you also learned how to copy and move files as well as how to create folders. Next, you saw how to work with files and folders in the Music folder window. You changed the rating of a music file and learned how to listen to a music file using the Windows Media Player. Finally, you gained knowledge of how to make a backup of files and restore the files, including how to copy, rename, and delete files and folders. The items listed below include all of the new Windows Vista skills you have learned in this chapter.

1. Open and Maximize the Computer Folder Window (WIN 152)
2. Display Properties for the Local Disk (C:) Drive in the Details Pane (WIN 153)
3. Display the Local Disk(C:) Properties Dialog Box (WIN 154)
4. Close the Local Disk (C:) Properties Dialog Box (WIN 155)
5. Switch Folders Using the Address Bar (WIN 155)
6. View the Contents of a Drive (WIN 158)
7. Preview the Properties for a Folder (WIN 159)
8. Display Properties for the Windows Folder in the Details Pane (WIN 160)
9. Display All of the Properties for the Windows Folder (WIN 161)
10. View the Contents of a Folder (WIN 163)
11. Search for a File and Folder in a Folder Window (WIN 164)
12. Return to the Computer Folder Window (WIN 165)
13. Search for Files Using Advanced Search (WIN 166)
14. Cascade Open Windows (WIN 169)
15. Make a Window the Active Window (WIN 170)
16. Undo Cascading (WIN 171)
17. Stack Open Windows (WIN 172)
18. Undo Show Windows Stacked (WIN 173)
19. Show Windows Side by Side (WIN 174)
20. Undo Show Windows Side by Side (WIN 175)
21. Copy Files to the Pictures Folder (WIN 177)
22. Create a Folder in the Pictures Folder (WIN 180)
23. Move Multiple Files into a Folder (WIN 182)
24. Refresh the Image on a Folder (WIN 183)
25. View and Change the Properties of a Picture (WIN 184)
26. Open a Picture in the Windows Photo Gallery (WIN 187)
27. Navigate through Your Pictures (WIN 188)
28. View Your Pictures as a Slide Show (WIN 189)
29. End a Slide Show (WIN 190)
30. E-Mail a Picture (WIN 191)
31. Open the Public Folder (WIN 194)
32. Return to the Music Folder (WIN 194)
33. Open the Sample Music Folder (WIN 195)
34. View Information about a Music File (WIN 195)
35. Reset the Rating for a Music File (WIN 198)
36. Play a Music File in Windows Media Player (WIN 199)
37. Pause a Music File (WIN 200)
38. Create a Backup on a USB Drive (WIN 201)
39. Rename a Folder (WIN 203)
40. Create a Backup on a CD (WIN 206)
41. Eject a CD (WIN 208)
42. Restore a Folder from a Backup (WIN 210)

Learn It Online

Test your knowledge of chapter content and key terms.

Instructions: To complete the Learn It Online exercises, start your browser, click the Address bar, and then enter the Web address scsite.com/winvista/learn. When the Windows Vista Learn It Online page is displayed, click the link for the exercise you want to complete and then read the instructions.

Chapter Reinforcement TF, MC, and SA
A series of true/false, multiple-choice, and short-answer questions that test your knowledge of the chapter content.

Flash Cards
An interactive learning environment where you identify chapter key terms associated with displayed definitions.

Practice Test
A series of multiple-choice questions that test your knowledge of chapter content and key terms.

Who Wants To Be a Computer Genius?
An interactive game that challenges your knowledge of chapter content in the style of a television quiz show.

Wheel of Terms
An interactive game that challenges your knowledge of chapter key terms in the style of the television show *Wheel of Fortune*.

Crossword Puzzle Challenge
A crossword puzzle that challenges your knowledge of key terms presented in the chapter.

Apply Your Knowledge

Reinforce the skills and apply the concepts you learned in this chapter.

File and Program Properties
Instructions: You want to demonstrate to a friend how to display the properties of a bitmap image, display the image using the Paint program instead of the Windows Photo Gallery program, and print the image. The **Paint program** is an application program included with Windows Vista to display and create images. You also want to demonstrate how to display the properties of an application program.

Perform the following tasks and answer the questions:

Part 1: Displaying File Properties
1. Click the Start button and then click Computer on the Start menu.
2. Double-click the Local Disk (C:) icon. If necessary, click Show the contents of this folder.
3. Double-click the Windows icon. If necessary, click the Show the contents of this folder link.
4. Search for the White_Chocolate picture file. If the White_Chocolate icon is not available on your computer, find the icon of another image file.
5. Right-click the White_Chocolate icon. Click Properties on the shortcut menu. Answer the following questions about the White_Chocolate file.
    a. What type of file is White_Chocolate? _____
    b. What program is used to open the White_Chocolate image? _____
    c. What is the path for the location of the White_Chocolate file? _____
    d. What is the size (in bytes) of the White_Chocolate file? _____
    e. When was the file created? _____

f. When was the file last modified? _____

g. When was the file last accessed? _____

Part 2: Using the Paint Program to Display an Image

1. Click the Change button in the White_Chocolate Properties dialog box. Answer the following questions.

   a. What is the name of the dialog box that displays? _____

   b. Which program is used to open the White_Chocolate file? _____

   c. Which other program(s) is recommended to open the file? _____

   d. List the other programs you can use to open the file? _____

2. Click the Paint icon in the Open With dialog box.

3. Click the OK button in the Open With dialog box.

4. Click the OK button in the White_Chocolate Properties dialog box.

5. Double-click the White_Chocolate icon to launch the Paint program and display the White_Chocolate image in the White_Chocolate – Paint window (Figure 3–91).

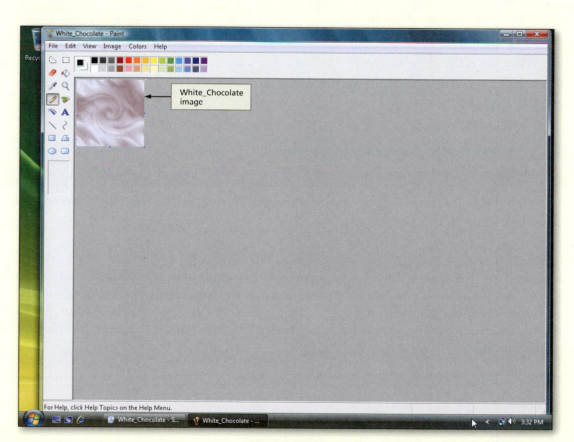

Figure 3–91

6. Print the White_Chocolate image by clicking File on the menu bar, clicking Print on the File menu, and then clicking the Print button in the Print dialog box.

7. Click the Close button in the White_Chocolate – Paint window.

Continued >

Apply Your Knowledge *continued*

Part 3:   Resetting the Program Selection in the Open With Dialog Box
1. Right-click the White_Chocolate icon. Click Properties on the shortcut menu. Answer the following question.

   a.   What program is used to open the White_Chocolate image? _____

2. Click the Change button in the White_Chocolate Properties dialog box.
3. If necessary, click the Windows Photo Gallery icon in the Open With dialog box to select the icon.
4. Click the OK button in the Open With dialog box.
5. Click the OK button in the White_Chocolate Properties dialog box.

Part 4:   Displaying Program Properties
1. Return to the Windows folder and scroll the right pane of the Windows folder window until the HelpPane icon displays. If the HelpPane icon does not appear, scroll to display another file.
2. Right-click the icon. Click Properties on the shortcut menu. Answer the following questions.

   a.   What type of file is selected? _____

   b.   What is the file's description? _____

   c.   What is the path of the file? _____

   d.   What size is the file when stored on disk? _____

3. Click the Cancel button in the Properties dialog box.
4. Close the Windows window.

Extend Your Knowledge

Extend the skills you learned in this chapter and experiment with new skills. You may need to use Help to complete the assignment.

Creating a Picture

Instructions: You want to use the Paint program to design a happy birthday image for a friend and then e-mail the message to the friend. The Paint program is an application program supplied with Windows Vista to display and create bitmap images. The file name of the Paint program is mspaint, but you do not know the location of the program on the hard drive. You first will use Search to find the mspaint file on the hard drive.

Perform the following tasks and answer the questions:

Part 1:   Searching for the Paint Program
1. Click the Start button and then click Computer on the Start menu.
2. Double-click the Local Disk (C:) icon.
3. Double-click the Windows folder icon.
4. Type mspaint in the Search box.

Part 2:   Creating a Bitmap Image
1. Double-click the mspaint icon in the Search Results window to launch Paint and display the Untitled – Paint window. *Hint*: The file type of the Paint program is Application (Figure 3–92).

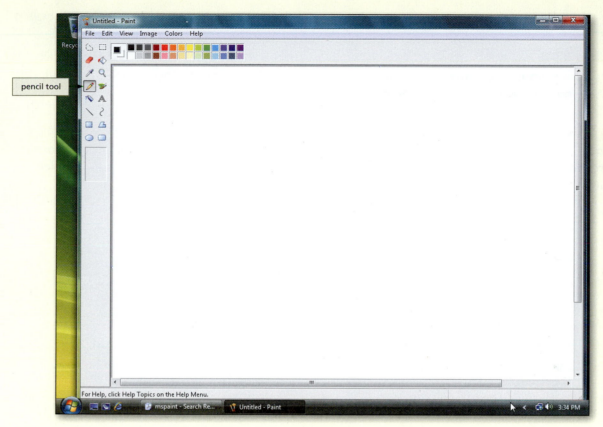

Figure 3–92

2. Use the Pencil tool shown in Figure 3–92 to write the message `Happy Birthday Stephen` in the Untitled – Paint window. *Hint:* Hold the left mouse button down to write and release the left mouse button to stop writing. If you make a mistake and want to start over, click Image on the menu bar and then click Clear Image to remove the image.

3. Click File on the menu bar and then click Save As. When the Save As dialog box displays, type `Happy Birthday` in the File name text box, and then click the Save button in the Save As dialog box to save the file in the Pictures folder.

4. Print the image.

5. Click the Close button in the Happy Birthday - Paint window.

6. Click the Close button in the Search Results window.

Part 3:   E-mail the Happy Birthday Image

1. Click the Happy Birthday icon in the Pictures window to select the icon.

2. Click E-mail on the toolbar.

3. Click the Attach button in the Attach Files dialog box.

4. Type your instructors e-mail address in the To text box. Type `Have a happy birthday!` in the message area.

5. Click the Send button on the toolbar.

Part 4:   Deleting the Happy Birthday Image

1. Click the Happy Birthday icon to select the file.

2. Click Organize on the toolbar, and then click Delete.

3. Click the Yes button in the Delete File dialog box.

4. Click the Close button in the Pictures window.

In the Lab

Using the guidelines, concepts and skills presented in this chapter to increase your knowledge of Windows Vista. Labs are listed in order of increasing difficulty.

Lab 1 Using Search to Find Picture Files

Instructions: You know that searching is an important feature of Windows Vista. You decide to use Search to find the images on the hard drive. You will store the files in a folder in the Pictures folder, print the images, and e-mail them to a friend.

Perform the following tasks and answer the questions:

Part 1: Searching for Files in the Search Results Window

1. If necessary, launch Microsoft Windows Vista and log on to the computer.
2. Click the Start button on the taskbar and then click Search on the Start menu. Maximize the Search Results window.
3. In the Search box, type Garden.jpg as the entry.
4. Copy the image to the Pictures folder.
5. Click the Close button in the Search Results window.

Part 2: Searching for Files from Another Window

1. Click the Start button on the taskbar and then click Computer on the Start menu.
2. Click the Search box.
3. Type Forest.jpg as the entry.
4. Copy the image to the Pictures folder.
5. Click the Close button in the Search Results window.

Part 3: Searching for Groups of Files

1. Click the Start button on the taskbar, click Search on the Start menu, and then click the arrow to the right of Advanced Search to expand the Advanced Search options. Maximize the Search Results window.
2. In the Name text box, type cr* as the entry. Click Search (Figure 3–93).
3. Answer the following question.
   a. How many files were found? _____
4. Click the Creek icon to select the icon. If the Creek icon does not display, select another icon.
5. Copy the image to the Pictures folder.

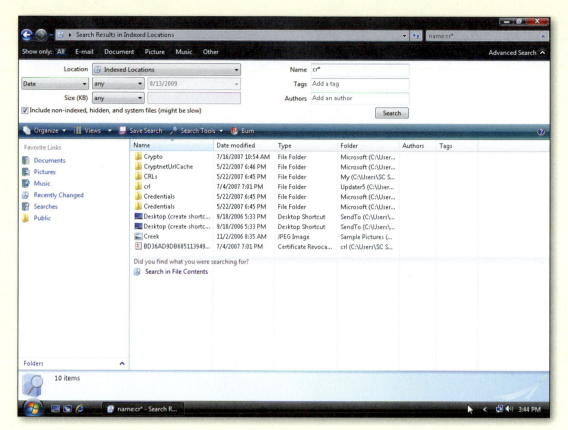

Figure 3–93

Part 4:   Creating the More Backgrounds Folder in the Pictures Folder

1. If necessary, open the Pictures folder window and make it the active window.

2. Make a new folder, type `More Backgrounds` in the icon title text box, and then press the ENTER key.

3. Select the icons of the images you copied to the Pictures folder.

4. Move the images to the More Backgrounds folder.

5. Refresh the thumbnail image on the More Backgrounds folder.

Part 5:   Printing the Images

1. Open the More Backgrounds folder.

2. Select the pictures.

3. Click Print on the toolbar to display the Print Pictures dialog box.

4. Use the scroll bar to select the Wallet option.

5. Click the Print button to print the pictures.

Part 6:   E-mail the Files in the More Backgrounds Folder

1. If necessary, click the More Backgrounds icon to select the icon.

2. Click E-mail on the toolbar.

3. Click the Attach button in the Attach Files dialog box.

4. Type `rayenger@yahoo.com` in the To text box. Type `I searched the computer to find these background images. I thought you might like to see them.` in the message area.

5. Click the Send button on the toolbar.

Continued >

In the Lab *continued*

Part 7: *Moving the More Backgrounds Folder to a USB Drive*
1. Insert a formatted USB drive into an open USB port.
2. Click the Pictures button on the Address bar.
3. Select the More Backgrounds icon in the Pictures window.
4. Right-click the More Backgrounds icon.
5. Click Send To and then click USB drive.
6. Click the Close button in the Pictures window.
7. Safely remove the USB drive from the computer.

In the Lab

Lab 2 Finding Pictures Online

Instructions: A classmate informs you that the Internet is a great source of photos, pictures, and images. You decide to launch the Internet Explorer program, search for well-known candy and drink logos on the Internet, and then save them in a folder. A **logo** is an image that identifies businesses, government agencies, products, and other entities. In addition, you want to print the logos and e-mail them to your instructor.

Perform the following tasks and answer the questions:

Part 1: *Launching the Internet Explorer Program*
1. Click the Start button and then click Computer on the Start menu.
2. Click the Folders button.
3. Expand the Local Disk (C:) folder.
4. Expand the Program Files folder.
5. Display the contents of the Internet Explorer folder.
6. Double-click the iexplore icon to launch Internet Explorer and display the Microsoft Internet Explorer window.

Part 2: *Finding and Saving Logo Images*
1. Type www.jellybelly.com on the Address bar in the Windows Internet Explorer window and then click the Go button.
2. Find the jelly belly bean man. Right-click the jelly belly bean man, click Save Picture As on the shortcut menu, type jelly belly logo in the File name text box in the Save Picture dialog box, and then click the Save button to save the logo in the Pictures folder.
3. Type www.jollyrancherfruitchews.com on the Address bar in the Windows Internet Explorer window and then click the Go button. Locate the Jolly Rancher picture that matches the one in Figure 3-94 and use the file name, Jolly Rancher logo, to save the Jolly Rancher logo in the Pictures folder.
4. Close the Internet Explorer window.
5. Click the Start button and then click Pictures. The Jelly Belly logo and Jolly Rancher image, display in the Pictures window (Figure 3–94). The logos in the Pictures window on your computer may be different from the logos shown in Figure 3–94 if the businesses have changed their logos.

Figure 3–94

Part 3: Displaying File Properties

1. Right-click each logo file in the Pictures folder window, click Properties, answer the question about the logo below, and then close the Properties dialog box.

    a. What type of file is the Jelly Belly logo file? _____

    b. What type of file is the Jolly Rancher logo file? _____

2. Click an open area of the Pictures folder window to deselect the Jolly Rancher logo file.

Part 4: Creating the Candy Logos Folder in the Pictures Folder Window

1. Make a new folder in the Pictures folder window, type `Candy Logos` in the icon title text box, and then press the ENTER key.

2. Click the Jelly Belly logo, hold down the CTRL key, and then click the Jolly Rancher logo.

3. Right-drag the icons to the Candy Logos icon and then click Move Here on the shortcut menu.

4. Refresh the image on the Candy Logos folder.

Part 5: Printing the Logo Images

1. Open the Candy Logos folder.

2. Select both of the logos.

3. Click Print on the toolbar to display the Print Pictures dialog box.

4. Click the Print button to print the pictures.

Continued >

In the Lab *continued*

Part 6:   E-mail the Files in the Candy Logos Folder
1. Click the Back button on the toolbar to display the Pictures folder window.
2. E-mail the pictures to your instructor with a brief message describing the pictures.
3. Click the Send button on the toolbar.

Part 7:   Moving the Candy Logos Folder to a USB Drive
1. Insert a formatted USB drive into an open USB port.
2. Copy the Candy Logos folders to the USB drive.
3. Safely remove the USB drive from the computer.
4. Delete the Candy Logos folder from the Pictures folder.

In the Lab

Lab 3 Managing Your Music

Instructions: You want to investigate the different ways you can organize the music stored on your computer. Once you determine which method of organizing your music you prefer, you decide that you want to add to your music collection. First you will learn about the copyright laws that pertain to digital music, and then you will research a few Web sites that allow you to download music files.

Perform the following tasks and answer the questions:

Part 1:   Organizing Your Music
1. Open the Start menu, and then open the Music folder window. Open the Sample Music folder, and answer the following questions.
   a.   How many files are there? _____
2. Group the files according to Artist.
   a.   How many groupings result? _____
   b.   How many songs are in the largest group? _____
3. Group the files according to Album.
   a.   How many groupings result? _____
   b.   How many songs are in the largest group? _____
   c.   Which method of grouping files do you prefer, and why? _____

Part 2:   Researching Copyright Laws Regarding Digital Music Files
1. Click the Internet Explorer icon on the Quick Launch toolbar. Type `www.mpa.org/ copyright_resource_center/` on the Address bar, and then press ENTER.
   a.   What copyrights exist concerning music files? _____
   b.   What should you know before downloading music files? _____
   c.   What are the legal ramifications of downloading and sharing illegal music files? _____
   _____

Part 3:   Finding Music Online

1. Type www.netmusic.com on the Internet Explorer Address bar and press ENTER.

   a.   What types of music can be downloaded from this Web site? _____

   b.   What are the fees? _____

   c.   Are there any free, legal downloads available? _____

   d.   Would you use this service? _____

2. Type music.yahoo.com on the Address bar of Internet Explorer and press ENTER.

   a.   What types of music can be downloaded from this Web site? _____

   b.   What are the fees? _____

   c.   Are there any free, legal downloads available? _____

   d.   Would you use this service? _____

3. Type www.apple.com/itunes on the Address bar of Internet Explorer and press ENTER.

   a.   What types of music can be downloaded from this Web site? _____

   b.   What are the fees? _____

   c.   Are there any free, legal downloads available? _____

   d.   Would you use this service? _____

Cases and Places

Apply your creative thinking and problem solving skills to design and implement a solution.

• Easier •• More Difficult

• 1 Finding Picture Files

Your seven-year old brother cannot get enough of the graphics that display on computers. Lately, he has been asking about what additional graphics come installed in Windows Vista beyond just the sample pictures. You finally have agreed to show him. Using techniques you learned in this chapter, display the icons for all the graphics image files that are stored on your computer. *Hint*: Graphics files on Windows Vista computers typically use the following file extensions of .bmp, .pcx, .tif, .jpg, or .gif. Once you have found the graphics files, display them and then print the three that you like best.

• 2 Advanced Searching

Your employer suspects that someone has used your computer during off-hours for non-company business. She has asked you to search your computer for all files that have been created or modified during the last ten days. When you find the files, determine if any are WordPad files or Paint files that you did not create or modify. Summarize the number and date they were created or modified in a brief report.

•• 3 Researching Backups

Backing up files is an important way to protect data and ensure that it is not lost or destroyed accidentally. You can use a variety of devices and techniques to back up files from a personal computer. Using Windows Help and Support, research the Backup and Restore Center. Determine the types of devices used to store backed up data, schedules, methods, and techniques for backing up data, and the consequences of not backing up data. Write a brief report of your findings.

•• 4 Researching Photo Printing Sites

Make It Personal

Now that you know how to work with the Pictures folder, you want to find Web sites where you can upload and print your photos. Using the Internet, search for three photo printing Web sites. Find the prices per 4 × 6 photo, the required file formats, and explore any other photo products that you would be interested in purchasing. Write a brief report that compares the three Web sites, and indicate which one you would use.

•• 5 Researching Data Security

Working Together

Data stored on disk is one of a company's most valuable assets. If that data were to be stolen, lost, or compromised so that it could not be accessed, the company could go out of business. Therefore, companies go to great lengths to protect their data. Working with classmates, research how the companies where you each work handle their backups. Find out how each one protects its data against viruses, unauthorized access, and even against such natural disasters such as fire and floods. Prepare a brief report that describes the companies' procedures. In your report, point out any areas where you find a company has not protected its data adequately.

4 Personal Information Management and Communication

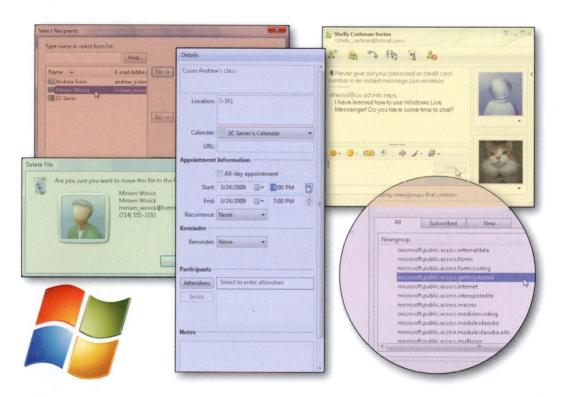

Objectives

You will have mastered the material in this project when you can:

- Open, read, print, reply to, and delete electronic mail messages
- Open a file attachment
- Compose and format an electronic mail message
- Attach a file to an e-mail
- Send an e-mail
- Add and modify a Windows Calendar event
- Add and delete a Windows contact
- Display and subscribe to a newsgroup

- Read and print newsgroup articles
- Unsubscribe from a newsgroup
- Locate and subscribe to an RSS feed
- Identify other communication methods available on the Internet
- Start and sign in to Windows Live Messenger
- Add and remove a Windows Live Messenger contact
- Send an instant message

4 | Personal Information Management and Communication

Introduction

In addition to the application programs discussed in earlier chapters, Windows Vista also includes programs that allow you to manage your personal information and communicate with other individuals via the Internet. These programs include Windows Mail, which allows you to send and receive electronic mail and to read and post messages to a newsgroup, Windows Calendar, which allows you to keep track of appointments and tasks, Windows Contacts, which allows you to capture detail contact information on your friends and associates, and Internet Explorer, which allows you to visit Web sites, subscribe to RSS feeds, and communicate using blogs, chat rooms, bulletin boards and forums, and groups. Previous versions of the Windows operating system included Windows Messenger, an application program that allowed you to communicate by sending and receiving instant messages. With Windows Vista, however, Microsoft moved this functionality from the operating system to the Web. In this chapter, you will use Windows Mail, Contacts, and Calendar for personal information management, along with Internet Explorer and Windows Live Messenger to explore other means of Web-based communications.

Overview

As you read this chapter, you will learn how to use Windows Mail, Contacts, Calendar, Internet Explorer, Windows Live Messenger, and how to communicate over the Internet (Figure 4-1), by performing these general tasks:

- Send and receive e-mail
- Schedule appointments and tasks
- Add and remove contacts
- Subscribe to and read newsgroup articles
- Subscribe to and read RSS feeds
- Send and receive instant messages

Plan Ahead

> **Internet Communication Guidelines**
> To communicate effectively, you should understand the general guidelines for using e-mail, instant messaging, and newsgroups. Before communicating via the Internet, consider these general guidelines:
>
> 1. **Determine the information you need.** The Internet provides access to a wealth of information, whether it is current news, a note from a friend stating whether she can join you for dinner Friday, or an instant message from a colleague who is asking a question for a customer at his desk. The type of information and the speed at which you need it will help you choose the most effective method of communication.
>
> *(continued)*

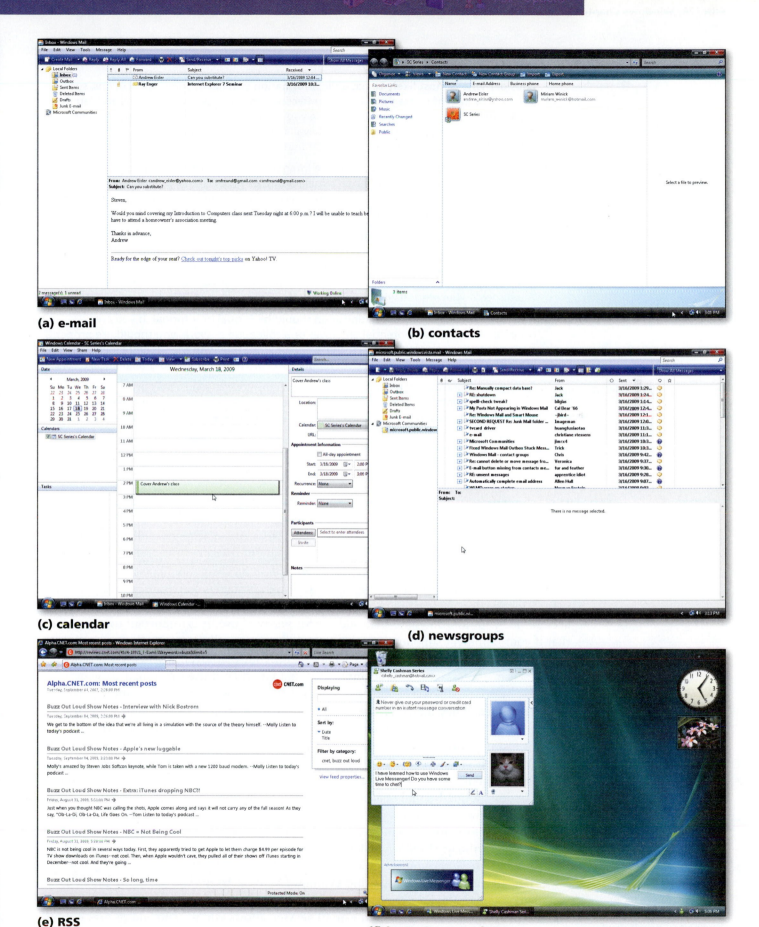

(a) e-mail

(b) contacts

(c) calendar

(d) newsgroups

(e) RSS

(f) instant messaging

Figure 4–1

**Plan
Ahead**

(continued)

2. **Consider who is most likely to have the information you need.** Some applications, such as e-mail or instant messaging, allow you to communicate easily with friends and family, while others, such as newsgroups, provide you with access to people you may not know. If the information you are seeking is not available from those who are close to you, you will need to use a communication method that enables you to reach a broader audience.

3. **Communicate with people you trust.** The Internet enables anyone to communicate with you. In fact, it is possible to receive a large amount of unsolicited communication as well as harmful e-mail attachments. Communicate with individuals you trust or through exchanges that you initiate, and be cautious when communicating with strangers.

4. **Do not open unsolicited file attachments.** If you receive a file via an e-mail or an instant message, do not open it unless you are expecting it from someone you know and trust. Some viruses that travel via file attachments are able to appear as if they originated from someone you know and trust, so it is especially important for you to be careful. If you receive a file that you suspect to be infected with a virus, contact the sender of the file immediately.

5. **Determine whether your communication should be formal or informal.** If you are communicating with a potential employer or a colleague at work, you should use proper spelling, grammar, and etiquette. If you are communicating with friends and family, you can be less formal, and you might not bother checking for spelling and grammatical errors.

6. **Gather e-mail and instant messaging addresses.** Before you can send e-mail or instant messages to your friends, family, and colleagues, you will need to obtain their e-mail or instant messaging addresses. Without this information, you will be unable to communicate with them.

Electronic Mail (E-Mail)

Electronic mail (e-mail) has become an important means of exchanging messages and files between business associates and friends. Businesses find that using e-mail to send files electronically saves both time and money. Parents with students away at college or relatives who are scattered across the country find that exchanging e-mail messages is an inexpensive and easy way to stay in touch with family members. In fact, exchanging e-mail messages is one of the more widely used features of the Internet. E-mail is so popular nowadays that many individuals have multiple e-mail accounts. For instance, you might have an e-mail account for your job, and an e-mail address for personal use. It is important to recognize that if your employer supplies you with an e-mail account, all messages sent to and from that account are the property of, and accessible by, your employer. If you plan to send personal e-mail messages, it is recommended that you do not use the e-mail account provided by your employer. Some individuals also find it useful to have multiple personal e-mail accounts. They may give one e-mail address to their friends and family, and use another e-mail address when signing up for mailing lists, filling out registration forms, or entering a sweepstakes. This way personal e-mail is kept separate from bulk or junk e-mail.

Microsoft Windows Mail is an e-mail program that allows you to receive and store incoming e-mail messages, compose and send e-mail messages, access your Contacts and your Windows Calendar, and read and post messages to Internet newsgroups. The Contacts folder in Windows Vista allows you to store information about individuals you frequently contact. This information might include their e-mail address, street address, telephone number, and birthday. Windows Calendar allows you to keep track of appointments and events that you have scheduled.

E-mail can be accessed by using Windows Mail, or by other e-mail programs installed on your computer, such as Microsoft Outlook or Eudora, or by using a Web-based e-mail service. A **Web-based e-mail service** allows you to send and receive e-mails by logging into a Web site, instead of installing an e-mail program on your computer. By using a Web-based e-mail service, you are able to check your e-mail on any computer that has an Internet connection and a Web browser. Free Web-based e-mail services include

BTW

POP Mail
You are able to configure Windows Mail to automatically retrieve e-mail messages from other e-mail accounts, such as Gmail, using the Post Office Protocol (POP). This feature is useful when you do not want to access your e-mail account using a Web browser.

Windows Live Hotmail (www.hotmail.com), Gmail (www.gmail.com), Yahoo! Mail (www.yahoo.com), and AIM Mail (www.aim.com). These companies are able to provide free Web-based e-mail services by placing advertisements on their Web sites or directly in the e-mail messages sent from their Web site. While all e-mail services offer the same basic functionality, such as sending and receiving e-mails and storing contact information, some features, such as the amount of storage space each service offers, may differ. Before choosing a Web-based e-mail service, compare the different options to determine which one might work best for you.

If you work for an employer who provides you with an e-mail account, you most likely access your e-mail account by using an e-mail program installed on your computer. Some companies also provide Web-based access to their e-mail system, enabling employees to send and receive e-mail messages from a location other than the office. It is common for the Web-based interface to resemble the interface of the e-mail program you use in the office to access your e-mail account. While the interfaces and functionality may be similar between Web-based e-mail services and e-mail programs installed on your computer, some differences do exist. For example, if you are accessing your e-mail account by using an e-mail program installed on your computer, the e-mail messages are transferred to and stored on your computer before you can read them. If you are accessing your e-mail account using a Web-based e-mail service, the e-mail messages are stored remotely on the e-mail server.

To Start Windows Mail

The following steps, which illustrate how to start Windows Mail, assume that you have an e-mail account configured in Windows Mail. For more information about configuring an e-mail account in Windows Mail, see your instructor.

1

- Display the Start menu.

- Click All Programs on the Start menu to display the All Programs list (Figure 4–2).

Figure 4–2

②

- Click Windows Mail to start the Windows Mail application.

- If necessary, maximize the Inbox - Windows Mail window (Figure 4–3).

Q&A

Why does my screen look different?

Because you are accessing your own e-mail account, Windows Mail will display different e-mail messages in the message list. However, you can still follow the steps presented in this chapter by using the e-mails displayed in your message list.

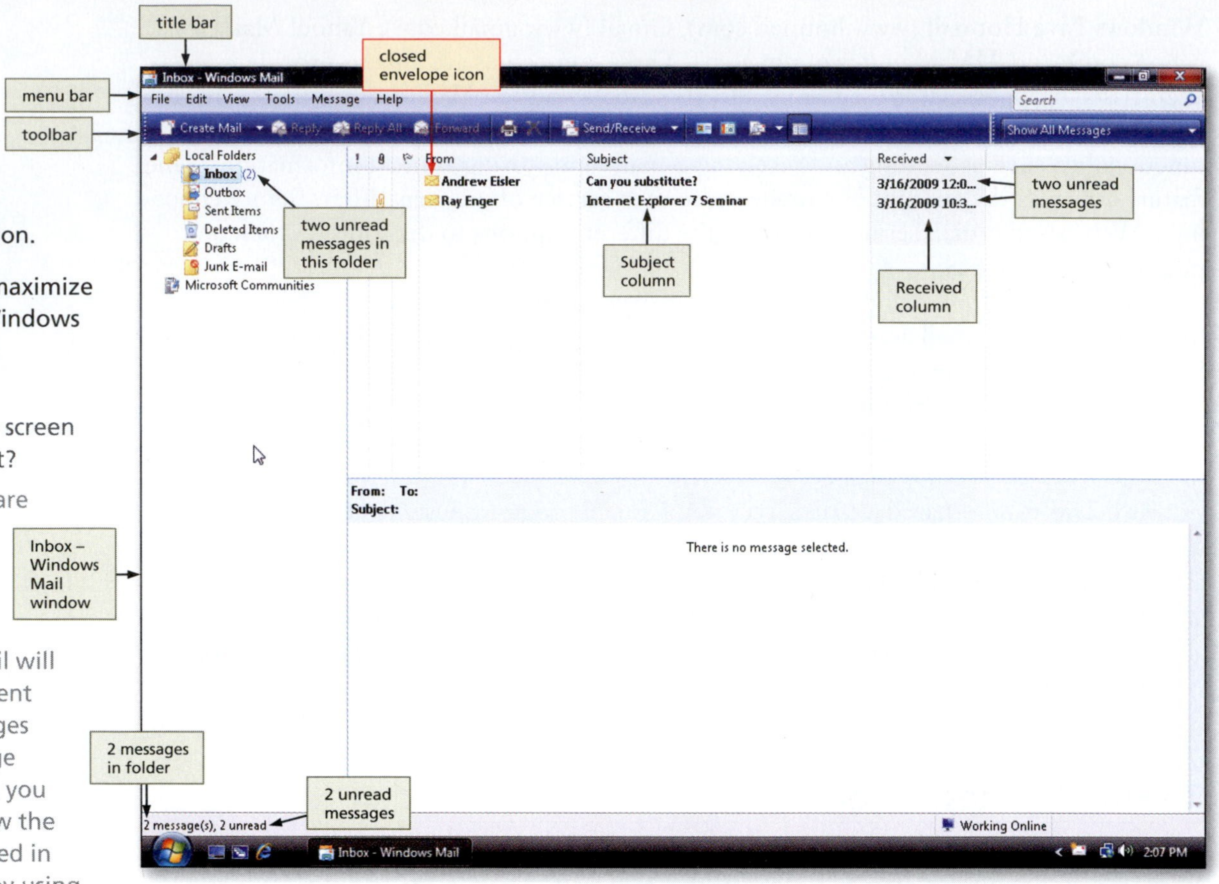

title bar

closed envelope icon

menu bar

toolbar

Inbox – Windows Mail window

two unread messages in this folder

Subject column

Received column

two unread messages

2 messages in folder

2 unread messages

Figure 4–3

Other Ways

1. Press CTRL+ESC, type `windows mail`, click Windows Mail

The Windows Mail Window

The Inbox - Windows Mail window shown in Figure 4–3 contains a number of elements. The title bar contains the folder name (Inbox) and the application name (Windows Mail). A toolbar below the title bar and menu bar contains buttons specific to Windows Mail (Create Mail, Reply, Reply All, Forward, and so on). Table 4–1 contains the toolbar buttons and a brief explanation of their functions.

Table 4–1 Toolbar Buttons and Functions	
Button	**Function**
Create Mail	Displays the New Message window used to compose a new e-mail message.
Reply	Displays a window used to reply to an e-mail message. The recipient's name, original subject of the e-mail message preceded by the Re: entry, and the original e-mail message appear in the window.
Reply All	Displays a window used to reply to an e-mail message. The names of all recipients, subject of the e-mail message preceded by the Re: entry, and the original e-mail message appear in the window.
Forward	Displays a window used to forward an e-mail message to another recipient. The original subject of the e-mail message preceded by the Fw: entry and the original e-mail message appear in the window.

Table 4–1 Toolbar Buttons and Functions (continued)

Button	Function
	Prints the highlighted e-mail message in the message list.
	Deletes the highlighted e-mail message in the message list by moving the message to the Deleted Items folder.
	Displays the Windows Mail dialog box, contacts the mail server, sends any e-mail messages in the Outbox folder, and places new e-mail messages in the Inbox folder.
	Displays the Contacts window containing a list of frequently used contacts.
	Displays the Windows Calendar, containing a list of appointments and tasks you may have scheduled.
	Displays the Find Message window that allows you to search for an e-mail message in the message list based on sender name, recipient name, e-mail subject, e-mail message, date, whether the e-mail has an attachment, and whether the e-mail is flagged.
	Displays or hides the Folder list in the left pane.

The Inbox - Windows Mail window is divided into three areas. The Folder list contains, in a hierarchical structure, the Local Folders folder and the six mail folders contained within it. The six standard mail folders (Inbox, Outbox, Sent Items, Deleted Items, Drafts, and Junk E-mail) are displayed when you first start Windows Mail. Although you cannot rename or delete these folders, you can create additional folders.

The Inbox folder in Figure 4–4 on the next page is the destination for incoming mail. The Outbox folder temporarily holds messages you send until Windows Mail delivers them. The Sent Items folder retains copies of messages that you have sent. The Deleted Items folder contains messages that you have deleted. As a safety precaution, you can retrieve deleted messages from the Deleted Items folder if you later decide you want to keep them. Deleting messages from the Deleted Items folder removes the messages permanently. The Drafts folder retains copies of messages that you are not yet ready to send. The Junk E-mail folder contains e-mail messages that have been flagged as junk e-mail. Windows Mail contains a feature that can automatically detect junk e-mail, otherwise known as unsolicited commercial e-mail, or spam. Although Windows Mail can identify most junk e-mail, it cannot detect it all. Similarly, Windows Mail may incorrectly flag an incoming message as junk e-mail. For this reason, it is important that you check your Junk E-mail folder regularly to ensure that no legitimate messages have been filed there.

Folders can contain e-mail messages, faxes, and files created in other Windows applications. Folders in bold type followed by a blue number in parentheses indicate the number of messages in the folder that are unopened. Other folders may appear on your computer in addition to the folders shown in Figure 4–4.

The contents of the Inbox folder automatically appear in the message list shown in Figure 4–4 when you start Windows Mail. The first three columns in the message list contain icons that provide information about the e-mail. The second three columns contain the e-mail author's name or e-mail address, subject of the message, and date and time the message was received. Collectively, these three entries are referred to as the message heading.

An exclamation point icon appearing in the first column indicates that the e-mail message has been marked high priority by the sender, suggesting that it should be read immediately. A paper clip icon appearing in the second column indicates that the e-mail message contains an attachment. In Figure 4–4, the second e-mail message in the message list (Ray Enger) contains an attachment, as indicated by the paper clip icon. A flag icon in the third column indicates the e-mail message has been flagged. You may choose to flag an important message that you want to revisit at a later time.

BTW

Mail Folders
You can create additional folders in the Local Folders folder. To do so, right-click the Local Folders icon, click New Folder, type the folder name in the Folder name text box, and then click the OK button.

BTW

Sorting E-mail Messages
You can sort e-mail messages in Windows Mail by sender, subject, date received, and more. To sort your e-mail messages by sender, for example, click the From column heading. E-mail messages can be sorted in ascending or descending order.

A closed envelope icon in the From column and a message heading that appears in bold type identifies an unread e-mail message. In Figure 4–4, the second e-mail message, from Ray Enger, contains a paper clip icon, a closed envelope icon, and a message heading that appears in bold type. The closed envelope icon and bold message heading indicate that the e-mail message has not been read (opened) and the paper clip indicates that the message has an attachment.

The first e-mail message, from Andrew Eisler, contains an opened envelope icon and a message heading that appears in normal type. The icon and message heading indicate that the e-mail message has been read. Because you will be accessing Windows Mail with a different e-mail account, other e-mail messages will display on your computer in place of these messages.

The closed envelope icon is one of several icons, called message list icons, that display in the From column. Different message list icons may display in the From column to indicate the status of the message. The icon may indicate an action that was performed by the sender or one that was performed by the recipient. The actions may include reading, replying to, forwarding, digitally signing, and encrypting a message. The Preview pane in Figure 4–4 contains the text of the highlighted e-mail message (Andrew Eisler) in the message pane. The message header is displayed at the top of the Preview pane and contains the sender's name and e-mail address, recipient's e-mail address, and the subject of the e-mail. The text of the e-mail message appears below the message header.

BTW

Column Headings
You can change the width of column headings in the message list by dragging the vertical line between two column headings.

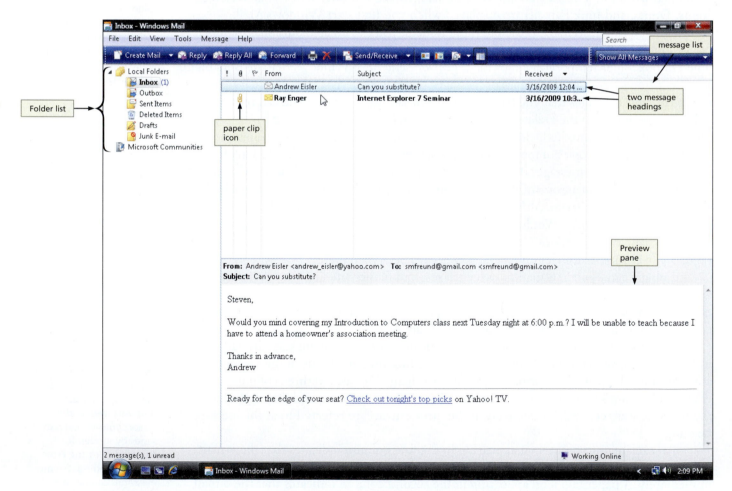

Figure 4–4

To Open (Read) an E-Mail Message

In Figure 4–4, the message headings for Andrew Eisler and Ray Enger are displayed in the message list. Double-clicking the closed envelope icon in either heading opens the e-mail message in a separate window, as opposed to opening it in the Preview pane. The following step opens an e-mail message in a new window so you can read it.

1

- Double-click anywhere on the message heading of the message from Andrew Eisler, which has the closed envelope icon. If the envelope icon for Andrew Eisler is not displayed in the message list, double-click another message with a closed envelope icon.

- Maximize the Can you substitute? window (Figure 4–5).

Q&A What should I do if I do not see the message from Andrew Eisler in the message list?

If you do not see the message from Andrew Eisler, double-click any message in the message list and then maximize the window that opens.

Q&A What happens to the Inbox after I open an e-mail message?

The closed envelope icon changes to an opened envelope icon, the message heading no longer appears in bold type, and the number of unread e-mails next to the Inbox folder in the Folder list decreases by one.

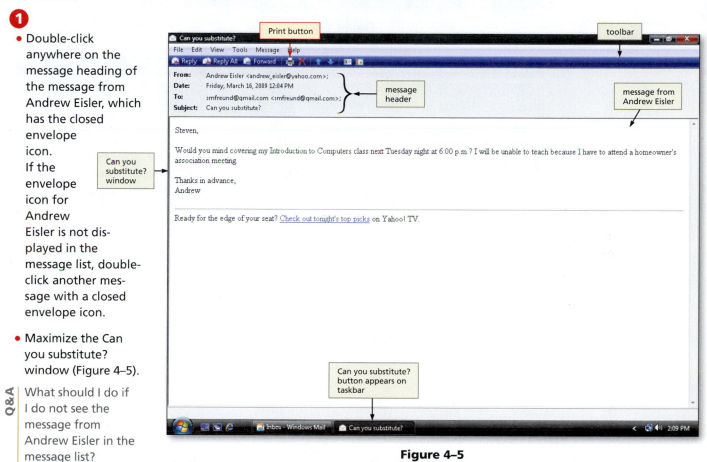

Figure 4–5

Other Ways

1. Right-click message heading with a closed envelope icon, click Open on shortcut menu
2. Click message heading with a closed envelope icon, on File menu click Open
3. Select message heading, press CTRL+O

Reading E-Mail Messages
Many people minimize the Inbox - Windows Mail window. When they receive a new e-mail message, an envelope icon is displayed in the status area on the Windows taskbar and a notification sound is played.

The Windows Mail toolbar (Figure 4–6) contains the buttons needed to work with opened e-mail messages (Reply, Reply All, Forward, and so on). Table 4–2 contains the toolbar buttons and a brief explanation of their functions.

Figure 4–6

Table 4–2 Toolbar Buttons and Functions	
Button	**Function**
Reply	Displays a window used to reply to an e-mail message. The e-mail address, original subject of the e-mail message preceded by the Re: entry, and original e-mail message appear in the window.
Reply All	Displays a window used to reply to an e-mail message. The e-mail addresses of all recipients, subject of the e-mail message preceded by the Re: entry, and original e-mail message appear in the window.
Forward	Displays a window used to forward an e-mail message to another recipient. The original subject of the e-mail message preceded by the Fw: entry and the original e-mail message appear in the window.
	Prints the e-mail message in the window.
	Deletes the e-mail message in the window by moving the message to the Deleted Items folder and displays the next e-mail message in the message list.
	Displays the previous e-mail message in the message list.
	Displays the next e-mail message in the message list.
	Displays the Contacts window containing a list of frequently used contacts.
	Displays the Windows Calendar containing a list of your appointments and tasks.

To Print an Opened E-Mail Message

You can print the contents of an e-mail message before or after opening the message. The following steps print an opened e-mail message.

1
• Click the Print button on the toolbar to display the Print dialog box (Figure 4–7).

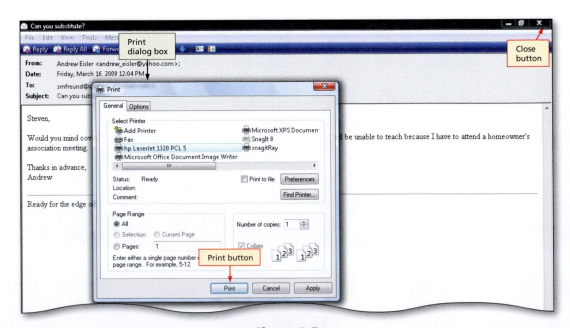

Figure 4–7

2

• Click the Print button
  in the Print dialog box
  (Figure 4–8).

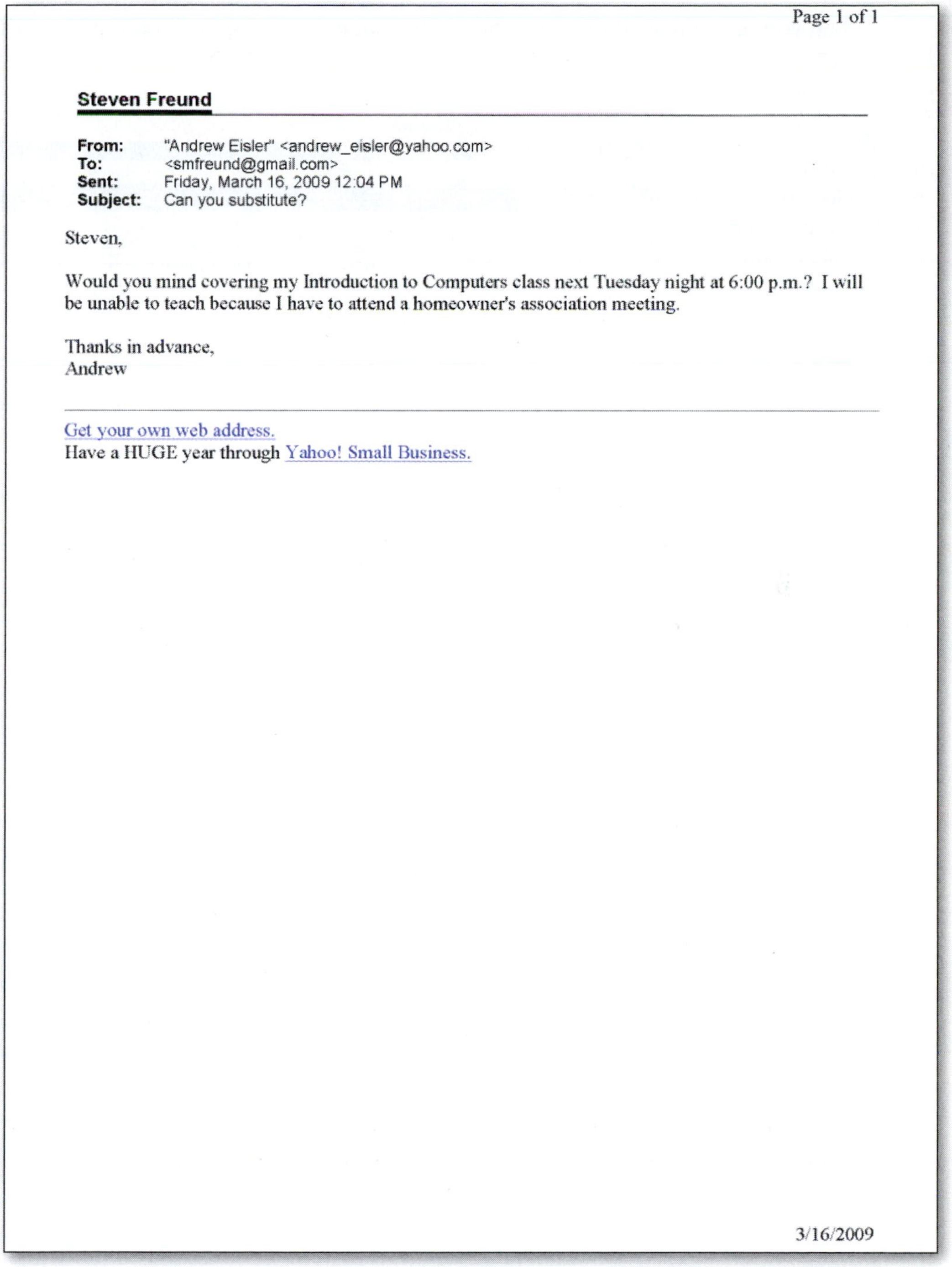

Steven Freund

From:	"Andrew Eisler" <andrew_eisler@yahoo.com>
To:	<smfreund@gmail.com>
Sent:	Friday, March 16, 2009 12:04 PM
Subject:	Can you substitute?

Steven,

Would you mind covering my Introduction to Computers class next Tuesday night at 6:00 p.m.? I will be unable to teach because I have to attend a homeowner's association meeting.

Thanks in advance,
Andrew

Get your own web address.
Have a HUGE year through Yahoo! Small Business.

3/16/2009

Figure 4–8

Other Ways

1. On File menu click Print, click Print button in Print dialog box

2. Press ALT+F, press P, press ENTER

3. Press CTRL+P, press ENTER

To Close an E-Mail Message

When you have finished opening and reading an e-mail message, you can close the window containing the message.

1

• Click the Close button on the title bar to close the window containing the e-mail message (Figure 4–9).

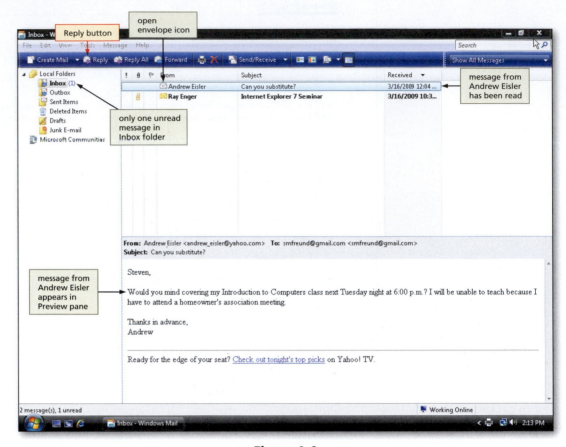

Figure 4–9

Other Ways
1. On File menu click Close   2. Press ALT+F4

To Reply to an E-Mail Message

One method of composing and sending an e-mail reply uses the Reply button, located on the toolbar. The Reply button opens a new message and pre-populates the To: text box with the e-mail address of the sender and the Subject: text box with the subject line of the original message preceded by Re: (regarding). The following steps compose and send an e-mail reply to a sender, in this case, Andrew Eisler, using the Reply button.

1

- Click the Reply button on the toolbar.

- Maximize the Re: Can you substitute? window (Figure 4–10).

Q&A

If I am replying to a message that was sent to multiple recipients, will each recipient see my reply?

No. Your reply only will be sent to the sender of the original message. If you want all recipients to see your reply, you click the Reply All button instead of the Reply button.

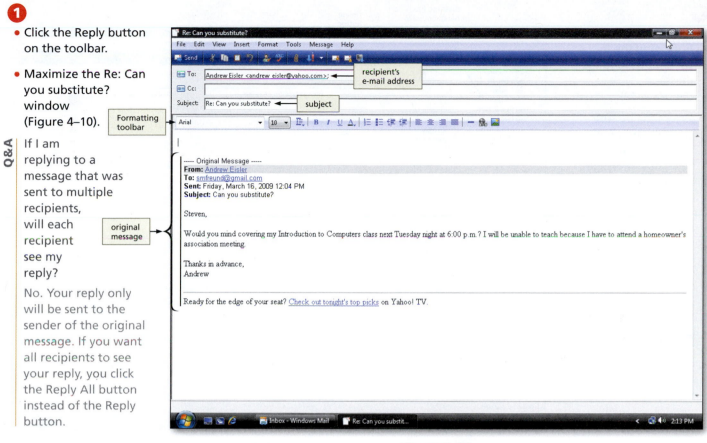

Figure 4–10

2

- Type I will be happy to cover your class. Please let me know what I will have to cover. (Figure 4–11).

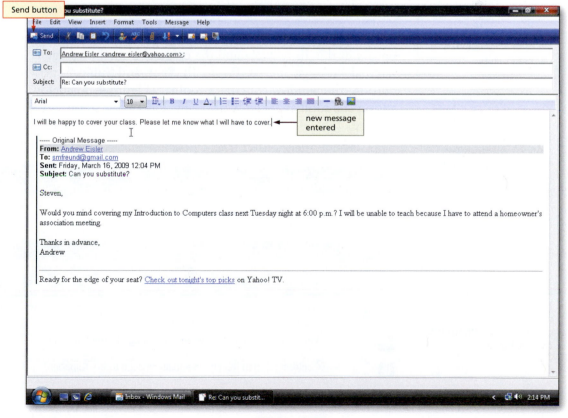

Figure 4–11

3
- Click the Send button on the toolbar to send the message (Figure 4–12).

Q&A

How can I be sure that the intended recipient will receive my e-mail message?

The best way to verify that the recipient has received your e-mail message is to ask him or her for a response. If an e-mail address is incorrect, you often will receive an e-mail stating that your message was unable to be delivered. If this happens, confirm the e-mail address of your recipient and try to send the e-mail message again.

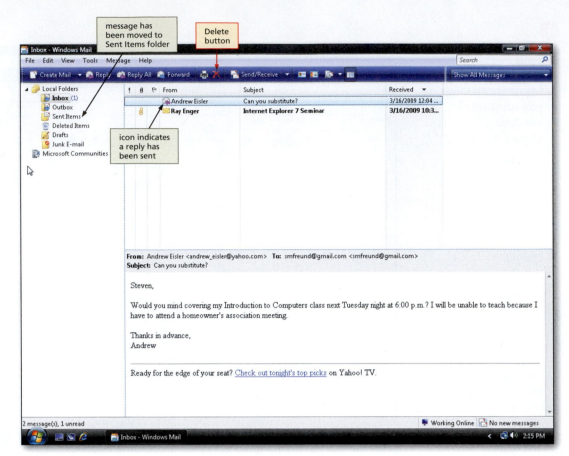

Figure 4–12

Other Ways

1. On Message menu click Reply to Sender
2. Press ALT+M, press R
3. Press CTRL+R

BTW

Replying to an E-Mail Message
Some people who receive reply e-mail messages find it awkward that the original e-mail message appears with the reply message. To remove the original message from all e-mail replies, the person who sends the e-mail replies should click Tools on the menu bar, click Options, click the Send tab, click to deselect the Include message in reply check box, and then click the OK button.

In Figure 4–11 on the previous page, the underlined Andrew Eisler name appears in the To text box and the original e-mail message is identified by the words Original Message and the From, To, Sent, and Subject entries in the message list. In addition, the window contains a toolbar (Figure 4–13) below the menu bar. The buttons on the toolbar (Send, Cut, Copy, Paste, and so on) are useful when replying to a message. Table 4–3 shows the toolbar buttons and their functions.

Figure 4–13

Table 4–3 Toolbar Buttons and Functions

Button	Function
Send	Places the e-mail message in the Outbox folder temporarily, sends the message and then moves the message to the Sent Items folder.
✂	Moves a selected item in an e-mail message to the Clipboard.
📋	Copies a selected item in an e-mail message to the Clipboard.
📋	Pastes an item from the Clipboard to an e-mail message.

Table 4–3 Toolbar Buttons and Functions (continued)

Button	Function
	Undoes the previous operation.
	Checks the recipient's name against the Contacts list.
	Spell checks the e-mail message.
	Attaches a file to the e-mail message.
	Sets the priority (high, normal, or low) of an e-mail message.
	Digitally signs an e-mail message, allowing the recipient to verify the sender's authenticity.
	Encrypts, or scrambles, an e-mail message, preventing someone other than the recipient from reading the message.
	Allows you to read and compose e-mail messages without being connected to the Internet.

To Delete an E-Mail Message

After reading and replying to an e-mail message, you may want to delete the original e-mail message from the Message list. Deleting a message moves it from the Inbox folder to the Deleted Items folder. If you do not delete unwanted messages, large numbers of messages in the Inbox folder make it difficult to find and read new messages; this also wastes disk space. The following step deletes the e-mail message from Andrew Eisler.

1

• If necessary, click the message from Andrew Eisler in the Message list to select it.

• Click the Delete button on the toolbar to delete the message from Andrew Eisler (Figure 4–14).

Q&A

What should I do if I accidentally delete an e-mail message?

If you accidentally delete an e-mail message, the message remains on your computer until you delete it from the Deleted Items folder. To retrieve a message from the Deleted Items folder, click the Deleted Items folder, and then drag the message to the Inbox folder.

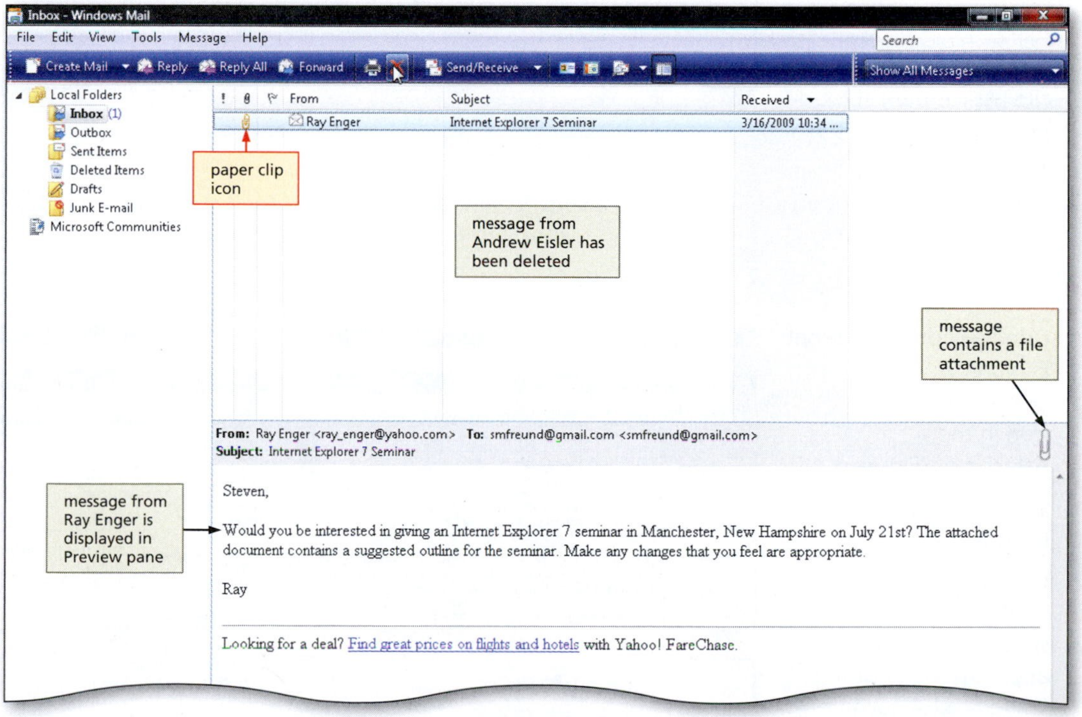

Figure 4–14

Other Ways
1. Drag e-mail message to Deleted Items folder in Folder list
2. On Edit menu click Delete
3. Right-click e-mail message, click Delete on shortcut menu
4. Press ALT+E, press D
5. Press CTRL+D

BTW

Mail Folders
If Windows Mail becomes slow or sluggish, you may be able to improve performance by removing old messages from the Inbox. You can either delete the messages or create a new folder and move messages from the Inbox into your new folder.

As you delete messages from the Inbox, the number of messages in the Deleted Items folder increases. To delete an e-mail message permanently, you should select the Deleted Items folder in the Folders list and then delete the message from that folder. Similarly, as you send and reply to messages, the number of messages in the Sent Items folder increases. To delete an e-mail message from the Sent Items folder, click the Sent Items folder icon in the Folders list, highlight the message in the message list, and then click the Delete button on the toolbar in the Sent Items - Windows Mail window.

To Open a File Attachment

The remaining message in the message list, from Ray Enger, contains a file attachment, as indicated by the paper clip icon displayed in the column below the second header. The following steps open the file attachment.

1

- Double-click the row containing the paper clip icon to the left of the Ray Enger name in the Message list.

- Maximize the Internet Explorer 7 Seminar window (Figure 4–15).

Q&A
Is it okay to open a file attachment if I do not know who has sent it to me?

You should never open a file attachment sent from an unknown source. It is usually best to only open file attachments when you are expecting them from a trusted source.

Figure 4–15

2

- Double-click the Internet Explorer 7 Outline.txt icon in the Attach box (Figure 4–16).

Q&A
What types of files can be attached to an e-mail?

File attachments can be anything from spreadsheets to pictures to application programs. If the Mail Attachment dialog box appears when you attempt to open an attachment, you can open the attachment by clicking the Open button.

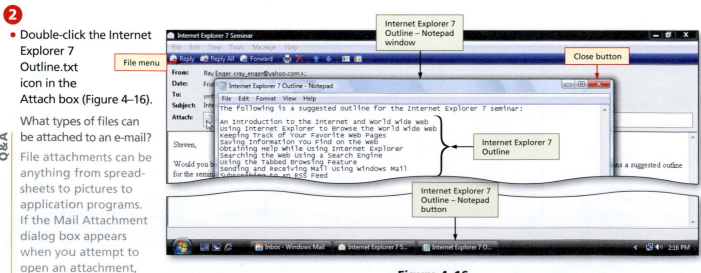

Figure 4–16

To Save and Close a File Attachment

After scanning the attachment in Notepad, you decide to save it to your computer to read at a later time. The following steps save and close the file attachment.

1 To display the Save As dialog box, click File on the menu bar and then click Save As.

2 If necessary, click the Browse Folders button and then click the Documents link to save the file to the Documents folder.

3 Click the Save button.

Q&A If I make changes to a file attachment before saving it, will the file attached to the original e-mail also change?

No. If you open the e-mail containing the attachment again, you will not see any of your changes. However, if you open the file that was saved to your computer, your changes will display.

4 Click the Close button in the Internet Explorer 7 Outline - Notepad window.

5 Click the Close button in the Internet Explorer 7 Seminar window.

Composing a New Mail Message

In addition to opening and reading, replying to, and deleting e-mail messages, you also need to compose and send new e-mail messages. When composing an e-mail message, you enter a brief one-line subject that identifies the purpose or contents of the message in the subject line, and type your text in the message area. You must know the e-mail address of the message recipient before you can send it.

You also can format e-mail messages to enhance their appearance. **Formatting** is the process of altering how a document looks by modifying the style, size, or color of its text, or by changing its background. One method of formatting an e-mail message is to select stationery. Using stationery allows you to add a colorful background image, unique text sizes and colors, and custom margins to an e-mail message. For example, the Shades of Blue stationery causes a decorative blue background and the text of the e-mail message to appear using the Arial 10-point font and black text. The Arial font is one of many fonts, or typefaces, available to format an e-mail message. In addition, any links within the e-mail message will be underlined and displayed in blue text. It is important to note that in a business environment, it may be inappropriate to apply stationery to e-mail messages. In most cases, work-related e-mail uses the default background and text colors (black text on a white background). If you are sending a personal or informal e-mail message, selecting a stationery may be more appropriate.

To Compose an E-Mail Message Using Stationery

The next steps compose an e-mail message to one of the authors (Steven Freund) of this book using the Shades of Blue stationery.

1

- Click the Create Mail button arrow on the toolbar to display the Create Mail menu (Figure 4–17).

Q&A

What are the three commands at the bottom of the Create Mail menu?

The three commands at the bottom of the menu allow you to select from a larger list of stationeries, choose not to use stationery, or send a Web page as an e-mail message.

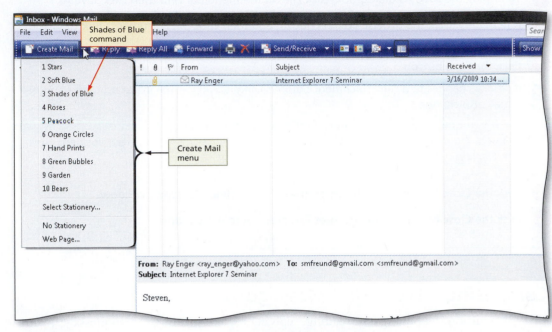

Figure 4–17

2

- Click Shades of Blue on the Create Mail menu to display the New Message window and apply the Shades of Blue stationery to the new message.

- Maximize the New Message window (Figure 4–18).

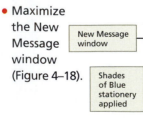

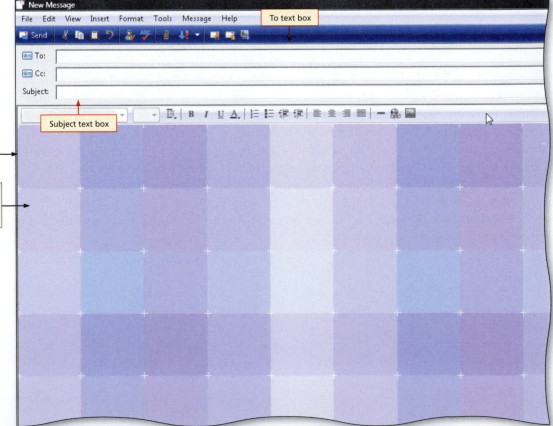

Figure 4–18

3

- Type smfreund@gmail.com in the To text box.

- Click the Subject text box.

- Type Internet Explorer 7 Seminar in the Subject text box (Figure 4–19).

Q&A

What should I use as a subject for e-mails that I send?

You should choose an e-mail subject that briefly describes the contents of the e-mail message. It is not good practice to leave the Subject blank, as some spam filters will mark your e-mail message as spam and it will not reach your intended recipient.

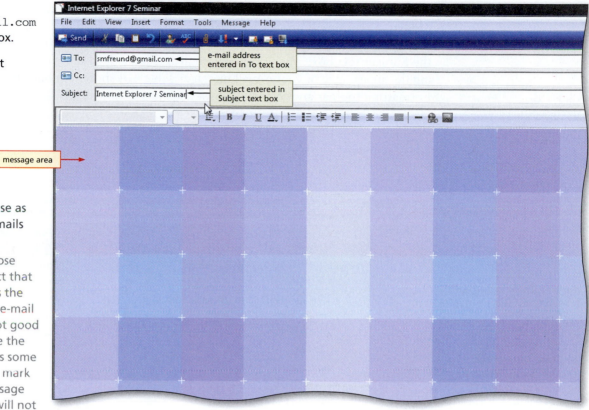

Figure 4–19

4

- Press the TAB key on the keyboard to move the insertion point into the message area of the Internet Explorer 7 Seminar window.

- Type Internet Explorer 7 Seminar and then press the ENTER key twice.

- Type There will be an Internet Explorer 7 Seminar in Manchester, NH on July 21st. Would you like to attend? Please see the attached file for more details. in the message area and then press the ENTER key twice.

- Type your name and then press the ENTER key (Figure 4–20).

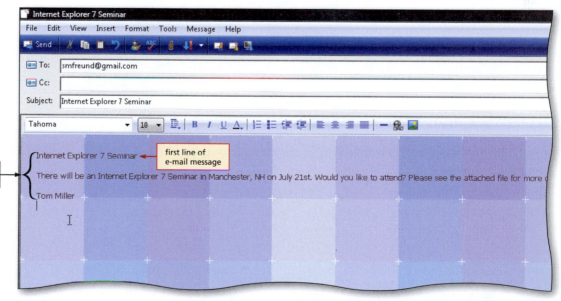

Figure 4–20

Formatting an E-Mail Message

The Internet Explorer 7 Seminar message window contains two toolbars. The toolbar containing buttons specific to replying to an e-mail or composing a new e-mail message is displayed below the menu bar. The Formatting toolbar is displayed below the Subject text box. The Formatting toolbar (Figure 4–21) contains options for changing the appearance of your e-mail message. Table 4–4 shows the buttons and boxes on the Formatting toolbar and their functions.

> **BTW**
> **Font Size**
> You change the size of text by selecting a font size. A **font size** is measured in **points**. One inch contains 72 points. Thus, a font size of 36 points is approximately one-half inch in height when printed.

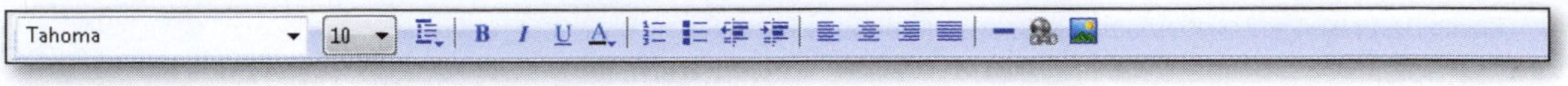

Figure 4–21

Table 4–4 Formatting Toolbar Buttons / Boxes and Functions

Button/Box	Function	Button/Box	Function
Tahoma	Changes the font of text in the message.		Decreases the indentation of a paragraph.
10	Changes the font size of text in the message.		Increases the indentation of a paragraph.
	Changes the paragraph style in the message.		Aligns text with the left margin.
B	Bolds text in the message.		Centers text between the left and right margins.
I	Italicizes text in the message.		Aligns text with the right margin.
U	Underlines text in the message.		Aligns text with the left and right margins.
A	Changes the color of text in the message.		Adds a horizontal line to the message.
	Creates a numbered list in the message.		Inserts a link in the message.
	Creates a bulleted list in the message.		Inserts a picture in the message.

> **BTW**
> **Adding Emotion to an E-Mail Message**
> One method of communicating emotion in an e-mail message is by using emoticons. Emoticons use the keys on your keyboard to express emotion. For example, the :-) smiley means I am happy / I am smiling, the :-(smiley means I am sad / I am unhappy, the :-D smiley means I am laughing, and the :-O smiley means I am surprised.

To Format an E-Mail Message

The following steps use the Formatting toolbar to center the text, Internet Explorer 7 Seminar, and format it using the 36-point font size.

1

- Select the phrase Internet Explorer 7 Seminar in the first line of the e-mail message by pointing to any word and then triple-click to select the entire phrase (Figure 4–22).

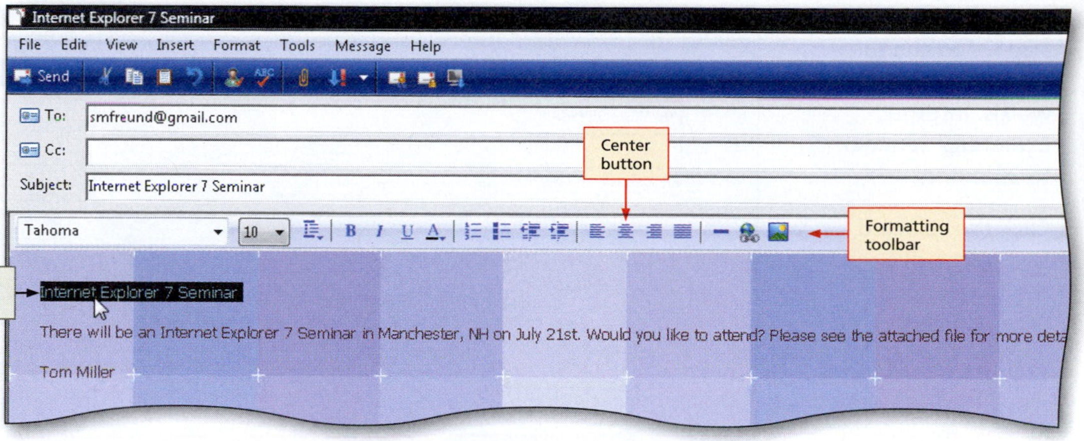

Q&A

I have never heard of triple-clicking. What does it mean to triple-click?

Similar to how double-clicking refers to clicking the mouse twice in rapid succession, triple-clicking refers to clicking the mouse three times in rapid succession.

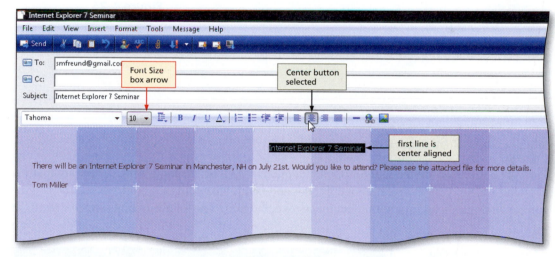

Figure 4–22

2

- Click the Center button on the Formatting toolbar to center the selected words, Internet Explorer 7 Seminar (Figure 4–23).

Figure 4–23

3

- Click the Font Size box arrow to display a list of available font sizes (Figure 4–24).

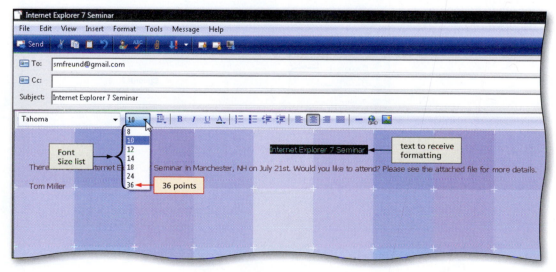

Figure 4–24

- Click 36 in the Font Size list to change the font size of the words, Internet Explorer 7 Seminar, to 36 points.

- Click the selected text to remove the highlight (Figure 4–25).

Q&A

Will the recipient of this e-mail message be able to view the formatting?

Many e-mail programs are capable of displaying e-mails formatted with various fonts, styles, and backgrounds. If this e-mail message is read with an e-mail program that does not support this formatting, the text of the e-mail message will be formatted as plain text.

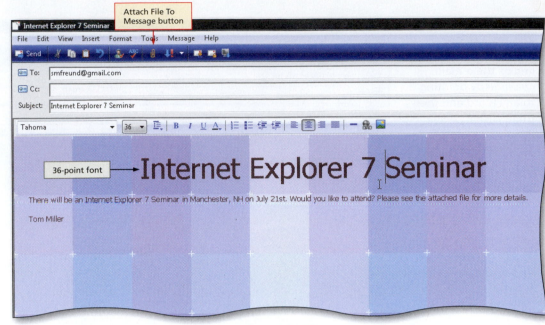

Figure 4–25

To Attach a File to an E-Mail Message

You may find it necessary to supplement your e-mail by attaching a file. There are many reasons why you might want to attach a file to your e-mail message: friends and family share pictures, students submit assignments to their instructors, and professionals send important documents to colleagues. The following steps attach a file to an e-mail message.

- Click the Attach File To Message button on the toolbar to display the Open dialog box (Figure 4–26).

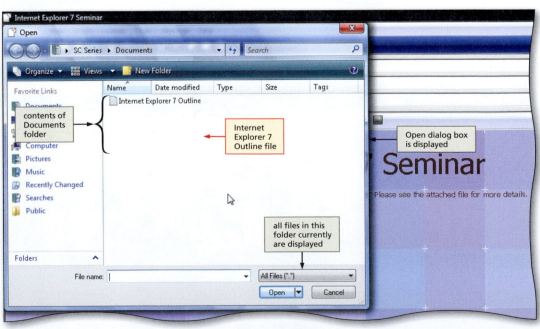

Figure 4–26

2

- Click the Internet Explorer 7 Outline file in the Open dialog box to select it (Figure 4–27). If the Internet Explorer 7 Outline file does not display, navigate to the folder containing the file.

Q&A

What types of files can I attach to my e-mail messages?

You can attach just about any type of file to an e-mail message, but you should make sure that the attachment is not too large in size. If you attach a large file, it may take the recipient a long time to download the attachment, or the recipient's e-mail program may reject the message.

Figure 4–27

3

- Click the Open button to attach the Internet Explorer 7 Outline file to the e-mail message (Figure 4–28).

Q&A

How do I know that my file has been attached?

After you click the Open button, the name and size of the file should display in the Attach box. If the file does not display, repeat the previous steps to try again.

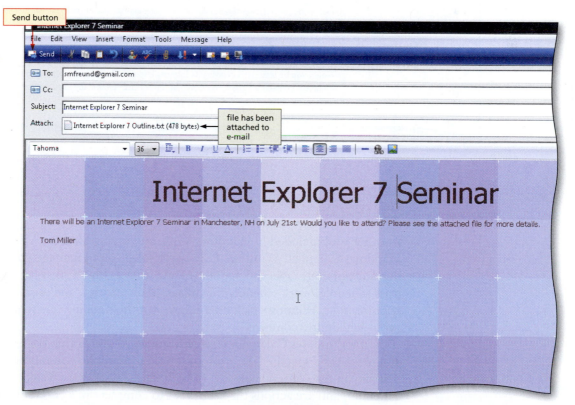

Figure 4–28

BTW

Abbreviations in E-Mail Messages
The use of abbreviations has become popular when composing informal e-mail messages. Examples include: ASAP for As soon as possible, CU for See you later, HTH for Hope this helps, NRN for No reply necessary, PLS for Please, and THX for Thank you.

To Send an E-Mail Message

After composing and formatting an e-mail message, send the message. The following step illustrates how to send an e-mail message.

 Click the Send button on the toolbar below the menu bar to send the e-mail message to Steven Freund. Sending the e-mail closes the Internet Explorer 7 Seminar window, stores the e-mail message in the Outbox folder temporarily while it sends the message, and then moves the message to the Sent Items folder (Figure 4–29).

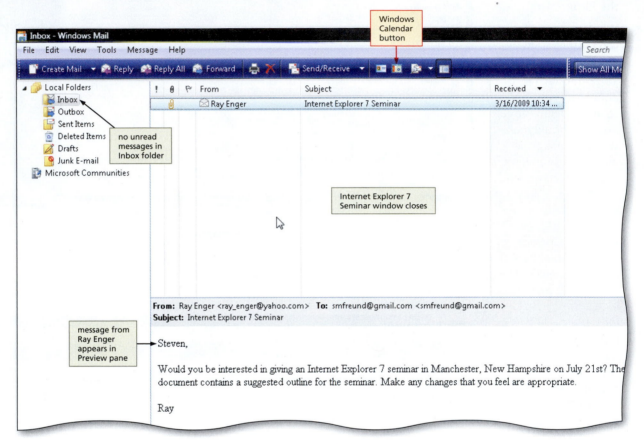

Figure 4–29

Windows Calendar

Another tool included in Windows Vista, and accessible from Windows Mail, is the Windows Calendar. Windows Calendar allows you to manage your schedule by keeping track of your tasks and appointments. In Windows Calendar, you can input your class schedule, work schedule, birthdays, anniversaries, and more. When you schedule an appointment, Windows Calendar blocks out the time in your schedule, helping you to avoid scheduling conflicts.

In Windows Calendar, **appointments** are events that occur at a particular time and place for a specified duration of time, for example, you might have a meeting on Tuesday in the conference room from 10:00 to 11:00 a.m. **Tasks** also are part of Windows Calendar, and are actions that you want to complete in a certain number of days. Tasks have start and end dates like appointments, but do not occur at a specific time.

To Add an Appointment in Windows Calendar

You have agreed to cover the class for Andrew, and you need to make an appointment in your calendar so that you have the time set aside for the class. The following steps open your calendar and add an appointment.

1
- Click the Windows Calendar button to open Windows Calendar.

- If necessary, maximize the Windows Calendar window (Figure 4–30).

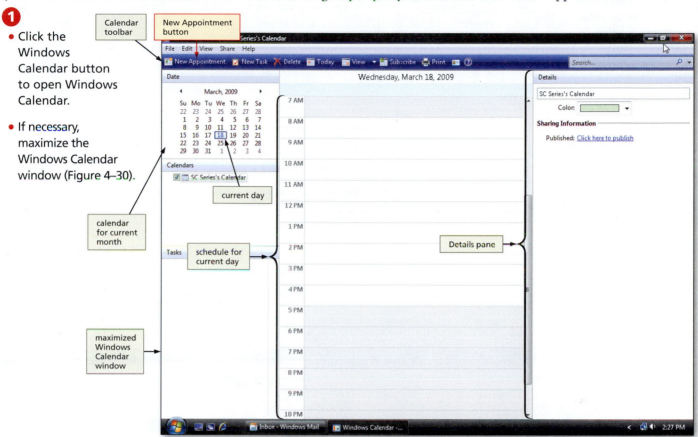

Figure 4–30

2
- Click New Appointment button on the Calendar toolbar to add a new appointment (Figure 4–31).

Q&A

Why did Windows Calendar assign a time to my new appointment ?

By default, Windows Calendar automatically schedules an appointment based on the current time. When you specifiy the details for the appointment, it is easy to change the time.

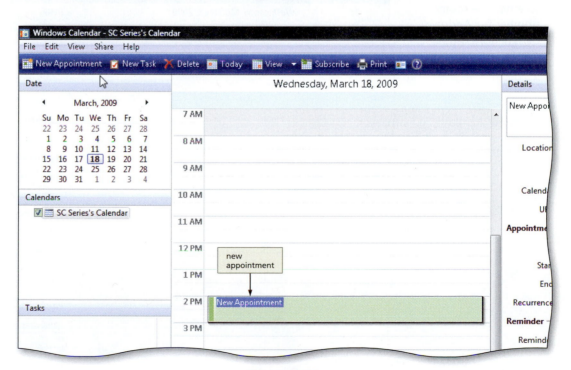

Figure 4–31

3

• Type Cover
Andrew's Class
and then press the
ENTER key to enter
a name for the
appointment
(Figure 4–32).

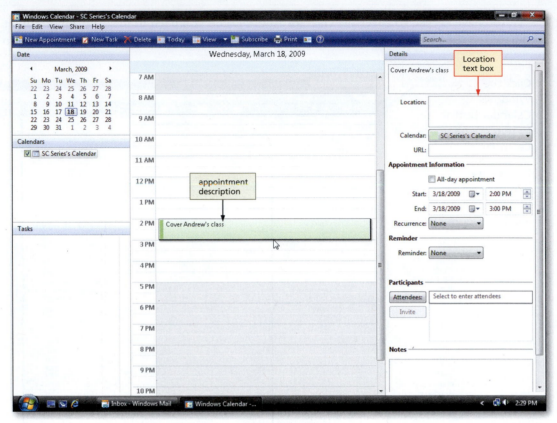

Figure 4–32

4

• In the Details pane,
type 3-301 in the
Location text box
to enter the room
number for Andrew's
class (Figure 4–33).

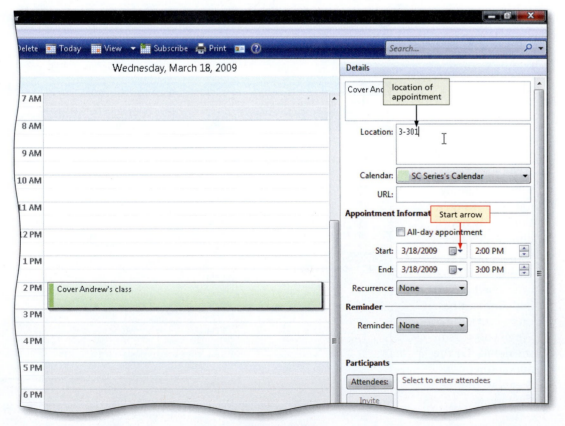

Figure 4–33

5

- Click the Start arrow to display the mini calendar (Figure 4–34). If necessary, use the arrows to display the month of March.

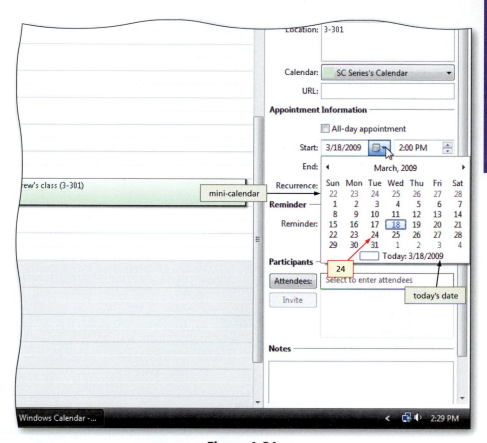

Figure 4–34

6

- Click 24 to select March 24 as the start date for the appointment (Figure 4–35).

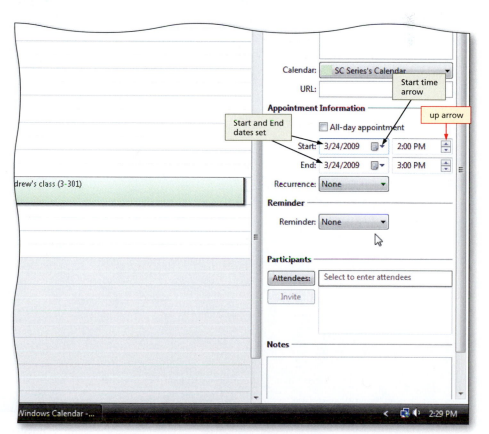

Figure 4–35

7

- Click the Start time hour to select the hour setting.

- Click the up arrow until it changes to 6 to set the hour to 6 (Figure 4–36).

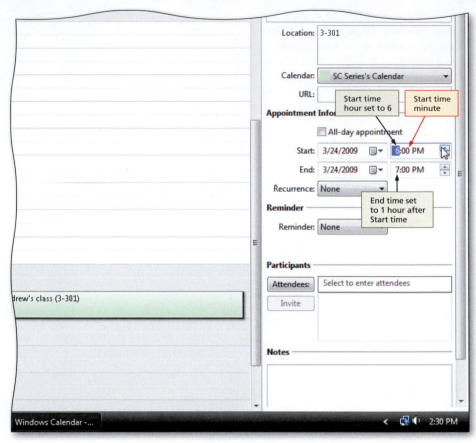

Figure 4–36

8

- If necessary, click the Start time minute to select the minute setting.

- Type 00 to set the minute to 00 (Figure 4–37).

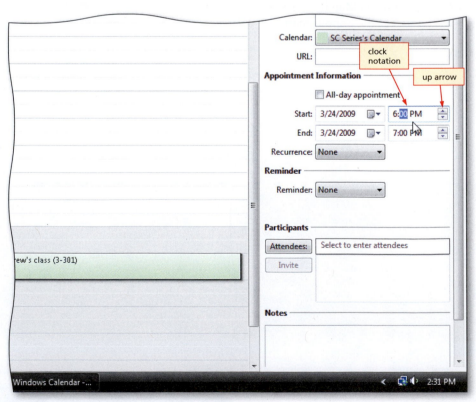

Figure 4–37

9

- If the Start time clock notation shows AM, click the Start time clock notation to select the AM/PM setting.

- Click the up arrow to change the AM to PM (Figure 4–38).

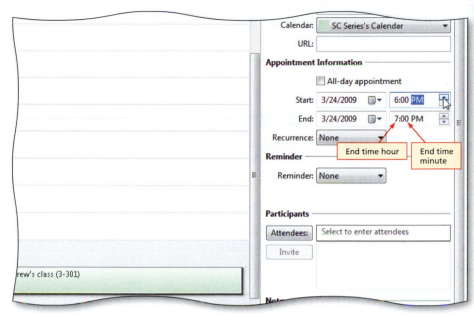

Figure 4–38

10

- Click the End time hour and click the up arrow until it changes to 8 to set the hour to 8.

- If necessary, click the End time minute.

- Type 00 to set the minute setting to 00 (Figure 4–39).

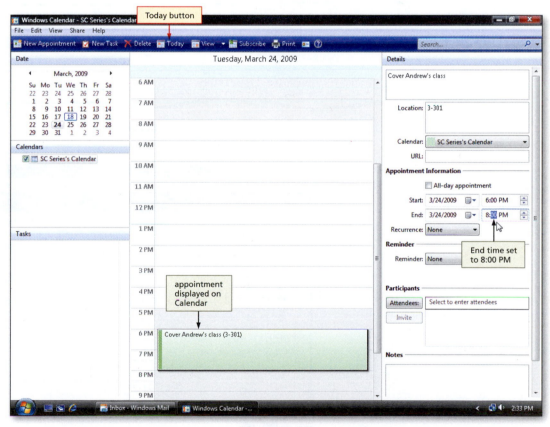

Figure 4–39

Other Ways	
1. Click File, click New Appointment, type Appointment Name, set Start date, set Start time, set End time	2. Press CTRL+N, type appointment name, set Start date, set Start time, set End time

To Add a Task to Windows Calendar

Besides adding an appointment to your calendar indicating that you will be covering Andrew's class on the 24th, you also may want to add a task to remind you to prepare for the class. Because this task begins today, you will leave the start date as today. For the end date, you will set it to the day you teach the class. The following steps add a task to Windows Calendar.

1

- Click the Today button on the Windows Calendar toolbar to switch the calendar back to today (Figure 4–40).

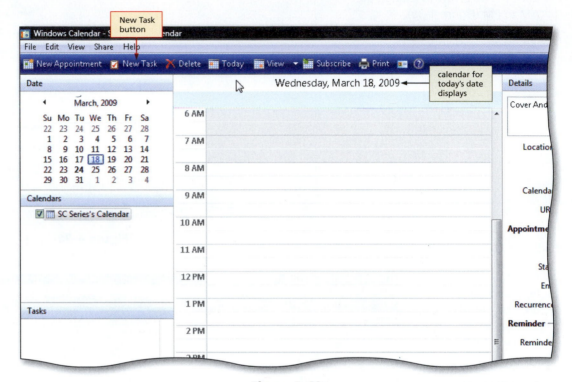

Figure 4–40

2

- Click the New Task button on the Windows Calendar toolbar to add a new task (Figure 4–41).

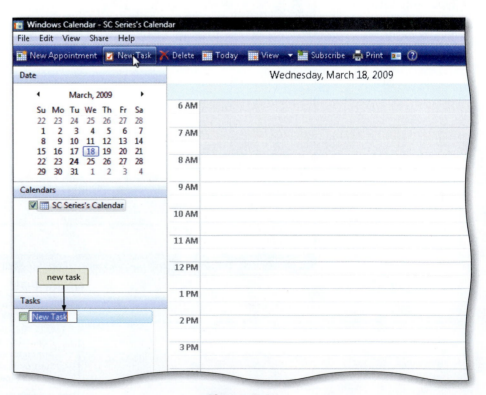

Figure 4–41

3

• Type `Prepare for Andrew's class` and press the ENTER key to enter a name for the task (Figure 4–42).

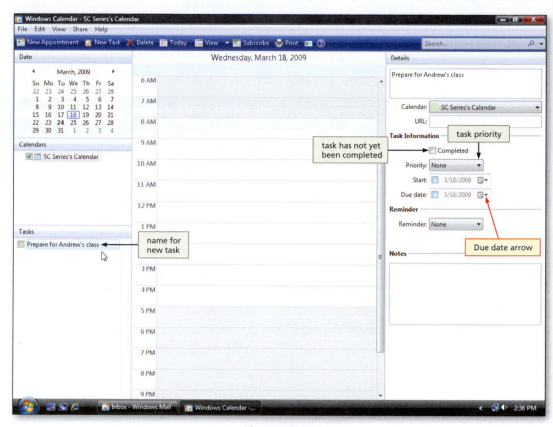

Figure 4–42

4

• Click the Due date arrow to display the calendar.

• Click March 24 to select March 24 as the end date (Figure 4–43).

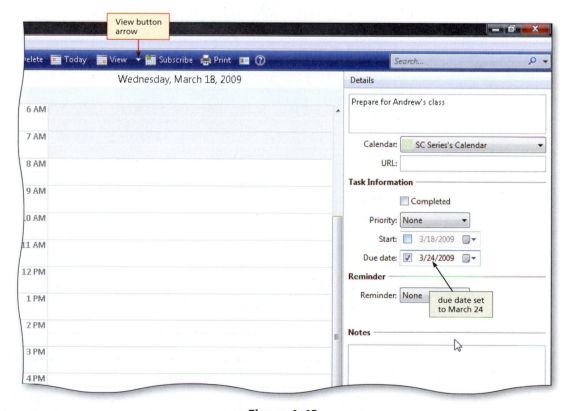

Figure 4–43

To Change the Calendar View

Now that you have added a task and an appointment, you would like to switch your view to Month view to look at your appointments for the next month and verify that you have entered the new appointment correctly. The following steps change the calendar view to Month view.

- Click the View button arrow to display the list of views (Figure 4–44).

🔍 **Experiment**

- There is more than one way to view your calendar. Click the View button to switch to the different views and see what they look like.

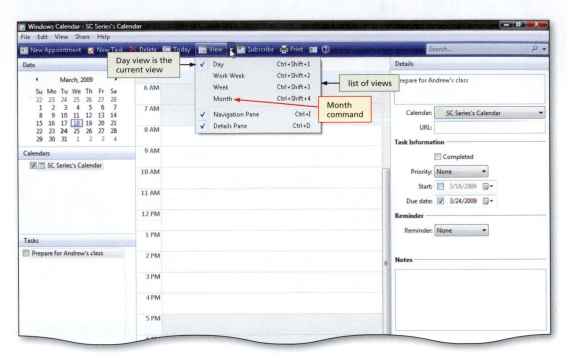

Figure 4–44

- Click the Month command to change the calendar view to Month view (Figure 4–45).

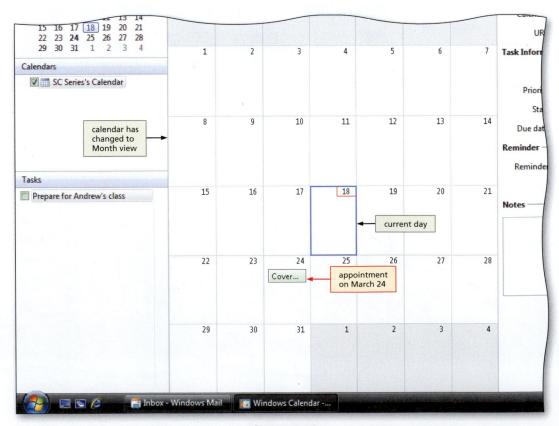

Figure 4–45

3

- Click the appointment on March 24 to display the appointment for covering Andrew's class in the Details pane (Figure 4–46). If March is not the current month on your computer, use the right and left arrow navigation buttons on the calendar to navigate to the month of March.

Q&A

Why does the task have a check box?

Once you complete a task, you can click the check box to add a check mark, which will indicate to you that the task has been completed.

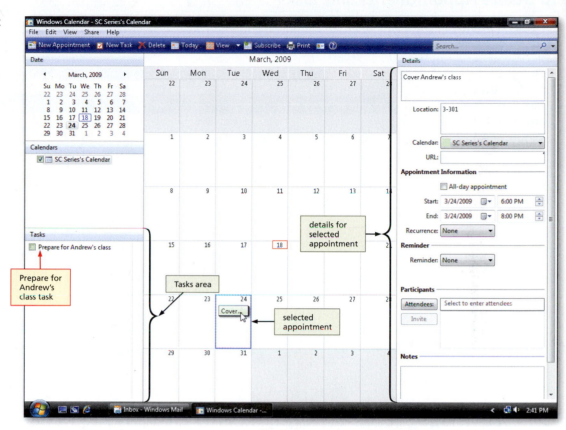

Figure 4–46

Other Ways

1. Click the View button three times, click the appointment

2. Click View on the Menu bar, click Month, click the appointment

3. Press CTRL+SHIFT+4, click the appointment

To Delete Appointments and Tasks

The following steps will delete the appointment and task for covering Andrew's class.

1

• Click the Prepare for Andrew's class task in the Tasks area to select it (Figure 4–47).

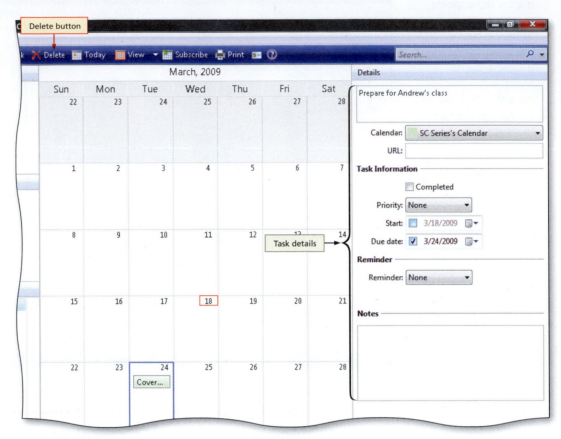

Figure 4–47

2

• Click the Delete button on the Calendar toolbar to delete the task (Figure 4–48).

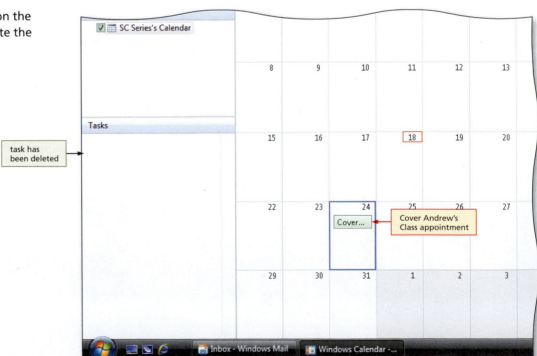

Figure 4–48

3
- Click the Cover Andrew's Class appointment in the Appointments area to select it (Figure 4–49).

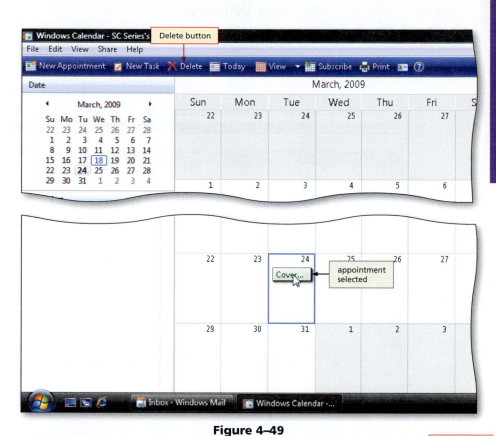

Figure 4–49

4
- Click the Delete button on the Calendar toolbar to delete the appointment (Figure 4–50).

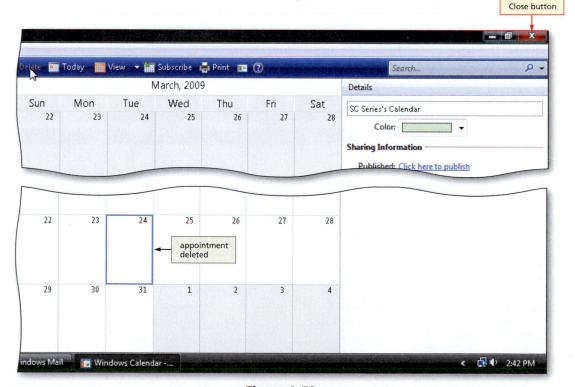

Figure 4–50

Other Ways	
1. Select task or appointment, click Edit menu, click Delete	2. Select task or appointment, press DELETE

To Close Windows Calendar

When you are done using Windows Calendar, you should close it.

1 Click the Close button to close Windows Calendar (Figure 4–51).

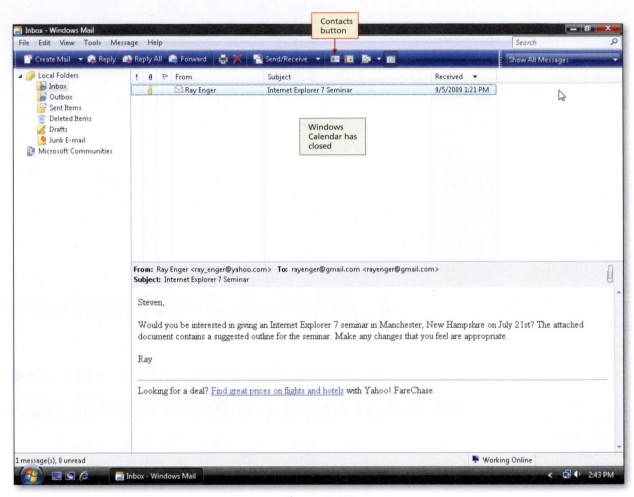

Figure 4–51

Windows Contacts

The Contacts feature included with Windows Vista allows you to store information about your family, friends, colleagues, and others. The information stored in the Contacts folder relating to an individual is referred to as a **contact**, and can include e-mail addresses, home and work addresses, telephone and fax numbers, digital IDs, notes, Web site addresses, and personal information such as birthdays or anniversaries.

Although most contact information is stored in the Contacts folder, Windows Vista also allows you to create additional folders in which to store groups of contacts, making it easy to send an e-mail message to a group of contacts, such as business associates, relatives, or friends, because you do not have to remember or type each person's e-mail address. The contents of the Contacts folder in Windows Vista not only are available to Windows Mail, but also to other applications that allow you to access your contacts.

To Add a Contact to the Contacts Folder

Before you can use the Contacts folder to send an e-mail to an individual, you need to add the contact information to the Contacts folder. The following steps add the contact information (first name, last name, e-mail address, home telephone, and business telephone) for Miriam Winick.

1

- Click the Contacts button on the toolbar in the Inbox - Windows Mail window to open the Contacts window.

- If necessary, maximize the Contacts window (Figure 4–52).

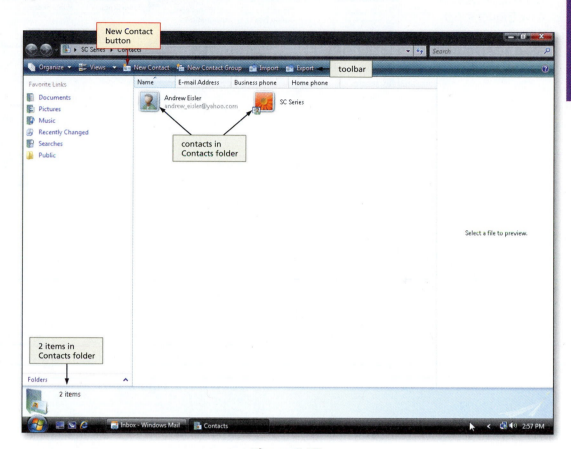

Figure 4–52

2

• Click the New Contact button on the toolbar to display the Properties window (Figure 4–53).

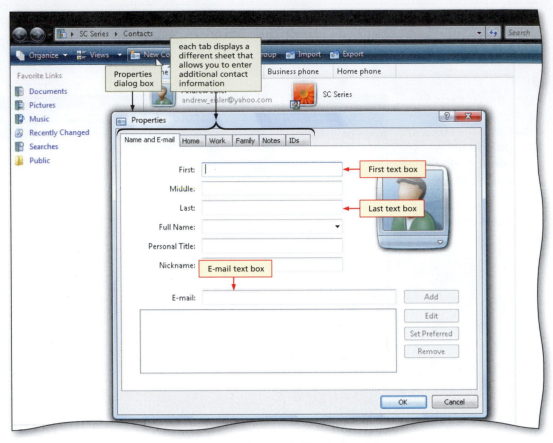

Figure 4–53

3

• Type `Miriam` in the First text box.

• Click the Last text box and then type `Winick` in the text box.

• Click the E-mail text box and then type `miriam_winick@hotmail.com` in the text box (Figure 4–54).

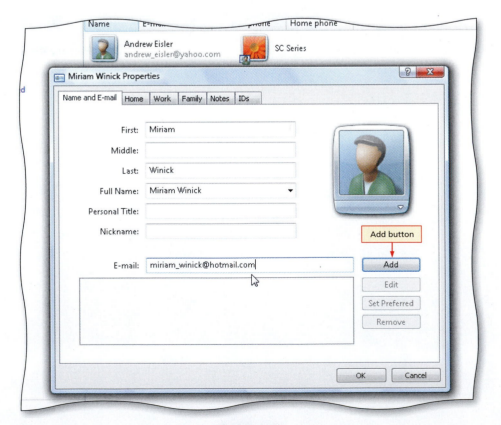

Figure 4–54

4

- Click the Add button in the Name and E-mail sheet to display the E-mail address in the E-mail list box (Figure 4–55).

Why do I have to click the Add button instead of just leaving the e-mail address in the E-mail text box?

Windows Vista can store multiple e-mail addresses for a single contact. The Add button allows you to add the e-mail address in the E-mail text box to the E-mail list box, and clear the E-mail text box so you can add another e-mail address.

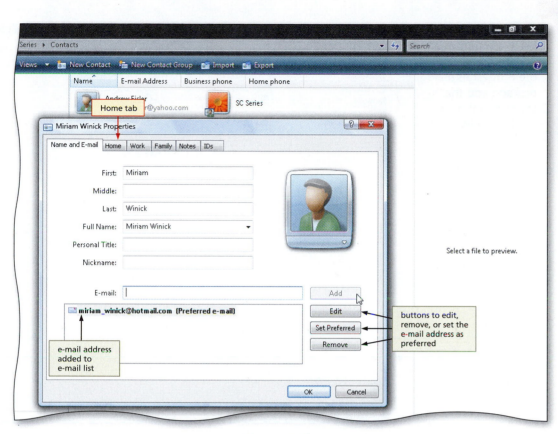

Figure 4–55

5

- Click the Home tab in the Properties dialog box.

- Type 17325 Winding Lane in the Street text box.

- Click the City text box and then type Brea as the name of the city.

- Click the State/Province text box and then type CA as the name of the state.

- Click the Postal Code text box and then type 92821 as the postal code.

- Click the Phone text box and then type (714) 555–3292 as the telephone number (Figure 4–56).

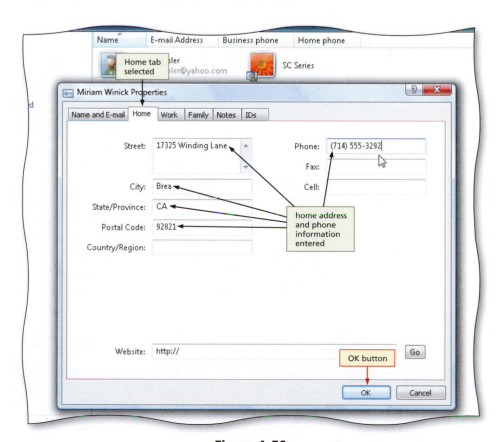

Figure 4–56

6

- Click the OK button in the Properties dialog box to close the Properties dialog box and add the contact to the Contacts folder (Figure 4–57).

- Close the Contacts window.

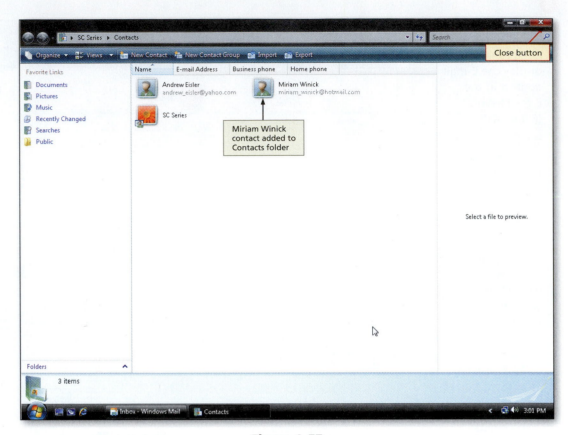

Figure 4–57

When you add a contact in Windows Vista, the Properties dialog box contains a series of tabs. Each tab allows you to store different types of information about the contact. If you are entering information for a business contact, you can enter business-related information on the Work tab. Clicking the Work tab shown in Figure 4–56 on the previous page allows you not only to enter the company's name and business address (street address, city, state/province, postal code, and country/region), but also business information (such as job title, department, and office), phone numbers (telephone, fax, and pager), and the URL of the company's Web page. By using the Family tab, you can enter personal information about your contact, such as spouse or partner's name, children's names and gender, and birthday and anniversary dates. Clicking the Notes tab allows you to enter notes about the contact. Clicking the IDs tab allows you to view the Digital IDs of a selected e-mail address. A **Digital ID** allows you to encrypt messages sent over the Internet and to prove your identity in an electronic transaction on the Internet in a manner similar to showing your driver's license when you cash a check.

To Compose an E-Mail Message Using the Contacts Folder

When you compose an e-mail message, you must know the e-mail address of the recipient of the message. Previously, you addressed an e-mail message by typing the e-mail address in the To text box in the New Message window. Now you use the Contacts folder to enter an e-mail address. The following steps compose an e-mail message to Miriam Winick using her e-mail address in the Contacts folder.

1

- Click the Create Mail button to display the New Message window.

- Maximize the New Message window (Figure 4–58).

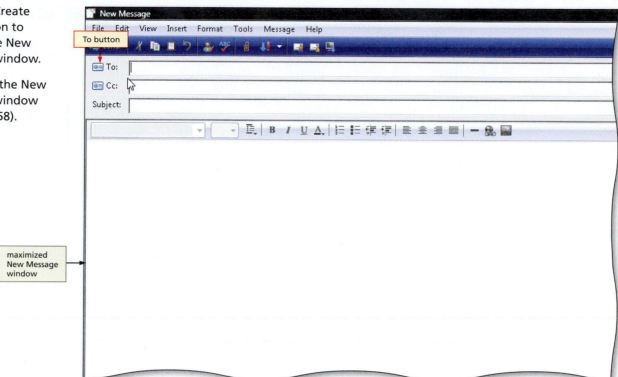

Figure 4–58

2

- Click the To button in the New Message window to display the Select Recipients dialog box.

- Click the Miriam Winick entry in the list box to select it (Figure 4–59).

Q&A

What is the difference between the Cc: field and the Bcc: field?

The names and e-mail addresses of recipients listed in the Cc: field will be visible to all recipients. However, the names and e-mail addresses of recipients listed in the Bcc: field will be hidden from all recipients.

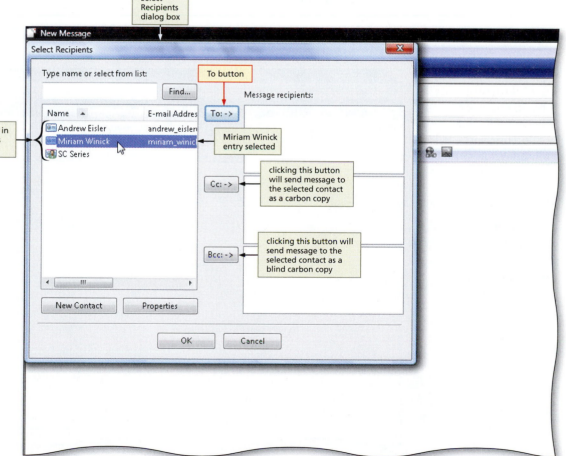

Figure 4–59

3

• Click the To button in the Select Recipients dialog box to add Miriam Winick to the Message recipients list (Figure 4–60).

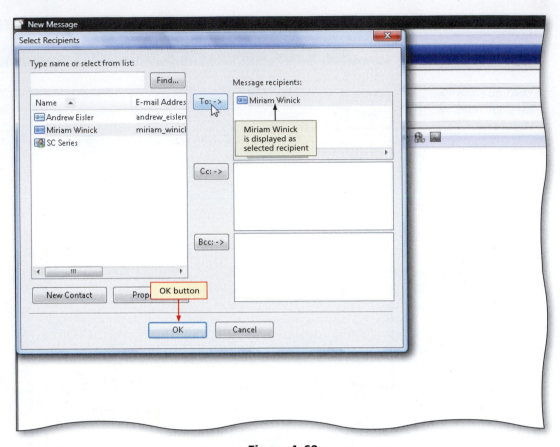

Figure 4–60

4

• Click the OK button in the Select Recipients dialog box to close the Select Recipients dialog box and add Miriam Winick's name and e-mail address to the To text box in the New Message window.

• Click the Subject text box and then type `Contacts Folder` in the text box (Figure 4–61).

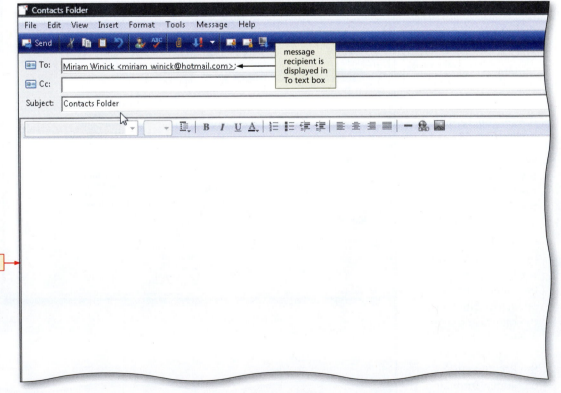

Figure 4–61

5

- Press the TAB key to move the insertion point to the message area.

- Type Great News! and then press the ENTER key twice.

- Type I have learned to enter an e-mail address using the Contacts folder. and then press the ENTER key twice.

- Type your name and then press the ENTER key.

- Select the words, Great News!, in the message area, click the Center button on the Formatting toolbar to center the text, click the Font size box arrow, and then click 36 in the Font Size list to increase the font size to 36 points.

- Click the selected text to remove the highlight (Figure 4–62).

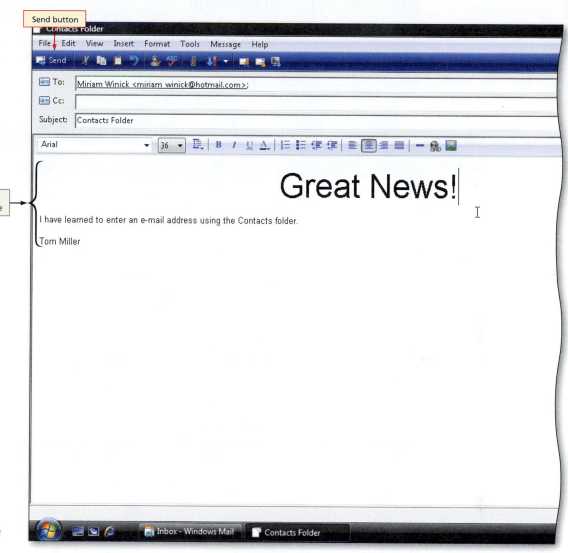

Figure 4–62

To Send an E-Mail Message

The following step sends the e-mail message.

1 Click the Send button on the toolbar to send the message (Figure 4–63).

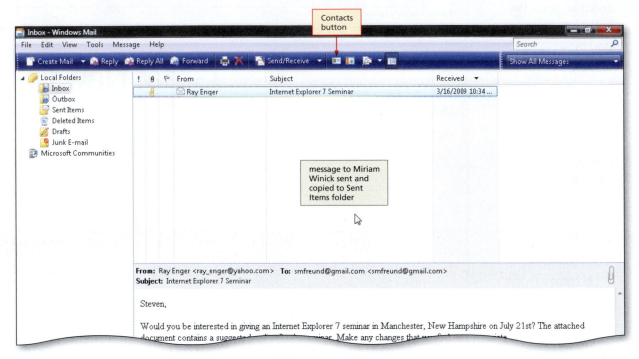

Figure 4–63

To Delete a Contact from the Contacts Folder

Occasionally, you will want to remove a contact from the Contacts folder. The following steps remove the Miriam Winick contact from the Contacts folder.

1

• Click the Contacts button on the toolbar to display the Contacts window.

• If necessary, maximize the Contacts window.

• Click the Miriam Winick entry in the Contacts folder (Figure 4–64).

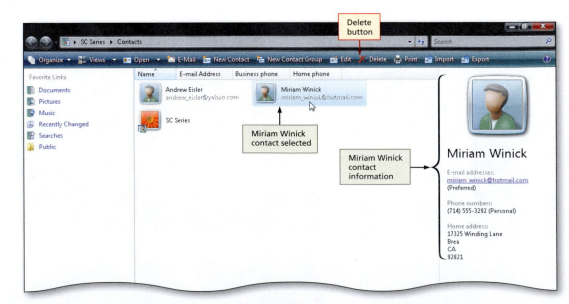

Figure 4–64

2

- Click the Delete button on the toolbar to display the Delete File dialog box (Figure 4–65).

Q&A

Why is the dialog box called the Delete File dialog box when I am deleting a contact?

Each contact in Windows Vista is stored as a file. When you delete a contact, you are moving the associated file to the Recycle Bin.

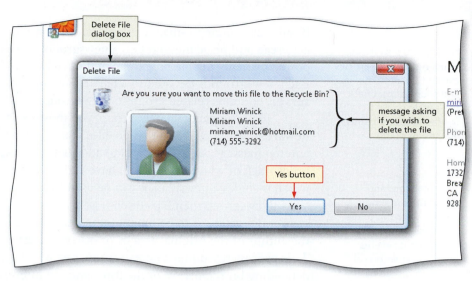

Figure 4–65

3

- Click the Yes button in the Delete File dialog box to delete the Miriam Winick contact (Figure 4–66).

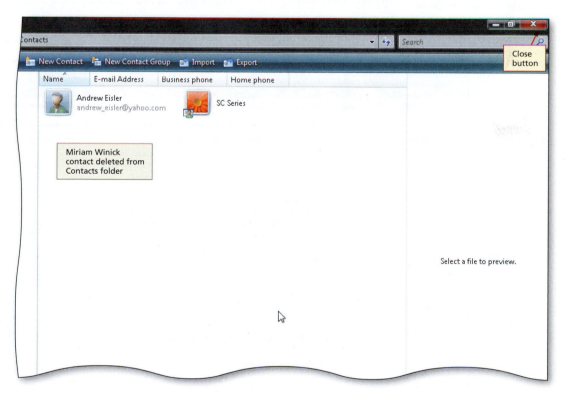

Figure 4–66

To Close the Contacts Window

The following step closes the Contacts window.

1 Close the Contacts window.

Other Ways

1. Click contact entry, on File menu click Delete, click Yes button

2. Right-click contact entry, click Delete on shortcut menu, click Yes button

Internet Newsgroups

BTW

Newsgroup Articles
Many newsgroup articles contain pictures, movies, and sound clips. Check the article name for the words, pictures, movies, or audio.

BTW

Local Newsgroups
Some colleges and universities maintain a local newsgroup to disseminate information about school events and answer technical questions asked by students. To locate your local newsgroup, search for the school's name in the list of newsgroup names.

Besides exchanging e-mail messages, another method of communicating over the Internet is to read and place messages on a newsgroup. A **newsgroup** is a collection of messages posted by many people on a topic of mutual interest that you can access via the Internet. Each newsgroup is devoted to a particular topic. A special computer, called a **news server**, contains related groups of newsgroups.

To participate in a newsgroup, you must use a program called a newsreader. The **newsreader** is a program that enables you to access a newsgroup to read a previously entered message, or **article**, and to add a new message, called **posting**. A newsreader also keeps track of which articles you have and have not read. In this chapter, Windows Mail, which includes a newsreader, will be used to read newsgroup articles.

Newsgroup members often post articles in reply to previous postings — either to answer questions or to comment on material in the original. These replies often prompt the author of the original article, or other interested members, to post additional articles. This process resembles a conversation, one which can be short-lived or go on indefinitely, depending on the nature of the topic and the interest of the participants. The original article and all subsequent related replies are called a **thread**, or **threaded discussion**. Figure 4–67 shows some articles and threads from a newsgroup called microsoft.public. windows.vista.mail.

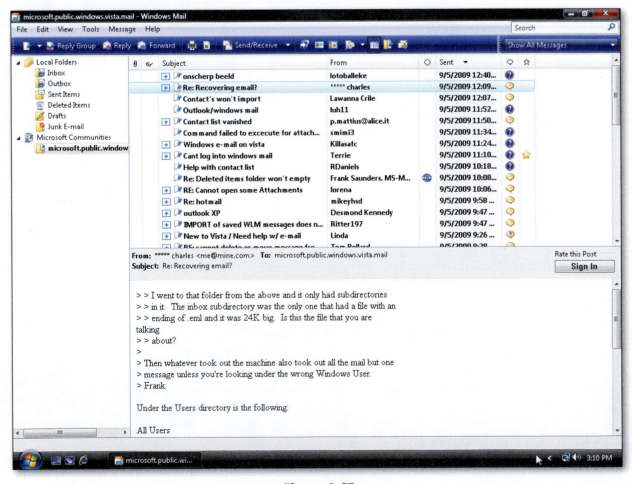

Figure 4–67

Newsgroups exist to discuss products, such as those from Microsoft and IBM; subjects such as recipes, gardening, and music; and just about any other topic you can imagine. A newsgroup name consists of a prefix and one or more subgroup names. For example, the comp.software newsgroup name consists of a prefix (comp), which indicates that the subject of the newsgroup is computers, a period (.), and a subgroup name (software), which indicates that the subject is further narrowed down to a discussion of software. A list of some prefix names and their descriptions is shown in Table 4–5.

Table 4–5 Prefix Names and Descriptions

Prefix	Description
alt	Groups on alternative topics
biz	Business topics
comp	Computer topics
gnu	GNU Software Foundation topics
ieee	Electrical engineering topics
info	Information about various topics
misc	Miscellaneous topics
news	Groups pertaining to newsgroups
rec	Recreational topics
sci	Science topics
talk	Various conversation groups

The newsgroup prefixes found in Table 4–5 are not the only ones used. Innovative newsgroups are being created every day. Some colleges and universities have their own newsgroups on topics such as administrative information, tutoring, campus organizations, and distance learning. A large corporation like Microsoft warrants its own prefix, microsoft.

In addition, some newsgroups are supervised by a **moderator**, who reads each article before it is posted to the newsgroup. If the moderator thinks an article is appropriate for the newsgroup, then the moderator posts the article for all members to read. If the moderator thinks an article is inappropriate, he or she may decide to delete the article without posting it.

To Subscribe to and Display a Newsgroup on the Microsoft News Server

Before you can access the articles in a newsgroup or post to a newsgroup, you first must establish a news account on your computer. A **news account** allows access to the news server. Several hundred newsgroups are listed in the Newsgroup Subscriptions dialog box. If you find a newsgroup that you particularly like and want to visit on a frequent basis, you should subscribe to it. **Subscribing to a newsgroup** permanently adds the newsgroup name to the Folders list and allows you to return to the newsgroup quickly instead of searching or scrolling to find the newsgroup name each time you wish to visit it. The following steps use Windows Mail to subscribe to and view the articles in the microsoft.public.windows.vista.mail newsgroup.

1
- Click the Microsoft Communities link in the Inbox - Windows Mail window to display the Windows Mail dialog box (Figure 4–68).

Figure 4–68

2
- Click the Show available newsgroups and turn on Communities link to download a list of available newsgroups on the Microsoft news server and display the list in the Newsgroup Subscriptions dialog box (Figure 4–69).

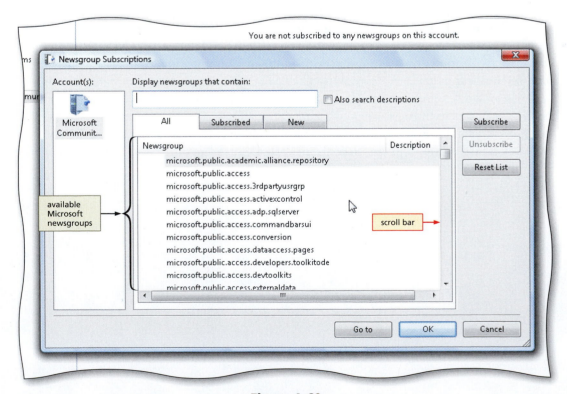

Figure 4–69

3
- Scroll to display the microsoft.public. windows.vista. mail entry in the Newsgroup list (Figure 4–70).

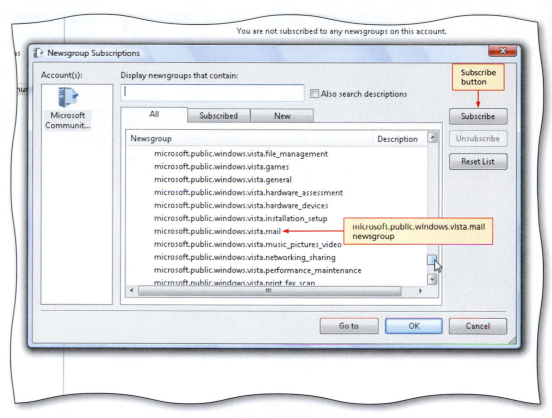

Figure 4–70

4
- Click the microsoft. public.windows. vista.mail entry in the Newsgroup list to select it, and then click the Subscribe button to subscribe to the newsgroup (Figure 4–71).

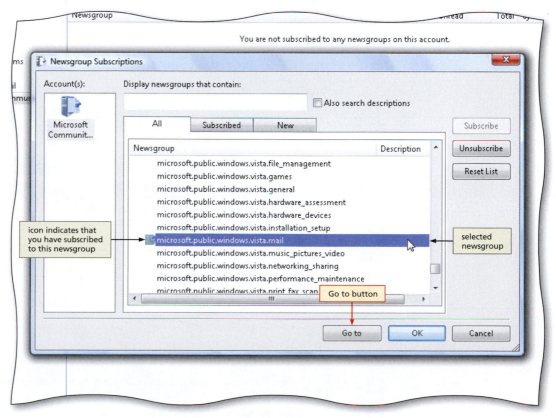

Figure 4–71

5
- Click the Go to button in the Newsgroup Subscriptions dialog box to close the dialog box and display the articles in the microsoft.public. windows.vista.mail newsgroup.

- If a horizontal scroll bar displays at the bottom of the Folder list, if necessary, drag the scroll bar to the left (Figure 4–72).

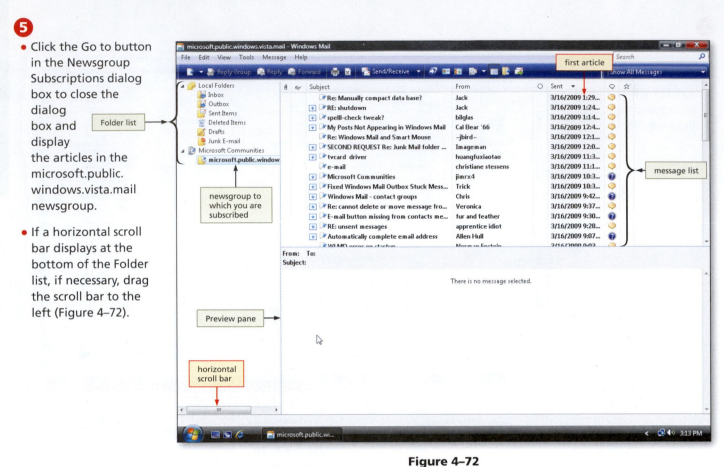

Figure 4–72

Newsgroup Functions

The toolbar below the menu bar shown in Figure 4–72 contains buttons specific to working with news messages (Write Message, Reply Group, Reply, and so on). Table 4–6 provides a brief explanation of the function of each button.

Table 4–6 Toolbar Buttons and Functions	
Button	**Function**
	Displays a window used to post an article to the newsgroup.
Reply Group	Displays a window that allows you to reply to all authors of articles in a newsgroup by e-mail.
	Displays a window that allows you to reply to the author of an article in a newsgroup by e-mail.
	Displays a window that allows you to forward an article in a newsgroup by e-mail.
	Prints the selected article in the message area.
	Stops the transfer of articles from a news server to the message area.
	Displays the Windows Mail dialog box, contacts the news server, and displays new news messages in the message area.
	Displays the Sign in to Microsoft Communities login screen.

Table 4–6 Toolbar Buttons and Functions (continued)

Button	Function
	Displays the Contacts folder containing a list of frequently used contacts.
	Displays the Windows Calendar.
	Displays the Find Message window that allows you to search for an article in the message area based on sender name, recipient name, subject, message, and date.
	Hides/shows the Folder list.
	Displays a dialog box that allows you to select a newsgroup on the current news server.
	Downloads more message headers from the news server.

BTW

Newsgroups
Instructors sometimes use newsgroups in courses taught over the Internet by posting a question and allowing students to respond by posting an article. Students can read the articles in the thread to be aware of all responses and subscribe to the newsgroup to return to it quickly.

To Read a Newsgroup Article

The entries in the Subject column in the message list allow you to review the subjects of a list of articles before deciding which one to read. The following step selects a newsgroup article to read.

1

- Click the first article in the message list to display the article in the Preview pane (Figure 4–73).

Experiment

- Click some of the other articles in the message list to display the contents in the Preview pane. Once you are done, click the first article in the message list.

Q&A

What do the plus signs indicate?

When a plus sign appears to the left of an article in the message list, the article is part of a thread and can be expanded. Expanding the thread displays the replies to the original article indented below the original article and changes the plus sign to a minus sign. After reading the replies within a thread, you may want to collapse the expanded thread. Collapsing the thread hides the replies from the thread, displays the original article in the Preview pane, and changes the minus sign to a plus sign.

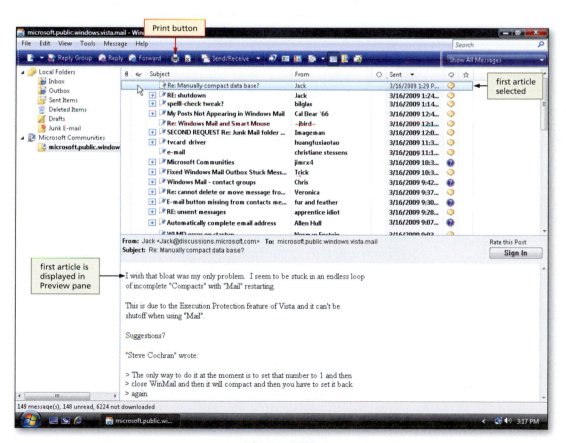

Figure 4–73

Other Ways
1. Press CTRL+< to read previous article   2. Press CTRL+> to read next article

BTW **Watching Conversations**
Windows Mail provides a feature that allows you to find all e-mail messages or newsgroup articles that are part of the same conversation. If you are viewing an e-mail message or newsgroup article and quickly wish to find the other messages in the conversation, select the Watch Conversation command on the Message menu.

To Print a Newsgroup Article

After reading an article, you may want to print it. The method of printing a newsgroup article is identical to how you print an e-mail message, with similar results (see Figure 4–7 on page WIN 234). The following steps print the contents of the first article in the newsgroup.

1. Click the Print button on the toolbar.
2. Click the Print button in the Print dialog box to print the newsgroup article (Figure 4–74).

Page 1 of 1

Steven Freund

From: "Jack" <Jack@discussions.com>
Newsgroups: microsoft.public.windows.vista.mail
Sent: Friday, March 16, 2009 1:29 PM
Subject: Re: Manually compact data base?

I wish that bloat was my only problem. I seem to be stuck in an endless loop of incomplete "Compacts" with "Mail" restarting.

This is due to the Execution Protection feature of Vista and it can't be shutoff when using "Mail".

Suggestions?

"Steve Cochran" wrote:

> The only way to do it at the moment is to set that number to 1 and then
> close WinMail and then it will compact and then you have to set it back
> again.
>
> I don't think compaction is as big an issue as it was in OE, as the messages
> are not in the database files any longer, so there is less bloat.
>
> steve
>
> "Bob" <luna5nospam@scsite.com> wrote in message
> news:utuI7RURHHA.1200@TK2MSFTNGP04.phx.gbl...
> > Is there a way to manually compact the data base in Mail? All I see is the
> > option to change the number of "runs" before it compacts automatically.
> > You could manually do it in OE.
> > Thanks,
> > Bob
>

Figure 4–74

Posting a Newsgroup Article

Once you become familiar with a newsgroup, you may want to post a reply to a newsgroup article. In order to be able to post to a newsgroup, you first need to be subscribed to it. After subscribing to the newsgroup and displaying the list of articles in the message list, click the Write Message button to display the New Message window to compose your newsgroup posting. The New Message window (Figure 4–75) contains menus, buttons, and text boxes that are specific to newsgroup postings. Once you type a subject and text for the posting, click the Send button to post the newsgroup article. Because many people will be able to read your posting, make sure that the posting is free from grammatical and spelling errors. If the newsgroup is moderated, postings may not appear immediately after sending them.

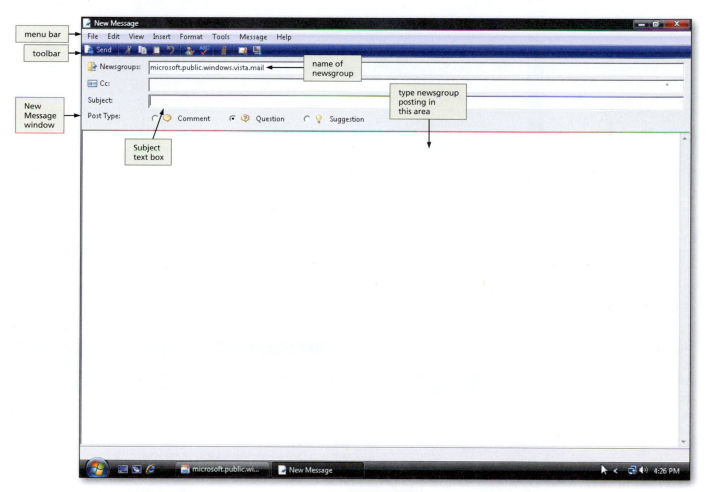

Figure 4–75

The buttons on the toolbar illustrated in Figure 4–75 on the previous page (Send, Cut, Copy, Paste, and so on) are useful when posting a new article. Table 4–7 shows the buttons on the toolbar and their functions.

Table 4–7 Toolbar Buttons and Functions	
Button	**Function**
	Sends the article in the New Message window to a news server.
	Moves a selected item in an article that has not yet been posted to the Clipboard and removes the item from the article.
	Copies a selected item in an article to the Clipboard.
	Pastes an item from the Clipboard to an article.
	Undoes the previous operation.
	Checks the recipient's name against the Contacts folder.
	Spell checks the article.
	Attaches a file to the article.
	Digitally signs an article, allowing the recipient to verify the sender's identity.
	Allows you to work without being connected to a news server (offline).

To Unsubscribe from a Newsgroup

When you no longer need quick access to a newsgroup, you can cancel the subscription to the newsgroup, or unsubscribe, and then remove the newsgroup name from the Folder list. The next steps unsubscribe from the microsoft.public.windows.vista.mail newsgroup.

1

• Right-click the microsoft.public. windows.vista.mail newsgroup name in the Folder list to display the shortcut menu (Figure 4–76).

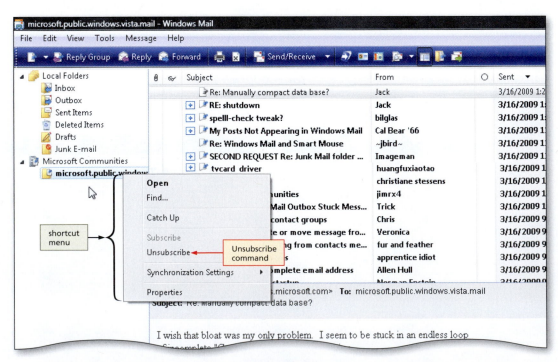

Figure 4–76

2

- Click Unsubscribe on the shortcut menu.

- If the Windows Mail dialog box appears, click the OK button in the dialog box to unsubscribe from the microsoft.public. windows.vista.mail newsgroup.

- If a second Windows Mail dialog box appears asking if you would like to view a list of available newsgroups, click the No button in the dialog box (Figure 4–77).

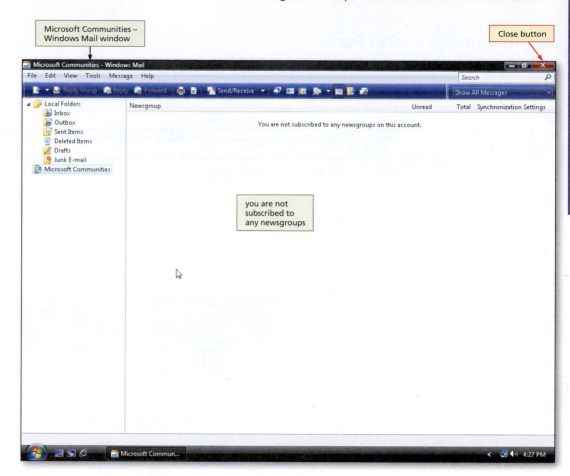

Microsoft Communities – Windows Mail window

Close button

you are not subscribed to any newsgroups

Figure 4–77

To Quit Windows Mail

Now that you have finished working with e-mails and newsgroups, the following step quits Windows Mail.

1 Click the Close button in the Microsoft Communities - Windows Mail window to quit Windows Mail.

Other Ways

1. Select newsgroup name in Newsgroup Subscriptions dialog box, click Unsubscribe button

2. Double-click newsgroup name in Newsgroup Subscriptions dialog box

Using Internet Explorer to Subscribe to RSS Feeds

Other ways of accessing information from the Internet go beyond simply typing a URL into the Address bar of Internet Explorer. One of the newer technologies on the Internet is **Really Simple Syndication (RSS)**. RSS allows Web page authors easily to distribute, or syndicate, Web content. If you frequently visit multiple Web sites that offer RSS feeds, you can subscribe to their RSS feeds, using Internet Explorer, which allows you to quickly review the feed content of all the Web sites in a simple list in your browser window, without having to first navigate to each individual site. For example, the CNN Web site contains two RSS feeds that allows people to view top stories and recent stories in one convenient location. By subscribing to an RSS feed using Internet Explorer, you will be able to access the feed by clicking the Feeds button in the Favorites Center. RSS feeds are typically found on news Web sites, discussion boards, blogs, and other Web sites that frequently update their content.

To Subscribe to an RSS Feed

Before you can view the contents of an RSS feed, you must subscribe to it. The following steps use Internet Explorer to subscribe to an RSS feed on the CNET.com Web site.

1

- Start Internet Explorer.

- Type www. cnet.com in the Address bar and then press the ENTER key to display the CNET.com Web page (Figure 4–78).

Figure 4–78

2

- Click the View feeds on this page button arrow to display a menu containing the available RSS feeds (Figure 4–79).

Figure 4–79

3

• Click the Buzz weekly (new) command on the menu to display the Buzz weekly RSS feed (Figure 4–80).

Figure 4–80

4

• Click the Subscribe to this feed link in the Alpha.CNET.com: Most recent posts - Windows Internet Explorer window to display the Internet Explorer dialog box (Figure 4–81).

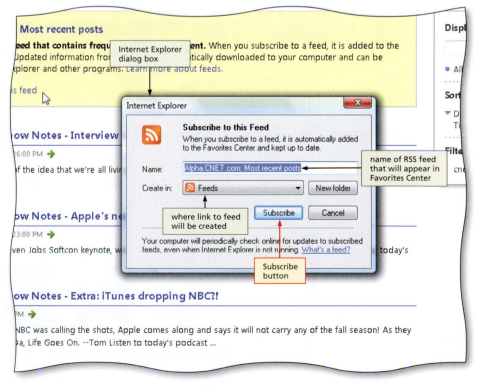

Figure 4–81

5

• Click the Subscribe button in the Internet Explorer dialog box to subscribe to the RSS feed (Figure 4–82).

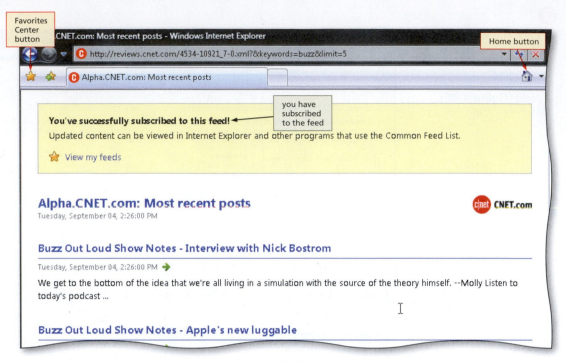

Figure 4–82

To View Your RSS Feeds in the Favorites Center

After you subscribe to an RSS feed, you are able to view the RSS feeds in the Favorites Center. The following steps display the RSS feeds to which you have subscribed in the Favorites Center.

**1**

• Click the Home button on the Command Bar to display your home page.

• Click the Favorites Center button to display the Favorites Center (Figure 4–83).

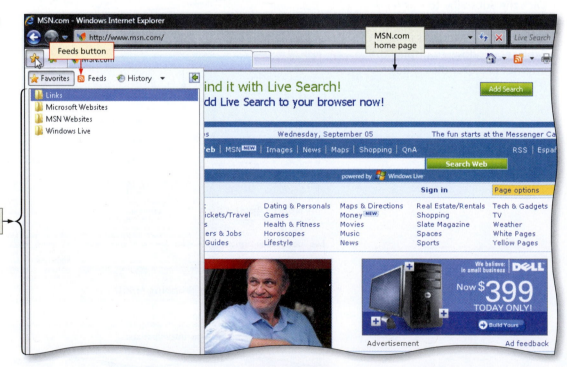

Figure 4–83

2

- Click the Feeds button in the Favorites Center to display the list of RSS feeds to which you have subscribed (Figure 4–84).

Figure 4–84

3

- Click the Alpha.CNET. com: Most recent posts link to display the RSS feed.

- If necessary, click the Close the Favorites Center button to close the Favorites Center (Figure 4–85).

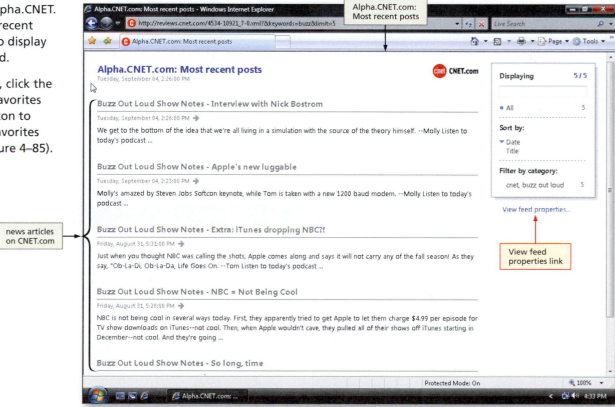

Figure 4–85

To Modify Feed Properties

Because RSS feeds disseminate frequently updated information, Internet Explorer automatically downloads updated RSS content every day. If you want Internet Explorer to download the RSS feeds more frequently so that you are sure that you are viewing the most up-to-date information, you can modify the feed properties. The following steps modify the properties for the Alpha.CNET.com: Most recent posts RSS feed so that the feed will update every four hours.

1

- Click the View feed properties link in the Alpha.CNET.com: Most recent posts - Windows Internet Explorer window to display the Feed Properties dialog box (Figure 4–86).

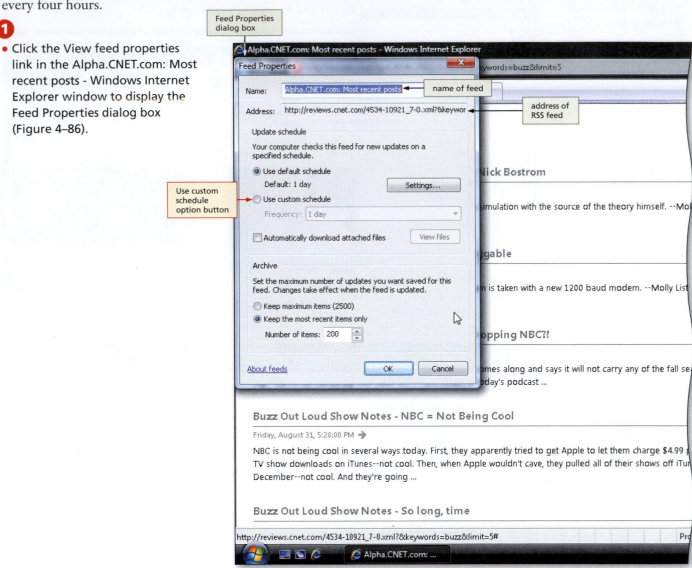

Figure 4–86

2
- Click the Use custom schedule option button in the Update schedule area of the Feed Properties dialog box (Figure 4–87).

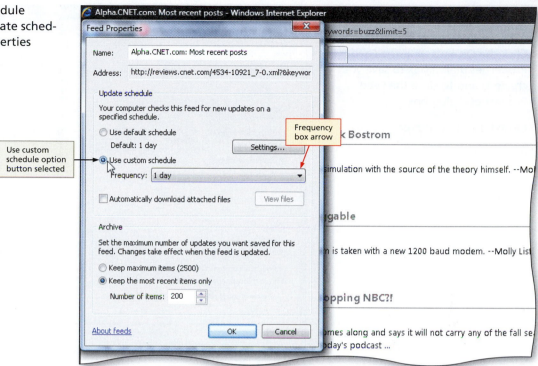

Figure 4–87

3
- Click the Frequency box arrow to display the Frequency list (Figure 4–88).

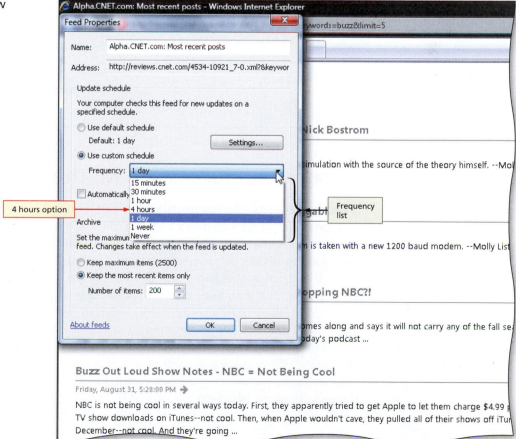

Figure 4–88

4

- Click 4 hours in the Frequency list (Figure 4–89).

- Click the OK button in the Feed Properties dialog box to save your changes and to close the Feed Properties dialog box.

- Close Internet Explorer.

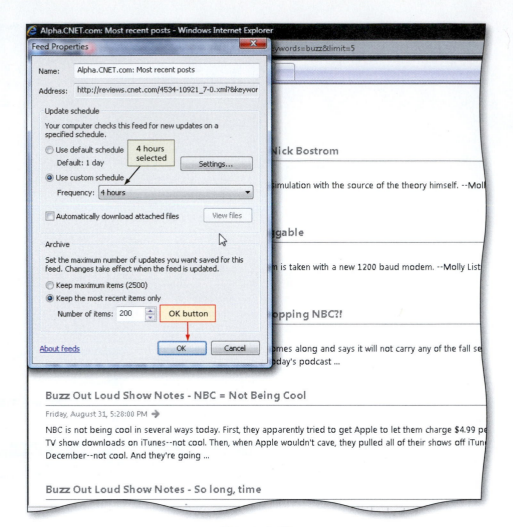

Figure 4–89

Other Communication Methods

This chapter has so far discussed how to communicate over the Internet by using e-mail, newsgroups, and RSS feeds. In addition to these methods, several other Web applications facilitate communication between individuals over the Internet, including wikis, blogs, online social networks, groups, chat rooms, and instant messaging.

Blogs, wikis, and online social networks are types of Web sites that allow one or more people to communicate directly with each other. Some Web sites, such as Google and Yahoo!, allow their visitors to communicate with others via groups. A **group** is a Web application that enables people to form an online community for discussion around specific topics, such as ballooning, Internet Explorer 7, or your favorite video game. You also can create Web pages inside your group. If you are unable to find a group that matches your interests, you can create a new group. Figure 4–90 shows the Google Groups Web site (http://groups.google.com).

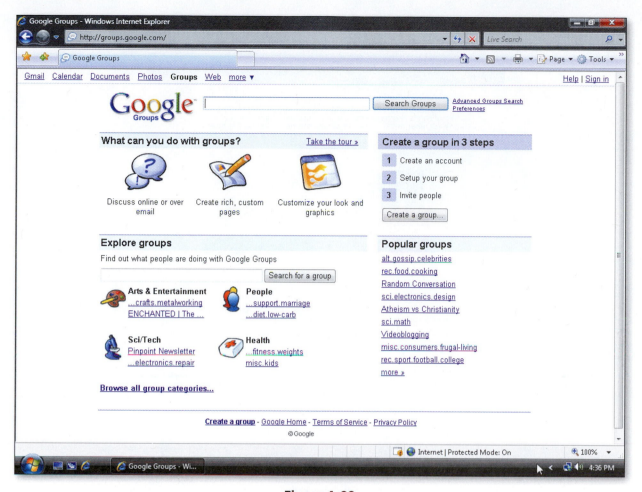

Figure 4–90

Similar to a group, a **chat room** application also allows people to communicate with each other. However, unlike a group, the communication that takes place in a chat room happens in real time. **Real-time communication** means that users participating in the communication must be online at the same time. For example, a telephone conversation is one type of communication that takes place in real time. If one person was not on the telephone, it would be impossible for the telephone conversation to take place. On the other hand, an e-mail conversation does not take place in real time because you are able to send someone an e-mail regardless of whether or not they are online. When you enter a chat room, messages that you send are viewable by everyone else who is in the same chat room. Some chat rooms are available via Web sites, and others are accessible only by first downloading a special program to your computer that allows you to enter and participate in chat rooms. Figure 4–91 on the next page shows a Web site that allows you to download a popular chat program called mIRC.

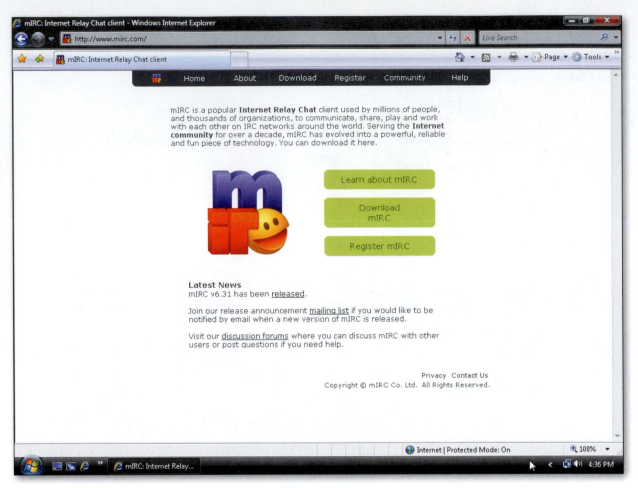

Figure 4–91

Another way by which people on the Internet can communicate is via a mailing list. A **mailing list** allows an individual to send the same e-mail to multiple recipients at the same time. For example, many colleges and universities allow instructors to communicate with their students outside of class by using a mailing list. At the beginning of the semester, students manually subscribe to the mailing list with their e-mail address or the instructor automatically subscribes them. When the instructor needs to disseminate information to the students, he or she sends a message to the mailing list, which is forwarded to everyone who has subscribed. In addition to schools using mailing lists, many companies also offer mailing lists to update their customers periodically about their products or services. If you have subscribed to a mailing list and no longer wish to receive e-mail from the list, you have to unsubscribe from it. Mailing lists offer different methods of unsubscribing, the instructions for which are usually located at the bottom of each e-mail sent to the list. If you are unable to find instructions for unsubscribing, contact the mailing list administrator. Figure 4–92 shows a Web page that contains a subscription form for a mailing list that distributes the DivX newsletter.

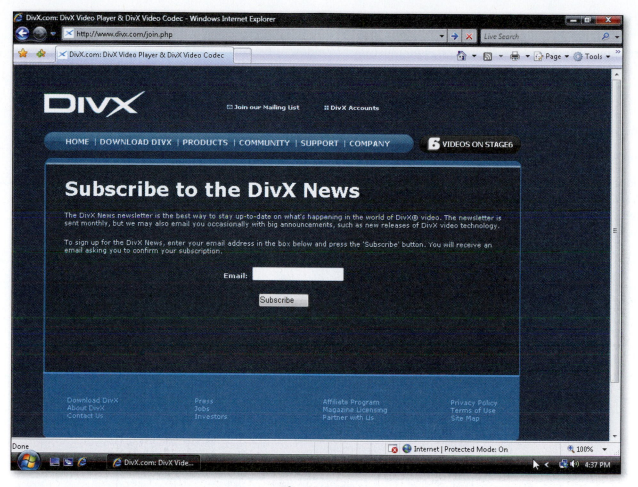

Figure 4–92

Windows Live Messenger and Instant Messaging

Another communication tool is instant messaging (IM). An **instant messaging application** allows two or more people who are online at the same time to exchange messages in real time. Windows Live Messenger, an instant messaging application, is available for free from the MSN.com Web site. Although Windows Live Messenger is not included with the Windows Vista operating system, many users choose to install it. The advantage of using Windows Live Messenger instead of e-mail is that once sent, your instant message appears immediately on the recipient's computer and they can reply immediately, while the disadvantage is that your recipient must be online and signed in to Windows Live Messenger to receive your message.

Windows Live Messenger users can perform a variety of functions, including adding a contact to the contact list; viewing a list of online and offline contacts; performing real-time communication with a single contact or a group of contacts; placing a telephone call from the computer and talking using the microphone and headset; sending files to another computer; sending instant messages to a mobile device; and inviting someone to an online meeting or to play an Internet game.

You sign into Windows Live Messenger using your Windows Live ID. Your Windows Live ID is a secure way for you to sign in to multiple Microsoft Web sites. If you have an MSN Hotmail, MSN Messenger, or Passport account, you already have a Windows Live ID. This section assumes that you already have Windows Live Messenger installed, and a Windows Live ID created. If you need a Windows Live ID, see your instructor for assistance. Before you will be able to send an instant message, your contact also must have a Windows Live ID and have the Windows Live Messenger software installed on their computer.

To Start Windows Live Messenger and Sign In

Before using Windows Live Messenger, you must start Windows Live Messenger and sign in using your Windows Live ID and password. The following steps, which assume that you have Windows Live Messenger installed on your computer, start and sign in to Windows Live Messenger.

- Display the Start menu.

- Display the All Programs list.

- Click Windows Live, and then click Windows Live Messenger on the All Programs list to start Windows Live Messenger (Figure 4–93).

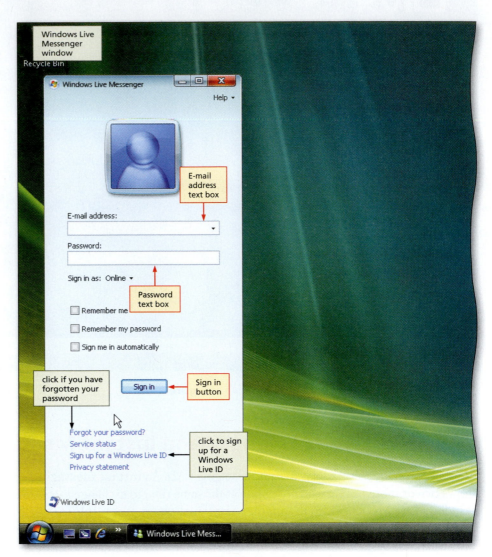

Figure 4–93

2

- Type your Windows Live ID into the E-mail address text box in the Windows Live Messenger window.

- Type your Windows Live password into the Password text box in the Windows Live Messenger window.

- Click the Sign in button to sign in to Windows Live Messenger and to display your Contact list (Figure 4–94).

- If the Today window displays, click the Close button to close the window.

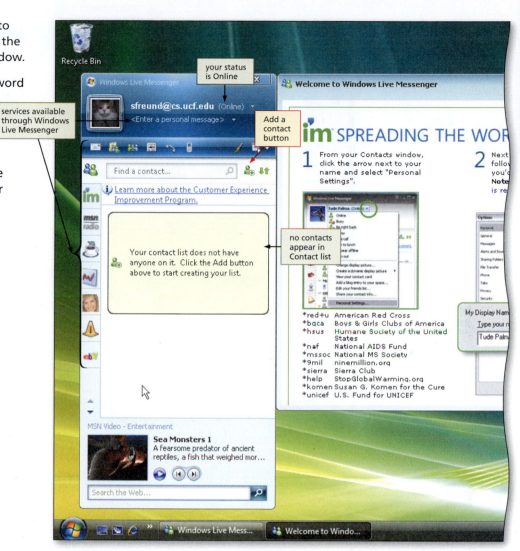

Figure 4–94

To Add a Contact to the Contact List

After starting Windows Live Messenger, you can add a contact to the contact list if you know their instant messaging address. A contact must have a Windows Live ID and have the Windows Live Messenger software installed on his or her computer. If you want to add a contact that does not meet these requirements, you can send the contact an e-mail invitation or text message on their mobile device that explains how to get a Windows Live ID and download the Windows Live Messenger software. The steps on the next page add a contact to the contact list using the e-mail address of someone you know who has signed in to Windows Live Messenger.

1

- Click the Add a contact button in the Windows Live Messenger window to display the Add a Contact dialog box (Figure 4–95).

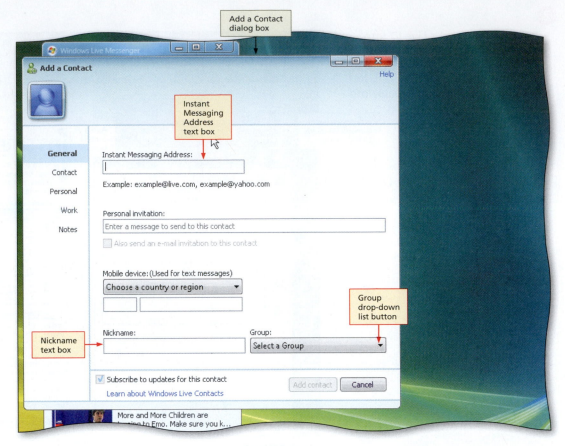

Figure 4–95

2

- Type `Shelly_Cashman@hotmail.com` in the Instant Messaging Address text box.

- Type `Shelly Cashman Series` in the Nickname text box.

- Click the Group drop-down list button to display a list of available groups (Figure 4–96).

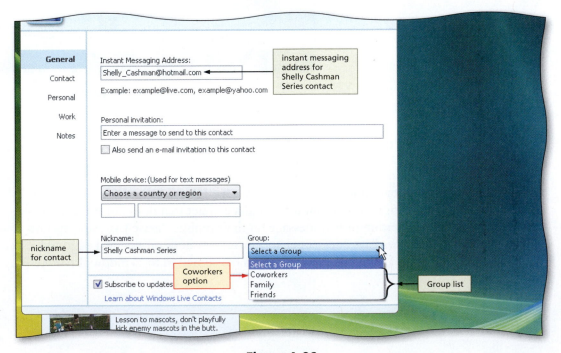

Figure 4–96

3

- Click the Coworkers option in the Group list (Figure 4–97). You may have different options than those listed in the Group list.

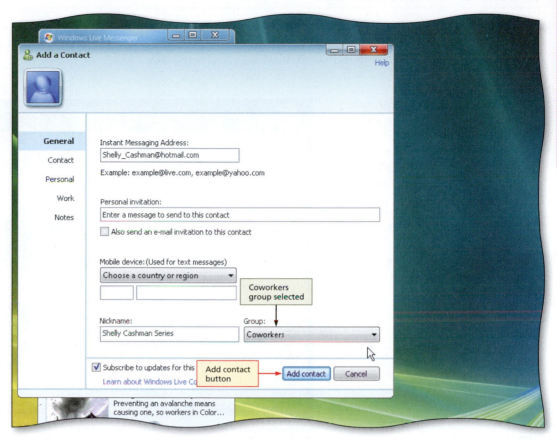

Figure 4–97

4

- Click the Add contact button to close the Add a Contact dialog box and add the Shelly Cashman Series contact to your contact list (Figure 4–98).

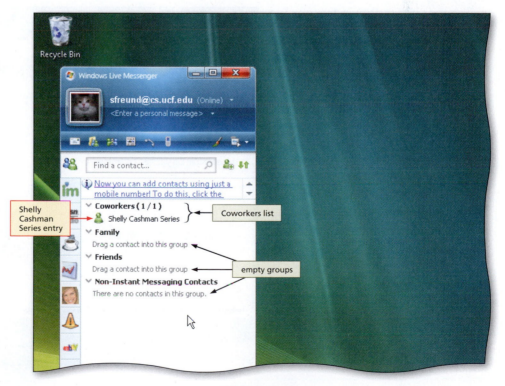

Figure 4–98

To Send an Instant Message

To use Windows Live Messenger, the person with whom you want to communicate must be online. The Online list shown in Figure 4–98 on the previous page displays the Shelly Cashman Series contact. The following steps send an instant message to the Shelly Cashman Series contact.

- Double-click the Shelly Cashman entry in the Coworkers group to display the Shelly Cashman Series window (Figure 4–99). If the Shelly Cashman contact is not online, double-click the name of another online contact.

- Type I have learned how to use Windows Live Messenger! Do you have some time to chat? in the Send text box.

Figure 4–99

- Click the Send button in the Shelly Cashman Series window to send the instant message (Figure 4–100).

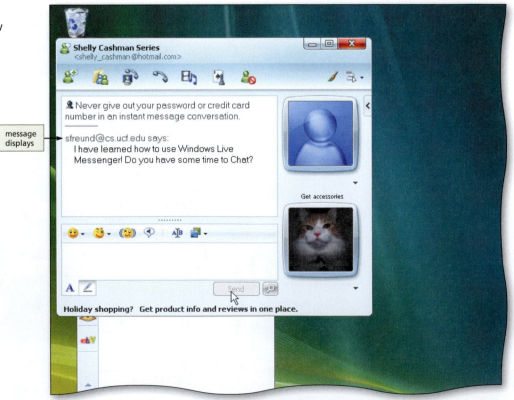

Figure 4–100

3

- The receiver of the message types and then sends a response (Figure 4–101).

Experiment

- Feel free to send additional messages to the Shelly Cashman Series contact or the contact you are communicating with in Windows Live Messenger.

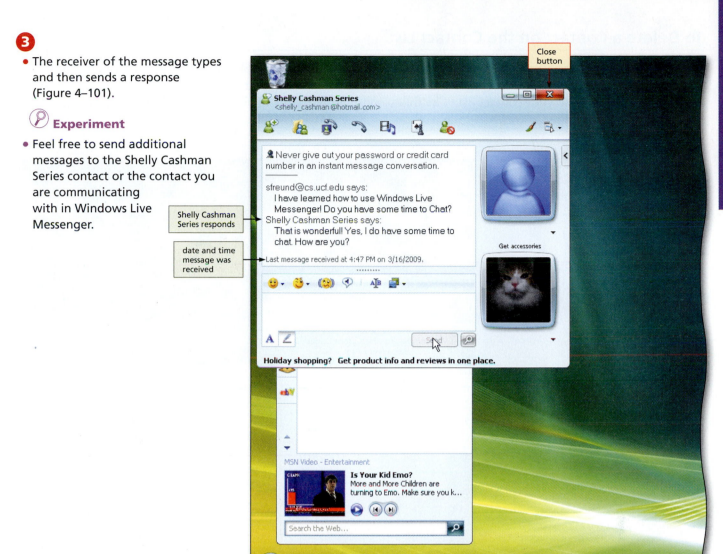

Figure 4–101

Other Ways

1. Right-click contact name, click Send an instant message on shortcut menu

To Close the Shelly Cashman Series Window

When you have finished with your conversation, you should close the instant messaging window to end the conversation. The next step closes the Shelly Cashman Series window.

1 Click the Close button in the Shelly Cashman Series window to close the instant messaging window.

To Delete a Contact on the Contact List

The Shelly Cashman Series contact remains on the contact list and the Shelly Cashman Series icon appears below the Coworkers heading in the Windows Live Messenger window. If you lose touch with a contact, you may want to delete them from your contact list. The following steps delete the Shelly Cashman Series contact and remove the entry from the Coworkers group.

1

• Right-click the Shelly Cashman Series entry under the Coworkers heading to display the shortcut menu (Figure 4–102).

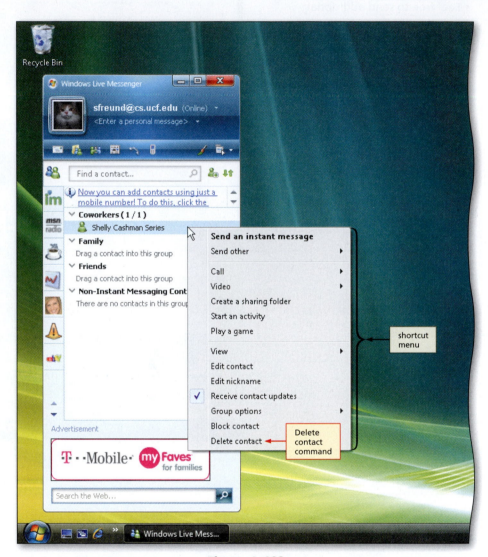

Figure 4–102

2

- Click Delete contact on the shortcut menu (Figure 4–103).

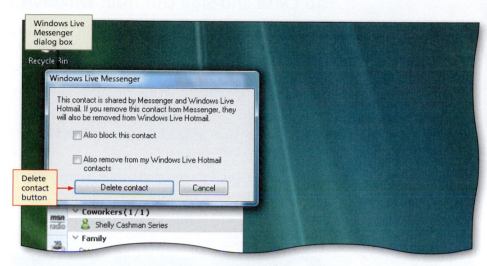

Figure 4–103

3

- Click the Delete contact button in the Windows Live Messenger dialog box to delete the Shelly Cashman Series contact and remove the Shelly Cashman Series entry from the Coworkers group (Figure 4–104).

Figure 4–104

To Close and Sign Out from Windows Live Messenger

When you have finished using Windows Live Messenger, close the Windows Live Messenger window. The following steps close the Windows Live Messenger window and signs out from the Windows Live Messenger service.

1 Click the Close button in the Windows Live Messenger window to close Windows Live Messenger (Figure 4–105).

2 Click the Windows Live Messenger - Signed In icon in the notification area on the Windows taskbar.

3 Click the Sign out command on the shortcut menu to sign out from Windows Live Messenger.

Figure 4–105

To Log Off from and Turn Off the Computer

After completing your work with Windows Vista, you first should close your user account by logging off from the computer, and then turn off the computer.

1 On the Start menu, click the arrow to the right of the Lock this computer button, and then click the Log Off command to log off from the computer.

2 On the Welcome Screen, click the Shut Down button to turn off the computer.

Chapter Summary

In this chapter, you have learned to use Windows Mail to read, write, format, and send e-mail messages, and to attach and view file attachments. You added and removed Windows Calendar appointments and tasks. You added and deleted contacts in the Contacts folder. You also used Windows Mail to subscribe to and read newsgroups. You used Internet Explorer to view RSS feeds. You learned about other Web applications including groups, mailing lists, and chat rooms. Finally, you used Windows Live Messenger to send an instant message. The following list includes all the new Windows Vista skills you have learned in this chapter.

1. Start Windows Mail (WIN 229)
2. Open (Read) an E-Mail Message (WIN 233)
3. Print an Opened E-Mail Message (WIN 234)
4. Close an E-Mail Message (WIN 236)
5. Reply to an E-Mail Message (WIN 236)
6. Delete an E-Mail Message (WIN 239)
7. Open a File Attachment (WIN 240)
8. Save and Close a File Attachment (WIN 241)
9. Compose an E-Mail Message Using Stationery (WIN 242)
10. Format an E-Mail Message (WIN 244)
11. Attach a File to an E-Mail Message (WIN 246)
12. Send an E-Mail Message (WIN 248)
13. Add an Appointment in Windows Calendar (WIN 249)
14. Add a Task in Windows Calendar (WIN 254)
15. Change the Calendar View (WIN 256)
16. Delete Appointments and Tasks (WIN 258)
17. Close Windows Calendar (WIN 260)
18. Add a Contact to the Contacts Folder (WIN 261)
19. Compose an E-Mail Message Using the Contacts Folder (WIN 264)
20. Send an E-Mail Message (WIN 268)
21. Delete a Contact from the Contacts Folder (WIN 268)
22. Close the Contacts Window (WIN 269)
23. Subscribe to and Display a Newsgroup on the Microsoft News Server (WIN 272)
24. Read a Newsgroup Article (WIN 275)
25. Print a Newsgroup Article (WIN 276)
26. Unsubscribe from a Newsgroup (WIN 278)
27. Quit Windows Mail (WIN 279)
28. Subscribe to an RSS Feed (WIN 280)
29. View Your RSS Feeds in the Favorites Center (WIN 282)
30. Modify Feed Properties (WIN 284)
31. Start Windows Live Messenger and Sign In (WIN 290)
32. Add a Contact to the Contact List (WIN 291)
33. Send an Instant Message (WIN 294)
34. Close the Shelly Cashman Series Window (WIN 295)
35. Delete a Contact on the Contact List (WIN 296)
36. Close and Sign Out from Windows Live Messenger (WIN 298)
37. Log Off from and Turn Off the Computer (WIN 299)

Learn It Online

Test your knowledge of chapter content and key terms.

Instructions: To complete the Learn It Online exercises, start your browser, click the Address bar, and then enter the Web address scsite.com/winvista/learn. When the Windows Vista Learn It Online page is displayed, click the link for the exercise you want to complete and then read the instructions.

Chapter Reinforcement TF, MC, and SA
A series of true/false, multiple-choice, and short answer questions that test your knowledge of the chapter content.

Flash Cards
An interactive learning environment where you identify chapter key terms associated with displayed definitions.

Practice Test
A series of multiple-choice questions that test your knowledge of chapter content and key terms.

Who Wants To Be a Computer Genius?
An interactive game that challenges your knowledge of chapter content in the style of a television quiz show.

Wheel of Terms
An interactive game that challenges your knowledge of chapter key terms in the style of the television show *Wheel of Fortune*.

Crossword Puzzle Challenge
A crossword puzzle that challenges your knowledge of key terms presented in the chapter.

Apply Your Knowledge

Reinforce the skills and apply the concepts you learned in this chapter.

Sending an E-Mail Message to Your Instructor
Instructions: You want to send an e-mail to the instructor of your course stating what you like best about his or her class. Use Windows Mail to send the e-mail.

Perform the following tasks:
1. Search for the home page for your college or university. Figure 4–106 shows the home page for Valencia Community College.
2. Find and write down the e-mail address of your instructor.
3. Start Windows Mail.
4. Click the Create Mail button on the Mail toolbar.
5. Using the e-mail address of the instructor you obtained in Step 2, compose a mail message to this instructor stating what you like best about his or her class.
6. Send the e-mail message to your instructor.

Figure 4–106

Valencia Community College home page

Extend Your Knowledge

Extend the skills you learned in this chapter and experiment with new skills. You may need to use Help to complete the assignment.

Posting a Newsgroup Article

Instructions: Locate a newsgroup on Windows Vista, and compose and post a message about a new feature to the newsgroup. After posting the article, find your message in the message pane, and then print the article.

Perform the following tasks:

1. Search for and subscribe to a newsgroup that contains articles about Windows Vista.
2. Locate and click the newsgroup name in the Folder list.

Continued >

Extend Your Knowledge *continued*

3. Click the Write Message button to display the New Message window (Figure 4–107).

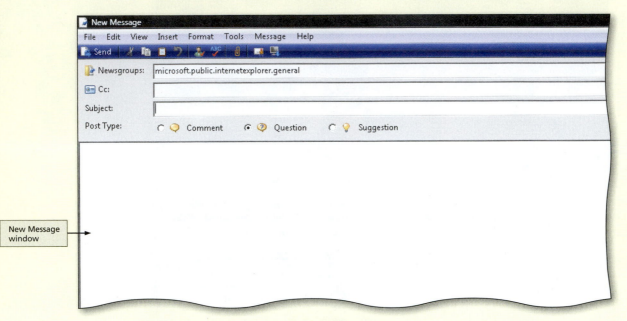

New Message
window

Figure 4–107

4. Compose and then post a message to the newsgroup that explains your favorite feature of Windows Vista.

5. Find your message in the Message list. Print the message, write your name on the printed message, and submit it to your instructor.

In the Lab

Use the guidelines, concepts and skills presented in this chapter to increase your knowledge of Windows Vista. Labs are listed in order of increasing difficulty.

Lab 1: Adding Your Friends to the Contacts Folder

Instructions: You want to use the Contacts folder in Windows Vista to keep track of the names, e-mail addresses, home addresses, and home telephone numbers of your favorite school friends.

Perform the following tasks:

1. Click the Contacts button on the toolbar to open the Contacts folder. If necessary, maximize the window (Figure 4–108).

2. Use the New Contact button on the toolbar to add the contacts listed in Table 4–8 to the Contacts folder.

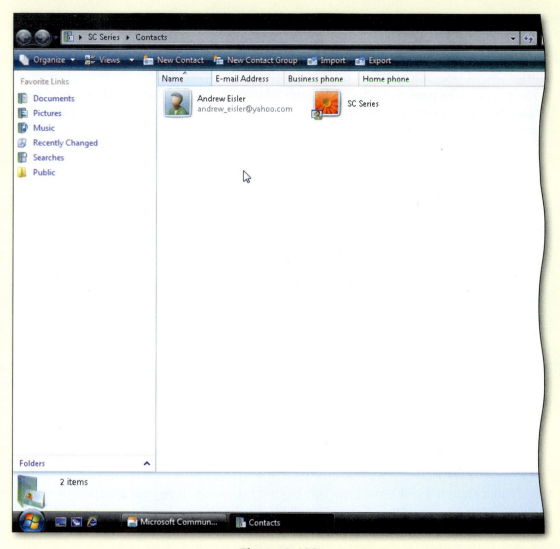

Figure 4–108

Table 4–8 Contact List for Contacts Folder

Name	E-mail Address	Address	Home Phone
Theresa Collins	tcollins@isp.com	8451 Colony Dr., Brea, CA 92821	(714) 555-2831
Sean Geftic	sgeftic@isp.com	3544 Clayton Rd., Placentia, CA 92871	(714) 555-1484
Jessica McEwen	jmcewen@isp.com	5689 State St., Fullerton, CA 92834	(714) 555-2318
Tami Newell	tnewell@isp.com	7812 Bennington Dr., Atwood, CA 92811	(714) 555-8622
Amanda Silva	asilva@isp.com	257 W. Wilson St., Yorba Linda, CA 92885	(714) 555-2782
Cherry Tran	ctran@isp.com	648 Flower Rd., Brea, CA 92821	(714) 555-6495

3. Print the information for each contact by right-clicking a contact name, clicking the Print command on the shortcut menu, and then clicking the Print button in the Print dialog box. Write your name on each printed contact.

4. Delete each contact by selecting the contact name and then clicking the Delete button on the toolbar.

In the Lab

Lab 2: E-Mailing Your Class Schedule as an Attachment

Instructions: You want to send your class schedule to your instructor as an attachment. Type your class schedule into a new Notepad document and save the file. Switch to Windows Mail, type an e-mail message to your instructor and attach the Notepad file containing your class schedule.

Perform the following tasks:

1. Type your class schedule into the Notepad document, organizing your classes using a method of your choosing. A sample Notepad document containing a class schedule is illustrated in Figure 4–109.

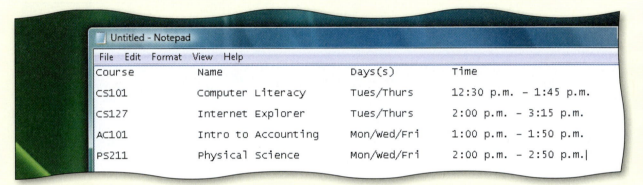

Course	Name	Days(s)	Time
CS101	Computer Literacy	Tues/Thurs	12:30 p.m. – 1:45 p.m.
CS127	Internet Explorer	Tues/Thurs	2:00 p.m. – 3:15 p.m.
AC101	Intro to Accounting	Mon/Wed/Fri	1:00 p.m. – 1:50 p.m.
PS211	Physical Science	Mon/Wed/Fri	2:00 p.m. – 2:50 p.m.|

Figure 4–109

2. Using your first and last name as the file name (put a space between your first and last names), save the Notepad document to your Documents folder.
3. In Windows Mail, compose a new e-mail message to your instructor. Type your instructor's e-mail address into the To text box. Type My Class Schedule for the Subject. For the body of the e-mail message, type I have created a document with Notepad that contains my class schedule. The file is attached to this e-mail message.
4. Press the ENTER key twice.
5. Type your name and then press the ENTER key.
6. Click the Attach File To Message button, navigate to the Documents folder, and then attach the Notepad file you created to the e-mail message.
7. Send the e-mail message.
8. Display the contents of the Sent Items folder to verify that your message was sent.

In the Lab

Lab 3: Using Windows Live Messenger

Instructions: Start and sign in to Windows Live Messenger. Add a new person to your Windows Live Messenger contact list. After adding the contact, send instant messages to each other, and then save and print the entire conversation.

Perform the following tasks:
Part 1: Add a Contact to the Contact List

1. Click the Add a contact button in the Windows Live Messenger window.
2. Type the Windows Live ID or Windows Live Hotmail e-mail address of a friend in the Instant Messaging Address text box, choose an appropriate nickname, and then click the Add contact button.

Part 2: Send an Instant Message

1. Double-click the icon of the contact you added in the contact list.

2. Type a message in the Message area, click the Send button, wait for the response, and type your response.

3. Continue conversing in this manner until you have typed at least four messages. Figure 4–110 shows a sample conversation.

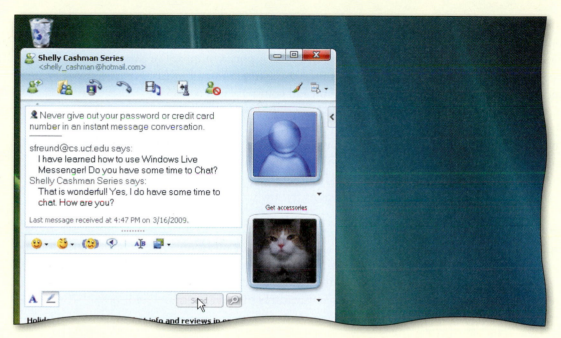

Figure 4–110

Part 3: Save the Conversation

1. Press ALT to display the menu bar.

2. Click File on the menu bar to display the file menu.

3. Click Save as on the File menu. If the Windows Live Messenger dialog box displays, click the OK button.

4. Save the file with the filename Conversation, to the Documents folder on your computer.

Part 4: Delete a Contact on the Contact List

1. In the Windows Live Messenger window, right-click the contact you want to delete.

2. Click Delete contact on the shortcut menu.

3. Click the Delete contact button in the Windows Live Messenger dialog box.

Part 5: Close Windows Live Messenger Window and Sign Out from the Windows Live Messenger Service

1. Click the Close button in the Windows Live Messenger window.

2. Right-click the Windows Live Messenger - Signed In icon in the notification area on the Windows taskbar.

3. Click Exit on the shortcut menu.

4. E-mail the Conversation file to your instructor as an e-mail attachment.

Cases and Places

Apply your creative thinking and problem solving skills to design and implement a solution.

● Easier   ●● More Difficult

● 1: Compare Windows Mail and Microsoft Office Outlook

Using computer magazines, advertising brochures, the Internet, or other resources, compile information about Windows Mail and Microsoft Office Outlook. In a brief report, compare the two programs. Include the differences and similarities, how to obtain the software, the function and features of each program, and so forth. If possible, test Microsoft Office Outlook and add your personal comments.

● 2: Discuss the Use of False Online Identities

Some people have expressed concerns that some users try to disguise their identities by displaying false information when signing up for a free e-mail account. In a brief report, summarize the reasons why you should identify yourself correctly on the Internet, what kinds of problems result when users disguise their identities, and offer some suggestions as to how to prevent this problem.

●● 3: Research E-mail Programs

Using computer magazines, advertising brochures, the Internet, or other resources, compile information about two e-mail programs other than Windows Mail and Microsoft Office Outlook. In a brief report, compare the two programs and the Windows Mail e-mail program. Include the differences and similarities, how to obtain the software, the functions and features of each program, and so forth. Submit the report to your instructor.

●● 4: Locate an RSS Feed

Make It Personal

Many Web sites provide their content via an RSS feed. Locate at least two news Web sites and at least two other Web sites that you are interested in that allow you to subscribe to an RSS feed. What are the advantages of subscribing to an RSS feed? Would you rather subscribe to an RSS feed or navigate directly to the Web site to view its content? Why or why not? Submit your answers to your instructor.

●● 5: Create a Google Group

Working Together

Groups are a popular way for people to communicate with each other about a certain topic via the Internet. Create a Google Group about a topic of your choice (http://groups.google.com) and have each team member post a message to the group to initiate a conversation. Wait two days to see if anyone outside of your team has signed up for your group. Find one other group that discusses a similar topic. How many people have joined that group? Discuss how you could attract more people to your group. Submit your answers to your instructor.

5 | Personalize Your Work Environment

Objectives

You will have mastered the material in this chapter when you can:

- Create, save, and delete a desktop theme
- Change the desktop background
- View sound settings
- Change mouse pointers
- Change the screen saver
- Add icons to the desktop
- Unlock, move, hide, and resize the taskbar
- Add, resize, and remove a toolbar on the taskbar

- Add and remove a shortcut on a toolbar
- Launch an application from a toolbar
- Use the Address toolbar to display folder content and search the Internet
- Customize the Start menu and notification area
- Change folder options and restore default folder options

5 | Personalize Your Work Environment

Introduction

One of the best ways to improve your productivity on the computer is to personalize your work environment. You can add a frequently used toolbar to your desktop in order to save time. If you use many different programs, you may want to modify the Start menu to show more recently used programs than it usually does. Similarly, people often personalize their computer by adding their own unique touches. This includes changing their desktop to display a family photo or changing the sounds that Windows plays when certain events occur. By personalizing their work environment, users feel more in tune with their computer, which can put users more at ease and lead to improved performance.

Overview

As you read this chapter, you will learn how to personalize your work environment by performing these general tasks:

- Opening and changing the desktop settings
- Reviewing your sound and mouse pointer selections
- Changing your screen saver
- Adding additional icons to your desktop
- Unlocking, moving, resizing, locking, and hiding the taskbar
- Modifying and adding shortcuts to the Quick Launch toolbar
- Adding and using the Address toolbar
- Customizing Start menu options
- Customizing the notification area

Plan Ahead

Working with the Windows Vista Desktop
Customizing and personalizing the Windows Vista desktop requires a basic knowledge of how to use Windows Vista, the appropriate permissions, access to sample files, and access to the Internet.

1. **Determine the permissions you have on the computer you will be using.** Each user account can have different rights and permissions. Depending on which rights and permissions have been set for your account, you may or may not be able to perform certain operations.

2. **Find out if you have access to the sample files installed with Windows Vista.** To complete the steps in this chapter, you will need access to the sample pictures and videos installed with Windows Vista.

3. **Determine whether you have Internet access.** For this chapter, you will be accessing the Internet to search for information. You will want to know if your computer has Internet access and if anything is required of you to use it.

Personalize Your Desktop

Windows Vista provides a variety of methods to modify the desktop with which you work. As introduced in Chapter 1, Windows Vista considers most items on the desktop, including the desktop itself, to be objects. Every object has properties, which are the defining characteristics of an object. In many cases, you can change an object's properties to fit your needs. You may be surprised at the many different preferences people have for their computer desktops. Some like quiet, cool colors while others like bright, glittery schemes. There is no single correct way to set up your desktop. Preferences are an individual matter, which is why Microsoft and other operating system designers offer the capability of customizing the desktop.

To Open the Personalization Window

A starting point for personalizing your work environment is to change the appearance of the desktop. Desktop appearance objects that you can modify include the choice of a desktop theme and background, which icons appear on the desktop and their size and color, how windows open on the desktop, and the choice of which screen saver to use. In order to change the desktop appearance, you first open the Personalization window. The following steps open the Personalization window.

- Right-click an open area of the desktop to display the shortcut menu (Figure 5–1).

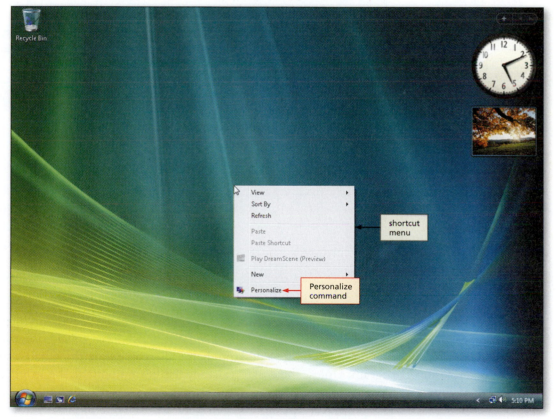

Figure 5–1

2

- Click the Personalize command to open the Personalization window (Figure 5–2).

Why does a shield appear next to Adjust font size (DPI)?

You can use the Adjust font size (DPI) link to increase the font size based upon the number of dots per inch (DPI) used to create the font. The shield appears because this action requires you to have correct authorization: if you click the link, Windows will display the User Account Control dialog box, requesting additional permission to perform this task. Additionally, changing the DPI will require you to reboot your computer for the changes to take effect.

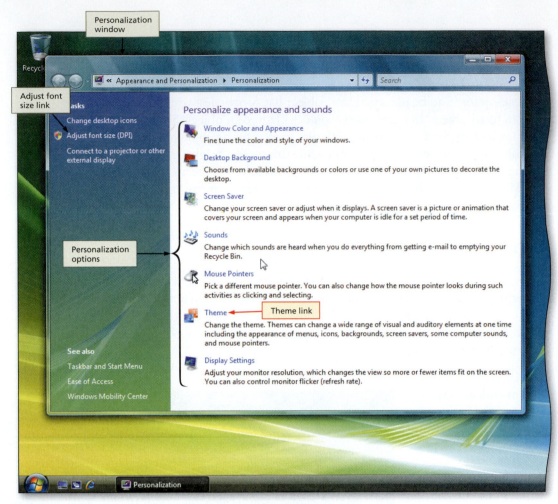

Figure 5–2

Other Ways

1. Open Start menu, click Control Panel command, click Appearance and Personalization link, click Personalization

To View the Current Theme

One method of changing the appearance of the desktop is to change the desktop theme. A **desktop theme** is a set of graphical elements that give the desktop a unified and distinctive look. In addition to determining the look of the various graphic elements on the desktop, a desktop theme also can define the sounds associated with events such as opening or closing a program. Unless the desktop already has been modified, the Windows Vista desktop theme displays when you launch Windows Vista.

If you wish to change the desktop appearance, you can make changes to your desktop using the various options available in the Personalization window. All of the changes you make will be added to the Modified Theme desktop theme. After you make changes, you can save the modified theme with a name of your choice using the Theme option in the Personalization window.

Before you begin making changes to your work environment, you should view and record which theme currently is in use by Windows Vista so that you can restore it later if you want to do so. In most cases, this will be the Windows Vista theme. The following steps display the current theme.

1

- Click the Theme link in the Personalization window to open the Theme Settings dialog box (Figure 5–3).

- Write down the name of the theme being used for future reference.

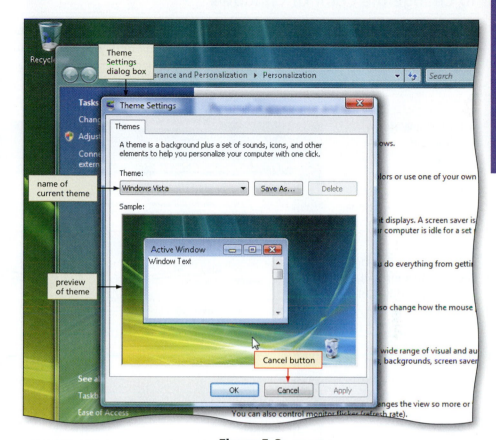

Figure 5–3

2

- Click the Cancel button to close the Theme Settings dialog box without making changes (Figure 5–4).

Figure 5–4

To Change the Color of Windows

One of the simplest ways that you can customize your desktop is to change the color and appearance of your windows. The Window Color and Appearance link in the Personalization window will allow you to change how your windows look. Windows Vista provides eight pre-set color options, and gives you the option of turning off the transparency effect. The following steps change the window color to red.

1

- Click the Window Color and Appearance link to open the Window Color and Appearance window (Figure 5–5).

Q&A

Why do I see the Appearance Settings dialog box instead of the Window Color and Appearance window?

Your computer may not be capable of using Aero or Aero may be turned off. Your computer must be using Aero in order to use the Window Color and Appearance window. To turn on Aero, if available, open the Appearance Settings dialog box and change the color scheme to Windows Aero. The Appearance Settings dialog box can be opened from within the Window Color and Appearance window by clicking the Open classic appearance properties for more color options link.

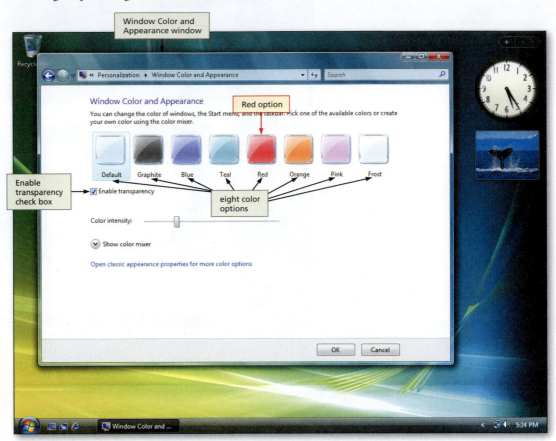

Figure 5–5

2

- Click the Red option to change the color of the windows to red (Figure 5–6).

Experiment

- There are several built-in color schemes for Aero. Click the different color options to see what they look like. After you have changed the color scheme, you also can turn on the transparency effect of Aero on and off by using the Enable transparency check box. Return to the Red color option and turn on the transparency effect when you are done.

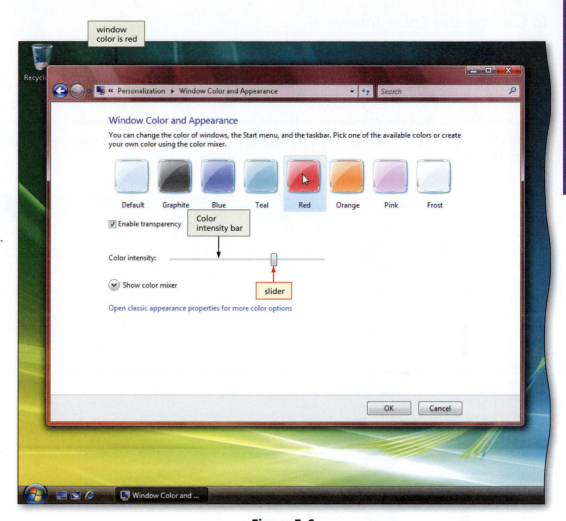

Figure 5–6

Other Ways

1. Press RIGHT ARROW until Red color scheme is selected

To Change the Color Intensity

Once you have selected a color scheme, you can adjust the intensity using the Color intensity bar. By moving the slider on the Color intensity bar to the left, you will make the window appear more transparent by decreasing the amount of color. If you move the slider more to the right, you will increase the amount of color and the window will appear less transparent. Although changing the color intensity affects how the Red color scheme appears on your desktop, it does not change the default setting of the Red color scheme. If you were to click the Red color scheme, the color intensity would return to the pre-set value. The following step changes the color intensity to its maximum value.

- Click and drag the slider on the Color intensity bar all the way to the right to increase the color intensity to its maximum value (Figure 5–7).

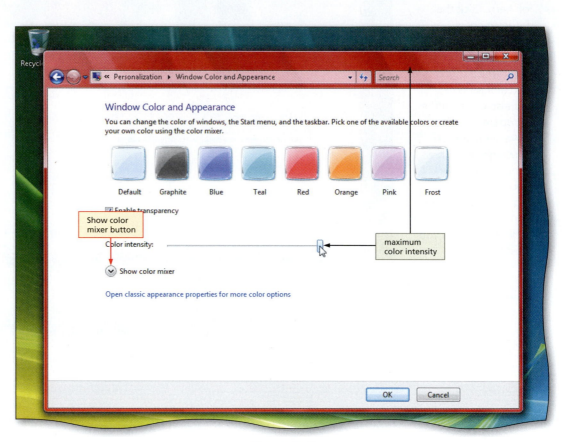

Experiment

- Move the slider around to see how changing the color intensity can change the appearance of your windows. Position the slider all the way to the right when you are finished.

Figure 5–7

Other Ways

1. Press TAB until Color intensity bar is selected, press RIGHT ARROW until slider is at its maximum value

To Show the Color Mixer

In addition to altering the intensity of color, the color scheme also can be adjusted by using the color mixer. The color mixer allows you to change the hue, saturation, and brightness of the color scheme. By changing the **hue**, you change the color. Changing the hue in the color mixer is a way to select a color that is different from the eight schemes provided by Windows Vista. **Saturation** refers to the distribution of the hue, and you can use the saturation bar to make a color more or less intense. **Brightness** determines how light or dark the hue and saturation appear.

You can use all three options to create a custom color scheme more to your taste. When you change these options, you are not changing the default settings of the Red color scheme. As with changes to the Color intensity bar, if you were to click on the Red color scheme, the color mixer options would change back to the default Red color scheme settings. The following step uses the color mixer to show the hue, saturation, and brightness of your color scheme.

1

- Click the Show color mixer button to display the color mixer (Figure 5–8).

Experiment

- Move the sliders for hue, saturation, and brightness to see how changing their values affects the color of your windows.

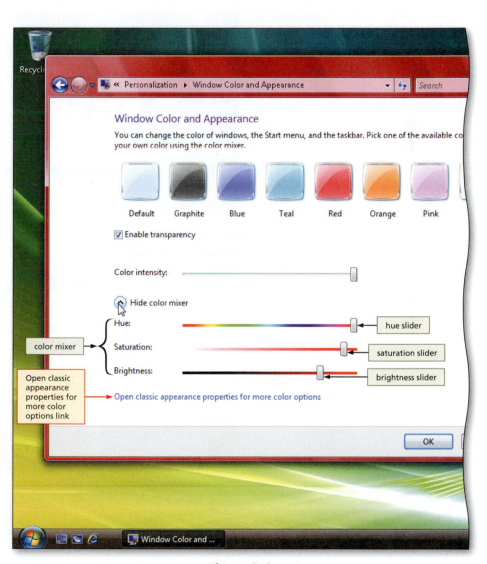

Figure 5–8

To View Classic Appearance Settings

Additional color modifications are available that you can make by using the classic Appearance Settings dialog box. For example, you can change your color scheme by selecting from a list of pre-set schemes, or you can change effects such as menu shadowing or showing window content when you move the window around on the desktop. Advanced appearance settings also can be accessed from the Appearance Settings dialog box; however, not all of the options can be applied to the Windows Aero scheme. Advanced appearance settings concerning color and size only can be applied if your theme or color scheme has been set to Windows Classic. The Windows Classic scheme displays the familiar desktop colors and appearance found on computers with a previous version of the Microsoft Windows operating system. The following step displays the Appearance Settings dialog box.

- Click the Open classic appearance properties for more color options link to display the Appearance Settings dialog box (Figure 5–9).

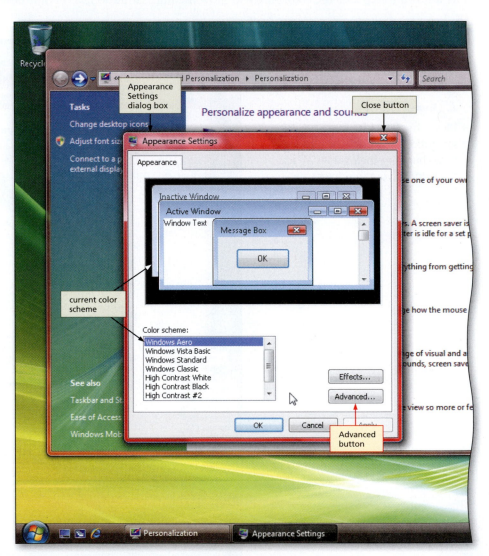

Figure 5–9

Other Ways
1. Press TAB until Open classic appearance properties for more color options is selected, press ENTER

To View the Advanced Appearance Settings

One of the items that you can adjust using the Advanced Appearance dialog box is the font for the icons on your desktop. If you look closely at the dialog box, you will notice that it states that changing color or size will not work for any color scheme other than the Windows Classic scheme. When you use Aero, the font property will be the only thing that you can change successfully. The following step displays the Advanced Appearance dialog box.

1
- Click the Advanced button to display the Advanced Appearance dialog box (Figure 5–10).

Q&A

What happens if I change one of the settings?

If you are using Aero, none of the changes actually will work, except for the font settings. If you are not using Aero, you can make changes to the sizes, and colors of various window features. This includes features such as title bars, buttons, hyperlinks, and icons.

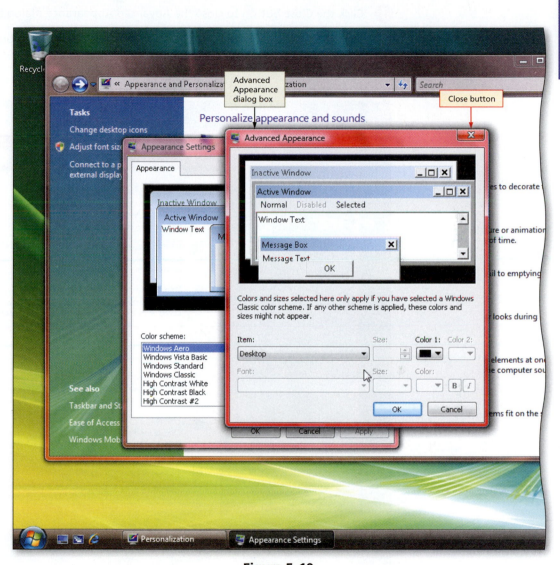

Figure 5–10

Other Ways

1. Press TAB until Advanced button is selected, press ENTER

To Close the Advanced Appearance and Appearance Settings Dialog Boxes

Now that you have finished exploring the Advanced Appearance dialog box and the Appearance Settings dialog box, you should close them. The following steps close both dialog boxes.

1 Click the Close button to close the Advanced Appearance dialog box.

2 Click the Close button to close the Appearance Settings dialog box (Figure 5–11).

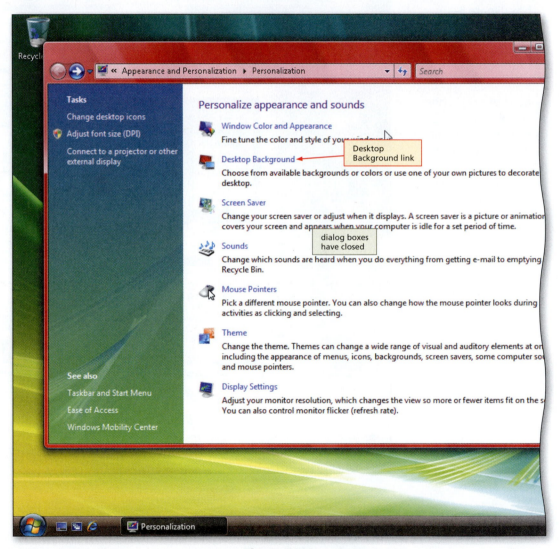

Figure 5–11

To Open the Desktop Background Window

Another element of a desktop theme is the desktop background. The **desktop background** is the pattern, picture, or wallpaper that displays on the desktop, appearing behind windows and icons. With Windows Vista, you even can use videos as your desktop background.

To change your desktop background from the Personalization window, you will need to open the Desktop Background window. The following step opens the Desktop Background window.

1

- Click the Desktop Background link to open the Desktop Background window (Figure 5–12).

Q&A

Can I use any image as my desktop background?

Yes. All you have to do is right-click the picture, select Set as Desktop Background, and then the picture will be used as your background. You can then open the Desktop Background window and set any additional settings you would like to use.

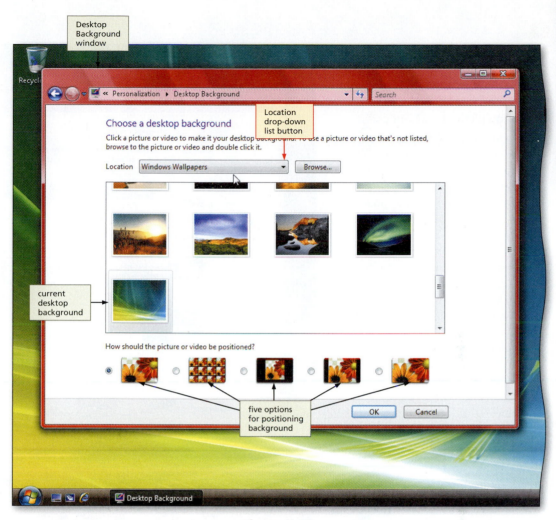

Figure 5–12

Other Ways

1. Press TAB until Desktop Background is selected, press ENTER

To Change the Desktop Background to a Video

When you work with Windows Vista and do not maximize the window you are using, the desktop background is the single most dominant feature of the computer screen. Your choice of background can affect your mood, the ease at which you can use your computer, and even can affect others who work nearby. Using a video as a background is a way to change your desktop background to something more dynamic than a simple picture. When a video is selected, Windows Vista automatically will select the appropriate positioning option for the height and width of the video. For the Butterfly video included in the sample videos with Windows Vista, the position will be set to Center. The steps on the following pages change the background to the Butterfly sample video.

1

- Click the Location drop-down list button to display the list of location options (Figure 5–13).

Q&A

What file formats are used for desktop pictures and videos?

You can use a photograph you took, a picture from the Pictures folder, a picture from any other folder on your computer, or a graphic image you found on a Web page as a desktop background. The file can be any of the following formats: bitmap file (.bmp), GIF file (.gif), JPEG file (.jpg), Microsoft PhotoDraw Picture file (.dib), Portable Network Graphics file (.png), or HTML file (.htm). You also can use videos as your desktop background. The videos need to be either in Windows Media Video (.wmv) format or MPEG (.mpg) format.

Figure 5–13

2

- Click the Public Videos option to select the Public Videos folder (Figure 5–14).

Q&A

What if I am unable to find the Public Videos folder?

The Public Videos folder is available for those using the Ultimate edition of Windows Vista. If you do not have Windows Vista Ultimate edition with the latest updates and extras, you will not see the Public Videos folder. In this case, please continue to read the steps without performing them.

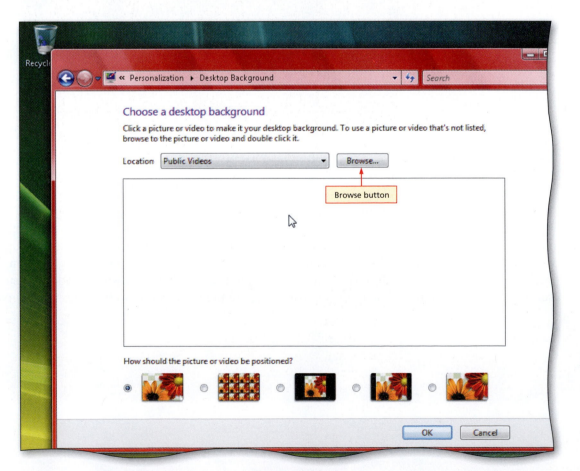

Figure 5–14

3

• Click the Browse
  button to open the
  Browse dialog box
  (Figure 5–15).

Figure 5–15

4

• Double-click the
  Sample Videos folder
  icon to open the
  Sample Videos folder
  (Figure 5–16).

Figure 5–16

5

● Click the Butterfly
video icon to select
the Butterfly video
(Figure 5–17).

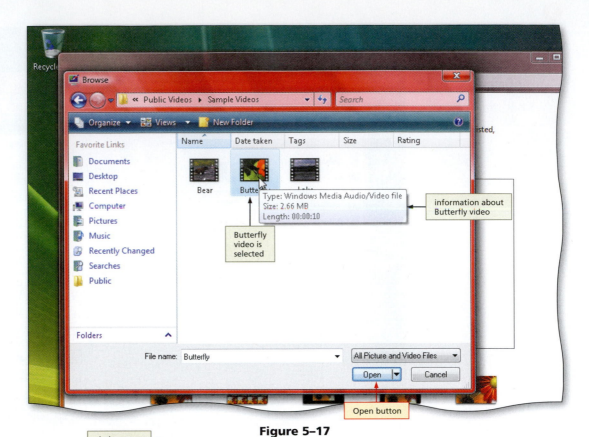

Figure 5–17

6

● Click the Open
button to set the
Butterfly video
as the desktop
background
(Figure 5–18).

Figure 5–18

- Click the OK button to return to the Personalization window.

- Click the Minimize button to minimize the Personalization window and view the new desktop background (Figure 5–19).

new desktop background

Personalization button

Figure 5–19

To Change the Screen Saver

Another element of a desktop theme that you can modify is the screen saver. A **screen saver** is a moving picture or pattern that displays on the monitor when you have not used the mouse or keyboard for a specified period of time. Originally, screen savers were designed to prevent the problem of **ghosting** (where a dim version of an image would permanently be etched on the monitor if the same image were to be displayed for a long time) by continually changing the image on the monitor. Although ghosting is less of a problem with today's monitors, people still use screen savers. Screen savers can be animations, designs, and other entertaining or fascinating activities that display on the screen after a period of time has passed without any computer activity. You can determine how long this interval should be. Screen savers stop executing when you press a key on the keyboard or move the mouse. Windows Vista provides a variety of screen savers from which you can choose. The steps on the following pages change the screen saver to Photos.

1

- Click the Personalization button on the taskbar to restore the Personalization window.

- Click the Screen Saver link to display the Screen Saver Settings dialog box (Figure 5–20).

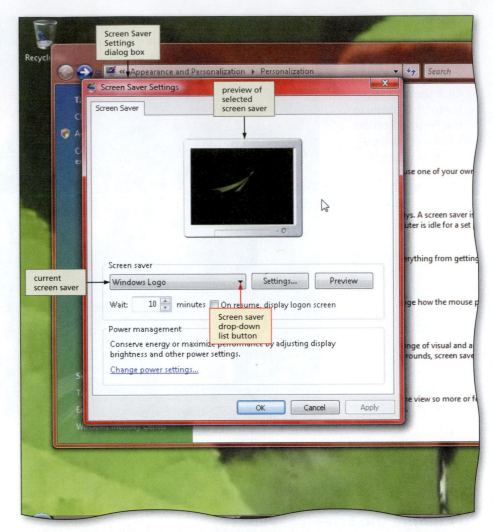

Figure 5–20

2

- Click the Screen saver drop-down list button to display the list of installed screen savers (Figure 5–21).

Figure 5–21

3
- Click the Photos list item to select the Photos screen saver (Figure 5–22).

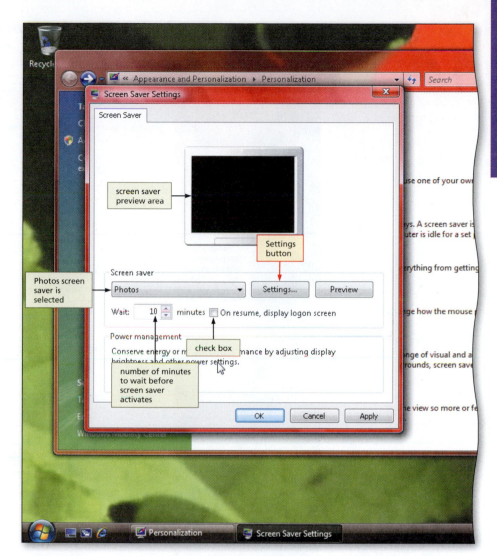

Figure 5–22

To Change the Screen Saver Settings and Preview the Screen Saver

After selecting the Photos screen saver, you can use the Settings button to browse and select pictures you would like the screen saver to use. Not all screen savers have settings that you can change. In the Photos Screen Saver Settings dialog box, you can choose to use all pictures from the Photo Gallery or to select them based upon tags and ratings. You also can use pictures and videos from a folder on your computer. The steps on the following pages add the pictures from the Sample Pictures folder in the Public Pictures folder to the Photos screen saver.

1

• Click the Settings button to display the Photos Screen Saver Settings dialog box (Figure 5–23).

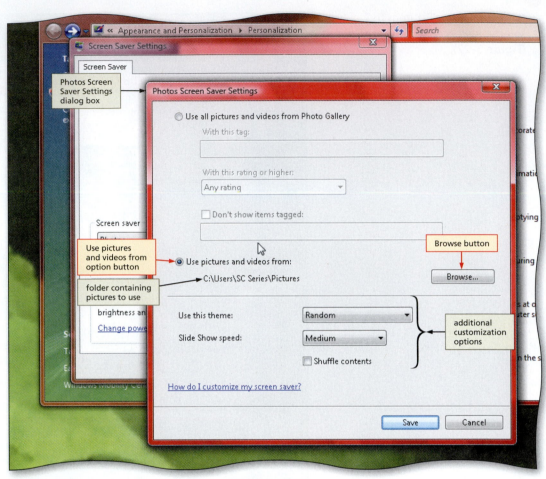

Figure 5–23

2

• If necessary, click the Use pictures and videos from option button.

• Click the Browse button to display the Browse For Folder dialog box (Figure 5–24).

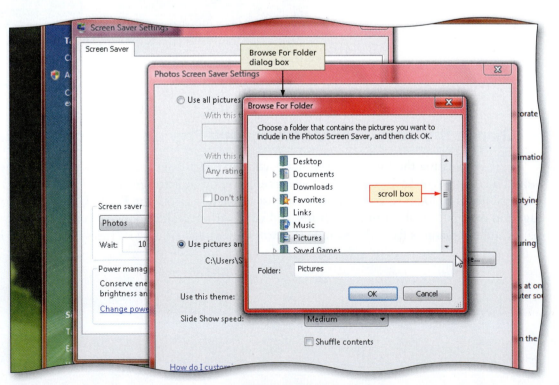

Figure 5–24

3

- Click and drag the scroll box down to display the Public folder.

- Click the Public folder to expand it (Figure 5–25).

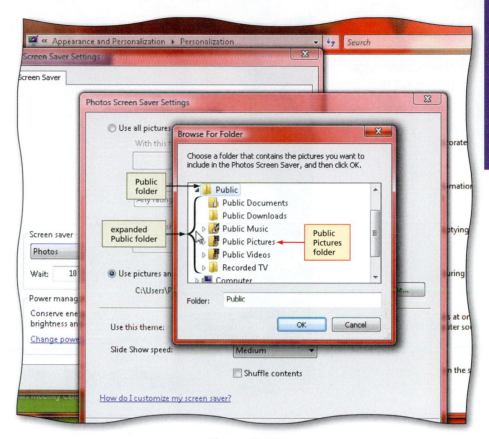

Figure 5–25

4

- Click the Public Pictures folder to expand it.

- Click the Sample Pictures folder to select it (Figure 5–26).

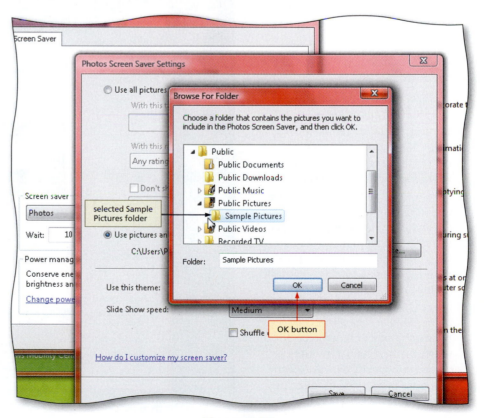

Figure 5–26

5

- Click the OK button to add the Sample Pictures folder to the Photos screen saver (Figure 5–27).

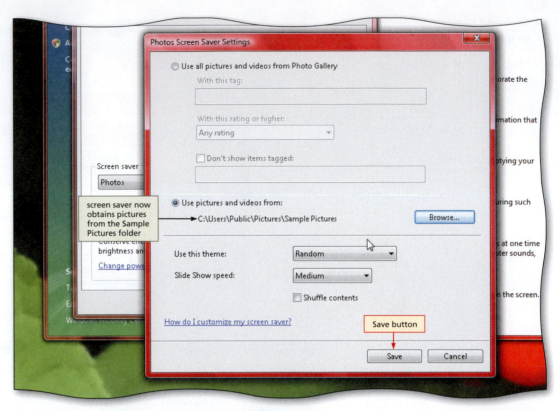

Figure 5–27

6

- Click the Save button to save the changes and return to the Screen Saver Settings dialog box (Figure 5–28).

What does changing the Wait or the power settings do?

The Wait setting controls how long the computer waits before turning on the screen saver. The default number of minutes to wait is set to ten. If the check box to the right of the Wait box contains a check mark, the Welcome screen will display when you resume using the computer after the screen saver has started running, and you may be required to enter a password to access the desktop. Clicking the Change power settings link in the Power management area allows you to select a power scheme and select the number of minutes or hours of inactivity that you want to elapse before the monitor or hard disk turns off and the system standby or system hibernation turn on.

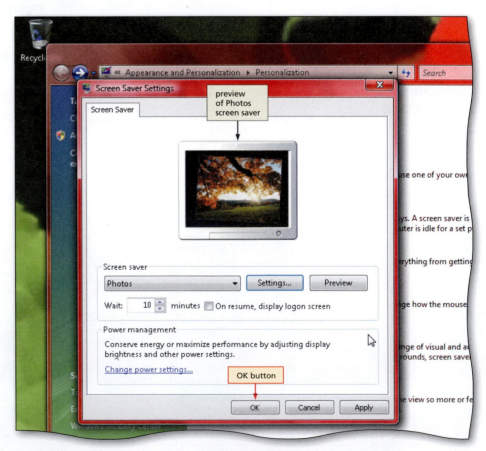

Figure 5–28

7

- Click the Preview button to preview the screen saver (Figure 5–29).

- Move the mouse to exit the preview.

Figure 5–29

8

- Click the OK button to return to the Personalization window (Figure 5–30).

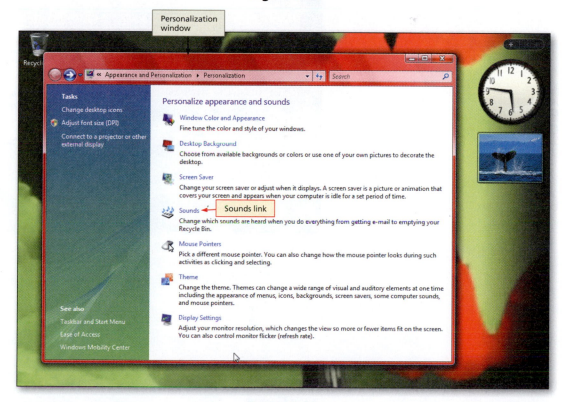

Figure 5–30

To View the Sound Settings

The Sounds link on the Personalization window allows you to view and change the sound settings, including the entire sound scheme, for Windows Vista. A **sound scheme** includes all the sounds that are played when Windows events occur, such as when the computer starts up or shuts down, when an error occurs, and when the Recycle Bin is emptied. Many people change the sound scheme so that they can hear clips from songs and movies that they like. You even can use sound schemes that you have created or downloaded from the Internet. The following steps will display the Sound dialog box.

1

• Click the Sounds link in the Personalization window to open the Sound dialog box (Figure 5–31).

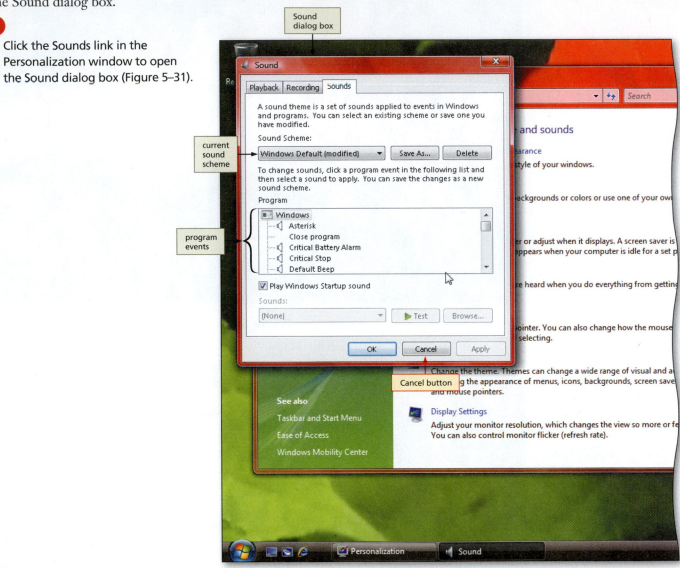

Figure 5–31

2

- After viewing the Sounds settings, click the Cancel button to close the Sound dialog box without making changes (Figure 5–32).

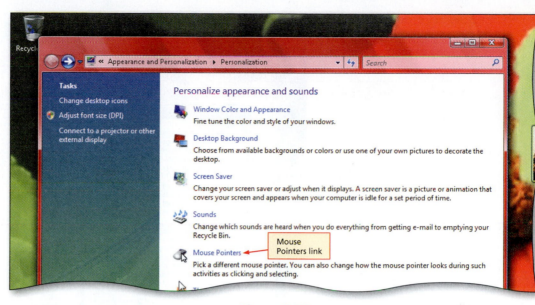

Figure 5–32

Other Ways

1. Press TAB until Sounds is selected, press ENTER

To Change the Mouse Pointers

You can change the way the mouse pointers appear by using the Mouse Pointers link on the Personalization window. You can customize the mouse pointers by selecting a new scheme or modifying a specific mouse event. After selecting the event, you use the Browse button to find mouse pointers that you either have created or downloaded from the Internet. Once you have customized the settings to your satisfaction, you can save the settings as a new scheme. You also can delete schemes that you no longer need. The following steps will display the Mouse Properties dialog box and change the mouse pointers scheme to Windows Aero (extra large) (system scheme).

1

- Click the Mouse Pointers link in the Personalization window to display the Mouse Properties dialog box (Figure 5–33).

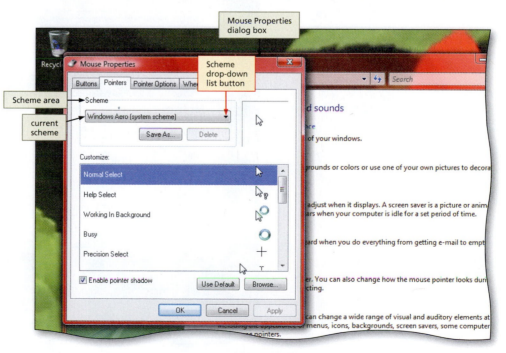

Figure 5–33

2

• Click the Schemes drop-down list button in the Scheme area to display the list of schemes (Figure 5–34).

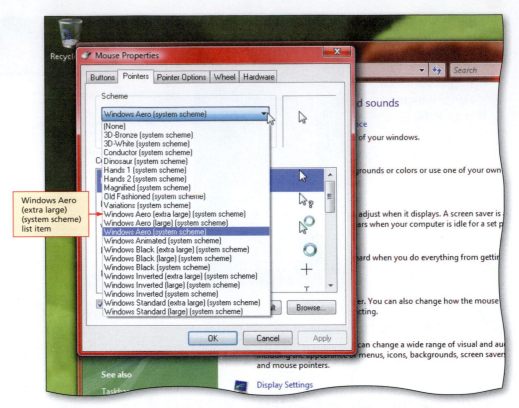

Figure 5–34

3

• Click the Windows Aero (extra large) (system scheme) list item to change the mouse pointers to extra large (Figure 5–35).

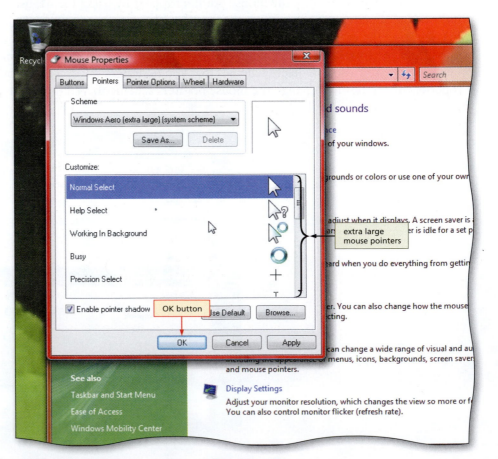

Figure 5–35

4

- Click the OK button to save the changes (Figure 5–36).

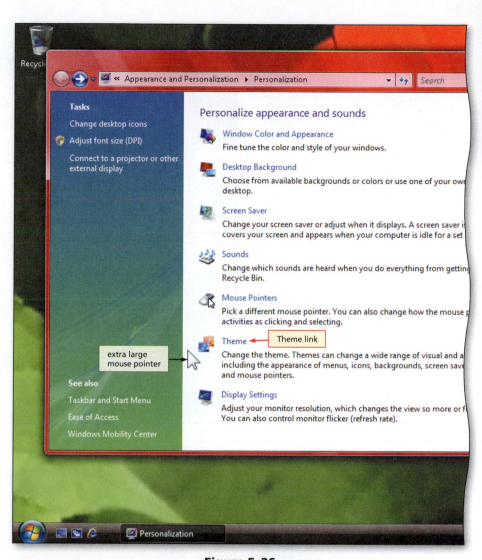

Figure 5–36

Other Ways		
1. Press TAB until Mouse Pointers is selected, press ENTER, press TAB until	Scheme button is selected, press DOWN ARROW until Windows Aero (extra	large) (system scheme) is displayed, press ENTER

To Save a Desktop Theme

Now that you have made all of these changes to your desktop settings, you can save your theme by using the Theme link in the Personalization window. Recall that by clicking on the Theme link, the Theme Settings dialog box is displayed. In the Theme Settings dialog box, you can change themes by using the Theme list button. The changes that you have been making have been saved in the Modified Theme. Each user can personalize their Windows Vista environment, and for each one, a Modified Theme will be created. If you were to switch to another theme such as Windows Vista or Windows Classic, all of your changes to Modified Theme will be lost. If you want to keep a copy of the theme that you have created, you can use the Save As button to save a copy to the Documents folder. The steps on the following pages save the Modified Theme as the SC Theme in the Documents folder.

1

• Click the Theme link in the Personalization window to open the Theme Settings dialog box (Figure 5–37).

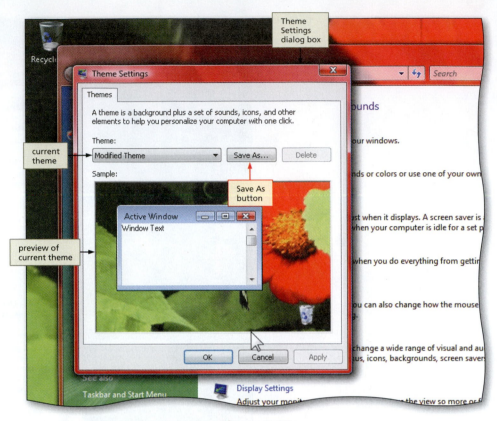

Figure 5–37

2

• Click the Save As button to display the Save As dialog box.

• Type SC Theme in the File name text box to enter the name for the theme (Figure 5–38).

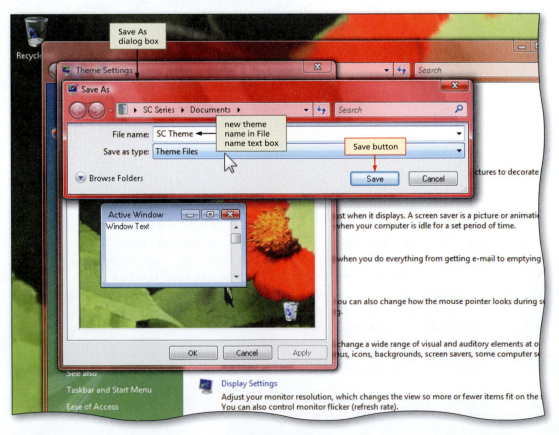

Figure 5–38

3

• Click the Save button in the Save As dialog box to save the SC Theme (Figure 5–39).

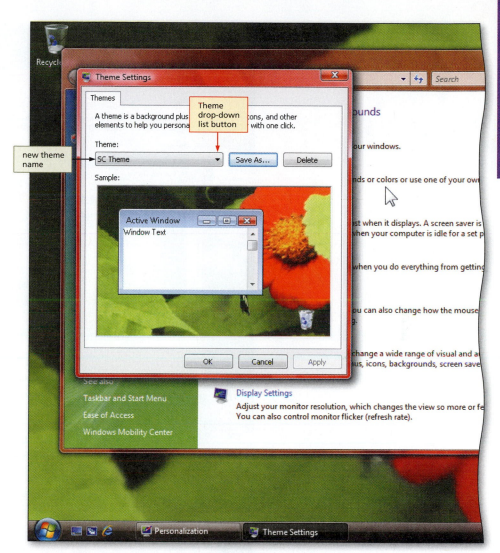

Figure 5–39

To Switch to a Different Desktop Theme

You can test your saved theme by switching to another theme and then back again. This will let you see that all of your changes were properly saved. The steps on the following pages change the desktop theme to Windows Vista and then back to the saved SC Theme.

①

- Click the Theme drop-down list button to display a list of themes (Figure 5–40).

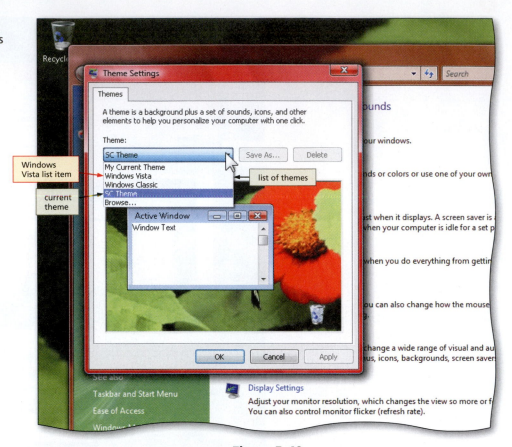

Figure 5–40

②

- Click the Windows Vista list item to select the theme (Figure 5–41).

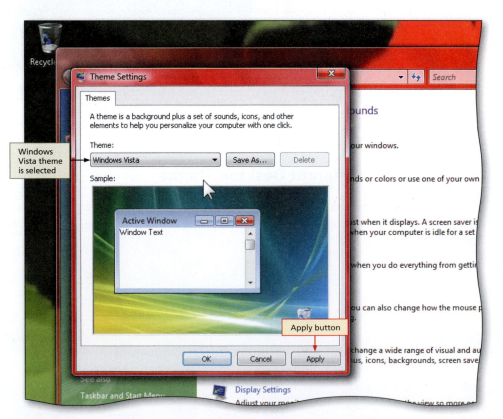

Figure 5–41

3
- Click the Apply button to change to the Windows Vista theme (Figure 5–42).
- Notice the changes in the desktop theme.

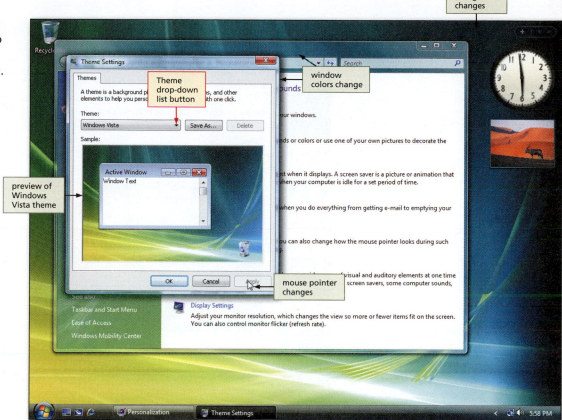

Figure 5–42

4
- Click the Theme drop-down list button to display a list of themes (Figure 5–43).

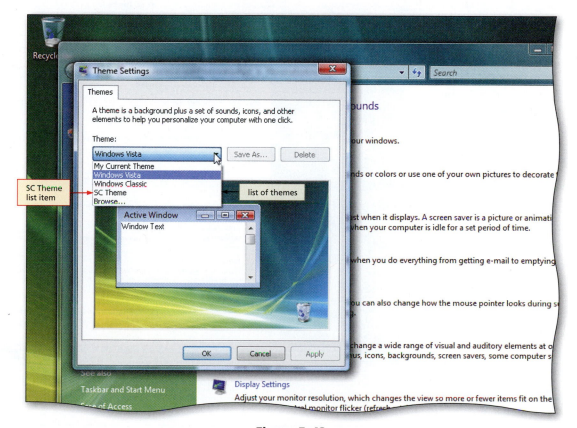

Figure 5–43

5

● Click the SC Theme list item to select the theme (Figure 5–44).

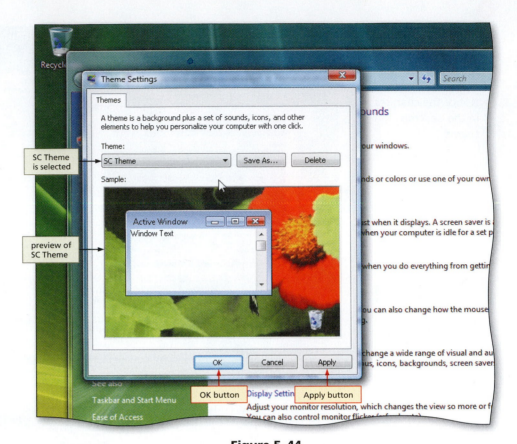

Figure 5–44

6

● Click the Apply button to change to the SC Theme.

● Click the OK button to close the Theme Settings dialog box (Figure 5–45).

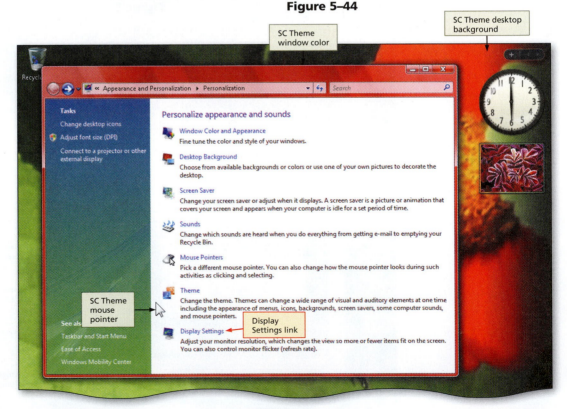

Figure 5–45

To View Display Settings

Another way to personalize your computer is to adjust the display settings for your monitor. You can use the Display Settings dialog box to control the display settings for your monitor, such as the size of the desktop or whether more than one monitor are in use. Typically, Windows Vista automatically chooses the best display settings, including screen resolution, refresh rate (also called monitor flicker), and color, based on your particular monitor and video card support. Your ability to change the display settings is limited to those supported by your monitor type. Options that are not supported by your monitor will appear dimmed, and you will not be able to change those settings.

For most monitors, you can set the Resolution and Colors settings. **Resolution** refers to the clarity of the text and images on your screen. The higher the resolution, the sharper and smaller the items will appear on your desktop. At a lower resolution, fewer items fit on the screen, but they are larger and easier to see. Depending upon whether you have an **LCD** (Liquid Crystal Display) or **CRT** (Cathode Ray Tube) monitor, the recommended resolution for your monitor will vary based upon the display size. The Colors setting allows you to set the color quality that your monitor displays. The **color quality** is determined by the number of colors the monitor can assign to a single **pixel**, which is the smallest part of a picture on your monitor. Computer monitors display pictures by drawing thousands of pixels in columns and rows. The more colors that your monitor can display, the better the color quality will be of the pictures that appear. To get the best color, set your Colors setting to the Highest (32 bit) color setting.

Using the Advanced button in the Display Settings dialog box, you can adjust the adapter settings, the monitor advance settings such as refresh rate, troubleshoot problems, and configure color management for your display. You only should change these options if necessary. Under normal circumstances, you should let Windows Vista configure these options for you. The following steps display the Display Settings dialog box.

1

- Click the Display Settings link to display the Display Settings dialog box (Figure 5–46).

Q&A What is the resolution I should use?

Notebook computers come with LCD monitors. Desktop computers mainly come with LCD monitors; however, some people still use a CRT monitor. For 15-inch monitors, the recommended resolution is 1024 × 768. A 17-inch or 19-inch monitor should use a 1280 × 1024 resolution. Larger monitors use a 1600 × 1200 resolution setting. You always can set your resolution to settings other than the recommended resolution. Reasons for using a non-recommended resolution can include using older programs with more limited display capabilites or creating screen captures to be published at a certain resolution.

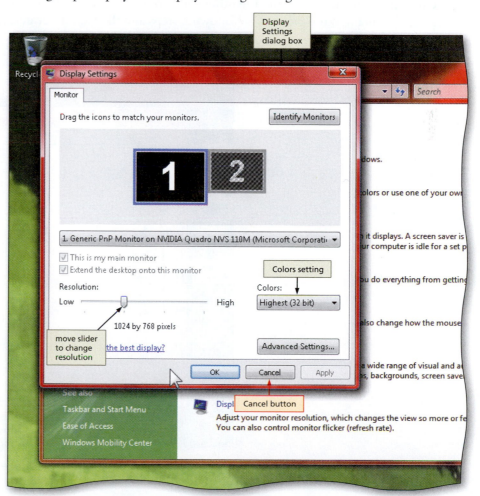

Figure 5–46

2

• After viewing the display settings, click the Cancel button to close the Display Settings dialog box without making any changes (Figure 5–47).

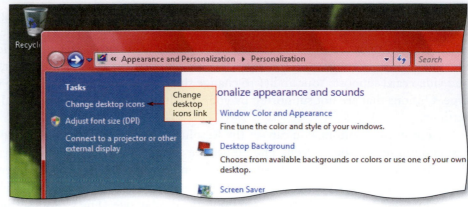

Figure 5–47

Other Ways

1. Press TAB until Display Settings is selected, press ENTER, press TAB until Cancel button is selected, press ENTER

To Add Desktop Icons

The default desktop icon in Windows Vista is the Recycle Bin. You can use the Change desktop icons link in the Personalization window to add the other standard desktop icons: Computer, User's Files, Network, Recycle Bin, and Control Panel desktop icons. The following steps add the Computer desktop icon to the desktop.

1

• Click the Change desktop icons link to display the Desktop Icon Settings dialog box (Figure 5–48).

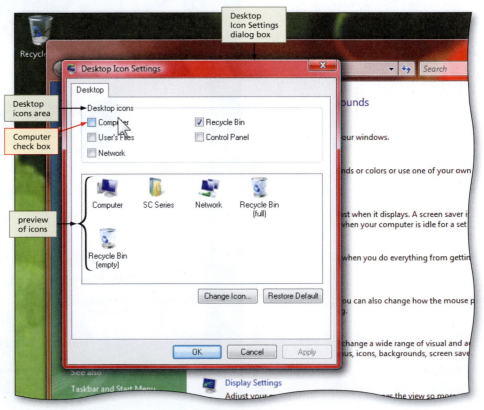

Figure 5–48

2

• Click the Computer check box to configure Windows to show the Computer desktop icon (Figure 5–49).

Can I change how these icons look?

Yes, you can change the icon image used for each of these icons by using the Change Icon button. Use the Restore Default button to change the settings back to their default appearance.

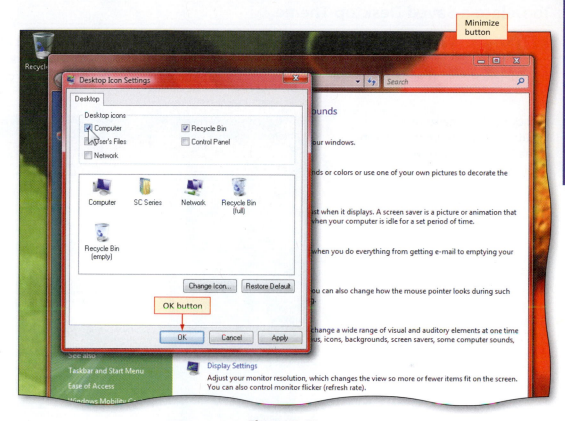

Figure 5–49

3

• Click the OK button to apply the changes and close the Desktop Icon Settings dialog box.

• Click the Minimize button on the Personalization window to minimize the window and view the desktop icon changes (Figure 5–50).

Figure 5–50

To Delete a Saved Desktop Theme

Now that you have finished using the new desktop theme you created and saved, you will remove it. You only can delete desktop themes that you have created and saved, not those provided by Windows Vista. The following steps delete the SC Theme and restore the original desktop theme you noted earlier in the chapter.

1

- Click the Personalization button on the taskbar to restore the Personalization window (Figure 5–51).

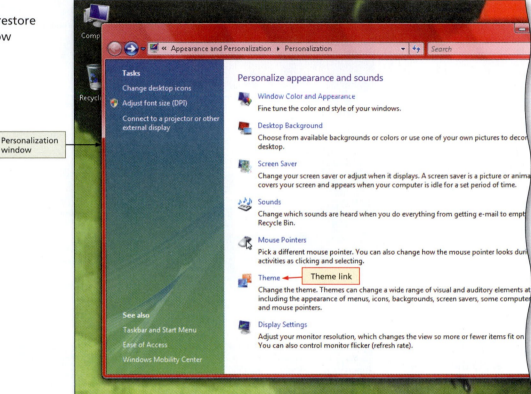

Figure 5–51

2

- Click the Theme link to display the Theme Settings dialog box (Figure 5–52).

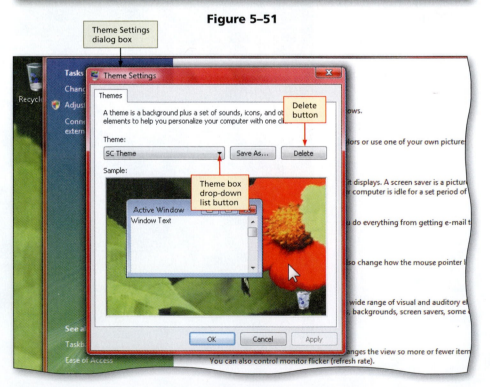

Figure 5–52

3

• If necessary, click the Theme drop-down list button and then select SC Theme to make sure that it is selected.

• Click the Delete button to delete the SC Theme (Figure 5–53).

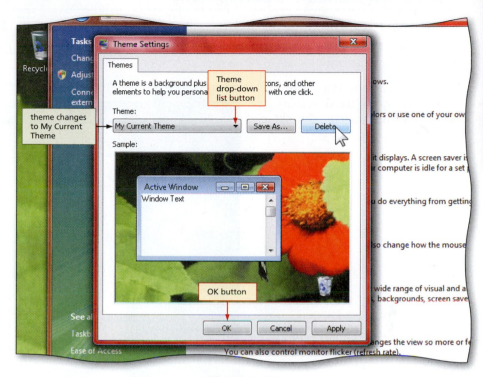

Figure 5–53

4

• Click the Theme drop-down list button to display the list of themes.

• Click the theme that you wrote down on page WIN 311 to restore the original desktop theme.

• Click the OK button to apply the theme (Figure 5–54).

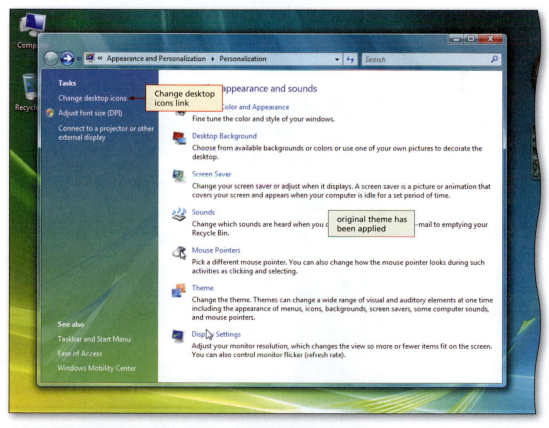

Figure 5–54

To Remove a Standard Desktop Icon

Because you are restoring the desktop back to its original state, you also should remove the Computer icon. The following steps remove the Computer icon from the desktop.

1
- Click the Change desktop icons link to display the Desktop Icon Settings dialog box (Figure 5–55).

Figure 5–55

2
- Click the Computer check box to remove the Computer icon from the desktop (Figure 5–56).

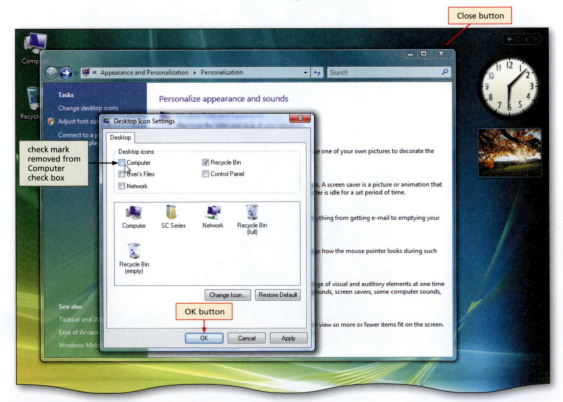

Figure 5–56

3
- Click the OK button to save and apply the changes.

- Click the Close button on the Personalization window to close the Personalization window and to view the desktop icon changes (Figure 5-57).

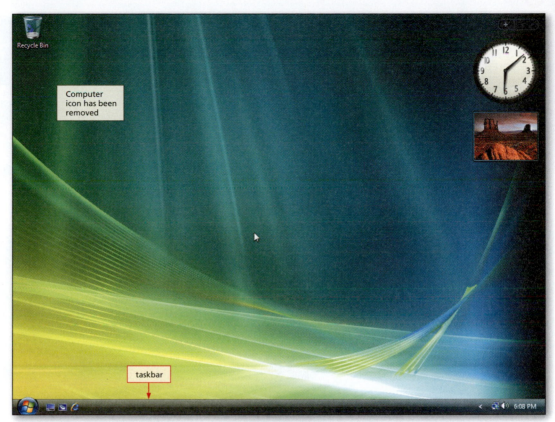

Computer icon has been removed

Recycle Bin

taskbar

Figure 5–57

Customizing the Taskbar

Another method of modifying the desktop work environment is to customize the taskbar at the bottom of the desktop. For example, you can move, resize, and hide the taskbar; add toolbars to the taskbar; change the appearance of the taskbar; and change the taskbar properties. The next sections will illustrate how to customize the taskbar and the toolbars on the taskbar.

To Unlock the Taskbar

By default, the taskbar is locked into position at the bottom of the desktop. Locking the taskbar prevents the taskbar from being moved to another location on the desktop and also locks the size and position of any toolbars displayed on the taskbar. Prior to moving or resizing the taskbar, you must unlock the taskbar. After moving or resizing, you may want to lock the taskbar in its new location so that you do not accidentally change the size and position of the taskbar. The steps on the following page unlock the taskbar.

• Right-click an open area of the taskbar to display a shortcut menu (Figure 5–58).

Figure 5–58

• Click the Lock the Taskbar command to remove the check mark and unlock the taskbar (Figure 5–59).

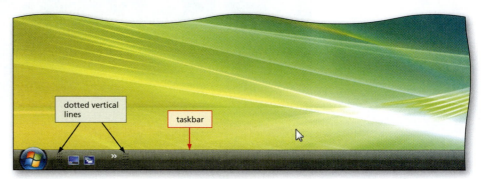

Figure 5–59

Other Ways

1. Right-click open area of taskbar, click Properties, click Lock the taskbar, click OK button

2. Right-click Start button, click Properties, click Taskbar tab, click Lock the taskbar, click OK button

---

To Move the Taskbar

When the taskbar is unlocked, dotted vertical bars appear. You now can change the size of the taskbar by dragging the border up or down. The dotted vertical bar on the left edge of the taskbar button area allows you to resize the Quick Launch toolbar. The dotted vertical bar to the right of the Start button defines the left edge of the Quick Launch toolbar. Other dotted vertical bars will display on the taskbar as toolbars are added to the taskbar. By default, the taskbar is docked at the bottom edge of the desktop, but it can be moved to any of the four edges of the desktop by dragging. The following steps move the taskbar to the top, left, and right edge of the desktop and then back to the bottom.

• Click an open area on the taskbar to select the taskbar (Figure 5–60).

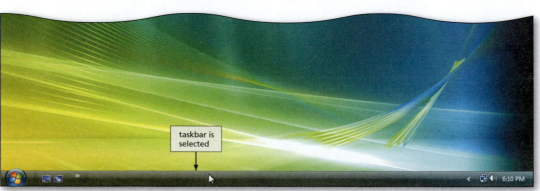

Figure 5–60

2

- Drag the taskbar to the top of the desktop to position the taskbar at the top of the desktop (Figure 5–61).

Q&A

Why am I unable to drag the taskbar?

If the dotted vertical bars do not appear, the taskbar still is locked.

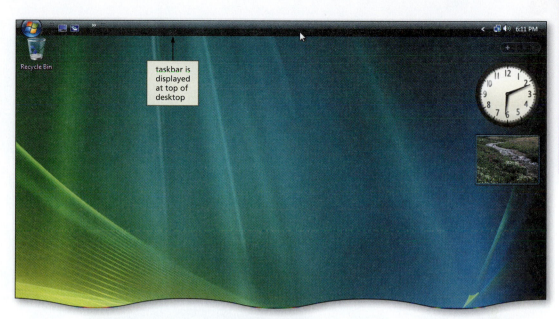

taskbar is displayed at top of desktop

Figure 5–61

3

- Drag the taskbar to the left to position the taskbar on the left side of the desktop (Figure 5–62).

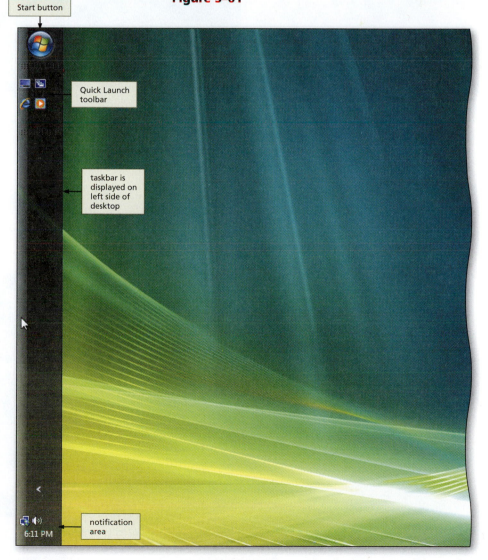

Start button

Quick Launch toolbar

taskbar is displayed on left side of desktop

notification area

Figure 5–62

- Drag the taskbar to the right side of the desktop to position the taskbar on the right of the desktop (Figure 5–63).

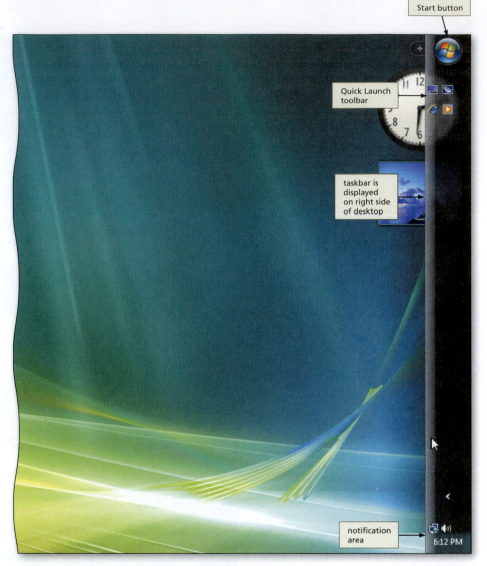

Start button

Quick Launch toolbar

taskbar is displayed on right side of desktop

notification area

6:12 PM

Figure 5–63

- Drag the taskbar back to the bottom of the desktop to return the taskbar to its original location (Figure 5–64).

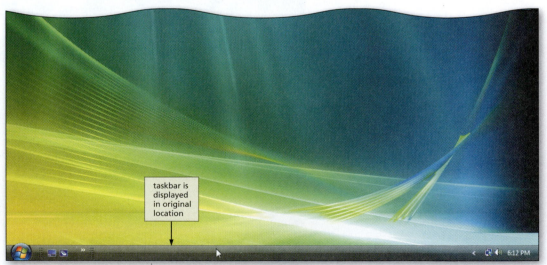

taskbar is displayed in original location

6:12 PM

Figure 5–64

To Lock the Taskbar

Now that you have returned the taskbar to the bottom of the desktop, you will lock the taskbar so that the position of the taskbar is fixed and cannot be changed. The following steps lock the taskbar.

1

- Right-click an open area of the taskbar to display the shortcut menu (Figure 5–65).

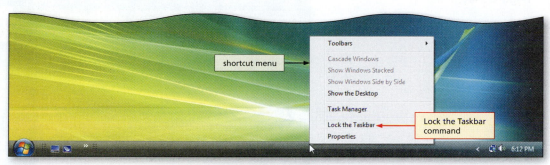

Figure 5–65

2

- Click the Lock the Taskbar command on the shortcut menu to lock the taskbar (Figure 5–66).

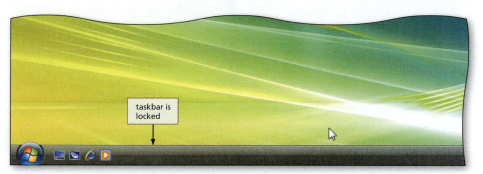

Figure 5–66

To Hide and Redisplay the Taskbar

Another way to customize the desktop is to hide the taskbar so that only its top edge is visible at the bottom of the desktop. When the taskbar is hidden, you must point to the top edge of the hidden taskbar to display it on the desktop. The taskbar will remain on the desktop as long as the mouse pointer hovers on the taskbar. The taskbar does not have to be unlocked to hide and redisplay the taskbar. The following steps hide and then redisplay the taskbar.

1

- Right-click an open area on the taskbar to display the shortcut menu (Figure 5–67).

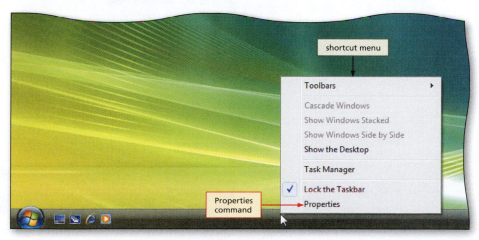

Figure 5–67

2

- Click the Properties command to display the Taskbar and Start Menu Properties dialog box (Figure 5–68).

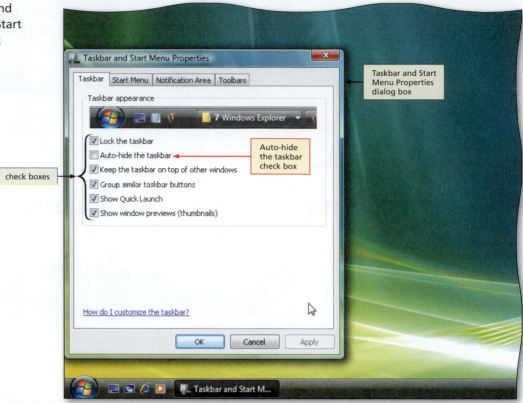

Figure 5–68

3

- Click the Auto-hide the taskbar check box to select it (Figure 5–69).

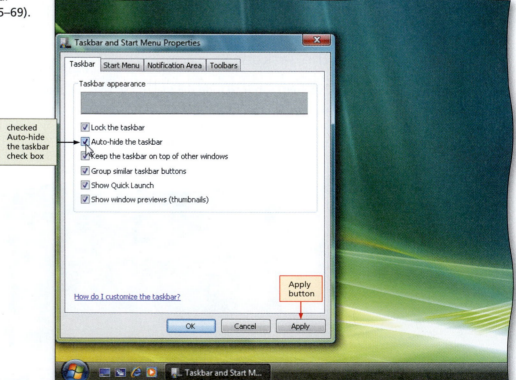

Figure 5–69

- Click the Apply button to apply the Auto-hide feature (Figure 5–70).

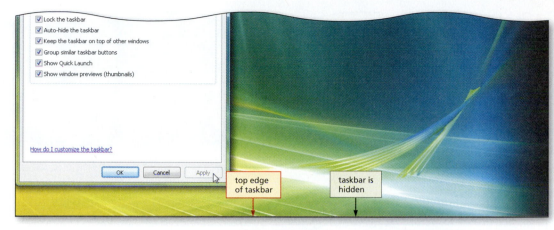

top edge of taskbar

taskbar is hidden

Figure 5–70

- Point to the top edge (thin horizontal line) of the taskbar to display the taskbar (Figure 5–71).

Q&A

Is there another way to display the hidden taskbar?

In addition to pointing to the top edge of the hidden taskbar to display the taskbar, you can display the taskbar and the Start menu at any time by pressing the WINDOWS key or pressing CTRL+ESC.

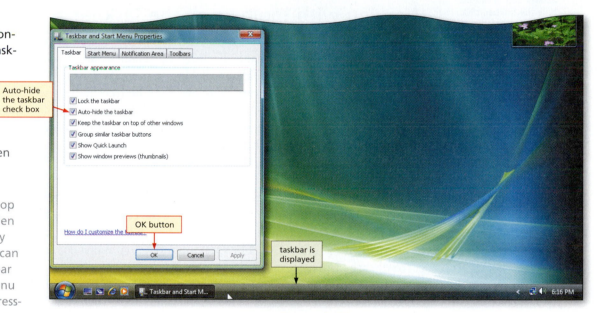

Auto-hide the taskbar check box

OK button

taskbar is displayed

Figure 5–71

6

- Click the Auto-hide the taskbar check box in the Taskbar and Start Menu Properties dialog box to deselect the option.

- Click the OK button to apply the changes and close the dialog box (Figure 5–72).

Figure 5–72

Other Ways

1. Right-click Start button, click Properties, click Taskbar tab, click Auto-hide the taskbar, click OK button

Working with Toolbars on the Taskbar

Windows Vista offers five toolbars that you can add to the taskbar, in addition to the Quick Launch toolbar that is displayed by default. The Quick Launch toolbar allows you to launch a program quickly by clicking an icon. Typically, it contains icons that allow you to view the desktop, activate Windows 3D Flip to switch between open windows on the desktop, launch the Web browser, and launch Windows Media Player (the Windows Media Player shortcut might not be added until you run Windows Media Player for the first time). The Address toolbar allows you to open a document, open a folder, launch an application program, and even search for a Web page. The Windows Media Player toolbar displays controls for playing music and other media, including the Play, Stop, and Pause buttons. The Links toolbar allows you to go to selected Web sites without first having to launch the Internet Explorer Web browser. The Tablet PC Input Panel toolbar allows you to get input from a tablet pen instead of from the keyboard, and is primarily designed to be used with a Tablet PC. The Desktop toolbar contains copies of all the icons that currently are displayed on the desktop.

In addition to adding one of these toolbars provided by Windows Vista, you also can create a custom toolbar and add it to the taskbar using the New Toolbar option. For example, you might create a Current Chapters toolbar containing the icons for all the applications and documents with which you currently are working. Sometimes, applications that you have installed on your computer will provide additional toolbars that you can display on the taskbar. For example, if you were to download Google Desktop from the Internet, a Google Desktop toolbar would be added to the list of available toolbars that you can place on the taskbar.

To Place a Shortcut on a Toolbar

As introduced in Chapter 1, a shortcut is defined as a link to any object on the computer or a network, such as a program, file, folder, disk drive, Web page, printer, or another computer. By default, three shortcuts are displayed on the Quick Launch toolbar when Windows Vista is installed. You can place additional shortcut icons on the Quick Launch toolbar to make launching other applications quick and easy. For example, you may want to add a shortcut icon for Help and Support on the Quick Launch toolbar to make it faster to launch the Help and Support program. The following steps place a shortcut icon to the Help and Support program on the Quick Launch toolbar.

1

- Display the Start menu (Figure 5–73).

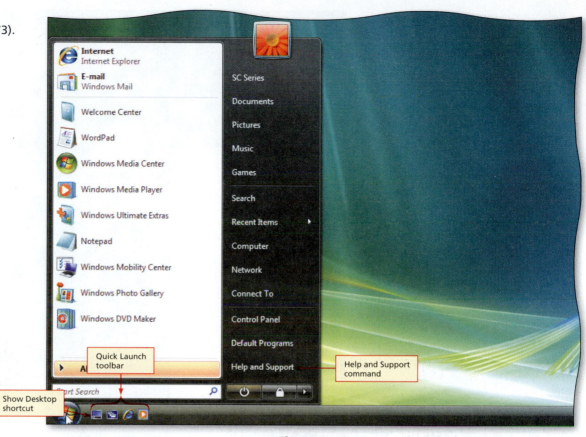

Figure 5–73

2

- Click and drag (without releasing the mouse) the Help and Support command to the Quick Launch toolbar until a vertical divider line displays to the right of the Show Desktop shortcut (Figure 5–74).

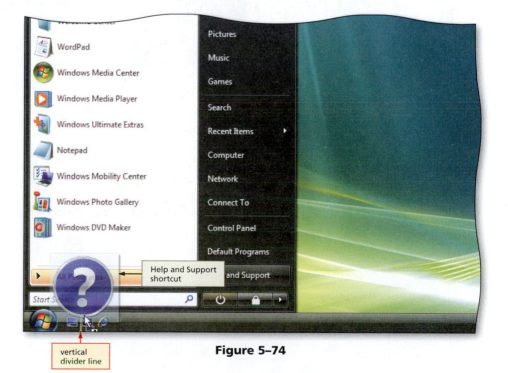

Figure 5–74

3

- Release the mouse button to add the Help and Support shortcut to the Quick Launch toolbar (Figure 5–75).

Figure 5–75

Other Ways

1. Right-drag command to Quick Launch toolbar, release mouse button, select Create Shortcuts Here

To Launch an Application on a Toolbar Using the Double Chevron

When there are more icons on the Quick Launch toolbar than can be displayed in the available space, a double-chevron appears to indicate the presence of additional shortcut icons. The following steps launch Windows Media Player using the double chevron on the Quick Launch toolbar.

1

• Click the double chevron on the Quick Launch toolbar to display a list of hidden shortcut icons (Figure 5–76).

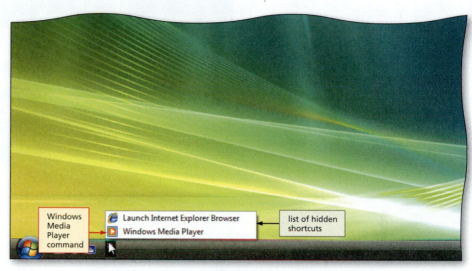

Figure 5–76

2

• Click the Windows Media Player command to launch Windows Media Player (Figure 5–77).

Q&A

What if the Windows Media Player icon does not appear on my Quick Launch toolbar?

If you have not run Windows Media Player, or you have removed the icon from the Quick Launch toolbar, click another shortcut of a program to launch it.

Figure 5–77

3

• Click the Close button to close Windows Media Player (Figure 5–78).

Windows Media Player closes

Figure 5–78

To Unlock the Taskbar

Although you can place a shortcut icon on a toolbar, and launch an application from a toolbar when the taskbar is locked, you cannot resize the toolbar until you unlock the taskbar. The following steps unlock the taskbar.

1 Right-click an open area of the taskbar to display a shortcut menu.

2 Click the Lock the Taskbar command on the shortcut menu to unlock the taskbar (Figure 5–79).

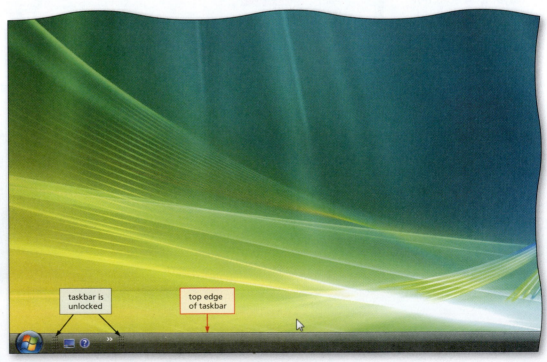

taskbar is unlocked

top edge of taskbar

Figure 5–79

To Resize the Taskbar

Another way to make a hidden shortcut icon on the Quick Launch toolbar visible is to resize the taskbar. The following steps resize the taskbar.

- Point to the top edge of the taskbar until a two-headed arrow displays.

- Click and hold the left mouse button to select the taskbar (Figure 5–80).

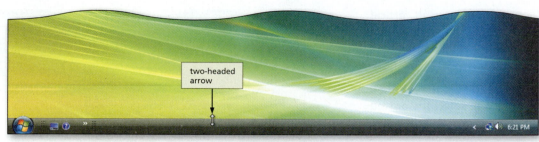

Figure 5–80

- Drag the top edge of the taskbar toward the top of the desktop until the taskbar on your desktop displays all of the shortcuts on the Quick Launch toolbar (Figure 5–81).

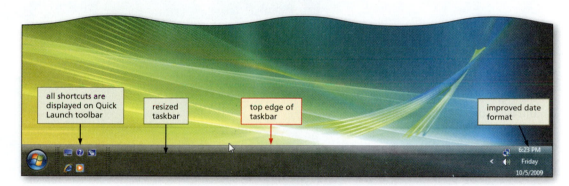

Figure 5–81

To Return the Taskbar to Its Original Size

The following steps return the taskbar to its original size.

1. Point to the top edge of the taskbar until a two-headed arrow displays.

2. Click and hold the left mouse button to select the taskbar.

3. Drag the top edge of the taskbar downward until the taskbar is back to its normal size (Figure 5–82).

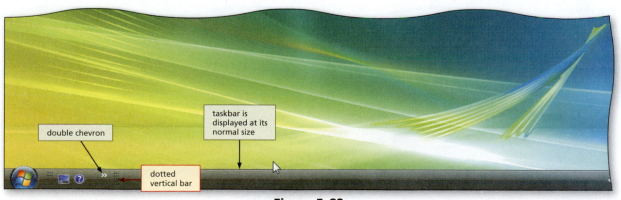

Figure 5–82

To Resize a Toolbar

A third method of making a hidden shortcut icon visible on the Quick Launch toolbar is to resize the toolbar horizontally. The following steps resize the Quick Launch toolbar by dragging the dotted vertical bar.

- Point to the dotted vertical bar to the right of the Quick Launch toolbar until a horizontal double-headed arrow displays.
- Click and hold the left mouse button to select the dotted vertical bar (Figure 5–83).

Figure 5–83

- Drag the dotted vertical bar to the right along the taskbar until the Windows Media Player icon is displayed on the Quick Launch toolbar (Figure 5–84).

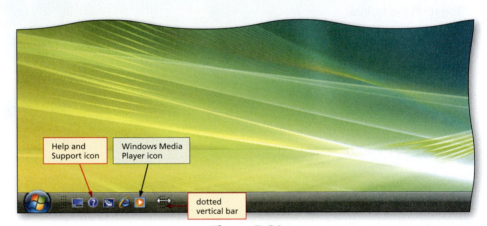

Figure 5–84

To Remove a Shortcut from a Toolbar and Resize a Toolbar

The following steps remove the Help and Support shortcut from the Quick Launch toolbar and resize the Quick Launch toolbar.

- Right-click the Help and Support icon on the Quick Launch toolbar to display a shortcut menu (Figure 5–85).

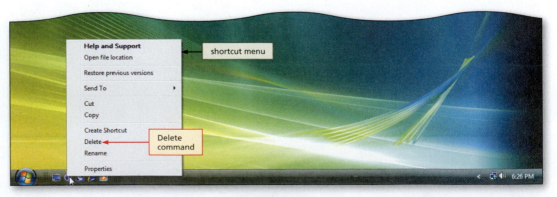

Figure 5–85

2
- Click the Delete command on the shortcut menu to delete the Help and Support shortcut (Figure 5–86).

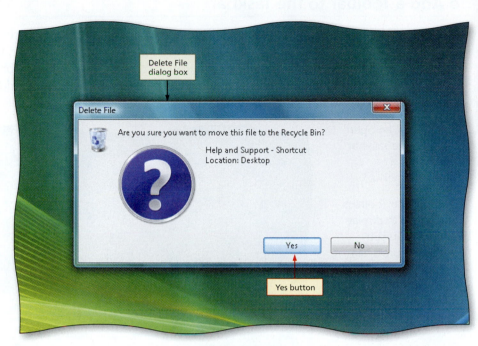

Figure 5–86

3
- Click the Yes button in the Delete File dialog box to confirm that you wish to delete the shortcut (Figure 5–87).

Figure 5–87

4
- Click and drag the dotted vertical bar to the right of the Quick Launch toolbar, moving it to the left along the taskbar to return the Quick Launch toolbar to its original size (Figure 5–88).

Figure 5–88

To Add a Toolbar to the Taskbar

In addition to the Quick Launch toolbar on the taskbar, you can add other toolbars (Address toolbar, Windows Media Player toolbar, Links toolbar, Tablet PC Input Panel toolbar, and Desktop toolbar) to the taskbar. The function of the Address toolbar is multi-faceted: it allows you to search for a Web page, launch an application program, open a document, and open a folder. The following steps add the Address toolbar to the taskbar.

1

- Right-click an open area of the taskbar to display a shortcut menu.

- Point to the Toolbars command to display the Toolbars submenu (Figure 5–89).

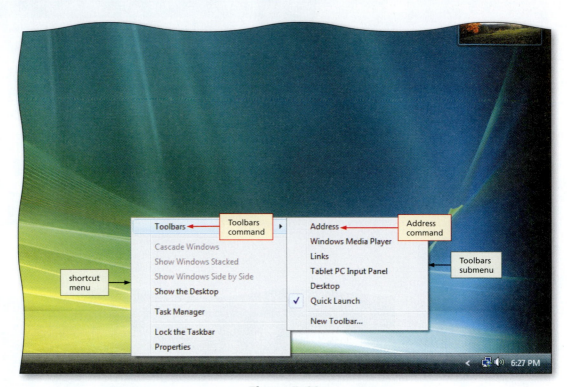

Figure 5–89

2

- Click the Address command to add the Address toolbar to the taskbar (Figure 5–90).

Q&A

Can I change the toolbar's appearance?

You can change the appearance of a toolbar by removing the toolbar title. Right-click the toolbar to display a shortcut menu and then click the Show Title command to remove or display the toolbar title.

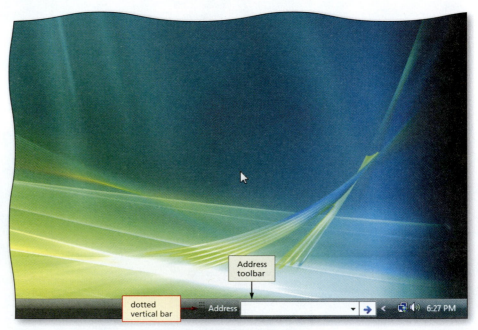

Figure 5–90

To Expand a Toolbar

When you add toolbars to the taskbar, the toolbars display in a collapsed form depending upon the available space on the taskbar. The following step expands the Address toolbar to its full size.

- Double-click the dotted vertical bar on the left side of the Address toolbar to expand the Address toolbar (Figure 5–91).

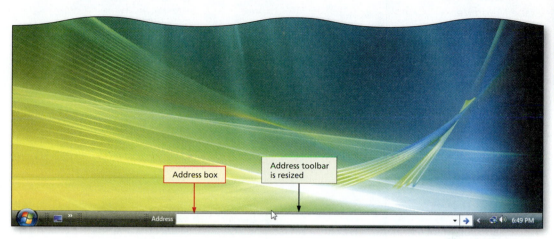

Address box

Address toolbar is resized

Figure 5–91

To Lock the Taskbar

After expanding the Address toolbar, you will lock the taskbar to keep the Address toolbar in its current position.

1 Right-click an open area of the taskbar to display the shortcut menu.

2 Click the Lock the Taskbar command on the shortcut menu to lock the taskbar.

To Display the Contents of a Folder Using the Address Toolbar

To display the contents of a folder using the Address toolbar, you must type the path of the folder in the Address box and then click the Go button. A **path** is the means of navigating to a specific location on a computer. To specify a path to a folder on a computer you must type the drive letter, followed by a colon (:), a backslash (\), and the folder name. For example, the path for the Windows folder on drive C is: C:\Windows. The following steps display the contents of the Windows folder.

- Type `c:\windows` in the Address box to specify the folder to be opened (Figure 5–92).

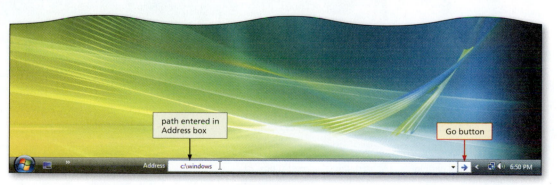

path entered in Address box

Go button

Figure 5–92

2

- Click the Go button to open the folder.

- If necessary, click the Maximize button to maximize the Windows folder window (Figure 5–93).

Q&A

Why am I unable to open the Windows folder?

On some computers, the Windows folder does not exist and the path for the Windows folder will cause an error message to display. In this case, use the path for the WINNT folder (C:\WINNT) for these steps.

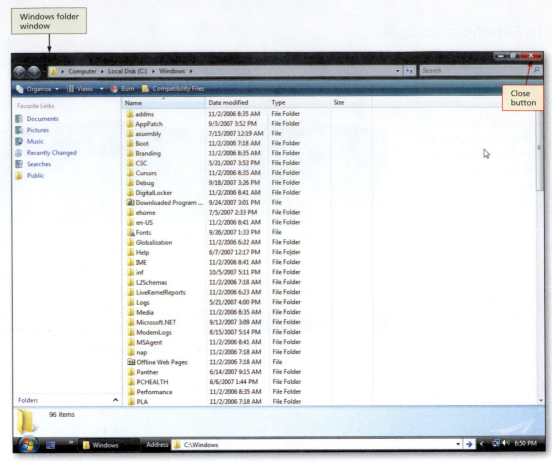

Figure 5–93

3

- After viewing the folder, click the Close button to close the window (Figure 5–94).

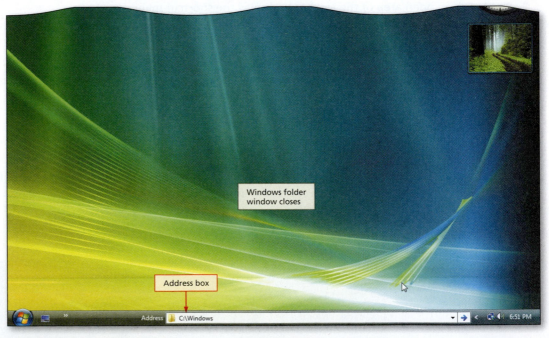

Figure 5–94

Other Ways	
1. Click Address drop-down list button, click path in Address list	2. Click Address box, type path until Address list box is displayed, click path in Address list

To Display a Web Page Using the Address Toolbar

To search for and display a Web page using the Address toolbar, you must type an address, or **Uniform Resource Locator** (URL), and then click the Go button. A URL provides a unique identifier for every Web page and Web site. The following steps enter the URL of the Microsoft Web page in the Address box, launch the Internet Explorer browser, and display the Microsoft Web page in a browser window.

- Click the text in the Address box to select it.

- Type www. microsoft.com in the Address box to enter the address for the Microsoft Web page (Figure 5–95).

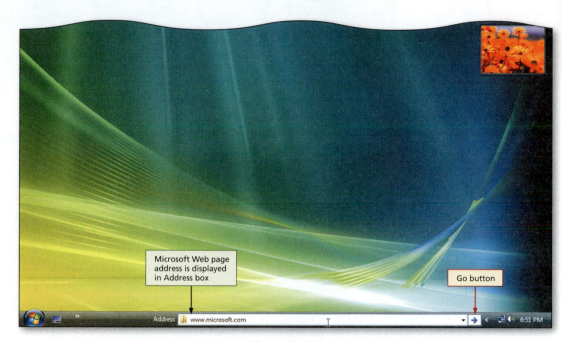

Figure 5–95

- Click the Go button to open the Microsoft Web page in the Internet Explorer Web browser window. If necessary, maximize the window (Figure 5–96).

Figure 5–96

3

- After viewing the Web page, click the Close button to close Internet Explorer (Figure 5–97).

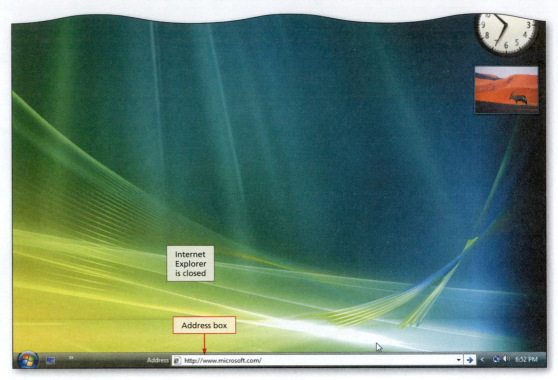

Internet Explorer is closed

Address box

Address 🔵 http://www.microsoft.com/ 6:52 PM

Figure 5–97

Other Ways

1. Click Address drop-down list button, click URL in Address list

2. Click Address box, type URL until Address list box is displayed, click URL in Address list

To Search for Information on the Internet Using the Address Toolbar

To search for information on the Internet using the Address toolbar, you type a keyword or phrase and then click the Go button. The following steps enter the phrase, national weather, in the Address box and display links to Web pages containing the phrase, national weather.

1

- Click the Address box.

- Type `national weather` in the Address box to specify the search keywords (Figure 5–98).

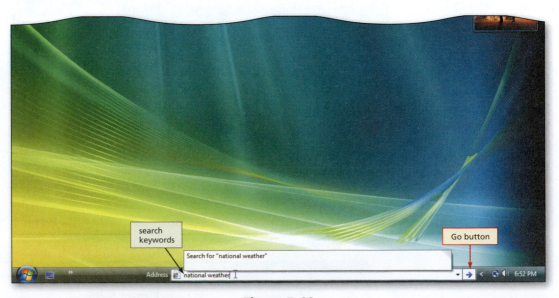

search keywords

Go button

Search for "national weather"

Address 🔵 national weather 6:52 PM

Figure 5–98

2

- Click the Go button to search the Internet (Figure 5–99).

Q&A

Do all search engines process search requests the same way?

Search engines that process search requests have their own rules for entering a search inquiry. On some, you may have to place the word AND between two words to find Web pages containing both words. With other search engines, you select a check box (Any of the words, All the words, and so on) to perform a search. To learn the rules for a search engine, look for a Tips or Help link and then click the link.

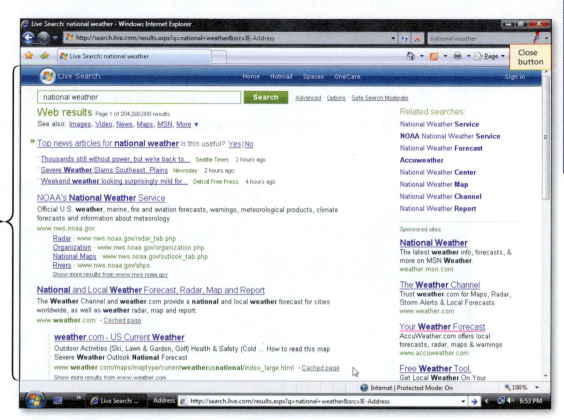

Figure 5–99

3

- After viewing the search results, close Internet Explorer (Figure 5–100).

Q&A

How can I launch an application by using the Address box?

To launch an application such as WordPad, type the application name (WordPad) in the Address box and then click the Go button. The Untitled - WordPad window will display on the desktop.

Figure 5–100

To Remove a Toolbar from the Taskbar

When you no longer want a toolbar on the taskbar, you can remove the toolbar. The following steps remove the Address toolbar from the taskbar.

1 Right-click an open area on the taskbar to display a shortcut menu.

2 Point to Toolbars on the shortcut menu to display the Toolbars submenu.

3 Click Address on the Toolbars submenu to remove the Address toolbar (Figure 5–101).

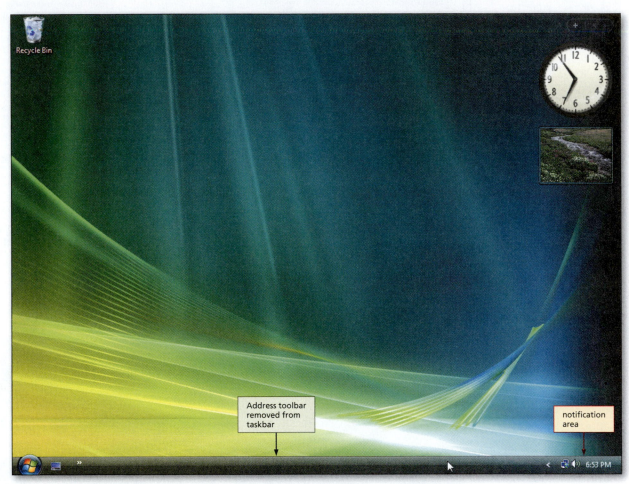

Figure 5–101

Customizing the Notification Area

Another method of modifying the desktop work environment is to customize the notification area. The **notification area** displays the time and also can contain shortcuts that provide quick access to programs which run in the background on your computer, such as Windows Live Messenger and Volume Control. Other shortcuts in the notification area provide information about the status of activities. For example, the Printer icon is displayed when a document is sent to the printer and is removed when printing is complete.

To Set the Notification Behavior of a Notification Item

The notification area shown in Figure 5–101 contains the Show hidden icons button, two notification icons, and the current time. The contents of the notification area may be different on your computer. You can customize the notification area by removing the clock, hiding inactive icons, and setting the notification behavior for the items in the notification area. By default, the clock is displayed and inactive icons are hidden from view. The following steps set the notification behavior for the Windows Live Messenger icon.

- Right-click an open area in the notification area to display a shortcut menu (Figure 5–102).

Figure 5–102

2

- Click the Customize Notification Icons command to display the Customize Notification Icons dialog box (Figure 5–103).

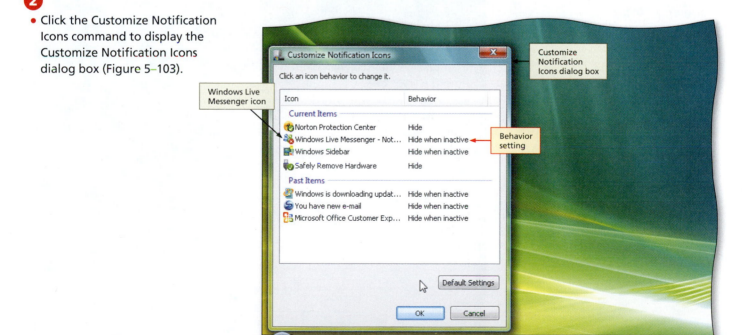

Figure 5–103

3

• Click the Behavior setting next to the Windows Live Messenger icon to display the Behavior list (Figure 5–104).

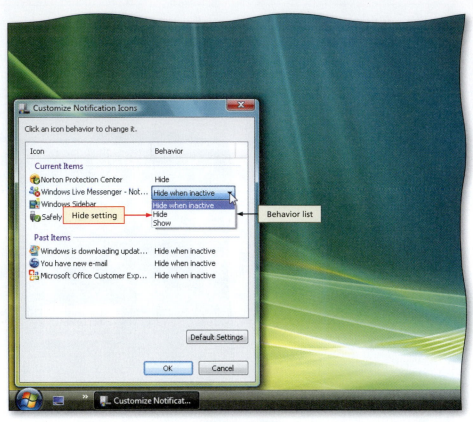

Figure 5–104

4

• Click the Hide setting in the Behavior list to hide the Windows Live Messenger all of the time (Figure 5–105).

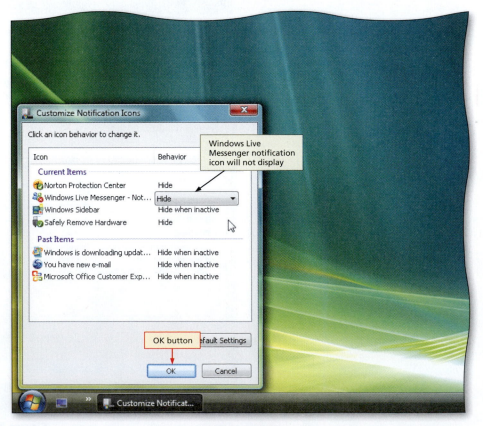

Figure 5–105

- Click the OK button in the Customize Notification Icons dialog box to close the dialog box (Figure 5–106).

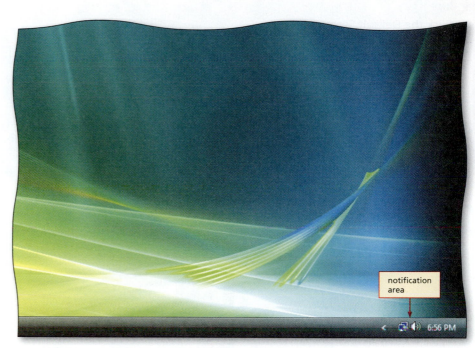

Figure 5–106

To Restore the Default Notification Behaviors

The following steps restore the original notification behavior for the Windows Live Messenger icon.

- Right-click an open area in the notification area to display the shortcut menu.

- Click the Customize Notification Icons command on the shortcut menu to display the Customize Notification Icons dialog box (Figure 5–107).

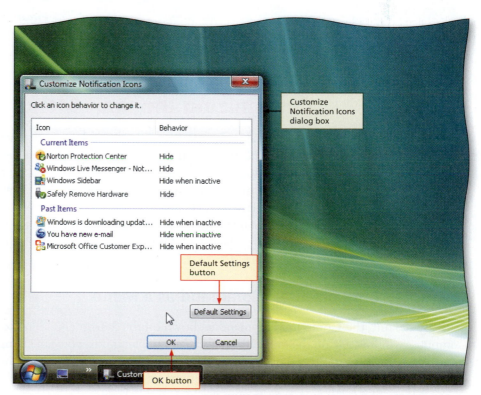

Figure 5–107

2

- Click the Default Settings button in the Customize Notifications dialog box to display the Hide when inactive behavior to the right of each current or past item (Figure 5–108).

- Click the OK button to close the Customize Notification Icons dialog box.

Figure 5–108

Customizing the Start Menu

Another method of personalizing the desktop work environment is to modify the appearance of the Start menu. Recall that in Chapter 2, you customized the Start menu by adding a shortcut to the Daily Reminders folder on the Start menu. In addition to adding a shortcut, you can select a different menu style (Windows Vista or Windows Classic), adjust privacy settings, change the number of menu items to display in the recent programs to display list, alter the look and behavior of menu items, add or remove items from the menu, and select different application programs for the default Web browser and e-mail programs.

To Display the Computer Command as a Menu

By default, the Computer command is shown on the Start menu. This command serves as a link to open the Computer window. Using the Customize Start Menu dialog box, you can change the behavior of the Computer command from a button to a menu. Now when you click the Computer command, instead of opening the Computer window, it will display a menu that shows the items normally appearing in the Computer window as menu items for you to select. The following steps change the look and behavior of the Computer command to a menu and display the new menu.

1

● Right-click the Start button to display a shortcut menu (Figure 5–109).

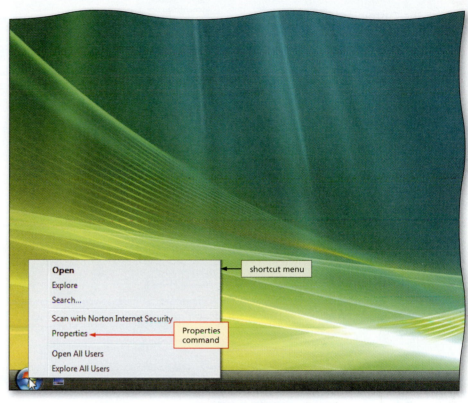

Figure 5–109

2

● Click the Properties command to open the Taskbar and Start Menu Properties dialog box (Figure 5–110).

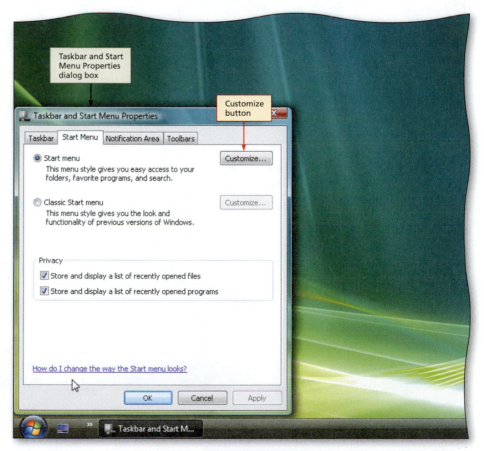

Figure 5–110

• Click the Customize button to open the Customize Start Menu dialog box (Figure 5–111).

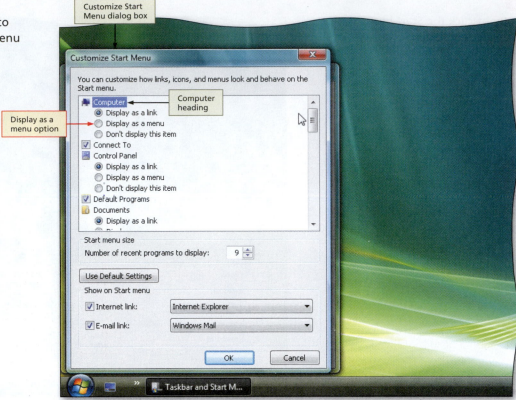

Figure 5–111

• In the customize list, click the Display as a menu option under the Computer heading to change the Computer command to look and behave like a menu (Figure 5–112).

• Click the OK button in the Customize Start Menu dialog box to close the dialog box.

• Click the OK button in the Taskbar and Start Menu Properties dialog box to close the dialog box.

Q&A

Can I change the default Web browser program and default E-mail program?

Yes. The default Web browser program and the default e-mail program shown in Figure 5–112 are Internet Explorer and Windows Mail, respectively. You can change either of these default settings by clicking either the Internet drop-down list button or the E-mail drop-down list button to display a list of available Web browser or e-mail programs and then selecting a program name. The list of Web browser programs may include Internet Explorer and Mozilla Firefox and the list of e-mail programs may include Microsoft Office Outlook, Hotmail, or Gmail.

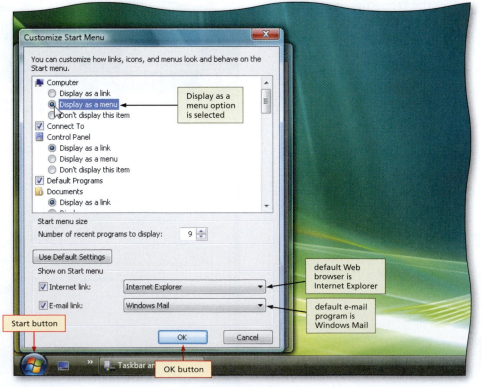

Figure 5–112

- Display the Start menu.

- Point to the Computer command to display the Computer menu (Figure 5–113).

- Click an open area of the desktop to close the Start menu.

Figure 5–113

To Set the Number of Recent Programs to Display

By default, the maximum number of programs that can appear on the recent programs to display list on the Start menu is nine. The steps on the following pages set the maximum number of programs that appear on the number of recent programs to display list to twelve.

- Right-click the Start button to display the shortcut menu.

- Click the Properties command to open the Taskbar and Start Menu Properties dialog box.

- Click the Customize button to open the Customize Start Menu dialog box (Figure 5–114).

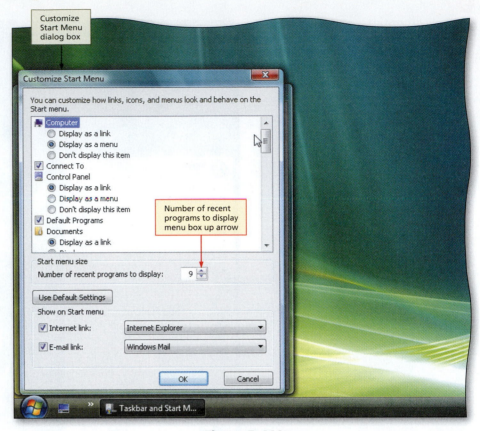

Figure 5–114

2

- Click the Number of recent programs to display menu box up arrow until the number 12 is displayed (Figure 5–115).

- Click the OK button in the Customize Start Menu dialog box to close the dialog box.

- Click the OK button in the Taskbar and Start Menu Properties dialog box to close the dialog box.

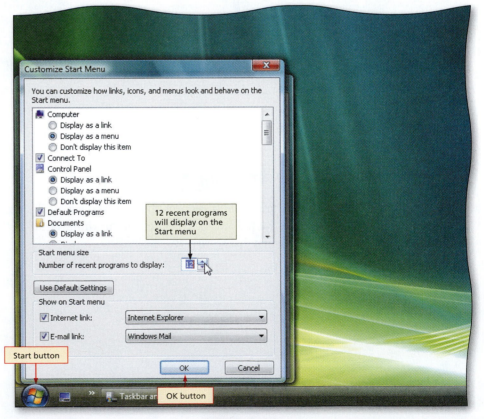

Figure 5–115

3

- Display the Start menu (Figure 5–116).

- Close the Start menu.

Figure 5–116

To Reset the Default Settings of the Start Menu

After changing the Computer command and the number of recent programs to display settings, you will revert to the original settings. The following steps reset the Start menu settings.

- Right-click the Start button to display the shortcut menu.

- Click the Properties command to open the Taskbar and Start Menu Properties dialog box.

- Click the Customize button to open the Customize Start Menu dialog box.

- Click the Use Default Settings button to reset the Start menu to default settings (Figure 5–117).

- Click the OK button in the Customize Start Menu dialog box to close the dialog box.

- Click the OK button in the Taskbar and Start Menu Properties dialog box to close the dialog box.

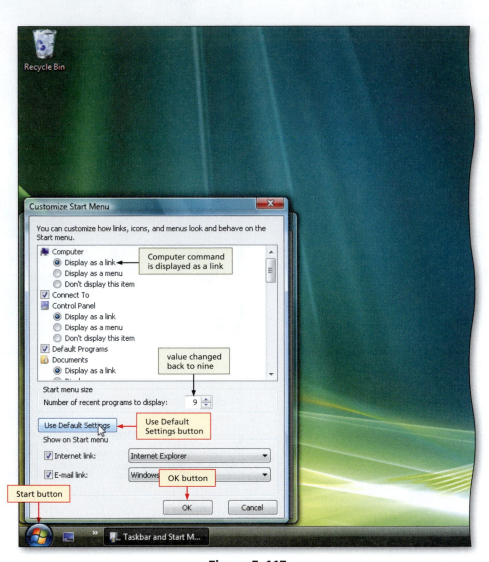

Figure 5–117

Changing Folder Options

In this chapter, you modified the desktop work environment by changing the desktop properties, customizing toolbars and the taskbar, customizing the Start menu, and customizing the notification area. In addition to these changes, you also can make changes to folders, windows, and the desktop by changing folder options. Folder options allow you to specify how you open and work with icons, windows, folders, and files on the desktop.

To Display the Folder Options Dialog Box

The following sections demonstrate how to customize folders, windows, and the desktop by changing folder options in the Folder Options dialog box. The following steps open the Computer folder and then display the Folder Options dialog box.

1

• Display the Start menu.

• Click the Computer command to display the Computer folder window.

• Click the Organize button in the Computer folder window to display the Organize menu (Figure 5–118).

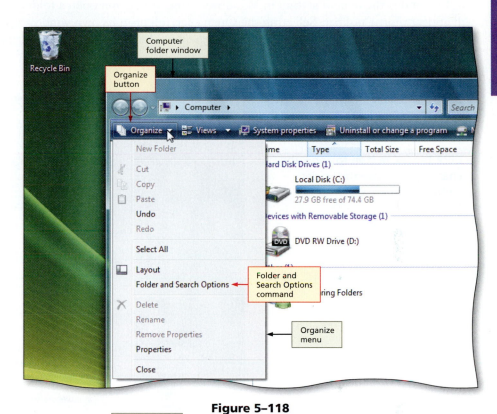

Figure 5–118

2

• Click the Folder and Search Options command to display the Folder Options dialog box (Figure 5–119).

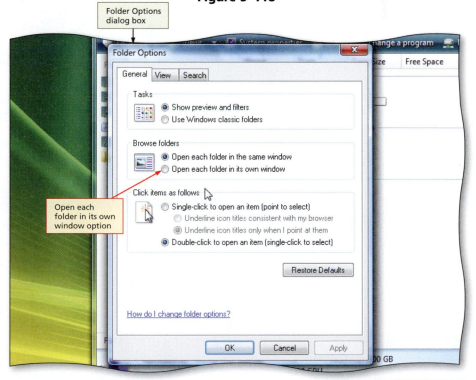

Figure 5–119

Other Ways
1. Press ALT+T, press O

To Select the Open Each Folder in Its Own Window Option

In previous chapters, each time you double-clicked a folder icon in an open window, the new folder window opened in the same window where the previously opened folder window was displayed. The process of opening a folder window in the same window as the previously opened folder is referred to as opening a folder in the same window, and is the default setting in Windows Vista. When you open a folder in the same window, a single button will appear on the taskbar. Selecting the Open each folder in its own window option will cause each folder to open in its own window, resulting in an additional open windows and additional buttons on the taskbar. The following steps turn on the Open each folder in its own window option.

- Click the Open each folder in its own window option to select it (Figure 5–120).

- Click the OK button to apply the changes and close the Folder Options dialog box.

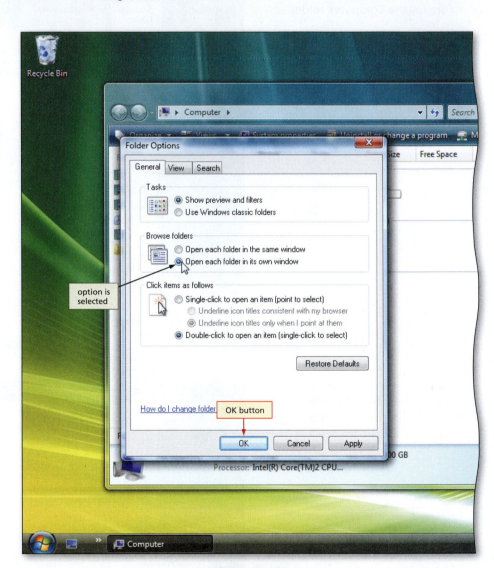

Figure 5–120

To Open a Folder in Its Own Window

The following steps open the Local Disk (C:) folder in its own window.

- Double-click the Local Disk (C:) icon in the Computer folder window to display the Local Disk (C:) folder in its own window (Figure 5–121).

- Click the Close button in the Local Disk (C:) window to close the window.

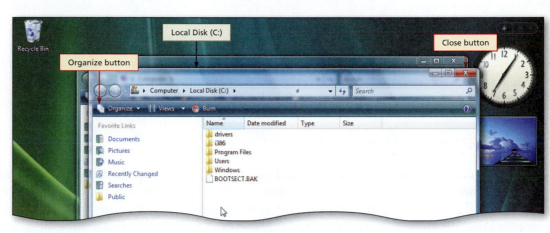

Figure 5–121

To Restore the Folder Options to the Default Folder Options

After changing one or more folder options, you can restore the default folder options you changed by clicking every option button you changed, or you can restore all the folder options to their default options by using the Restore Defaults button. The following steps restore the changed folder options to their default folder options.

- Click the Organize button in the Computer folder window to display the Organize menu.

- Click the Folder and Search Options command to display the Folder Options dialog box.

- Click the Restore Defaults button to restore the folder defaults (Figure 5–122).

- Click the OK button to close Folder Options dialog box, and then click the Close button to close the Computer folder window.

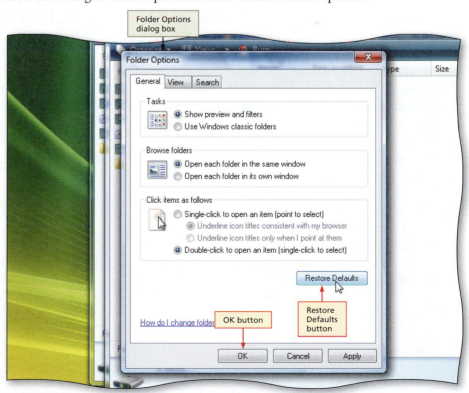

Figure 5–122

To Log Off from and Shut Down the Computer

After completing your work with Windows Vista, you first should close your user account by logging off from the computer, and then turn off the computer.

1 On the Start menu, click the Shutdown options button, and then click the Log Off command to log off from the computer.

2 On the Welcome screen, click the Shut Down button to turn off the computer.

Chapter Summary

In this chapter, you learned to customize and personalize the desktop. You modified desktop properties by selecting a desktop theme, creating a new desktop theme, and changing the mouse pointers and screen saver. You personalized the taskbar by moving, resizing, and hiding the taskbar, adding toolbars to the taskbar, and adding a shortcut icon to a toolbar. You customized the Start menu by changing the Computer command on the Start menu and customized the notification area by changing the behaviors of items. Finally, you selected and turned on folder options, viewed the results of turning on folder options, and restored folder options. The items listed below include all the new Windows Vista skills you have learned in this chapter.

1. Open the Personalization Window (WIN 309)
2. View the Current Theme (WIN 310)
3. Change the Color of Windows (WIN 312)
4. Change the Color Intensity (WIN 314)
5. Show the Color Mixer (WIN 315)
6. View Classic Appearance Settings (WIN 316)
7. View the Advanced Appearance Settings (WIN 317)
8. Open the Desktop Background Window (WIN 318)
9. Change the Desktop Background to a Video (WIN 319)
10. Change the Screen Saver (WIN 323)
11. Change the Screen Saver Settings and Preview the Screen Saver (WIN 325)
12. View the Sound Settings (WIN 330)
13. Change the Mouse Pointers (WIN 331)
14. Save a Desktop Theme (WIN 333)
15. Switch to a Different Desktop Theme (WIN 335)
16. View Display Settings (WIN 339)
17. Add Desktop Icons (WIN 340)
18. Delete a Saved Desktop Theme (WIN 342)
19. Remove a Standard Desktop Icon (WIN 344)
20. Unlock the Taskbar (WIN 345)
21. Move the Taskbar (WIN 346)
22. Lock the Taskbar (WIN 349)
23. Hide and Redisplay the Taskbar (WIN 349)
24. Place a Shortcut on a Toolbar (WIN 352)
25. Launch an Application on a Toolbar Using the Double Chevron (WIN 355)
26. Resize the Taskbar (WIN 357)
27. Resize a Toolbar (WIN 358)
28. Remove a Shortcut from a Toolbar and Resize a Toolbar (WIN 358)
29. Add a Toolbar to the Taskbar (WIN 360)
30. Expand a Toolbar (WIN 361)
31. Display the Contents of a Folder Using the Address Toolbar (WIN 361)
32. Display a Web Page Using the Address Toolbar (WIN 363)
33. Search for Information on the Internet Using the Address Toolbar (WIN 364)
34. Set the Notification Behavior of a Notification Item (WIN 367)
35. Restore the Default Notification Behaviors (WIN 369)
36. Display the Computer Command as a Menu (WIN 370)
37. Set the Number of Recent Programs to Display (WIN 373)
38. Reset the Default Settings of the Start Menu (WIN 376)
39. Display the Folder Options Dialog Box (WIN 377)
40. Select the Open Each Folder in Its Own Window Option (WIN 378)
41. Open a Folder in Its Own Window (WIN 379)
42. Restore the Folder Options to the Default Folder Options (WIN 379)

Learn It Online

Test your knowledge of chapter content and key terms.

Instructions: To complete the Learn It Online exercises, start your browser, click the Address bar, and then enter the Web address `scsite.com/winvista/learn`. When the Windows Vista Learn It Online page is displayed, click the link for the exercise you want to complete and then read the instructions.

Chapter Reinforcement TF, MC, and SA

A series of true/false, multiple-choice, and short-answer questions that test your knowledge of the chapter content.

Flash Cards

An interactive learning environment where you identify chapter key terms associated with displayed definitions.

Practice Test

A series of multiple-choice questions that test your knowledge of chapter content and key terms.

Who Wants To Be a Computer Genius?

An interactive game that challenges your knowledge of chapter content in the style of a television quiz show.

Wheel of Terms

An interactive game that challenges your knowledge of chapter key terms in the style of the television show *Wheel of Fortune*.

Crossword Puzzle Challenge

A crossword puzzle that challenges your knowledge of key terms presented in the chapter.

Apply Your Knowledge

Reinforce the skills and apply the concepts you learned in this chapter.

Creating and Saving a Desktop Theme

Instructions: A friend, who owns a tropical fish store, showed you the creative desktop theme she created for the computers in her store. The desktop looked like an aquarium. You own a travel agency and want to create a unique desktop theme for the computers in your agency, instead of using the default Windows Vista desktop theme.

Perform the following tasks:
Part 1: Select the Windows Vista Desktop Theme
1. Right-click the desktop and then click Personalize on the shortcut menu to open the Personalization folder window. Click Theme to open the Theme Settings dialog box.

2. In the space provided, write down the desktop theme name that displays in the Theme box on the desktop of your computer. After you write it down, close the Theme Settings dialog box.

_____

Part 2: Change the Desktop Background
1. Click the Desktop Background link.

2. Change location to the Sample Pictures folder on your computer, and then select the Garden picture. If the Garden Picture is not available, select another background and use this background for the remainder of this assignment.

3. Center the background and then click the OK button to close the Desktop Background folder window.

Part 3: Add Icons to the Desktop

1. Click the Change desktop icons link to display the Desktop Icon Settings dialog box.

2. Click User's Files and Computer in the Desktop icons area.

3. Click the OK button in the Desktop Icon Settings dialog box.

Part 4: Change the Screen Saver

1. Click the Screen Saver link to display the Screen Saver Settings dialog box.

2. Click the Screen saver drop-down list button and then click Aurora in the Screen saver list.

3. Click the Preview button to display the screen saver on the desktop. Move the mouse to remove the screen saver.

4. Click the OK button in the Screen Saver Settings dialog box.

Part 5: Change the Color Scheme

1. Click the Window Color and Appearance link.

2. Click the Orange color option.

3. Click the OK button to save and apply the color scheme (Figure 5–123).

Figure 5–123

Part 6: Save the Desktop Theme

1. Click the Theme link.

2. Click the Save As button.

3. Type Garden Paradise for in the File name box, press the SPACEBAR, type your first name, press the SPACEBAR, and then type your last name.

4. Click the Save button to save the new desktop theme.

5. Click the OK button in the Theme Settings dialog box. Click the Close button in the Personalization window.

Part 7: Printing the Desktop

1. Double-click the Computer icon on the desktop to display the Computer folder window. Resize the Computer folder window so that the Computer folder window and the desktop icons (Computer and User's files) are visible on the desktop.

2. Press the PRINT SCREEN key on the keyboard to place an image of the desktop on the Clipboard, a temporary Windows storage area.

3. Display the Start menu, click All Programs, click Accessories, and then click Paint.

4. Maximize the Untitled – Paint window.

5. Click Edit on the menu bar and then click Paste on the Edit menu to copy the image from the Clipboard to the Paint window.

6. Click File on the menu bar, click Print on the File menu, and then click the Print button in the Print dialog box to print the Paint document.

7. Click the Close button in the Untitled – Paint window and then click the Don't Save button in the Paint dialog box to quit the Paint program.

8. Click the Close button in the Computer folder window to close the window.

Part 8: Deleting the Desktop Theme

1. Right-click an open area on the desktop and then click Personalize on the shortcut menu.

2. Click the Theme link.

3. Verify that the name of the desktop theme (Garden Paradise for…) you created earlier displays in the Theme box.

4. Click the Delete button.

5. Click the Theme drop-down list button.

6. Click the desktop theme name in the Theme list you wrote down in Step 2 of Part 1.

7. Click the OK button in the Theme Settings dialog box.

Part 9: Deleting the Icons on the Desktop

1. Click the Change desktop icons link in the Personalization window.

2. Remove the check marks from the User's Files and Computer check boxes in the Desktop Icon Settings dialog box.

3. Click the OK button in the Desktop Icon Settings dialog box.

4. Click the Close button in the Personalization window.

5. Submit the printed Paint document illustrating your desktop theme to your instructor.

Extend Your Knowledge

Extend the skills you learned in this chapter and experiment with new skills. You may need to use Help to complete the assignment.

Researching Power Plans and Folder Options

Instructions: Your friend has asked for your input about how best to personalize the power plan and folder options on her computer to meet her needs. Not knowing much about these two topics, you decide to research them further.

Perform the following tasks and answer the questions.

Part 1: Learn about Power Options

1. Right-click the desktop and then click Personalize on the shortcut menu to display the Personalization window.

2. Click the Screen Saver link. Click the Change power settings link to display the Power Options window (Figure 5–124).

Figure 5–124

3. Answer the following questions about energy management using the question mark button in the Power Options window.

   a. What is a power plan? _____

   b. Which plans are available in Windows Vista? _____

   c. Which plan is the best for a laptop? A desktop PC? _____

4. Answer the following questions about power plans using the figure and Windows Help and Support.

   a. What power plans display in the Preferred plans area? _____

   b. Click Change plan settings link for the Power saver power plan. What does the entry in the Turn off the display box indicate?

   _____

   c. Click the Change advanced power settings link. What does the entry for Hard disk indicate?

   _____

   d. What does the entry for Sleep indicate? _____

5. Click the Cancel button in the Power Options dialog box, click the Close button in the Edit Plan Settings window, click the Cancel button in the Screen Saver Settings dialog box, and then click the Close button in the Personalization window.

Part 2: Learn about Folder Options

1. Display the Start menu, click the Computer command, click the Organize button, and then click Folder and Search Options.

2. Click the View tab in the Folder Options dialog box.

3. Answer the following questions about the advanced settings. You may have to use Windows Help and Support to find the answers.

   a. What does the Reset Folders button do? _____

   b. How many advanced settings are active? _____

   c. Which setting is active for hidden files and folders? (A selected option button indicates an active setting.) _____

   d. What does the Restore Defaults button do? _____

4. Click the Cancel button in the Folder Options dialog box, and then click the Close button in the Computer folder window.

In the Lab

Using the guidelines, concepts and skills presented in this chapter to increase your knowledge of Windows Vista. Labs are listed in order of increasing difficulty.

Lab 1: Working with Folder Options

Instructions: You recently took an operating system course at school. The instructor spent an entire hour demonstrating how to change folder options, but there was no time left at the end of the class to practice in the computer lab. You want to practice changing folder options on your home computer.

Perform the following tasks:

Part 1: Recording the Current Folder Options

1. Display the Start menu and then click the Computer command.

2. Click the Organize button on the toolbar and then click Folder and Search Options.

3. In the space provided, record which option buttons in the Folder Options dialog box are selected.

   _____

4. Click the Cancel button in the Folder Options dialog box.

5. Click the Close button in the Computer folder window.

Part 2: Displaying Icons on the Desktop

1. Right-click an open area of the desktop and then click Personalize.

2. Click the Change desktop icons link.

3. Click User's Files and Computer in the Desktop Icon Settings dialog box. Change the icon for User's Files and Computer to a different icon of your choosing (Figure 5–125).

4. Click the OK button in the Desktop Icon Settings dialog box.

5. Click the Close button in the Personalization window.

Figure 5–125

Part 3: Turning on the Single-click to Open an Item (Point to Select) Option

1. Double-click the Computer icon on the desktop to open the Computer folder window.

2. Click the Organize button and then click Folder and Search Options.

3. Click Single-click to open an item (point to select) in the Click items as follows area. If necessary, click Underline icon titles consistent with my browser.

4. Click the OK button in the Folder Options dialog box.

Part 4: Opening a Folder by Single-Clicking

1. Click the Pictures link in the Computer folder window.

   a. Does the Pictures folder window open in its own window? _____

2. Click the Close button in the Pictures folder window.

Part 5: Printing the Desktop

1. Click the Computer icon on the desktop, click the Local Disk (C:) icon in the Computer folder window, and then click the Windows (or WINNT) icon in the Local Disk (C:) folder window.

2. Press the PRINT SCREEN key on the keyboard to place an image of the desktop on the Clipboard, which is a temporary Windows storage area.

3. Display the Start menu, type `paint` in the Search box, and then click Paint in the results list under Programs.

4. Maximize the Untitled – Paint window.

5. Click Edit on the menu bar and then click Paste on the Edit menu to copy the image from the Clipboard to the Paint window.

6. Click File on the menu bar, click Print on the File menu, and then click the Print button in the Print dialog box to print the Paint document.

7. Click the Close button in the Untitled – Paint window and then click the Don't Save button in the Paint dialog box to quit the Paint program.

8. Close all open windows.

Part 6: Removing the Icons on the Desktop
1. Right-click an open area on the desktop and then click Personalize.

2. Click the Change desktop icons link.

3. Click User's Files and Computer in the Desktop Icon Settings dialog box.

4. Click the OK button in the Desktop Icon Settings dialog box.

5. Click the Close button in the Personalization window.

Part 7: Resetting the Folder Options
1. Display the Start menu, click the Computer command, click the Organize button, and then click Folder and Search Options.

2. Click the option buttons in the Folder Options dialog box that correspond to the settings you recorded in Step 3 of Part 1 and then click the OK button.

3. Click the Close button in the Computer folder window.

4. Submit the printed Paint document illustrating the open windows on the desktop to your instructor.

In the Lab

Lab 2: Using the Address Toolbar to Search the Internet

Instructions: You decide to use your newly acquired Internet searching skills to earn money during the summer vacation. You take a part-time job in the Information Technology department to assist an instructor doing research on searching techniques. You decide to use the Address toolbar as a means of searching the Internet.

Perform the following tasks:
Part 1: Unlocking the Taskbar and Adding the Address Toolbar to the Taskbar
1. Right-click an open area of the taskbar.

2. Click Lock the Taskbar on the shortcut menu to unlock the taskbar.

3. Right-click an open area of the taskbar, point to Toolbars, and then click Address.

4. Double-click the dotted vertical bar to the left of the Address title.

Part 2: Locking the Taskbar

1. Right-click an open area of the taskbar.

2. Click Lock the Taskbar on the shortcut menu to lock the taskbar (Figure 5–126).

Figure 5–126

Part 3: Using the Address Toolbar to Display Folder Content

1. Type c:\users in the Address box and then click the Go button.

    a. What folder displays on the desktop? _____

2. Type documents in the Address box and then click the Go button.

    a. What folder displays on the desktop? _____

3. Type pictures in the Address box and then click the Go button.

    a. What folder displays on the desktop? _____

4. Close all open windows.

Part 4: Using the Address Toolbar to Display a Web Page

1. Type www.course.com in the Address box and then click the Go button. Print the Web page using the Print button.

2. Type www.espn.com in the Address box and then click the Go button. Print the Web page using the Print button.

3. Type www.youtube.com in the Address box and then click the Go button. Print the Web page using the Print button.

Part 5: Using the Address Toolbar to Search for Information

1. Type university of miami in the Address box and then click the Go button. A list of Web sites will display. Click an appropriate link to display the associated Web page, and print the Web page using the Print button.

2. Type hybrid cars in the Address box and then click the Go button. A list of Web sites will display. Click an appropriate link to display the associated Web page, and print the Web page using the Print button.

3. Type video podcasts in the Address box and then click the Go button. A list of Web sites will display. Click an appropriate link to display the associated Web page, and print the Web page using the Print button.

Part 6: Removing the Address Toolbar on the Taskbar
1. Right-click an open area of the taskbar and then point to Toolbars on the shortcut menu.
2. Click Address on the Toolbars submenu.
3. Close all open windows.
4. Submit the printed Web pages to your instructor.

In the Lab

Lab 3: Using the Personalization Window

Instructions: Your boss appoints you to design a desktop that all employees within your company will use. Experiment with the options in the Personalization window (Figure 5-127) until you have decided on the perfect desktop theme, background, desktop icons, mouse pointers, screen saver, color scheme, and font size. Write down all settings. Make sure after this exercise that you reset the computer to its original settings.

Figure 5–127

Perform the following tasks:
1. Select a picture, from the Sample Pictures folder, from the Internet, or from your own photos, for the background.
2. Add at least two new desktop icons and change their icons.
3. Change the theme of the mouse pointers.
4. Change the screen saver to an appropriate choice and change the wait time to 20 minutes.
5. Change the folder options so that all folder windows display contents in details view.
6. Change the font size to a larger font size.
7. Save this as the Company Desktop theme.

Cases and Places

Apply your creative thinking and problem solving skills to design and implement a solution.

● Easier   ●● More Difficult

● 1: Finding Screen Savers

Although several screen savers are included with Windows Vista, many more are available for download online, and various organizations give them away. Using your favorite search engine, locate five free screen savers from different Web sites. In a brief report, describe each screen saver, state the source from which you can obtain the screen saver, and the contents of the screen saver.

● 2: Finding Desktop Themes

Besides screen savers, themes for the desktop often are available for purchase and download online. Find three Web sites that have Windows Vista desktop themes available. How much do the themes for sale cost? For both the free and for sale themes, how much hard disk space do they require? Which ones would you consider using? Is creating your own theme better than purchasing one? Write a brief report containing your findings.

●● 3: Researching Advanced Search Techniques

In this chapter, you typed a keyword or phrase in the Address toolbar to search for information on the Internet. In addition, you can perform advanced searches using compound search criteria in which the words, AND, OR, and NOT, control how individual keywords are used. You also can specify which keywords are more important and can cause multiple keywords to be treated as a phrase. Use the Internet, Windows Help and Support, computer articles, and your own opinions to find out as much information as you can about advanced search techniques. Summarize your findings in a brief report and provide examples of some advanced searches that you created. Include sample output from running the advanced searches.

●● 4: Customizing the Taskbar

Make It Personal

The taskbar is a central part of the Windows Vista desktop. As such, it is important to organize the taskbar, and the toolbars on the taskbar, to best fit your individual needs. Make a list of items you would like to have appear on your desktop and on the Sidebar. In addition, think about what color scheme you might prefer to use while working in Windows. Design the taskbar and toolbars to meet your needs. Write a brief report summarizing your experience.

●● 5: Constructing the Optimal Desktop for Workplace Efficiency

Working Together

Colors, patterns, and the arrangement of the workplace can have a significant effect on worker productivity. These factors might draw attention to some objects, de-emphasize others, speed the completion of tasks, or even promote desirable moods and attitudes. Working with classmates, visit the Internet, a library, or other research facility to find out how colors, patterns, and arrangements can impact a work environment. Using what you have learned, together with the concepts and techniques presented in this chapter, create the Windows Vista desktop that you think would help workers be more efficient. Write a report describing your desktop and explaining why you feel it would enhance productivity.

6 Customizing Your Computer Using the Control Panel

Objectives

You will have mastered the material in this chapter when you can:

- Open the Control Panel window and switch to Classic View

- View system information and hardware properties

- Add and remove a printer

- Customize the mouse configuration

- Install and uninstall a program

- Explain account privileges and view account information

- Create and configure a new user account

- View and change the date, time, and time zone

- Adjust Ease of Access Center settings

6 Customizing Your Computer Using the Control Panel

Introduction

As you have learned, personalizing your work environment can lead to improved productivity. In Chapter 5, you modified desktop properties by creating a new desktop theme, personalizing the taskbar, and customizing folder options. However, there are other ways to customize Windows Vista so that you can get the most from your computer. Technology works best when it supports our lifestyles, providing the tools we need to accomplish the tasks set before us.

The Control Panel window contains categories that allow you to change the properties of an object and thus customize the Windows Vista environment (Figure 6-1). In addition, the Control Panel provides links to other windows that contain settings allowing you to further customize your computer. In this chapter, you will learn how to add a software program, make the computer more usable for physically challenged individuals, add a printer to the computer, use a troubleshooter to solve a hardware problem, and view the properties of the hardware devices attached to the computer. In addition, you will use the Control Panel to customize the mouse, keyboard, date and time, and time zone.

You will not be able to perform some tasks in this chapter unless you have proper User Account Control access. **User Account Control (UAC)** controls the access rights granted to all users. A **standard user account** is a collection of information that Windows Vista needs to know about a computer user. This information includes the user name, password, picture, the workgroups in which the user has membership, and the rights and permissions the user has for accessing a computer or computer network. User accounts make it possible for each user to log on to the computer, keep information confidential and computer settings protected, customize Windows Vista, store files in a unique Documents folder, maintain a personal list of favorite Web sites, and allow other users access to the computer without having to close any open programs.

Normally, all accounts, even administrator accounts, operate in standard user mode. A standard user cannot install software that affects other users or change system settings that affect security. An **administrator account** has full control over the computer and operating system, and can change user permissions, install software that affects all users, and change system settings that affect security. When a task requires administrator access, User Account Control prompts you to authorize the task. Once authorized, the user has temporary administrator privileges. After the task is finished, the user returns to standard user mode. User Access Control is designed to prevent malicious software from being inadvertently installed, even by administrators. For standard user accounts, the user will need to know an administrator account user name and password to authorize User Account Control. Administrators only will be prompted to continue.

Figure 6–1

In the Control Panel window, a shield will be displayed to indicate that a task requires User Account Control access. Some of the steps in this chapter require administrative privileges. If you do not have administrative privileges, read the steps instead of performing them.

Overview

As you read this chapter, you will learn how to customize your computer by performing these general tasks:

- Viewing and monitoring your system
- Adding and removing a hardware device
- Customizing your mouse functionality
- Installing and uninstalling software
- Creating, using, and deleting a user account
- Accessing and configuring Ease of Access features

Plan Ahead

Customizing Your Computer Using the Control Panel

Customizing your computer using the Control Panel window requires the appropriate permissions to make changes to your computer, familiarity with the keyboard and mouse, and access to the Internet.

1. **Determine the permissions you have on the computer you will be using.** Each user account can have different rights and permissions. Depending on which rights and permissions have been set for your account, you may or may not be able to perform certain operations.

2. **Identify the type of keyboard and mouse you will be using.** Sections in this chapter will make changes to your keyboard and mouse settings. If you are using a touchpad or a mouse with a scroll wheel, different options may be available to you. If your keyboard lacks a numeric keypad, you will be instructed not to perform certain steps.

3. **Determine if you have Internet access.** For this chapter, you will be accessing the Internet to search for infomation. You will want to know if your computer has Internet access and if anything is required of you to use it.

System and Maintenance

You can use the System and Maintenance window to open the Welcome Center window, schedule backups (covered in Appendix D), configure Windows Update, change your energy-saving settings, troubleshoot most software and hardware problems by searching for solutions, and use other administrator tools. Each option provides different opportunities for you to fine-tune your computer. However, be aware that many of the advanced system and maintenance options will require User Account Control authorization.

To Open the Control Panel Window

The following step opens the Control Panel window.

- Display the Start menu.

- Click the Control Panel command to display the Control Panel window (Figure 6–2).

Figure 6–2

To Switch to Classic View

By default, the Control Panel window displays in Category View. Category View offers the various Control Panel options organized into ten functional categories and appears in the right pane of the window. Links to common tasks are provided below each category name. The Classic View link in the Control Panel window allows you to display the popular Classic View that was common in previous versions of the Windows operating system. Classic View displays all of the individual Control Panel icons in alphabetical order instead of organized into categories. The following steps switch to Classic View and then back to Category View.

1

- Click the Classic View link in the Control Panel window to switch to Classic View (Figure 6–3).

Q&A
Why might I want to use Classic View?

Some users prefer Classic View because they feel that the commands in the Control Panel are easier to find. In addition, individuals who are familiar with previous versions of Windows may be more comfortable using Classic View.

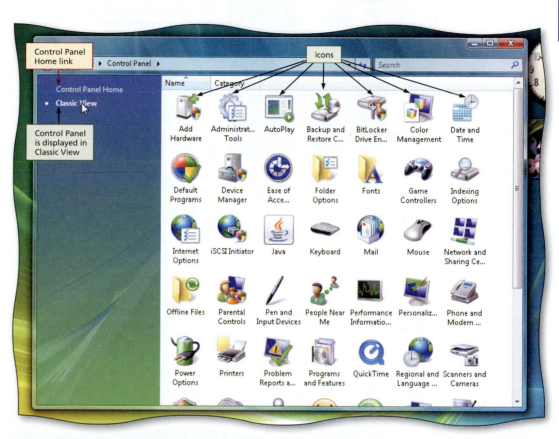

Figure 6–3

2

- Click the Control Panel Home link to return Control Panel to Category View (Figure 6–4).

Figure 6–4

To Open the System and Maintenance Window

The step on the following page opens the System and Maintenance window.

1

• Click the System and Maintenance link to open the System and Maintenance window (Figure 6–5).

Q&A Why do my links differ from those shown in the figure?

If your computer has an Internet connection, Microsoft may display different links and offers in the Welcome Center.

Figure 6–5

To Open the Welcome Center Window and View the Get Started Topics

You can learn about some of the basic getting started features of Windows Vista in the Welcome Center window. The Welcome Center window provides links for everything from basic computer details to using the Control Panel. The following steps open the Welcome Center and display the Get started with Windows topics.

1

• Click the Welcome Center link to open the Welcome Center (Figure 6–6).

Q&A Why do my links differ from those shown in the figure?

If your computer has an Internet connection, Microsoft may display different links and offers in the Welcome Center.

Figure 6–6

2
- Click the Show all 14 items link to show all of the Get started with Windows links (Figure 6–7).

 Experiment
- Click a sampling of links to view the summary information that is displayed in the Welcome Center.

Q&A Why does my link show a different number of items?

Depending upon your edition and installation of Windows Vista, the Welcome Center may show a different number of links and options.

Figure 6–7

3
- Click the Back button to return to the System and Maintenance window (Figure 6–8).

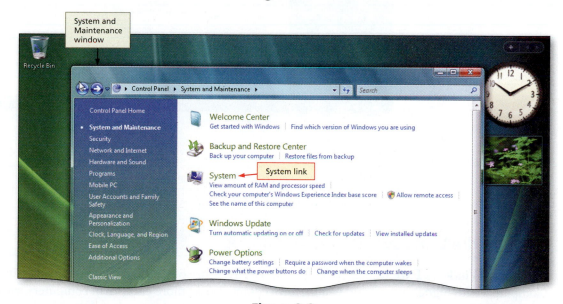

Figure 6–8

Other Ways

1. Open Control Panel, click Get started with Windows
2. Open Control Panel, click Classic View, double-click Welcome Center icon
3. Display Start menu, click All Programs, click Accessories, click Welcome Center

To View System Information

The System window displays summary information about your computer. You can access the Device Manager, adjust remote access settings, change advanced system settings, view the Windows Experience Index, change network settings, and update Windows Vista registration information using the System window. The following step opens the System window.

1
- Click the System link to open the System window. If necessary, click the Maximize button to maximize the window (Figure 6–9).

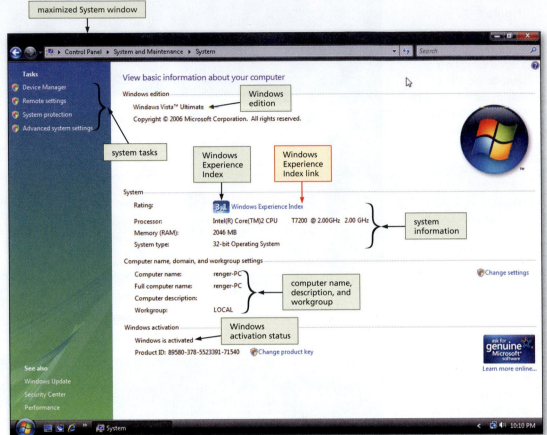

Figure 6–9

Other Ways

1. Open Control Panel, click Classic View, double-click System icon
2. Open Welcome Center, click View computer details, click Show more details
3. Open Computer window, click System properties

To View the Windows Experience Index

The **Windows Experience Index** provides a base score of your computer's hardware and software configuration. Computers with higher base scores will perform complex tasks more easily than computers with lower scores. To calculate the Windows Experience Index, each hardware component is scored, and the lowest score becomes your base score. When buying software, you can use the base score to determine if your computer can support the new software. Changing your hardware components will require you to recalculate your Windows Experience Index. Microsoft says that for now, the base scores can range from 1 to 5.9; however, this range may expand in the future as technology advances. You can view the complete details of your score or update your score in the Performance and Tools window. The following steps display the complete Windows Experience Index information.

1
- Click the Windows Experience Index link to open the Performance Information and Tools window (Figure 6–10).

Figure 6–10

2
- After viewing your score information, close the Performance Information and Tools window (Figure 6–11).

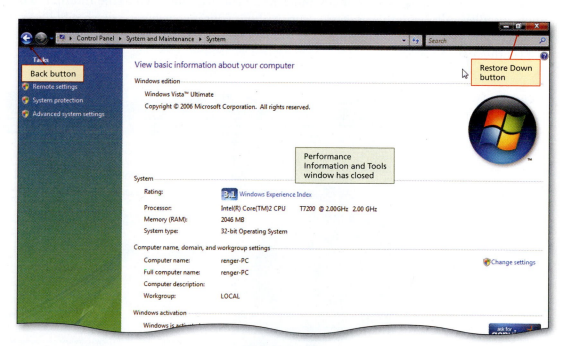

Figure 6–11

3
- Return to the System and Maintenance window.

- Click the Restore Down button to restore the System and Maintenance window (Figure 6–12).

Figure 6–12

To View Installed Updates

Windows Update is turned on by default when Windows Vista is installed. Windows Update automatically searches online for updates to your computer while you are connected to the Internet. These updates are then routinely installed. Although this process occurs without your involvement, you should be aware of the updates that are installed on your computer, and from time to time, review the list. The following steps open Windows Update and display the update history.

1

- Click the Windows Update link to open the Windows Update window (Figure 6–13).

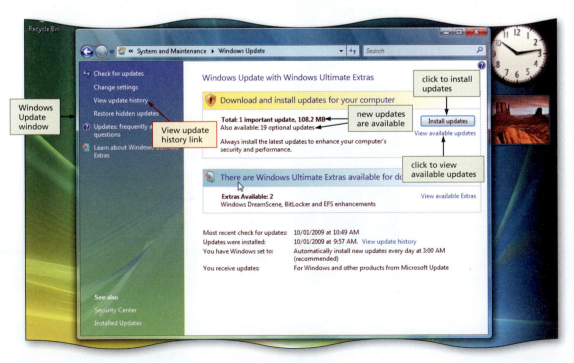

Figure 6–13

2

- Click the View update history link to open the View update history window (Figure 6–14).

Q&A

Why are there different types of updates?

Microsoft offers three different levels of updates based upon how critical the update is. An update that is identified as Important is a critical update and usually is a security update, a bug fix, or both. Recommended updates are non-critical updates, but can improve performance. Optional updates also are non-critical, and are not installed automatically.

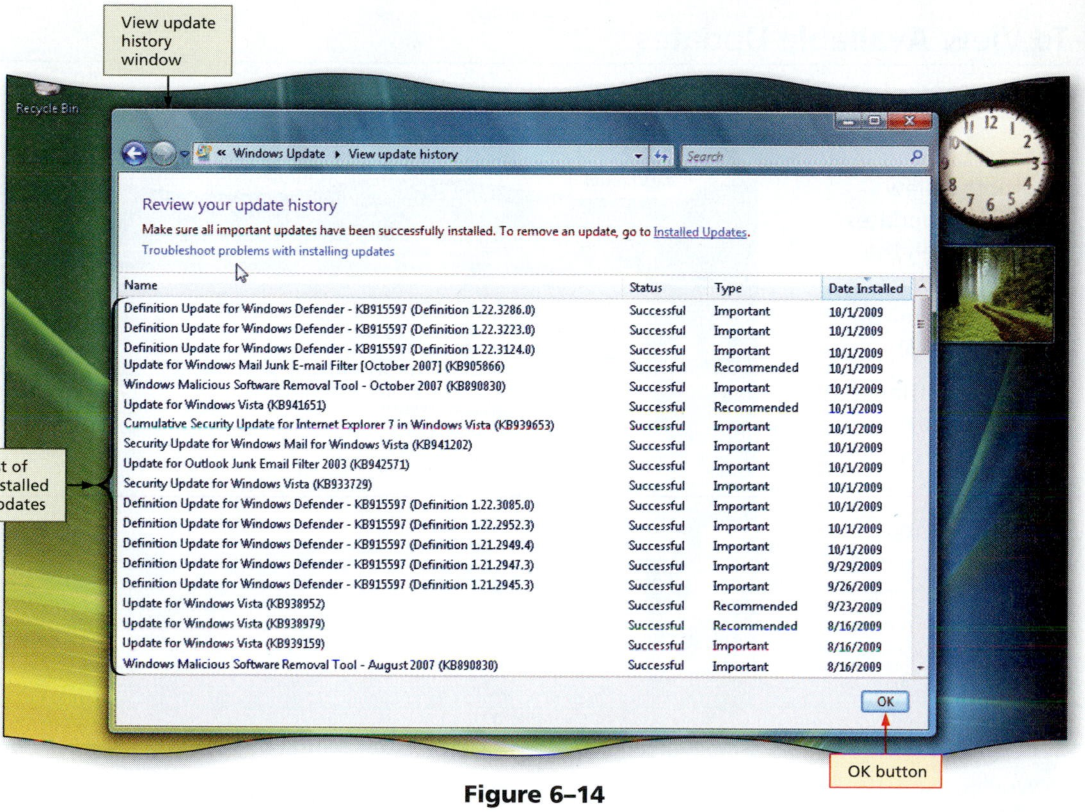

Figure 6–14

3

- Click the OK button to return to the Windows Update window (Figure 6–15).

Q&A

What happens if an update fails?

If the automatic update feature is turned on, Windows Vista will continue trying to install the update. If the update still fails, you can use the Troubleshoot problems with installing updates link to find solutions to the installation problems.

Figure 6–15

Other Ways

1. Open Control Panel, click Classic View, double-click Windows Update icon, click View update history

To View Available Updates

The following steps display the list of available updates for Windows Vista.

1

- Click the View available updates link to open the View available updates window (Figure 6–16).

Q&A Why does the Install updates button not appear on my computer?

If your computer is up-to-date and requires no updates at the present time, the Install updates button will not appear.

Q&A Why do I see a different list of available updates?

The list of available updates is determined by your edition of Windows Vista, the software that you have installed, and the updates you already have installed.

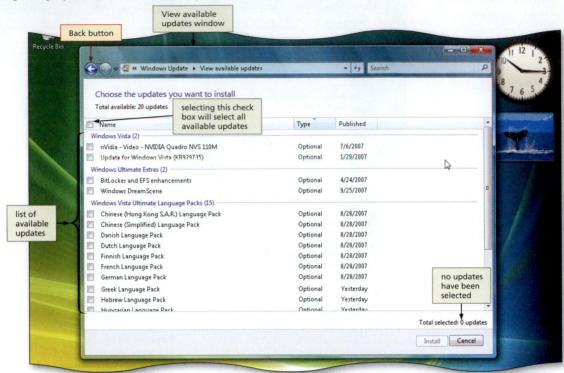

Figure 6–16

2

- After viewing the available updates, click the Back button to return to the Windows Update window (Figure 6–17).

Q&A How do I install an update?

Click the View available updates link, and then select the updates that you would like to install. After selecting the updates, click the Install button to install them. Depending on the update, you may be instructed to restart your computer.

Figure 6–17

3

- Return to the System and Maintenance window (Figure 6–18).

Figure 6–18

Other Ways

1. Open Control Panel, click Classic View, double-click Windows Update icon, click View available updates

To View Power Options

Windows Vista offers three preset power plans. A **power plan** is comprised of hardware and system settings that manage how your computer uses power. The balanced power plan provides full performance when you are actively using the computer, and saves power when your computer is inactive. The power saver power plan is designed to save the most power it can by decreasing system performance. Using the power saver power plan, laptop computer users can extend the amount of time they can use the computer while it is running on battery power. Computers not running on battery power can take advantage of the high performance power plan, which maximizes system performance by using more power. Laptop users only should use this option when they are not running on battery power. The following step opens the Power Options window.

1

- Click the Power Options link to open the Power Options window (Figure 6–19).

Q&A

Can I customize the power plan to meet my needs?

You can use the Change plan settings link for the plan your computer is using and adjust the settings. You also can click the Create a power plan link to create your own customized power plan.

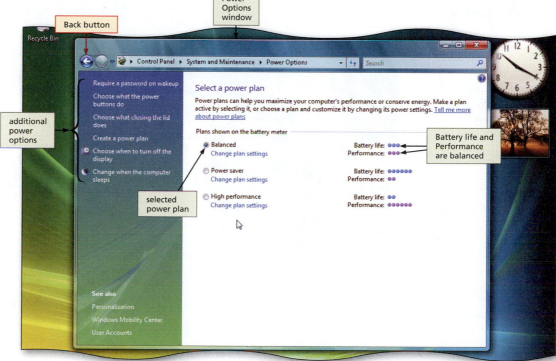

Figure 6–19

● Return to the System
and Maintenance
window (Figure 6–20).

Figure 6–20

To View Problem Reports and Solutions

The Problem Reports and Solutions window offers solutions for problems that you have experienced, and provides links to information on those problems for which Windows Vista currently does not have solutions. For example, if Internet Explorer does not work properly on your computer, Windows Vista will detect the problem and report it to Microsoft, if you allow it. Once the problem has been addressed or resolved, you will see a change in status in the Problem Reports and Solutions window. The following step opens the Problem Reports and Solutions window.

● Click the Problem
Reports and
Solutions link to
open the Problem
Reports and
Solutions window
(Figure 6–21).

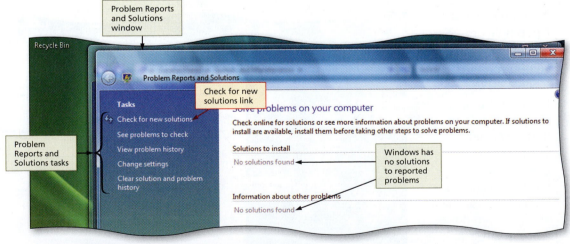

Figure 6–21

To Check for New Solutions

Normally, Windows Vista automatically locates solutions, unless this feature is turned off. If you have outstanding problems, you can check for new solutions manually. The following steps check for new solutions.

1

• Click the Check for new solutions link to check for new solutions (Figure 6–22).

Figure 6–22

2

• After the check finishes, the results display in the Problem Reports and Solutions dialog box (Figure 6–23).

Q&A

What happens if Windows Vista finds a solution?

If a solution is found for an outstanding problem, you will be notified of the actions you should take. These actions could include changing the way a program runs or installing an update.

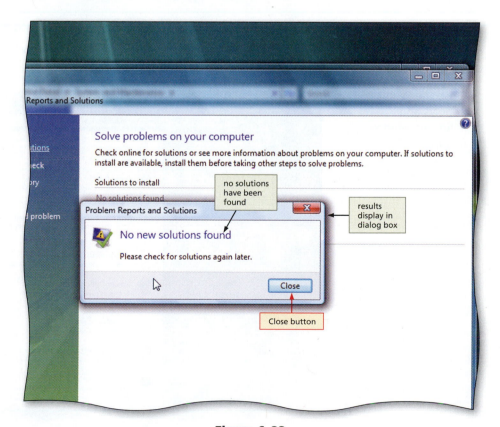

Figure 6–23

● Click the Close
button to close the
Problem Reports and
Solutions dialog box
(Figure 6–24).

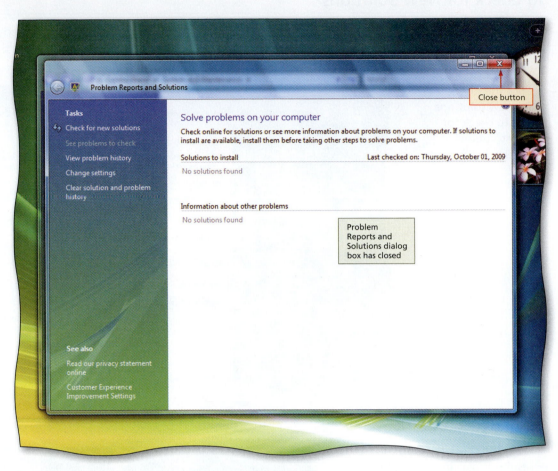

Figure 6–24

● Close the Problem
Reports and
Solutions window
(Figure 6–25).

Figure 6–25

To Open the Device Manager

The Device Manager allows you to display a list of the hardware devices installed on your computer and also allows you to update device drivers, view and modify hardware settings, and troubleshoot problems. The following steps open the Device Manager.

1

• Scroll down in the System and Maintenance window until the Device Manager link appears (Figure 6–26).

Figure 6–26

2

• Click the Device Manager link to open the Device Manager (Figure 6–27).

• If necessary, click the Continue button in the User Account Control dialog box.

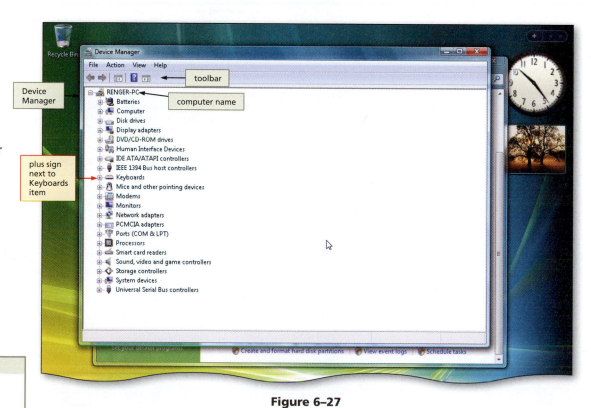

Other Ways

1. Open Control Panel, click Classic View, double-click Device Manager icon

Figure 6–27

To View the Properties of a Device

You can use Device Manager to see the properties of the devices installed on your computer. Normally, device drivers are included in the automatic updating that Windows Vista performs. A **device driver** is a program used by the operating system to control the hardware. You can view the driver details in the Device Properties dialog box for the particular device. If necessary, you can update the device driver manually. You also can rollback the driver to a previous working version if the current driver fails to work properly, or disable the device if you wish to prevent users from accessing it. The following steps display the properties and driver information for the keyboard.

- Click the plus sign next to the Keyboards item to expand the list of installed keyboards (Figure 6–28).

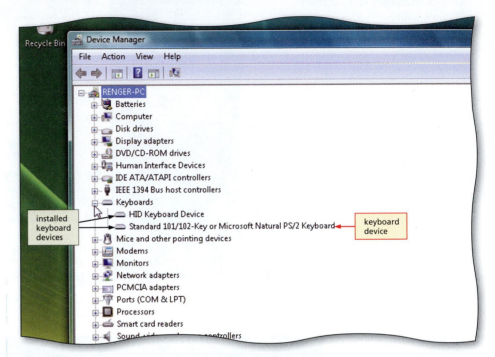

Figure 6–28

- Double-click the installed keyboard device to open the Keyboard Device Properties dialog box (Figure 6–29).

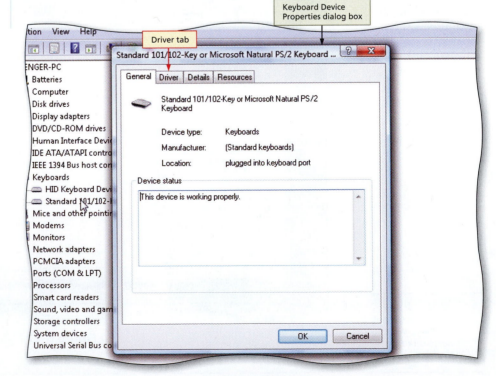

Figure 6–29

3

• Click the Driver tab to display the Driver sheet (Figure 6–30).

• After viewing the driver information, click the OK button to close the dialog box.

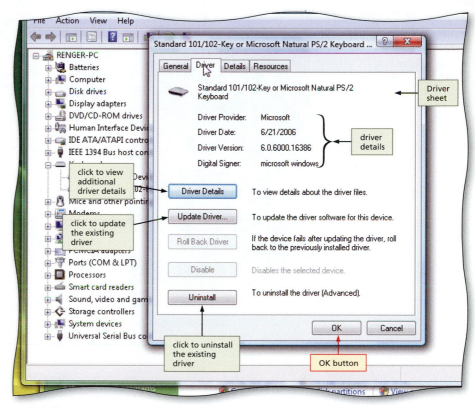

Figure 6–30

4

• Close the Device Manager (Figure 6–31).

Figure 6–31

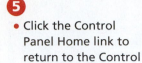

5
- Click the Control Panel Home link to return to the Control Panel window (Figure 6–32).

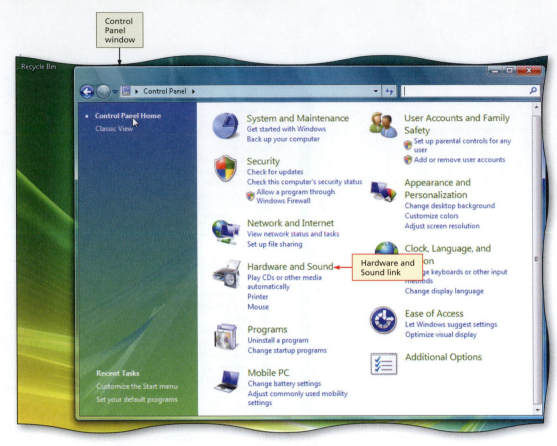

Figure 6–32

Hardware and Sound

You can install printers, configure AutoPlay, configure the mouse, configure scanners and cameras, adjust Tablet PC settings, and more, from the Hardware and Sound window. Because there are multiple paths to the various system windows, you also will find that you can go to the Power Options window, the Personalization window, and the Device Manager window, from the Hardware and Sound window.

When you add a printer, scanner, camera, keyboard, mouse, or any other hardware device, Windows Vista usually will install and configure it automatically. If you want to install it manually or configure it after it is installed, you can use the Hardware and Sound window to access the appropriate controls.

To Add a Printer

The procedure to add a printer to a computer depends upon whether the printer is a local printer or network printer. A **local printer** is a printer directly attached to the computer. A **network printer** is a printer attached to another computer or directly attached to the network. New printers generally support the Plug and Play standard, which makes adding a new printer easy because Windows Vista automatically finds the correct driver to use and adds the printer to your list of printers. Older printers may not support Plug and Play.

Windows Vista also allows you to add printers manually. To add a local printer, you must know which port to use to connect the printer to the computer, and then decide whether the printer should be designated as the default printer. A **port** is a socket on the back of a computer used to connect a hardware device to the computer. You typically use the LPT1 printer port to connect a printer to the computer. The **default printer** is the printer to which all printed documents are sent. Most likely, a printer already is attached to the computer on which you are working and that printer is designated as the default printer. Therefore, you should not designate the printer you add to the computer in the following steps as the default printer. The following steps use the Add Printer Wizard to add the HP Deskjet 6940 series printer to the computer as a local printer.

1
- Click the Hardware and Sound link to open the Hardware and Sound window (Figure 6–33).

Figure 6–33

2
- Click the Printers link to open the Printers window (Figure 6–34).

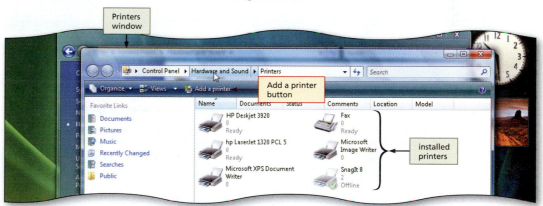

Figure 6–34

3
- Click the Add a printer button to start the Add Printer Wizard (Figure 6–35).

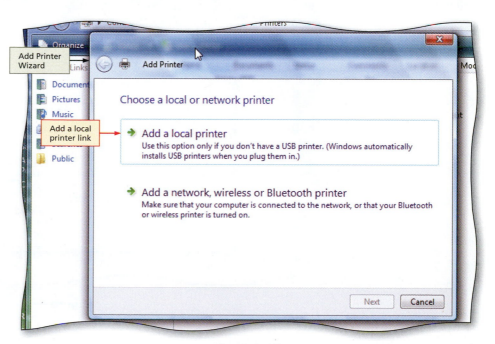

Figure 6–35

4

- Click the Add a local printer link (Figure 6–36).

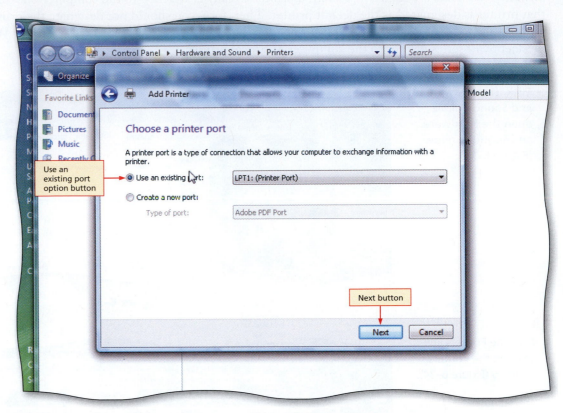

Figure 6–36

5

- If necessary, click the Use an existing port option button.

- Click the Next button to continue (Figure 6–37).

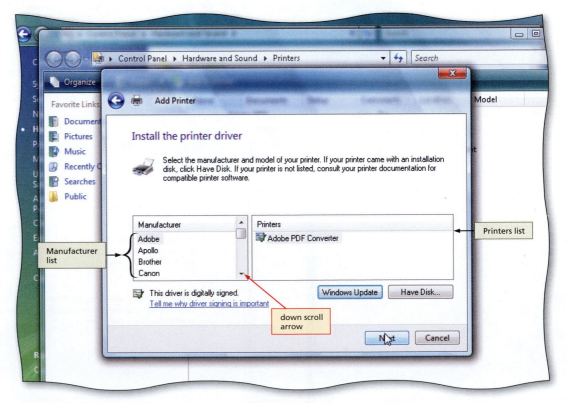

Figure 6–37

6

- Scroll down in the Manufacturer list to display HP.

- Click HP to display a list of HP printers in the Printers list (Figure 6–38).

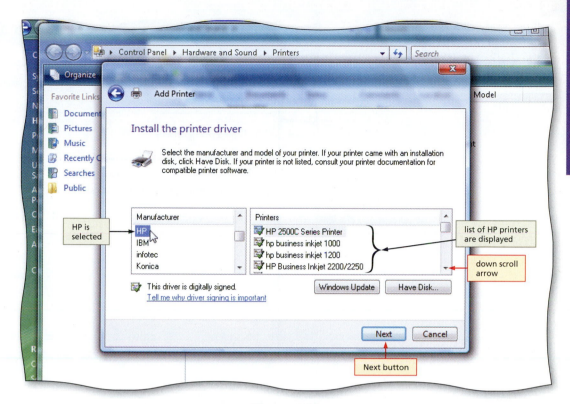

Figure 6–38

7

- Scroll down in the Printers list until the HP Deskjet 6940 series appears.

- Click HP Deskjet 6940 series to select it (Figure 6–39).

- Click the Next button to continue.

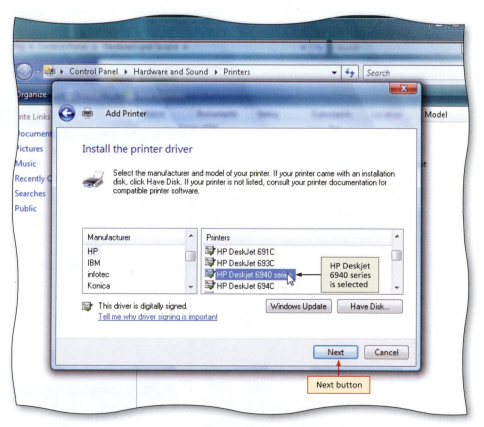

Figure 6–39

8

- If necessary, click the Set as the default printer check box to remove the check mark (Figure 6–40).

- Click the Next button to continue.

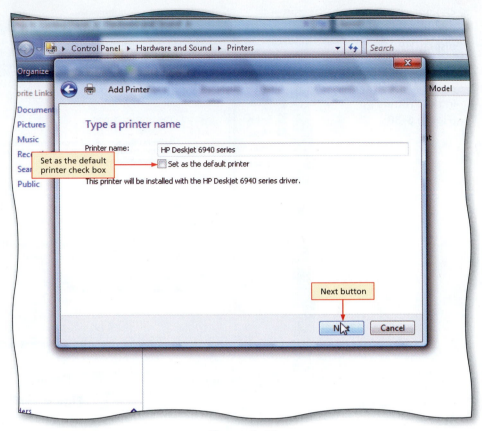

Figure 6–40

9

- The Installing printer message appears, indicating the progress of the installation (Figure 6–41).

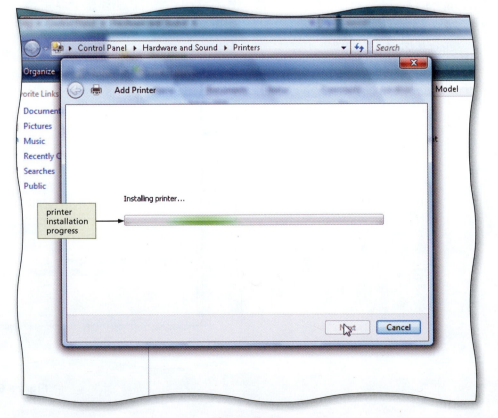

Figure 6–41

10

- After the installation is complete, the You've successfully added HP Deskjet 6940 series message is displayed (Figure 6–42).

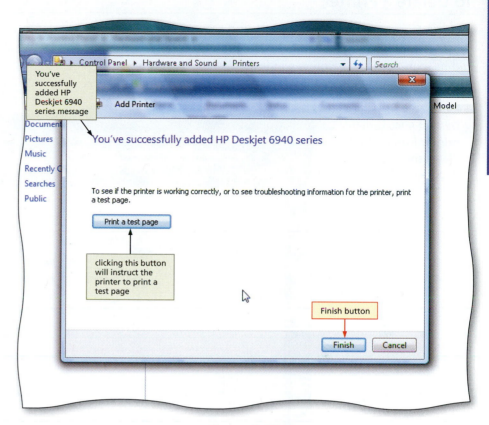

Figure 6–42

11

- Click the Finish button to exit the wizard (Figure 6–43).

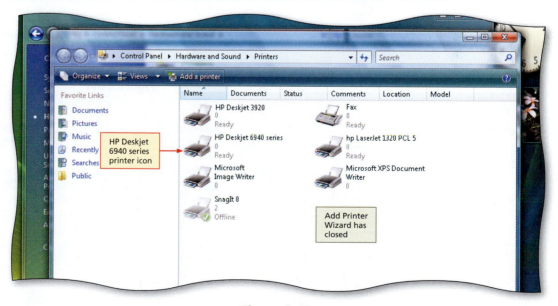

Figure 6–43

Other Ways
1. Open Control Panel, click Printer, click Add a printer 　 2. Open Control Panel, click Classic View, double-click Printers icon, click Add a printer

To Delete a Printer

When you disconnect a printer and have no plans to reconnect the printer in the future, you should delete the printer from the Printers window. The following steps delete the HP Deskjet 6940 series printer from the computer and its icon from the Printers window.

1

• Right-click the HP Deskjet 6940 series printer icon to display a shortcut menu (Figure 6–44).

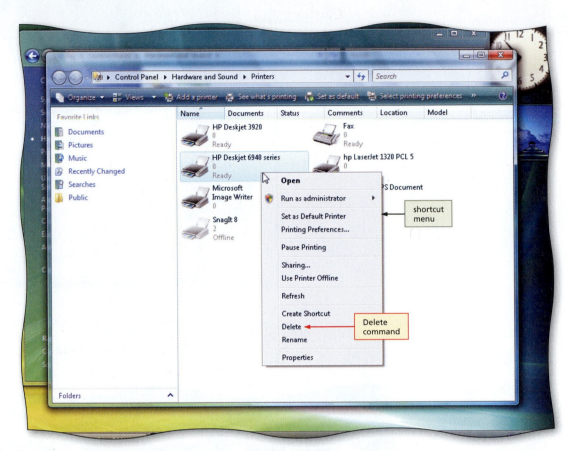

Figure 6–44

2

• Click the Delete command on the shortcut menu to display the Printers dialog box (Figure 6–45).

Figure 6–45

3

- Click the Yes button in the Printers dialog box to confirm that you want to delete the printer (Figure 6–46).

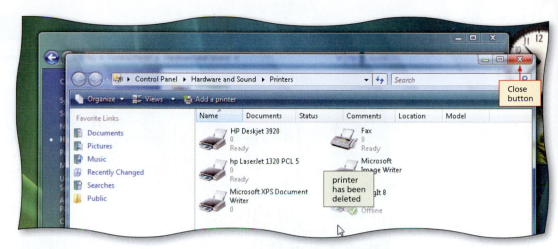

Figure 6–46

4

- Close the Printers window and return to the Hardware and Sound window (Figure 6–47).

Figure 6–47

To Adjust AutoPlay Settings

Windows Vista allows you to customize the AutoPlay features for your computer. **AutoPlay** refers to the default action that occurs when media and devices are inserted into your computer. You already have seen AutoPlay in action when you used a USB drive. In that case, Windows Vista asked you what you would like to do. Using the AutoPlay window, you can view and modify the settings for all media and devices inserted into your computer. Once set, the new action will be used the next time you insert the media or device. The steps on the following pages open the AutoPlay window and change the action for the Software and games setting to the Open folder to view files using Windows Explorer action.

1
• Click the AutoPlay link to open the AutoPlay window (Figure 6–48).

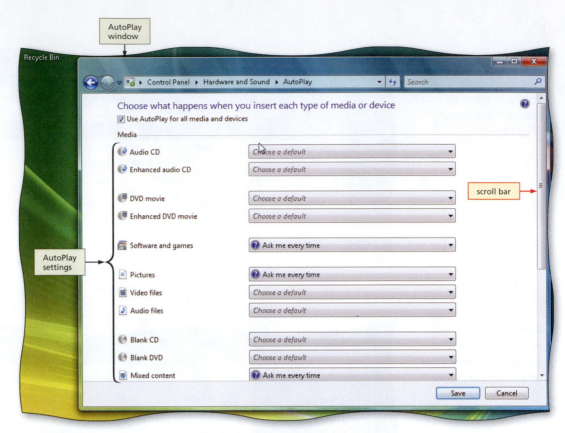

Figure 6–48

2
• Scroll down to view the remaining AutoPlay settings (Figure 6–49).

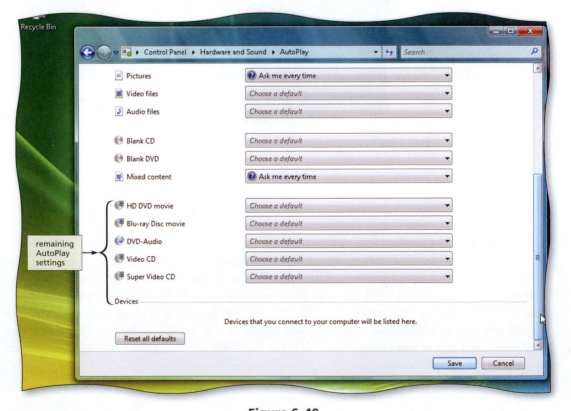

Figure 6–49

3

- If necessary, scroll up until the Software and games setting is visible.

- Click the Software and games drop-down list button to see a list of available actions (Figure 6–50).

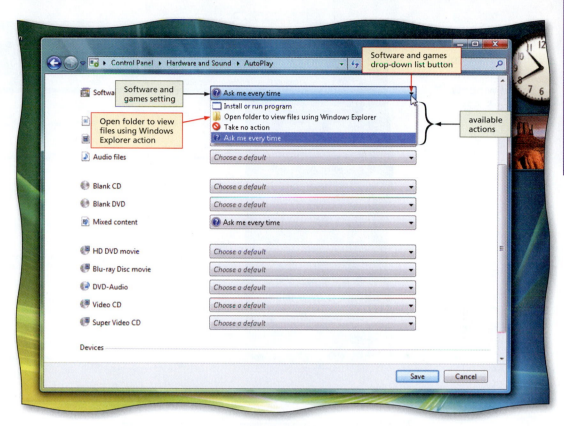

Figure 6–50

4

- Click the Open folder to view files using Windows Explorer action to change the action for Software and games (Figure 6–51).

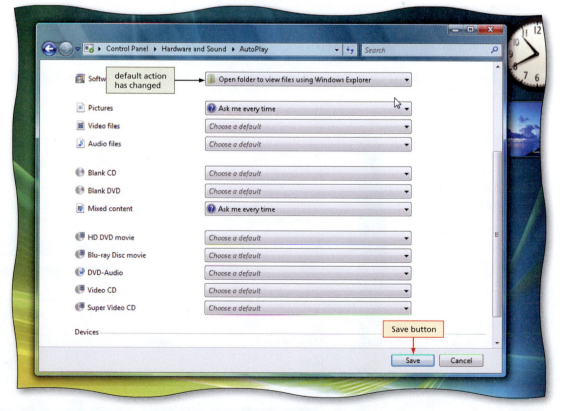

Figure 6–51

● Click the Save
button to save the
changes and return
to the Hardware and
Sound window
(Figure 6–52).

Figure 6–52

To Revert an AutoPlay Setting

The following steps open the AutoPlay window and change the Software and games action back to Ask me
every time.

● Click the Change
default settings for
media or devices
link to open the
AutoPlay window.

● Click the Software
and games drop-
down list button
to display a list of
available actions
(Figure 6–53).

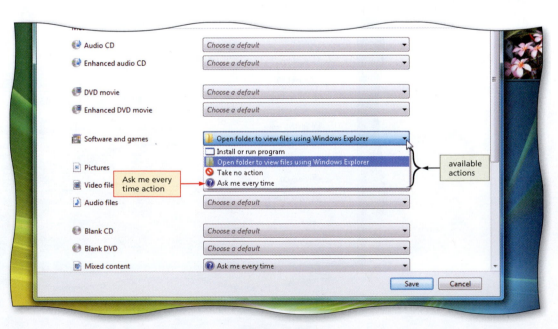

Figure 6–53

2

- Click the Ask me every time action to change the default action (Figure 6–54).

- Save the changes and return to the Hardware and Sound window.

What if Ask me every time was not the original action set for Software and games on my computer?

Click the action that was selected before you changed the action. Your lab administrators may have set a different default action for Software and games or may have set no action at all.

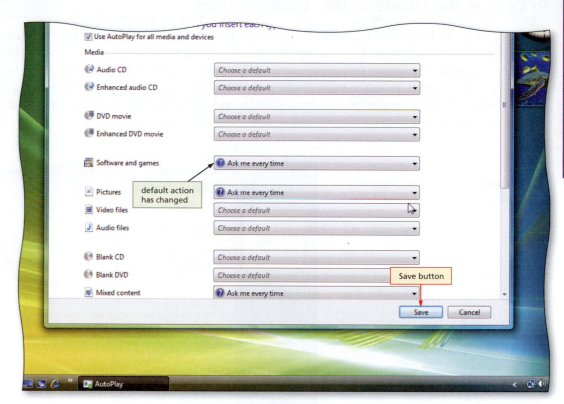

Figure 6–54

Customizing the Mouse

The mouse is another hardware device that Windows Vista allows you to customize. In Chapter 5, you changed the mouse pointers scheme to Windows Aero (extra large), which increased the size of the mouse pointers. Among the other mouse properties you can customize are the functions of the left and right mouse buttons, the double-click speed, and the pointer speed. You also can turn on ClickLock and Snap To functionality, as well as add pointer trails. If you have a mouse with a scroll wheel, you can adjust how far a page scrolls each time you move the mouse wheel one notch. You use the Mouse Properties dialog box to change all of these properties.

BTW

Touchpad

If you have a computer that has a touchpad, you will see options in the Mouse Properties dialog box that specifically pertain to touchpads. For instance, you might see options to change the functions of the touchpad's mouse buttons or to adjust the sensitivity of the touchpad for recognizing a mouse click when you tap your finger. Some touchpad software programs, as well as other custom mouse software, can completely change the appearance of the Mouse Properties dialog box. Once this software is installed, the only way to return the Mouse Properties dialog box to its original state may be to uninstall the touchpad or custom mouse software.

To Change the Mouse Button Configuration

Typically, the left mouse button is the primary button, which performs the operations of selecting and dragging, and the right mouse button is the secondary button, which performs the aptly named right-clicking and right-dragging. If you are left-handed, you may find it more convenient to change the button configuration, by switching the selecting and dragging operations to the right mouse button and the right-clicking and right-dragging operations to the left mouse button. The following steps switch the primary and secondary buttons and then change the buttons back to the original configuration.

- Click the Mouse link to display the Mouse Properties dialog box (Figure 6–55).

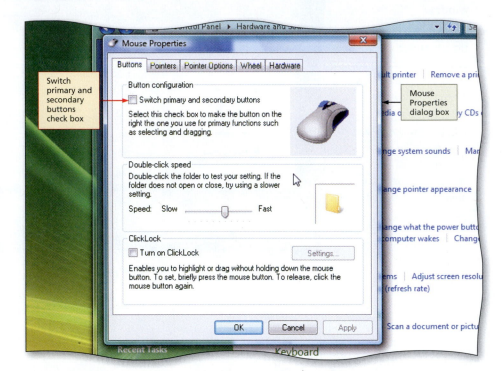

Figure 6–55

- Click the Switch primary and secondary buttons check box to select it (Figure 6–56).

- Experiment with the left and right mouse buttons until you are comfortable with this configuration. Return to the Mouse Properties dialog box when you are done.

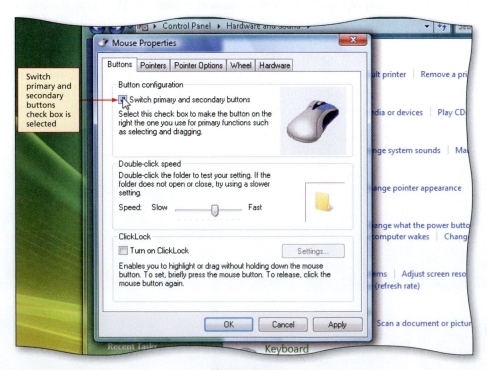

Figure 6–56

3

- Using the right mouse button, click the Switch primary and secondary buttons check box to deselect it (Figure 6–57).

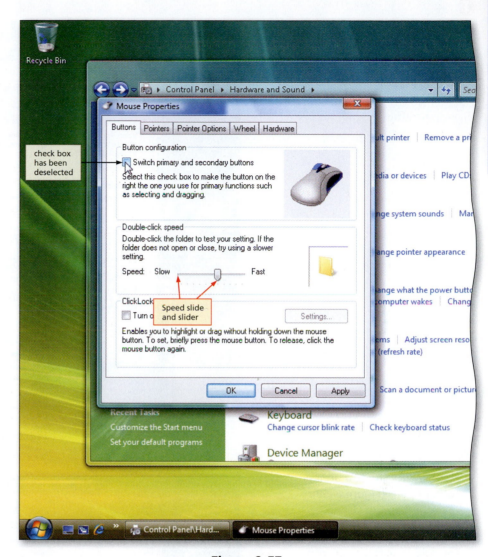

check box has been deselected

Speed slide and slider

Figure 6–57

Other Ways

1. Open Control Panel, click Classic View, double-click Mouse icon, click Switch primary and secondary buttons
2. Open Control Panel, click Mouse link, click Switch primary and secondary buttons

To Adjust the Double-Click Speed

Windows Vista measures the amount of time that occurs between clicking the mouse button once and then clicking the same button again. This time interval, called **double-click speed**, determines whether Windows Vista recognizes when a mouse button is clicked twice as a double-click or two single clicks. If you click a mouse button twice, and the second click does not fall within the double-click time interval, Windows Vista treats the action as two single clicks, not as a double-click. The steps on the following page adjust and test the double-click speed.

1

- Drag the Double-click speed slider in the Double-click speed area to the right end of the slide to select the fastest Double-click speed (Figure 6–58).

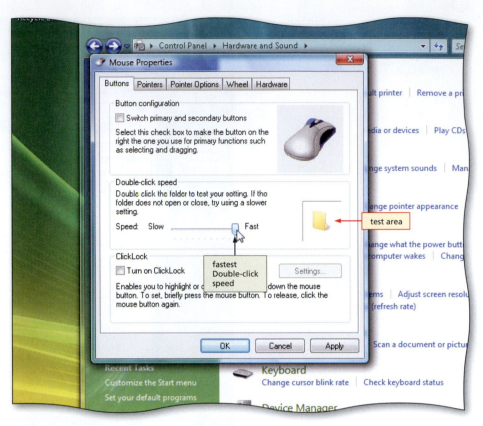

Figure 6–58

2

- Double-click the test area until the folder opens (Figure 6–59).

- If the folder does not open, drag the speed slider to the left until the folder opens when you double-click the test area.

Q&A

Why was I unable to open the folder when the speed slider was set all the way to the right?

Setting the double-click speed to its fastest speed may make it impossible for you to double-click an object. The speed at which individuals can double-click a mouse can vary.

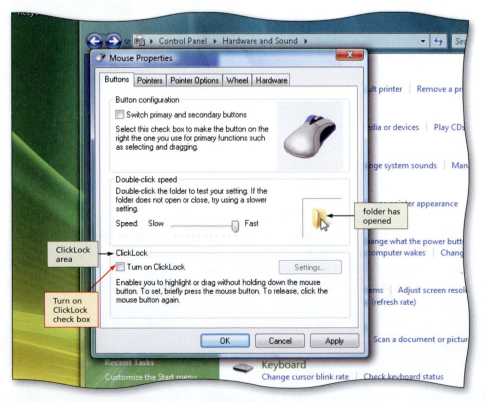

Figure 6–59

To Turn On and Use ClickLock

The ClickLock feature allows you to select or drag text without continuously holding down the mouse button by locking the button. Once the ClickLock feature is turned on, you activate it by holding the mouse button down for a few second to 'lock' the mouse click. You simply click the mouse button again to 'unlock' the button. The following steps turn on ClickLock, create a simple text document, lock the mouse click, and then highlight text in the document.

1

- Click the Turn on ClickLock check box in the ClickLock area in the Mouse Properties dialog box to select it (Figure 6–60).

- Create and open a new document in Notepad.

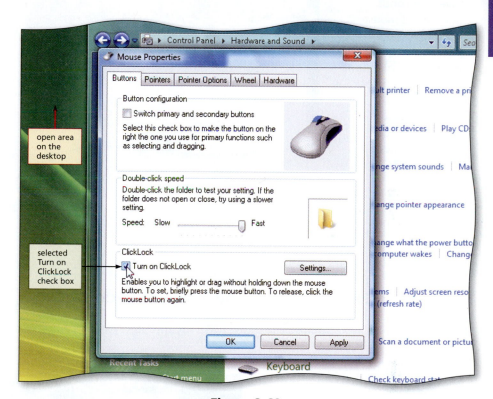

Figure 6–60

2

- Type ClickLock allows you to lock a mouse button and select or drag text. in the New Text Document - Notepad window (Figure 6–61).

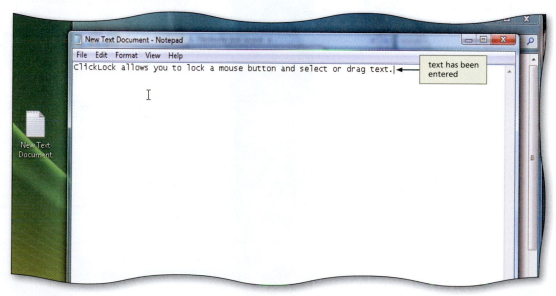

Figure 6–61

3

- Position the mouse pointer to the left of the word, ClickLock, in the document, hold down the left mouse button for several seconds, release the mouse button, move the insertion point to the right to highlight the word, ClickLock, and then click the left mouse button to select the word, ClickLock (Figure 6–62).

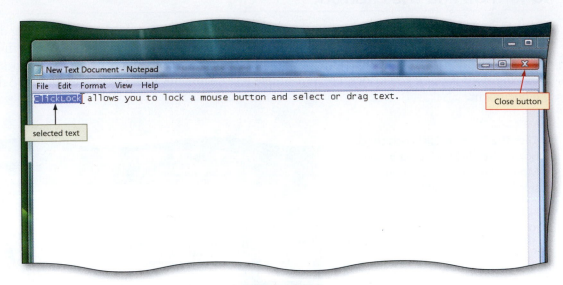

Figure 6–62

Other Ways
1. Open Control Panel, click Classic View, double-click Mouse icon, click Turn on ClickLock   2. Open Control Panel, click Mouse link, click Turn on ClickLock

To Close the Text Document and Turn Off ClickLock

The following steps close the New Text Document - Notepad window and turn off ClickLock.

1

- Close the New Text Document - Notepad window.

- Click the Don't Save button in the Notepad dialog box to discard the changes to the document (Figure 6–63).

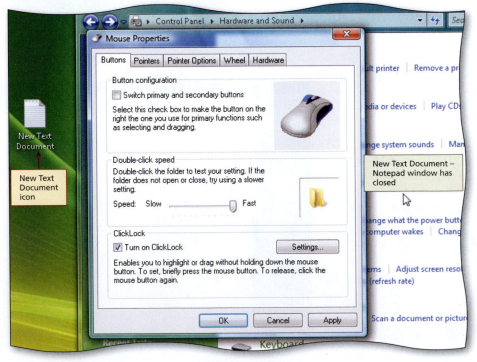

Figure 6–63

2

• Delete the New Text Document icon by moving the file to the Recycle Bin (Figure 6–64).

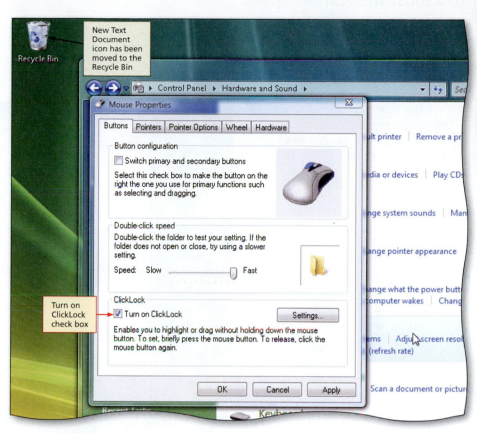

Figure 6–64

3

• If necessary, click the Mouse Properties button on the taskbar to make the Mouse Properties dialog box active.

• Click the Turn on ClickLock check box to remove the check mark (Figure 6–65).

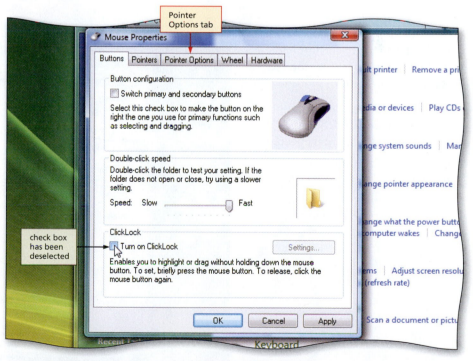

Figure 6–65

To Adjust the Pointer Speed

You can adjust the pointer speed from the Pointer Options sheet in the Mouse Properties dialog box. The **pointer speed** is the speed at which the mouse pointer travels across the desktop when you move the mouse. The following steps adjust the pointer speed.

 1

- Click the Pointer Options tab in the Mouse Properties dialog box to display the Pointer Options sheet (Figure 6–66).

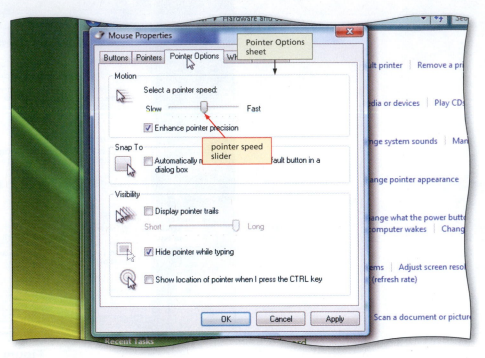

Figure 6–66

 2

- Drag the pointer speed slider in the Motion area to the left end of the slide to select the slowest setting (Figure 6–67).

- Move the mouse pointer around the desktop and notice the difference in the pointer speed.

Q&A

Do I need to click the Apply button?

Because moving the slider adjusts the pointer speed immediately, it is not necessary to click the Apply button.

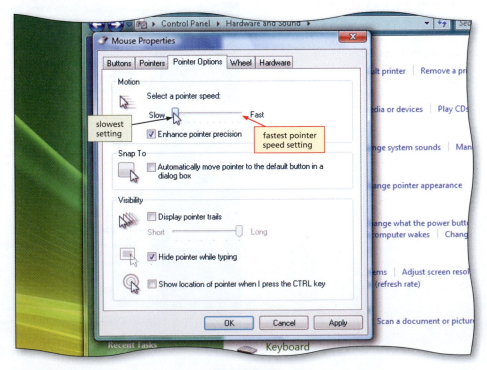

Figure 6–67

3

- Drag the pointer speed slider to the right end of the slide to select the fastest setting (Figure 6–68).

- Move the mouse pointer around the desktop and notice the difference in the pointer speed.

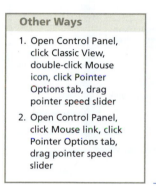 **Experiment**

- Experiment with the pointer speed until you find the pointer speed that works best for you.

Other Ways

1. Open Control Panel, click Classic View, double-click Mouse icon, click Pointer Options tab, drag pointer speed slider

2. Open Control Panel, click Mouse link, click Pointer Options tab, drag pointer speed slider

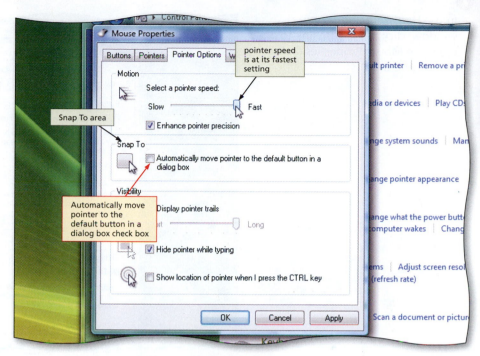

Figure 6–68

To Turn On Snap To

Normally when a dialog box appears on the desktop, the mouse pointer remains where it was before the dialog box appeared. However, you can change the settings so that the mouse pointer will automatically 'snap to' the default button in any dialog box. The following steps turn on Snap To and cause the mouse pointer to point to the default (OK) button in the Mouse Properties dialog box.

 1

- Click the Automatically move pointer to the default button in a dialog box check box in the Snap To area to select it (Figure 6–69).

- Apply the changes, and close the Mouse Properties dialog box.

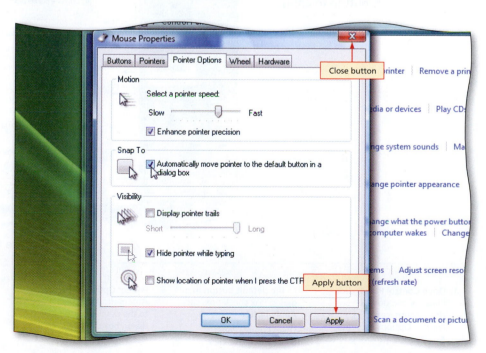

Figure 6–69

2

- In the Hardware and Sound window, click the Mouse link to open the Mouse Properties dialog box (Figure 6–70).

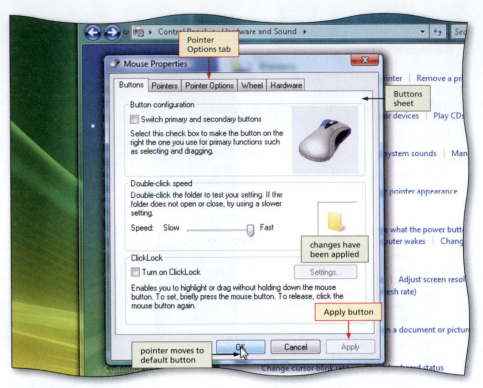

Figure 6–70

3

- Click the Pointer Options tab to display the Pointer Options sheet.

- Click the Automatically move pointer to the default button in a dialog box check box to remove the check mark (Figure 6–71).

- Click the Apply button to apply the changes.

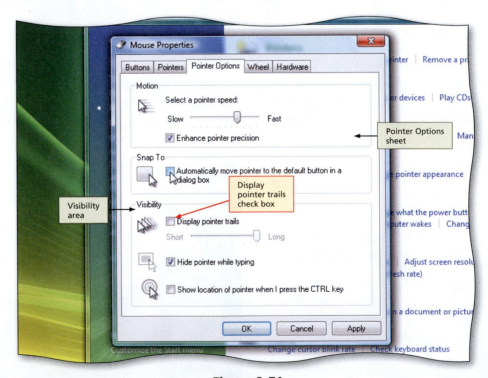

Figure 6–71

Other Ways

1. Open Control Panel, click Classic View, double-click Mouse icon, click Pointer Options tab, click Automatically move pointer to the default button in a dialog box check box, click Apply button

2. Open Control Panel, click Mouse link, click Pointer Options tab, click Automatically move pointer to the default button in a dialog box check box, click Apply button

To Display a Pointer Trail

When the mouse pointer moves across the desktop, it can be difficult to see where it is on the desktop. To improve the visibility of the mouse pointer, you can display a pointer trail, or trail of mouse pointers, on the desktop as you move the mouse. The following steps display a pointer trail.

- Click the Display pointer trails check box in the Visibility area to select it (Figure 6–72).

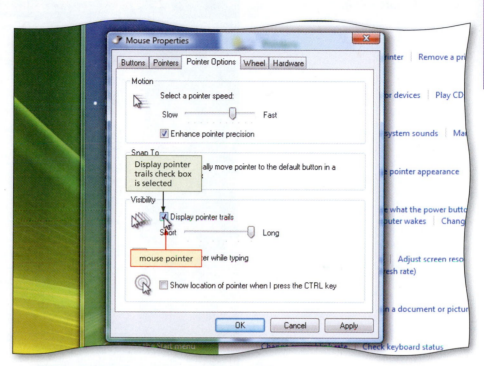

Figure 6–72

2

- Move the mouse and then watch the trail of mouse pointers that appear as the mouse moves across the desktop (Figure 6–73).

🔎 Experiment

- Experiment with the length of the pointer trail by dragging the pointer trails slider until you find the best length for you.

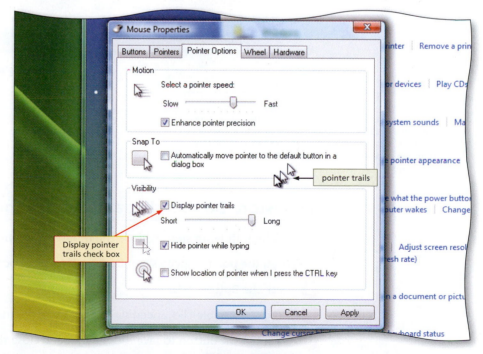

Figure 6–73

• When you have finished viewing the pointer trails, click the Display pointer trails check box to deselect the pointer trails option (Figure 6–74).

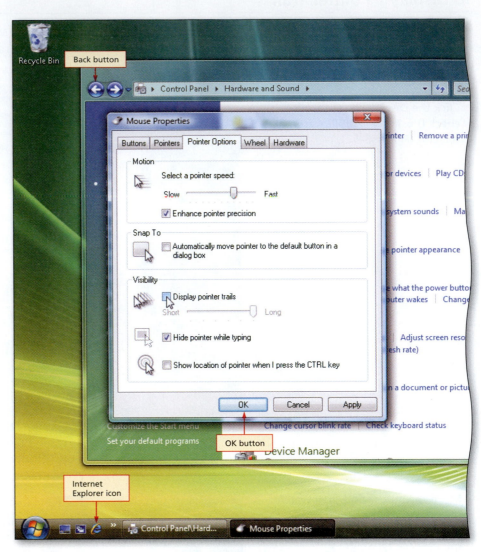

Figure 6–74

Other Ways

1. Open Control Panel, click Classic View, double-click Mouse icon, click Pointer Options tab, click Display pointer trails

2. Open Control Panel, click Mouse link, click Pointer Options tab, click Display pointer trails

To Restore Double-click and Pointer Speed

The following steps restore the mouse functionality back to its original settings.

1 Drag the pointer speed slider back to its original position.

2 Click the Buttons tab.

3 Drag the Double-click speed slider back to its original position.

4 Click the OK button to save the changes and close the Mouse Properties dialog box.

5 Return to the Control Panel window.

Programs

The Programs window brings together all of the tools you need when working with the various programs on your computer. From the Programs window, you can uninstall programs, configure older programs to run in Vista, and turn a variety of Windows features on and off. You also can access Windows Defender (covered in Appendix B), set your default programs, configure a second display device using SideShow, work with the Sidebar (which you learned about in Chapters 1 and 2), and access the Windows Marketplace online. In this section, you will install and uninstall a program as these are among the most common program tasks that users perform.

BTW

Windows SideShow
Windows SideShow enables you to connect a Windows SideShow-compatible device to your computer, which will access information from your computer. For example, you can configure Windows SideShow to display your e-mail messages from Windows Mail on a secondary display device.

To Install a Program

In previous versions of Windows, you could install a program using the Control Panel. In Windows Vista, you install a program by inserting the CD, DVD, or USB device that has the program you wish to install and running its install program, or you can download and install a program from the Internet. When installing programs, you will be required to provide the proper User Account Control authorization. If you are not using an account with administrator privileges or do not have the user name and password of an administrative account, you will be unable to install a program. The following steps install Microsoft Silverlight, a Web browser plug-in that allows you to view high definition media files on the Internet. It is important to note that due to different computer configurations, and because Web sites on the Internet frequently change, the steps required to download Microsoft Silverlight may vary slightly from the steps below. If you are having difficulty locating the Microsoft Silverlight program online, contact your instructor. If you do not have administrative privileges or you do not have access to administrative login information, read the following steps without performing them.

- Start Internet Explorer.

- If necessary, maximize the Windows Internet Explorer window (Figure 6–75).

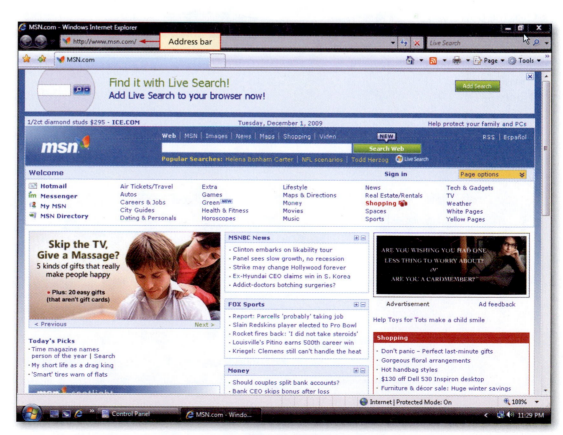

Figure 6–75

2

● Type http://www.
microsoft.com/
silverlight/ in
the Address bar
and then press
the ENTER key to
display the Microsoft
Silverlight Web page
(Figure 6–76).

Figure 6–76

3

● Click the Download
Silverlight Now
link to display the
Microsoft Silverlight
download page
(Figure 6–77).

Figure 6–77

4
- Click the Windows link to display the download page for the Windows version of Microsoft Silverlight (Figure 6–78).

Why do I have to click the Windows link?

When installing software, you should install only those programs that are compatible with your operating system. Most programs are compatible with specific operating systems and versions.

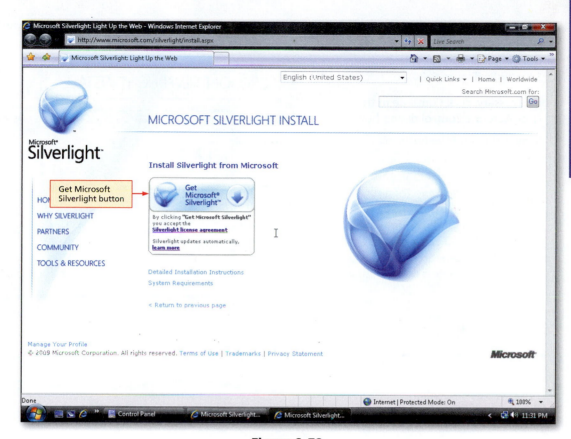

Figure 6–78

5
- Click the Install Now button to display the File Download - Security Warning dialog box (Figure 6–79).

Figure 6–79

6

- Click the Run button in the File Download dialog box to download and install Microsoft Silverlight (Figure 6–80).

- If necessary, click Continue in the User Account Control dialog box.

Q&A   Why is there a Save button?

If you do not trust the source of the software program, you should save it first and then run a virus check on the downloaded file. After verifying its safety, you can install it. You also can save a downloaded software program so that you can create a backup copy.

Figure 6–80

7

- After installing, the Microsoft Silverlight Web browser window changes to indicate that the installation was a success by displaying an ani-mated media file (Figure 6–81).

Q&A   What if the installation failed?

Depending upon the error message displayed, you may have to retry the installation or seek help from your instructor.

Figure 6–81

8

- Close both Internet Explorer windows.

- If necessary, click the Control Panel button on the taskbar to make it the active window (Figure 6–82).

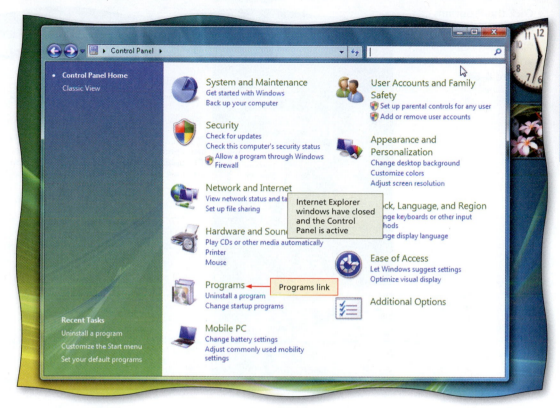

Figure 6–82

To Uninstall a Program

Some programs include uninstall options as a part of their installation. For example, some programs, when installed, add a program group to the Start menu which includes an uninstall command that you can use to run the uninstall program. Other programs do not offer an uninstall option or a program group on the Start menu. Instead, a menu command is available during the installation process to uninstall the software. Other software must be removed by deleting the files that comprise the software. Although you can remove software by dragging the software's folder to the Recycle Bin, it is recommended that you uninstall the software program using the Programs and Features window. This ensures that the software is completely removed from the system without leaving any miscellaneous files to potentially interfere with the normal processes of the computer. Most of the programs you install can be uninstalled from the Programs and Features window as well. The following steps uninstall the Microsoft Silverlight plug-in using the Programs and Features window.

1

- Click the Programs link in the Control Panel to display the Programs window (Figure 6–83).

Figure 6–83

2

● Click the Programs
and Features link to
open the Programs
and Features window
(Figure 6–84).

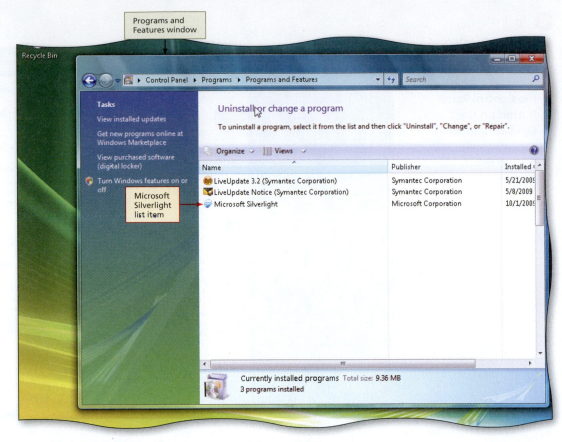

Figure 6–84

3

● Click the Microsoft
Silverlight list
item to select it
(Figure 6–85).

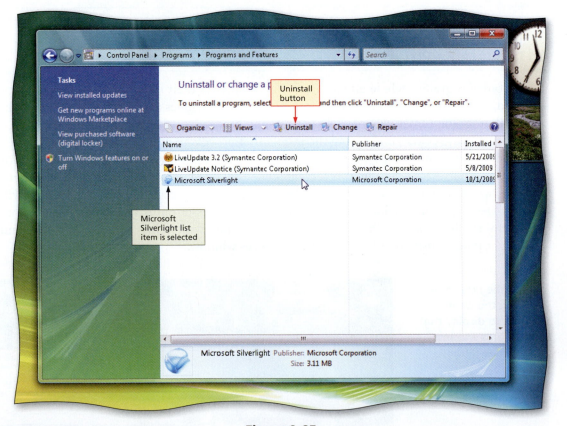

Figure 6–85

4

- Click the Uninstall button to display the Programs and Features dialog box (Figure 6–86).

Figure 6–86

5

- Click the Yes button to confirm that you want to uninstall Microsoft Silverlight (Figure 6–87).

- If necessary, click Allow in the User Account Control dialog box.

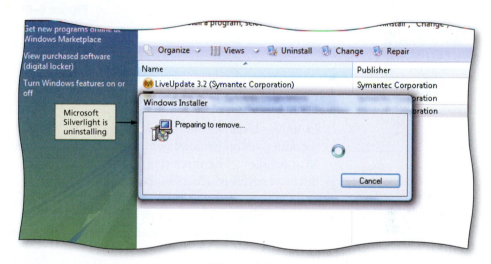

Figure 6–87

6

- After a short amount of time, the uninstall process finishes (Figure 6–88).

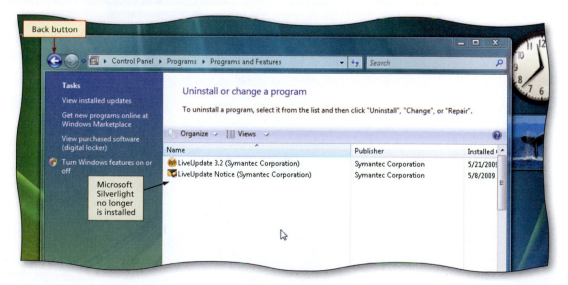

Figure 6–88

7
- Return to the Programs window.

- Return to the Control Panel window (Figure 6–89).

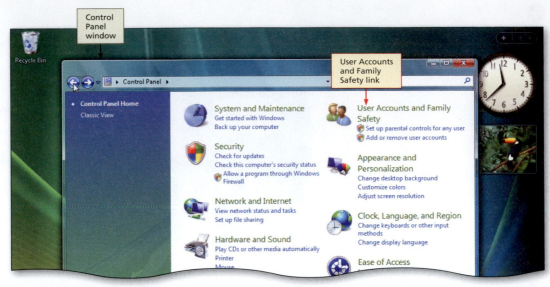

Figure 6–89

BTW

Windows CardSpace
Windows CardSpace is used to create and manage a set of digital identities, similar to phone book entries, that can be shared with Web sites that support the technology. These cards can be used to replace the user names and passwords you use to register and log on to Web sites.

User Accounts and Family Safety

From the User Accounts and Family Safety window, you can create and manage user accounts, set up parental controls for accounts, configure Windows CardSpace, and set up Mail profiles. The three types of user accounts (Administrator, Standard, and Guest) have different levels of access to the computer. The privileges of the Administrator, Standard, and Guest user accounts are summarized in Table 6-1. For Standard accounts that will be used by children, you also can set up parental controls so that the user is restricted from performing certain actions such as playing games with certain ratings or browsing the Internet for too long.

Table 6–1 User Accounts and Privileges

User Accounts	Privileges
Administrator	• Creates, changes, and deletes user accounts and groups • Installs programs • Sets folder sharing • Sets permissions • Accesses all files • Takes ownership of files • Grants rights to other user accounts and to themselves • Installs or removes hardware devices • Logs on in Safe Mode
Standard	• Changes the password and picture for their own user accounts • Uses programs that have been installed on the computer • Views permissions • Creates, changes, and deletes files in their Document folders • Views files in shared document folders

Table 6–1 User Accounts and Privileges (continued)

User Accounts	Privileges
Guest	• Same as Standard account, but cannot create a password • Is turned off by default, you must turn it on before it can be used

To View Account Information

If you have administrative privileges you can do more than simply view account information for all user accounts. You also can change a user account, create a new user account, and change the way users log on or off. You also can turn User Account Control on and off; however, it is not recommended that you turn it off. If you do not have administrative privileges, only information about your account will be visible. The following steps display your account information.

• Click the User Accounts and Family Safety link in the Control Panel window to display the User Accounts and Family Safety window (Figure 6–90).

Figure 6–90

2
- Click the User Accounts link to display the User Accounts window (Figure 6–91).

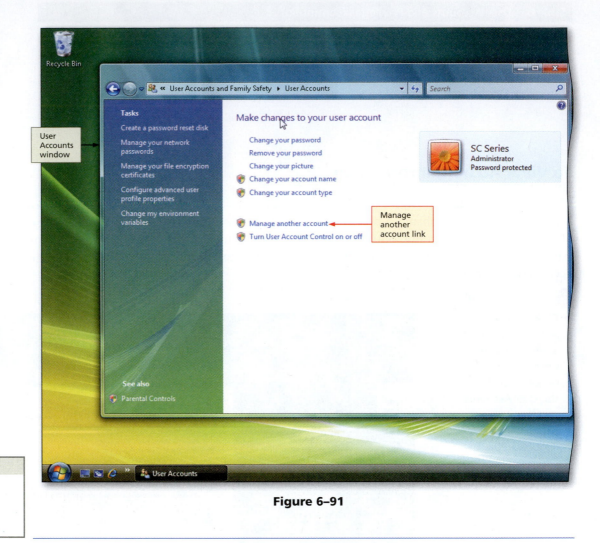

Figure 6–91

Other Ways

1. Open Control Panel, click Classic View, double-click User Accounts icon

To Create a User Account

If you have administrative privileges, you can create a new user account. When you create a new user account, if you use the defaults, Windows Vista will create a standard account with no password. To make the account more secure after you create it, you can view the account information and then add a password. The following steps create the SCStudent user account as a standard account and display its information.

1

- Click the Manage another account link to display the Manage Accounts window (Figure 6–92).

- If necessary, click the Continue button in the User Account Control dialog box.

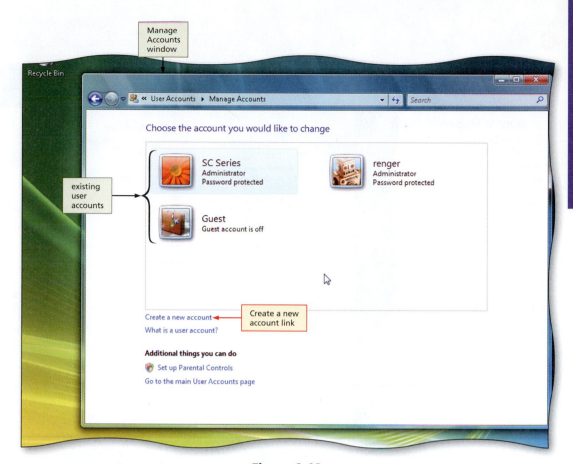

Figure 6–92

2

- Click the Create a new account link to create a new user account (Figure 6–93).

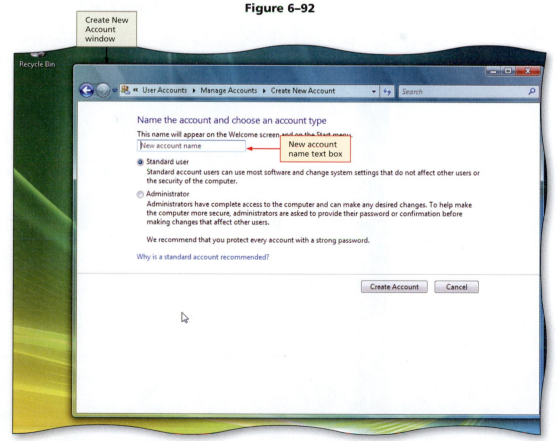

Figure 6–93

3
- Type `SCStudent` in the New account name text box to name the new account SCStudent (Figure 6–94).

- If necessary, click the Standard user option button.

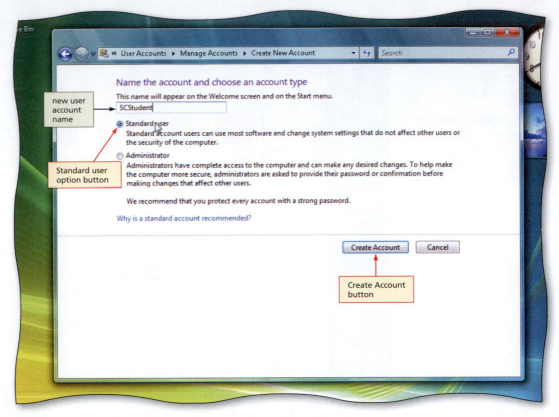

Figure 6–94

4
- Click the Create Account button to create the SCStudent account (Figure 6–95).

Figure 6–95

5

- Click the SCStudent icon to view the SCStudent account information and options (Figure 6–96).

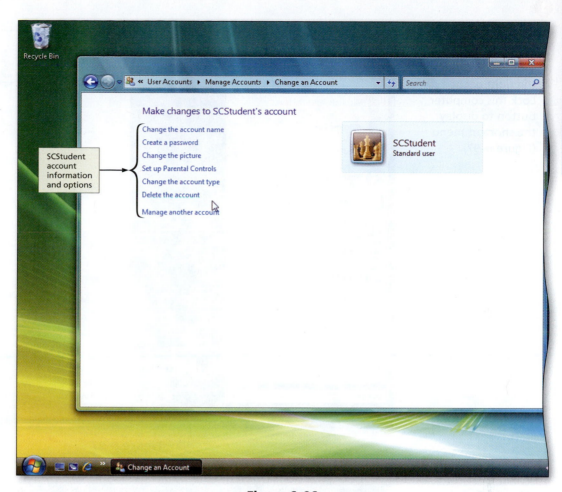

Figure 6–96

Other Ways	
1. Open Control Panel, click Add or remove user accounts link	2. Open Control Panel, click Classic View, double-click User Accounts icon, click Manage another account link

To Switch to a Different User

Even though you currently are logged on as SC Series, you can switch to a different user account without logging off of the SC Series account. In fact, you do not even have to close any open windows when switching to a different user account, as Windows Vista will maintain separate desktops for each user. The steps on the following pages switch to the SCStudent account, and then log off and return to the SC Series user account.

1

- Display the Start menu.

- Click the arrow to the right of the Lock this computer button to display the shortcut menu (Figure 6–97).

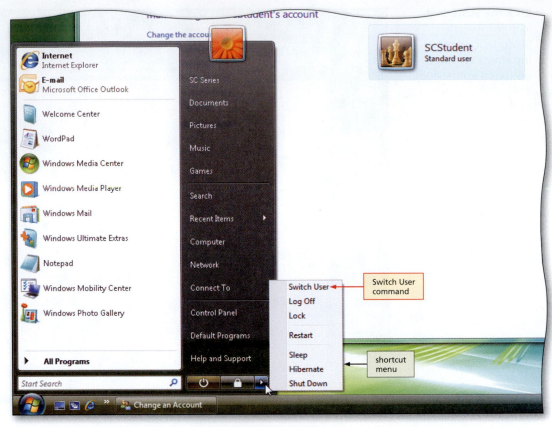

Figure 6–97

2

- Click the Switch User command to display the Welcome Screen (Figure 6–98).

- Click the SCStudent icon to log in.

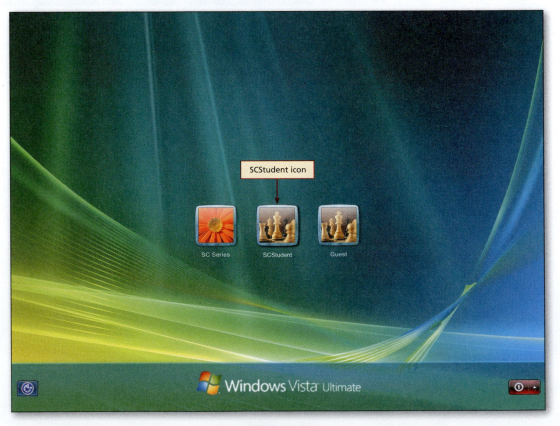

Figure 6–98

3

- After the Preparing Your Desktop message disappears, the SCStudent desktop is displayed and the Welcome Center window appears (Figure 6–99).

Figure 6–99

4

- After reviewing the desktop for SCStudent, display the Start menu.

- Click the arrow to the right of the Lock this computer button to display the shortcut menu (Figure 6–100).

- Click the Log Off command to log off and display the Welcome Screen.

Figure 6–100

5

- Click SC Series icon (or your icon) to switch back to the SC Series user account (Figure 6–101).

- If necessary, enter your password.

Figure 6–101

6

- Click the arrow button to display the SC Series desktop (Figure 6–102).

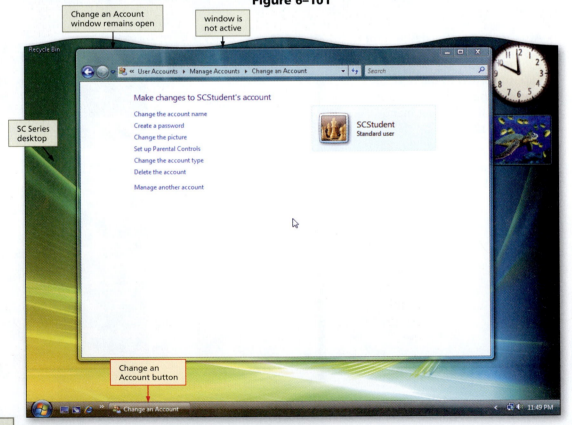

Figure 6–102

Other Ways

1. Press Windows logo key + L

To Delete a User Account

When you no longer have a need for a particular user account, perhaps because that user no longer will be using your computer, you should delete it from your computer. The following steps delete the SCStudent account.

- If necessary, click the Change an Account button on the taskbar to make the Change an Account window the active window.

- Click the Delete the account link to display the Delete Account window (Figure 6–103).

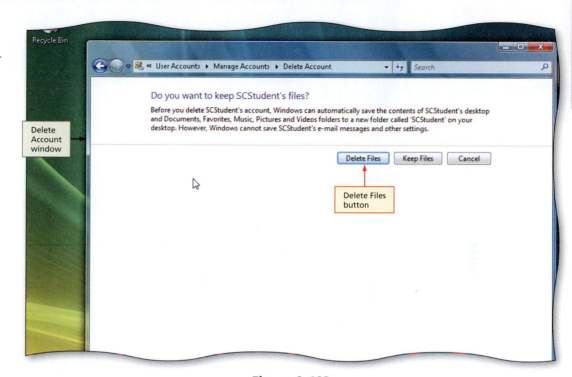

Figure 6–103

- Click the Delete Files button to delete the files associated with the SCStudent user account and display the Confirm Deletion window (Figure 6–104).

Do I have to delete the files?

You can keep a copy of the files associated with the user account you are deleting, but because the SCStudent account was created for demonstration purposes, there is no need to keep the files.

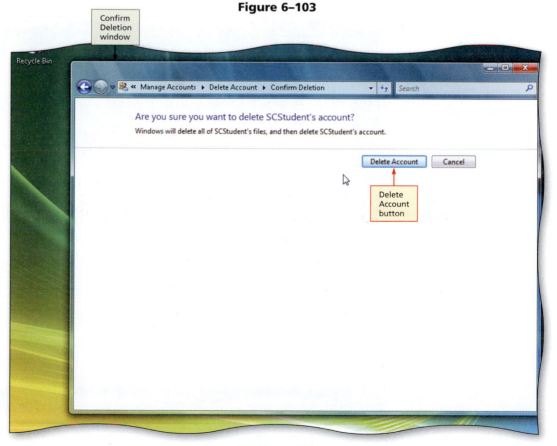

Figure 6–104

3

- Click the Delete Account button to confirm that you want to delete the user account and return to the Manage Accounts window (Figure 6–105).

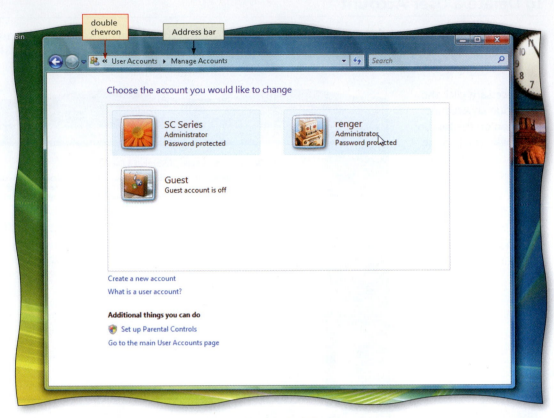

Figure 6–105

4

- Click the double chevron in the Address bar to display a list of locations (Figure 6–106).

- Click the Control Panel command to return to the Control Panel window.

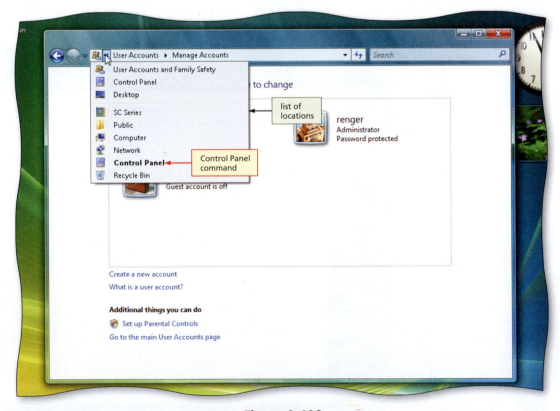

Figure 6–106

Clock, Language, and Region

The Clock, Language, and Region window includes the controls for setting the date and time and adjusting the Regional and Language options. The date and time dialog box is where you can change the date, time and time zone, add additional clocks, and alter Internet time settings. The Internet time settings automatically synchronize the time and date on the computer with the time and date on an Internet time server. The Regional and Language dialog box is where you can change and customize data formats, change the country, change keyboards and languages, and make other administrative changes related to the language you choose to use with Windows Vista.

BTW

Time Servers
If you always want the date and time on your computer to be correct and have an Internet connection, you might consider retrieving this information from an Internet time server. When you configure Windows Vista to synchronize the date and time with a time server (the default time server is time.windows.com), your computer periodically will check its date and time against the time server to make sure that it is correct.

To Change the Date and Time

Changes to the date and time are made in the Date and Time Settings dialog box. Administrative privileges are required to change the date and time. The following steps change the date and time, and then cancel the changes. If you do not have administrative privileges, read the following steps without performing them.

1

- Click the Clock, Language, and Region link in the Control Panel window to display the Clock, Language, and Region window (Figure 6–107).

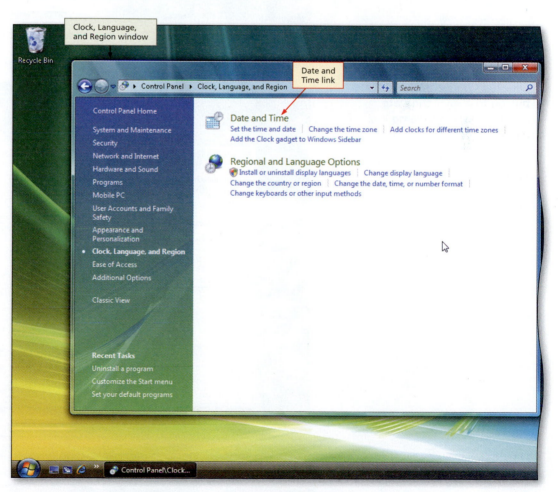

Figure 6–107

2

• Click the Date and Time link to display the Date and Time dialog box (Figure 6–108).

Q&A Do I need to manually adjust the clock for daylight savings time?

No. Windows Vista will automatically change the time for daylight savings time.

Q&A Should I change the time or the time zone if I travel?

If you travel to a different time zone, you can use the Change time zone button to update the day and time on your computer so that the clock displays the correct time, or you can configure an additional clock to display the time and date of your destination.

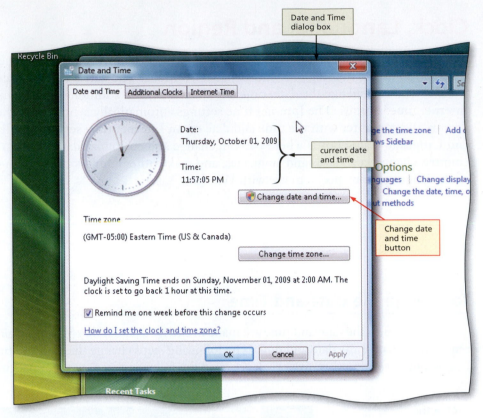

Figure 6–108

3

• Click the Change date and time button to display the Date and Time Settings dialog box (Figure 6–109).

• If necessary, click the Continue button in the User Account Control dialog box.

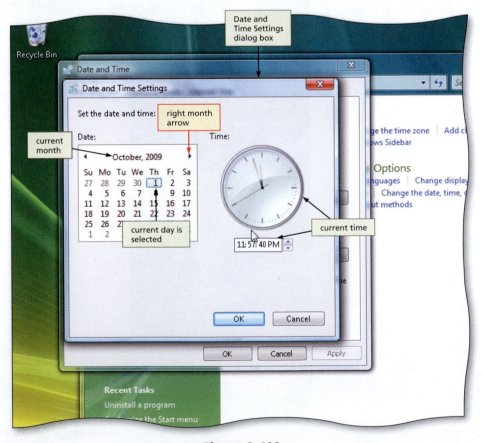

Figure 6–109

● Click the right month arrow until the month changes to November (Figure 6–110). If November already is the current month, you do not need to click the right month arrow.

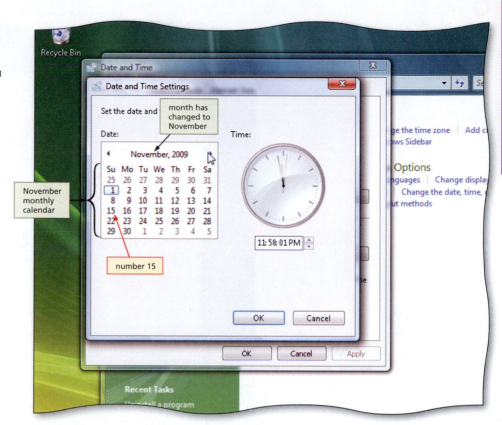

Figure 6–110

5

● Click the number 15 in the monthly calendar to select November 15 (Figure 6–111).

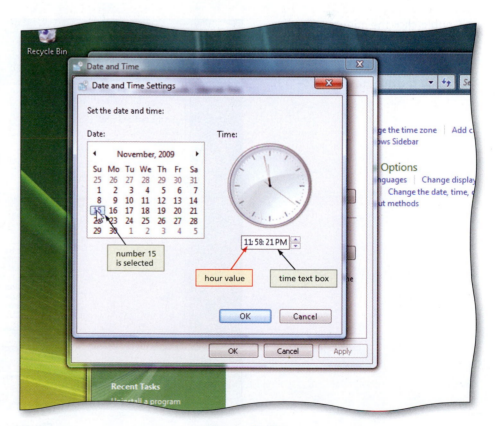

Figure 6–111

6

● Double-click the hour value in the time text box, and then type 9 as the new value to change the hour (Figure 6–112).

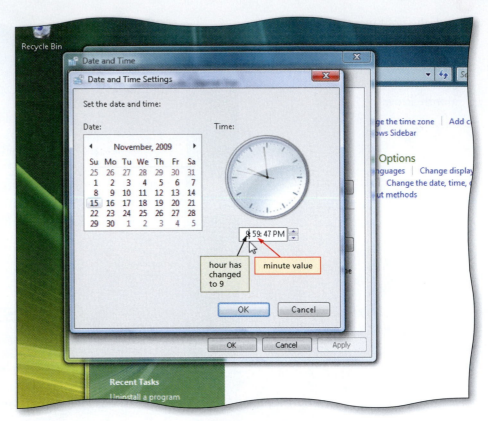

Figure 6–112

7

● Double-click the minute value in the time text box.

● Type 00 as the new value to change the minute (Figure 6–113).

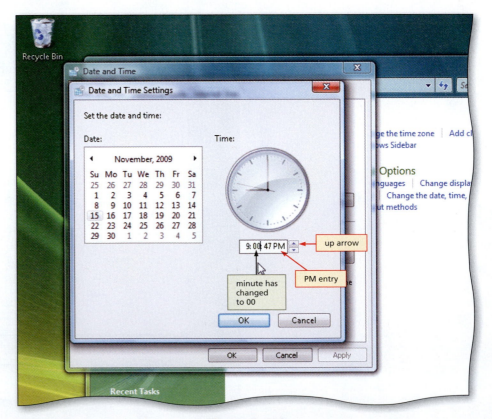

Figure 6–113

8

- If the PM entry displays in the time text box, click the PM entry and then click the up arrow to display the AM entry (Figure 6–114).

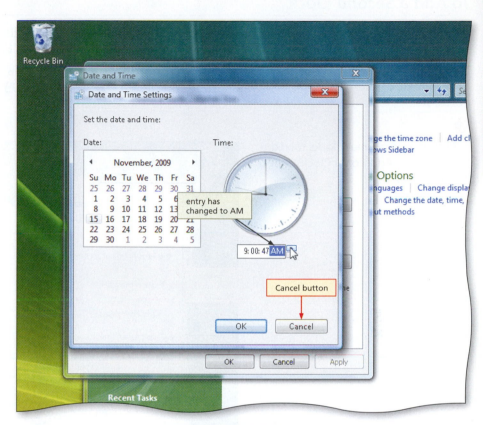

Figure 6–114

9

- Click the Cancel button to cancel the changes and return to the Date and Time dialog box (Figure 6–115).

Q&A

What if I want to save the date and time changes?

If you wish to save the date and time changes, you should click the OK button instead of the Cancel button.

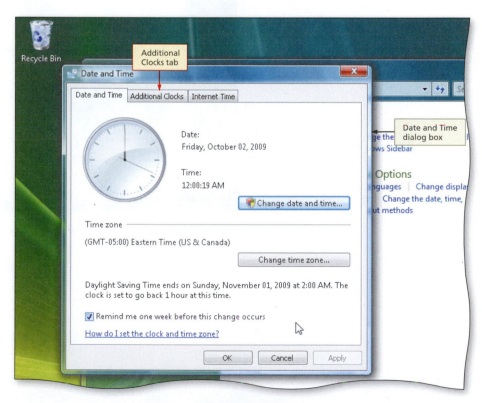

Figure 6–115

Other Ways

1. In Notification area, right-click time, click Adjust Date/Time
2. Open Control Panel, click Classic View, double-click Date and Time icon

To Add a Second Clock

Windows Vista can display several clocks besides the default clock in the Notification area. Each clock that you add can show the time for a different time zone. International students, business travelers, and tourists might find it useful to have a clock to show the time in the location they are visiting, as well as the time in their home location. The following steps add a second clock to show Hawaii time, display it in the Notification area, and then delete it.

- Click the Additional Clocks tab to display the Additional Clocks sheet (Figure 6–116).

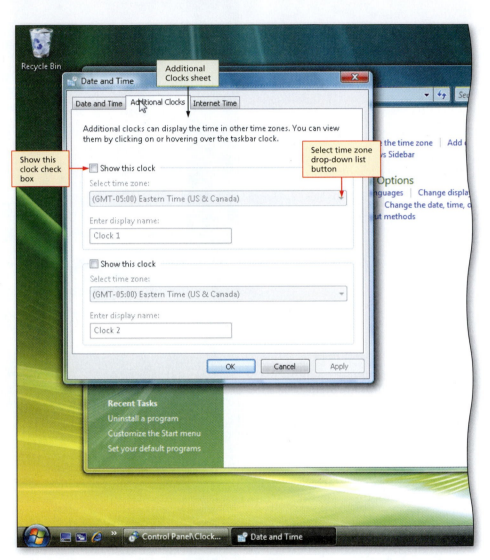

Figure 6–116

2

- Click the first Show this clock check box to enable it.

- Click the Select time zone drop-down list button to display a list of time zones.

- Scroll up until you see the Hawaii list item (Figure 6–117).

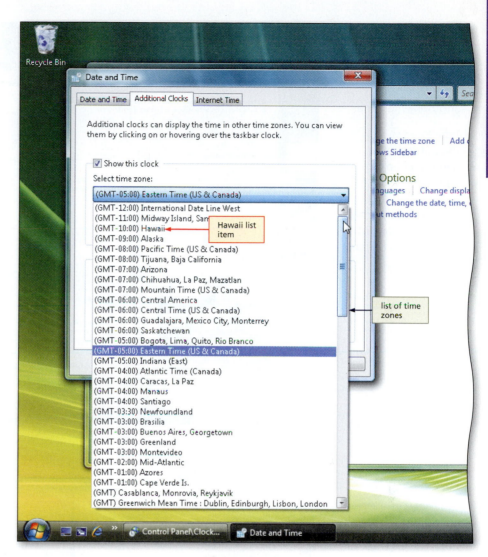

Figure 6–117

3

- Click the Hawaii list item to select it. If your time zone already is set for Hawaii, select another time zone.

- Type `Hawaii` in the Enter display name text box to name the clock (Figure 6–118). If you selected a different time zone, enter an appropriate name for the clock.

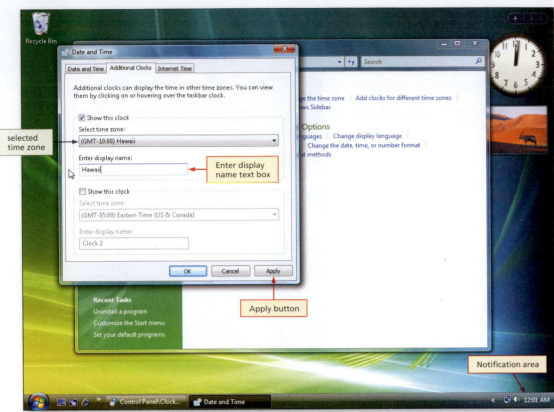

Figure 6–118

4

- Click the Apply button to apply the changes.

- Point to the clock in the Notification area to display the additional clock (Figure 6–119).

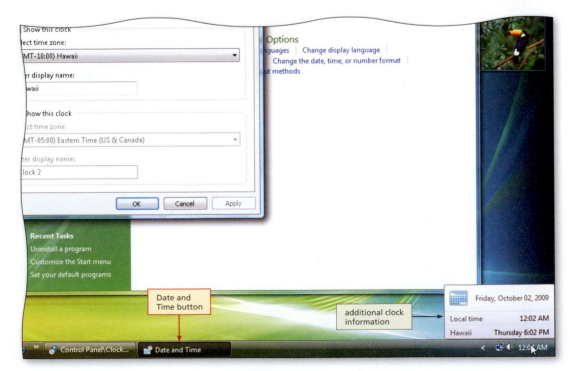

Figure 6–119

5

- Click the Date and Time button on the taskbar to activate the Date and Time dialog box.

- Type `Clock 1` in the Enter display name text box.

- Change the time zone back to the Eastern Time, (US and Canada) setting, or your original time zone.

- Click the Show this clock check box to disable it (Figure 6–120).

- Click the OK button to apply the changes and close the Date and Time dialog box.

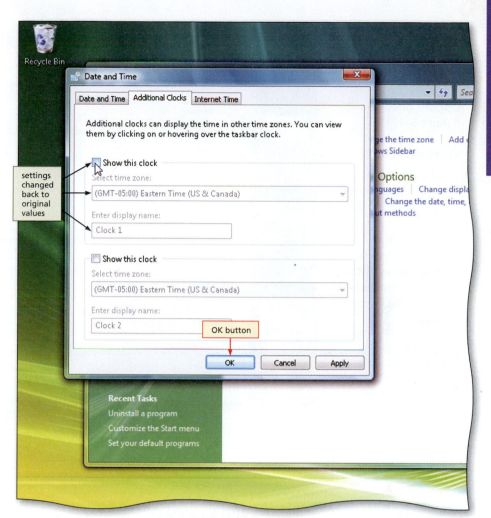

Figure 6–120

Other Ways	
1. In Notification area, right-click time, click Adjust Date/Time	2. Open Control Panel, click Classic View, double-click Date and Time icon

To View the Data Formats

Windows Vista is designed to work in many regions of the world and in many different languages. Computer users in other countries often have different conventions for displaying their dates, time, and currency. For example, many countries in Europe use the 24-hour clock when displaying time. You can use the Regional and Language Options dialog box to view the formats that Windows Vista uses to display data. If you are planning to visit other countries, you can change the data formats so that they will match the formats used by the countries you visit. The steps on the following page display the Regional and Language Options dialog box.

1

- Click the Regional and Language Options link to display the Regional and Language Options dialog box (Figure 6–121).

Experiment

- Try changing the current format selection. Review the different data formats that are used by other countries. Note that Windows Vista can be customized to match the various formats.

- After viewing the data formats, click the Cancel button to close the dialog box.

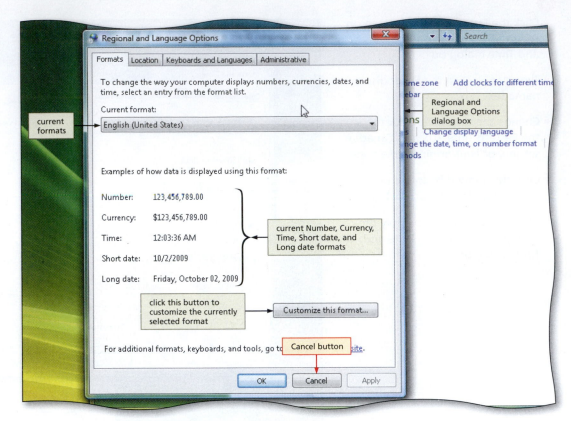

Figure 6–121

Other Ways

1. Open Control Panel, click Classic View, double-click Regional and Language Options icon

BTW

Windows Vista Accessibility Features
For more information about the Accessibility Features of Windows Vista, visit the Windows Vista Accessibility Web Page (scsite.com/winvista/access).

Ease of Access

In the previous sections, you customized the mouse by changing the button configuration, adjusting the double-click speed, turning on ClickLock, altering the pointer speed, turning on Snap To, and displaying pointer trails. These changes make it easier for some users to work in the Windows Vista environment. Windows Vista also provides additional tools, known as **accessibility features**, which make it easier for people who are mobility, hearing or vision impaired, to use Windows Vista. All of the accessibility features can be found in the Ease of Access Center. New to Windows Vista, the Ease of Access Center consolidates all of the accessibility features in one location.

People who have restricted movement and cannot move the mouse (**mobility impaired**) have the option of using Mouse Keys that allow them to use the numeric keypad to move the mouse pointer, click, double-click, and drag. People who are deaf or hard of hearing (**hearing impaired**) can enable Sound Sentry, which generates visual warnings when the computer makes a sound and can turn on captions when a program speaks or makes sounds, if captions are available. People who have difficulty seeing the screen (**vision impaired**) can use the High Contrast feature. High Contrast changes the desktop color scheme to the High Contrast Black (Large) color scheme. This color scheme increases the size of text on the desktop, which improves a person's ability to read the text. Windows Vista also offers Narrator, which translates text to speech, and Magnifier, which creates a separate window to display a magnified part of the screen.

These are just a few of the accessibility features that are available in Windows Vista. From the Ease of Access Center, you also can access a questionnaire that will allow Windows Vista to determine the right accessibility features for you. If you are unsure of where to begin, start with the questionnaire. The following section demonstrates some of the accessibility features.

To View Accessibility Options

The following steps open the Ease of Access Center.

1

- Click the Ease of Access link in the left pane to open the Ease of Access window (Figure 6–122).

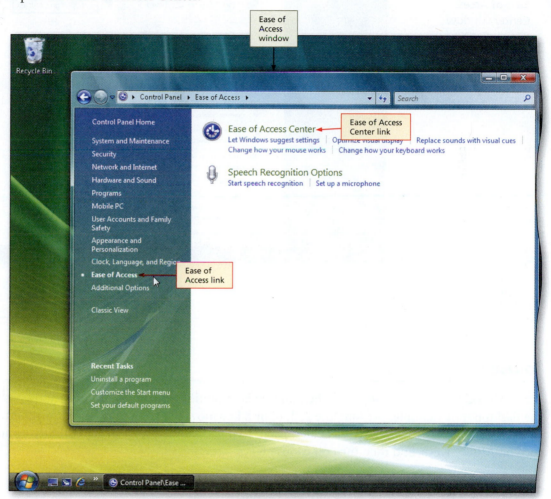

Figure 6–122

2

- Click the Ease of Access Center link in the Ease of Access window to open the Ease of Access Center window.

- If necessary, maximize the Ease of Access Center window (Figure 6–123).

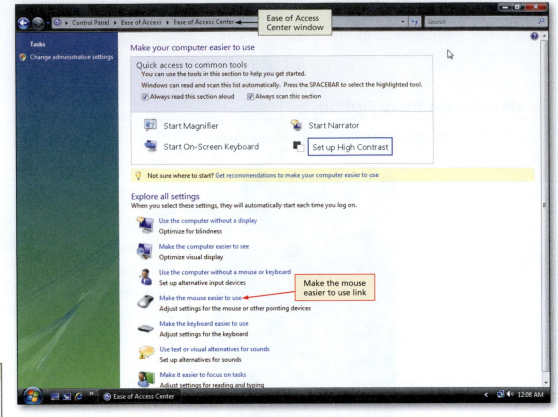

Figure 6–123

Other Ways

1. Press WINDOWS + U

2. Open Control Panel, click Classic View, double-click Ease of Access Center icon

To Use Mouse Keys

Mouse Keys allows you to use the numeric keys on the keypad, instead of a mouse, to move the pointer across the desktop. For example, pressing the 2, 4, 6, or 8 key moves the mouse pointer down, left, right, or up, respectively, while the 5 key is used to select an object. To illustrate the use of an accessibility option, the following steps turn on Mouse Keys, and then turn off Mouse Keys.

1

• Click the Make the mouse easier to use link to open the Make the mouse easier to use window (Figure 6–124).

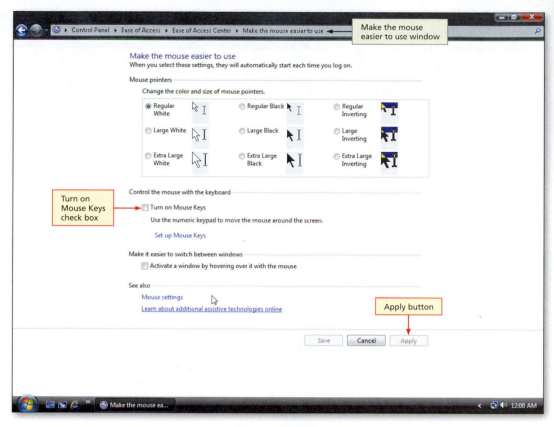

Figure 6–124

2

• Click the Turn on Mouse Keys check box to turn on Mouse Keys (Figure 6–125).

• Click the Apply button to apply the changes.

Q&A

What if I do not have a numeric keypad on my keyboard?

Mouse Keys requires that the keyboard have a numeric keypad. If you do not have a numeric keypad, you will not be able to use Mouse Keys.

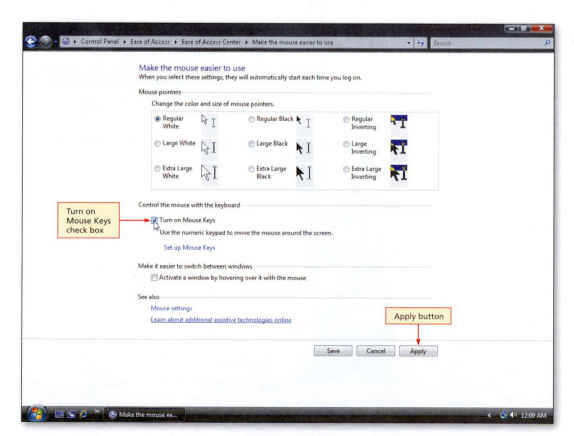

Figure 6–125

- Use the 1, 2, 3, 4, 6, 7, 8, and 9 keys on the numeric keypad to move the mouse pointer to the Turn on Mouse Keys check box.

- Press the 5 key to remove the check mark from the check box (Figure 6–126).

- Using the numeric keys on the numeric keypad, move the mouse pointer to the Apply button.

- Press the 5 key to simulate clicking the Apply button to turn off Mouse Keys.

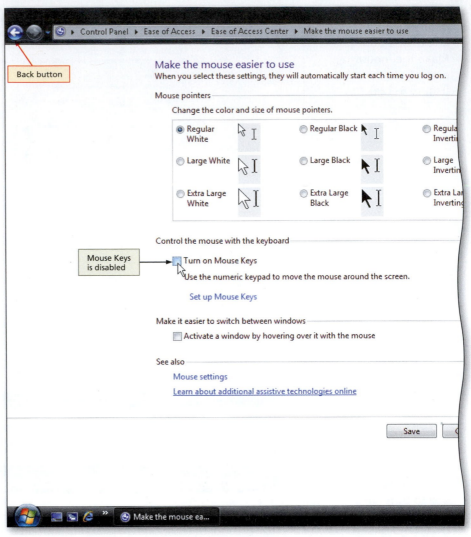

Figure 6–126

- Return to the Ease of Access Center window (Figure 6–127).

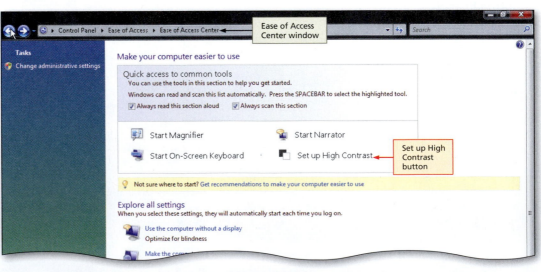

Figure 6–127

Other Ways

1. Open Control Panel, click Classic View, double-click Ease of Access Center icon, click Make the mouse easier to use, click Turn on Mouse Keys, click Apply button

2. Press left ALT+left SHIFT+NUM LOCK

To Turn On High Contrast

High Contrast is designed for individuals who are visually impaired. The following steps turn on High Contrast.

● Click the Set up High Contrast button to display the Make the computer easier to see window (Figure 6–128).

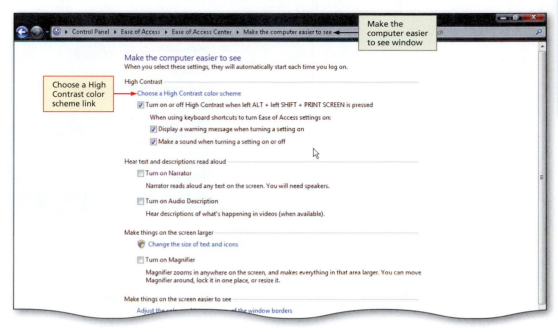

Figure 6–128

2

● Click the Choose a High Contrast color scheme link to display the Appearance Settings dialog box (Figure 6–129).

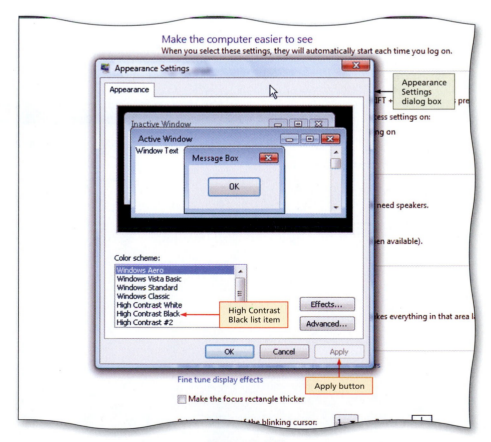

Figure 6–129

- Click the High Contrast Black list item to select it (Figure 6–130).

- Click the Apply button to apply the changes.

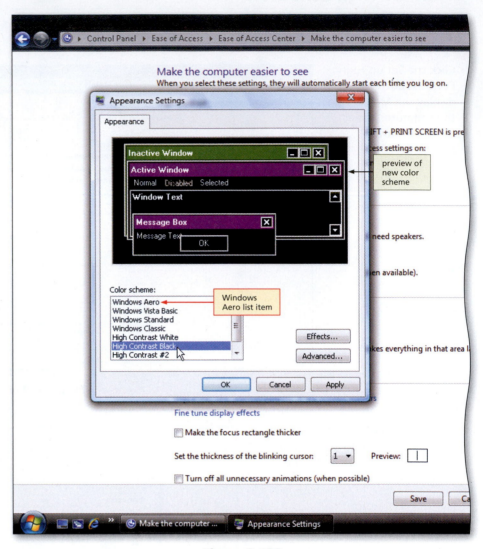

Figure 6–130

To Turn Off High Contrast

After turning on High Contrast and applying the High Contrast Black color scheme, remove the color scheme by switching back to the Windows Aero color scheme. The following steps turn off High Contrast.

1

- Click the Windows Aero list item to select it (Figure 6–131).

- Click the Apply button to switch back to Windows Aero color scheme.

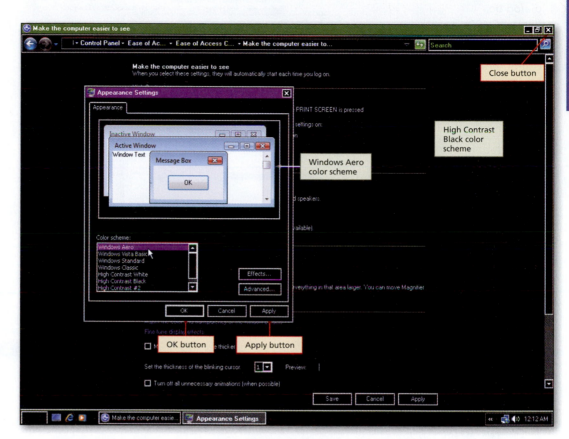

Figure 6–131

2

- Click the OK button to close the Appearance Settings dialog box (Figure 6-132).

- Close the Make the computer easier to see window.

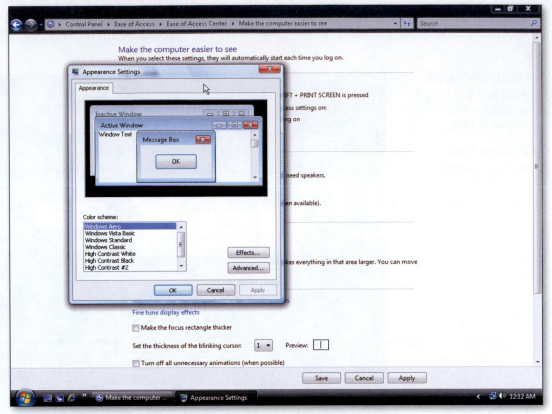

Figure 6–132

Other Ways

1. Press left ALT+left SHIFT+PRINT SCREEN

To Log Off from and Shut Down the Computer

After completing your work with Windows Vista, you first should close your user account by logging off from the computer, and then turn off the computer.

1 On the Start menu, click the arrow to the right of the Lock this computer button, and then click the Log Off command to log off from the computer.

2 On the Welcome Screen, click the Shut Down button to turn off the computer.

Chapter Summary

In this chapter you have learned how to customize Windows Vista using various links from the Control Panel window. You customized the keyboard, mouse, and date and time. You installed and removed a software program, added and deleted a printer, viewed installed updates, and viewed the properties of the hardware devices attached to the computer. Using the Ease of Access Center, you made adjustments to the computer for mobility and visibility impaired users. You also created a new user account, switched users while logged into an account, and deleted a user account. The following list includes all the new Windows Vista skills you have learned in this chapter.

1. Open the Control Panel Window (WIN 394)
2. Switch to Classic View (WIN 395)
3. Open the System and Maintenance Window (WIN 395)
4. Open the Welcome Center Window and View the Get Started Topics (WIN 396)
5. View System Information (WIN 398)
6. View the Windows Experience Index (WIN 398)
7. View Installed Updates (WIN 400)
8. View Available Updates (WIN 402)
9. View Power Options (WIN 403)
10. View Problem Reports and Solutions (WIN 404)
11. Check for New Solutions (WIN 405)
12. Open the Device Manager (WIN 407)
13. View the Properties of a Device (WIN 408)
14. Add a Printer (WIN 410)
15. Delete a Printer (WIN 416)
16. Adjust AutoPlay Settings (WIN 417)
17. Revert an AutoPlay Setting (WIN 420)
18. Change the Mouse Button Configuration (WIN 422)
19. Adjust the Double-Click Speed (WIN 423)
20. Turn On and Use ClickLock (WIN 425)
21. Close a Text Document and Turn Off ClickLock (WIN 426)
22. Adjust the Pointer Speed (WIN 428)
23. Turn On Snap To (WIN 429)
24. Display a Pointer Trail (WIN 431)
25. Install a Program (WIN 433)
26. Uninstall a Program (WIN 437)
27. View Account Information (WIN 441)
28. Create a User Account (WIN 442)
29. Switch to a Different User (WIN 445)
30. Delete a User Account (WIN 449)
31. Change the Date and Time (WIN 451)
32. Add a Second Clock (WIN 456)
33. View the Data Formats (WIN 459)
34. View Accessibility Options (WIN 461)
35. Use Mouse Keys (WIN 462)
36. Turn On High Contrast (WIN 465)
37. Turn Off High Contrast (WIN 467)

Learn It Online

Test your knowledge of chapter content and key terms.

Instructions: To complete the Learn It Online exercises, start your browser, click the Address bar, and then enter the Web address scsite.com/winvista/learn. When the Windows Vista Learn It Online page is displayed, click the link for the exercise you want to complete and then read the instructions.

Chapter Reinforcement TF, MC, and SA
A series of true/false, multiple-choice, and short-answer questions that test your knowledge of the chapter content.

Flash Cards
An interactive learning environment where you identify chapter key terms associated with displayed definitions.

Practice Test
A series of multiple-choice questions that test your knowledge of chapter content and key terms.

Who Wants To Be a Computer Genius?
An interactive game that challenges your knowledge of chapter content in the style of a television quiz show.

Wheel of Terms
An interactive game that challenges your knowledge of chapter key terms in the style of the television show *Wheel of Fortune*.

Crossword Puzzle Challenge
A crossword puzzle that challenges your knowledge of key terms presented in the chapter.

Apply Your Knowledge

Reinforce the skills and apply the concepts you learned in this chapter.

Add a Printer

Instructions: You decide to try your friend's suggestion and add a CANON Inkjet PIXMA iP8500 printer using the Add Printer Wizard. You must have administrative privileges for this exercise.

Perform the following tasks:
Part 1: Install the CANON Inkjet PIXMA iP8500 Printer
1. Display the Start menu and then click Control Panel.
2. Click the Hardware and Sound icon in the Control Panel window.
3. Click Printers to open the Printers window (Figure 6–133).

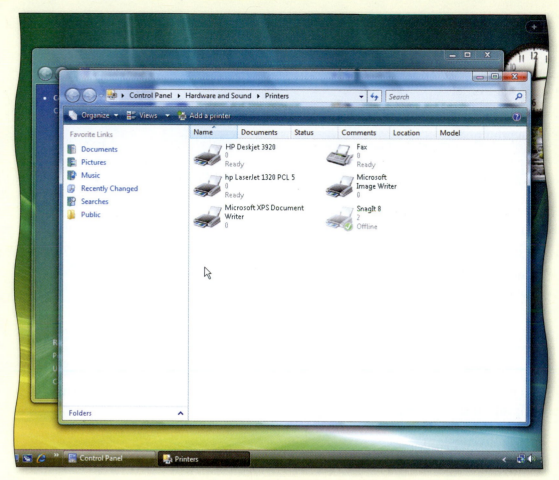

Figure 6–133

4. Click Add a printer to run the Add Printer Wizard.

5. Add CANON Inkjet PIXMA iP8500 as a local printer on LPT1.

Part 2: Printing the Contents of the Printers Window

1. Maximize the Printers window.

2. Press the PRINT SCREEN key on the keyboard to place an image of the desktop on the Clipboard.

3. Display the Start menu, click All Programs, click Accessories, and then click Paint.

4. Maximize the Untitled – Paint window.

5. Paste the image from the Clipboard to the Paint window.

6. Print the Paint document.

7. Quit the Paint program, and do not save the file.

Part 3: Display the Properties of the CANON Inkjet PIXMA iP8500 Printer

1. Right-click the CANON Inkjet PIXMA iP8500 icon and then click Properties on the shortcut menu to display the CANON Inkjet PIXMA iP8500 Properties dialog box. Using the tabs in the dialog box, answer the following questions.

   a. Is the printer always available?

Continued >

Apply Your Knowledge *continued*

   b. What is the orientation of the paper?

   _____

   c. What is the page order?

   _____

   d. What is the print quality?

   _____

2. Click the OK button to close the CANON Inkjet PIXMA iP8500 Properties dialog box.

Part 4: Delete the CANON Inkjet PIXMA iP8500 Icon
1. Right-click the CANON Inkjet PIXMA iP8500 icon, and then click Delete on the shortcut menu.
2. Click the Yes button in the Printers dialog box to delete the CANON Inkjet PIXMA iP8500 icon.
3. Close the Printers and Hardware and Sound windows.
4. Submit the printed Paint document and the answers to the questions to your instructor.

Extend Your Knowledge

Extend the skills you learned in this chapter and experiment with new skills. You may need to use Help to complete the assignment.

Troubleshoot Hardware Problems

Instructions: Use Windows Vista troubleshooters to answer the following questions.

Perform the following tasks:
1. Display the Start menu, click Help and Support, click Troubleshooting (Figure 6–134).

   a. Your document does not print at all. How do you troubleshoot it? What suggestions does Windows offer that might help fix your printing problem?

   _____

   b. You are having trouble with the new USB keyboard you purchased. What should you do?

   _____

   c. You are having trouble with turning on automatic updating. What should you do?

   _____

   d. You are having driver troubles with a hardware device. You decide to see what Windows Vista recommends. What are some of the tips that Windows Vista gives you?

   Tip 1:

   _____

   Tip 2:

   _____

   Tip 3:

   _____

   Tip 4:

   _____

   Tip 5:

   _____

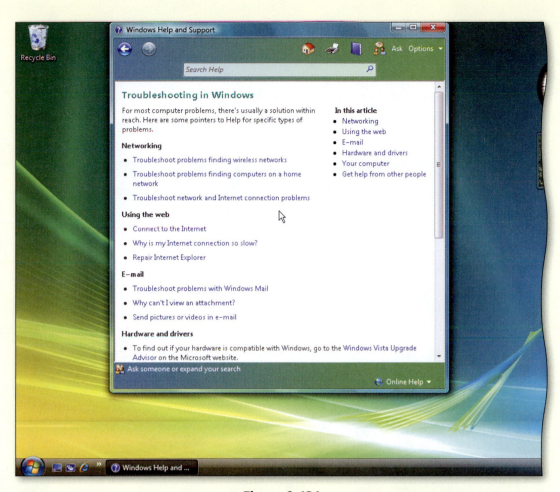

Figure 6–134

In the Lab

Use the guidelines, concepts and skills presented in this chapter to increase your knowledge of Windows Vista. Labs are listed in order of increasing difficulty.

Lab 1: Developing a Control Panel Guide

Instructions: Although most people like to use the Category View when working with the Control Panel, your boss favors the Classic View (Figure 6–135). Your boss asks you to create a Control Panel guide so that other employees can familiarize themselves with the Classic View and the Control Panel icons. Using WordPad, create a guide with a title and description of the following icons in the Control Panel window: Add Hardware, Windows CardSpace, People Near Me, and Tablet PC Settings.

Continued >

In the Lab *continued*

Perform the following tasks:

Part 1: Launching the WordPad Application

1. Open the Control Panel window, and click Classic View (Figure 6–135).

2. Open WordPad, and maximize the Document - WordPad window.

Figure 6–135

Part 2: Entering Text

1. Type `The Control Panel Window (Classic View)` as the title.

2. Type a brief statement about how Classic View is different from the normal Windows Vista Control Panel.

3. Type `Add Hardware` and then type a brief description of the Add Hardware wizard.

4. Type `Windows CardSpace` and then type a brief description of Windows CardSpace.

5. Type `People Near Me` and then type a brief description of how People Near Me can be used.

6. Type `Tablet PC Settings` and then type a brief description of the various Tablet PC Settings.

Part 3: Finishing, Saving and Printing the Control Panel Guide

1. Save the completed document on a USB drive using the file name, Control Panel Guide.

2. Print the completed document using the Print button.

3. Close WordPad and the Control Panel window.

4. Safely remove the USB drive.

5. Submit the Control Panel Guide to your instructor.

In the Lab

Lab 2: Customizing the Computer Using the Ease of Access Center

Instructions: You are volunteering at the local senior center, and you have noticed that a number of the residents have difficulty reading the text on the desktop and using the keyboard to type text. You decide to change the settings to help them access the computer more easily. You will make the screen easier to read and make it easier to type in WordPad. After seeing how these changes helped some of the seniors to use the computer, you decide to explore additional accessibility options.

Perform the following tasks:
Part 1: Using Microsoft Magnifier
1. Open the Ease of Access Center (Figure 6–136).

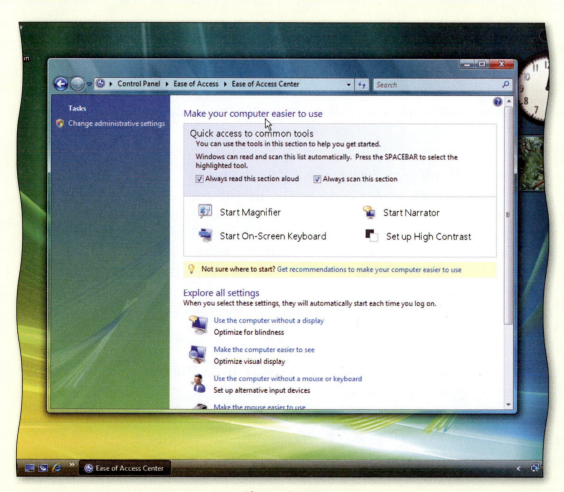

Figure 6–136

Continued >

In the Lab continued

2. Click Start Magnifier to start the Microsoft Magnifier and open the Magnifier dialog box. Microsoft Magnifier displays a separate window at the top of the desktop that contains the magnified text and objects that display near the mouse pointer.

3. Point to the text in the Magnifier dialog box.

   a. What is displayed in the window at the top of the desktop?

   _____

4. Point to the Help button in the Magnifier dialog box.

   a. What is displayed in the window at the top of the desktop?

   _____

5. Click the Minimize button in the Magnifier dialog box.

   a. What is displayed in the window at the top of the desktop?

   _____

6. Point to the Recycle Bin icon on the desktop, double-click the Recycle Bin icon, point to the Magnifier button on the taskbar, right-click the button, and then click Close on the shortcut menu.

7. Close the Recycle Bin window.

Part 2: Using On-Screen Keyboard

1. Click Start On-Screen Keyboard in the Ease of Access Center. The On-Screen Keyboard allows you to type text in a document window using the mouse.

2. If necessary, drag the On-Screen Keyboard window to position the window at the bottom of the desktop.

3. Open WordPad.

4. Resize and position the WordPad window at the top of the desktop.

5. Using the mouse pointer and On-Screen Keyboard, type the following sentence: It is easy to type using the On-Screen Keyboard. and then click the ENTER key twice on the On-Screen Keyboard. *Hint:* To type using the On-Screen Keyboard, click the key on the On-Screen Keyboard corresponding to the character you want to type. Click the shift key on the On-Screen Keyboard to capitalize text. Click the SPACEBAR on the On-Screen Keyboard to insert a blank space.

6. Using the mouse pointer and On-Screen Keyboard, type your first and last name and then click the ENTER key.

7. Print the document.

8. Close the On-Screen Keyboard window, and close WordPad. In the WordPad dialog box, click the Don't Save button to discard your changes.

Part 3: Letting Windows Help You Configure Settings

1. Open the Personalization window from the Control Panel window, and write down the theme that is displayed in the Theme box in the Theme Settings dialog box.

   _____

2. Click the Get recommendations to make your computer easier to use link in the Ease of Access Center, and experiment with the accessibility questionnaire. As you answer the questions, select the appropriate options as if you had a visibility and hearing impairment.

3. After you complete the questionnaire, turn on the suggested options.

Part 4: Working with Accessibility Settings

1. Display the Start menu.

    a. What color is the background color on the Start menu?

    _____

    b. Did the size of the commands on the Start menu change? If so, how?

    _____

    c. Is each icon on the Start menu fully visible?

    _____

2. Open and maximize the Control Panel window.

    a. Are the icons in the Control Panel window easy to see?

    _____

3. Close the Control Panel window.

Part 5: Restoring the Default Settings

1. Restore the Theme to the original theme you noted in Part 3, Step 1.

2. Turn off the options you turned on in the Ease of Access Center.

3. Hand in the printed WordPad document and the answers to the questions to your instructor.

In the Lab

Lab 3: Creating an Account with Parental Controls

Instructions: Your skills with Windows Vista are becoming well known. Your neighbor asks for help in setting up parental controls for her children. Before your make changes to your neighbor's computer, you decide to research how to use parental controls, and then you create an account to test them.

Perform the following tasks:

Part 1: Understanding Parental Controls

1. Open Windows Help and Support.

2. Answer the following questions concerning Parental Controls.

    a. What are Web restriction levels? Can you block file downloading?

    _____

    b. Can you control when and how long a child can use the computer? If so, how?

    _____

    c. What can you adjust concerning games that a child can play on the computer?

    _____

    d. Can you limit the programs that a child can use? If so, how?

    _____

    e. What type of reporting features does Parental Controls have?

    _____

Part 2: Create a User Account and Turn on Parental Controls

1. Open User Accounts and Family Safety, click Add or remove user accounts, and then click Continue.

Continued >

In the Lab *continued*

2. Create a new standard user account with `kidFriendly` as the user name. Add `safety123` as the password. Change the user icon to the fireworks icon.

3. After creating the account, return to User Accounts and Family Safety, click Parental Controls (Figure 6–137), and then click Continue.

Figure 6–137

4. Click kidFriendly to set up parental controls for the kidFriendly account from the User Controls window.

5. Click On, enforce current settings to turn on parental controls.

6. Switch to the kidFriendly account.

Part 3: Testing Parental Controls

1. Open Internet Explorer.

2. Visit `www.msn.com`. Was anything blocked?

_____

3. Visit `www.google.com`. Was anything blocked?

_____

4. Close Internet Explorer, log off kidFriendly and switch to your regular account.

5. In the User Controls window for kidFriendly, click View activity reports.

6. When was the most recent logon for kidFriendly?

_____

7. What Web sites did kidFriendly visit last?

_____

8. What content, if any, was blocked?

_____

Part 4: Restore Default Settings
1. Return to the User Controls window.
2. Turn off parental controls.
3. Delete the kidFriendly user account.
4. Submit your answers for this lab to your instructor.

Cases and Places

Apply your creative thinking and problem solving skills to design and implement a solution.

• EASIER   •• MORE DIFFICULT

• 1 Helping a Friend

A friend recently purchased a new computer. She would like to customize the mouse and keyboard. She wants to change the mouse pointer to add a drop shadow to the pointer to make it easier to see on the desktop, and slow down the cursor blink rate to make it easier to see the insertion point while word processing. She is left-handed and has trouble using the left mouse button. She asks if you would write down the instructions for these changes so she can make the changes herself. You agree to write the instructions and print a copy for her.

• 2 Researching USB Devices

Windows Vista supports the use of USB hardware devices. Using the Internet, computer magazines, or other resources, collect information about USB hardware devices. Prepare a brief report describing how USB devices work, who developed the USB specifications, and the problems the new devices solved. Include a list of three USB devices currently available for sale, the cost of the devices, and where you can purchase them.

•• 3 Configuring Accessibility Options

Your physically challenged friend asks you to help him set up his computer and customize the keyboard to his specific needs. He is unable to hold down the ALT, CTRL, or SHIFT key while pressing another key and would prefer to use the keyboard instead of the mouse. He also would like to control the mouse pointer using the keys on the numeric keypad. List two accessibility options you can use to help your friend. Summarize each accessibility option, including how you use the keyboard with and without the option.

•• 4 Troubleshooting Your New Hardware

Make it Personal

On a Thursday night, you purchase and install a new DVD burner and video card on the computer. The process involves installing the devices and their device drivers. Friday morning, you turn on the computer and nothing happens. The Windows Vista operating system will not launch. You assume it must be a problem resulting from last night's installations. Instead of calling technical support, you call a friend. Your friend suggests you investigate the problem using Safe Mode to launch the computer. Windows Help and Support contains information about Safe Mode and other features that allow you to repair a system. Write a brief report explaining these features.

•• 5 Researching Networking Usage Standards

Working Together

Many companies maintain a Standards and Procedures manual to outline the standards for using a computer on their network. Topics often include the procedures for adding new hardware, adding and removing application programs, and customizing a company computer. Working with classmates, research a small, medium, and large company online to find out if, and how, each company handles employee standards and procedures. Prepare a brief report summarizing the standards and procedures developed for each company. Include the procedures for adding new hardware, adding and removing application programs, and customizing the computer. In the report, make recommendations for each company based on what you found.

Appendix A

Comparison of the New Features of Windows Vista Editions

The Microsoft Windows Vista operating system is available in a variety of editions. The six editions that you most likely will encounter are Windows Vista Starter, Windows Vista Home Basic, Windows Vista Home Premium, Windows Vista Business, Windows Vista Ultimate, and Windows Vista Enterprise. Because not all computers have the same hardware or are used for the same functions, Microsoft provides these various editions so that each user can have the edition that meets his or her needs. The new features of Windows Vista are listed in Table A–1. Windows Vista Ultimate, the most complete version of Windows Vista, is used as a baseline for clarifying the features of the other editions. Windows Vista Starter is not included in this table as it only contains the core Windows Vista features and only is available in developing countries.

Table A–1 Windows Vista New Features and Comparison of Editions

Ultimate Features	Home Basic	Home Premium	Business	Enterprise
.NET Framework 3.0	✓	✓	✓	✓
64-bit processor support	✓	✓	✓	✓
Ad hoc backup and recovery of user files and folders	✓	✓	✓	✓
Anti-phishing tools	✓	✓	✓	✓
Application Compatibility features	✓	✓	✓	✓
Automatic hard disk defragmentation	✓	✓	✓	✓
Complete PC Backup and Restore			✓	✓
Control over installation of device drivers			✓	✓
Desktop deployment tools for managed networks			✓	✓
Ease of Access Center	✓	✓	✓	✓
Encrypting File System			✓	✓
File tagging	✓	✓	✓	✓

Table A–1 Windows Vista New Features and Comparison of Editions *(continued)*

Ultimate Features	Home Basic	Home Premium	Business	Enterprise
File-based image format (WIM)	✓	✓	✓	✓
Games Explorer	✓	✓	✓	✓
I/O prioritization	✓	✓	✓	✓
Improved file and folder sharing	✓	✓	✓	✓
Improved peer networking	✓	✓	✓	✓
Improved power management	✓	✓	✓	✓
Improved VPN support	✓	✓	✓	✓
Improved wireless networking	✓	✓	✓	✓
Instant Search	✓	✓	✓	✓
Internet Explorer 7	✓	✓	✓	✓
IPv6 and IPv4 support	✓	✓	✓	✓
Maximum RAM (32-bit system)	4 GB	4 GB	4 GB	4 GB
Maximum RAM (64-bit system)	8 GB	16 GB	128+ GB	128+ GB
Multiple user interface languages				✓
Native DVD playback		✓		
Network Access Protection Client Agent			✓	✓
Network and Sharing Center	✓	✓	✓	✓
Network Diagnostics and troubleshooting	✓	✓	✓	✓
New premium games		✓	Optional	Optional
Next-generation TCP/IP stack	✓	✓	✓	✓
Offline Folder support			✓	✓
Parental Controls	✓	✓		
Performance and Hardware Tools	✓	✓	✓	✓
Pluggable logon authentication architecture	✓	✓	✓	✓
Policy-based QOS for networking			✓	✓
Scheduled, networked, incremental and automatic backup		✓	✓	✓
Service Hardening	✓	✓	✓	✓
Shadow Copy			✓	✓
Simultaneous SMB peer network connections	5	10	10	10
Small Business Resources			✓	Optional
Speech Recognition	✓	✓	✓	✓
Stacking and Group By View	✓	✓	✓	✓
Subsystem for UNIX-based applications				✓
Sync Center	✓	✓	✓	✓
System image–based backup and recovery			✓	✓
Themed slide shows		✓		
Two processors support			✓	✓
Universal game controller support	✓	✓	Optional	Optional
Updated games	✓	✓	✓	✓

Table A–1 Windows Vista New Features and Comparison of Editions *(continued)*

Ultimate Features	Home Basic	Home Premium	Business	Enterprise
User Account Control	✓	✓	✓	✓
Welcome Center	✓	✓	✓	✓
Windows Aero experience		✓	✓	✓
Windows BitLocker Drive Encryption				✓
Windows Calendar	✓	✓	✓	✓
Windows CardSpace	✓	✓	✓	✓
Windows Defender	✓	✓	✓	✓
Windows Display Driver Model (WDDM)	✓	✓	✓	✓
Windows Experience Index	✓	✓	✓	✓
Windows Fax and Scan (optional for Ultimate)			✓	Optional
Windows Firewall	✓	✓	✓	✓
Windows HotStart	✓	✓	✓	✓
Windows Mail	✓	✓	✓	✓
Windows Media Center		✓		
Windows Media Player 11	✓	✓	✓	✓
Windows Meeting Space	View only	✓	✓	✓
Windows Mobility Center	Partial	Partial	✓	✓
Windows Movie Maker	✓	✓	✓	✓
Windows Photo Gallery	✓	✓	✓	✓
Windows ReadyBoost	✓	✓	✓	✓
Windows ReadyDrive	✓	✓	✓	✓
Windows Rights Management Services (RMS) Client			✓	✓
Windows Security Center	✓	✓	✓	✓
Windows Sidebar	✓	✓	✓	✓
Windows SideShow		✓	✓	✓
Windows SuperFetch	✓	✓	✓	✓
Windows Tablet PC		✓	✓	✓
Windows Update	✓	✓	✓	✓
Windows Vista Basic experience	✓	✓	✓	✓
Wireless network provisioning			✓	✓
XPS Document support	✓	✓	✓	✓
Years of product support	5	5	10	10

Appendix B

Windows Vista Security

Windows Vista Security Features

Windows Vista has been engineered to be the most secure version of Windows ever, according to Microsoft. It includes a number of new security features that help you accomplish three important goals: to enjoy a PC free from malware, including viruses, worms, spyware, and other potentially unwanted software, to have a safer online experience, and to understand when a PC is vulnerable, and how to make it more secure from hackers and other intruders.

Malware, short for malicious software, are computer programs designed to do harm to your computer whether just showing inappropriate Web sites to performing identity theft. Examples of malware include viruses, worms, and spyware. A **virus** is a computer program that attaches itself to another computer program or file so that it can spread from computer to computer, infecting programs and files as it spreads. Viruses can damage computer software, computer hardware, and files. A **worm** copies itself from one computer to another by taking advantage of the features that transport files and information between computers. A worm is dangerous because it has the ability to travel without being detected and to replicate itself in great volume. For example, if a worm copies itself to every name in your e-mail address book and then the worm copies itself to the names of all the e-mail addresses of each of your friends' computers, the effect could result in increased Internet traffic that slows down business networks and the Internet. **Spyware** is software that is installed on your computer that monitors the activity that takes place to gather personal information and send it secretly to its creator. Spyware also can be designed to take control of the infected computer.

A **hacker** is an individual who uses his or her expertise to gain unauthorized access to a computer with the intention of learning more about the computer or examining the contents of the computer without the owner's permission.

The Windows Security Center

The **Windows Security Center** can help you to manage your computer's security by monitoring the status of several essential security features on your computer including firewall settings, Windows automatic updating, anti-malware software settings, Internet security settings, and User Account Control settings. Table B–1 contains a list of the four security features and their descriptions.

Table B–1 Security Features and Descriptions	
Security Feature	**Description**
Windows Firewall	Windows Firewall monitors and restricts information coming from the Internet, prevents access without your permission, and protects against hackers.
Automatic Updating	Automatic updating indicates whether Windows Update is turned on. Windows Update checks the Windows Update Web site for high-priority updates that can help protect a computer against attacks. High-priority updates include security updates, critical updates, and service packs.
Malware Protection	Malware protection includes virus, spyware, and other security threat protection. It includes making sure you are using virus protection software.
Other Security Settings	This is where you can view and adjust other security settings including Internet security settings.

To Display the Windows Security Center

The following steps display the Windows Security Center.

- Click the Start button on the taskbar to display the Start menu (Figure B–1).

Figure B–1

2

• Click the Control Panel command on the Start menu to open the Control Panel (Figure B–2).

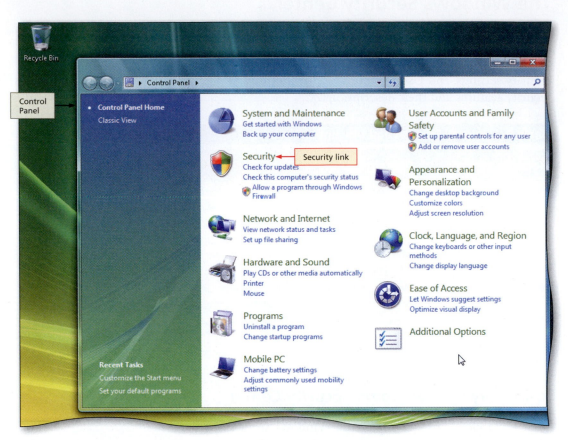

Figure B–2

3

• Click the Security link to display the security features (Figure B–3).

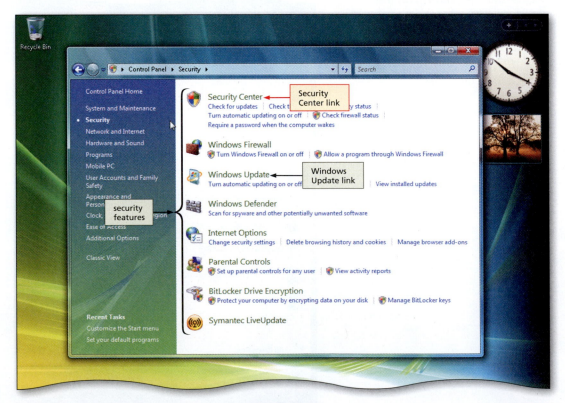

Figure B–3

4

- Click the Security Center link in the right pane of the Control Panel window to display the Windows Security Center.

- If necessary, maximize the Windows Security Center window (Figure B–4).

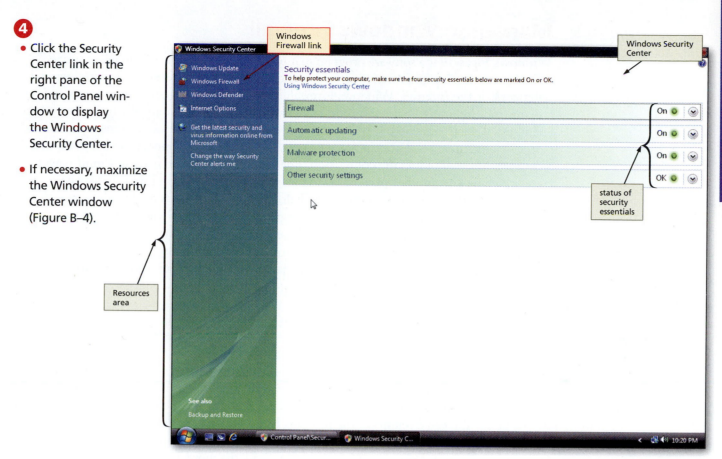

Figure B–4

The right pane provides a snapshot of the four security essentials that Microsoft believes should be turned on and up-to-date. These essential features are Firewall, Automatic updating, Malware protection, and Other security settings. Clicking the down arrow to the right of a security area will expand the area to show additional detail, while clicking the up arrow will collapse the area, hiding the details. User Account Control prompts you for permission to perform many of the operations in this appendix. Status values appear next to the arrow button: "On" and "OK" indicate that the security feature is turned on and working; "Off" means that the security feature is turned off and you should turn it on; and "Check Settings" means that although the feature is turned on, you need to change the settings to what Microsoft recommends for that security feature. It is important to have the On or OK status value showing for each of these features.

On the left pane of the Windows Security Center window is the Resources area containing six links that allow you to open Windows Update to view available updates, open Microsoft Firewall to view and configure firewall features, open Windows Defender to view and configure malware protection options, open Internet Options to view and configure Internet properties, view the latest security and virus information online from Microsoft, and change the way Security Center alerts you to potential issues in the Windows Security Center dialog box.

Managing Windows Firewall

Windows Firewall is a software program that protects your computer from unauthorized users by monitoring and restricting information that travels between your computer and a network or the Internet. Windows Firewall also helps to block computer viruses and worms from infecting your computer. Windows Firewall is automatically turned on when Windows Vista is launched. It is recommended that Windows Firewall remain turned on.

If someone on the Internet or on a network attempts to connect to your computer, Windows Firewall blocks the connection. For example, if you are playing a multiplayer network game and another player asks to join the game, Windows Firewall displays a Windows Security Alert dialog box. The dialog box contains buttons that allow you to block or unblock the connection. If you recognize the player and choose to unblock the connection and allow the player to join the game, Windows Firewall adds an exception for the player to the Windows Firewall Exceptions list. An **exception** is an adjustment made to the firewall settings so that the player can join the game now and in the future.

To Add a Program to the Windows Firewall Exceptions List

You can add a program to the Windows Firewall Exceptions list manually, without waiting for the program to communicate with you. Windows Firewall also limits access by some programs that depend on low security settings. A program that has low security settings requires more access to the operating system than Windows Vista normally allows a program to have. When you run a program with low security settings, you would be prompted many times to allow the program to perform its tasks. You can circumvent the prompts by adding the program to the Exceptions list.

However, with every program you add to the Windows Firewall Exceptions list, the computer becomes easier to access and more vulnerable to attacks by hackers. The more programs you add, the more vulnerable the firewall. To decrease the risk of security problems, only add programs that are necessary and recognizable, and promptly remove any program that is no longer required. The following steps add the Hearts program to the Windows Firewall Exceptions list.

- Click the Windows Firewall link in the Resources Area of the Windows Security Center window to display the Windows Firewall window (Figure B–5).

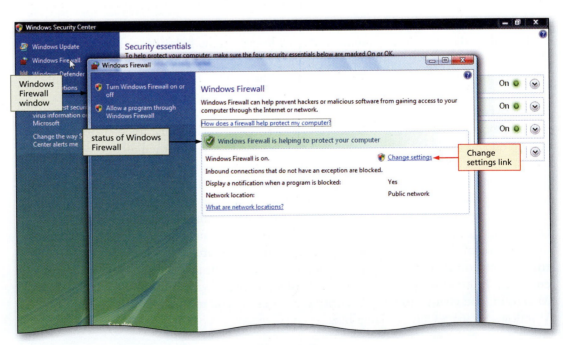

Figure B–5

2
- Click the Change settings link to display the User Account Control dialog box (Figure B–6).

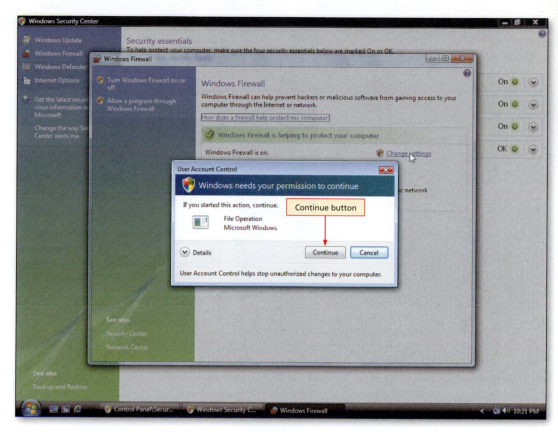

Figure B–6

3
- Click the Continue button to authorize Windows Vista to display the Windows Firewall Settings dialog box (Figure B–7).

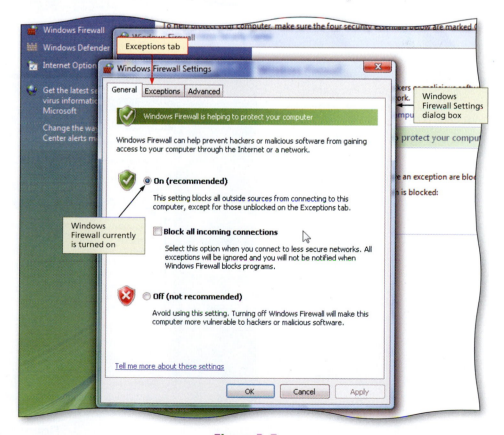

Figure B–7

● Click the Exceptions tab to display a list of Windows Firewall exceptions (Figure B–8).

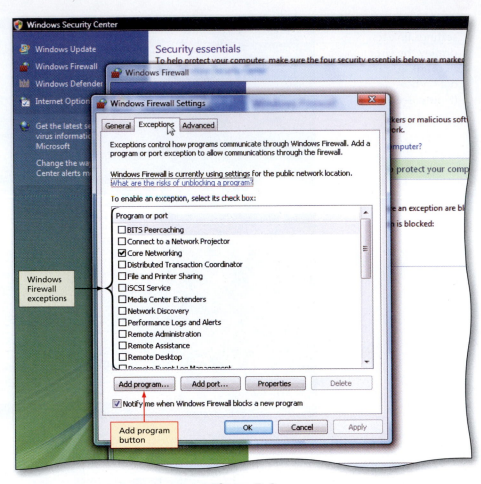

Figure B–8

● Click the Add program button to display the Add a Program dialog box. If necessary, scroll the Programs list box to view the Hearts program (Figure B–9).

Figure B–9

6

- Click the Hearts program in the Programs list box to select the Hearts program (Figure B–10).

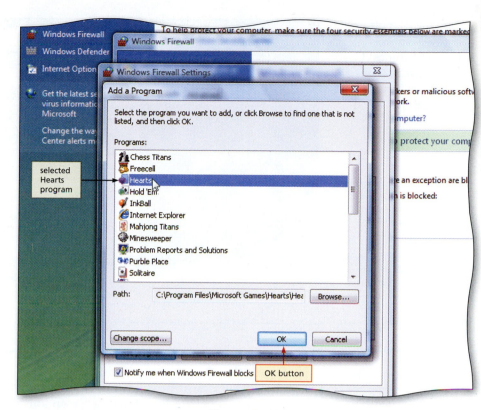

Figure B–10

7

- Click the OK button in the Add a Program dialog box to add the Hearts program to the list of exceptions (Figure B–11).

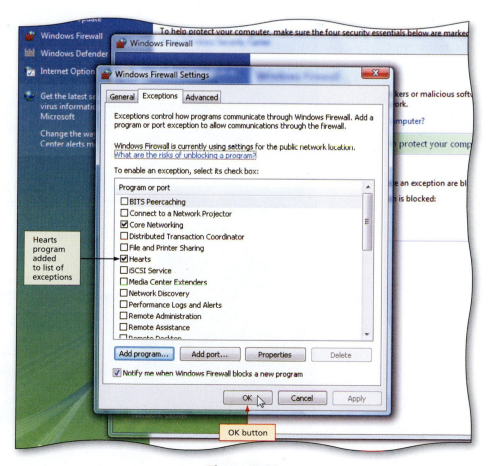

Figure B–11

8

● Click the OK button in the Windows Firewall Settings dialog box to close the dialog box (Figure B–12).

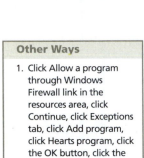

Other Ways

1. Click Allow a program through Windows Firewall link in the resources area, click Continue, click Exceptions tab, click Add program, click Hearts program, click the OK button, click the OK button.

Figure B-12

To Remove a Program from the Exceptions List

After adding the Hearts program to the Windows Firewall Exceptions list, you now will remove the program from the Windows Exceptions list. The following steps remove a program from the Exceptions list.

1

● Click the Change settings link to display the User Account Control dialog box (Figure B–13).

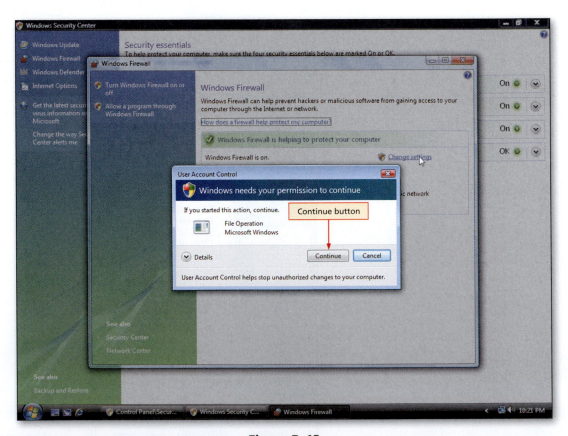

Figure B–13

2

• Click the Continue button to authorize Windows to display the Windows Firewall Settings dialog box (Figure B–14).

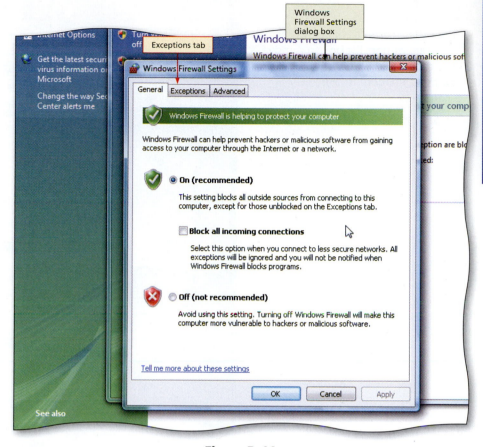

Figure B–14

3

• Click the Exceptions tab to display the list of exceptions.

• If necessary, scroll down to display the Hearts program (Figure B–15).

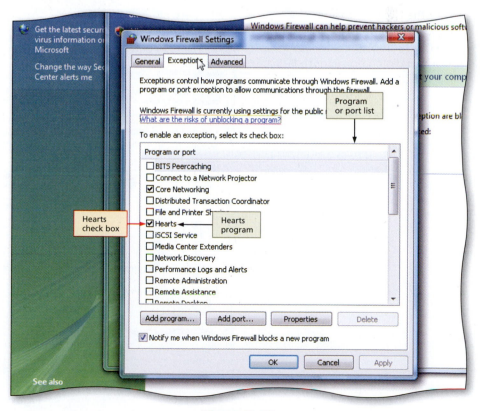

Figure B–15

● Click the Hearts check box in the Program or port list box to remove the check mark and to disable the exception (Figure B–16).

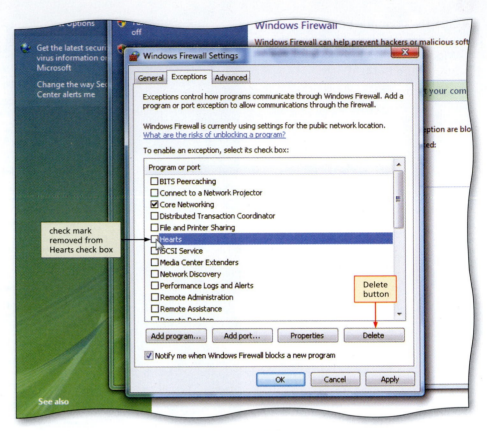

Figure B–16

● Click the Delete button in the Windows Firewall Settings dialog box to display the Delete a Program dialog box (Figure B–17).

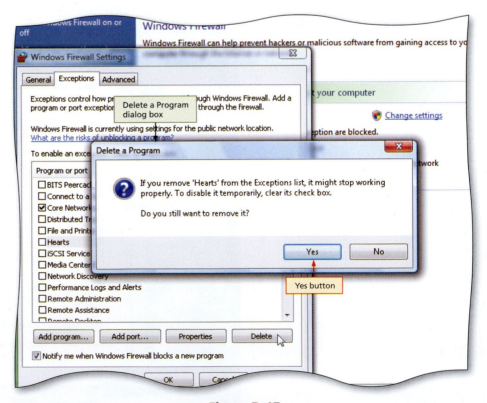

Figure B–17

6
- Click the Yes button in the Delete a Program dialog box to remove the Hearts program from the list of exceptions (Figure B–18).

What does the warning in the dialog box mean?

Some programs that you install cannot function properly unless they are placed in the Program or port list. Hearts is not such a program; therefore, you can ignore the warning and delete it from the list. Normally, before removing a program from the Program or port list, you should know whether this will affect its performance. This information is usually found in the program's documentation or help files.

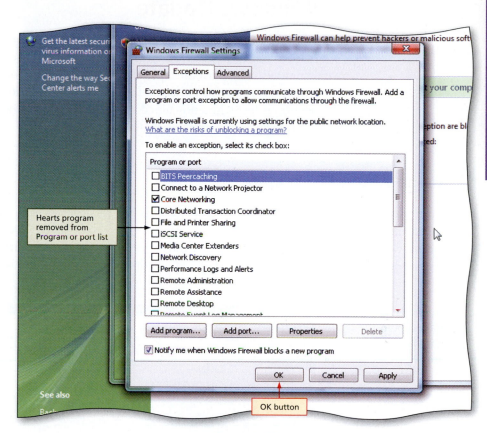

Figure B–18

7
- Click the OK button in the Windows Firewall Settings dialog box (Figure B–19).

8
- Click the Close button to close the Windows Firewall window.

Figure B–19

Windows Update

Windows Update helps to protect your computer from viruses, worms, and other security risks. When Windows Update is turned on and the computer is connected to the Internet, Windows Vista periodically checks with the Microsoft Update Web site to find updates, patches, and service packs, and then automatically downloads them. If the Internet connection is lost while downloading an update, Windows Vista resumes downloading when the Internet connection is available.

To Set an Automatic Update

You want to make sure that Windows Update runs once a week, so you decide to set it to run on a specific day and at a specific time. Once you set the day and time for every Friday at 6:00 AM, Windows Vista will check with the Microsoft Updates Web site to find updates and service packs, and then automatically download any available updates and service packs. The followings steps set an automatic update for a day (Friday) and time (6:00 AM).

1

- Click the Windows Update link in the Windows Security Center window to display the Windows Update window (Figure B–20).

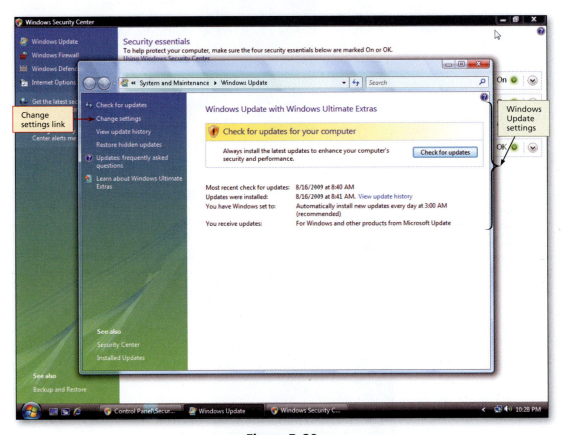

Figure B–20

2

● Click the Change settings link to display the Change settings window (Figure B–21).

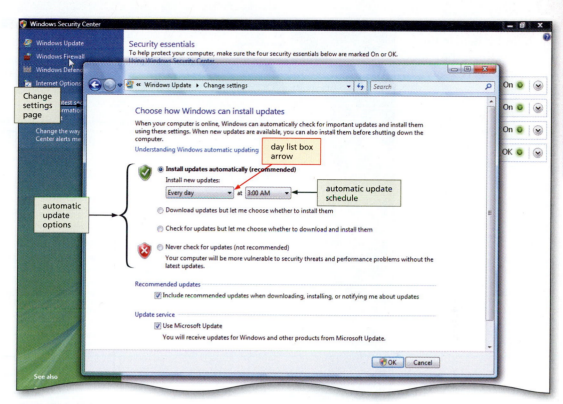

Figure B–21

3

● Click the day list box arrow to display a list of day options (Figure B–22).

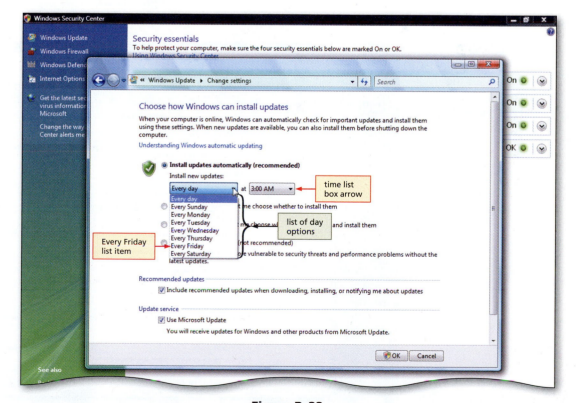

Figure B–22

4

- Click the Every Friday list item in the list box to set the update day to Every Friday.

- Click the time list box arrow to show the list of time options (Figure B–23).

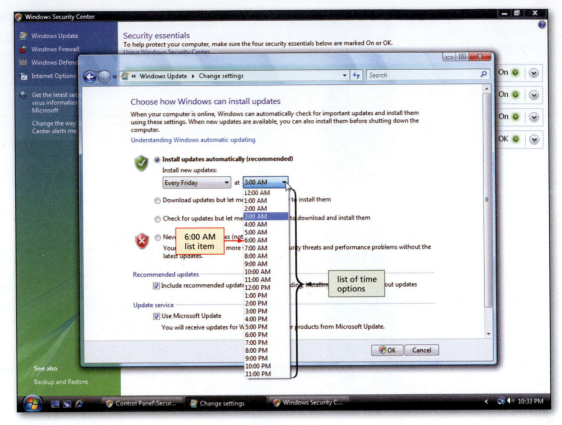

Figure B–23

5

- Click the 6:00 AM list item in the time list box to set the update time to 6:00 AM (Figure B–24).

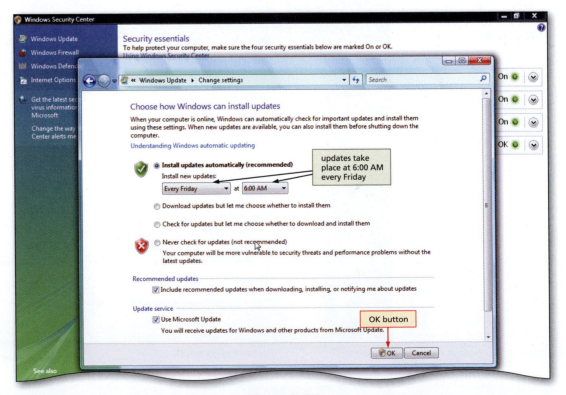

Figure B–24

6

- Click the OK button in the Change Settings window to display the User Account Control dialog box (Figure B–25).

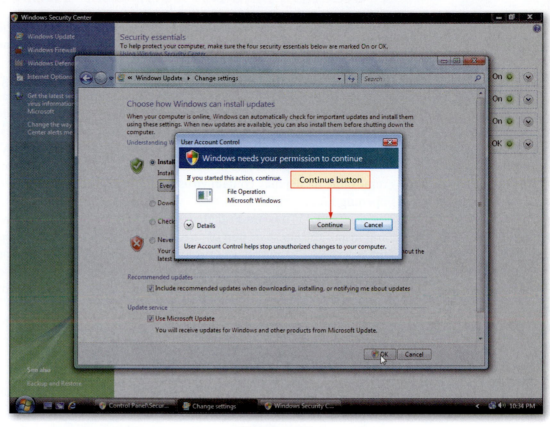

Figure B–25

7

- Click the Continue button in the User Account Control dialog box to authorize the changes (Figure B–26).

Q&A

What does my screen say that Windows is up to date?

If you already have turned on automatic updates, or recently have updated your computer, it is possible that no additional updates are available for download at this time.

Figure B–26

8

- Verify that your update is scheduled for every Friday at 6:00 AM.

- Click the Close button to close the Windows Update window.

Protecting Against Computer Viruses

Most computer magazines, daily newspapers, and even news broadcasts warn us of computer virus threats. Although these threats sound alarming, a little common sense and a good antivirus program can ward off even the most malicious viruses.

You can protect your computer against viruses by following these suggestions. First, educate yourself about viruses and how they are spread. Downloading a program from the Internet, accessing an online discussion board, or receiving an e-mail message may cause a virus to infect your computer. Second, learn the common signs of a virus. Observe any unusual messages that appear on the computer screen, monitor system performance, and watch for missing files and inaccessible hard disks. Third, recognize that programs on removable media may contain viruses, and scan all removable media before copying or opening files.

Finally, Windows Vista does not include an antivirus program. You should purchase and install the latest version of an antivirus program and use it regularly to check for computer viruses. Many antivirus programs run automatically and display a dialog box on the screen when a problem exists. If you do not have an antivirus program installed on your computer, you can search online for antivirus software vendors to find a program that meets your needs.

To Search for Antivirus Software Vendors

The following steps display an online list of Microsoft approved antivirus software vendors.

1

- Click the Internet Explorer icon on the Quick Launch toolbar to open the Windows Internet Explorer window (Figure B–27).

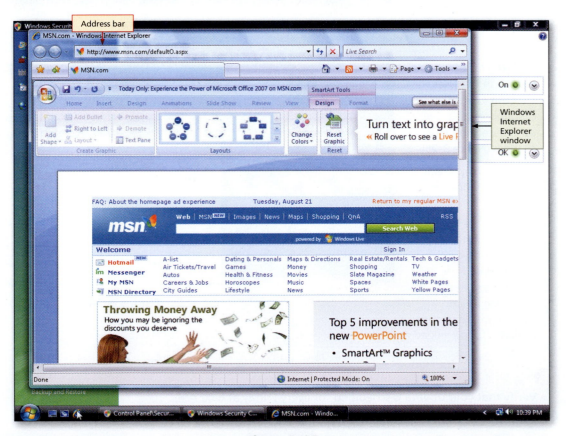

Figure B–27

2

- Type www.
microsoft.com/
protect/viruses/
vista/av.mspx
in the Address bar
and then press the
ENTER key to display
the Windows Vista
Security Software
Providers Web page
(Figure B–28).

- Read the list of
vendors and visit a
few links to learn
more about some
of the vendors and
their products.

Figure B–28

3

- When you have finished, click the Close button on the Windows Internet Explorer window to
close the Windows Internet Explorer window.

Protecting Against Malware

It is important to run anti-malware software whenever you are using your computer. Malware
and other unwanted software can attempt to install itself on your computer any time you
connect to the Internet or when you install some programs using a CD, DVD, or other
removable media. Potentially unwanted or malicious software also can be programmed to run
at unexpected times, not just when it is installed.

Windows Defender is installed with Windows Vista. Windows Defender uses
definitions similar to those used by antivirus programs. A **definition** is a rule for Windows
Defender that identifies what programs are malware and how to deal with them. Windows
Defender scans your computer regularly to find malware and remove it.

To keep up with new malware developments, Windows Defender uses Windows
Update to check regularly for definition updates. This helps you to ensure that your
computer can handle new threats. It is recommended to allow Windows Defender to run
using the default actions.

To View the Windows Defender Settings for Automatic Scanning

The following steps display the automatic scanning settings in Windows Defender.

1

• Click the Windows Defender link in the Windows Security Center to start Windows Defender (Figure B–29).

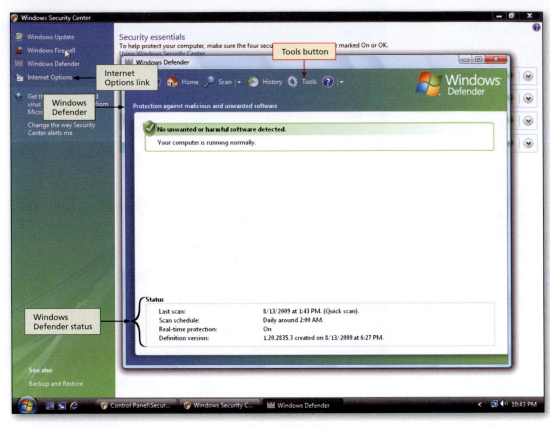

Figure B–29

2

• Click the Tools button on the tool-bar to display the Windows Defender Tools and Settings (Figure B–30).

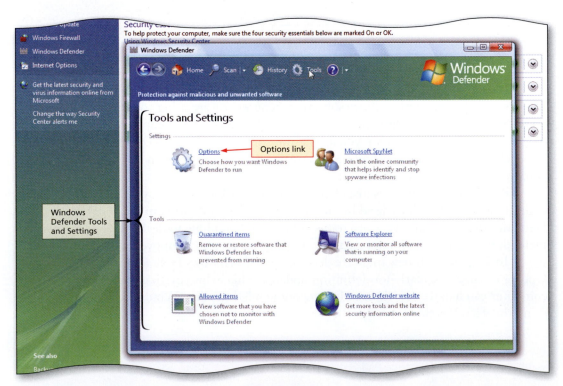

Figure B–30

3

- Click the Options link to view the Windows Defender settings for Automatic scanning (Figure B–31).

- Click the Close button to close the Windows Defender window.

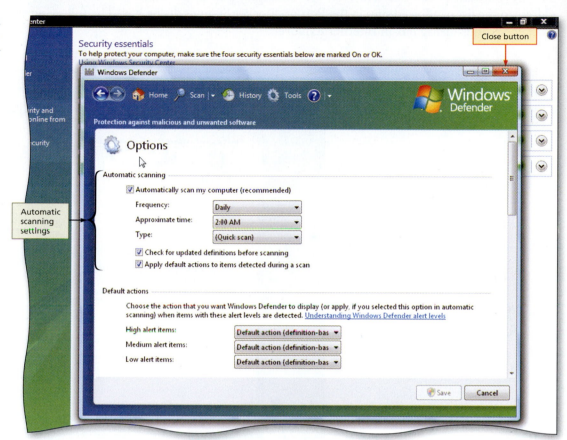

Figure B–31

Security Settings in Internet Explorer

In addition to the security features shown earlier in this appendix, Windows Vista also enhances the security features of Windows Internet Explorer. These enhanced security features protect the computer while you browse the Internet or send and receive e-mail. The new Internet Explorer security settings protect the computer, the computer's contents, and the computer's privacy by preventing against viruses and other security threats on the Internet.

To View Pop-up Settings

One new security feature in Internet Explorer is the Pop-up Blocker. **Pop-up Blocker** prevents annoying **pop-up ads**, advertising products or services, from appearing while you view a Web page. Pop-up ads can be difficult to close, often interrupt what you are doing, and can download spyware, which secretly gathers information about you and your computer, and sends the information to advertisers and other individuals.

By default, Pop-up Blocker is turned on by Internet Explorer and set to a Medium setting, which blocks most pop-up ads. Pop-up Blocker also plays a sound and displays an Information Bar in the Internet Explorer window when a pop-up ad is blocked.

If you want to allow certain Web sites to display pop-up ads when you visit the site, you can add the Web site address to the list of allowed sites in the Pop-up Blocker Settings dialog box. The following steps display the Pop-up Blocker Settings dialog box in Internet Explorer.

• Click the Internet Options link in the Windows Security Center window to display the Internet Properties dialog box (Figure B–32).

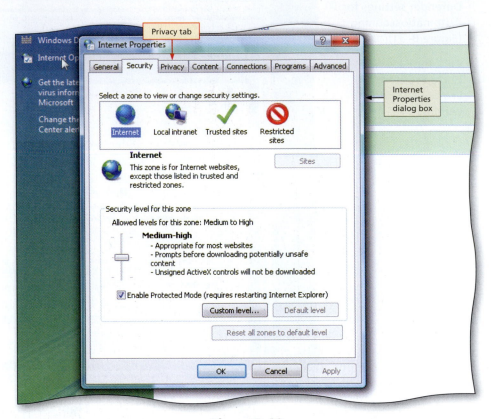

Figure B–32

2

• Click the Privacy tab in the Internet Properties dialog box to display the Privacy sheet (Figure B–33).

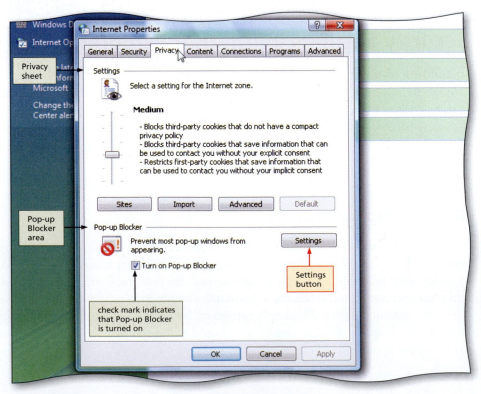

Figure B–33

3

• Click the Settings button in the Pop-up Blocker area to display the Pop-up Blocker Settings dialog box (Figure B–34).

Q&A

How do I block all pop-ups?

If you want to block all pop-ups, click the Filter level list box arrow, and then click High: Block all pop-ups (CTRL+ALT to override) in the Filter level list box. If you want to allow more pop-up ads, click the Filter level list box arrow, and then click Low: Allow pop-ups from secure sites in the Filter level list box.

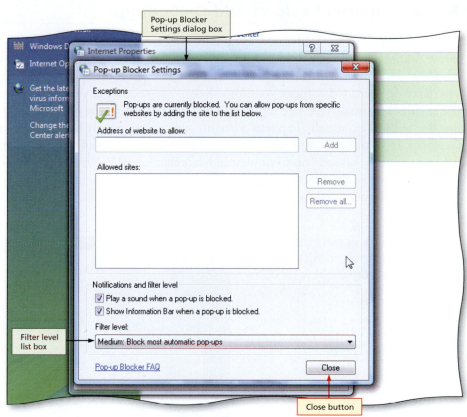

Figure B–34

4

• After viewing the Pop-up Blocker Settings dialog box, click the Close button to close the Pop-up Blocker Settings dialog box (Figure B–35).

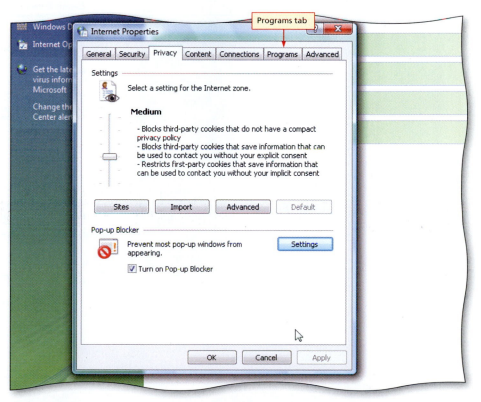

Figure B–35

To View Internet Explorer Add-On Settings

Internet Explorer **add-ons** add functionality to Internet Explorer by allowing different toolbars, animated mouse pointers, and stock tickers. Although some add-ons are included with Windows Vista, thousands are available from Web sites on the Internet. Most Web site add-ons require permission before downloading the add-on, while others are downloaded without your knowledge. Some add-ons do not need permission at all.

Add-ons usually are safe to use, but some may slow down your computer or shut down Internet Explorer unexpectedly. This usually happens when an add-on was poorly built, or created for an earlier version of Internet Explorer. In some cases, spyware is included with an add-on and may track your Web surfing habits. The Manage Add-ons window allows you to display add-ons that have been used by Internet Explorer or that run without permission, enable or disable add-ons, and remove downloaded ActiveX controls.

The following steps display the add-on settings.

1

• Click the Programs tab in the Internet Properties dialog box to show the Programs sheet (Figure B–36).

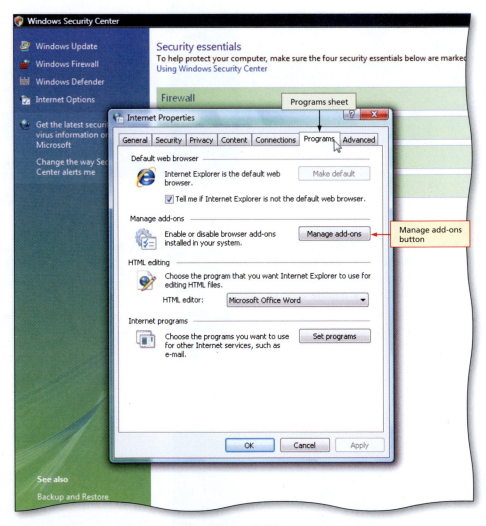

Figure B–36

2

- Click the Manage add-ons button in the Manage add-ons area to display the Manage Add-ons dialog box (Figure B–37).

3

- When finished viewing the add-ons, click the OK button in the Manage Add-ons dialog box to close the Manage Add-ons dialog box.

- Click the OK button in the Internet Properties dialog box to close the Internet Properties dialog box.

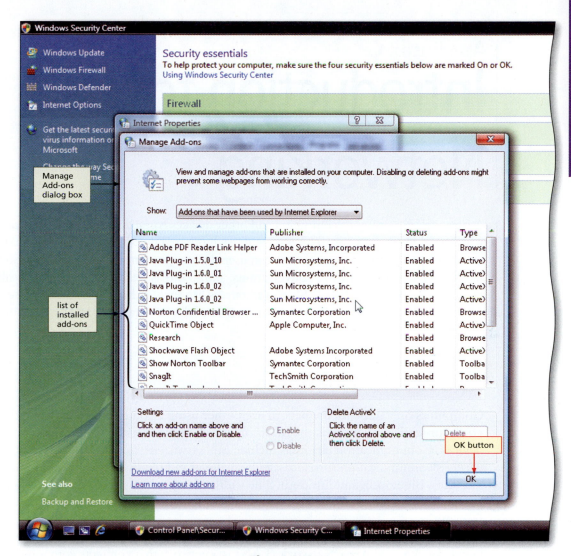

Figure B–37

To Close the Windows Security Center and the Control Panel

Now that you have finished reviewing some highlights of the Windows Security Center, you will close the Windows Security Center window and the Control Panel.

1 Click the Close button in the Windows Security Center window to close the Windows Security Center. Click the Close button in the Control Panel window to close the Control Panel.

Summary

Security is an important issue for computer users. You need to be aware of the possible threats to your computer as well as the security features that can be used to protect your computer. The Windows Vista Security Center allows you to view and configure the security features that will help you keep your computer safe.

Appendix C

Introduction to Networking

A **network** is a group of computers and other devices connected by a communications link, which enables the devices to interact with each other. The advantages of using a network are simplified communications between users (e-mail, instant messenger, chat rooms, newsgroups, video and voice conversations, and so on) as well as the ability to easily share resources across the network. Shared resources can include hardware (printers, scanners, cameras, and so on), data and information (files, folders, databases, and so on), and programs.

Setting Up a Network

Computers on a network connect to each other using a communication channel. A **communication channel** is the means by which information is passed between two devices. Communication channels include cable (twisted-pair, coaxial, and fiber-optic) and wireless communication (broadcast radio, cellular radio, microwaves, communications satellites, Bluetooth, and infrared). The width of the communication channel is called **bandwidth**. The higher the bandwidth, the more data and information the channel can transmit.

Computer networks can be classified as either local area networks or wide area networks. A **Local Area Network (LAN)** is a network that connects computers and devices in a limited geographical area such as a home, school computer laboratory, office building, or closely positioned group of buildings. A LAN enables people in a small geographic area to communicate with one another and to share the computer resources connected to the network. Each device on the network, such as a computer or printer, is referred to as a **node**. Nodes can be connected to the LAN via cables, however a **Wireless LAN (WLAN)** is a LAN that uses no physical wires. Instead of wires or cables, WLANs use wireless media, such as radio waves. A **Wide Area Network (WAN)** is a network that covers a large geographic area (such as a city or state) and uses many types of media such as telephone lines, cables, and airwaves. A WAN can be one large network or consist of two or more LANs that are connected together. The Internet is the world's largest WAN.

If you have multiple computers in your home or small office, you can connect all of them together with a home or small office network using software included with Windows Vista. The advantages of a home or small office network include sharing a single Internet connection, sharing hardware devices, sharing files and folders, and communicating with others. Today, because of competition in the hardware industry and lower computer prices, most homes have one or more computers and a connection to the Internet. Three types of networks that are suitable for home or small office use include Ethernet networks, phoneline networks, and wireless networks.

Understanding Wired Networks

Wired networks use cables to connect devices together (Figure C–1). Ethernet is the most popular type of network connection, because it is relatively inexpensive and fast. There are two types of Ethernet cables: **coaxial cable**, which resembles the cable used for televisions and rarely is used, and **unshielded twisted pair cable (UTP)**, which looks like telephone cable but with larger connectors at each end. Category 5 (Cat5) or Category 6 (Cat6) UTP cable typically is used for networking. A network based on Cat5 UTP requires an additional piece of hardware, called a hub, to which all computers on the network connect.

Another type of wired network is a phoneline network. A **phoneline network** takes advantage of the existing telephone wiring to connect the computers on a network. This technology is supported by a group of industry experts called the Home Phoneline Networking Alliance (HomePNA). The network takes advantage of the unused band-width of the telephone lines, while still allowing them to be used for telephone conversations. The only equipment needed for this type of network is a phoneline network adapter for each computer, as well as telephone cable long enough to connect each computer to a telephone jack.

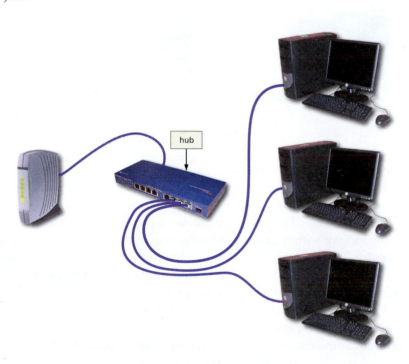

Figure C–1

Understanding Wireless Networks

A wireless network is the easiest type of network to install. Each computer uses a special network adapter that sends wireless signals through the air (Figure C–2 on the next page). Any computer located within range that also has a network adapter can send and receive through floors, ceilings, and walls. The distance between computers limits this connection, and the hardware required for the system is relatively inexpensive. Most hardware devices implement the Wi-Fi (Wireless Fidelity) standard, which was developed by the Wi-Fi Alliance to improve the interoperability of wireless products.

Several companies and industry groups have come together to create standards for wireless networking. The leader is the Wi-Fi Alliance, which certifies the interoperability of Wi-Fi (IEEE 802.11) products, offers speeds of up to 11 Mbps (Megabits per second), with that speed increasing as technology advances. The two types of Wi-Fi networks are ad hoc and infrastructure. In an **ad hoc** network, every computer with a wireless network adapter communicates directly with every other computer with a wireless network adapter. Although the range varies by manufacturer, ad hoc networks work best when connecting computers are within 100 feet of each other.

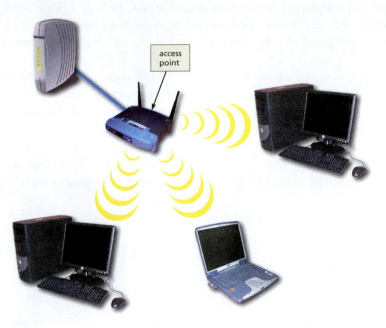

access point

Figure C–2

An **infrastructure network** is based on an access point connected to a high-speed Internet connection. An **access point** functions as a bridge between two different types of networks, such as a wireless network and an Ethernet network. The access point allows for a much greater range than an ad hoc network because a computer needs to be within range of the access point and not within range of the other computers. This network is best when connecting more than two computers that are more than 100 feet apart and commonly is used in wireless networks that simultaneously share a single Internet connection.

Some infrastructure networks use a router to share an Internet connection between computers on the network. A **router** is a hardware device that can connect a cable or DSL modem to a network, allowing several computer users to simultaneously use the same Internet connection. Some network hardware manufacturers combine the access point and router in a device called a **wireless router**. A wireless router can function as a bridge between two different types of networks and allows all computers on the network to access the same Internet connection.

Putting It All Together

Each computer on a network must have a **network adapter** to connect to the network. Both internal network adapters and external network adapters are available. Most computers come with internal network adapters. An **internal network adapter** plugs into a Peripheral Components Interconnect (PCI) slot or Industry Standard Architecture (ISA) slot inside the computer. Before purchasing an internal network adapter, check to be sure that the computer has an extra slot, and then determine if the slot is a PCI or ISA slot. Newer computers have PCI slots, and older computers have ISA slots. Because a PCI slot is more likely to be Plug and Play compatible, select a PCI slot when possible. Instead of an internal network adapter that plugs into a PCI or ISA slot, some new computers have an internal network adapter integrated with the motherboard. An **external network adapter** plugs into a serial, parallel, or USB port on the computer. If the computer has a USB port, select the USB adapter because it is Plug and Play compatible and easier to install, although using a USB port may restrict the speed of the network.

A **modem** is used to connect to an Internet access provider. Common Internet access providers include cable service providers, phone service providers, and satellite service providers. The modem is connected to the router which is then used to connect to the nodes on the network. A USB, Cat5, or Cat6 cable connects the modem to wired computers. If the network is wireless, the computers connect using wireless network adapters and an access point. Many home networks use a wireless router and support wired and wireless connections (Figure C–3).

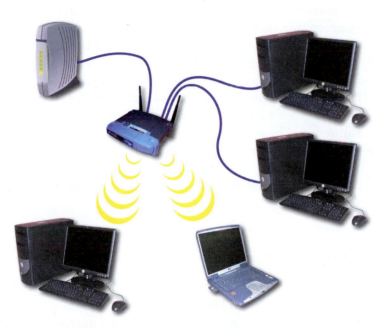

Figure C–3

Wireless Security Issues

Whether you connect a single computer to the Internet or connect computers on a home or small office network to the Internet, problems can develop if you do not protect computers that are connected to the Internet. Hackers scan the Internet looking for unprotected computers. When an unprotected computer is found, a hacker can access and/or damage files on the computer and release harmful computer viruses that can render the computer unusable.

You can protect computers on a network from hackers, viruses, and other malicious attacks by using a firewall. A firewall is a security system intended to protect a network from external threats, such as the Internet. A firewall commonly is a combination of hardware and/or software that prevents computers on the network from communicating directly with computers that are not on the network and vice versa. Many routers come with integrated firewalls. Windows Vista also comes with a built-in firewall (see Appendix B).

Setting Up Wireless Security

Wireless networks require extra thought as they introduce some security concerns that wired networks do not. Because the signal travels through the air, anyone with the proper equipment can intercept the signal. As a result, a wireless network should use extra precautions to prevent unauthorized access. When you purchase a wireless router, it may include a program that allows you to set up security on your wireless network. If the wireless router does not include a program that can set up security, Windows Vista can configure it using the Setup a wireless router or access point wizard.

The key to securing a wireless network successfully is to use a multi-pronged defense. For best results, use more than one of the following recommended security measures. First, make sure that the wireless router's user name and password are changed from the defaults so that the hacker is unable to use the default user name and password found in the device's documentation (often kept on the manufacturer's Web site for public access). Secondly, you can turn on wireless encryption. This can include Wired Equivalent Privacy (WEP), Wi-Fi Protected Access (WPA), or 802.1X authentication. Encryption ensures that only those with the right encryption key will be able to understand the information being sent across the network. Thirdly, you can set up the wireless router to not broadcast its **SSID (Service Set Identifier)**, the network name for the wireless router. This will make it more difficult for hackers to see your router. Next, you can change the SSID from its default value. The most secure SSIDs are a combination of letters and numbers, and do not include any part of your name or location. Finally, you can turn on MAC Address Control, so that only devices with authorized MAC addresses would be allowed to connect. A **MAC address** is an address that uniquely identifies each device that is connected to the Internet.

Using the Network and Sharing Center

Normally when you turn on your computer, Windows Vista will detect available networks and prompt you to set up a connection. However, you manually can set up a connection by using the Network and Sharing Center. The Network and Sharing Center is designed to provide you with all of the tools that you need to connect to a network and share information. From the Network and Sharing Center, you can view available connections, connect to a network, manage a network, set up a network, and diagnose and repair network problems. The Network window displays the available computers and shared devices once you are connected to the network.

To Open the Network and Sharing Center

When first opened, the Network and Sharing Center will show your current network connection and the properties for that connection. If you are not connected to a network, then you will be shown what networking options are available to you. The following steps open the Network and Sharing Center.

1

- Display the Start menu.

- Click the Network command to open the Network window (Figure C–4).

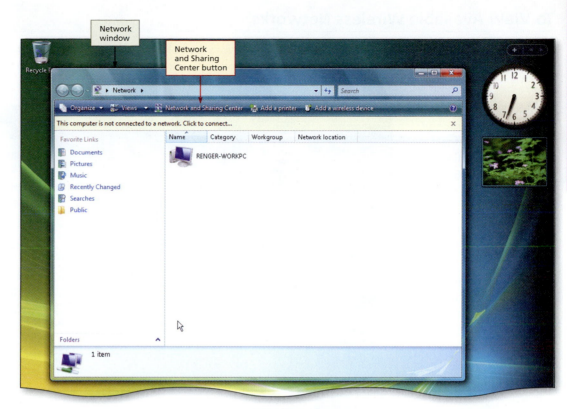

Figure C–4

2

- Click the Network and Sharing Center button to open the Network and Sharing Center (Figure C–5).

Other Ways

1. Right-click networking icon in notification area on the taskbar, click Network and Sharing Center

2. Open Control Panel, click Network and Internet, click Network and Sharing Center

3. Open Control Panel, click Classic View, click Network and Sharing Center

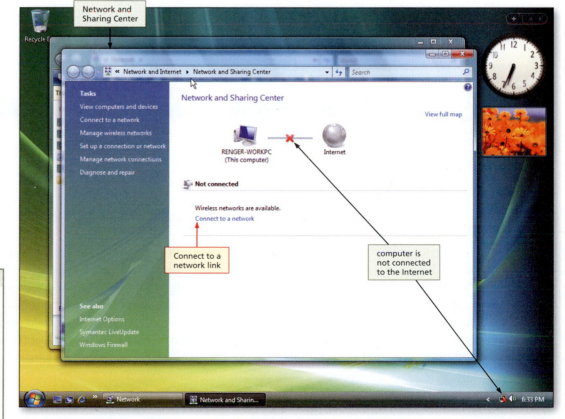

Figure C–5

To View Available Wireless Networks

If there are wireless networks available, the Network and Sharing Center will display a message stating that they are available. The following step displays the list of available wireless networks.

- Click the Connect to a network link to display the Connect to a network dialog box (Figure C–6).

Q&A

Why do I see a different list of networks?

Because your computer will show the wireless networks that are near your physical location, the list of available wireless networks will be different from those shown in the figure.

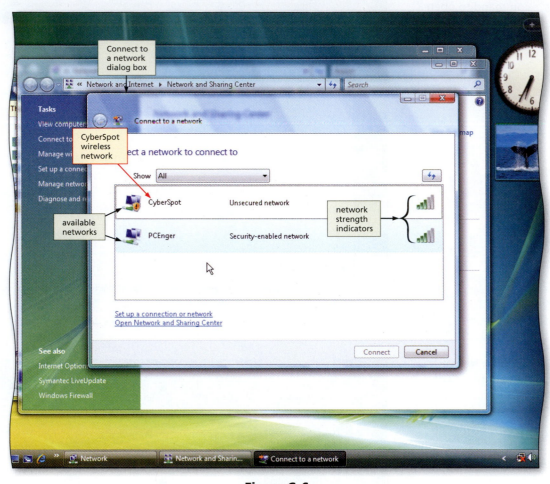

Figure C–6

Other Ways

1. Right-click networking icon in notification area on the taskbar, click Connect to a network
2. Open Control Panel, click Classic View, double-click Network and Sharing Center, click Connect to a network link

To Connect to a Public Network

When connecting to a network, you should be aware of the information that is necessary to connect. You first should determine whether the network is secure or unsecure. Secure wireless networks typically use WPA or WEP encryption, while unsecure networks are not encrypted. Secondly, you should know whether the network location should be classified as home, work, or public. Windows Vista automatically will configure it as a public location. For public locations, **network discovery**, which is the capability of network devices to identify your computer when connected, is turned off. With your computer hidden, hackers will have a more difficult time finding it. The following steps connect the computer to a wireless network and allows Windows Vista to configure all of the settings.

1

- Click the CyberSpot entry, or the entry corresponding to a wireless network available in your area, to select the wireless network (Figure C–7).

Q&A

How can I locate public wireless networks?

When you view network connections, any public wireless networks should display. Some cities and towns sponsor public Wi-Fi, many public libraries, schools, hotels and airports offer Wi-Fi, and occasionally, cafes and coffeehouses will offer free Wi-Fi.

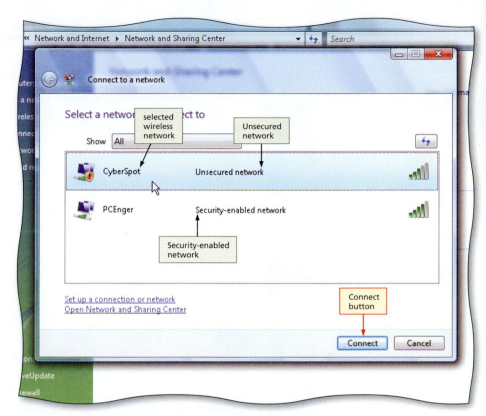

Figure C–7

2

- Click the Connect button to connect to the network (Figure C–8).

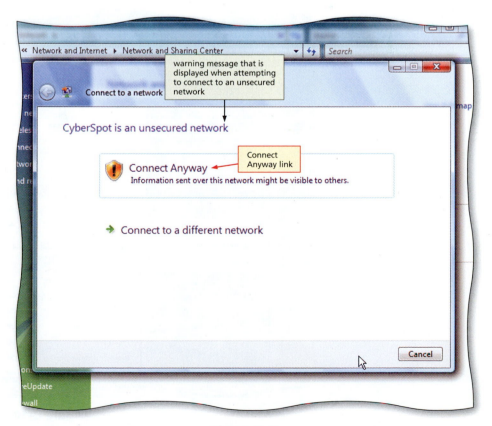

Figure C–8

3
- Click the Connect Anyway link to connect to the public unsecured wireless network (Figure C–9).

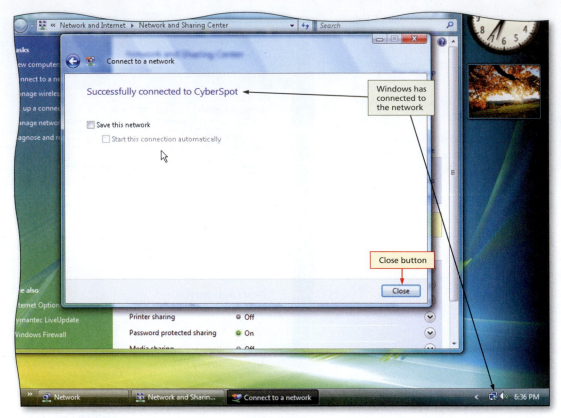

Figure C–9

4
- Close the Connect to a network dialog box (Figure C–10).

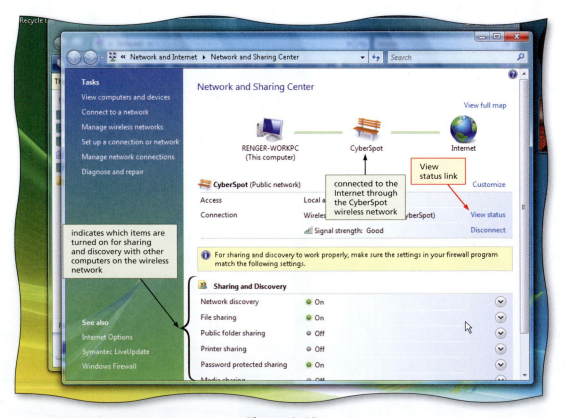

Figure C–10

To View the Status of a Connection

You can view the status of the connection from the Network and Sharing Center. The Wireless Network Connection Status dialog box shows the properties of the connection and allows you to adjust the properties of the connection manually, disable the connection, and diagnose problems with the connection. The following steps display the connection status.

1
• Click the View status link to display the Wireless Network Connection Status dialog box (Figure C–11).

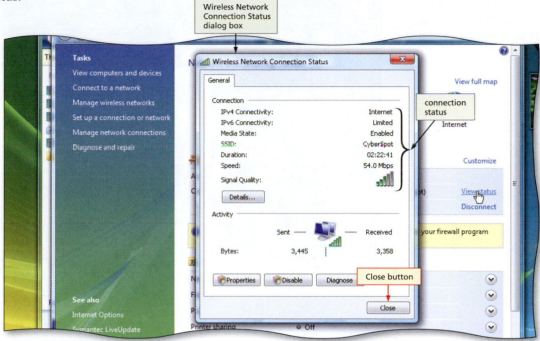

Figure C–11

2
• After viewing the connection status, click the Close button to close the dialog box (Figure C–12).

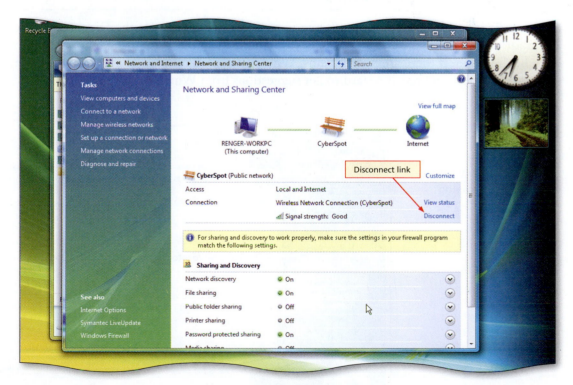

Figure C–12

To Disconnect from a Network

The following step disconnects the computer from the public network.

- Click the Disconnect link to disconnect from the public network (Figure C–13).

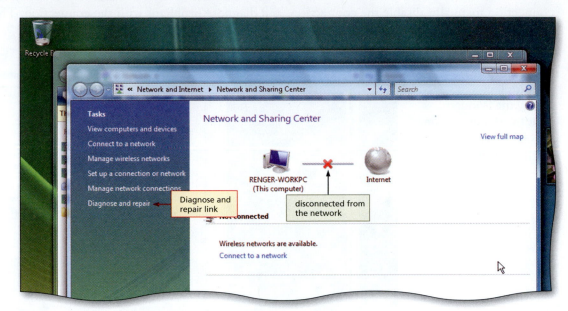

Figure C–13

To Use Diagnose and Repair

If a network connection is not functioning properly, you can use the Diagnose and repair wizard to let Windows Vista detect problems and suggest solutions to you. If Windows cannot determine a solution, a message will be displayed. If there are no problems, Windows also will display an appropriate message. The following steps run the Diagnose and repair wizard to get suggestions from Windows Vista about how to connect to a network.

- Click the Diagnose and repair link to display the Windows Network Diagnostics dialog box (Figure C–14).

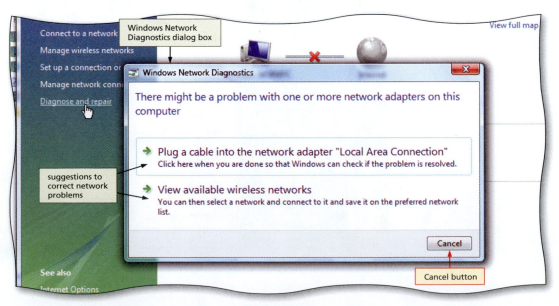

Figure C–14

- After viewing the suggestions, click the Cancel button to close the Windows Network Diagnostics dialog box (Figure C–15).

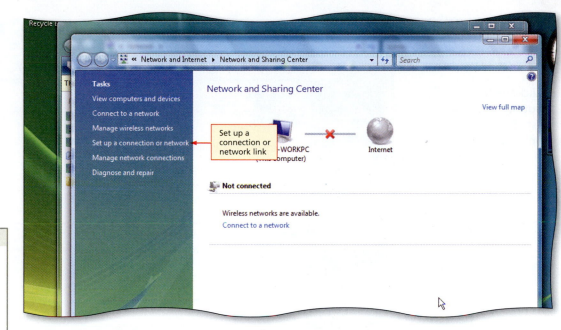

Figure C–15

Other Ways

1. Right-click networking icon in notification area on the taskbar. Click Diagnose and repair

2. Open Control Panel, click Classic View, double-click Network and Sharing Center, click Diagnose and repair

To Connect to a Home Network

When connecting to a network, you also can use the Set up a connection or network wizard. In this case, because the network is a home network, the location type should be set to Private. The following steps connect the computer to a wireless network and change the location type to Private.

- Click the Set up a connection or network link to run the Set up a connection or network wizard (Figure C–16).

Figure C–16

2
- Click Connect to the Internet to select the Connect to the Internet option.
- Click the Next button to view a list of connection options (Figure C–17).

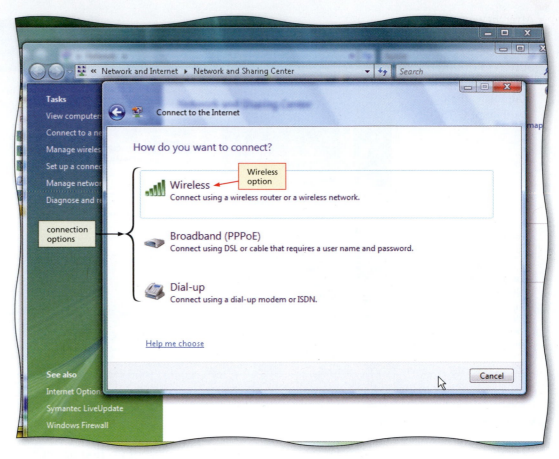

Figure C–17

3
- Click the Wireless option to view a list of available wireless networks (Figure C–18).

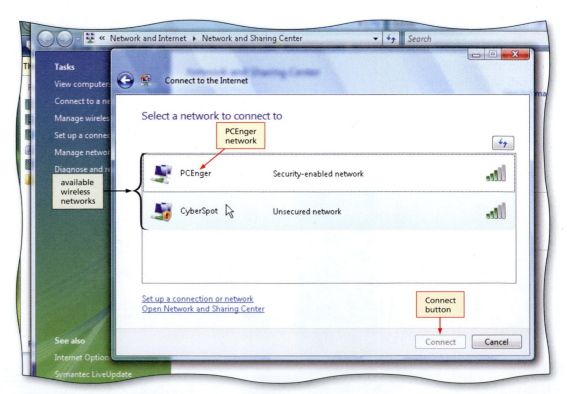

Figure C–18

4

- Click the PCEnger network, or your local security-enabled network, to select it.

- Click the Connect button to begin connecting to the network (Figure C–19).

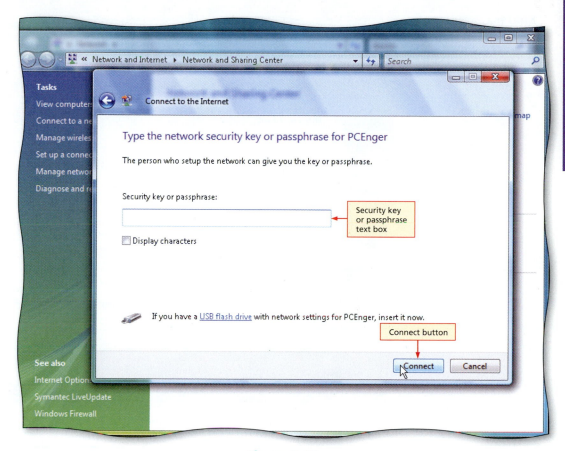

Figure C–19

5

- Type your security key or passphrase into the Security key or passphrase text box.

- Click the Connect button to connect to the network (Figure C–20).

Q&A

What is my security key or passphrase?

The security key or passphrase will be provided either by your network administrator (if at school or at work) or by your wireless router software (if at home).

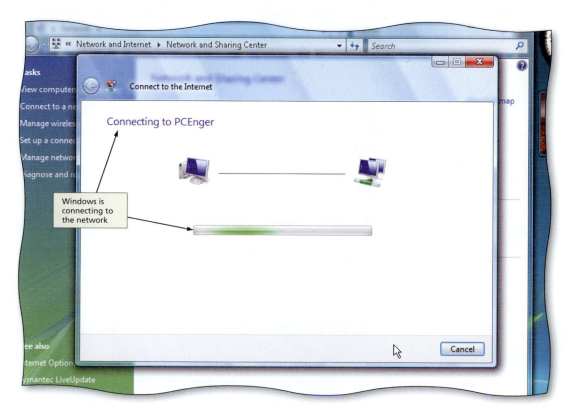

Figure C–20

6

• After the connection is established, a successful connection message is displayed (Figure C–21).

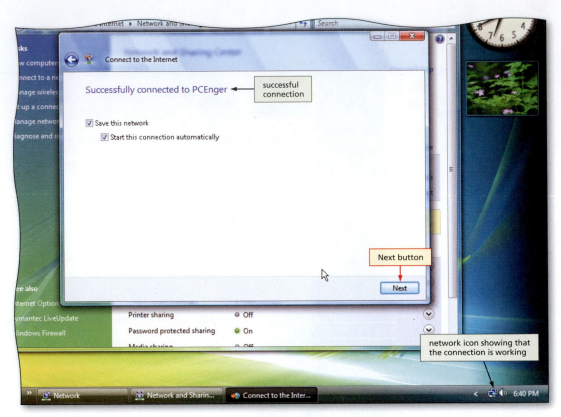

Figure C–21

7

• Click the Next button to test the network connection (Figure C–22).

Q&A

Why does Windows Vista test the connection?

Windows will test the connection to make sure that you can communicate on the network. It is possible to be connected to a network and still be unable to communicate.

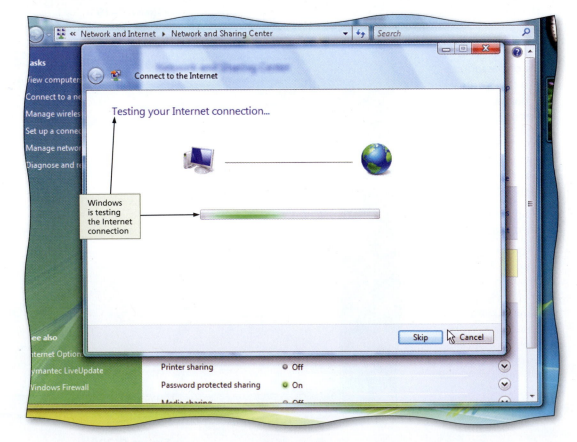

Figure C–22

8

- After a short pause, the You are connected to the Internet message appears (Figure C–23).

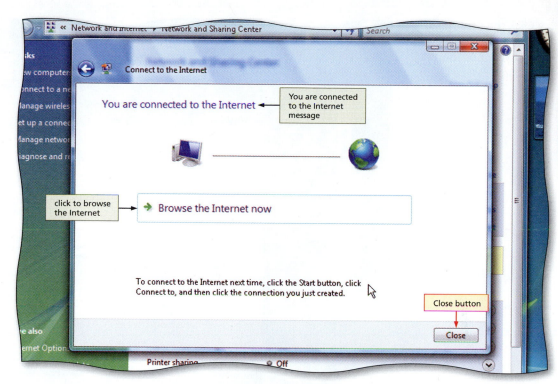

Figure C–23

9

- Click the Close button to close the wizard and return to the Network and Sharing Center (Figure C–24).

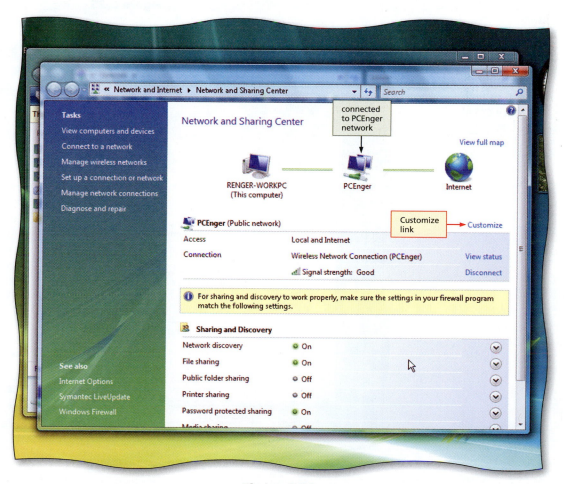

Figure C–24

10
- Click the Customize link to open the Set Network Location wizard (Figure C–25).

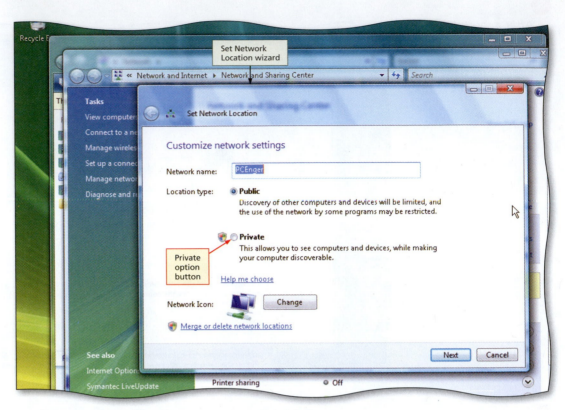

Figure C–25

11
- Click the Private option button to select the private location type (Figure C–26).

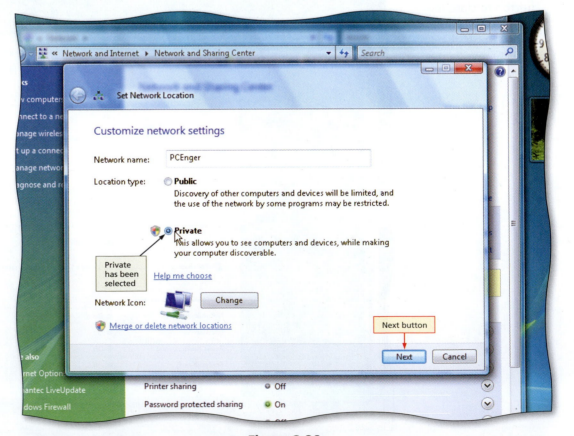

Figure C–26

12

- Click the Next button to change the location type to Private.

- If necessary, click Continue in the User Account Control dialog box to authorize the change (Figure C–27).

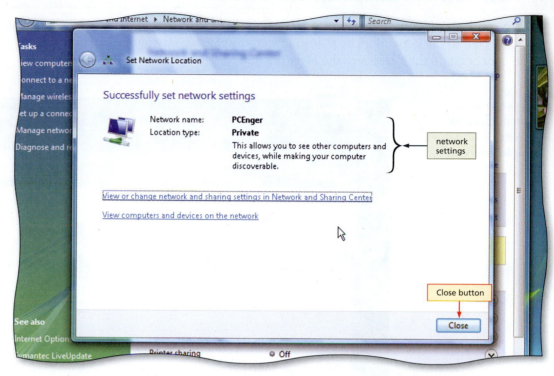

Figure C–27

13

- Click the Close button to close the wizard (Figure C–28).

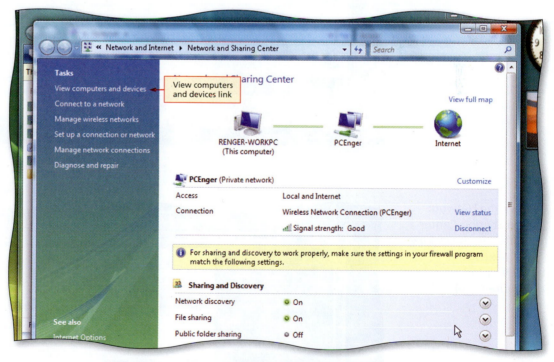

Figure C–28

Other Ways

1. Right-click networking icon in notification area on the taskbar, click Connect to a network, click Setup a connection or network link

To View Network Computers and Devices

Now that the location type of the network is set to Private, you can see the other computers and devices that are connected to the network. The following steps display the computers and devices that are connected to the home network, and then return to the Network and Sharing Center.

1

• Click the View computers and devices link to open the Network window (Figure C–29).

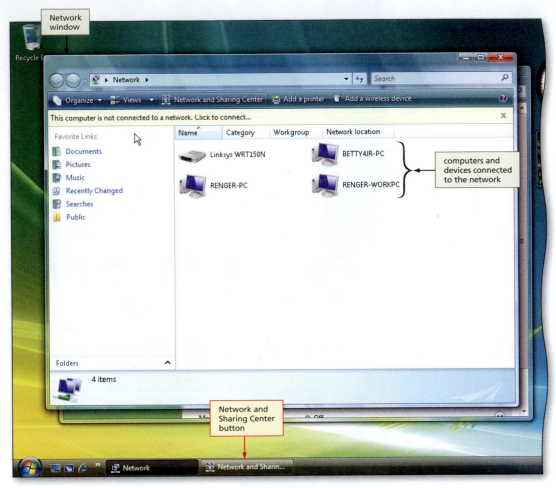

Figure C–29

2

• Click the Network and Sharing Center button in the taskbar to make it the active window (Figure C–30).

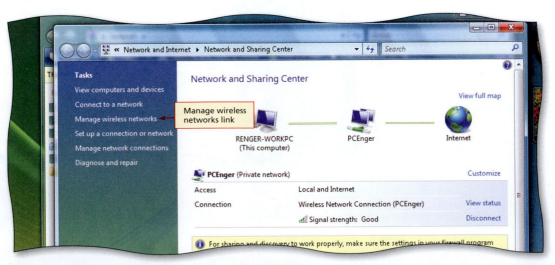

Figure C–30

Other Ways

1. Display Start menu, click Network

To Remove a Wireless Network Connection

You sometimes may need to delete wireless network connections. The following steps remove the Private network wireless connection you just created.

1

• Click Manage wireless networks to open the Manage Wireless Networks window (Figure C–31).

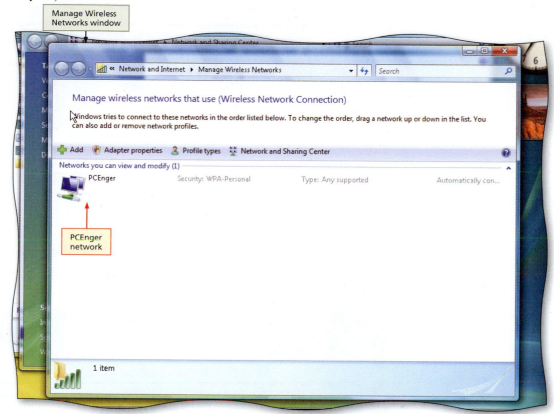

Figure C–31

2

• Click the PCEnger network, or your local network, to select it (Figure C–32).

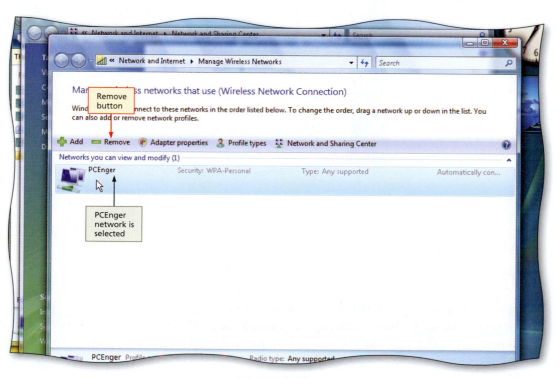

Figure C–32

3

- Click the Remove button to remove the PCEnger wireless network (Figure C–33).

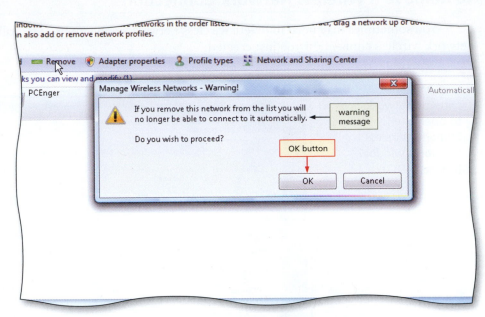

Figure C–33

4

- Click the OK button to confirm that you no longer want to connect to this wireless network automatically (Figure C–34).

5

- Close the Manage Wireless Networks window.

- Close the Network and Sharing Center.

- Close the Network.

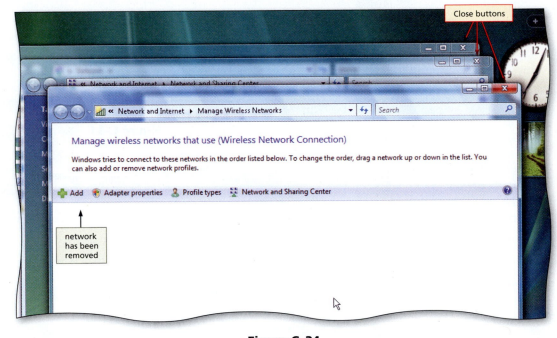

Figure C–34

Summary

Being able to connect to a network is essential in today's society where people use portable computers more often and in more locations. Once connected, you should be aware of what type of network you are using and how secure the network is so that you and your computer are protected whether at home or in public.

Appendix D
Maintaining Your Computer

Backing up and Restoring Files

It can be frustrating to lose data. Almost everyone has heard a story about someone who lost a file and spent hours trying to recover it. In addition, hard disks fail more often than any other component on a computer. When a hard disk fails, it is extremely difficult to recover the data on the drive without obtaining professional help at a hefty price.

Even if a hard disk never fails, errors made while using the computer can result in the loss of a file or group of files. If you are not careful when you save a file, you could lose the file by saving a new file with the original file's name, or by accidentally clicking the wrong button in a dialog box and wiping out the contents of the file. In either case, you most certainly are going to lose some data. If a hard disk failure occurs, all of the files you have created or saved since the last backup may be gone for good. To avoid the loss of data, you should get into the habit of backing up the data on a regular basis.

Although Windows Vista cannot prevent you from losing data on your hard disk, taking proper steps will ensure that you can recover lost data when an accident happens. To protect data on a hard disk, you should use a backup program. A **backup program** copies and then automatically compresses the files and folders from the hard disk into a single file, called a **backup file**. The backup program stores the backup file on a **backup medium**, which can be a hard disk, CD or DVD, shared network folder, USB drive, or even on another computer on the network.

To Open the Backup and Restore Center

Windows Vista includes powerful backup utilities. The Backup and Restore Center allows you to back up selected files or your entire computer, restore selected files or your entire computer, create a restore point, and repair Windows Vista by using the restore option. Note that Windows Vista Home and Home Premium editions do not offer the option of backing up your entire computer. The following steps open the Backup and Restore Center.

- Display the Start menu, and then open the Control Panel window.

- Click the System and Maintenance link to open the System and Maintenance window (Figure D–1).

Figure D–1

2

- Click the Backup and Restore Center link to open the Backup and Restore Center window (Figure D–2).

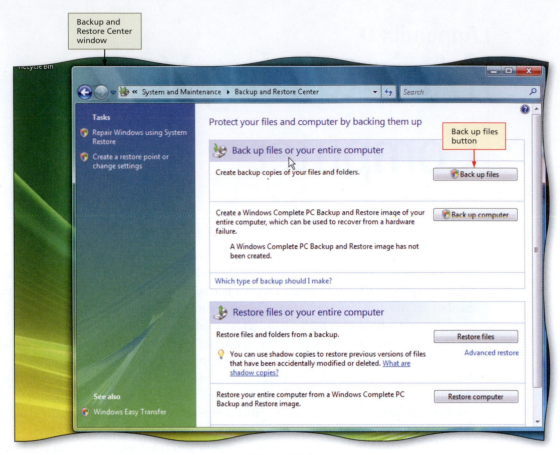

Backup and Restore Center window

Back up files button

Figure D–2

Other Ways

1. Open Control Panel, click Classic View, double-click Backup and Restore Center

To Back Up Selected Files

The Back Up Files wizard allows you to select the files and folders that you wish to back up. You can back up files such as music files, pictures, documents, and game data files. The Back Up Files wizard will not let you back up program files, system files, Web e-mail that has not been downloaded onto your hard disk, anything in the Recycle Bin, any temporary files, user profile settings, or files encrypted using the **Encrypting File System (EFS)**. EFS is an encryption format only supported in Windows Vista Business, Enterprise, and Ultimate editions. Another limitation is that you only can back up files stored on disks formatted with the NT File System (NTFS). The **NT File System (NTFS)** was developed first for Windows NT, and then improved upon as future versions of Windows were developed, including Windows Vista. You will not be able to use the wizard to back up any files stored on disks formatted with the File Allocation Table (FAT) system. The **File Allocation Table (FAT) system** is the file system used in older versions of Windows and is not as secure as NTFS.

When backing up files, you can choose to back up your files on CD or DVD, a hard disk (internal or external), or a network location. You also can choose the frequency, day, and time the backups occur. It is recommended that you back up your files weekly. The first time that you use the Back Up Files wizard, you will be asked these questions and a first backup will be created. The amount of time that a backup takes depends upon the options you choose when you select the backup settings. It can take from a few minutes to one hour or more. The following steps schedule a backup of all picture files to an external USB hard disk that will occur weekly on Saturday at 11:00 PM and create the first backup file.

1

- Click the Back up files button to display the Back Up Files wizard (Figure D–3).

- If necessary, click the Continue button in the User Account Control dialog box.

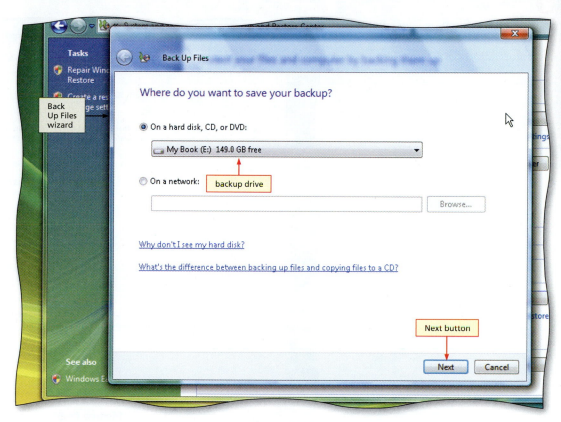

Figure D–3

2

- Select the hard disk My Book (E:) as the location for the backup. If the My Book (E:) drive does not appear, choose the desired drive where you want to back up your files.

- Click the Next button to display list of files to back up (Figure D– 4).

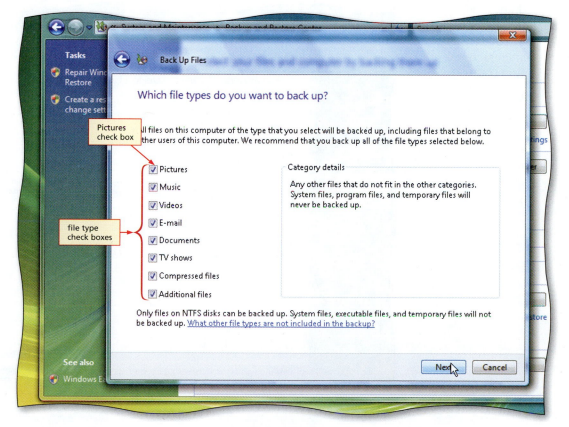

Figure D–4

- Click all the file type check boxes, except for the Pictures check box, to uncheck them (Figure D–5).

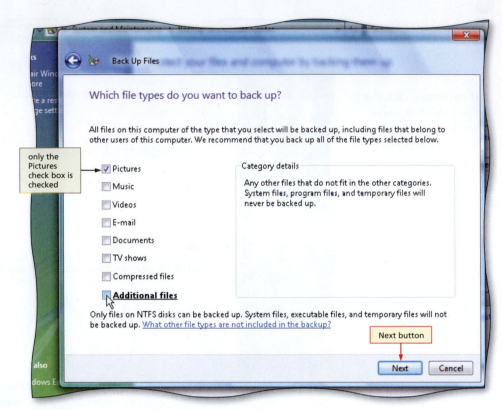

Figure D–5

4

- Click the Next button to display the frequency, day, and time settings (Figure D–6).

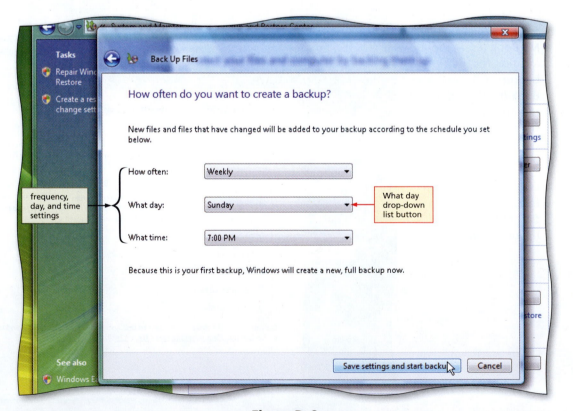

Figure D–6

5

- Click the What day drop-down list button to display the list of days (Figure D–7).

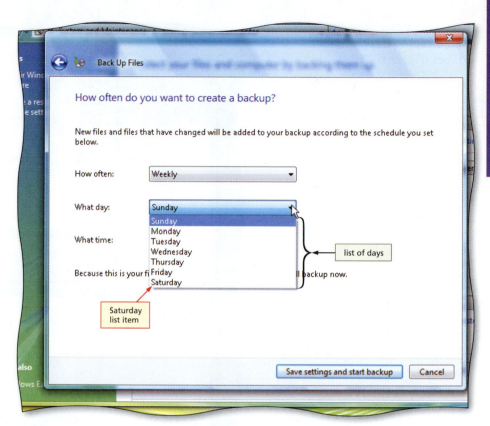

Figure D–7

6

- Click the Saturday list item to change the backup day to Saturday (Figure D–8).

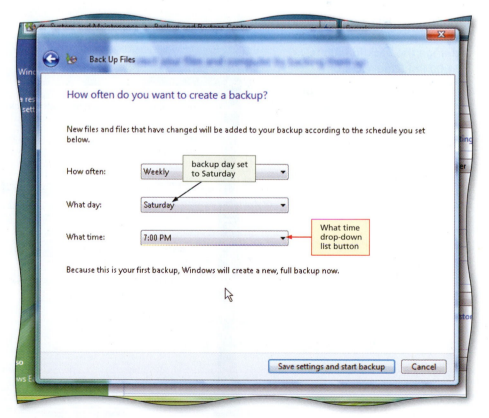

Figure D–8

7

● Click the What time drop-down list arrow to display the list of times (Figure D–9).

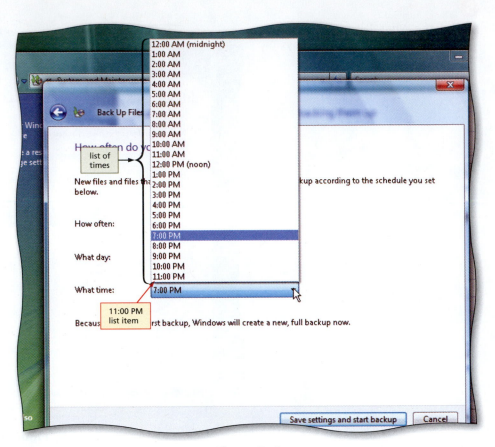

Figure D–9

8

● Click the 11:00 PM list item to change the backup time to 11:00 PM (Figure D–10).

Q&A

How do I change the backup schedule once it has been created?

After the wizard runs for the first time, you can use the Change settings link to open the Back Up Files wizard. You then can change the backup schedule as well as which files are backed up.

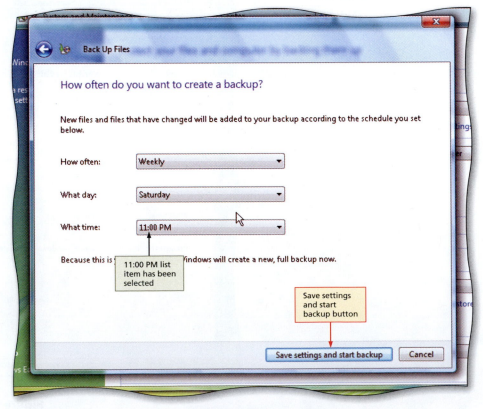

Figure D–10

9

- Click the Save settings and start backup button to save the settings and start the backup process (Figure D–11).

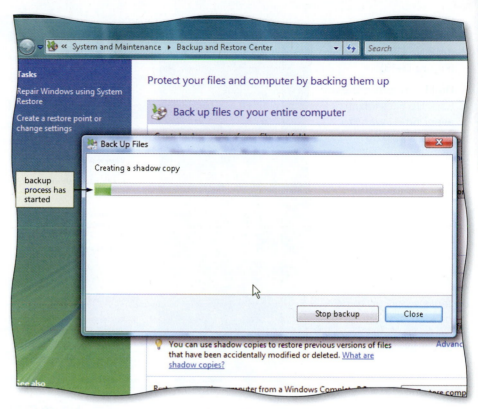

backup process has started

Figure D–11

10

- After the backup is created, the Back Up Files dialog box displays a message indicating that the backup has finished successfully (Figure D–12).

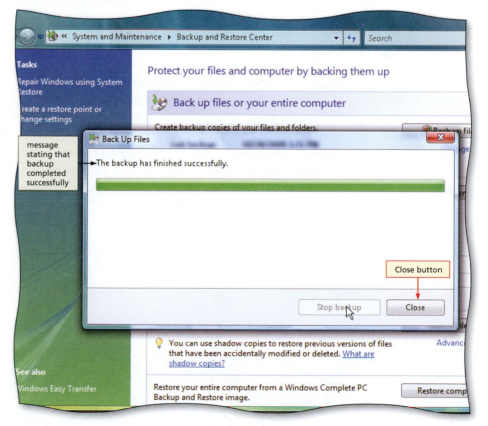

message stating that backup completed successfully

Close button

Figure D–12

11
• Click the Close button to exit the Back Up Files wizard (Figure D–13).

Q&A

Do I have to use the Back Up Files wizard every time I want to create a backup?

No, you do not have to run the Back Up Files wizard. After the wizard creates the initial backup, simply clicking the Back up files button in the Backup and Restore Center will cause a backup to be created. If you wish to change which files and folders are backed up, then you will need to use the Back Up Files wizard or click the Change settings link.

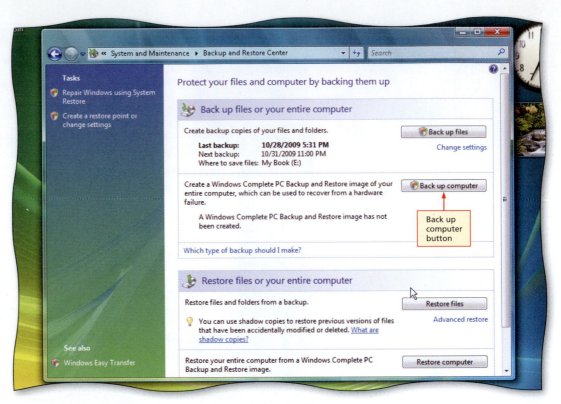

Figure D–13

To Back Up the Entire PC

The Backup and Restore Center contains a link to the Windows Complete PC Backup wizard, which only is available in Windows Vista Business, Enterprise, and Ultimate editions. You can perform a complete PC backup to most external storage devices, or to a CD or DVD. When you back up an entire computer, the Windows Complete PC Backup image contains copies of your programs, system settings, and files. This results in a very large backup file that you can use to restore the contents of your computer if your hard disk or entire computer fails. Microsoft recommends that you back up your entire PC once when you first set up your PC, and then once every six months. A complete PC backup can take anywhere from 30 minutes to an hour or more depending upon the size of the backup. The following steps create a complete backup of the computer.

1

• Click the Back up computer button to display the Windows Complete PC Backup wizard (Figure D–14).

• If necessary, click the Continue button in the User Account Control dialog box.

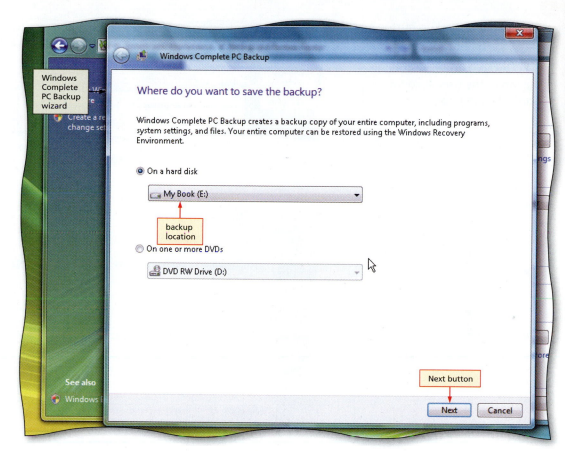

Figure D–14

2

• Verify that the My Book (E:) drive, or your preferred backup location, is selected.

• Click the Next button to continue through the wizard (Figure D–15).

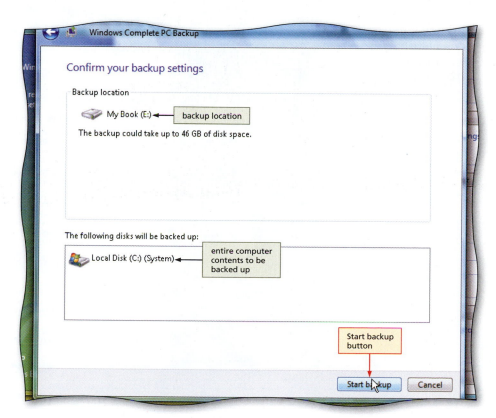

Figure D–15

3

- Click the Start backup button to start the backup (Figure D–16).

- If necessary, click the Continue button in the User Account Control dialog box.

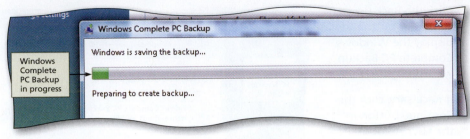

Figure D–16

4

- When the backup completes, the Windows Complete PC Backup window displays a message stating that the backup has completed successfully (Figure D–17).

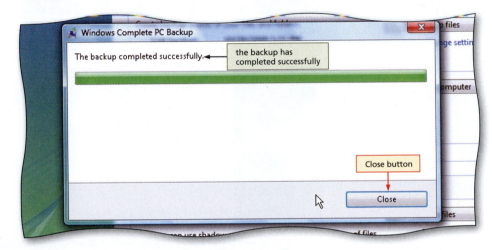

Figure D–17

5

- Click the Close button to close the Windows Complete PC Backup wizard window (Figure D–18).

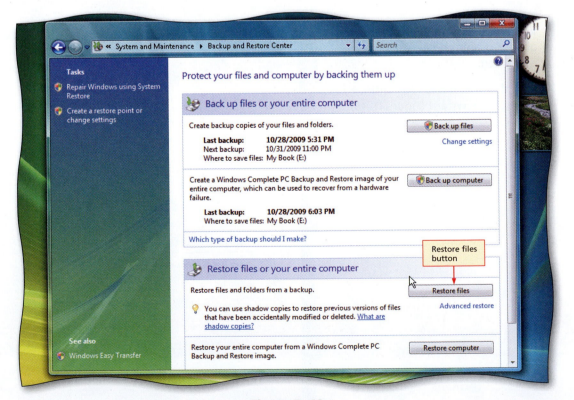

Figure D–18

To Restore Files from a Backup

There may be occasions when you need to restore files from a backup. The Restore Files wizard will allow you to restore individual files and folders. The following steps restore the Creek.jpg file from the most current backup.

1
● Click the Restore files button to start the Restore Files wizard (Figure D–19).

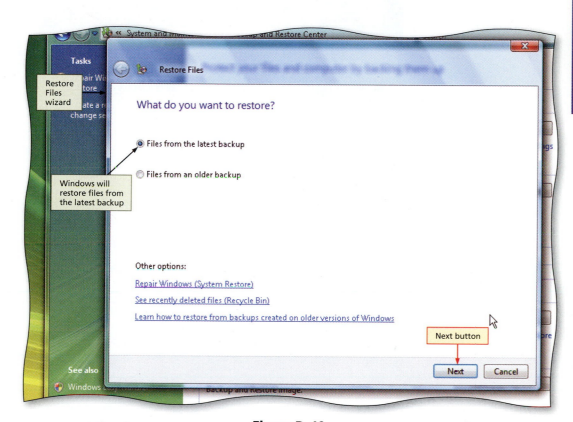

Figure D–19

2
● Click the Next button to display options for selecting files and folders to restore (Figure D–20).

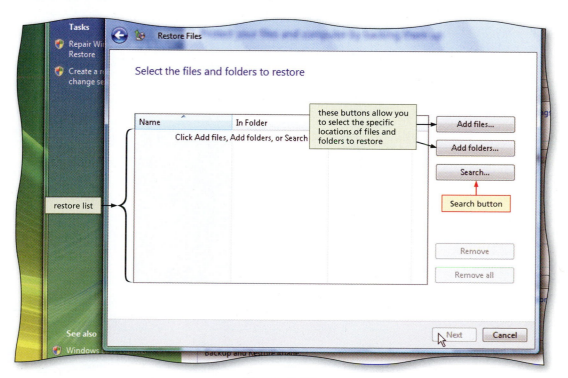

Figure D–20

● Click the Search button to start the Search for files to restore wizard (Figure D–21).

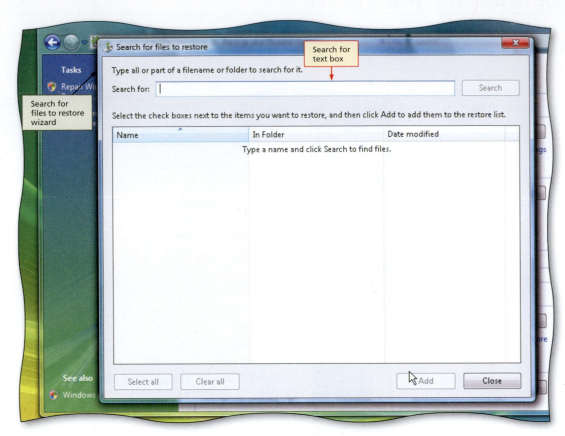

Figure D–21

● Type `creek.jpg` in the Search for text box to enter the file name to find (Figure D–22).

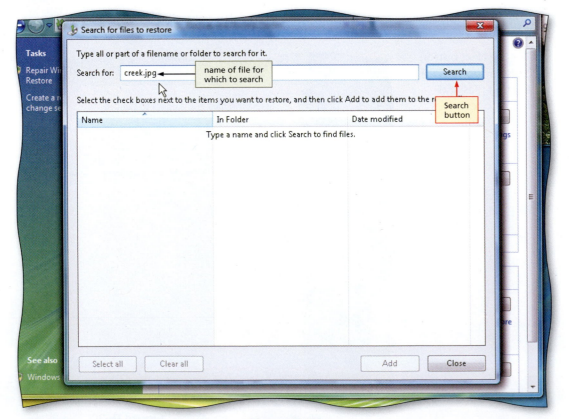

Figure D–22

5

- Click the Search button to search for the file (Figure D–23).

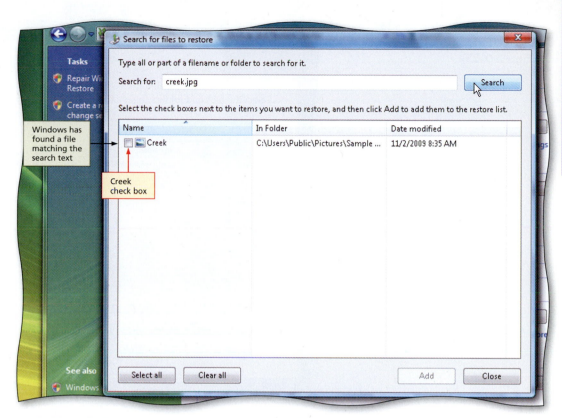

Figure D–23

6

- Click the Creek check box to select it (Figure D–24).

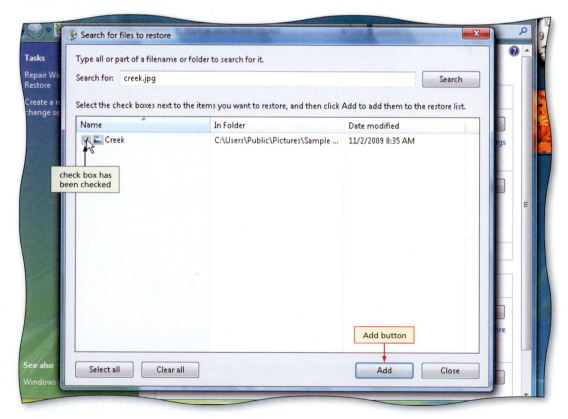

Figure D–24

7

- Click the Add button to add the file to the restore list (Figure D–25).

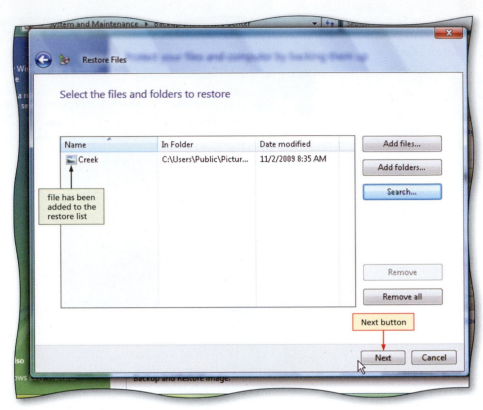

Figure D–25

8

- Click the Next button to continue the restoration (Figure D–26).

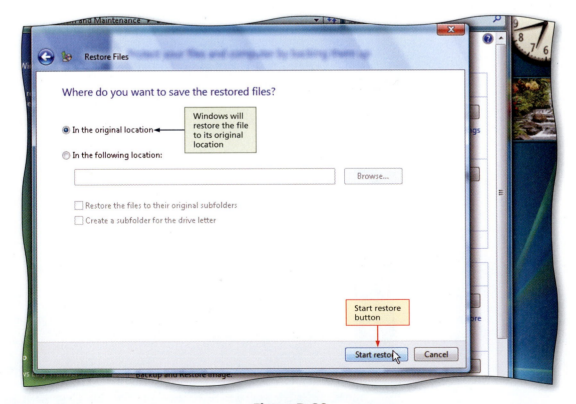

Figure D–26

9
- Click the Start restore button to start the restoration (Figure D–27).

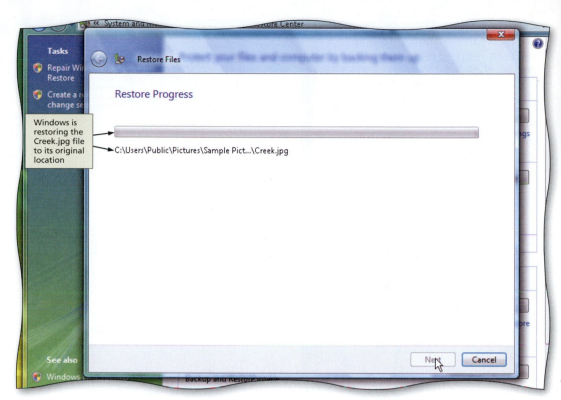

Windows is restoring the Creek.jpg file to its original location

Figure D–27

10
- After the Restore Progress message is displayed, the Copy File dialog box appears (Figure D–28).

Q&A

Why does the Copy File dialog box appear?

The Copy File dialog box appears because there already is a file in Windows Vista with the same name. From this dialog box, you can choose to replace the existing file with the file from the backup, keep the original file, or keep both files.

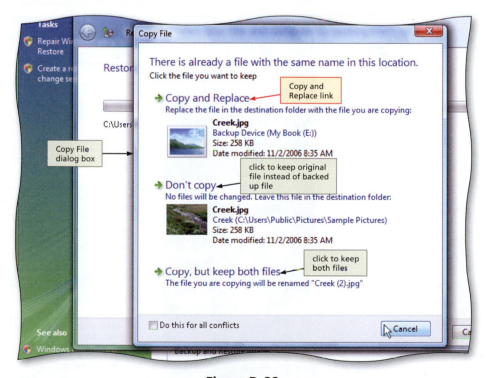

Copy File dialog box

Figure D–28

11

● Click the Copy and Replace link to replace the existing Creek.jpg with the restored backup copy (Figure D–29).

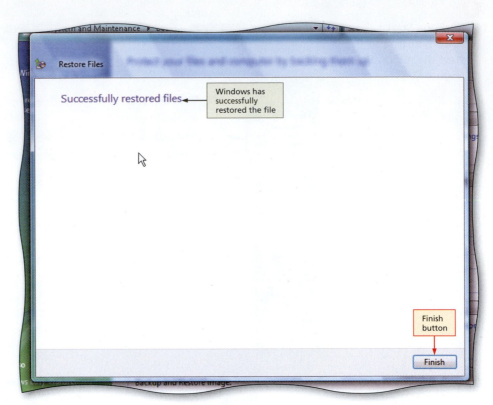

Figure D–29

12

● Click the Finish button to exit the Restore Files wizard (Figure D–30).

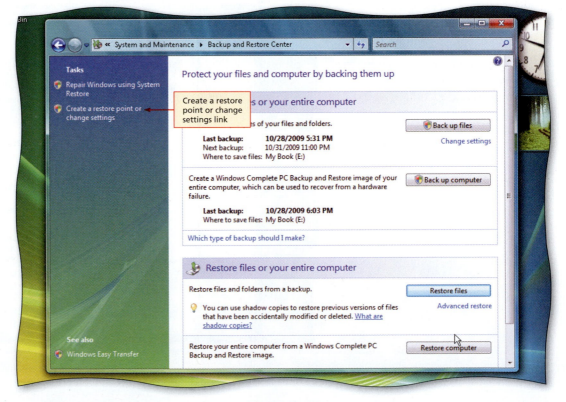

Figure D–30

To Create a Restore Point

Another safeguard for preventing damage to a computer is System Restore. System Restore is a tool that tracks changes to the computer and automatically creates a restore point when it detects the beginning of a change. A **restore point** is a representation of a stored state of the computer. System Restore automatically runs in the background and monitors changes to files, folders, and settings that are essential to the correct operation of the operating system.

System Restore creates an initial restore point when you install or upgrade to Windows Vista. At regular intervals, System Restore creates a restore point to capture the current configuration of the computer and stores the configuration in the registry. Restore points are created when you install an unsigned device driver, install an application using an installer program that is compatible with System Restore, install a Microsoft Update or patch, restore a prior configuration using System Restore, and restore data from a backup set created with the Backup program. In addition, System Restore creates a restore point every 24 hours if you leave the computer running. If you shut down the computer, System Restore creates a new restore point when you restart, if the most recent restore point was created more than 24 hours ago.

System Restore can help correct problems that occur when you install device drivers or software that conflict with other device drivers or software on the computer, when you update device drivers that cause performance or stability problems, or when the computer develops performance or stability problems. However, System Restore does not monitor the page file, the hibernation file, any files stored in personal data folders (Documents, Favorites, Cookies, Recycle Bin, Temporary Internet Files, History, or Temp), image, music or graphics files, files with extensions associated with data files (.docx, .xlsx, .accdb, .pdf, and so on), or e-mail files. In addition, System Restore cannot protect the computer from viruses, worms, and Trojan horse programs. An antivirus program is your best defense against these malicious threats.

In addition to automatically creating restore points, System Restore also allows you to create and name a restore point. Restore points commonly are set prior to making changes to the computer, such as when you install new hardware, install software, or download device drivers. If, after setting a restore point, you determine that the hardware, software, or device drivers do not work properly, you can select the appropriate restore point and reset the computer to the state it was in when you set the restore point, without the fear of losing personal files (documents, Internet favorites, e-mail messages, and so on) that would have been lost if you needed to reformat the hard disk and reinstall Windows Vista. The following steps manually set a restore point called Restore Point - October 28.

1

- Click the Create a restore point or change settings link to open the System Properties dialog box with the System Protection tab selected (Figure D–31).

- If necessary, click the Continue button in the User Account Control dialog box.

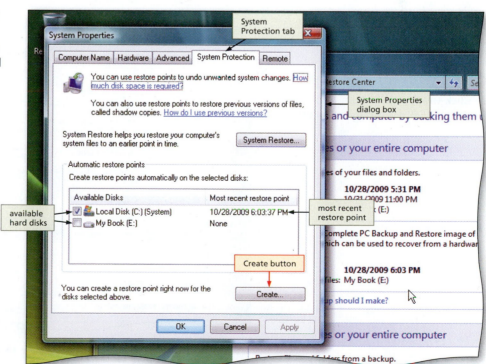

Figure D–31

2

● Click the Create button to display the System Protection dialog box (Figure D–32).

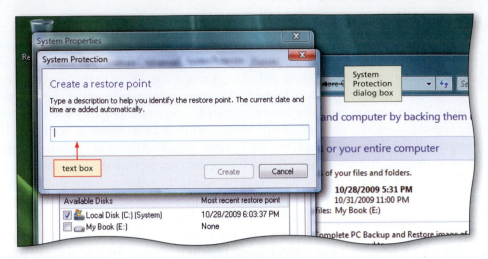

Figure D–32

3

● Type `Restore Point – October 28` in the text box to enter the description (Figure D–33).

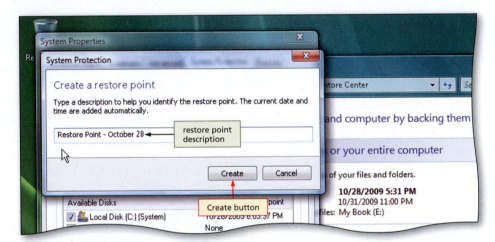

Figure D–33

4

● Click the Create button to create the restore point (Figure D–34).

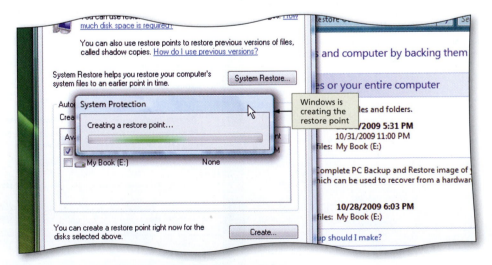

Figure D–34

5

- The System Protection progress indicator will animate. When the restore point has been created, System Protection will display a message stating that the restore point was created successfully (Figure D–35).

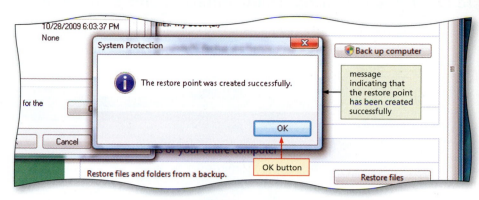

Figure D–35

6

- Click the OK button to close the System Protection dialog box (Figure D–36).

- Click the OK button to close the System Properties dialog box.

- Close the Backup and Restore Center.

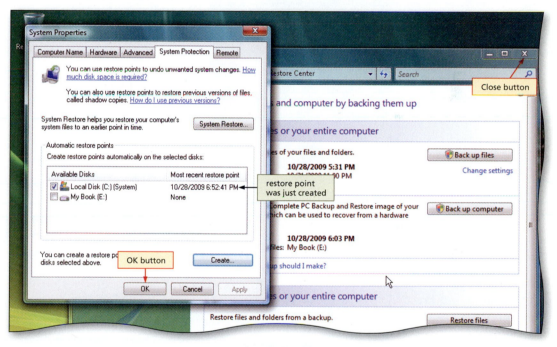

Figure D–36

Performance Information and Tools

After a long period of usage and especially after installing software and saving and deleting files, you might notice changes in your system performance. Your computer may not do what it is supposed to do or it may run slower than usual. These changes mean that your computer is not functioning as it did when Windows Vista first was installed. By performing some system maintenance, you greatly can improve the performance of your computer.

To Open the Performance Information and Tools Window

The Performance Information and Tools window contains the links to most of the tools that you will need to improve system performance. The following steps open the Performance Information and Tools window.

1
- Display the Start menu, and then open the Control Panel window.

- Open the System and Maintenance window (Figure D–37).

Figure D–37

2
- Click the Performance Information and Tools link to open the Performance Information and Tools window (Figure D–38).

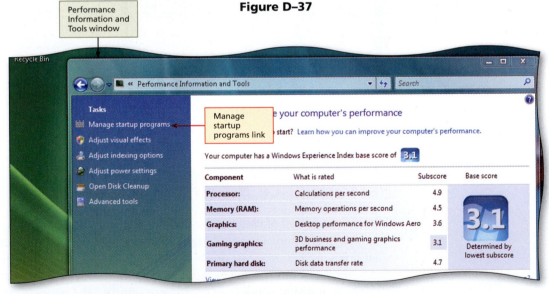

Figure D–38

Other Ways

1. Open Control Panel, click Classic View, double-click Performance Information and Tools

To Manage Startup Programs

One way to improve performance is to review and manage the programs that your computer runs at startup. Windows Defender allows you to view the list of startup programs on your computer, allowing you to disable those programs that you do not want to run automatically. Before disabling a startup program, you should be sure that you no longer need it to run when the computer starts. The following steps open Windows Defender for you to view startup programs.

1

• Click the Manage startup programs link to open Windows Defender displaying the Startup Programs category (Figure D–39).

Q&A

Why is my list of startup programs different?

Because your computer may have different applications and devices installed, the list of startup programs may be different.

Figure D–39

2

• After reviewing the startup programs, close the Windows Defender window (Figure D–40).

Figure D–40

To Open the Reliability and Performance Monitor Window

It is often unclear what is making your computer or program run slowly. To research this problem, you can open the Reliability and Performance Monitor window. The Reliability and Performance Monitor allows you to view data logs indicating the performance of your computer. The following steps open the Reliability and Performance Monitor window.

1

- Click the Advanced tools link to open the Advanced Tools window (Figure D–41).

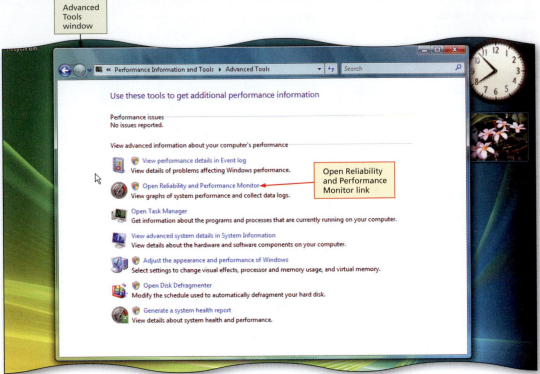

Figure D–41

2

- Click the Open Reliability and Performance Monitor link to open the Reliability and Performance Monitor window (Figure D–42).

- If necessary, click the Continue button in the User Account Control dialog box.

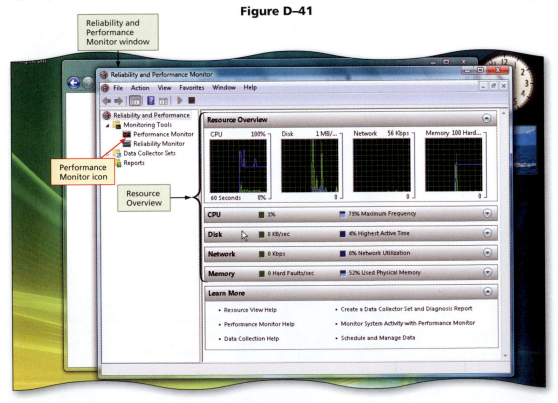

Figure D–42

To View the Performance Monitor

The Performance Monitor displays the processor utilization over time. This can be helpful to see if the processor is being tasked too hard during a particular time period. This can help shed light on why system performance may be slow. If there are particular times when the processor is extremely busy, you can then examine what programs were running at that time. Also, if the processor is always busy, then this can be a sign that a program may not be functioning properly or that you possibly need to add more memory to your computer (if your programs are running as they should be). The following step displays the Performance Monitor.

- Click the Performance Monitor icon to view the Performance Monitor data (Figure D–43).

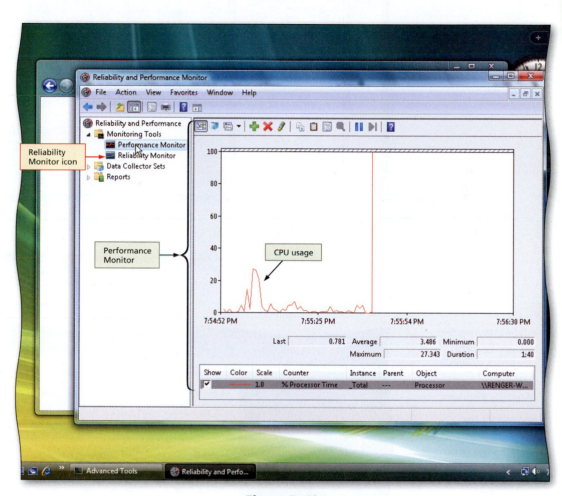

Figure D–43

To View the Reliability Monitor

The Reliability Monitor displays system reliability over time. From here, you can view which programs caused the system to fail. This will help you determine which programs may need to be repaired or removed from the system. If a program needs to be repaired or removed, it will show up as having failed in the reliability monitor. You then can attempt to reinstall or repair the software or just remove it. The steps on the following page display the Reliability Monitor.

1

● Click the Reliability Monitor icon to view the Reliability Monitor data (Figure D–44).

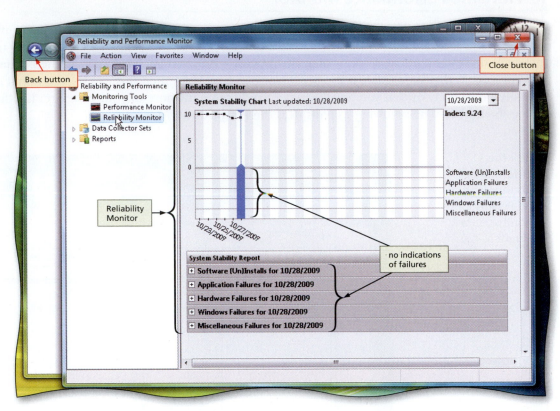

Figure D–44

2

● After viewing the reliability data, close the Reliability and Performance Monitor window.

● Return to the Performance Information and Tools window (Figure D–45).

Figure D–45

To Run Disk Cleanup

Whenever you launch an application program, delete a file using the Recycle Bin, view a Web page, or download a file from a Web site, files are stored on the hard disk. As a result, the hard disk contains many unnecessary files that reduce the amount of free space. If the free space falls too low for the operating system, error messages may display when you run programs. Removing the unnecessary files and increasing the amount of free space on the hard disk will increase the performance of your computer.

The easiest method to delete unnecessary files and make more free space available is to use Disk Cleanup. Disk Cleanup searches the hard disk, lists the files that you can delete safely, allows you to select the type of files to delete, and then deletes the files from the hard disk. Files you can select for deletion include, temporary Internet files, downloaded program files, temporary files, and files in the Recycle Bin. The following steps run Disk Cleanup.

1
- Click the Open Disk Cleanup link to open the Disk Cleanup Options dialog box (Figure D–46).

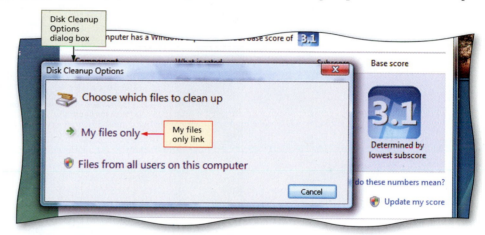

Figure D–46

2
- Click the My files only link to display the Disk Cleanup : Drive Selection dialog box (Figure D–47).

 Why am I not shown a Disk Cleanup : Drive Selection dialog box?

The dialog box will appear if you have more than one hard disk installed. If you only have one, scanning will begin right away.

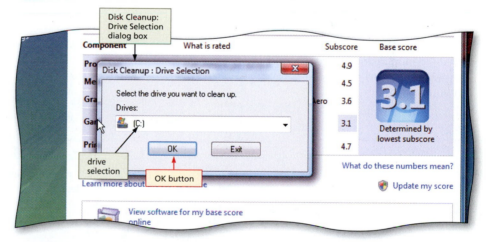

Figure D–47

3
- Click the OK button to search for files to clean up (Figure D–48).

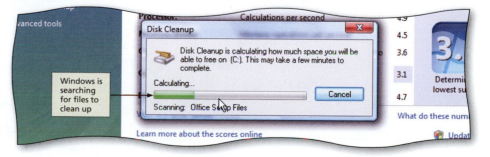

Figure D–48

4

• When Disk Cleanup finishes scanning the computer, the Disk Cleanup for (C:) dialog box appears (Figure D–49).

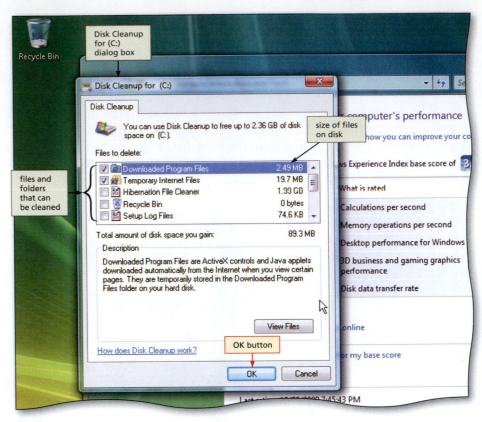

Figure D–49

5

• Click the OK button to display the Disk Cleanup dialog box confirming that you want to delete the files (Figure D–50).

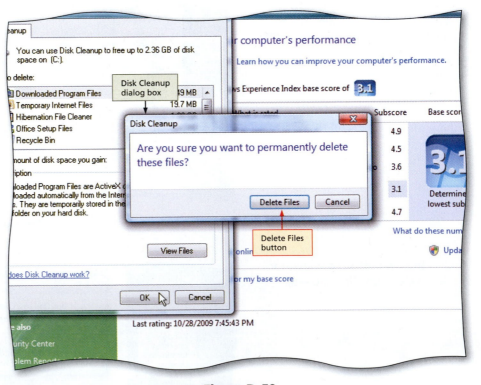

Figure D–50

- Click Delete Files button to confirm the deletion (Figure D–51).

Figure D–51

To Open Disk Defragmenter

When you delete a file from a disk, the locations on the disk used by the deleted file become free disk space on the disk, and the next file the operating system stores on the disk may use all or part of those locations. When new files are repeatedly added and deleted, the disk locations, called **clusters**, for a single file are not always located together on the hard disk, which creates a **fragmented file**. For your computer to run more efficiently these clusters need to be periodically rearranged so that each file's clusters are together. This process is called **disk defragmentation**. Disk Defragmenter, an administrative tool included with Windows Vista, rearranges the files on the hard disk in contiguous blocks with no fragmentation. In Windows Vista, disk defragmentation automatically is scheduled to occur on a regular basis. You can change the schedule, but you should leave automatic disk defragmentation enabled. The following steps open the Disk Defragmenter to allow you to view the settings.

- Click Advanced tools to open the Advanced Tools window (Figure D–52).

Figure D–52

2

● Click the Open Disk
Defragmenter link
to open the Disk
Defragmenter dialog
box (Figure D–53).

● If necessary, click the
Continue button in
the User Account
Control dialog box.

Figure D–53

3

● After viewing
options, click the
Close button to
close the dialog
box (Figure D–54).

● Close the Advanced
Tools window.

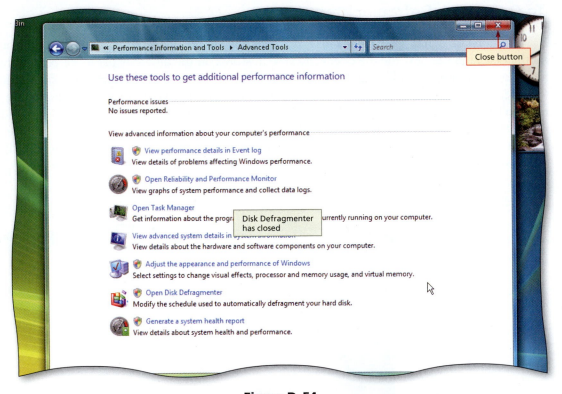

Figure D–54

To View ReadyBoost Options

In addition to the tools available in the Performance Information and Tools window, Windows Vista offers
other methods to improve system performance. Two such methods are ReadyDrive and ReadyBoost. ReadyDrive
is a hybrid hard disk that includes flash memory as part of the hard disk. Windows Vista can use ReadyDrive, when
it is available, to increase performance and battery life of a mobile PC. ReadyDrives are relatively new, so you may
or may not have a system with a ReadyDrive installed. ReadyBoost uses storage space on certain removable media

devices, such as selected USB drives, to increase your computer's speed. This option only will work with the newer USB drives with fast flash memory. Your USB drive must have at least 256 MB of space available for ReadyBoost to work properly, and it only will run while the USB drive is connected to the computer. The following steps select ReadyBoost to display the available ReadyBoost options for a USB drive.

1

• Insert your compatible USB drive to display the AutoPlay dialog box (Figure D–55).

Q&A Why does my dialog box show a different drive letter?

The drive letter assigned to a USB drive depends on the computer where it is inserted. Your drive letter may be different.

Figure D–55

2

• Click the Speed up my system option to display the Removable Disk (H:) Properties dialog box (Figure D–56).

3

• After viewing the options, click the Cancel button to close the dialog box without enabling ReadyBoost.

• Safely remove the USB drive.

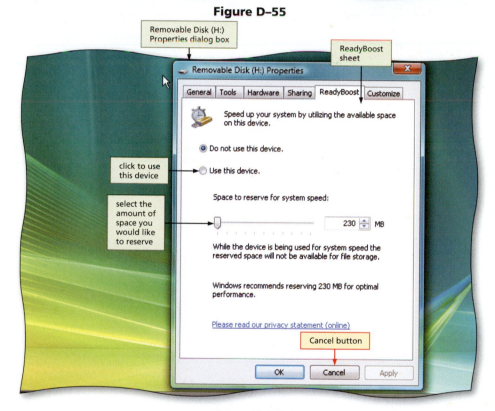

Figure D–56

Summary

Being able to maintain your computer is very important. An essential part of security is making sure that your computer functions properly. Part of the process of maintenance that people often overlook is making proper backups. By using backups, you protect yourself and your computer from valuable data loss.

Index